Contemporary Spanish Politics

D0076120

Having been fully revised and updated to reflect the considerable changes in Spain over the last decade, José M. Magone gives a fresh insight into the formal and informal workings of this dynamic southern European democracy. Thoroughly examining Spain's historical background, political culture, core political institutions and foreign policy-making, each chapter provides a research-based overview of the studied topic which can then be used as the basis for further research by students.

Key themes of the book include:

- Recent history of Spain after Franco's death
- Spain's political culture, institutional framework and political economy
- Foreign policy-making; the reaction to the global anti-terrorist coalition and the Madrid bombings
- Policy-making process and the system of interest intermediation
- Party system and electoral process
- The dynamics of regional/territorial politics and the Basque problem
- External relations with the European Union, the Mediterranean and Latin America
- Constitutional reform
- Immigration

Chapters new to this edition:

- Interest groups and civil society
- Media and politics

Richly illustrated with maps and biographical details of key actors and presenting large amounts of statistical and quantative data, this book is an indispensable source of information for students, academics and the wider public interested in Spanish politics.

José M. Magone is Professor in Regional and Global Governance at the Berlin School of Economics. He was Reader in European Politics at the University of Hull. Among his publications are *Politics of Southern Europe* (2003), *The Developing Place of Portugal in the European Union* (2004) and *The New World Architecture* (2006).

Contemporary Spanish Politics

Second edition

141.- 93

José M. Magone

Routledge
Taylor & Francis Group

LONDON AND NEW YORK

First published 2004
Second edition, 2009
by Routledge
2 Park Square, Milton Park, Abingdon, Oxon OX14 4RN

Simultaneously published in the USA and Canada
by Routledge
270 Madison Ave, New York, NY 10016

*Routledge is an imprint of the Taylor & Francis Group,
an informa business*

© 2004, 2009 José M. Magone

Typeset in Times New Roman by Keyword Group Ltd
Printed and bound in Great Britain by CPI Antony Rowe, Chippenham, Wittshire

British Library Cataloguing-in-Publication Data
A catalogue record for this book is available
from the British Library

Library of Congress Cataloging-in-Publication Data
Magone, José M. (José María), 1962–
    Contemporary Spanish politics / José M. Magone. – 2nd ed.
        p. cm.
    Includes bibliographical references and index.
    1. Spain–Politics and government–1975- I. Title.
    JN8210.M33 2008
    320.946–dc22   2008012658

ISBN10: 0-415-42188-8 (hbk)
ISBN10: 0-415-42189-6 (pbk)
ISBN10: 0-203-89077-9 (ebk)

ISBN13: 978-0-415-42188-1 (hbk)
ISBN13: 978-0-415-42189-8 (pbk)
ISBN13: 978-0-203-89077-6 (ebk)

Dedicated to
My dear sister Mari, Helder and Nuno
A great Spanish family

Tales los hombres sus fortunas vieron;
En un dia nacieron y expiraron,
que pasados los siglos horas fueron.

(Pedro Caldero'n de la Barca, 1660–81)

Llamó mi atención, perdida por las flores de la vereda, un pajarillo lleno de luz, que, sobre el humedo prado verde, abria sin cesar su preso vuelo policromo. Nos acercamos despacio, yo delante, Platero detrás…

(Juan Ramón Jimenez, Platero y yo)

Contents

List of tables

List of figures

Preface to the first edition

Contemporary Spanish Politics is a research-based introduction into the workings and processes of one of the most diverse democracies of the European Union. After almost four decades of authoritarian rule, Spain moved towards democracy and created a unique political system which today has matured to an extraordinary laboratory of democratic experiments. Such a diversity and complexity after two and a half decades of democracy is difficult to contain in several, let alone one. In this sense, this book can be only an introduction to a much more complex reality. In recent years political science has blossomed in Spain, producing very interesting and, in some cases, innovative studies on different aspects of political life. In this book, I am very keen to include the latest developments of these efforts of Spanish political science. This is naturally complemented by the growing research communities on Spanish politics across the world.

The book consists of nine chapters. The first chapter is intended to give an overview of the historical legacy of contemporary Spanish politics. It goes back to the end of the fifteenth century, when Spain emerged as an actor in global politics. Chapter 2 gives an overview of the political culture, or rather political cultures, of the country and maps out the present challenges for Spanish democracy. Chapters 3, 4 and 5 discuss the core political institutions, the political party system and the political systems of the autonomous communities. This is followed by, Chapter 6 on the impact of the European Union on Spanish public policy and Chapter 7 on the Spanish political economy. In the penultimate chapter Spanish foreign policy is discussed at length. Last but not least, Chapter 9 makes some concluding remarks on the quality of democracy in Spain by using some socio-economic indicators.

I want to thank my friends Jose Ramon Montero and Martha Peach for welcoming me always very warmly to the Centre for Advanced Studies of Social Sciences of the Juan March Institute and allowing me to use its excellent library during my research trips to Spain. The idea for the book came from the senior politics editor at Routledge, Craig Fowlie, who asked me if I would be interested in writing such an introductory book. From the very beginning I was thrilled at the prospect of writing a book on contemporary Spanish politics, after a decade of intensive research and teaching on the subject. It was a great privilege to work with Craig and his assistants Zoe Botterill and Jennifer Lovel and I want to thank them all for their support during the conception and actual writing of the book.

José M. Magone

Preface to the second edition

This book has been so far a great success. I received excellent feedback from my fellow colleagues in the United Kingdom and Spain after the publication of the first edition. I just want to mention the feedback from a young academic Rafael Vasquez from the University of Granada, who said that the first chapter of the book on the historical legacy of present Spanish politics is well liked by American students, because of its conciseness. I also had very supportive feedback from César Colino when we bumped into each other in Helsinki during a political science gathering there. He wrote a very positive review in the prestigious Spanish *Revista de Estudios Politicos* (Review of Political Studies) which is published by the Centre for Political and Constitutional Studies in Madrid.

In view of the success of the first edition, senior editor Craig Fowlie asked me to write a second edition, a challenge which I accepted with joy. It was an opportunity to widen the scope of the first edition to more aspects of Spanish politics. On the one hand, it was important to expand and update the present text to include the achievements of the Zapatero government between 2004 and 2008, on the other hand, it allowed for new chapters to be included. New chapters on the media and its relationship to politics and on interest groups and Spanish civil society are designed to show new developments in Spanish politics.

I want to thank everybody who directly or indirectly helped me in my enquiries related to aspects of Spanish politics. First of all, I want to thank my students in Hull, who have been a source of inspiration over the past $14^1/_2$ years. Their critical spirit and constant questions about Spain contributed to the nature of issues that are tackled in the book. I also want to thank the University of Hull for being so generous in providing me with research leave for the autumn semester of 2007/8. This free time allowed me to dedicate myself completely to the writing of the second edition. I obtained a professorship in regional and global governance in the Berlin School of Economics in October 2007, which led to some interruptions in the move from Hull to Berlin. All my books are still in the many boxes that were transported from the UK to Germany.

At last, I finished the book, which is substantially updated and has two brand new chapters. I want to thank my friend and mentor in many ways José Ramón Montero, who has been always so kind and supportive in my research on Spain. I also want to thank the Centre for Advanced Studies in Social Sciences at the

Institute Juan March, Berlin, for allowing me to use its excellent library whenever I am in Madrid. It is always a pleasure to talk to many of the students that work quite hard there, for example Alvaro, who I met at Easter time 2007, working hard on his PhD. Naturally, my greatest joy is always to meet Martha Peach, who is the chief librarian and has remained an excellent friend over the years. She always tells me with enthusiasm about the new projects in which the library has been engaged. Indeed, the digitalisation of the news archive of Juan Linz has to be regarded as a great achievement. Over the years I gained many academic friends in Spain, including Irene Delgado, Esther del Campo, Ivan Llamazares, Miguel Jerez, Fernando Jimenez Manuel Sanchez Diós and Mariano Torcal. Special thanks go to my Catalan friends, Francesc Morata, Pere Vilanova, Joan Subirats and Francesc Pallarés, who have helped me to understand better the complexity of Spanish politics from a Catalan perspective. I profited very much discussing Spanish issues with my friends from the United States. I want to thank particularly Kerstin Hammann, Juan Linz, Richard Gunther, Sebastian Royo and Peter McDonough. A very special thanks goes naturally to Nancy Bermeo, who has been always very supportive of my work in Iberian and European politics. Last but not least, I want to thank Alda Mercedes and Juan Antonio Ramos Gallarin for sending me a great book on intergovernmental relations in Spain, which helped me to improve substantially the relevant section in Chapter 5.

Although I have certainly improved some sections and was able to fill some gaps in this edition, Spanish politics is so complex that certainly other areas are still under-researched. It means that any remaining or emerging gaps or mistakes are fully my responsibility.

I want to thank Craig Fowlie for being so supportive over the years. I would also like to thank his assistant, Natalja Mortensen, for responding promptly to all my queries and giving support throughout the writing process. Many thanks go also to the copy-editor Mickey Munns and the project manager Jais K. Alphonse for his support during the copy-editing and production process.

José M. Magone
Berlin

Abbreviations

ANC	*Acuerdo Interconfederal para la Negociación Colectiva* (Interconfederal Agreement for Collective Negotiation)
ANE	*Acuerdo Nacional de Empleo* (National Agreement of Employment)
ANV	*Acción Nacional Vasca*/Basque National Action
AP	*Alianza Popular* (People's Alliance)
AVT	*Associación de Victimas del Terrorismo*/Association of the Victims of Terrorism
BBVA	*Banco Bilbao y Vizcaya Argentaria*
BEPG	Broad Economic Policy Guidelines
BNG	*Bloque Nacional Galego* (National Galician Block)
CAP	Common Agricultural Policy
CARCE	*Conferencia para Asuntos Relacionados con las Comunidades Europeas* (Conference for Affairs related to the European Communities)
CC	*Coalición Canaria*
CCOO	*Comisiones Obreras* (Workers' Commissions)
CD	*Coalición Democrática* (Democratic Coalition)
CDC	*Convergencia Democrática de Catalunya* (Democratic Convergence of Catalonia)
CDS	*Centro Democrático y Social* (Democratic and Social Centre)
CEDA	*Confederación de las Derechas Autonomas* (Confederation of Autonomous Rights)
CEDSP	Common European Defence and Security Policy
CEOE	*Confederación Española de Organizaciones Empresariales* (Spanish Confederation of Business Organisations)
CEPYME	*Confederación Española de Pequeñas y Medias Empresas* (Spanish Confederation of Small- and Medium-Sized Enterprises)
CESID	*Consejo Superior de Informacion de la Defensa* (Higher Council of Defence Information)
CFP	Common Fisheries Policy
CFSP	Common Foreign and Security Policy

CHA	*Chunta Aragonesista* (Aragonese Junta)
CIAC	*Comisión Interministerial para Asuntos Comunitários* (Interministerial Committee for Community Affairs)
CiU	*Convergencia i Unió* (Convergence and Union)
CNAG	*Confederación Nacional de Agricultores y Ganaderos* (Nacional Confederation of Arable and Livestock Farmers)
CNI	*Consejo Nacional de Inteligencia* (National Council of Inteligence)
CNJA	*Confederación Nacional de Jovenes Agricultores* (National Confederation of Young Farmers)
CNMV	*Comisión Nacional de Mercados de Valores* (Nacional Commission of Stock Markets)
CNT	*Confederación Nacional del Trabajo* (National Confederation of Labour)
COAG	*Coordinadora de Organizaciones de Agricultores y Ganaderos del Estado Español* (Coordinating Body of Arable and Livestock Farmers in the Spanish State)
COREPER	Committee of Permanent Representatives
COSAC	*Comité' des Organs Specialisés' en Affaires Communautaires* (Committee of Bodies Specialising in Community Affairs)
CSPJ	*Consejo Superior del Poder Judicial* (Higher Council of Judiciary Power)
CSU	Christian-Social Union
EA	*Eusko Alkartasuna* (Basque Solidarity)
EC/EU	European Community/European Union
EE	*Euskadiko Ezquerra* (Basque Left)
EFC	Economic Financial Committee
EH	*Eusko Herritarrok* (Basque Nation)
EMU	Economic and Monetary Union
EPC	Economic Policy Committee (Chapter 6)
EP	European Political Cooperation (Chapter 8)
ERC	*Esquerra Republicana de Catalunya* (Republican Left of Catalonia)
ESDI	European Security and Defence Identity
ETA	*Euskadi Ta Askatasuma* (Basque Country and Freedom)
ETUC	European Trade Union Confederation
EURES	European Service of Employment
FCI	Fondo de Compensacion' Inter-territorial
GAL	*Grupos Anti-Terroristas de Liberación'* (Anti-terrorist Liberation Groups)
GDP	Gross Domestic Product
HB	*Herri Batasuna* (Basque Homeland and Freedom Party)
IC	*Iniciativa per Catalunya* (Initiative for Catalonia)
ILO	International Labour Organisation

INI	*Instituto Nacional de Industria* (National Industry Institute)
IU	*Izquierda Unida* (United Left)
LGS	*Ley General de Sanidad* (General Law of Health)
LOAPA	*Ley Organica de Armonización del Proceso Autonómico* (Organic Law on the Harmonisation of the Autonomy Process)
LOCE	*Ley Orgánica de Calidad en Educación* (Organic Law of Quality in Education)
LOFPP	*Ley Orgánica de Financiación a los Partidos Politicos* (Organic Law for the Financing of Political Parties)
LOREG	*Ley Orgánica del Regime Electoral General* (Organic Law of the General Electoral Regime)
MAE	*Ministério de Asuntos Exteriores* (Ministry of Foreign Affairs)
MP	Member of Parliament
NATO	North Atlantic Treaty Organisation
NGO	Non-Governmental Organisation
OCCAR	Joint Cooperation Organisation in the Field of Armament
OECD	Organisation for Economic Cooperation and Development
OLAF	Office for the Fight Against Corruption
OMC	Open Method of Coordination
OSCE	Organisation for Security and Cooperation in Europe
PA	*Partido Andalucista* (Andalusian Party)
PAR	*Partido Aragonés'* (Aragonese Party)
PCE	*Partido Comunista Español* (Spanish Communist Party)
PNV-EAJ	*Partido Nacionalista Vasco/Eusko Alderdi Jeltzalea* (Basque Nationalist Party)
PP	*Partido Popular* (People's Party)
PR	*Partido Riojano* (Rioja Party)
PRC	*Partido Regionalista de Cantabria* (Regionalist Party of Cantabria)
PCTV	*Partido Comunista de las Tierras Vascas* (Communist Party of the Basque Country)
PSOE	*Partido Socialista Obrero Español* (Spanish Socialist Workers' Party)
REPER	Permanent Representation of Spain to the EU in Brussels
SEAE	*Secretaria de Estado para Asuntos Europeos* (State Secretariat for European Affairs)
SEM	Single European Market
SEPI	*Sociedad Estatal de Participaciones Industriales* (State Consortium of Industrial Enterprises)
UA	*Unión Alava* (Alavan Union)
UCD	*Unión del Centro Democratico* (Union of Democratic Centre)
UGT	*Unión General de Trabajadores* (General Workers' Union)
UM	*Unión Mallorquina* (Mallorcan Union)

UNICE	*Unión des Conféderations de Industrie et Employeurs* (Union of Confederations of Industry and Employers)
UP	*Unión Patriótica* (Patriotic Union)
UPN	*Unión Popular de Navarra* (People's Union of Navarre)
TVE	*Television Española* (Spanish State Television)
ZUR	*Zonas de Urgente Reindustrialización* (Zones of Urgent Reindustrialisation)

1 The transformation of Spanish politics

A review of the historical legacy

The rise and decline of the Spanish empire: the politics of the ancien regime (1492–1814)

Any understanding of contemporary Spanish politics has to take into account the historical trajectory of this important European country. For many centuries Spain was a kingdom consisting of several regions, each one characterised by linguistic and cultural differences. It took centuries to bring all these different political and economic sub-units into a coherent larger whole. Even today, the emphasis on the regional differences of Spain is a major element of the identity of the country. Indeed, one can speak of Spains (*Españas*) in terms of politics, economics, culture and geography. Since the unification of the two main kingdoms of Spain in 1492 under the *Reyes Catolicos* (Catholic monarchs), Ferdinand of Aragon and Isabella of Castile, the country was able to unleash energies which led to its unification by conquering the southern kingdom of Granada controlled by the Moors, the discovery and colonisation of America and the expansion of the Spanish kingdom to the largest empire ever reaching from Lisbon to the Middle East under Charles V (1517–56) and Philip II (1556–98).

This unique expansion at the beginning of modern European history had its price. The empire established in the sixteenth century by Emperor Charles V and consolidated by his son Philip II became the target of attacks from the other emerging powers, France, England and later on the Netherlands.

Charles V clearly fitted in more in the category of a medieval monarch always on the move from one part of the empire to the other. His successor Philip II, less keen to travel around the empire, decided to make Spain its centre. He laid the foundations for the modern bureaucratic state, being very concerned about all its aspects (Bernecker, 2002: 47–8; Braudel, 1949: 940–1).

In spite of establishing the first modern bureaucratic administration, the vast empire was always suffering from lack of financial means to sustain its expansion. In particular, wars against the Ottoman empire, against the main European enemies and naturally the war in the Netherlands led to major financial problems. His successors inherited this problem of empire-building. Silver and gold from the Spanish colonies had to be sent to the centres of finance in the Netherlands, so that the funding for wars could be secured. Moreover, the selling of offices to the nobility, particularly at local and regional level, was a common form of raising funds for the state in most European countries (Braudel, 1949: 535–9). The empire was declared bankrupt several times in the sixteenth and seventeenth centuries. The main reason was that the kingdom of Castile was carrying most of the financial burden to sustain the huge empire throughout the sixteenth and seventeenth centuries. This was not so much spent on the administration of the territory, but in undertaking wars against its main competitors. This was reinforced by a very inefficient underdeveloped economy, which clearly was not very industrious. The population tended to imitate the behaviour of the upper classes, the hidalgos, who clearly felt that work was below their dignity. This led to a two-tier society which tended to allow high levels of poverty and brigandage (Williams, 1999: 76–9).

Only in the eighteenth century were reforms undertaken to achieve a more even share of the burden by the other main kingdom of Aragón. This was achieved mainly by a greater nation-state building effort by the Bourbons, the new dynasty which had replaced the Habsburgs during the war of Spanish succession, conducted between France and Habsburg Austria in the early eighteenth century. The accession of Philip V (1700–46), the French candidate, instead of Archduke Charles, the Habsburg candidate, at the end of the war of Spanish succession, led ultimately to the end of the claims of the kingdom of Aragón, and within it, Catalonia, to achieve independence. The alliance of the Aragonese and Catalan aristocracy to the Habsburg candidate, Archduke Charles, was regarded as treason by the new king, leading in the end to the full integration into the Spanish nation-state. Philip V emulated naturally the way the French nation-state was built, by achieving a high level of centralisation and the creation of a modern administration based on a system of intendants in the newly created provinces of Spain. The intendants were representatives of the monarchy at provincial level, who had full administrative powers and followed direct orders from Madrid. As in France, this new administrative structure was established against the old order based on medieval principles of job allocations. This effort to undermine the local power of the nobility did not fully succeed. Philip V and his successors Ferdinand VI (1746–59) and Charles III (1759–88) tried to strengthen the role of the state by introducing more regulations in public life, which in turn led to revolts of the population. This became quite clear during the revolts against Prime Minister Esquilache, during the reign of Charles III. Meanwhile, Spain had fallen considerably behind the Netherlands, France and England in terms of economic development. Attempts to follow the French example of setting up manufacturers led to an improvement, but nevertheless the economic gap remained. One positive development was the economic rise of Catalonia which was able to profit from the national integration of the Spanish market introduced by Philip V and continued by his successors.

The French Revolution became a major threat to the absolute monarchy. Indeed, only by reviving the old institution of the Inquisition was it possible to control the dissemination of the ideas of the Enlightenment and the French Revolution. The Napoleonic invasion, which put Napoleon's brother, Joseph Bonaparte, on the

Spanish throne, sparked a major resistance movement in Spain. In 1812, the opposition met at Cadiz and promulgated a new constitution which clearly was influenced by the ideas of the French Revolution. It enshrined popular sovereignty, universal male suffrage and a vast catalogue of personal and political rights. The so-called 'Constitution of the Spanish Nation' was to remain a reference document of Spanish liberalism throughout the nineteenth century, leading to a continuous opposition to the return of an absolute monarchy. In spite of that, after the end of the Napoleonic wars, the Bourbon dynasty was restored and a new king, Ferdinand VII (1814–33), re-established an absolute monarchy.

The discontinuous road to democracy: from constitutional monarchy to the Spanish Civil War (1814–1939)

From absolutist to constitutional monarchy (1814–74)

The restoration of the absolute monarchy of Ferdinand VII was not achieved peacefully. Between 1814 and 1820 several military groups tried to reverse the process by *pronunciamientos*, coup attempts at local or regional level. Such *pronunciamientos* were able to rely on some sort of popular support. Among the emerging democratic political elites, it was the liberals who clearly tried to revive the spirit of the Constitution of Cadiz, which defined that sovereignty resided with the Spanish nation, represented both in the Spanish motherland as well as in the colonies of Latin America. Quite important was the *pronunciamiento* of 1820, which started in Cabezas de San Juan on 1 January and soon spread across the whole country. Such liberal movements could be witnessed in all European countries. The liberals could count on the support of the colonies which themselves staged an uprising. Although Ferdinand VII was forced to swear loyalty to the Constitution of Cadiz, soon after the support of the Holy Alliance, which had achieved the return of the absolute monarchy in Europe, helped Ferdinand VII to crush the rebels and re-establish his authority (Sanchez-Albornoz, 1998: 6–7, 16–28). Liberalism was to continue to be a major force for the establishment of a constitutional monarchy throughout the nineteenth century. It also was clearly linked to the principles of the Constitution of Cadiz, which already enshrined the principle of universal male suffrage. After the death of Ferdinand VII, the country was once more in turmoil, due to the fact that a civil war between different pretenders to the throne erupted. Ferdinand's brother Charles did not want to recognise the so-called pragmatic sanction which was proclaimed in the Cortes of 1789 and allowed for female children to follow in the succession of the throne. In this case, Ferdinand wanted his daughter Isabella to become queen of Spain after his death. Maria Cristina, the wife of Ferdinand VII, was to act as regent for Isabella until she was old enough to become the new queen of Spain. This led to a war which became synonymous with the struggle between liberalism and absolutism. While Charles represented the forces of absolutism, Maria Cristina and Isabella opened up the inherited absolutist regime and allowed the establishment of a moderate constitutional monarchy with support of the liberals. The so-called first Carlist War (1833–39) led to the establishment of the *Estatuto Real* (Royal Statute) in 1834, which provided for a moderate constitutional monarchy. The so-called *Abrazo de Vergara* (Embrace of Vergara) in 1839 achieved a ceasefire, but not the end of the war.[1]

Although the *Estatuto Real* was accepted by the moderate liberals (*moderados*), it remained a reason for conflict and contest for the progressive liberals (*progresistas*). While the former represented the upper classes of the bourgeoisie and the land oligarchy, the latter relied on a broader social basis of the growing lower-middle classes. The *progresistas* wanted a far-reaching constitution based on the principles of the Constitution of Cadiz which included separation of powers, popular sovereignty and democratisation of local power. In contrast, the *moderados* supported the *Estatuto Real* which clearly did not envisage a separation of powers. It resided in the principle of dual sovereignty of the monarchy and the nation, did not allow a democratisation of local power, and last but not least, still retained a restricted electorate, based on a property qualification. In the midst of the Carlist War, Maria Cristina and Isabella had to deal with this growing opposition of the *progresistas* who clearly had the support of the population and the military at local level. A compromise was struck leading to the Constitution of 1837 which clearly restored the principle of popular sovereignty, but kept the census electoral system at a low level and still based on property. It kept the bicameral parliament which was already part of the *Estatuto Real*. The *Estatuto Real* of 1834 and the Constitution of 1837 remained the two reference documents of the constitutional monarchy. Most of the contents were to remain important until the end of the monarchy in 1931 (Viadel, 1989).

In 1844 the 13-year-old Isabella II (1844–68) became the new queen of Spain. Maria Cristina had to move to exile in France, after uprisings against her regency. During Isabella's reign the struggle between *moderados* and *progresistas* was further exacerbated. The political infightings and intrigues of politicians led to a conflictive alternation in power, which clearly tended to eradicate everything that the previous government had achieved before. The *moderados* abolished the 1837 constitution and replaced it with a new one based on the *Estatuto Real* in 1845. Furthermore, they reduced the number of people eligible to vote by raising the property qualification. In spite of the second Carlist War (1847–49), the infighting between *moderados* and *progresistas* contributed to a climate of instability, in which reforms such as the desamortisation of Church land and its redistribution could not be successfully implemented. Clearly, the main problem of the constitutional monarchy was the high level of political corruption and manipulation of the political process. Sooner or later, the positions of the *moderados* and *progresistas* would harden and become uncompromising. Other social movements such as republicanism and socialism were beginning to join the cause of the *progresistas*. A last successful attempt to strengthen the constitutional monarchy was undertaken by Guillermo O'Donnell who founded a new party, the Liberal Union (*Unión Liberal*) designed to overcome the gap between *progresistas* and *moderados*. He was able to stay in power between 1858 and 1863, thus allowing a period of political stability. One of the characteristics of the Liberal

Union government was the manipulation of elections through the Ministry of the Interior, something that was picked up by Canovas del Castillo later, who was working at that time as a secretary (Carr, 1999: 254–60). It meant that elections were normally rigged and manipulated to produce a majority for the government in power. Eventually, the majority of O'Donnell's Liberal Union disintegrated, leading to political and economic instability in the second half of the1860s. The revolutionary momentum was mounting among the *progresistas* with the eventual support of the emerging republicans who were organised in the democratic party (Carr, 1999: 284–96).

Between 1868 and 1873 Spain witnessed a period of revolutionary turmoil, more or less imposed by uprisings of democrats at local level. Under great difficulties, the dominant oligarchy consisting of *unionistas* and *progresistas* was able to achieve a compromise with the *democratas* on the Constitution. The Constitution of 1869 introduced many democratising elements, but the final demand of the democrats relating to the establishment of a republic was resisted successfully by the dominant political class. Due to the fact that the old monarchy was discredited, a new king, Amadeo of Savoy, was brought from abroad. In spite of these changes the revolutionary anti-clerical republican movement continued to create major problems for the political establishment. One faction of the *democratas* was against any compromise with the monarchy and clearly wanted the full establishment of a republic. The new monarchy under King Amadeo of Savoy lasted only 3 years, and was replaced by the First Spanish Republic in 1873–74. The king's widespread unpopularity and the continuing infighting between *progresistas, unionistas* and *democratas* were the main reason for the establishment of the republic, which was the preferred option for the radical democrats. The abdication of King Amadeo in February 1873 opened the way for the proclamation of the republic. Nevertheless, the Republican movement was divided into unitary and federalist Republicans, leading to more infighting and violence between these two groups. The dominance of the federalist Republicans led to opposition from the right at local level. By early 1874 the republic had lost its credibility (Carr, 1999: 317–26). Throughout the year the Carlists were able to revive their movement and start the third Carlist War. They hoped to put Don Carlos Maria, Duke of Madrid, on the throne. The stronghold of the Carlists was in the Basque country. In this situation of political and economic instability, the return of the Bourbon king, Alfonso XII, son of Isabella II, was regarded as a viable solution to achieve law and order in the country. Instrumental in convincing the upper classes of Catalonia and Madrid was Antonio Canovas del Castillo, who used a propaganda offensive throughout the year to bring Alfonso XII, as a representative of the pre-revolutionary Bourbon dynasty, to the throne. By the end of the year, the monarchy was restored, while the republic was discredited for at least a generation (Carr, 1999: 326–31).

Rise and fall of the Restoration system (1874–1923)

Antonio Canovas del Castillo became the central architect of the Restoration which lasted until the proclamation of Primo de Rivera's dictatorship in September 1923.

He created the most stable constitutional monarchy, which was highly conservative in character. He became the undisputed leader of the Restoration.

The new constitutional monarchy established after 1875 created a party system called *turno pacifico* (peaceful alternation), in which two parties would alternate peacefully in government under a liberal constitutional framework. The two parties which dominated political life in this period were the Conservative Liberal Party (*Partido Liberal Conservador* – PLC) under the leadership of Antonio Canovas del Castillo, and the Fusionist-Liberal Party (*Partido Liberal-Fusionista* – PLF) whose leader was Praxedes Mateo Sagasta. The re-election of these two parties in government was ensured by an electoral machine. Although the suffrage was steadily extended to other social groups, the vast majority of the population was still illiterate and living in rural areas. These factors contributed substantially to control the electorate by this electoral mechanism centred in the Ministry of Public Administration (*Ministerio de Gobernación*). Canovas del Castillo's ideological predisposition was towards the abolition of competitive politics and the concretisation of what he called broadness (*amplitud*). This meant nothing else but the inclusion of all relevant groups into a system of clientelism and patronage (Kern, 1974: 31). The so-called *caciques*,[2] important local notables, ensured that the right candidates supported by the government would be elected. The highly centralised Spanish state based its strength on a network of provincial governors who reported regularly to the Ministry of Public Administration in Madrid about the political situation in the corresponding province. The provincial governor was an important link between the government, the regional party leader and the local and regional *cacique*. He normally based his influence on negotiations with all relevant actors, so that he would achieve in the end the election of a governmental candidate. The regional or local party leader was less scrupulous in using violence and other forms of intimidation to ensure the election of the candidate. The *cacique* groomed their voters to vote for the governmental candidate (Tusell Gomez, 1976: 3–5). At the top of the hierarchy was the Minister of Public Administration, who set up the list of governmental candidates to be elected in the provinces. A so-called *encasillado*, a pigeonholing of candidates in the different provinces, was the normal ritual of the Minister of Public Administration. This was achieved after many months of negotiations at local, regional and national levels. Such a system was established by the first Minister of the Interior of the Restoration, Romero Robledo, who increased the level of centralisation of the administration. This so-called *romeroroblismo* became a synonym for the overall system of systemic corruption carried out during the Restoration. Only Catalonia and Valencia were able to resist successfully against this clientelistic and patronage system. On the other end of the spectrum one can mention Andalusia, where *caciquismo* was a widespread system (Kern, 1974: 33–9).

In this period Spain experienced a boom in railway construction and foreign investment in different new industrial sectors. Until 1923, the social structure would change considerably, leading to the rise of a modest working class and the Canovite political system became less sustainable from the turn of the century onwards.

Although discontent with the Canovite system became louder throughout the 1890s, the main event which triggered growing protest and criticism of political corruption of the *turno pacifico* was the loss of Cuba, the Philippines and Puerto Rico after a war with the United States in 1898. The so-called 'Disaster' affected strongly the national psyche of the country. The criticisms of the Canovite system came from the old political forces such as the radical liberals as well as new forces such as the republicans, socialists and later on anarchists. Quite important became the criticisms of *caciquismo* and oligarchical corruption by Joaquin Costa (1898). The main grievance was the degeneration and corruption of the *turno pacifico*. According to Costa, an iron surgeon was needed to operate on the sick body of the Spanish nation. Such an operation should be carried out by a strong personality within the framework of democratic politics. Such an analogy was to be used and abused by Primo de Rivera's dictatorship after 1923. He believed that he was the required iron surgeon for Spain (Clemente, 1998). The rise of the anti-systemic forces contributed to an increase of discontent in the first two decades of the century. Steadily, these new social movements were able to count on a broader social support due to the transformation of the social structure.

The decay of the two-party system started with the deaths of Canovas del Castillo (1897) and Sagasta (1903), the protagonists of the rigged two-party system, leading inevitably to the collapse of the two main parties into factions. The main reason was the lack of cohesion of political parties which relied very much on the electoral machine, but had no concrete party organisations. The personal nature of Spanish politics, which was quite common in other Latin countries, tended to put personal differences, likes and dislikes above party and national interest.

The emergence of other parties changed the composition of parliament. It became more fragmented. The first socialist MP was elected in 1910. This was possible because the government had to extend the suffrage to new classes.

In Catalonia, the cultural *renaixença* of the nineteenth century became translated into political action in the early twentieth century. The foundation of the *Lliga Regionalista* by Fernando Cambó in 1901 pushed the cause for Catalan autonomy. This party widely supported by the Catalan bourgeoisie contributed in some way to the foundation of a republican working-class party by Alejandro Lerroux, who opposed the *Lliga*, as being the representative of the Catalan upper bourgeoisie. In 1906 the Catalan parties founded a coalition called *Solidaridad Catalana* (Catalan Solidarity) in Barcelona against the *turno pacifico* parties (Garcia-Nieto, 1973: 19–28). Similarly in the Basque Country regionalist-nationalist parties became a growing force. The foundation of the National Basque Party (*Partido Nacionalista Vasco* – PNV) in 1898 clearly strengthened Basque nationalism, which was supported by the regional bourgeoisie. Their ideology was based on the writings of Sabino Arana, who clearly advocated a more racist exclusionist interpretation of the Basque nation. This exclusionist nature of Basque nationalism was to remain the main difference between Basque and Catalan nationalism (Garcia-Nieto, 1973: 29–30; Conversi, 1997).

An attempt to regenerate the Canovite political system by Prime Minister Antonio Maura between 1907 and 1909 failed, because *caciquismo* and clientelism were already too inbred in local politics. Instead, political violence in Spain increased in this period. The centres of continuing violence were Catalonia and Andalusia, where the anarchists, and later on, anarchosyndicalists, wanted to overthrow the government. The climax of this social revolt was the so-called 'Tragic Week' at the end of July 1909. Maura wanted to send troops to Morocco to defend some Spanish mining concessions against an attack by the native *harkas*. The ill-organised call-up of reservists, which included soldiers who had served during the Spanish-American war, led to a major revolt across Catalonia. Barcelona was the main port of embarkation for Morocco, so that it became the centre of action. *Solidariedad Obrera* (Workers' Solidarity), a new party founded in 1907, used the momentum to call for a general strike against the government. This led to a general anti-clericalist revolt, of which the outcome was the burning of twenty-one churches and forty convents (Ulman, 1968). Maura was dismissed as prime minister.

In 1910, José Canalejas became the new prime minister. He attempted to incorporate the working class into the *turno pacifico* system by making social concessions, similar to what the Italian Prime Minister Giovanni Giolitti tried to do in Italy. This policy of accommodation failed completely, because of the growing number of strikes and working-class mass organisation. He was assassinated in November 1912. Canalejas's 2 years in government achieved only little to improve the image of the decaying Canovite political system. The last years before the First World War clearly showed signs of demise and impossibility of reform. The two prime ministers before 1914 were appointed by the king, without conducting elections.

During the War social uprisings and discontent increased considerably. The political order was steadily undermined by the new social movements of republicanism, socialism and anarchosyndicalism. Moreover, the Spanish Cortes was suspended several times. Between 1917 and 1923, the Restoration system was confronted with several challenges imposed by the First World War and upcoming militant social movements. Political violence was mainly undertaken by the anarchosyndicalist movement, the National Confederation of Labour (*Confederación Nacional del Trabajo* – CNT), which was founded in 1910 and became the strongest working-class movement both in Catalonia as well as in Andalusia (Casas, 1986: 47–67; Maurice, 1990). On the eve of the collapse of the Restoration system the CNT was the strongest movement with 750,000 members and a major force in destabilising the political system. They clearly surpassed the more moderate socialist General Workers' Union (*Union General de Trabajadores* – UGT) and the Spanish Socialist Workers' Party (*Partido Socialista Obrero Español* – PSOE) in terms of membership. In this period Spain experienced fifteen governments, the growing political apathy of the electorate and the recurrence of violent politics.[3] The Russian Bolshevik Revolution of October 1917 was a major catalyst for similar revolutionary situations in many European countries such as Germany, Italy and, naturally, Spain. The so-called *triennium bolchevista* between 1918 and 1921 contributed to the creation of the myth of the 'red scare' among the upper-middle classes. Indeed, the centre of the *triennium bolchevista* was Barcelona, the capital of Spanish anarchosyndicalism. The Catalan upper bourgeoisie felt threatened during this period of turmoil and instability and advocated a radical authoritarian solution to deal with the revolutionaries.

After November 1917 the new captain-general of Barcelona clearly used a policy of white terrorism to crush the anarchosyndicalist revolt. In spite of that, anarchosyndicalist violence and terrorism did not stop. Indeed, in March 1921, Prime Minister Dato was assassinated, creating further tensions in the late phase of the Restoration system. This was further exacerbated by a disaster in Morocco, where Spanish forces were defeated by the Kabyle population (*Riff*) in 1921 after a decade of exhaustive efforts to keep control of the country. The humiliation of the military led to recriminations by the political class which clearly wanted to attribute responsibilities for the debacle. The growing discontent on the part of the military paved the way to the successful coup d'état of General Miguel Primo de Rivera, who clearly was able to count on the support of King Alfonso XIII, similar to what happened in Italy in 1922 when King Victor Emmanuel asked Mussolini to form a government. The conservative system of the *turno pacifico* came to an end due to a *pronunciamiento* on 12 and 13 September 1923 of General Primo de Rivera. From the beginning he established an authoritarian developmental dictatorship.

The dictatorship of Miguel Primo de Rivera (1923–31)

The political model of General Primo de Rivera was related to the modernisation of Spain. He was supported by the upper-middle classes of Catalonia and Madrid. He proclaimed himself the iron surgeon who would cure Spain from all its vices and diseases in analogy with the ideas of Joaquin Costa. It attempted to promote economic development, by preserving a Spain of small towns and wealthy farmers. It became the best example of a development dictatorship which established high protectionist tariffs to protect Spanish industry and agriculture. It also developed a vast programme of public works to curb internal demand. In this period, Primo de Rivera was successful in integrating the leaders of the socialist General Workers' Union (*Unión General de Trabajadores* – UGT) into the political system. So-called *comités paritários* (parity committees) gave voice to working-class representatives intended to build up a corporatist form of interest intermediation. The intention was to establish an harmonious society and overcome class conflict (Martin, 1990). Indeed, the political system tended to support the grievances of workers against their employers creating at some stage alienation from the dictatorship. He founded a single party, the Patriotic Union (*Unión Patriotica* – UP) which in 1927 had over 1.3 million members, but then declined to 700,000 in 1929 (Ben-Ami, 1983: 384). The UP, the military and the Church became the three pillars upon which Primo de Rivera's dictatorship was built. Although Primo de Rivera was originally very keen to fight against clientelism, patronage and corruption established by the political class of the former constitutional monarchy, he soon replaced it by one centred around the military and the UP (Ben-Ami, 1983: 90–4, 133–8). Although Primo de Rivera was able to get a National Assembly approved by the king on 5 September 1927, which consisted of personally appointed people close to the UP and representatives of the main institutions of society, he was not able to make a case for his new constitution. King Alfonso XIII wished to get rid of the dictator, and Primo Rivera resigned and went into exile in late 1929. Primo de Rivera died some months later alone in a hotel in Paris (Ben-Ami, 1983: 389–92). After his death General Berenguer attempted to return to the Canovite constitution of 1876 by dismantling the whole state established by his predecessor, but without success. On 14 April 1931 the king, who had supported the regime of Primo de Rivera, decided to leave the country.

The Second Republic and the Civil War (1931–39)

The Second Republic was proclaimed on a wave of hope and optimism. It was called *la niña bonita* (the pretty girl). The imagery of the failed First Republic had faded away completely. In the local elections of 12 April 1931, the Republicans received an overwhelming majority. This started the process towards the Second Spanish Republic. The Republic can more or less be divided into three main periods. The first period can be characterised as the 2 years of reforms (*bienio de reformas*, 1931–33), the second period as the 2 black years (*bienio negro*, 1934–36) and the third period the Popular Front government of 1936. The Second Republic was defeated in 1939 by the Nationalist victory in the Spanish Civil War.

The first 2 years were controlled by the Republican left which attempted to implement an ambitious reform programme in the education, social policy and agricultural fields. The Republican elite was quite intolerant of any party that wanted to challenge the Republican constitution. This so-called *bienio de reformas* (biennium of reforms, 1931–33) was replaced by a *bienio negro* (black biennium, 1934–36) which targeted the reversal of the social reforms introduced previously by the Republican left. The constitution was highly anti-clerical as were the first governments under the Republican left. Indeed, a special law of defence of the Republic was approved by the Cortes which permitted the persecution of anybody who publicly uttered opinions or conducted actions against the Republic. This law was very much influenced by the Law for the Defence of Democracy introduced in 1925 by the Weimar Republic in Germany. This naturally led to the persecution of right-wing parties. The Republican Left's 2 years of reforms were quite ambitious. These included the separation of Church and state, severe restrictions on Catholicism by an aggressive policy of closing down Catholic private schools, the extension of public education, an aggressive land reform, a major reform of the armed forces and regional autonomy. The end results of these first 2 years were not very positive, because policies tended not to be well thought out. They tended also to alienate potential moderate centre-right supporters of the Republic. The most impressive part of the reforms was the expansion of public education sector by more than 10,000 schools across the country. These were naturally small schools with low resources and not very well-paid staff. Nevertheless, they represented the will of the Republican government to raise the levels of education of the population, due to the fact that, in 1930, 25 per cent of the country was still illiterate. Regional autonomy was conceded to Catalonia on 9 September 1932, but not to the Basque Country (Payne, 1993: 81–125).

Growing opposition was mounting to the pace of reforms and the one-sided position of the government of Manuel Azaña. This led to the development of right-wing party organisations influenced by the Zeitgeist dominated by fascism and corporatism. The more moderate Confederation of the Autonomous Right (*Confederación de las Derechas Autonomas* – CEDA) became the pivotal organisation to change the political climate towards the right. In the early elections of November 1933, the CEDA became a major player in the government. After a phase of parliamentary support of a radical republican government under the leadership of Alejandro Lerroux, it joined the coalition in October 1934. Three ministers became part of the Lerroux government, which led subsequently to the left-wing insurrection of 4–5 October 1934 in different parts of the country, particularly in Catalonia and Asturias. In Catalonia, Lluis Campanys, the President of Generalitat, proclaimed the independence of the Catalan state leading to major violence throughout the region. In Asturias, the miners started an insurrection on 4 October which lasted until the twentieth of the same month. The insurrection led to 1,200 fatalities. This insurrection of 1934 was regarded as one of the seeds of the forthcoming Civil War of 1936 (Payne, 1993: 200–23; Diaz-Nosty, 1976). The consequences were the suspension of Catalan autonomy and growing polarisation between left and right. Throughout 1935 the previous Republican reforms were either modified or nullified. Moreover, government instability continued to be a major feature of the political system leading to six governments throughout the year. In the end, early elections had to be called for in 1936. The legislative elections of 16 February 1936 led to an overwhelming victory of the left which was campaigning as a united Popular Front. The whole process of transition from the previous to the new government was done very hastily without waiting for the final results 3 days later. It showed the inability of the political elites from the different ideological sides of the spectrum to cooperate. This was reinforced by a growing level of political violence originating from right-wing and left-wing paramilitary groups. Moreover, results were altered in favour of the left by a very arbitrary electoral review committee (*comisión de actas*) set up to look at irregular cases during the legislative elections (Payne, 1993: 296–300). Again, the tendency of the Republican governments was to tolerate the violence of left-wing groups such as the anarchosyndicalists and hit hard at the right-wing groups such as the Falange of José Antonio Primo de Rivera, the eldest son of the former dictator. The consequence was a growing discontent of the military. In order to reduce the contagious nature of political violence, newspapers were censored without success. Between May and July the situation became quite unbearable. The number of political killings was rising by the day. Indeed, shortly before the military uprising under General Francisco Franco, José Calvo Sotelo, a major leader of the monarchist right, was assassinated by a member of the Republican Assault Guard on 13 July 1936 (Payne, 1993: 324–57). Six days later, the military uprising started the Civil War. In the period between

14 April 1931 and 18 July 1936, the beginning of the Civil War, the Republic experienced nineteen cabinets and eight prime ministers. The average duration of the cabinets was 101 days (Linz, 1994: 171). The legislatures were unstable, because only about 7 per cent of the members of parliament were re-elected to all three legislatures of the Second Republic (Linz, 1994: 170). The overall number of political killings, according to Stanley Payne, was 2,225 (1993: 362). The lessons of the failure of the Second Republic were learned by the political elite of the transition to democracy between 1975 and 1978. All parties used moderate and compromising language to achieve a consensual settlement which led to today's Spanish Constitution.

The uprising led by General Franco in July 1936 started off a Civil War, which lasted until his victory in April 1939. The Civil War itself between the right-wing Nationalists supporting General Franco and the Republicans supporting the legitimacy of the Second Republic was not only a bloody war between the two Spains; beyond that, it was an international war, a prelude to the Second World War. The intervention of Italy and Nazi Germany on behalf of Franco contributed to the internationalisation of the conflict. In different countries, particularly France, several combatants joined the forces of the Republic in the so-called International Brigades. It became a symbol of the struggle of republican democratic Europe against the rise of the authoritarian and totalitarian regimes. Of the many combatants of the International Brigades, one has to mention George Orwell and Ernest Hemingway whose work was shaped by this conflict. The Civil War lasted 3 years. Until early 1937, the Nationalists had one-third of Spanish territory under their control. With the help of the German and Italian air support, they were able to move forward and to gain the western part of the country. By early 1938, they had conquered the northern provinces including the Basque Country. Pablo Picasso painted an extraordinary testimony to this with his *Guernica* featuring the bombing of this hallowed town of the Basque Country (26 April 1937). Throughout 1938, Nationalist troops were able to make gains against the Republican government which was now confined to Catalonia and Madrid. Nevertheless, by March 1939 the Nationalists had finally taken Barcelona and an uprising in Madrid put an end to Republican control of the capital (Bernecker, 2002: 167–8; Thomas, 1984; Brenan, 1995: 316–40).

From authoritarianism to restoration of democracy

The legacy of authoritarianism (1939–75)

The regime of General Franco after the Civil War was very much influenced by Primo de Rivera's dictatorship. The only major difference was that Franco did not intend, at least in the beginning, to restore the monarchy. Many of the ideological foundations had been developed during the Second Republic, but Franco himself was not an ideologue. He was interested in maintaining his power. Therefore, the first measures of Francoism were directed towards the creation of a totalitarian state, which culminated in a policy of elimination of his enemies. He pursued a policy of hunting down and exterminating all Republican enemies, who were all regarded, without differentiation, as communists.

The rebuilding of the country was the primary task of the dictator, who was internationally isolated. Therefore, Franco adopted an autarkic economic policy. This first phase of Francoism lasted until 1953. The only major ally Franco could count on was Portuguese dictator António de Oliveira Salazar, who had been in power in Portugal since 1932. Both signed an Iberian pact in 1943 in order to protect the Iberian peninsula against eventual enemies. The relationship of Franco to the axis powers Germany and Italy cooled also, and he was able to keep Spain out of the European conflict.

In this first phase, Franco was also very keen to reduce the power of eventual challengers to his newly gained power. The loyal right-wing opposition, particularly the Falange, was streamlined by the dictator. Although the Falange became the single party of the regime, after 1945 Franco forced it to merge with other political forces that were supportive of the dictator into a new broader Francoist Party. The so-called National Movement (*Movimiento Nacional* – MN) founded in 1956 was a way to neutralise the ambitions of the radical Falange and other right-wing groups (Ellwood, 1987: 95–8; Robinson, 1975: 19).

The regime was naturally supported by the Catholic Church, which was one of the most intransigent national churches until the 1960s. It was difficult to introduce the reforms of the second Vatican Council in Spain. Franco used very much national Catholicism established by the Catholic monarchs to legitimise his regime. National Catholicism prevented dissent within the Catholic organisation. Apart from the Church and the single party, he relied naturally on the military. Throughout the period of the dictatorship one could see how Franco remunerated the upper echelons of the military with positions of power in the state sector.

In constitutional terms, Franco never drafted a new constitution. Instead, several Fundamental Laws were approved which structured the political system. The most important of them was the succession of the Chief of State, which became the main document legitimising the succession of King Juan Carlos I after his death on 20 November 1975. Other Fundamental Laws were on the Principles of the National Movement (1958), on Labour (1938/1967), on the Spanish People (1945/1967), on the Referendum (1945) and on the Establishment of the Cortes (1942/1946/1967). In some way, Franco moved towards the idea that the dictatorship was a prelude to a new monarchy.[4] This is the reason why Prince Juan Carlos, son of the legitimate heir to the throne of Spain Don Juan, Count of Barcelona, was educated and prepared as successor by Franco. The Cortes was transformed into a rubber stamp parliament within the majority appointed procuradores. Twenty per cent were elected by the heads of families. It meant that elections under the authoritarian regime were controlled by Franco.

In some way, he neutralised the right-wing revolutionary dynamics of political groups, which saw the military dictatorship as a prelude to the establishment of a genuine fascist state.

Indeed, it was Franco's general tendency to de-fascistise the state after the end of the Second World War, which contributed also to the beginning of an opening up to the international community, in particular to to the United States. One has also to understand that the policy of economic autarky was contributing to poverty and stagnation of the Spanish economy. It was essential to integrate the country into the international economy without giving up on political power. After 1948, the world became bipolar. The United States and the Soviet Union were now fierce enemies initiating the period of the Cold War. This was a fortunate coincidence for Franco, who clearly was a fierce anti-communist and agreed with the new international relations of the American establishment. The alliance with the United States allowed for international integration and US financial support for the development of the country. Spain became a full member of the United Nations in 1955. Before that, Spain received a grant of US$ 86.5 million from the Import-Export Bank of the United States and by end of September 1953 economic relations between the United States and Spain were established via a Hispano–American agreement, the so-called *Pactos de Madrid* (Powell, 1995: 22–6).

This steady conversion of the economy experienced its climax during the 1960s. A new elite of technocrats was recruited from the Opus Dei, a religious organisation close to the Catholic Church, which propagated the idea of building up elitism based on Catholic principles and values. These technocrats promoted the ideology of *desarollismo* (developmentalism) which clearly gave priority to the quantitative exponential growth of the economy. On average, the yearly growth of the gross national product of Spain was around 7 per cent, the yearly productivity rate 6 per cent and national income per capita rose from 400 in 1961 to US$ 2,000 in 1974 (Bernecker, 1984: 124).

This industrialisation and modernisation of the economy could be characterised as a Spanish miracle. Within two decades major social transformations took place. The decline of the agricultural sector, emigration from the rural regions to the main urban centres and several European countries such as the United Kingdom, Belgium, Switzerland and Germany, and the expansion of the working and middle classes contributed to a complete transformation of the social structure upon which the Francoist political system relied.[5] The Minister of Information, Manuel Fraga Iribarne, liberalised also the media sector with a new press law in 1966 (Law of 18 March 1966). Media, tourism, emigration and rising living standards contributed to the erosion of the social support for the regime. In the mid-1970s the political structure no longer matched the more complex structures of the economy and society. Finally, the economic and social transformation required a political transformation. Protest and dissent in civil society expanded in the late 1960s and 1970s. In particular the working class, supported by the trade union movement, and the students spearheaded the new political culture against Francoism (Maravall, 1978; Lopez Pina and Aranguren, 1976). The number of political strikes, political demonstrations and dissent increased in this period. The dissent of the working class came principally from the classic centres of left-wing dissent of the Second Republic such as Asturias, Barcelona, the Basque Country and Madrid (Maravall, 1978: 48–54). Moreover, the regionalist movements in Catalonia and the Basque Country were able to gather momentum before Franco's death. In the Basque Country, a terrorist organisation Basque Country and Freedom

(*Euskadi ta Askatasuma* – ETA) created major problems for the regime. The violent acts against prominent members of the regime contributed to political instability. The assassination of the number two in the regime, Prime Minister Admiral Luis Carrero Blanco, by a car bomb in Madrid in December 1973 was a major blow for Franco. It led to the execution of several ETA members and to negative publicity for the regime in the world community. In Catalonia, the regionalist forces organised meetings resisting the policies of centralisation of the government. Economically, the situation in Spain was deteriorating due to the oil crisis of 1973. Similar to other European countries, the boom of the 1960s came to an abrupt halt (Carr and Fusi, 1979).

The death of General Franco on 20 November 1975 led to the end of the moribund authoritarian dictatorship. It opened the way towards democratisation, similar to what had happened in Portugal and Greece in the previous year.

The Spanish transition to democracy (1975–82)

In many ways, the Spanish transition to democracy was extremely influenced by the negative Portuguese experience. On 25 April 1974, a coup d'état led to a revolutionary situation in Portugal. For a year and a half Portugal was in a situation of turmoil and political instability. The whole process of transition to democracy was dominated by the Portuguese Armed Forces Movement (MFA), which was split into different factions with different views fragmented on the future of democracy in the country. The political elite was subaltern to the whole revolutionary process. Only after the founding elections of 25 April 1975 and support from the international community did Portugal move towards a constitutional settlement and a liberal democracy. The Spanish political elite was very keen to avoid such a situation of revolutionary turmoil and instability (Cervelló, 1993: 331–412). Instead, the transition to democracy in Spain became known as a *ruptura pactada* (pacted break) between the Francoist political elites and the main opposition parties (Share, 1987). The smooth succession from Franco to Juan Carlos I helped to prevent a revolutionary situation and move towards an evolutionary consensual solution. Although Prime Minister Arias Navarro, the successor of Carrero Blanco, was confirmed in his position by King Juan Carlos, it soon became evident that he was unable to lead a process towards opening up and democratisation. By July 1976 the king appointed Adolfo Suarez, who clearly was a man of the regime and this led to major disappointment among the forces who wanted a democratisation of the regime. In reality, Suarez became a clever operator in terms of bringing together the Francoist political elites who wanted *aperturismo* (opening up) and democracy, and the opposition parties, which wanted an end to the regime and the move towards democratic conditions.

The main opposition groups were led by the Communist Party (*Partido Comunista Español* – PCE) and the Socialist Workers' Party (*Partido Socialista Obrero Español* – PSOE). In early 1976, both had formed the Democratic Junta (*Junta Democrática*) and the Democratic Platform (*Plataforma Democraticá*) respectively with other smaller parties and trade union organisations. They decided to join forces by creating Democratic Coordination (*Coordinación Democraticá*). Although the opposition was able to confront the Francoist political elites as a united front, the divergences between Communists and Socialists remained a major difficulty throughout the transition process. Among the Francoist elites, the most supportive of the whole process was the *tácito* group. Already before the death of the dictator, they had established contacts with the major opposition parties. They clearly contributed massively towards the dialogue between regime and opposition. Adolfo Suarez's government consisted overwhelmingly of members of the *tácito* group. Their main objective was to achieve the transition towards democracy by legal means (Powell, 1990: 263–4). This led to the elaboration of a Law of Political Reform, which was presented to the Francoist Cortes. Basically, Suarez was asking the Cortes to dissolve itself and allow for the election of a Constituent Assembly, which would draft a new constitution. It also defined the design of the new Cortes as being bicameral and elected by universal suffrage. This was overwhelmingly approved by the Cortes in October 1976. In a referendum in December 1976, the law was also approved by the population with 94.2 per cent of the vote. The highest levels of abstention were registered in Catalonia and the Basque Country.

The most difficult problem that Prime Minister Adolfo Suarez had to tackle was the legalisation of the Communist Party. The military hierarchy regarded this as a provocation. The anti-communist nature of the regime was challenged by the Suarez government. The memory of the Civil War prevented many higher-ranking officers from accepting this necessity for the democratisation of the regime. Indeed, they regarded democratisation with suspicion. Suarez tried to achieve the legalisation by a judiciary ruling, but this was refused, so that he had to legalise the Communist Party by decree in April 1977.

The elections to the Constituent Assembly on 15 June 1977 led to a victory of Suarez's party, the Democratic Centre Union (*Unión del Centro Democrático* – UCD), which got 39.9 per cent of the vote. The PSOE received 28.8 per cent and the PCE only 9.2 per cent. The more conservative faction of the authoritarian regime formed the People's Alliance (*Alianza Popular* – AP) which achieved only 8.2 per cent of the vote. This naturally was a vote for the moderate parties, against the more extreme ones. The result for the Communist Party was regarded as quite interesting, because everybody assumed that they would do better due to their established party organisation in relation to the Socialist Party. Apart from these main parties, regionalist parties and other smaller parties were also represented.

The constitutional settlement became a central issue for Suarez's government. After a conflictive violent history bound up with ill-designed or imposed constitutions, this was the first time the main Spanish forces were able to negotiate and find common ground on all aspects of the constitution. The consensualism presented throughout the Spanish constitutional settlement contributed to a new political culture, which was to become essential for the organisation of politics after approval of the constitution. Two main issues were at stake, which were only partially resolved in the previous constitutional settlements. These were the form of government, republic or monarchy, and the organisation of the country, unitary or decentralised. In the end, after long deliberations and negotiations, the Spanish constitution became a historical compromise. Indeed, Spain became a monarchy, but it would submit completely to popular sovereignty. This meant that the monarch had only formal powers of representation and appointment. The centre of legitimacy shifted to the Cortes. This naturally led to the establishment of a republican monarchy. Moreover, the monarchy was not supposed to be a continuation of the Bourbon monarchy which finished abruptly in 1931, but a new restored monarchy.

On the second issue, related to the organisation of the country, a further compromise was reached, allowing for a limited autonomy of the historical regions Catalonia, the Basque Country and Galicia, but also the possibility through referendum to establish new autonomies. The so-called state of autonomies (*estado de autonomias*) was a concession to the Francoist elites, which were afraid of a disintegration of the unity of Spain. Soon after the constitution was approved by the Cortes and overwhelmingly by a referendum on 6 December 1978, a dynamic process of creation of autonomies took place. By 1983, there were seventeen autonomous communities (*Comunidades Autonomas* – CCAA) which clearly were and are a major contribution to the democratisation of the country.

Economically, Suarez was able to bring the main parties together to accept austere economic measures to put the Spanish economy back on track. This was done by the *Pactos de Moncloa* which were signed by the main parties with the tacit support of the main trade union confederations, the General Workers' Union (*Unión General de Trabajadores* – UGT) and the Workers' Commissions (*Comisiones Obreras* – CCOO). The pact included limitation of wage increases for the year 1978 to 20 per cent, when the index of consumption prices did not exceed 25 per cent. These measures led to the fall of inflation to 16.5 per cent in 1978 and 15.6 per cent in 1979, but unemployment rose considerably and the economic growth declined from 3.1 per cent to 1.5 per cent in this period (Antoni, 1981: 183; Gunther, Sani and Shabad, 1988: 124–6; Share, 1986: 30).

In the legislative elections of 1979, Suarez's UCD was able to win again with 35 per cent. Nevertheless, the PSOE was able to improve its share of the vote to 30.5 per cent, making it a real contender. Both the PCE and AP were not able to change their small party status. Between 1979 and 1982, Spain experienced a difficult period which was characterised by a weak economic situation with rising unemployment prospects, growing left-wing, right-wing and Basque terrorism and the rumours of a potential coup d'etat by the military. Already in 1978 the government had discovered a military conspiracy called *Operación Galaxia*. The possibility that such an attempt could happen again was a major concern for the government (Agüero, 1995). Although the government committed the UGT and the CCOO to sign a National Agreement on Employment (*Acuerdo Nacional de Empleo* – ANE) leading to freezing of wage increases to a figure lower than inflation, unemployment still continued to rise.

The resignation of Prime Minister Adolfo Suarez and his replacement by Leopoldo Calvo Sotelo could only be understood as a reaction to the process of disintegration of the UCD, which clearly collapsed during 1981. On 23 February 1981, before Calvo Sotelo could be invested as the new prime minister,

Colonel Antonio Tejero stormed the Cortes and held the members of parliament hostage. Tejero tried to gain support for his action from other garrisons of the country and the king. Nevertheless, it is to the credit of King Juan Carlos that he stood firm in support of democracy and ordered the insurgents to give themselves up. Soon, Tejero had to surrender. This was the crucial moment for the full acceptance of democracy by the Francoist military bunker (Powell, 2001: 292–320).

One major factor that led to the uprising was the growing demands of the regionalist-nationalist parties. The devolution process acquired a dynamic of its own. Still under the government of Adolfo Suarez, both the UCD and the PSOE supported the Law for the Harmonisation and Ordering of the Autonomy Process (*Ley Organica de Armonización del Proceso Autonómico* – LOAPA) in June 1981, which foresaw a restrictive interpretation of the Basque, Catalan and Galician statutes and reduced considerably the powers of the regional parliaments, making them highly dependent on the Cortes in Madrid in terms of legislation. This naturally led to generalised protest among the representatives of the autonomous communities (Graham, 1984: 262–5; Newton, 1983: 124–5, 127–9).

The new Calvo Sotelo government was not able to halt the disintegration of his party, which relied too much on the governmental structures. This was reinforced by a general feeling of disenchantment (*desencanto*) with the politicians and the political situation. In the October elections of 1982, the UCD vote collapsed to 6.8 per cent, while the PSOE was able to achieve an absolute majority of 48.2 per cent. Many UCD voters chose the Socialists and the AP. The latter was able to improve its share of the vote to 26 per cent. The vote of PCE also collapsed – to 4.1 per cent (Caciagli, 1993; Huneeus, 1985; Hopkin, 1993).

The politics of patrimonial socialism: the Spanish Socialist Workers' Party in power (1982–96)

The leader of the PSOE, Felipe Gonzalez, entered the electoral campaign with the slogan of change (*cambio*). Already in 1979, he was able to push the party towards a more moderate stand. Indeed, he persuaded the party to abandon a dogmatic position towards Marxism. His main intention was to broaden the appeal of the party towards the new middle classes. The strategy of Gonzalez clearly paid off, because the party was able to stay in power for 14 years. The agenda of the PSOE was one of reform, particularly in the education sector, defence, health and women's affairs.

The absolute majority allowed the party to implement most of the reforms throughout the 1980s. Although the PSOE was keen to reinforce redistributive policies, it clearly learned from the mistake committed by other Socialist governments which tried to achieve reforms far too fast. The best example was the French Socialist government which pursued nationally oriented policies and tried to counteract against the internationalisation and globalisation of the economy. The emergence of the Thatcherite paradigm of neoliberalism discredited considerably the French Socialists by 1983 (Sassoon, 1996: 552).

The strategy of the PSOE was to open up Spanish markets to competition, but at the same time restructure the main parts of the economy. Such a strategy was quite risky after decades of protectionism by the Francoist regime, but it followed very much the growing importance of the neoliberal approach. After a first phase of opening up, there was hope that the dividends of such an endeavour could finance redistributive policies. This economic strategy was quite important, because Spain wanted to become a full member of the European Community. The quest for competitiveness was quite important for the PSOE. They hoped that they could gain access to the emerging markets of Latin America (Boix, 1996). In spite of a restructuring of the public industrial sector, the policies of the Socialist Party did not lead to a fall in unemployment. In fact, unemployment remained high between 17 and 23 per cent throughout this period. In spite of early support by its sister trade union organisation UGT, by 1986 disenchantment with the party was growing rapidly (Gillespie, 1990).

Major reforms of the PSOE helped to democratise the country. Among them, one has to include the reform of the higher education sector, which was now opened up. Low-income families were able to receive scholarships to send their children to university. Moreover, the health sector expanded considerably. The PSOE was also very keen to improve the situation of women in society after decades of the repressive Francoist regime, which idealised the paternalist family. A system of benefits and an extension of rights, including the establishment of public clinics for abortion, was set up to strengthen their role in Spanish society.

Internationally, Gonzalez gave a new status to Spain. After decades of isolation, Spanish foreign policy and diplomacy became quite expansive and dynamic. Spain was very keen to strengthen its links with the Spanish-speaking Latin American countries. Finally, after years of concerted negotiation the first Ibero–American summit took place in 1991. Eleven such meetings have been held since then (Grugel, 1995: 144–5).

The most delicate issue was related to Spain's membership in the North Atlantic Treaty Organisation (NATO). Although the Socialist Party fought the elections of 1986 on an anti-NATO ticket, Gonzalez organised a referendum on membership in 1986, which was held in a climate of strong anti-Americanism. During the campaign he supported the continuation of membership, which was followed by an overwhelming 'yes' by the population (Rodrigo, 1995: 53–63).

A key event for the prospects of Spanish democracy was naturally the integration into the European Community/European Union (EC/EU) on 1 January 1986. The relationship between Spain and the European Union started in the 1960s, but the nature of the regime prevented the country's full membership. Spain was only able to achieve a free trade agreement with the European Community/European Union up to 1977. In 1977, Adolfo Suarez submitted Spain's application to the European Community/European Union.

After a favourable response by the European Commission and support by the Council of Ministers negotiations were started. The main adversary of Spain's membership was France, which saw Spanish membership as a major competitor in the agricultural sector. It took almost a decade to sort out all aspects of Spain's bid for entry. Nevertheless, on 12 June 1985 Spain became a full member of the European Union (Pereira Castañares and Moreno Juste, 2002). Naturally, Felipe Gonzalez's government had to sacrifice many items on the wish list to achieve the agreement of the French to Spain's accession. In a first period until 1992, one has to acknowledge that Spain was not able to benefit completely from accession. This changed only after 1992, when Spain became a hard bargainer in the Edinburgh summit along with the southern European countries, Germany and Ireland in relation to the doubling of the structural funds, the so-called Delors II package.

During Gonzalez's ministry two presidencies of the Council of the European Union were held by Spain. In 1989, Gonzalez pushed forward issues of the so-called Social Europe leading up to the Charter of Fundamental Workers' Rights. This was quite a prestigious and important achievement for the Spanish government, which wanted to become an active player both in the European integration process as well as on the world stage (Story and Grugel, 1991). The second presidency in 1995 spearheaded an even more ambitious project which was looming for a long time in the foreign ministries of Italy and Spain. In November 1995, Spain organised a major conference in Barcelona which inaugurated the Euro-Mediterranean partnership designed to help improve the situation in the southern rim of the Mediterranean. It was also a socioeconomic strategy to counteract against Islamic fundamentalism and the growing south–north emigration. The so-called Barcelona process is still a major external policy of the EU, though characterised by many problems and challenges (Gillespie, 1997).

Although the Socialist government was able to stay in power until 1996, it became more difficult to sustain an absolute majority from election to election. In the elections of 1986, it was able to achieve 44.06 per cent of the votes without any party being able to challenge the PSOE in power. The second largest party, the AP/CD, was not able to overcome their electorate threshold of 26 per cent. This also became evident in 1989, when the PP received only 25.83 per cent of the votes. Nevertheless, the electoral fortunes of the PSOE began also to wane, because it gathered only 39.55 per cent of the popular vote. Indeed, between 1989 and 1996 the PSOE lost the ability to repeat its absolute majorities. Simultaneously, with the emergence of a new leader in the PP, José Maria Aznar, the electoral fortunes of this second largest party began to change considerably, leading finally to the victory of the PP over the PSOE by 1 per cent in 1996 (Amodia, 1996).

The reasons for the decline of the PSOE during this period are manifold, the main one being the wish of the population for renewed change. The PSOE government was involved in several political scandals related to the abuse of power, corruption and clientelism. An American political scientist, James Petras, called it patrimonial socialism. It meant that the socialist political class was more interested in keeping in power and cultivating its contacts with the financial oligarchy, than improving the social conditions of the population. It also referred to practices of clientelism and corruption which in the end led to a discrediting of the government (Petras, 1990; Petras, 1993). Most of the scandals broke out after the elections of 1989. The most famous one was the case of Juan Guerra, the brother of Deputy Prime Minister

Alfonso Guerra, who was using the official government departments for private dealings. The deputy prime minister's activities naturally had an impact on public opinion which was naturally concerned about unemployment. Another scandal was related to the involvement of the Ministry of the Interior in recruiting Portuguese and French mercenaries to kill family members of alleged ETA terrorists. This naturally led to the suspicion that Felipe Gonzalez was fully aware of this initiative by Minister José Barrionuevo. Gonzalez denied until this day that he knew about this illicit initiative of the CESID, the former Spanish Secret Services (Rubio and Cerdán, 1997).

Other scandals soon amounted throughout the 1990s. Further cases were the misappropriation of funds by Luis Roldán, at that time chief of the Guardia Civil, the corruption of officers in the Spanish National Bank, the intransparency of funds flowing to the PSOE from the private sector and the collapse of the Banesto Bank of Mario Conde, who was strongly protected by leading members of the Socialist Party . This naturally was no longer possible, when it was found out that Banesto was insolvent (Heywood, 1994a; 1995b; Delgado Sotillos and Lopez-Nieto, 1995: 475–6; Jimenez, 1998).

This was naturally reinforced by the fact that the PSOE was not able to solve the main problem of Spanish society – unemployment. Prime Minister Gonzalez was unable to obtain the social partners for a constructive dialogue. This naturally contributed to a deterioration of the Spanish economy. After Alfonso Guerra left government, factionalism inside the party grew considerably leading to infighting between the left-wing supporters of Guerra, the *Guerristas*, and the supporters of Gonzalez, the *renovadores* (Gillespie, 1994).

Alternation in power: the rise of the People's Party after 1996

The rise of the PP as the largest party in Spain was certainly related to this negative image of the Socialist government which had to call early elections in December 1995, when it failed to get the budget bill approved. Gonzalez had to wait until the end of the presidency of the Council of the European Union to allow early elections to take place. Already in October 1995, Convergence and Union (*Convergencia i Unió* – CiU), which was supporting the last Socialist minority government, decided to withdraw support for the PSOE, in fear that the close relationship might jeopardise the forthcoming elections in Catalonia, which was Pujol's main power base. This growing isolation of the Socialists began to be more evident in the elections for the European Parliament in 1994 and in the autonomous communities in 1995, from which the PP emerged as the largest party. In March 1996, PP won the elections by 1 per cent. Although Aznar and his party were ideologically opposed to a further decentralisation by giving more powers to the autonomous communities, in the end the election results forced the leader of the PP to negotiate with the regionalist parties to achieve a stable majority for the new legislative period. This was quite difficult, because during the electoral campaign the PP had attacked vehemently the most important of the regionalist parties, the Catalan CiU. Aznar was then forced to negotiate a consensus formula with these parties. An important mediator was Manuel Fraga Iribarne, the former Minister of Information under Franco, but also president of the Galician Xunta, the regional government of Galicia. It took 3 months to achieve a compromise formula. Although Aznar had to form a minority government, it could now count on the support of most regionalist parties, thus preventing an overdominance of CiU. This deal may be regarded as historical, because it brought the highly centralistic conception of the PP towards a regionalist position. Aznar's government was able to rely on the support of the regionalist parties throughout the full legislature period. In this period, the regionalist catalogue of demands, particularly related to the devolution process in administrative and financial terms, led to an extension of the decentralisation process in Spain (Balfour, 1996; Roller, 2001).

One of the big achievements of the first Aznar government was to revive the social dialogue between the main trade union confederations UGT and CCOO and the main employers' organisation, the Spanish Confederation of Business Organisations (*Confederación Española de Organizaciones Empresariales* – CEOE). The social dialogue led to some social pacts, which clearly targeted the deregulation of the labour market in order to make the Spanish economy more competitive (Magone, 2001: 241–6). In the pursuit of the stability pact, Aznar also froze wage increases and inflation adjustments in public administration leading in 1996 and 1997 to major protests and demonstrations of the relevant trade unions. He also was more radical and consistent in the process of privatisation of public sector firms (Castañer, 1998: 93–100). All these measures led to a considerable improvement of the economy within 1 year. Unemployment decreased considerably. In the late 1990s, the rate of unemployment had fallen from 17–23 per cent to 13–15 per cent. Nevertheless, one problem of the Spanish economy remained: the low level of research and development investment in the Spanish economy. Investment in research and development continued to be among the lowest of the European Union. This meant that Aznar was not able to develop policies counteracting the low investment culture of business enterprises and the country remains extremely dependent on direct foreign investment (Magone, 2001: 197–9).

One of the major problems of the first term in office was the revived terrorism of ETA. Although it declared a ceasefire during 1998, by December 1999 it had started a new terror campaign against political representatives of the two main parties in the Basque Country and in other autonomous communities. Such a terror campaign not only led to the stronger resolve of the government to fight against Basque terrorism in its entirety, but Aznar could count on the support of the population which went several times on the streets of the main towns in their millions shouting the slogan '*ETA, basta ya*' (ETA, it is enough!) (Gillespie, 1999a; Delgado Sotillos and Lopez-Nieto, 2001: 416–7).

In contrast to the internationalism of Felipe Gonzalez, Aznar was more interested in promoting the Spanish national interest in international relations. Although he participated fully in Ibero–American European Union summits, he was clearly always keen to preserve the national interest. This became evident during the negotiations of the structural funds for the period 2000–06. Aznar was able to secure the largest financial share of the structural funds.

In the 2000 elections, Aznar could present really concrete positive results from his first government. The PSOE was not able to present an alternative to Aznar. Party leader Joaquin Almunia was not charismatic enough to challenge Aznar. Indeed, the PSOE had another candidate as prime minister, Joan Borrell, but he had to withdraw due to corruption charges. In the end, Almunia was a half-hearted solution. He also made the mistake of joining forces with the United Left (*Izquierda Unida* – IU), which consisted of the Communist Party and other smaller parties. The electorate clearly did not like this alliance and voted for Aznar. He achieved an absolute majority, which allowed him to be independent from regionalist parties support. This new situation allowed Aznar to undertake further liberalisation measures of the economy. Nevertheless, the support of the main trade union confederations began to wane, due to the fact that the working conditions of Spanish workers did not improve substantially during the Aznar period.

The mandate of the electorate led to an intensification of the fight against terrorism, which after 11 September 2001 gained even more international support. Policies of the European Union were synchronised from October 2001 to achieve a common European strategy against terrorism. Aznar was able to achieve the support of the PSOE under the new leader José Luis Rodriguez Zapatero. This meant that Aznar added the political wing of ETA (*Herri Batasuna* – HB) and all associated legal activities to the list of illegal organisations. In the summer of 2002, *Herri Batasuna* and several other Basque organisations linked to ETA were forced to close. It was a strategy to cut the financial support of legal organisations to ETA. This naturally led to controversies in the Basque Country within the regionalist-nationalist vote. In particular, the Basque Nationalist Party (*Partido Nacionalista Vasco* – PNV) was able to win the moderate vote in the Basque elections of 13 May 2001 against a growing campaign of Aznar against the whole regionalist-nationalist Basque vote (*El Pais*, 15 May 2001).

Another problem that Aznar solved with a heavy-handed approach was immigration. Spain is one of the countries of the northern Mediterranean coast that is most exposed to illegal immigration from North African countries. The two enclaves of Ceuta and Melilla in Morocco as well as the Canary Islands are a target for illegal immigrants from the whole of Africa. Many immigrants with the help of illegal traffickers cross the Straits of Gibraltar in small boats and reach the Spanish coast and many just die in this attempt. Aznar decided to tighten up the immigration laws (*Ley de Extranjeria*), preventing illegal immigrants from being hired by employers, particularly in the agricultural sector. This was regarded as a means to discourage immigrants to come to the country illegally. The immigration laws led to controversies among civil rights organisations and other civil society organisations.

A further reform was undertaken in the education sector. Aznar's Minister of Education, Pilar del Castillo, herself an excellent political scientist, introduced a bill to reform the higher education sector. The main rationale was to bring the Spanish system closer to those of other European countries. It also wanted a full modernisation of the research culture of Spanish universities, introducing competitive elements in the overall education system. This proposed reform was contested by the students, teachers, the PSOE and the trade union confederations throughout September and December 2001. Nevertheless, Pilar del Castillo was very keen to push through the higher education bill without support from the opposition. The new reforms in the education sector were to be introduced in the academic year 2003–04.

Aznar's decision to join the coalition of the willing in the Iraq War alongside US President George W. Bush and British Prime Minister Tony Blair was quite controversial in Spain. The overwhelming majority of the population was against the War which was felt to be based on flawed reasons. Any military support was also opposed by the opposition parties. The leader of the opposition, José Luis Rodriguez Zapatero, rejected completely the reasons to go to war. In spite of this resistance, Aznar confirmed the Spanish support of the US-led war by taking part in the summit of the Azores hosted by Portuguese Prime Minister José Durão Barroso on March 2003. Spain contributed with troops to the coalition of the willing.

However, in the autonomous communities and local elections the PP was able to contain the losses. Its victory in both the autonomous community as well as the capital city symbolically far offset the real losses in other parts of the country. The most charismatic leader of PP, Alberto Ruiz-Gallardón, run successfully to become mayor of the capital. Although the PSOE won the elections in terms of absolute votes and many other Spanish cities such as Barcelona and Sevilla, they could not disguise their disappointment by not winning Madrid. Moreover, they were not able to get a relative majority in the Community of Madrid, but the PP under the leadership of Esperanza Aguirre was not able to win an absolute majority. Socialist leader Rafael Simancas hoped to form a coalition with the United Left, but they were surprised by a defection of two of their MPs, thus preventing a working majority. It meant that elections for the autonomous community Madrid had to be repeated on 26 October 2003 when the PSOE lost in votes and seats and the PP was able to win an absolute majority and form a government. (Campmany, 2005: 158–62).

One of the main issues within the PP has been the question of the replacement of José Maria Aznar. After Aznar confirmed that he did not intend to be prime minister for more than two legislative periods, speculations started during the party conferences of 2002 and 2003 about who could succeed Aznar as leader. The list of potential successors of Aznar were refined to seven. These were Rodrigo Rato, the former minister of economy and responsible for the good economic situation; Marcelino Mayor Oreja, who had lost of its charisma after being defeated by the nationalist PNV in the Basque elections of October 2001; the Interior Minister Manuel Acebes, Javier Arenas; Eduardo Zaplana, the Spokesman of the government; and the Vice-President of Government Mariano Rajoy. Aznar delayed as long as possible his choice for successor. Finally, on 30 August when he returned from summer holidays he named Mariano Rajoy as his successor. This was confirmed by the executive council on 2 September 2003 (Campmany, 2005: 196–7). Mariano Rajoy started from that moment his campaign in order to catch up in relation to the advanced campaign of the PSOE with its candidate José Luis Rodriguez Zapatero.

Until the end of the year, the elections to the autonomous community of Catalonia became the focus of the main parties. Long-standing Regional President Jordi Pujol of the right-centre nationalist CiU decided to retire after 23 years and his *conceller en cap* (First-Minister), Artur Mas, became the official candidate to succeed him. Although CiU won the elections of 16 November 2003, Artur Mas was not able to achieve an absolute majority. He hoped to form a coalition with the left-wing nationalists, the Catalan Republican Left (Ezquerra Republicana de Catalunya – ERC), which surprisingly decided to form coalition with Pascual Maragall's Socialist Party and the Green–Communist coalition ICV–EUiA. After 1 month of negotiations, a government was formed on 20 December 2003. This was a boost for the Socialist Party, which began to focus on the legislative elections of 2004 (Davis, 2004).

The 2004 elections and the emergence of the Socialist government under José Luis Zapatero

On 9 January 2004, Eduardo Zaplana, spokesman of the Aznar government, announced that the date of the legislative elections would be on 14 March. On 20 January the formal decree of dissolution of the Cortes was issued in order to allow for new elections. The official campaign period for the elections started on 27 February and ended on 12 March 2004. Since Mariano Rajoy was announced as the candidate to the presidency of government in August 2003, the PP has been consistently leading the opinion polls. This lead was between 5–10 percentage points. The distance widened to 10 percentage points, when it was discovered by the newspaper *ABC* that the Lluis Josep Carod-Rovira, the *conceller en cap* of the new Catalan government had met with ETA representatives in Perpignan, France, allegedly to negotiate a deal in which ERC would announce that it supports the right of people to self-determination in exchange for ETA to refrain from terrorist acts in Catalonia. This secret information obtained by the government from the secret service National Centre de Intelligence (*Central Nacional de Inteligencia –* CNI) was allegedly leaked to the press for electoral political purposes by the government in order to gain party political advantage in the forthcoming elections. This led to a major cooling-off of the relations between the intelligence services and the government (Garcia-Abadillo, 2005: 169–73). This led to the resignation of Carod-Rovira after a phone call of Zapatero to regional president Pascual Maragall. However, the gap between the two parties began to narrow during the campaign period. According to Juan Campmany on 8 March 2004 it was a tie between the two main parties, each one with 41 per cent. It seems that after this date the PSOE was leading and shortly before the tragic events of 11 March 2004, opinion polls predicted a win for this party. (Campmany, 2005: 257–60; Lago and Montero, 2006: 8).

The tragic train bombings in Madrid perpetrated by Al Qaeda during the early morning of 11 March 2004 led to an interruption of the electoral campaign.

Although the elections took place on 14 March, on 12 and 13 March parties ceased all party political activities. According to official figures, 191 persons died and 2,000 were hurt. From the start the Aznar government identified ETA as being behind the perpetrated atrocities. Between 11 and 14 March, prominent PP politicians and members of the governments, including Mariano Rajoy, gave this same message. Aznar achieved a condemnation of ETA by the United Nations security council on 11 March and Interior Minister Manuel Acebes was keen to repeat this information. However, it became clear that the way the bombings were organised, the explosives and detonators used and later on a van containing a tape with verses from the Koran pointed to Al Qaeda. The police was investigating this line of enquiry which was ignored by the PP government. This misinformation was an important factor in enhancing the victory of the PSOE on the 14 March elections. On 12 March there were several demonstrations of the population condemning terrorism and the terrorist acts perpetrated in Madrid. The most important was around the Atocha train station. One day later, during the day of reflection in which no campaign publicity should be undertaken, several people went to the main PP offices and protested against the misinformation of the PP. Mariano Rajoy protested against these demonstrations and felt that they were orchestrated by the PSOE.

On 14 March 2004, the PSOE won the elections and José Luis Rodriguez Zapatero became president of government. Although he had only a relative majority, he was able to rely on the regionalist parties and United Left to have a workable majority in parliament. The gap between PSOE and PP had reached five points. According to Ignacio Lago and José Ramon Montero, one factor was that elections are in last instance the most important event to make politicians accountable. This accountability dimension was quite important in the electoral behaviour of Spaniards that day (Lago and Montero, 2006: 24). On the same day, regional elections in Andalucia took place which led to an absolute majority victory of the Socialist Party. This naturally allowed Socialist President Manuel Chaves to govern alone after 8 years of coalition government with the regionalist Andalucian Party (*Partido Andalucista* – PA) (Delgado and Lopez-Nieto, 2005: 1193).

Zapatero's government contrasted heavily with the previous government. One of the first decisions when Zapatero became prime minister in the second half of April was to withdraw the troops from Iraq. This was a fulfilment of a promise he had given to the population in a television interview during the electoral campaign. This decision was overwhelmingly supported by the population and required considerable courage to stand up to pressures from the US President George Bush, and British Prime Minister Tony Blair to stay the course. This decision consolidated the support of the population for the Socialist government. The troops were withdrawn within the next few months. This also led to a cooling of the relations between the Zapatero government and the US administration. Attempts to improve relations by foreign minister Miguel Moratinos were only partially successful.

The introduction of a law allowing same-sex marriages in 2005 was also quite controversial. This led to protests from the Catholic Church and the PP, which argued that marriages were only designed for a man and a woman. In spite of considerable protests across the country, the law was approved with the votes of other left-wing parties. In this sense, Spain became one of the most progressive countries in this issue. It joined a small number of European countries such as the Netherlands (2000), and Germany (2002) and also Canada (2003). Other countries such as France and the United Kingdom improved also the legislation in this matter towards a civil partnership. Similar discussions in Italy led to the collapse of the fragile left-wing coalition of Prime Minister Romano Prodi in 2006–7. After 30 years of democracy Spain became a more secularised country. The population overwhelmingly supported the policies of the government. It showed an increase in tolerance in relation to these issues. The conflict with the hierarchy of the Catholic Church extended to other areas in which the Socialist government wanted to introduce reforms such as the teaching of religion in public schools, further de-penalisation of abortion, fast-track of divorce within 10 days, controlled use of mother-cells and euthanasia. Furthermore, the government was also proposing a change of the funding of the Church by the state, because the present formula was not working (*El Pais*, 8 November 2004, 30–2).

Another controversy was the suspension of the education law introduced by the Aznar government in 2001 which came into force in the academic year 2003–4. The main issue was that the law made a selection of students destined for academic studies or vocational training at an early stage. Moreover, the Socialists proposed a review of the module religion by not making it compulsory and offering alternative modules. There was a major demonstration organised by the Catholic Confederation of Families' Parents and Pupils' Parents (*Confederación Católica de Padres de Familia y Padres de Alumnos* – CONCAPA) on 12 November 2005, in which six archbishops and members of the PP such as former Education Minister Pilar del Castillos took place. The organisation claimed that 2 million people went to the streets, but the official figures of the police were 407,000. (*El Pais*, 13 November 2005, pp. 20–1). The tension between the PSOE and the Catholic Church continued up until the elections of 9 March 2008. The government made attempts to improve the relationship with the Vatican but the tense national situation related to same-sex marriages, the law on education and the fast-track divorce were obstacles to this effect. (*El Pais*, 18 February: 21; *El Pais*, 1 March 2006: 25). In July 2007, the Spanish Episcopal Conference protested against the introduction of a module on citizenship and human rights in the school curriculum as an alternative to the module religion. The conference asked for a boycott of the new module by the associations closed to the Catholic Church. Prime Minister Zapatero contested that Spain is a lay state and aconfessional (*El Pais*, 13 July 2007: 36; 23 July 2007: 22).

One of the pledges of the Socialist Party during the electoral campaign was to achieve a consensus for a revision of the constitution. This was also linked to a review of the statutes of the seventeen autonomous communities. The Zapatero government looked for a consensus with all political parties, but mainly with the PP in order to undertake this revision of the constitution. The Socialist Party was willing to move to a fully fledged federalist model similar to that of the Federal Republic of Germany: this was rejected by the PP. In spite of attempts to revive this issue throughout his term, Prime Minister Zapatero had to concede that such revision was not possible during this term. (*El Pais*, 13 January 2006: 18).

However, Zapatero was quite successful in pushing forward the review of the statutes of the seventeen autonomous communities. For the first time in the history of the new democracy, the prime minister organised a conference with the regional presidents (*conferencia de los presidentes*) in the Spanish Senate on 28 October 2004 and this was quite successful. Any agreement achieved during the meetings was to be converted into law. Among the top priorities was a new model of financing in order to overcome the difficulties caused after the decentralisation of the Spanish National Health Service to the regions, the review of the participation of the autonomous communities in the European Union, including the right to file complaints to the European Court of Justice (*El Pais*, 29 October 2004: 21–7). Between 2005 and 2008, several autonomous communities started major revisions of their statutes (regional constitutions). Probably, the most difficult and controversial was the Catalan statute which the PSOE had to negotiate with the nationalist parties the ERC and the CiU. Such negotiations started during 2005 leading to agreement of the tripartite coalition government in Catalonia and CiU. It was adopted in the Catalan parliament on 30 September 2005 and then sent to the Spanish Cortes for approval. On 2 November 2005, the Cortes decided to accept it with 197 votes against the 146 votes of PP and one abstention. The negotiations in the Cortes led to a further watering-down of the concept of the 'nation' and other articles that were deemed inconstitutional. Finally, on 30 March 2006, it was approved with the votes of all parties, except ERC and PP. Afterwards, it was submitted to a successful referendum on 18 June 2006, in which 50.59 per cent of the electorate abstained, but an overwhelming 73.9 per cent approved it. (*Anuario El Pais*, 2007: 93). Moreover, the tripartite coalition government under new socialist leader José Montilla was able to get an absolute majority in the Catalan elections on 1 November 2006, in spite of the victory of main party CiU. (*Anuario El Pais*, 2007: 96). Although the Basque Country statute was rejected in 2005, the statutes of Valencia, Catalonia and Andalucia were approved by the Cortes during 2006.

All this was part of the dynamics created by the Zapatero government to create a new territorial model in Spain. Some of the statutes were quite unproblematic in terms of their review, such as the one of the Valencian Community, but others led to considerable discussion such as the Andalucian statute which included in its preamble the notion of a historical nationality.

In 2005, regional elections in Galicia and in the Basque Country led to a strengthening of the position of the PSOE which was able to improve by 11.54 percentage points to 33.64 per cent since the last elections in 2001, while the PP declined by 6.74 percentage points to 44.11 per cent, thus losing the absolute majority that the party had since the autonomous community was created. The Galician National Block (*Bloque Nacional Galego* – BNG) got 19.16 per cent and four seats, thus losing 3.94 percentage points and one seat (*Anuario El Pais*, 2006). In Galicia, after the electoral results of 20 June 2005, the Socialists formed a coalition with the nationalist Galician National Block (*Bloque Nacional*

Galego – BNG) and replaced the PP government led by long-standing president, Manuel Fraga Iribarne. Counting of the vote was not completed until one week later, because the result was so close and only the vote of expatriates could change the tie in favour of the PSOE (Diegues and Pinheiro, 2006)

In the Basque Country regionalist elections of 26 September 2005, the nationalist PNV–EA coalition government lost 2.76 percentage points achieving only 40.66 per cent and eleven seats and was only able to hold on to power due to the support of the communist coalition United Left which also lost slightly but could hold on to 5.51 per cent and one seat. The big winner of the elections was the Socialist Party, which was able to improve from 18.06 per cent to 23.45 per cent and increased its number of seats from four to six. In contrast, the big loser was the PP which went from 23.45 per cent to 17.47 per cent and got five seats, one less than in 2001. However, a new political formation called Communist Party of the Basque Country (PCTV–EHAK), in which many sympathisers and politicians of the forbidden party *Batasuna* took part was able to get 9.9 per cent of the vote and two seats. PP regarded PCTV–EHAK as *Batasuna* with a different name and criticised the government for allowing this political formation to take part in elections.

In the regional and local elections of 25 May 2007, the PSOE was able to win the municipal elections with 35.65 per cent against 34.93 per cent of PP. However, the picture was more mixed in relation to the autonomous communities. The PSOE was not able to win in both the autonomous community of Madrid and the city of Madrid, but it made inroads in Navarra, Baleares and Canarias. After the elections, eight autonomous communities were dominated by PP governments and eight by the PSOE. Only the Basque Country had a nationalist government.(*El Pais*, 28 May 2007: 20). In Navarre, there was a possibility for the PSOE to form a coalition with the nationalist party *Nafarroa Bai*, because the Union of the Navarran People (*Union del Pueblo Navarro* – UPN) which is a regional branch of the People's Party, lost the absolute majority. Negotiations broke down in mid-July, because the nationalists did not agree with the coalition formula of the PSN to include independents nominated by both parties. (*El Pais*, 19 July 2007: 16) Therefore, PSN leader Fernando Puras committed himself to support the UPN minority government of Miguel Sanz. (*El Pais*, 24 July 2007: 17). However, at the end of July negotiations between PSN and *Nafarroa Bai* were resumed and in early August an agreement was reached. Due to the previous agreement with the UPN, the national leadership of the PSOE vetoed this late agreement with the nationalists and demanded that the Navarran socialist party give up on the plan to form a government with *Nafarroa Bai*. (*El Pais*, 2 August 2007: 15; 3 August 2007: 15) This decision was taken, because the PSOE wanted to avoid confrontation with the PP and jeopardise its chances in the forthcoming legislative elections in early 2008.

The aftermath of the Madrid bombings on 11 March 2004 was dominated by a reinforcement of the fight against Islamic terrorism. In the Cortes, a committee of inquiry on the bombings of 11 March 2004 was established. This uncovered most of the failings which allowed such tragic events to occur, particularly related to the delayed circulation between the agencies. This led to considerable tensions between the Socialist government and the main party of the opposition, the People's Party (*Partido Popular* – PP). The judiciary and police investigation was directed by judge Juan del Olmo, who was able to discover all the different connections and networks related to the execution of the attacks on 11 March 2004. During 2006 and 2007, the trials of the twenty-nine indicted perpetrators of the Madrid bombings took place, leading to their conviction on 24 July 2007. In October, the twenty-nine convicted perpetrators were given prison sentences between maximum 40 and minimum 7 years (*El Pais*, 25 July 2007: 16).

On 22 March 2005, the Basque Terrorist organisation ETA declared a permanent ceasefire. This was welcomed by the government and 3 months later it agreed to enter negotiations with ETA in order to achieve an end to the violence. They started in October, although there was a considerable opposition by PP and the Association of Terrorism Victims (*Asociación de Victimas del Terrorismo* – AVT). The latter organised demonstrations October and November against the dialogue initiated by the government. Moreover, in the Basque Country the youth movement of ETA continued a campaign of street violence. A bombing of the car park in the Madrid airport Barajas on 30 December by ETA led to the death of two Ecuadorian immigrants, who were working in Spain (*El Pais Anuario*, 2007: 82–3). The Zapatero government had to acknowledge that the whole process of negotiations had come to an end, and would not resume as long as ETA would not give up violence for good. This setback was used by main leader of the opposition Mariano Rajoy to criticise the government as being soft on terrorism. The climax of such policy was when PP declined to take part in demonstrations of solidarity against ETA terrorism on 13 January 2007,which was organised by the National Federation of the Associations of Ecuadorians in Spain (*Federación Nacional de Associaciones de Equatorianos en España* – FENAEE) and joined by the trade union confederations UGT and CCOO and the main the political parties except PP. Demonstrations of over 170,000 and 80,000 took place in Madrid and Bilbao respectively. Moreover, other demonstrations were staged in Zaragoza, Pamplona and Santiago. (*El Pais*, 14 January 2007: 26–36). On 15 January 2007, Prime Minister Zapatero addressed parliament asking for support from the political parties for the anti-terrorism pact, which should also include the Basque Nationalist Party (*Partido Nacionalista Vasco* – PNV). However, main leader of the opposition, Mariano Rajoy was not willing to sign up to this new pact, asking from Prime Minister Zapatero an apology for the mistaken policy of dialogue. (*El Pais*, 15 January 2007: 1, 18–19).

This was also used by Mariano Rajoy in the local and regional elections on 28 May 2007. However, the Zapatero government was able to change this perception by achieving spectacular successes in dismantling the structure of the organisation. The Spanish government was able to rely on a close cooperation with the French security forces which was able to arrest several leaders of ETA in France. According to figures from the French prime minister between the end of the ceasefire of ETA and end of July 17 Etarras were arrested in France. Moreover, the French police was able to dismantle the logistical apparatus which provided weapons and explosives to the commandos of ETA in Aveyron(*El Pais*, 27 July 2007: 14; *El Pais*, 28 July 2007: 14). In spite of these successes, ETA perpetrated a new bombing in the headquarters of the police force Guardia Civil of the Basque Country in Durango nearby Bilbao. Allegedly, they were able to rely on an infrastructure in Portugal to carry out the bombing. A further attempt 2 days later was foiled by the police. (*El Pais*, 25 August 2007: 17; 28 August 2007: 16–17).

Internationally, the Zapatero government was very keen to be at the centre of the European integration process along with Germany and France. The withdrawal of troops from Iraq strengthened the position of the Franco-German alliance, which had opposed the US-led military intervention from the start. Prime Minister Zapatero was more flexible in negotiating the Constitutional Treaty than former Prime Minister Aznar during 2004. The population approved the European Constitutional Treaty in a referendum on 20 February 2005 with an overwhelming majority of 76.96 per cent, in spite of a 41.8 per cent turnout. (Delgado and Lopez Nieto, 2006: 1266) Moreover, Spain was also more flexible in the negotiation of the EU budget for the period 2007–13 at the Brussels European Council of 17–18 December 2005. Spain will be a net payer to the EU budget at the end of the period. Last but not least, Spain was among the countries that supported the efforts of the German presidency under the leadership of Angela Merkel, which took place during the first half of 2007, to revive the Constitutional Treaty by making the appropriate changes in order that it could be approved by national parliaments. This meant also the scaling down of some of the more controversial issues. The Zapatero government was a strong supporter of the Lisbon Treaty, which was agreed under the Portuguese presidency in December 2007. In sum, the Zapatero government followed a very pro-European policy which returned to the approach of dialogue and negotiating flexibility of former Socialist Prime Minister, Felipe Gonzalez. On 9 March 2008, Prime Minister Zapatero and the Socialist Party won the elections with 43.46 per cent and 169 seats, while PP was a close second 40.11 per cent and 153 seats. This result shows how polarised between left and right the country is. The Socialist victory contributed to the further consolidation of Prime Minister Zapatero which was able to form a new single minority government with the parliamentary support of the regionalist parties represented in the Cortes. In contrast, in the PP several leaders such as the president of the Madrid Community Esperanza Aguirre started a campaign to challenge PP leader Mariano Rajoy. However, Rajoy was able to respond successfully to these challenges and remained leader of the party.

Conclusions

The transition to Spanish democratic politics took longer than in most other west European countries. The whole history of Spain was characterised by the struggle to preserve the unity of the country. Spain emerged as a product of empire-building between 1492, the unification of the two main kingdoms of Castile and Aragón and the discovery of America, and 1598, when Philip II died. From then on, the decline of the Spanish empire led to the loss of power and influence of the country in world politics. The disaster of 1898 caused the loss of the last remnants of the empire. In the nineteenth and twentieth centuries, Spain was highly divided in two main groups. On the one hand, the oligarchical group consisting of the Andalusian landowners and the Castilian and Catalan upper classes wanted to keep the democratic experiment at an absolute minimum, while on the other, the new emerging working classes and the middle classes were very keen to promote development towards a genuine democracy. This conflict was only resolved after a bloody civil war and a long authoritarian dictatorship. After the transition to democracy between 1975 and 1978, the new Spain is regarded as an important laboratory of democratic politics. In the past 30 years, Spain was able to move from one of the most centralised and undemocratic countries to one of the most decentralised and democratic polities of the world. This was achieved through long-term policy-making which increased the level of autonomy of the different autonomous communities. Such achievement is a collective effort of successive governments. The governments led by José Maria Aznar until 2004 and José Luis Zapatero have only continued this process which started in the 1970s.

Although Islamic and Basque terrorism have tried to undermine the democratic structures of the country, they were not able to succeed. The solidarity of the population and political parties with the victims of terrorism has contributed to a weakening of both forms of terrorism. Instead, tolerance of otherness has become a central value of the vast majority of Spaniards. The vast majority of the 600,000 Muslim population remains an important part of democratic Spain, thus defying the indoctrinating capacities of Al Qaeda and other radical Islamic organisations. However, there are worrying signs that the ghosts of the past may re-emerge. The polarisation between the two main parties is creating rifts among the Spanish population. The role of the Catholic Church in this respect cannot be underestimated. The recent militant attitude of the Archbishop's Conference in relation to the Zapatero government has created considerable tensions in society. Moreover, the issue of terrorism has been politicised by the major opposition party. The victims of the Civil War on both sides and how to rehabilitate them, have become part of the divisive political discourse. The Church has played a major role in exacerbating this conflict.

In spite of these worrying signs, Spain has created the state of autonomies which has become the worldwide model for the establishment of new democracies. Although many problems remain, Spain is now among the most influential countries of the world.

2 The main features of contemporary political culture

Social change and moderation of Spanish politics

In the past 30 years Spanish society has experienced considerable social changes. According to the Spanish Institute National of Statistics (*Instituto Nacional de Estadística* – INE) between 1975, the year of dictator Francisco Franco's death and 1 January 2006 Spanish population has grown by 8.7 million, giving a total of 44.7 million persons. (*Anuario El Pais*, 2007: 115) Although the birth rate among Spaniards is declining in Spain, as in most countries, immigration has been a major factor to offset the loss of population. Spain is one of the countries with the highest level of immigration along with other west European countries such as the United Kingdom, France, Germany and Italy. On 1 January 2005, 3.7 million were immigrants working and well-integrated in Spanish society; they represented 8.5 per cent of the population. (Fundación Encuentro, 2006: 219). This contrasts heavily with the postwar period during the Franco period, for which Spain was known as a emigration country to the more industrialised countries of Western Europe such as Belgium, Switzerland, the United Kingdom, France and Germany. It is estimated that between 1961 and 1970 1.7 million Spaniards emigrated to western Europe representing at that time 6.3 per cent of the population. Due to the recession of the mid 1970s in most west European countries, emigration declined considerably after 1973–4 (Cazorla-Perez and Montabes Pereira, 1983: 185; Cazes, Domingo and Gauthier, 1985: 76–7). Today, Spain is a destination for immigrants around the world, particularly Latin America and the Maghreb.

Most Spaniards live in the main urban centres or around them. Such a level of urbanisation was due to the migration from the small rural villages to the main urban centres from the 1950s. According to figures from José Cazorla Perez and J. Montabes Pereira there was an internal migration of 6 millions between 1960 and 1975 (Cazorla Perez and Montabes Pereira, 1983: 185; Bradshaw, 1972). Today, many Spaniards living in the main urban centres such as Madrid and Barcelona are moving out to the outskirts. Spain is a highly urbanised country which naturally shapes the way of life of most of its citizens (*El Pais*, 27 July 2002: 24–5) (see Figure 2.1).

One of the main characteristics of the new Spain is the level of moderation in political discourse. In some way, the historical past of violence, political instability

Figure 2.1 Distribution of Spanish population according to autonomous communities – 1 January 2006 in percentages.

Source: Own graph and calculations based on figures from the Spanish National Institute of Statistics (INE) quoted in *Anuario El Pais* 2007: 115.

and conflict influenced the way Spaniards approach politics today. History reminds Spaniards of the human cost that positions of political intransigence may lead to. Urbanisation has led also to the expansion of the education system during the PSOE governments of the 1980s and 1990s. The PP government under José Maria Aznar between 1996 and 2004 continued this concern with the education sector, even if its approach was more conservative and led to major protests from parts of the population in 2003.The Zapatero government also focused on reform of the education sector. However, the proposed reforms particularly the downgrading of the religious module in the school curriculum, found considerable resistance from the Church hierarchy and conservative interest groups such as the Catholic Confederation of Family Pupils' Parents (CONCAPA) which led to tensions with the Church hierarchy, conservative interest groups such as the Catholic Confederation of Family and Pupils' Parents (COCAPA) and the main opposition party PP. This democratisation of education has created a highly educated society which is proud of its institutions. The higher education sector has expanded considerably in the past three decades with public and private universities in all autonomous communities. The opening up of the education sector was an important step towards democratisation of society and was directed against the elitist nature of higher education during the Françoist regime. In some way, the genetic code of the transition to democracy was disseminated and spread within society leading to a more tolerant and peaceful society. The belligerent tendencies of the past are less visible among Spaniards of today, although political subcultures may still emerge from time to time as in the case of the conflict with Morocco, over the Perejil rock off the Moroccan coast, in 2003. The occupation of this small rock by Morocco led to nationalist feelings in the government and some parts of the population. Although it was difficult to assert to whom this rock belonged, this led to major discussions and nationalist sentiment (see Chapter 8), or, as already mentioned, in relation to secondary education and the public funding of Catholic schools. It is seldom that Spaniards become intolerant. However some cases of violent xenophobic outbursts against North African immigrants were registered in Andalusia in El Ejido in 1999, but no right-wing extreme group was able to profit from them. On the contrary, the overwhelming majority of the population votes for moderate parties. There are violent right-wing extremist groups which comprise a tiny number of 10,000 members and are extremely influenced by American co-generis. Volksfront, Honour and Blood and Hammerskin have recruited supporters among the declassés of Spanish society such as the unemployed and the less qualified working-class. They are united by a xenophobic ideology against immigrants, of the supremacy of the white race and of law and order. According to the police, no leader was able to unite the scattered movements so that these movements remained tiny and insignificant. They remain concentrated in certain parts of the country such as Madrid, Catalonia, Castellón, Valencia, Zaragoza and some parts of Castilla-León. Only the Platform for Catalonia (*Plataforma de Catalunya*) was able to achieve representation at council level (*El Pais*, 8 October 2006: 18).

Although the PSOE has been at the forefront of this modernisation, or rather post-modernisation of Spanish policies through targeted policies such as the overcoming of the Francoist patriarchal society by supporting the emancipation of woman through a 'state feminism' which is only known in the Scandinavian countries such as Norway (Valiente, 2000), one cannot ignore the contribution of the PP in this process. The Aznar period between 1996 and 2004 led also to further democratisation, particularly in the development of the state of autonomies. In the end, this has been so far a collective effort of politicians and the population. Although the Church and Catholic interest groups are quite supportive of the PP, the party was able to remain an important moderate alternative on the right-centre, an important balance to many radical reforms of the PSOE. Although tensions and conflicts may emerge between the two main political parties, this has to be regarded as a sign of maturity of Spanish democracy. It means that Spanish politicians are no longer afraid of conflict and have overcome the trauma of the Civil War.

The moderation of Spanish society was very much induced by the consensualism produced by the political elites during the transition to democracy. The cooperation between the opposition and the Francoist elites shaped the way problems were solved during the consolidation and institutionalisation of Spanish democracy. The Spanish model is based on the reconciliation between left and right and the recognition that going back to past forms of behaviour is to go back towards patterns of national self-destruction. The new Spain is learning very much from history, so that it should avoid the mistakes of the past. The creation of a new genetic code became an essential element of creating a moderate political culture and society. As Laura Eddles clearly recognised, in terms of symbol and ritual the transition to democracy represented mainly a new beginning which would lead to democracy through national reconciliation (*convivencia*) and learning from the Civil War of the 1930s, the latter regarded as the symbolic opposite of the intended outcome of the transition. This naturally was not possible without the support of civil society, which already in the 1960s and 1970s was mobilising against Francoism. The evolutionary process towards democratisation was characterised by lack of paramilitary violence, with the exception of the Basque terrorist organisation ETA. This provided the conditions for a dissemination of the basic rules of the politics of consensus (Eddles, 1998: 8, 41–9).

The control of the whole process of transition by the political elites clearly allowed for an evolutionary establishment of the new democracy. Although social movements were active during the transition process, they did not have the same effect as in neighbouring Portugal (Magone, 1996: see Chapter 6). After the end of the transition process, some kind of *desencanto* (disenchantment) and disappointment became widespread leading to a demobilisation of civil society. Indeed, this element is still quite widespread in Spain. The democratisation process did not lead eventually to a stronger active organised civil society. Although civil society returned at different levels of the political system, it is still quite weak to challenge the policy-making process or other decisions taken by the political elites. The demobilisation and weakening of protest behaviour among Spaniards since the 1970s show that moderation and political apathy are becoming major features of Spanish society (Kraus and Merkel, 1998: 57–60; Perez-Diaz, 1993; Rodriguez Ibañez, 1987; Haubrich, 1998).

Similar to other countries Spanish political culture has changed considerably in the past 30 years from an ideological left–right and centre–periphery system of divisions to an instrumental individualised mode of participation (McDonough, Barnes and Lopez Pina, 1998: 166). However, since the beginning of second term of former Prime Minister José Maria Aznar, there are worrying signs of a return of divisions between left and right in Spanish politics and society. The absolute majority government of Prime Minister Aznar adopted a new Education law without the support of the opposition creating the beginning of a polarisation between the two parties. Although both parties agreed on anti-terrorism pact against ETA and its legal and illegal institutional networks and a pact to reform the justice system, the tensions remained high. The re-emergence of the Church as a political actor in this polarisation process further exacerbated the process. The new Zapatero government did not contribute to a dissuasion of the tensions. On the contrary, the adoption of a very radical agenda such as the legalisation of gay marriages, the adoption of fast-track divorces and a new education law in which the module religion lost its compulsory status in the curriculum kept the polarisation between the two main parties at high levels. Also quite relevant was the inability of the opposition to accept the victory of the Socialist party in the 14 March elections of 2004. Particularly, former Prime Minister José Maria Aznar played a major role in discrediting the new government in the United States and in Spain (Baumer, 2007: 153–7). Moreover, the lack of cooperation between the two main parties in relation to finding the truth about the 11 March events, in which 190 people died and almost 2,000 people were injured contributed further to this exacerbation of the discourse.

Probably, the most difficult issue has been the need to recover the historical memory. Many Spanish families still do not know where some of their relatives, who were victims of the authoritarian regime, are buried. These 'forced disappearances' have become the centre of a civil society movement to find out about the whereabouts of many of these victims. This bottom-up social movement is forcing the political class to go a step further in the process of reconciliation by allowing the truth about the Civil War and the authoritarian regime to come out. While democratic transition was designed to suppress conflict between the different ideological families – the so-called *pacto del olvido* (pact of forgetting) made in order to prevent a Civil War – the new bottom-up social movement is keen to have a honest debate and conflict about the authoritarian regime and its crimes. Such a process of reconciliation is similar to those that have happened in South Africa, Chile and other countries.

In an excellent article Georgina Blakeley regards this process towards recovering the historical memory as a new qualitative phase after the conciliation during the democratic transition period. After political conciliation in the 1970s, Spain is experiencing a period of social reconciliation, in which civil society groups want to achieve 'transitional justice' for their own relatives who died during the Civil War, were killed by the authoritarian regime or simply disappeared. Such movement began to emerge in the 1990s and took off in the new millennium. While conciliation establishes a working relationship between two sides, which remain differentiated, reconciliation means the overcoming and solving these differences between these two sides. (Blakeley, 2005: 53). This analysis by Blakeley seems to suggest that at present civil society has already advanced qualitatively one step further than the political class. Over twenty-six mass graves were found up until August 2003. Funding was required in order to make a proper exhumation of the bodies. The former Aznar government refused to allocate funding in the 2003 budget for these purposes, by arguing that this should be done by the local and regional authorities. However, the former Aznar government continued to fund the Francisco Franco foundation, which continued to give a glorified account of the authoritarian regime, and the Ministry of Defence funded the recovery of soldiers of the Blue Division who died in Russia fighting on the side of Nazi Germany (Blakeley, 2005: 47, 55).

Meanwhile, several civil society organisations, related to aspects of the historical memory, sprang up, which put the former Aznar government under pressure. Among them is the Association for the Recovery of Historical Memory

(*Asociación para la Recuperación de la Memória Histórica* – ARMH) founded by Santiago Macfas and Emilio Silva in December 2000. ARMH submitted a file of sixty-four forced disappearances to the UN Working Group on Forced Disappearances in New York on 20 August 2002. It led to a recommendation by the Working Group to the Spanish government to investigate at least two cases that had happened after 1945. The resolution named four duties of the Spanish state: proper exhumation of the bodies with all available modern techniques (such as DNA identification); return of the bodies to the family members, proper burying of the bodies and a judicial investigation of the facts surrounding the disappeared (Blakeley, 2005: 48, 50). A belated recognition by the political class of this new movement in civil society was the unanimous condemnation of the 18 April 1936 military coup by parliament on 20 November 2002 (Blakeley, 2005: 50).

The successive Socialist government under Prime Minister José Luis Zapatero tried with other left-wing parties to adopt a law of the historical memory in order to honour all those who suffered during Francoism. In July 2006, the Zapatero government introduced in the Spanish parliament the 'Law of Reparation to the Victims of the Civil War and Francoism' (*Ley de Reparación a las Victimas de la Guerra Civil y Franquismo*) also known as the 'Law of Historical Memory' (*Ley de Memoria Histórica*). Such law was a major demand of the constituencies of the PSOE, IU, ERC, PNV and CiU. However, disagreements about what should be included in the bill led to considerable delays. IU wanted to ensure that one could persecute former perpetrators or do retrospective justice. This was rejected by the PSOE, which wanted only to include a formal but general rejection and condemnation of the authoritarian regime. The PNV demanded compensation for the lost patrimony after the Civil War and the return of the archives related to the Basque Country from the University of Salamanca to the autonomous community. Already in 2006, the archives of the Catalan Generalitat had been returned to Catalonia. The government refused to allow this for the Basque Country. In spite of attempts to come to an agreement, the law was still being discussed in October 2007 and time was running out to achieve approval before end of the legislature. One major issue is also to change the role of the Valle de los Caídos, a major monument in honour of Franco and his state, from one of glorification of the authoritarian regime to one of education against fascist regimes, through the creation of a foundation dedicated to the issues raised in the bill. Proposals also include the removal of the bodies of Franco and Falange founder José Antonio Primo de Rivera from their prominent burial sites in the Valle de los Caídos to less prominent places. The law was extremely opposed by the PP, which regarded this as a danger to the consensus culture established during democratic transition and observed in the past 30 years (*El Pais*, 23 September 2007: 23; *El Pais*, 2 October 2007: 26).

The role of the Church in this matter has been also biased towards the authoritarian regime and against the Law of Historical Memory. Instead, it contributed to the exacerbation of the polarisation between left and right through the mass beatification of 498 persons referred as 'martyrs' in the Vatican on 28 October 2007 because they were persecuted during the Second Spanish Republic (*El Pais*, 29 October 2007).

Political mobilisation will always depend on how much citizens are interested in taking part in certain actions. This instrumentalisation of Spanish politics is quite common among all advanced democracies which are more than ever embedded in a political culture of market behaviour. The media play a major role in this process of transformation. In sum, the decline of the divisions, which were almost intransigent and rigid until the 1950s, has created a more individualised mass politics which is quite instrumental in its approach towards politics and politicians (Montero and Torcal, 1995). This became quite evident when José Maria Aznar's People's Party (*Partido Popular* – PP) was able to win the legislative elections of 1996 and 2000 after almost two decades of being identified with the former authoritarian regime. It showed that both PP as well as the electorate had changed considerably and no longer could be manipulated in terms of left-right divisions. There was a tendency for the PSOE in the elections of 1986, 1989, 1993 and 1996 to discredit the PP as the representative of the former authoritarian regime. In 1996, this strategy no longer worked and in 2000 the PP even won an absolute majority, because the PSOE under Joaquin Almunia made the historical mistake of joining forces with the United Left, the communist coalition. In terms of political attitudes, one has to acknowledge that politics is not a priority for most Spaniards. It remains at the bottom of several other priorities.

The most important aspect of life for Spaniards is the family, followed by friends and work. At the bottom are religion and politics. (see Figure 2.2.)

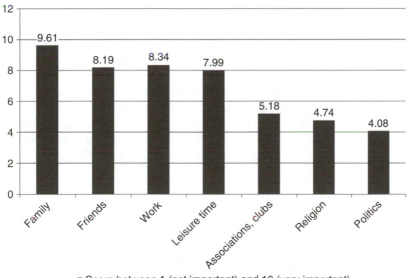

■ Score between 1 (not important) and 10 (very important)

Figure 2.2 Priorities of Spaniards in April 2007

Source: CIS, Monthly survey nr. 2700, April 2007, question 10: Please could you tell which of these aspects are the most important for you?(Average score) posted on website of Centro de Investigaciones Sociologicas, http://www.cis.es accessed on 7 September 2007.

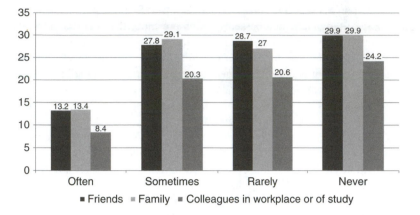

Figure 2.3 How often Spaniards discuss politics.

Source: CIS, Monthly survey nr. 2700, April 2007, question 11 posted on website of Centro de Investigaciones Sociologicas, http://www.cis.es accessed on 7 September 2007.

This lack of importance of politics shows also in another question on how often they discuss politics with the family, friends and colleagues in the workplace. Spaniards discuss moderately about politics, a large majority discusses rarely or never politics with friends, family members or even less with colleagues at work or of study. (see Figure 2.3.).

If asked about their sentiments towards politics, only a small minority of Spaniards are interested (12.2 per cent), while the vast majority either distrusts it, is indifferent towards it or find it boring. If we include the people who are irritated by it we have a staggering majority of 73.4 per cent of Spaniards who are not positively inclined towards politics (Figures 2.4, 2.5). According to several studies on the political attitudes of Spaniards, the main characteristics of Spanish political culture are based on indifference towards politics, distrust and a feeling of political impotence. This pattern of attitudes have been labelled as 'democratic cynicism' or 'political and institutional disaffection' (Bonet, Martin and Montero, 2006: 107).

Satisfaction with national democracy and institutional disaffection

Spaniards are in their overwhelming majority satisfied with democracy and their institutions. Their pattern of support for national institutions is similar to most other western European countries. This becomes quite evident when trust in political parties may vary between 19 and 30 per cent among survey respondents, while 60 to 70 per cent distrust them. Although there is a mistrust of political parties, overall satisfaction with Spanish democracy has improved considerably throughout the 1990s according to Eurobarometer studies. The low point was during the late phase of the PSOE government between 1993 and 1996. This can be explained by the

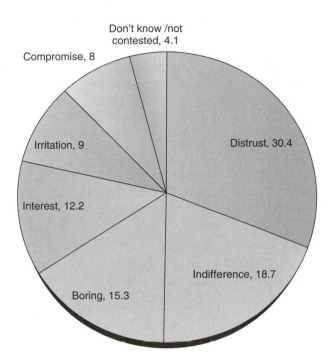

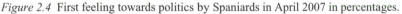

Figure 2.4 First feeling towards politics by Spaniards in April 2007 in percentages.

Source: CIS, Monthly survey nr. 2700, April 2007, question 14 posted on website of Centro de Investigaciones Sociologicas, http://www.cis.es accessed on 7 September 2007.

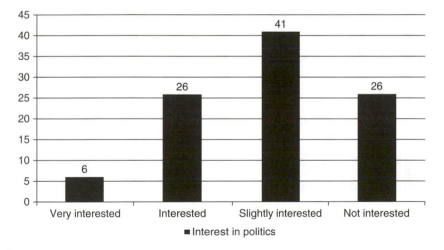

Figure 2.5 Interest in politics in January–February 2005.

Source: CIS, Boletin de Opinión 37, January–February 2005 posted on website of Centro de Investigaciones Sociologicas, http://www.cis.es accessed on 7 September 2007.

inertia of the PSOE government and the political corruption scandals associated with it (Magone, 2003). Although Spain has one of the highest support levels for national democracy, support for institutions is lower than in other European countries, particularly in older democracies such those in the Nordic countries, the Netherlands and Switzerland. The Eurobarometer data of recent years show a stable strong support for how national democracy works above the EU average but with countries such as Denmark, Luxembourg, Finland, Ireland, the Netherlands and Austria having higher figures. However, Spain has the highest support figures of all larger countries (Figure 2.6). In this issue Spain deviates from the southern European pattern, because Greece, Italy and Portugal are actually among the less satisfied nations with national democracies. In terms of trust in national institutions, there is a general confidence in parliament and the civil service, but less so in the judiciary (Figure 2.7). It is interesting that a growing number of people trust nongovernmental organisations, while the traditional intermediary organisations such as political parties and trade unions are in decline. The Church is also in decline, although the military and the police are held in high esteem. This naturally confirms the previous findings on the increasing importance of NGOs in Spanish society.

According to a study by Mariano Torcal, José Ramon Montero and Joan Teorell, Spaniards have a lower level of institutional affection, when compared with the more advanced and established democracies. Spain is closer to central and eastern European countries and in some cases to Portugal in terms of trust for political institutions. According to them citizens have the strongest confidence in government and the local councils and less confidence in parliament and

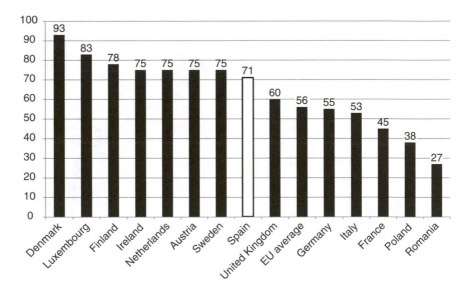

Figure 2.6 Satisfied with how national democracy works in March–May 2006.

Source: Eurobarometer, 65, March–May 2006, published in January 2007.

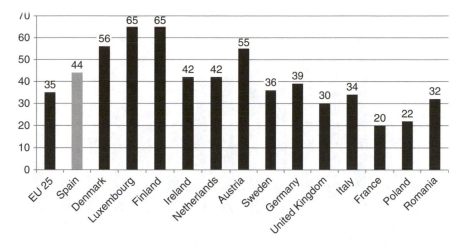

Figure 2.7 Trust in government (2006).

Source: eb.65, 2006: March–May 2006, QA10.3, published in January 2007.

political parties (Bonet, Martin and Montero, 2006: 113–6). This seems to be confirmed by Eurobarometer studies. In 2006, Spain was far behind the Scandinavian countries in terms of trust of government, parliament, justice system and political parties. However, decline of support in established democracies of west and central Europe such as France and Germany has contributed to similar figures in those countries. Positively, Spain is far from the values of some of the central and eastern European countries such as Poland, which clearly is dominated by a strong sense of democratic cynicism.

A more detailed study on the perception of the role of parliament in the Spanish political system shows that overall the majority of Spaniards find this institution important or very important, although a majority is aware of the low level of power in relation to the government. Such perception of the role of the Spanish Cortes in the political system has not changed very much in the past two decades (Delgado Sotillos, Martinez and Oñate, 1998). If we look at the level of satisfaction with the work of parliament, a slight majority finds that it is working well, but a strong minority has a negative perception of parliamentary work, leading to an evenly split verdict on the overall performance among the Spanish population (Castillo and Crespo, 2000: 412) (Figure 2.8).

Even in terms of trust in political parties, Spain fares well against the long-established democracies of Sweden, Germany, France, Italy and the United Kingdom (Figure 2.10). However, trust in the judiciary system is lower than most of the other selected countries, only the central and eastern European countries and understandably Italy have lower figures than Spain (Figure 2.9).

The lack of engagement in politics is also expressed in a generally low-perceived internal political efficacy by citizens, meaning the ability to influence politicians.

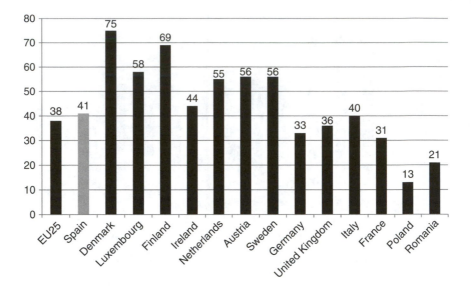

Figure 2.8 Trust in parliament (2006).

Source: eb.65, 2006: March–May 2006, QA10.4, published in January 2007.

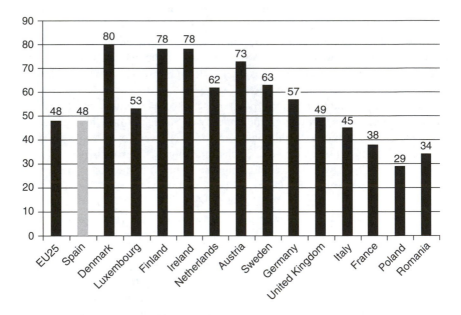

Figure 2.9 Trust in justice system (2006–).

Source: eb.65, March–May 2006, QA10.1, published in January 2007.

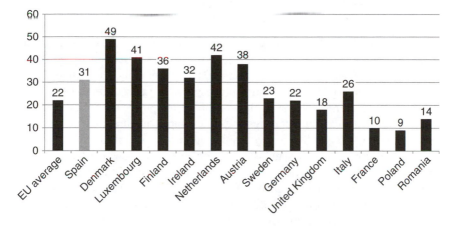

Figure 2.10 Trust in political parties (2006).

Source: eb.65, 2006: March–May 2006, QA10.2, published in January 2007.

Simultaneously, Spaniards perceive their representatives which corresponds to a low-perceived external efficacy by citizens, meaning the level of receptiveness of ideas by politicians. In both forms of efficacy, Spain is quite low in relation to most west and central European countries, however higher in relation to central and eastern European countries (Bonet, Martin and Montero, 2006: 113–22).

Among all institutions, it is the monarchy that achieves the highest scores in the past two decades. King Juan Carlos is held in high esteem among the Spanish population. His defence of democracy against the coup attempt of Colonel Tejero on 23 February 1981 strengthened the position of the monarchy in Spain, after a very negative record during the nineteenth and early twentieth centuries. The royal family has clearly a very good relationship with the population and the state institutions. King Juan Carlos was able to present the new monarchy created during the transition to democracy as a symbol of national unity, in spite of the regional diversity emerging out of the democratic process (*El Pais*, Special Issue on Juan Carlos, 22 November 2000: 4).

In sum, Spanish political culture is characterised by a vast majority of citizens being only little interested in politics. Although most Spaniards are happy with the way the political system works, they show moderate trust levels towards the political institutions and a high level of distrust and distance towards the political class. It means also that political parties dominate and structure political life. The penetration of state and society by political parties is certainly a factor which led to this overwhelming passive political culture (Matuschek, 2003: 341). Probably, the legacy of the former authoritarian regime which aimed at demobilising society and the elitist transition to democracy are important historical factors shaping today's Spanish political culture.

The secularisation of society: the consolidation
of the non-denominational state

One of the main controversial issues of the past remains the relationship of the left to the Church and religion. The Catholic Church was regarded as part of the political establishment of the Restoration period and the Francoist regime. It was one of the most intransigent national churches up until the end of the 1950s. The Catholic Church along with the Army was one of the pillars of the authoritarian regime. Protected by the Francoist regime, it developed an ultramontane 'national Catholicism', which translated into a quite oppressive socialisation of society. Nevertheless, urbanisation and industrialisation led to social change and to a more liberal society. In some way, the Church hierarchy was not able to prevent new social groups from achieving change from the bottom up. The second Vatican Council, liberation theology in Latin America and the left-wing Zeitgeist of the 1960s had its impact upon the Church. After 1975, the Catholic Church was no longer able to count on the special relationship with the new democratic regime. On the contrary, freedom of religion transformed the Catholic Church into a representative of one confession among others. It had to compete with New Age groups and other new churches, most of them originating in the United States or Latin America. Furthermore, the democratisation of education, the emergence of new life styles and the decline of the extended family led to a less rigid Catholic code among most Spaniards. Somehow this led to the erosion of the Catholic subculture (Brassloff, 1998). According to a survey in 2002, 80.8 per cent of Spaniards declared themselves as Catholic, but only 18.5 per cent go to church every Sunday, in contrast to 46 per cent who never go to church. On the one hand, the number of practising Catholics has decreased from 95 per cent in 1960 to 29 per cent in 2002, and non-practising Catholics increased from 5 to 50 per cent (Figure 2.11). The highest levels of practising Catholics can be found in the less developed regions of Spain such as Extremadura, Castilla La Mancha, Murcia, Castilla León, Cantabria, Andalusia and La Rioja. The lowest levels of practising Catholics can be found in the regions where the population is highly urbanised, has a high level of education and a strong interest in politics – such as Madrid, Catalonia and the Basque Country (*El Pais*, Domingo, 8 December 2002: 6). In some way, Spain is following the pattern of most other European countries, where religion is becoming less relevant. The extreme cases of a considerable decline of religiosity and church-going can be found in the Scandinavian countries and the United Kingdom. Spain clearly fits into a southern European pattern along with Portugal, Greece and Italy. The whole process of secularisation is slower in Spain, but is nevertheless advancing in the direction of the changes which have already taken place in other European countries. This is also leading to the decline of the patriarchal family which was so common in most west European societies until the 1960s. Slower than in other countries, Spain is becoming a diverse society with different family forms, including single-parent and same-sex families (Castells, 2000: 138–56).

According to Miguel Requena, the slower pace of decline of Spanish Catholicism is due to the ageing of the population and the low birth rate. It is among the older

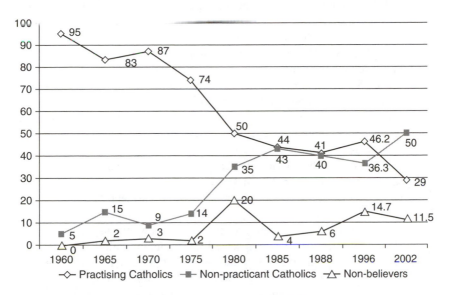

Figure 2.11 The decline of Catholicism in Spain, 1960–2002.

Source: *El Pais*, Domingo, 8 December 2002: 6 (years 1960 and 1970); Diaz, 1997: 311 (year 1996, Fundación Sistema); Diaz-Salazar, R., 1993: 133 quoted from Pérez-Agote, Santiago-Garcia, 2005: 10 (years 1965; 1975; 1980; 1985; 1988); Requena, 2005: 377–8.

population that Catholicism is strongest and were also religious practices prevail. The other variable is gender, women are twice as likely to go regularly to church as men are. Such a difference remains stable in spite of other interfering variables like educational attainment, habitat and employment (Requena, 2005: 380–1).

An excellent study by José Ramon Montero and Kerman Calvo also provides evidence of a decline in the relationship between religiosity and voting. In several studies, they found out that the more religious voters tend to vote for the right, but such connection has been blurring over time. It means that religion just explains a tiny part of electoral voting. Montero and Calvo differentiate between two kinds of religious voters which tend to voter for the two main parties PP and PSOE respectively. Voters with a 'traditional understanding of religiosity' in which moral principles defined by the Church and regular attendance at mass, condition their behaviour, tend to vote for the PP, while voters with an 'individualistic understanding of religiosity' and a pick-and-choose, sort of '*à la carte*' approach to religion, who are not bound by the Catholic moral teachings, vote for the PSOE (Montero and Calvo, 2000: 134). In spite of the eroding value of religion as explanation for voting, the elections of 2000 led to a re-emergence of the religious vote which benefitted the PP. According to the authors, religion played a role in two ways. Firstly, it acted as a reinforcing factor to the high levels of volatility from the PSOE to PP, particularly among the more religious voters of the former. Secondly, it was an important orientation source for voters, in lieu of the missing ideological differentiation between the main parties, which function today more as cartel parties. (Calvo and Montero 2002: 42–51). The importance of religion as a reinforcing or orientation factor in terms of ideology is confirmed by a study of Pérez-Agote, Alfonso and José A Santiago-Garcia based on the 2002 CIS survey on the religious situation in Spain. According to them in the 2000 elections 34 per cent of PP voters, 16.3 per cent of PSOE voters and 6.3 per cent voters went weekly to church. (Perez-Agote and Santiago-Garcia, 2005: 79–80). A cross-tabulation showed that the more a respondent was to the right, the more likely it was that he/she attended mass quite regularly, while the more to the left, he/she would be less inclined to do so (see Figure 2.12.)

This slow erosion of the religious factor, which seems to be more resilient than ideology, has led to the loss of power of the Catholic Church and as Miguel Requena writes to the 'constitutional consolidation of the non-denominational state' (Requena, 2005: 373).

A further step in this direction was the law on gay marriages which was approved by all political parties represented in parliament with the exception of PP in April 2005. This allowed for homosexual couples to have equal rights of inheritance and pension with heterosexual ones. This led to considerable protests from the PP, the Church and adjacent Catholic organisations during June 2005. The law was supported by over 70 per cent of the population in a survey in 2004 (Bernecker, 2006: 413). This high level of tolerance is particularly widespread among the younger population. Spain is now among the few countries that allows gay marriages, along with Canada, Belgium and the Netherlands. Other countries such as France, the United Kingdom and Germany allow civil partnerships.

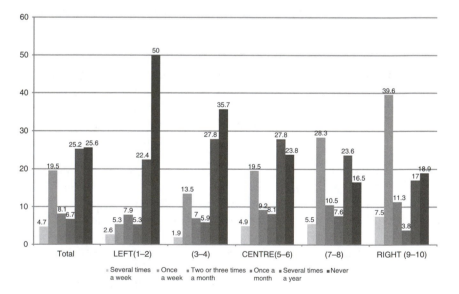

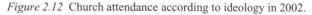

Figure 2.12 Church attendance according to ideology in 2002.

Source: Perez-Agote and Santiago-Garcia, 2005: 78 based on CIS Survey nr. 2443, January 2002, Figures include tiny group of believers in other religions (1.4 per cent).

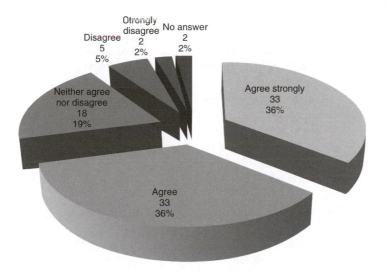

Figure 2.13 Gays and lesbians should have freedom to live as they like in percentage (2002).

Source: Calvo and Montero, 2005: 165.

Opinion surveys clearly confirm this overwhelming tolerant approach towards homosexuality (see Figure 2.13).

According to Ronald Inglehart and Christian Welzel, Spain is now among the most advanced countries in a worldwide cultural transition from modernity or industrial society based on survival consumerist values to post-modernity or post-industrial society which emphasise self-expressive non-consumerist values, meaning more human autonomy and choice. Such transition means also that hierarchical rigid institutions are being replaced by flat, flexible networks which are global in nature. According to them tolerance of homosexuality is one of the strongest signs of this advanced stage in the worldwide process. In their worldwide study conducted in 2000 conducted in 77 countries, only in nine countries more than 50 per cent of the population approved homosexuality: the Netherlands, Sweden, Iceland, Denmark, Switzerland, Germany, Spain, Canada, Luxembourg (Inglehart and Welzel, 2005: 40–1). In a Eurobarometer study carried out in September–October 2006 on the social attitudes of Europeans, there were also some questions related to homosexuality. On the question on homosexual marriages, 56 per cent of Spaniards supported it, well above the EU average of 44 per cent. On the question on adoption of children by homosexual marriages, Spaniards supported it with 43 per cent, well above the EU average of 32 per cent. However, the attitudes of Spaniards are still considerably behind the more open societies of the Netherlands, Sweden and Denmark. Other countries which are open to homosexuality and some of its issues are Austria, Germany, France, the Czech Republic, the United Kingdom and Finland. All of them are still above the EU average (Eurobarometer, 65, 2007: 43, 45).

Political mobilisation will always depend on how much citizens are interested in taking part in certain actions. This instrumentalisation of Spanish politics is quite common among all Western democracies, which are more than ever embedded in a political culture of market behaviour. The media play a major role in this process of transformation. In sum, the decline of the divisions which were almost intransigent and rigid until the 1950s has created a more individualised mass politics which is quite instrumental in its approach towards politics and politicians (Montero and Torcal, 1995). This became quite evident when José Maria Aznar's People's Party (*Partido Popular* – PP) was able to win the legislative elections of 1996 and 2000 after almost two decades of being identified with the former authoritarian regime. It showed that both PP as well as the electorate had changed considerably and no longer could be manipulated in terms of left–right divisions. There was a tendency for the PSOE in the elections of 1986, 1989, 1993 and 1996 to discredit the PP as the representative of the former authoritarian regime. In 1996, this strategy no longer worked and in 2000 the PP even won an absolute majority, because the PSOE under Joaquin Almunia made the historical mistake of joining forces with the United Left, the communist coalition.

Multiple identities: local, regional and national

One of the major transformations that Spain experienced was the establishment of the seventeen autonomous communities. After decades of repression of ethnic minorities in Spain, different historical autonomies are flourishing under the new democratic regime. Although the constitution was originally very restrictive about the possibilities to move towards autonomy, between 1978 and 1983 seventeen autonomous communities emerged, which made the country culturally more diverse. This diversity naturally shows that it is nonsensical to speak of political culture in the singular. Indeed, it is wiser to speak of political culture in the plural. All these different autonomous communities developed their own regional subcultures and clearly shape the overall atmosphere of national political culture. Spanish society has several identities: local, regional, national and European. Some of them are stronger than others, but in general terms one can clearly state that they exist simultaneously. (Marks and Llamazares, 2006: 252–6). Spain resembles in many ways Belgium, which also has multiple identities. Although the main historical regions have their own language such as the Basque Country, Catalonia and Galicia, other autonomous communities have their own political cultures as well. Andalusia clearly can draw part of its identity from the Arab past, which is architecturally visible in most cities such as Granada, Seville or Malaga. Andalusian Spanish is not a separate language, but represents a way of thinking about life that is quite different from that of the Castilians or Catalans. The Balearics and Valencia also declared Mallorcan and Valencian, which are similar to Catalan, as their own regional languages. This great achievement of the new Spanish democracy shows that decentralisation is contributing to a diversity of political cultures. In terms of divisions, the centre–periphery division is still the most salient one in electoral terms, while the left–right ideological division is more or less eroding due to social transformation and the impact of political marketing and the media. However, as Eva Anduiza Perea found out for the European elections of 1999, both cleavages are becoming axis of competition due to the increasing inter-block volatility in both cases. (Anduiza Perea, 2000: 250–65). This may show a growing integration of both nationalist-regionalist parties and centralist parties in the multi-level party system. The main parties have adopted regionalist strategies for the party branches in each individual autonomous community and the nationalist-regionalist parties have become more involved in national politics by supporting minority governments in the 1990s and after 2004 (Hamann, 1999).

After more than two decades of the state of autonomies, one can assert that the new Spanish territorial organisation is well accepted among the population. A majority tends to have a dual identity comprising of loyalty to the corresponding autonomous community and the Spanish state. This naturally varies considerably among the autonomous communities. On one side of the scale, the lowest levels of identification with the Spanish national state can be found in the Basque Country and Catalonia. In these autonomous communities one can also find the most intense regionalist-nationalist feelings. On the other side of the scale is Madrid, which has the highest awareness of Spanish national identity. Such a pattern of asymmetrical regional consciousness has been quite constant over the past three decades. The only major change has been the reduction of polarisation and radicalisation and a growing support for moderate regionalist-nationalist feelings. Galicia has been quite an interesting case in this context. Although regionalist-nationalist parties emerged in the 1980s and were able to achieve representation both at regional, local and national level, it was only when regionalist-nationalist Xosé Manuel Beiras emerged on the political scene, that a stronger moderate regionalist-nationalist subculture began to be more successful in political terms. Nevertheless, Galicians are extremely supportive of the state of autonomies and their regionalist-nationalist consciousness is completely adverse to those of the Basque Country and Catalonia, which present tendencies towards complete independence or further autonomy respectively. In this sense, the Spanish state of autonomies has led to asymmetrical regional consciousness, which is quite strong in the historical regions of the Basque Country, Catalonia, Galicia and Navarre, but less so in Madrid, Castilla-León, Castilla La Mancha and Extremadura. All the other regions are in between these two poles of low and high regional consciousness. In this sense, we have to speak of political culture in the plural, depending on the level of regional consciousness, economic development, social structure and linguistic proficiency. It is not without reason that the highest levels of regional consciousness in the periphery can be found in the Basque Country and Catalonia, which are also among the economically most developed autonomous communities in Spain. Other autonomous communities such as Galicia, Andalusia and the Valencian Community will use regional consciousness to achieve advantages in the financial redistribution mechanisms of the Spanish state, such as the Territorial Compensation Fund (*Fundo de Compensación Territorial* – FCT) (Garcia-Ferrando *et al.*, 1994: 11–33; Maldonado Gago, 2002: 94–5; Martinez-Herrera, 2002) (see Chapter 5).

Even more interesting is the fact that the primary identification of Spaniards is actually with their own village or city. Throughout the 1990s, this was the main primary territorial unit of identity for 45 per cent of the population, while only around 15 per cent referred to the autonomous community as the first primary source of identification. Higher than the village or city in which the citizens live, the source of primary territorial identification is naturally Spain, as the national identity, but even so this has declined since the 1980s from around 30 per cent to 20 per cent. This shows that Spanish society is extremely localist in their sources of identification (Hernandez de Frutos, 1997: 368).

In terms of linguistic identity and proficiency we see that this is used to strengthen the identity of the autonomous community vis-à-vis the Spanish state. This is naturally quite obvious in the Basque Country, where people have to learn Basque to get a job in the autonomous community administration. This led to major protests from Spaniards who moved to the Basque Country, because they felt discriminated against. In any case, about one-third of the population of the Basque Country speaks Basque, while the other parts of the population may speak some Basque or not at all. This is creating major problems in this part of Spain. In some way, it reinforces an existing division of the country into the core Basque nationalists, the moderate Basque nationalists and the supporters of so-called *españolismo*, meaning Spanishness in terms of the present constitution (Moreno del Rio, 2000; Mata, 1998). The regional elections of 13 May 2001 in the Basque Country clearly heightened awareness of this polarisation between the three subcultures. Such polarisation continued to play a major role in the regional elections of 26 September 2005. Basque terrorism through the terrorist organisation Basque Country and Freedom (*Euskadi Ta Askatasuma* – ETA) contributed to the terror campaign for almost 50 years to keep these divisions in the Basque Country. The moderate Basque Nationalist Party (*Partido Nacionalista Vasco* – PNV) is caught between the two other subcultures. Officially, the bourgeois right-centre PNV condemns violence and wants to achieve independence through peaceful means, which includes the holding of a referendum. The so-called 'Ibarretxe plan', named after the regional president and presented after the regional elections of 2001, envisaged a road map towards such independence, which would entail a transitional association with Spain. The 'Ibarretxe plan' was rejected in the Cortes in Madrid in 2004. There is some support within the PNV for ETA, which makes the position of the leadership quite ambiguous and ambivalent in some cases. However, the Zapatero government was very keen to integrate PNV and the regionalist parties in the anti-terrorist pact developed by Aznar. The crackdown by the Aznar government on Basque terrorism with support of the PSOE led to further polarisation of the positions in the Basque Country. In spite of starting negotiations with ETA during 2006, the return to violence in December the Zapatero government continued to work with the French authorities to reduce the organisational and logistics capacity of ETA. In this sense, ETA is weakened considerably and is trying to build alternative structures in Portugal, so that it can continue its 40-year terrorist campaign (*El Pais*, 25 of August 2007: 17; 28 August 2007: 16–17). The resignation of PNV chairman,

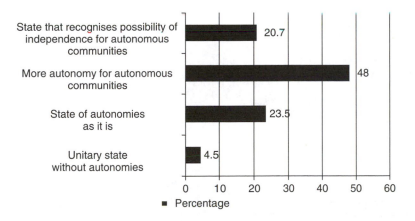

Figure 2.14 State preference of Spaniards, 2005.

Source: CIS Survey, 2610 to be found on website of Centro de Investigaciones Sociologicas, http://www.cis.es accessed on 7 September 2007.

Josu Jon Imaz, on 12 September 2007 who was supportive of Zapatero's efforts to unite all moderate forces against ETA terrorism, showed that there are still radical nationalist factions inside the PNV which tend to reject cooperation with the main national Spanish parties. Both Prime Minister José Luis Zapatero as well as main leader of the opposition Mariano Rajoy were surprised by Imaz's resignation. In the end, PNV decided to appoint compromise candidate Iñigo Urkullu to replace Imaz and contribute to the unity and cohesion of the party, which is split between the radical and moderate supporters of Basque independence (*El Pais*, 13 September 2007: 16–18; *El Pais*, 14 September 2007: 16–17; *El Pais*, 15 September 2007: 20).

This divided nationalist sector is expressed in the way Basques want the state organisation to evolve. In regular surveys the state of autonomies is supported by a vast majority in most autonomous communities. However, in the Basque country the figures are much lower and divided among different preferences. In 2006, 31.6 per cent wanted to have the possibility to move towards independence, in Catalonia this figure is only 16.6 per cent. (see Figures 2.14–2.15). In 2006, 25.2 per cent expressed an only Basque identity and 19.6 per cent more Basque than Spanish. It means that exclusionary Basque identity is strong, but not strong enough to offset the multiple identities of most of the population of this autonomous community. (see Figures 2.16–2.17.) This may be one of the reasons for the use of political violence to achieve its aims.

In Catalonia, an estimated 80–90 per cent of the population speak Catalan, which is easier for Spanish speakers to learn than Basque, because it is a language related to French and Spanish. The Catalans clearly have a more integrative, less exclusionist regional nationalism and language (Conversi, 1997). The language contributes to a high level of regional consciousness. In spite of the fact that there are demands for a stronger role for Catalonia within

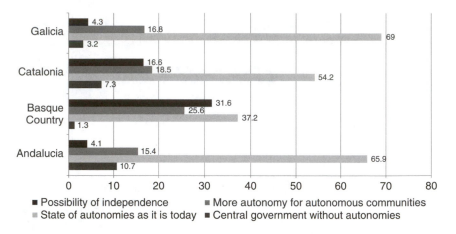

Figure 2.15 State organisation preferences in Galicia, Catalonia, the Basque Country and Andalucia 2006.

Source: OPA, 2006: 78–9.

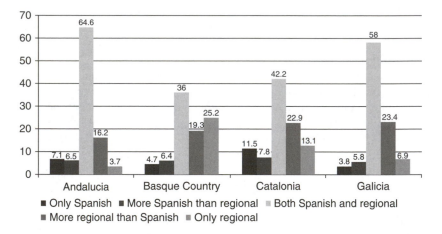

Figure 2.16 Subjective nationalist identity 2002.

Source: OPA, 2003: 35.

Spain, leading sometimes for calls for the establishment of a dual-nationality state, Spain and Catalonia, by Jordi Pujol, the former president of the regional government of Catalonia (*Generalitat*), most of it remains a verbal radical demand without concrete implications. Since the regional elections of 2003 and reconfirmed in 2006, the Socialist party in coalition with the Catalan Republican Left (*Esquerra Republicana Catalana* – ERC) and the United Left–Greens (EUiA) have broken the dominance of CiU in the Catalan political system. Due to the programme of constitutional reform of the Socialist government under

Prime Minister Zapatero, they were able to achieve a compromise in the revision of the regional statute. Many of the more radical proposals had to be rejected by the Cortes in Madrid, but the compromise and the positive referendum show that the nationalist cause is no longer monopolised by the nationalist parties.

Galician is widely spoken among the population, because it is an important element of regional consciousness, although never instrumentalised for this purpose. In contrast to Catalonia and the Basque Country, language was part of the culture, but not of a political agenda. The language is close to Portuguese, but there were never large movements asking for integration into Portugal. On the contrary, Galicians are happy to be in the Spanish state of autonomies. The highly conservative autonomous community has only recently embraced with more conviction moderate regionalism symbolised by the National Galician Bloc (*Bloco Nacional Galego* – BNG). The ecological catastrophe in October–November 2002 caused by the sinking of the oil tanker Prestige close to the Galician coast led to protests of fishermen and the wider regional population against the regional and central government for not supporting them and trying to cover up the mismanagement of the responsible authorities. The regional elections of 28 June 2005 led to a weakening of the BNG. Anxo Quintana, leader of the party, pursues a moderate pragmatic strategy in order to become a central party in Galicia. This contrasts heavily with previous charismatic leader Xosé Manuel Beiras who contributed to the prominence of the party. Power struggles inside the party sidelined Xosé Manuel Beiras (*El Pais*, 28 May 2005: 22; *El Pais*, 3 June 2005: 19)

In Valencia, the Balearics and Navarre language is not instrumentalised for political purposes. On the contrary, it is part of the culture, but it does not lead to a high level of regional consciousness in terms of nationalism.

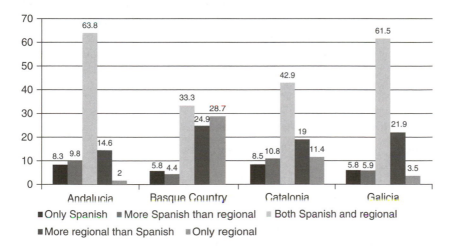

Figure 2.17 Subjective nationalist identity 2006.
Source: OPA, 2006: 80–81.

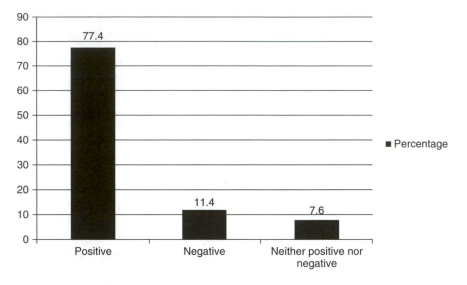

Figure 2.18 Evaluation of state of autonomies (2005).

Source: CIS Survey, 2610 to be found on website of Centro de Investigaciones Sociologicas, http://www.cis.es accessed on 7 September 2007.

The overwhelming majority of Spaniards confirm that the state of autonomies has been a positive thing for Spain. (Figure 2.18), although they are a bit more critical in the way it works (Figure 2.19).

In sum, the state of autonomies is certainly well accepted across all autonomous communities. The support for it against the alternatives of a federal state and full independence has been decreasing in the past three decades (Figures 2.14 and 2.2). This shows that, apart from a minority in the Basque Country, the Spanish state of autonomies is gaining more and more legitimacy and support. There is also surprisingly a growing interest in federalism, but this still remains a minority. This further confirms the consolidation and moderation of Spanish politics.

Patriotic constitutionalism and federalism

The current major issues in electoral politics are the different conceptions of how to move forward in terms of constitutional politics. After 30 years of the constitution, the People's Party and the Socialists presented different proposals to adjust the constitution to the developments and dynamics created by the state of autonomies. The regionalisation and decentralisation of the former unitary Spanish state led to the emergence of a federal state, which is not enshrined in the constitution. This naturally is leading to pressure to reform the constitution, so that the new reality is fully recognised. In this respect, two positions emerged which are clearly contrary to each other. While PP under former Prime Minister

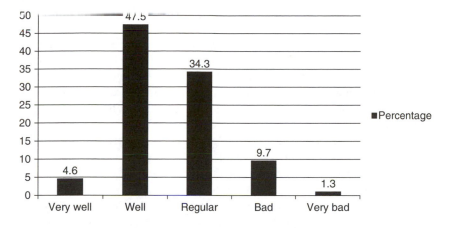

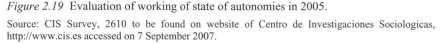

Figure 2.19 Evaluation of working of state of autonomies in 2005.

Source: CIS Survey, 2610 to be found on website of Centro de Investigaciones Sociologicas, http://www.cis.es accessed on 7 September 2007.

José Maria Aznar clearly wanted the constitution to remain untouched as a kind of magna carta, there are calls from the Socialists and the regionalist-nationalists to move towards a federal structure. Aznar clearly presented his so-called patriotic constitutionalism (*constitucionalismo patriotico*) – a concept originally coined by German philosopher Jürgen Habermas to characterise the affective relationship of citizens towards the German Basic Law – in the national electoral campaign of 2000 against the proposal of the PSOE, at that time under the leadership of Joaquin Almunia, to move towards fully fledged federalism. The question on the constitution gained renewed importance during the preparation for the autonomous and local elections of 2003 which included proposals from regionalist-nationalist parties as well. The PP feared that any change in the constitution would lead to the opening up of a Pandora's box leading to calls for further asymmetrical federalism and even independence (*El Pais*, 19 January 2003: 17–22). This is one of the reasons why Aznar was quite opposed to the regionalist-nationalists in the Basque Country under *Lehendekari* (Regional President) Juan José Ibarretxe, who was able to win a strong majority in the regional elections of 13 May 2001 (*El Mundo*, 15 May 2001: 5). Ibarretxe was pushing for a referendum towards self-determination. On 27 September 2002, he proposed a model of free association with Spain, which would lead in the end to full independence. This was utterly rejected by the two main parties (*El Pais*, 9 July 2002: 15; *El Pais*, 1 September 2002: 15; *El Pais*, 29 September 2002: 24–7; *El Pais*, 6 October 2002: 22). At the end of September 2007, Ibarretxe revived his plan, which led to splits inside the party. Furthermore, Prime Minister José Luis Zapatero rejected the plan as being unconstitutional (*El Pais*, 22 September 2007: 20; *El Pais*, 1 October 2007: 21–2).

The Galician Nationalist Bloc (*Bloc Nacionalista Galego* – BNG) put forward its own proposals. Its main idea is to refound the state on a plurinational and confederal basis recognising the four nations of Spain – Galicia, the Basque Country, Catalonia and Spain. The left-wing regionalist-nationalist Catalans want secession, while the right-wing Catalans under Jordi Pujol want a privileged relationship between Spain and Catalonia (*El Pais*, 27 October 2002: 15; *El Pais*, Domingo, 5 January 2003: 5).

This debate shows that the Spanish devolution process is not finished yet. There are still outstanding questions about the final form of territorial organisation and more important than that, how to create a fair representation of the autonomous communities in the Spanish political system. The reform of the second parliamentary chamber, the Senate, is still awaiting a final decision, in spite of discussions since 1993 (Roller, 2002b). Comparing this elitist discussion with the data from the OPA opinion polls quoted above, there is strong support for some change, although in the Basque Country strong minorities are supporters of federalism and even full independence and in Galicia federalism is the preferred form of state organisation by a majority (Figure 2.15). Nationally, almost half of the population are willing to grant more autonomy to the regions, while more than one-fifth want to allow regions to seek independence. Only a quarter of Spaniards are happy with the status quo (Figure 2.14).

Prime Minister José Luis Zapatero was instrumental in putting the revision of the constitution on the agenda. He started his term of office with an ambitious constitutional reform programme which entailed better relations with the regions through the establishment of the conference of presidents, generous support for a review of regional statutes, particularly in relation to Catalonia and a fairer allocation of funding. Although this generosity towards the regions has been painted by the People's Party as weakness of the government, Zapatero believes that his approach will in the end strengthen Spain. The increase of investment funding for Catalonia which matches the amount for Andalusia is a good example of this policy, which tries to overcome resentments between the regions (*El Pais*, 23 September 2007: 22).

In spite of these good relations between the centre and the periphery, Prime Minister Zapatero was not able to secure support from the People's Party to review the constitution. It means that at the end of the Zapatero legislature, the constitutional issue remains untouched. He was already quite pessimistic about it at the beginning of 2006. The main aspects of the reform are the inclusion of the denominations of the autonomous communities, which did not exist when the constitution was approved in 1978, the reform of the Senate to a genuine territorial chamber, the adaptation to the most recent developments of European integration (originally to the Constitutional Treaty) and the lifting of any discriminatory regulations preventing the succession to the throne by a female member of the royal family (*El Pais*, 13 January 2006: 18).

Decline of institutionalised mobilisation and the rise of cognitive sporadic mobilisation

One of the characteristics of present Spanish political culture is the low level of continuous participation in political and civil organisations. Spain is still part of a southern European pattern of participation, which can be specified by a low density of organisations of civil society. This does not mean that Spaniards do not take part in political protest or demonstrations, but they remain sporadic events which are not followed by more permanent movements. Indeed, social movements almost disappeared from Spanish politics. Society is becoming much more individualised, following a pattern across most developed European democracies. Both political parties and trade unions have low memberships. The membership of parties is difficult to estimate, because each party tends to present inflated numbers. Nevertheless, according to official figures the PP has 600,000 members and PSOE 400,000 (*El Pais*, 12 November 2001: 21; *El Pais*, 28 April 2002: 16). The other parties have smaller memberships, so one could estimate the number of people involved some way in political parties as not more than 1.5 million, which is about 3–4 per cent of the population. This means that party membership figures have been stagnant or even declining in the past three decades. The same can be said about the two main trade union confederations, which represent not more than 18 per cent of the working population, which is one of the lowest in western Europe. Naturally, Spanish trade unionism is very much influenced by the fact that it is subsidised by the state and is defined by the regular electoral results which take place every 4 years and will in the end determine the financial strength of the corresponding trade union confederation. Nevertheless, these figures are quite low by any standards.

The organisations that Spaniards, particularly the younger generation, feel attracted to are nongovernmental organisations (NGOs) dedicated to all possible international causes. Such organisations have gained importance over the past two decades. It clearly appeals to one of the most fundamental values of Spanish society – solidarity. This may sometimes sound too idealistic, but clearly constitutes a part of Spanish culture. One of the reasons for the importance of solidarity, even if it is sometimes reduced to taking part in a demonstration for a couple of hours, is probably the past history of Francoist authoritarian repression. The newly won freedom is used to advance the causes of other countries or international organisations. Naturally, this is not only related to external causes such as international development issues, but also to national causes such as the peaceful protest against Basque terrorism of the *Basta Ya*! movement, which even led the heir to the throne, Prince Felipe, to take part in demonstrations in Brussels. It also led to huge demonstrations in the main cities of the country.

Another case was the protest of students, university teachers, trade unions, PSOE and IU against the introduction of the Law of Quality in Higher Education, which aimed to introduce a more competitive and research-oriented university system similar to that of the United Kingdom. This led to major demonstrations in December 2001 and continuing protest in 2002 (*El Pais*, 2 December 2002: 22; *El Pais*, 14 November 2001; *El Pais*, 12 March 2002: 24; *El Pais*, 13 March 2002: 28). Street demonstrations and protest are also used by conservative associations such as the Catholic Confederation of Family and Pupils' Parents which took place in 2004 and 2005 against the law allowing same-sex marriages and changing the status of the school module religion to one among other optional ones, including the citizenship module.

This spontaneous participation in politics is naturally related to the overall transformation of participation patterns among Spaniards and populations in other west European democracies. Spain is among the countries with the lowest levels of associationism with only one in four Spaniards being part of any civil organisation. Although this is better than in Portugal and Greece, nevertheless it is far behind most other major countries in western Europe such as the United Kingdom, Germany and France (Funes Rivas Maria Jesus, 1997: 515–16). Membership of civil organisations increases among the parts of the population with higher levels of education. The most common associations which Spaniards belong to are neigh-bours' associations, followed by cultural associations, parents' associations, sports associations, charity or religious associations. More politicised associations such as human rights associations, consumers associations, professional associations, ecological and pacifist organisations and women's associations have a low level of association below the 8 per cent threshold (Funes Rivas, 1997: 522). Although there has been an increase in associationism in the past three decades, Spaniards continue to be far behind the more advanced democracies in terms of taking part in activities of associations. Several studies have been confirming the still weak engagement of Spanish citizens. According to a comparative survey of thirteen European countries analysed by Laura Morales and Fabiola Mota participation in associations by Spaniards is still quite low in contrast to more development democracies such as Norway, Switzerland, Denmark, Sweden or Holland. The highest level of any involvement of citizens has been registered in Norway with 96 per cent, while in Spain it is 49 per cent. Only Russia (28 per cent), Romania (20 per cent) and Moldavia (20 per cent) have lower figures. Morales and Mota called it the southern syndrome (*sindroma meridional*) which can be found in France, Greece, Italy and Portugal. (Morales and Mota, 2006: 80).

The study confirms also the findings of Maria Funés Rivas one decade earlier, that citizens take part in recreational associations and less in politically and socially inspired ones. According to Morales and Mota the largest number of members can be found in Sport associations, parents' associations, trade union confederations, pensioneers' and retired associations, defence of human rights and humanitarian cooperation in this sequence. (Morales and Mota, 2006: 85–6; see Figure 2.23.) This is reinforced by a low multi-associationism. The average of engaged Spanish citizens is involved in maximum one or two associations, it means that Spain is at the bottom of studied countries in this survey. In Switzerland the figure is 5.4, in Norway 5.2 and in the Netherlands 4.4. At the other end of the scale, engaged Romanians participate in 1.5 associations, Portugal's citizens in 2 (like Spain's) and Slovenia's in 2.3 (Morales and Mota, 2006: 85). However, Laura Morales has found out that membership of associations cannot be equalled with corresponding activism. Although in southern Europe membership of associations is lower, the intensity of activism is quite high. According to her, based on the European Social Survey of 2002–03, more than 50 per cent of all Spanish association members are actively engaged. The most active members are young, have a university degree and have left-wing ideological tendencies (Morales; 2005: 249–50, 2006: 67). This naturally leads to a different ranking in terms of activism. Figure 2.20 shows

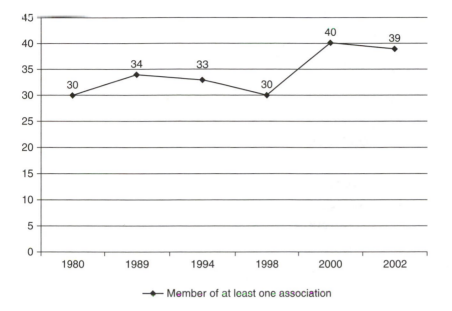

Figure 2.20 Membership of at least one association in Spain in percentage, 1980–2002.
Source: Morales and Mota, 2006: 80.

a more mixed figure, in which no clear region of Europe dominates the picture. The Nordic countries are below the European Social Survey average, and Portugal and Hungary manage to be above. Spain takes a middle-ranking position among the larger countries. While France, the United Kingdom and Germany have a very active membership, which is above the ESS average and far ahead of Spain, Italy and Poland occupy the bottom places in these number of selected countries (Figure 2.21).

Although chequebook associationism based on donations has become an important feature of most European democracies, including Spain, most associations in Spain have very small budgets which range between €6,000 (£4,000; $8,000) and €30,000 (£20,000; $40,000): this is quite modest in relation to other European countries. Moreover, most of these associations are confined to local areas. Larger associations with national and international reach can only be found in the larger metropolitan centres of the country. It means that the Spanish third (voluntary) sector is extremely dependent on state funding. Most associations have no permanent staff on pay roll, however occasional state funding may allow for the hiring of temporary assistants (Mendez and Mota, 2006: 210; 215–6). Particularly, social services and public services organisations are quite dependent on state funding (Mendez and Mota, 2006: 219).

In spite of low levels of membership and permanent activism, NGOs are held in high esteem among the Spanish population. This becomes evident, because many Spaniards believe that NGOs will increase in importance in the future.

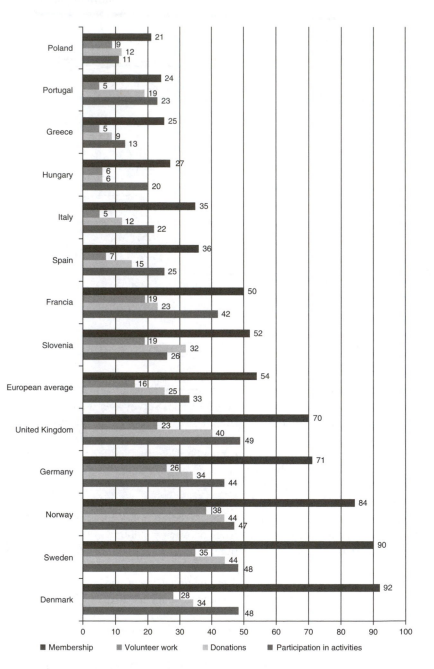

Figure 2.21 Level of associationism in Europe (2002–2003) based on European Social Survey.

Source: Morales, 2005: 242; Morales, 2006: 68 for own compilation of selected countries based on European Social Survey 2002–2003.

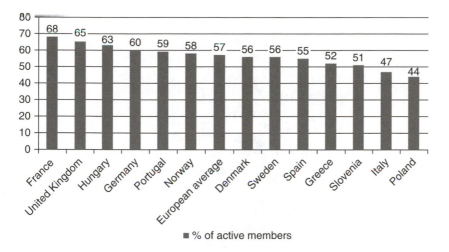

Figure 2.22 Percentage of active members within associations in Spain and selected European countries based on European Social Survey 2002–2003.

Source: Morales, 2005: 249; Morales, 2006: 69.

The main question is whether the NGOs are well equipped and prepared for this challenge. According to a major study sponsored by the PP government, the picture is rather bleak. The study organised by *Fundación Lealtad* wanted to create a guide for accountability and good practice within the NGOs. It was found out that 30 per cent of all NGOs are neither economically nor in terms of management fully accountable. Although more or less all NGOs fulfil most of the principles set up by the study, there is considerable concern that most of the finance is coming from the public sector, while the private sector is not donating enough to NGOs. It is estimated that 60 per cent or more is coming from public sources, making Spanish NGOs strongly dependent on the state. It is estimated that only 25 per cent or less of the budget is financed by donations. This is reinforced in some cases by lack of accountability in the control and use of funds (*El Pais*, 21 January 2003: 26).

The low level of associativism is naturally also conditioned by the fact that it is unevenly distributed across the Spanish autonomous communities. According to a study by Fabiola Mota and Joan Subirats the highest levels of associativism can be found in the richest and economically more developed regions of the north-east (Catalonia, the Basque Country, Navarre and Aragon) and Madrid. This is naturally reinforced by the fact that most of the population with a higher level of education is concentrated in these regions. This means there are similarities in Spain to the findings of Robert Putnam in Italy in his *Making Democracy Work* in which there is a correlation between the performance of different regional governments, their dependence on history and their economic development. Indeed, Mota and Subirats suggest cautiously that the reason for this higher level of social capital in the north-east is related to the historical trajectory of the kingdoms of Castile and

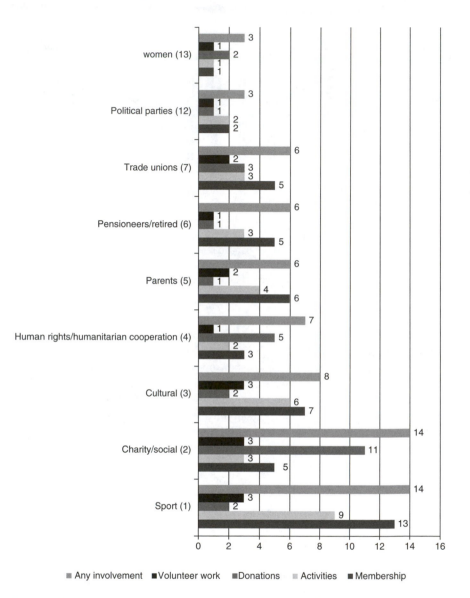

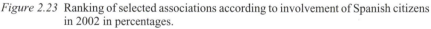

Figure 2.23 Ranking of selected associations according to involvement of Spanish citizens in 2002 in percentages.

Source: Morales and Mota, 2006: 86.

Aragon-Catalonia in contrast to the southern kingdom of Granada which became, after 1492, an integral part of the kingdom of Castile. All this makes us look hard at associativism in Spain in terms of the level of civic culture inherited through the centuries (Mota and Subirats, 2002: 113–8).

The role of the mass media, particularly television, in shaping politics has also increased in the past 25 years. According to a study on the 1993 elections, the strong impact of television on the coverage of political campaigns can be recognised. Although the quality of television coverage is much higher than in American television channels, nevertheless it shows a growing expansion of television as the main source of information (Gunther, Montero and Wert 1999: 38–55). Indeed, this naturally fits into a pattern of development towards a fully fledged political market behaviour of the electorate, which is approaching politics in a more individualised and utilitarian manner. One has to take into account that, since the early 1990s, Spanish television is no longer controlled by the state through their two channels TVE-1 and TVE-2. Today's Spanish population can resort to several channels with different positions towards the government. This has naturally led to fierce competition for audience quotas. In spite of that, TVE-1 is able to hold on to 18–19 per cent of the audience quota and Tele 5, which is owned by Silvio Berlusconi's media empire, 21 per cent. Antena 3 has a regular quota of 18–19 per cent and is owned mainly by Telefonica and the Spanish banks. La 2, the second channel of TVE, reaches only 4–5 per cent of the quota. Other channels are channel four (*cuatro*) with 7.8, channel six (*la sexta*) 2.8 per cent. The channels of the autonomous communities achieve together a audience share of 14–15 per cent. These figures show that the national television channels have lost considerable share of audience in the past two decades, while the television of the autonomous communities has stabilised a respectable share (*El Pais*, 14 January 2007: 81).

One should not underestimate the regional television stations which were established in the 1980s. Overall they achieve 18 per cent of the quota. The eight television stations in the autonomous communities are subsidised by the state, but they have difficulties in keeping their accounts in the black. Indeed, the Basque EITB or Catalan TV3 and C33 are quite expensive, because they want to translate many series and programmes into Basque and Catalan, which makes it impossible to sell them to other Spanish and international television channels. This is less problematic for the Valencian Community which has produced some programmes that became successful in other regions, due to the fact that they decided to make them in Spanish. The competition clearly affects TVE, currently the main national public broadcasting corporation, which has an annual deficit of 700 million and receives only 66.3 million annually from the state. The rest of the budget has to be financed through television advertising and the selling of their products (Spangenberg, 1998; *El Pais*, 28 July 2002: 22; *El Pais*, 1 December 2002: 61; *El Pais*, 7 February 2002: 26).

As Figure 2.24 shows, the vast majority of Spaniards either listen to radio or watch television to get information on politics. The vast majority watch or listen the regular daily news. A smaller minority read the political newspapers or watch further programmes on politics in radio or on television. Quite interesting is the fact that the Internet is still an almost virgin land in terms of getting information on politics for almost three-quarters of Spaniards. It means, that the vast majority of Spaniards is dependent on the information provided by the different channels, which are known to have different ideological tendencies.

The importance of television in Spanish society contributes to a simplification of the political message. The socialisation into a political market behaviour, which looks at politics in terms of personalisation and presidentialisation of the candidates, shows that the former left–right divisions are being replaced by more fluid forms of identity within an individualised society. Such Americanisation of Spanish politics thus gives a useful explanation for the lack of cohesion and permanence of social movements. The divisions are created from election to election according to different issues that may lead to polarisation along a left–right spectrum. The instrumentalisation of more such fluid catch-all strategies by political parties is naturally related to the fact that political parties in Spain are in reality cartel parties, meaning that they are more office-seeking and office-maintaining than ideological representations of the historical divisions. In this sense, membership is less important, while access to mass media becomes quite essential (Torcal and Chhiber, 1995). Indeed, they tend to me more *ad hoc* and less longterm than any in the past history of Spain. This has consequences for social movements, because the individualisation of society has also eroded the level of collective solidarity. Instead, social protest is sporadic and opportunistic, but not long term. Samuel H. Barnes calls this cognitive mobilisation in contrast to social mobilisation. Spain is an ideal country to understand this transformation from social to cognitive mobilisation, which is spreading across the developed countries of the world:

> Social mobilisation refers to elite-mass linkages through networks such as unions, social class and religious ties, and the like. Political mobilisation involves connections with political organisations, especially political parties and movements. Cognitive mobilisation emphasises the capabilities of individual citizens. They can gather and evaluate information on their own; they hold views concerning their interests and the best ways of advancing them; they become involved in politics in many ways; they may be active in traditional parties and political movements or they may seek out innovative forms of political involvement. In short, they possess the ability to function politically whether through traditional organisations or in other ways. The cognitive mobilisation does not mean the end of political mobilisation patterns or even of social mobilisation patterns. Rather it means that many well-educated and well-informed citizens are freed from dependence on these earlier forms of mobilisation and hence possess fewer incentives to use them. Such a view implies that cognitive mobilisation grows in importance among citizens with high levels of education and extensive communication networks. These are the people who have historically been shown in many comparative studies to be associated with high levels of political involvement.
>
> (Barnes, 1998: 128)

This summarises quite clearly what is going on in Spain. The emergence of cognitive mobilisation is related to the decline and erosion of divisions, the loss of importance of traditional organisations such as the Church and political parties and consequently the growing individualisation of society.

Although the level of associativism is lower in Spain, the experience with rigid authoritarian vertical structures during Francoism led to a fast transition of Spaniards towards less hierarchical forms of political engagement. This would imply that Spain is in midst of the worldwide transition from being a society based on survival values, such as gender inequality, strong faith in science and technology, low interpersonal trust and relatively low on environmental activism and low tolerance of outgroups to one based on self-expressive values, such as gender equality, environmental consciousness, tolerance of outgroups and a critical approach to science and technology. One of the most important aspects in the self-expressive post-material societies is that rigid institutions are being replaced by more flexible organisations which allow political activists more autonomy and self-expression (Inglehart and Welzel, 2005: 262). According to the typology of Ronald Inglehart and Christian Welzel, Spain is still considerably behind in relation to the Nordic countries, Germany, the Netherlands and other western European countries, but far ahead of most central and eastern European countries and other parts of the world (Inglehart and Welzel, 2005: 57).

In sum, associativism in Spain is still underdeveloped in comparison to other more advanced European countries. However, the lower number of activists is compensated by a more intense participation of its members. The low level of associativism can also be explained by the fact, that a possible worldwide transition from survival values to self-expressive societies is taking place and that Spain is in the midst of it but still without making the final big leap towards the latter.

Support for European union integration

One of the main features of Spanish political culture is that it is overwhelmingly pro-European, when we compare it with the Scandinavian countries, Austria and the United Kingdom. The main reason is that the European Union was always regarded as a means to democratise Spanish politics after decades of authoritarianism. Even during the Francoist dictatorship membership of European Community/European Union was something to strive for. Indeed, the opinion polls conducted by the Centre of Sociological Research (*Centro de Estudios Sociologicos* – CIS) based in Madrid show that since the late 1960s the population supports European integration as a way to converge on the EC countries in terms of economic, social and political modernisation and naturally democratisation (CIS, 1985). During and after democratic transition, the political elites and the population regarded the European Union as an external link[1] to achieve a stable, functioning democracy and naturally the modernisation of the Spanish economy and society (Whitehead, 1991). There are no relevant groups opposing the process towards European membership which started with the submission of the application in 1977 and led, after 8 years of difficult negotiations, to membership in 1986. Becoming part of the EC/EU was an important factor, to overcome an existing inferiority complex of Spaniards in relation to the dynamics of European integration. Francoism tried to lull the population into the idea that Spain is different in terms of culture, meaning that it is closer to the countries of Latin America than to Europe. This Francoist paradigm meant also a tendency towards the glorification of Spanish historical exceptionalism against any hint of Europeanisation (Pereira Castañares and Moreno Juste, 2000: 341–3).

Such an ambiguous cultural distinction became less and less viable with the modernisation of Spain throughout the 1960s and 1970s. Most of the Spaniards were more interested in European affairs, than the distant identity with Latin America (Pereira Castañares and Moreno Juste, 2000; 338). The consensual position of the political elites was supported by the population. All main political parties endorsed European Union membership, even if the communist coalition of parties, United Left (*Izquierda Unida* – IU), was moderately critical of some issues. In spite of the opposition of France due to the fact that Spain would be a major competitor in the agricultural sector, Spanish membership was regarded as a major success for the political class (Alvarez-Miranda, 1996).

Support for European integration has become probably one of the most salient features of Spanish political culture. Spain features among the countries that has the highest degrees of satisfaction with democracy in the European Union. This has not changed substantially throughout the 1990s. In 1999 it had the highest degree of satisfaction with the European Union and most recently it had the second highest degree of satisfaction (Figure 2.24)

Other indicators confirm this positive assessment of the European Union. The Spanish population has been overwhelmingly supportive of EU membership throughout the 1980s and 1990s. The lowest level of support was in 1994, when it fell to 40 per cent. Since then it has been above the EU average. More critical has been the question as to whether Spain has benefited from EU membership. There is a pattern which follows clearly the economic cycle in Spain. In difficult economic periods, there is a majority of Spaniards who believe that they have not benefited from EU membership, while in periods of economic growth the percentage of Spaniards who find that Spain has benefited from European Union membership increases considerably to between 45 and 60 per cent. This means that perception of benefit is closely linked to the performance of the economy. In spring 2007, two decades after joining the European Union, 75 per cent of Spaniards agreed that Spain had benefited from membership well above the EU27 average of 59 per cent (Magone, 2002: 230–1; Eurobarometer, 65, 2007: 18). Furthermore, 73 per cent of Spaniards support membership of the European Union, the highest score along with those of the Netherlands (77 per cent), Ireland (76 per cent) and Luxembourg (74 per cent) and Belgium (70 per cent). This contrasts heavily with other southern European countries – Portugal (55 per cent), Greece (55 per cent) and Italy (51 per cent) – all below the EU27 average of 57 per cent (Eurobarometer, 65, 2007: 17).

Spaniards are extremely proud of being Europeans. This is naturally related to their general support for EU membership. Spain is among the countries with the scores above the EU average (Figure 2.25).

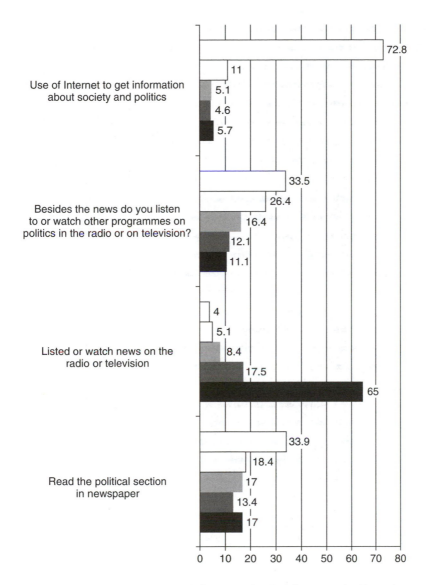

Use of Internet to get information about society and politics
- 72.8
- 11
- 5.1
- 4.6
- 5.7

Besides the news do you listen to or watch other programmes on politics in the radio or on television?
- 33.5
- 26.4
- 16.4
- 12.1
- 11.1

Listed or watch news on the radio or television
- 4
- 5.1
- 8.4
- 17.5
- 65

Read the political section in newspaper
- 33.9
- 18.4
- 17
- 13.4
- 17

□ Never □ With less frequence ▨ 1–2 days a week ▮ 3–4 days a week ▪ Every day

Figure 2.24 Media used by Spaniards to get information on politics.

Source: CIS Survey nr. 2700, April 2007, Question 12 to be found on http://www.cis.es accessed on 7 September 2007.

Figure 2.25 Satisfaction with how democracy works in the European Union (Spring 2006)–
Source: Eurobarometer, 65, Spring 2006, published January 2007: 48.

Nevertheless this does not mean that there is unconditional support for further European integration. In the past decade, Spaniards became more intergovern-mentalist in relation to the process of European integration. Over 60 per cent feel that the last word in any decision should belong to the member-states, only about 20 per cent advocate a supranational position, in which the European Union would take all decisions. According to policy areas the picture becomes more differentiated (Szmolka, 1999: 120–5). Environment, EMU, foreign policy in relation to third world countries, industrial policy, immigration and political asylum are regarded as policy areas that should be decided at supranational level, while education, culture, information, workers' rights in relation to employers, and media regulation should remain a domain of the member-state. In relation to defence and security the population is evenly split, but still slightly in favour that this should remain a domain of the member-states (Szmolka, 1999: 129–30). Spaniards in their vast majority want their government to work closely with the European Union in the most important problems such as unemployment, terrorism, immigration, pensions, research and development and support for regions with economic difficulties (Eurobarometer, 2007: 67: Spanish national survey: 13).

The cautious position of Spaniards towards intergovernmentalism does not mean that Spaniards are not supportive of further European integration. On the contrary, they normally are among the most pro-European peoples of the European Union, advocating a European constitution and further European unification for the future. For example, a less publicised news during the ratification process of the Constitutional Treaty during 2005, is that Spaniards approved it overwhelmingly with 76.96 per cent in a referendum which took place on 20 February 2005, in spite of a low turnout of 41.98 per cent (Delgado, Sotillos and Lopez-Nieto, 2006: 1266). Prime Minister José Luis Zapatero and the Spanish government has been so far a strong supporter of further European integration and continuing reform of the European Union. He represents a considerable change of attitude in relation to the more intergovernmentalist position of former Prime Minister José Maria Aznar. This shift of approach has certainly contributed to an increase in influence by the Spaniards in European Union affairs.

In spite of all this, Spain is also among the countries with the lowest levels of perceived knowledge of the European Union and the European institutions. This is naturally a major problem across most member-states, but affecting some countries more than others. In sum, Spaniards are overwhelmingly positive about the European Union, in spite of the fact that a continuing knowledge deficit of what happens at the supranational level leads us to a more moderate critical assessment of the quality of such endorsement to European integration.

Challenge to Spanish society and political culture: the growing importance of immigration

In the past 25 years Spain has experienced a fast pace of change which led to the opening up of the country. The country was ruled for 36 years by a more or less closed authoritarian regime. Spanish transition and consolidation to democracy coincided with a global transition from industrial to financial capitalism which is still not completed. Spain clearly became quite vulnerable to these global changes which also led to the emergence of other phenomena such as the globalisation of criminality and international movements of immigration and international terrorism.

Spanish political culture is currently confronted with several challenges which are affecting and will affect the country. The main one is immigration which has contributed to a substantial growth of the Spanish population, meaning that Spain is becoming more and more a multicultural society. Today, Spain has still the lowest percentage of foreigners among the EU member-states along with Portugal and Greece. All these three countries were traditional emigration countries. Now Spain is becoming an immigration country and there are still problems coping with this new role. According to figures from the National Institute of Statistics, on 1 January 2005 there were 3.73 million legalised foreigners in Spain, a more than seven times increase from the 49,973 of 1995 and a tripling of the 1.1 million of 2001. It corresponds to 8.5 per cent of the Spanish population. However, according to the figures of the Permanent Observatory on Immigration (*Observatorio Permanente de la Inmigración* – OPI) attached to the Spanish Labour ministry, the figures are much lower. OPI estimated that on 1 April 2005 2,054,453 foreigners had legal residence in Spain and this corresponded to 4.75 per cent of the population. These two figures show already the difficulties to find reliable data on the level of immigration in Spain. However the figures of 30 June 2007 which are 3,536,347 are closer to the 2005 figures of the National Institute of Statistics. In spite of the lower figures, one can agree that immigration to Spain has increased considerably. The reason for the different figures is related to different methods of calculation. Particularly, the figures of the Institute National of Statistics may include registered workers, who are no longer in employment or left the country. This leads to inflated figures. There is also consensus about the distribution of immigration in the main Spanish urban centres. The vast majority of foreign workers are concentrated in the more urbanised autonomous communities of Catalonia, Madrid, the Valencian Community and Andalucia. (Figures 2.26–2.28). In 2007, between them all are concentrated 65.2 per cent of all foreign workers. The remaining 34.8 per cent is distributed among 13 autonomous communities (Figure 2.28).

A large share of the foreign population come from the EU-27, particularly Romania and Bulgaria in the past seven years. However, one-third are inmigrants from Latin America, particularly from Colombia, Ecuador and Peru. A further quarter of the immigrants originate from Africa, particularly North Africa. Among them, the Moroccans are the most important community. (Figure 2.28; *El Pais*, 27 April 2005: 21) (Figure 2.29).

The vast majority of legal immigrants who pay into social insurance, work in the services sector, doing all kinds of jobs (61.6 per cent), construction (17.7 per cent), industry (9 per cent) and agriculture (11.7 per cent) (Fundación Encuentro, 2006: 237). Immigrants are concentrated in certain regions depending on the particular sector. Moroccans tend to work in the agricultural sector in Andalucia and Murcia, while Latin American female immigrants are normally domestic workers particularly in Madrid. In the tourism industry and construction we can find immigrants from all nationalities, with a slight predominance of male workers

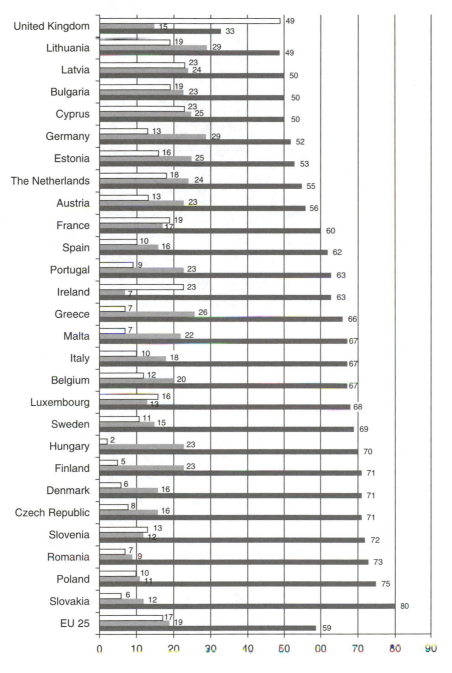

	I do not feel European	Not proud	Proud
United Kingdom	49	15	33
Lithuania	19	29	49
Latvia	23	24	50
Bulgaria	19	23	50
Cyprus	23	25	50
Germany	13	29	52
Estonia	16	25	53
The Netherlands	18	24	55
Austria	13	23	56
France	19	17	60
Spain	10	16	62
Portugal	9	23	63
Ireland	7	23	63
Greece	7	26	66
Malta	7	22	67
Italy	10	18	67
Belgium	12	20	67
Luxembourg	16	13	68
Sweden	11	15	69
Hungary	2	23	70
Finland	5	23	71
Denmark	6	16	71
Czech Republic	8	16	71
Slovenia	13	12	72
Romania	7	9	73
Poland	10	11	75
Slovakia	6	12	80
EU 25	17	19	59

□ I do not feel European ■ Not proud ■ Proud

Figure 2.26 Proud to be European in Autumn 2006.

Source: Eurobarometer, 65, Autumn 2006, published September 2007: 116.

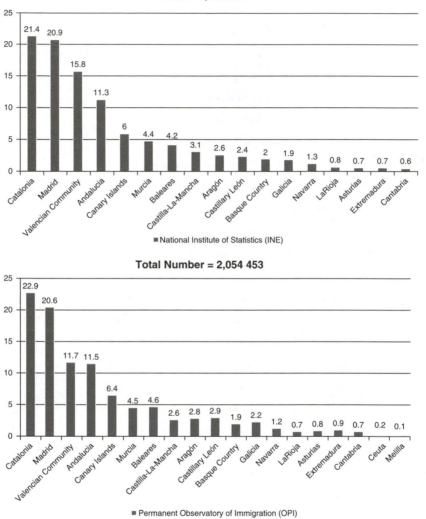

Total = 3,730.610

■ National Institute of Statistics (INE)

Total Number = 2,054 453

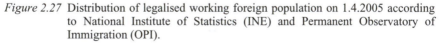

■ Permanent Observatory of Immigration (OPI)

Figure 2.27 Distribution of legalised working foreign population on 1.4.2005 according
to National Institute of Statistics (INE) and Permanent Observatory of
Immigration (OPI).

Source: Fundación Encuentro, 2006: 260; *El Pais*, 27 April 2005: 24.

from Latin America (Fundación Encuentro, 2006: 253). The Aznar government
tried to control immigration by adopting one of the toughest immigration laws
(*Ley de Extranjeria*) of the European Union in 2001. Such a policy was regarded
as essential by the government to deter potential immigrants from entering the
country illegally. Most illegal immigrants attempt to enter the country through

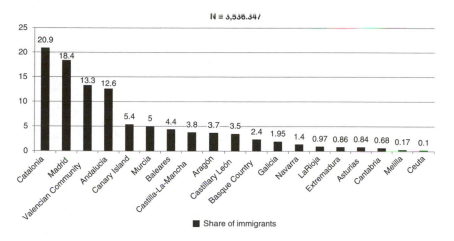

Figure 2.28 Distribution of legalised workers in the autonomous communities on 30 June 2007.

Source: Figures according to the Permanent Observatory of Immigration attached to the Ministry of Labour and Social Affairs, Ministerio del Trabajo y Asuntos Sociales, 2007: 4.

the two enclaves of Ceuta and Melilla in Morocco or through the Canary Islands.

According to Ministry of Interior figures over 18,517 illegal immigrants were detained in Gibraltar and the Canary Islands when they tried to enter the country illegally in 2001. In the process of catching them over 362 traffic networks were disbanded by the police. Spain was also tough in expelling and repatriating illegal immigrants who came mainly from Morocco, Senegal, Romania, Nigeria, Algeria and Ecuador. Rejection of entry on the border (particularly airports) targeted particularly Colombians, Moroccans and Ecuadorians. In 2001, 44,841 persons were denied entry to the country, expelled and repatriated (*El Pais*, 25 April 2002: 20; *El Pais*, 24 September 2002: 20; *El Pais*, 6 October 2002: 8; *El Pais*, 2 June 2003: 28). The number of estimated illegal immigrants was 462,957 – the so-called *sin papeles* (without documents) – and according to immigration law they are no longer allowed to legalise their situation (*El Pais*, 18 March 2003: 33). They remained in Spain in a permanent illegal situation, due to the fact that any employer who is caught employing illegal immigrants faces penalties. Somehow these immigrants are confronted with slave-like exploitation in the black market (economia submergida) which accounted for 28.7 per cent of Spanish GDP in the early first decade of the millenium. Aznar's policy was supported by the PSOE while it was in opposition up until mid-2002 (*El Pais*, Domingo, 16 June 2002: 2; *El Pais*, 24 September 2002: 21). Therefore, there was a growing conflict between the PP government and the opposition. The PP is very keen to push for stricter immigration laws, which is opposed by the PSOE and certain groups of civil society, in particular the Church (*El Pais*, 7 June 2002: 26; *El Pais*, 27 July 2002: 13).

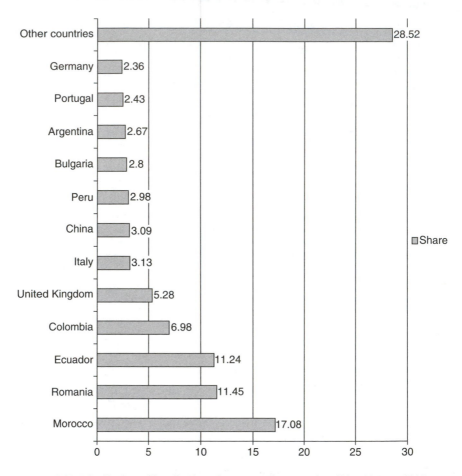

Figure 2.29 Distribution of legalised workers according to nationalities 30 June 2007.
Source: Ministerio de Trabajo y Asuntos Sociales, 2007: 3.

The government of José Luis Zapatero adopted a more or less similar policy, although it has emphasised more positive integrative aspects towards immigration, allowing for many illegal immigrants to legalise their status up until 7 May 2005. An official extraordinary period of legalisation was not firstly introduced by the Socialist government. In fact, from 1986 onwards this was the sixth such period of amnesty to legalise their immigrant status. Legalisation periods took place in 1986, 1991, 1996, 2000, 2001 and 2005. During the Aznar period there were three such processes of legalisation. In the last two in 2000 – 153,465 and in 2001 – 184,016 were able to legalise their working situation. The scale of the immigration phenomenon became quite apparent in 2005, when 550,136 immigrants were able to legalise their situation by the end of the year (Fundacion Encuentro, 2006: 235). It is estimated that this process of legalisation achieved to reduce the number of people working in the informal economy (*economia submergida*) by half-a-million at the end of 2005 (Fundación Encuentro, 2006. 235).

Zapatero's government was able to achieve a consensus of all parties, except the People's Party, on a package of proactive measures which includes reinforcement of border security forces, financial support for the border infrastructure and manpower of the countries from where immigrants are coming. Moreover, the European Union is also supporting these efforts of Spain in the context of the joint policing of the EU borders (*El Pais*, 17 February 2005: 33; *El Pais*, 2 June 2006: 24). A new border police called Frontex began to operate alongside Spanish forces in the second half of 2005. The Zapatero government avoided to use the populist card and through the amnesty of 2005 achieved a separation of those immigrants who are hard-working and want to build a new future in Spain, and those who may be involved in illegal and criminal activities and terrorism. Nonetheless, immigration from non-EU countries and the new EU member-states Romania and Bulgaria is still a major headache for the government. Quite problematic are the immigrants coming from Africa, who, in their desperation, cross the Atlantic ocean from the northwestern African coast to come to the Canary Islands and from Morocco and Algeria to the Spanish mainland. However, the government was successful in reducing considerably the number of immigrants through this concerted policy with the African countries and the European Border Police Frontex. For example, the cooperation with Algeria was reinforced. Four more maritime police brigades are to be created to intercept illegal immigrants. According to the figures of the Algerian police 2,600 illegal people were detained in 2007 (*El Pais*, 5 February 2008: 24). There has been a decline of boats (*pateras*) and immigrants by about 15 per cent between 2004 and 2005. This has been accompanied by a tough regime of deportations (repatriation) in cooperation with the African states. (*El Pais*, 19 May 2005: 30). Allegations of maltreatment and deceit by the Spanish and Senegalese authorities came forward in the case of the first group of repatriations to Senegal (*El Pais*, 2 June 2006: 24).

The PSOE government is very keen not to alienate the large Muslim population in Spain, because they need their support in the war against terrorism. In contrast to Germany, France, the Netherlands and the United Kingdom, the Muslim population is still quite small with estimates reaching from 300,000 (0.7 per cent) to 750,000 (1.5 per cent) of the overall population and 20–25 per cent of the foreign population. The moderate integrative policies of the PSOE government have helped so far to prevent a radicalisation of the Spanish Muslim population. There are naturally fears from more conservative politicians that the propaganda of Al Qaeda which speaks about the reconquest of Al-Andalus, meaning the whole Iberian Peninsula, is taken seriously by some extreme groups. Al Andalus is an period idealised by Al Qaeda: it is when Spain was dominated by different Muslim Khalifs between 710AD and 1269AD. The March 11, 2004 events are a strong reminder that the Spanish state needs the support of the Spanish Muslim community to undermine the power of these extremist Islamic terrorist groups. In fact, some more conservative analysts speak of immigration as a strategy of penetration of Al Qaeda to achieve the reconquest of Al-Andalus. (Aristegui, 2005: 262–3).

Most recently, the PSOE has hardened its immigration policies by being more proactive in fighting illegal immigration, but it has simultaneously sought a reform of the immigration law in order to depoliticise this issue (*El Pais*, 7 October 2006; *El Pais*, 11 October 2006). The PP very much uses a language which is tough on immigration, and which certainly attracts part of the electorate. The outcome is that PP has occupied this space, which under other circumstances would have been seized by new populist right-wing parties. In terms of party programmes, one can say that there are almost no differences, both parties support an orderly immigration policy to offset the ageing of the population (Partido Popular, 2004: 44–6; PSOE, 2004: 124–5). The only difference is probably one of style: the PSOE is perceived as soft on immigration and it seeks an all-party consensus in this particular policy, while the PP tends to present a tougher uncompromising position. Traditionally, the United Left tends to support the immigrants and their integration in society. In terms of the population, it seems that the strategy of the Socialist party to depoliticise the immigration issue has been working. The vast majority of the population regards immigration as a positive thing, but the share of support has been declining particularly after 11 March 2004 (see Figure 2.30).

According to figures from Eurobarometer, the population is split over the question of the contribution of immigrants. A slight majority does not agree that immigration is making a contribution to the country. (see Figure 2.31).

This tense situation creates major problems for the integration of immigrants which affects in particular children of non-EU countries. According to the Ministry of Education in school year 2006–07 the number of foreign pupils in Spanish

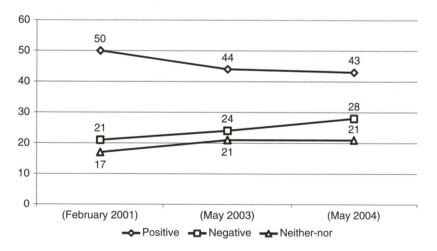

Figure 2.30 Immigration, a positive or negative thing?

Source: CIS, Datos de Opinion, Boletin 36: La Opinion de los barometros de 2004, September–December 2004, CIS, Datos de Opinion, Boletin 32, May–August 2003.

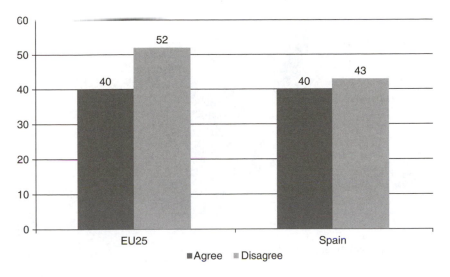

Figure 2.31 Does immigration contribute to your country? (2006).

Source: Eurobarometer 65, September–October 2006.

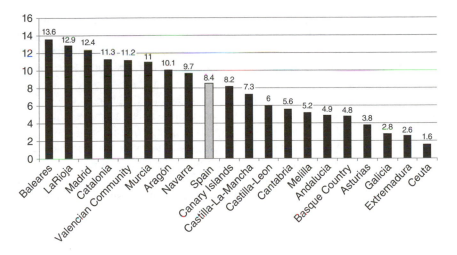

Figure 2.32 Percentage of foreign pupils in Spanish schools 2006–07.

Source: Ministerio de Educacion y Ciencia, 2007b: 8.

schools was 8.4 per cent. Most of them are in kindergarten, primary and secondary school.

This means that in the future a new generation will contribute to a more multicultural society in Spain. There is also a strong minority of North African children in Spanish schools. In most parts of Spain integration has been easy,

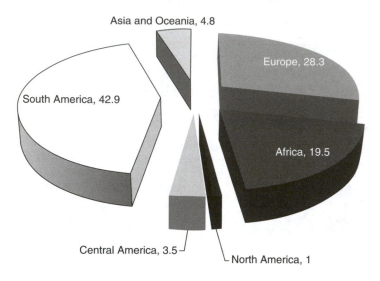

Figure 2.33 Foreign pupils in Spanish schools according to world regions 2006–07.
Source: Ministerio de Educación y Ciencia, 2007b: 8.

but sometimes it has led to conflict. For example, in Madrid there was a dispute between a school, which wanted to prohibit the wearing of the veil by a Moroccan girl, and the girl's parents. In the end the decision of the school was overturned by the Ministry of Education (*El Pais*, 17 February 2002: 22; *El Pais*, 2 June 2003: 34). Spaniards in their overwhelming majority are very tolerant. The relationship of parents with children is overwhelmingly liberal, even if there are always some tensions between the generations. This naturally shows that authoritarianism and intolerant attitudes are no longer strong in Spanish society. Indeed, this is evident by the fact that Spaniards do not vote for extreme right-wing parties. In spite of racist outbursts in Andalusia against immigrants in the village of Ejido in 1999, normally any form of xenophobic behaviour is condemned in Spanish society. This is indeed a precondition for any positive integration of foreigners into Spanish society.

Conclusions

The transformation of political culture in Spain from authoritarianism to democratic moderation and tolerance has been one of the greatest achievements of the new consensual constitution. The state of autonomies is well consolidated in the Spanish psyche. Although there are calls for fully fledged federalism, the population is quite content with the status quo according to opinion polls. Spaniards are not very keen to become members of political parties, trade unions or nongovernmental organisations, but they mobilise themselves on an *ad hoc* basis to support certain issues. The demonstrations against war in Iraq in March and

April 2003, in which over 3 million persons participated, far more than in London, shows that Spanish society may be mobilised *en masse on certain occasions*. Other examples of such mass demonstrations can be found in relation to the fight against Basque terrorism in the *Basta Ya!* movement, the protest against the Law of Quality in Higher Education (*Ley de Cualidad*) presented by Education Minister Pilar del Castillo in 2001, the demonstration on 12 March 2004 against the Madrid bombings perpetrated by Al Qaeda around the Atocha train station the previous day or the mobilisation of conservative interest groups against gay marriages and the change of the law on education by the Socialist party in 2005. Spain is moving from what were patterns of political mobilisation which involve traditional ideological commitment to political parties through membership and political action to patterns of cognitive mobilisation which are more characterised by more flexible individual and informed commitment to social movements without being clearly linked through membership to a particular political or social group. Spanish society is extremely supportive of European integration, although it is keen to preserve the power of the member-states against an overall dominance at the supranational level. Nevertheless, Spaniards are supportive of further European integration. Spanish society is being challenged today by constitutional issues and the exponential growth of immigration, of what was once traditionally an emigration country. However, after decades of consensual politics, old styles of polarisation between left and right have created new divisions in Spanish society. The future will show if these issues can be mastered by this tolerant and moderate society. Other challenges continue to shape Spanish political culture: Basque terrorism, international Al Qaeda terrorism and naturally the permanent feature of unemployment. All these are issues that we will return to in subsequent chapters.

3 The core Spanish institutions

The Spanish constitution at thirty: a successful framework for politics

After two centuries of political instability and regime discontinuity the settlement of the present Spanish constitution has to be considered a great success. Between 1812 and 1978, Spain had seven different constitutions which had been imposed either by the Right or the Left (Table 3.1). Moreover, we can count nine documents if we include a further two constitutional projects, the one of 1856 inspired by the *liberal progressistas* was approved but not ratified and the project of the constitution of the First Republic in 1873. In total, 166 years had to pass by between the first democratic constitution of Cadiz approved in 1812 and the 1978 constitution, in order for Spain to enjoy a stable and strong democracy. According to the constitutionalist Roberto Blanco Valdés, Spanish constitutionalism evolved like a pendulum which moved back and forth between progressism and conservatism. According to his calculations, Spain experienced 68 years of 'oligarchical, closed-minded and anti-democratic constitutionalism', further 62 years of 'radical negation of constitutionalism' (the 6 years of absolutist rule between 1814 and 1820, the dictatorship of Primo de Rivera between 1923 and 1931 and the dictatorship of Francisco Franco between 1939 and 1975), but barely three decades of progressism and democracy (Blanco Valdés, 2006b: 26).

Such regime instability led to the polarisation of Spanish politics culminating in civil wars throughout the nineteenth century up until 1939. The long authoritarian regime under Franco was clearly a major factor in moderating the positions between left and right. It allowed the emergence of a new generation which was no longer trapped in the politics of polarisation. The consensualism around the Spanish constitution of 1978 acquired over time a mystique around it, because it had achieved the conciliation of left-wing and right-wing Spaniards. More than that, it symbolised a new beginning. The images of the fratricidal Civil War haunted the minds of all the participants in the constitutional settlement. Consensualism was the creation of a new language to avoid even a return to a civil war situation.

The constitutional settlement took an extremely long time to achieve. It showed the genuine attempt of the negotiating political elites of avoiding the behaviour of the past. After the Law of Political Reform was passed by the Francoist Cortes on

Table 3.1 Constitutional development, 1812–1978

Constitution	Period	Ideological orientation
Constitution of Cadiz	1812–1814; 1820–1823	Constitutional Monarchy, Liberal, progressive
Six years of absolutist rule (1814–1820)		
Royal Statute	1834	Constitutional Monarchy, Conservative
Constitution of 1837	1837–1945	Constitutional Monarchy, Reform of Cadiz Constitution, Liberal, progressive
Constitution of 1845	1845–1956; 1958–1969	Constitutional Monarchy, Conservative
Constitution of 1869	1869–1873	Constitutional Monarchy, Liberal, progressive
First Republic (1873–1874)		
Constitution of the Restoration	1876–1923	Constitutional Monarchy, Conservative
Dictatorship of General Miguel Primo de Rivera (1923–1931)		
Constitution of 1931	1931–1939	2nd Republic, progressive, social constitution
Dictatorship of General Francisco Franco (1939–1975)		
Constitution of 1978	1978–	Constitutional Monarchy, Social-democratic

18 November 1976, a legal transition from the authoritarian regime to democracy was initiated. In the referendum on 15 December 1976, an overwhelming majority approved the Law of Political Reform. After the considerable courage of Prime Minister Adolfo Suarez, of which the climax was the legalisation of all political parties, including the Communist Party, in spite of considerable opposition from the Francoist ultraconservative military bunker, legislative elections took place on 15 June 1977. Although Suarez' party was able to gain a relative majority, his party the Union of Democratic Centre (*Unión del Centro Democratico* – UCD) was only able to get a relative majority. Nonetheless, it became the pivotal party in terms of negotiating the constitutional settlement. There were thirteen parties represented in the Cortes, but only eight were at the forefront of the constitutional settlement: Union of Democratic Centre, Socialists (PSOE), Communists (PCE), the neo-Francoist People's Alliance (AP), the Democratic Pact for Catalonia (PCD), Catalan Republican Left (ERC), Basque Nationalist Party (PNV) and the Basque Left (EE).

The whole process started on 22 July 1977 with the creation of a Committee for Constitutional Affairs and Public Freedoms. On 2 August the Committee created a subcommittee which was to consist of eight members according to the strength of the parliamentary groups: two members from the UCD, two members from PSOE, one from PCE, one from AP, one from the PCD and one from the PNV. However, the PNV decided to boycott the whole process, so that the subcommittee was reduced to seven members. The overall process of negotiations was quite informally based, according to Roberto Blanco Valdés, on gentlemen's agreements, and took half a year to complete. Over 1,000 amendments were presented to the proposed constitutional project. Further deliberations took place separately in the Congress and Senate, before a joint bicameral committee ironed out the discrepancies of the versions of the two houses. Finally, the constitution was approved in the Congress with 325 votes out of 350, only six MPs, mainly coming from AP and the Basque Left, voted against, fourteen abstained, including members of the PNV and there were five absences. In the Senate, 226 out of 248 approved it, five voted against, eight abstained and nine were absent. It meant that 94 per cent of MPs and Senators voted positively for the new constitution (see Table 3.2). A referendum on 6 December led to an overwhelming support of 88 per cent of the population (Blanco Valdés, 2006: 38–9), only in the Basque Country was there a considerable level of abstention, because it was felt the constitution did not go far enough in terms of regional autonomy. Overall, the new constitution had five readings and took a considerable amount of time, before it gained this high level of approval (Cascajo and Bustos, 2001: 102). (see Figure 3.1)

Table 3.2 Position of parties before the Constitutional Referendum on 6 December 1978

For the constitution	*Against the constitution*	*Abstention*
Parliamentary parties		
• Union of Democratic Centre (UCD) • Spanish Socialist Workers' Party (PSOE) • Spanish Communist Party (PCE) • Democratic Pact for Catalonia • Democratic Left	• National Spanish Union • Spanish Democratic Action	• Basque Nationalist Party (PNV) • Catalan Republican Left (ERC) • Basque Left (EE)
Extra-parliamentary parties		
• Carlist Party • Liberal Citizen Action • Liberal Party • Revolutionary Organisation of Workers	• Spanish Phalanx (FE de la JONS) • Traditionalist Communion • *Herri Batasuna* (political arm of ETA) • Communist Revolutionary League (LCR) • Feminist groups	• Organisation of the Communist Left • Spanish Workers' Communist Party • United Canary People

Source: Esteban, 1989: 298.

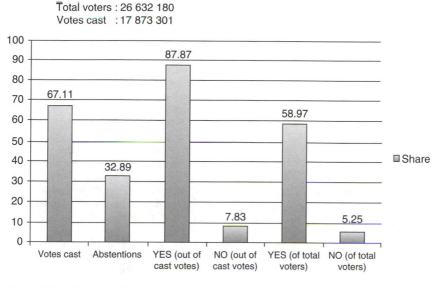

Total voters : 26 632 180
Votes cast   : 17 873 301

Figure 3.1 Referendum on Spanish Constitution on 6 December 1978.
Source: Own graph based on *El Pais*, 22 December 1978 quoted in Esteban, 1989: 246.

The most important single issue of the constitutional settlement was the form of state. In the succession laws of the authoritarian regime, it was enshrined that King Juan Carlos should succeed Franco when he died. Such a peaceful succession allowed for a similar peaceful transition to democracy. There was opposition from the Socialist Party and other smaller socialist parties against the restoration of the monarchy. They were profoundly republican and could not bear the return of the monarchy. For the communists, who were regarded as the arch-enemies of the former authoritarian regime, it was more important to achieve again a democratic order than reject the constitutional monarchy (Ramirez, 1989: 69–70). The leader of the Communist Party, Santiago Carrillo, was aware that the situation was too delicate to push the boundaries of the possible. The communists termed the situation a *ruptura pactada* (negotiated break), meaning that any break with the authoritarian regime had to be done in agreement with all political forces, in particular the Francoist supporters, otherwise the delicate situation could again lead to the breakdown of the process (Prego, 2000: 68). Carrillo was also very much part of a Eurocommunist movement, which had distanced itself from the Soviet Union and advocated an integration into peaceful national politics. According to Adolfo Suarez, the main architect of the new democratic system, the Law of Political Reform (*Ley de la Reforma Politica*) had given enough popular legitimacy to avoid a proper referendum on the form of the Spanish state. In the Law of Political Reform, designed to end the former authoritarian regime legally and open up the process towards democratic transition, the word 'king' appeared five times.

Table 3.3 Structure of Spanish Constitution

Preamble		
Preliminary Title	Art. 1–9	Legal, Social and Political Foundations of the Spanish State **Article 1 (State Principles, Sovereignty, Form)** (1) Spain constitutes itself into a social and democratic state of law which advocates liberty, justice, equality, and political pluralism as the superior values of its legal order. (2) National sovereignty belongs to the Spanish people from whom emanate the powers of the state. (3) The political form of the Spanish State is the parliamentary Monarchy. **Article 2 (National Unity, Regional Autonomy)** The Constitution is based on the indissoluble unity of the Spanish nation, the common and indivisible homeland of all Spaniards, and recognises and guarantees the right to autonomy of the nationalities and regions which make it up and the solidarity among all of them.

Title I
  Basic Rights
  and Duties
	Art. 10–55	Chapter 0: (Art. 10) Human Dignity and Human Rights
		Chapter 1: Spaniards and Aliens
		Chapter 2: Rights and Freedoms
		Chapter 3: Guiding Principles of Economic and Social Policy
		Chapter 4: Guarantees and Fundamental Rights
		Chapter 5: Suspension of Rights and Liberties

Title II The Crown	Art. 56–65	

Title III
  Parliament
  (*Cortes Generales*)
	Art. 66–96	Chapter 1: Chambers
		Chapter 2: Preparation of Laws
		Chapter 3: International Treaties

Title IV
  Government and
  Administration
	Art. 97–107	

Title V
  Government and
  Parliament
	Art. 108–116	

Title VI Judicial Power	Art. 117–127	
Title VII Economy and Finance	Art. 128–136	

Table 3.3 Continued

Preamble		
Title VIII Territorial Organisation	Art. 137–158	Chapter 1: General Principles Chapter 2: Local Administration Chapter 3: Autonomous Communities
Title IX Constitutional Court	Art. 159–165	
Title X Constitutional Amendment	Art. 166–169	
Additional Provisions	1–4	Guarantee of historical rights (*fueros*)
Transitional Provisions	1–9	Possibility of Navarre to become part of Basque Country
Repeal Provision		Repeal of Francoist Laws
Final Provision		Date of entering into force

Source: Institute for Constitutional Law, database.

The king was the executor of the transition to democracy, so that the greater part of the Law of Political Reform gave enough legitimacy for the restoration of the monarchy (Prego, 2000: 46–7). In the end, the abstention of the socialists and other republican parties in the Cortes and the support of the communists led to agreement over the form of the state. The constitution also expresses in Article 1, paragraph one, that national sovereignty belongs to the Spanish people, from which all powers of the state emanate. It means that the constitutional monarchy was established by the people and it is dependent on its approval. Spain can be called, according to Roberto Blanco Valdés, paraphrasing the constitutionalist Georg Jellinek a 'Republic with a hereditary chief of state' (Blanco Valdés, 2006b: 75) (see Table 3.3).

The second most important issue was the future territorial organisation of Spain. After decades of repression, the historical regions of Catalonia, Basque Country and Galicia clearly wanted a return to normalcy. The main difficulty was to find a compromise between the Francoist elites, who wanted to preserve a centralised unitary state, fearful of regionalist demands which would lead eventually to the break-up of Spain, and the opposition, dominated by socialists and communists, who wanted a restoration of autonomous governments in the historical regions. In the end, the compromise became the state of autonomies (*estado de autonomias*) which today is well accepted by the population. The constitution allowed for an open-ended outcome to this question by allowing two ways of achieving autonomy: a faster (Art. 143) and a slower route (Art. 146). The outcome was the establishment of seventeen autonomous communities by 1983. This so-called regional dynamics was unpredicted by the actors of the constitutional settlement, but for UCD politicians it was the best way to neutralise the over-dominance of Catalonia or the Basque Country in this devolution process. In the end, the state of autonomies was accepted by all participants. Originally, the left-wing parties had an ambitious agenda of constitutionalising Spain into a federal state, but the consensual process led to the formula of the 'state of autonomies'. In this sense, this crucial question was watered down and delayed in the indefinite future (Cascajo and Bustos, 2001: 102). Nevertheless, there was an attempt by the more conservative sectors of the UCD, with support from the Socialist Party, to curb the dynamics of the autonomy process by wanting to gain centralised control over the whole process. The Organic Law for the Harmonisation of the Autonomy Process (*Ley Organica para la Armonización del Proceso Autonómico* – LOAPA) was introduced by the UCD government in July 1981, in order to prevent the autonomous communities, apart from the Basque, Catalan and Galician ones, from being able to upgrade their autonomy statutes to the same more comprehensive level. However, the Constitutional Court decided against the government and for the autonomous communities in the legendary sentence STC 76/1983. There, the Constitutional Court upheld a constitutional guarantee of autonomy against any centralist interpretations of the UCD and other right-wing parties (Cascajo and Bustos, 2001: 115).

In 1992, the Socialist government and the People's Party were able to come to an agreement about the further process of autonomy. One important decision was to achieve a levelling of the competences between the different autonomous communities and reduce the existing asymmetrical federalism which advantaged the historical regions. Organic Law 9/1992 of 23 December translated the agreement into law. However, in 2004 a 'second decentralization' (*segunda decentralización*), in which several autonomous communities started to reform of the statutes, re-created the asymmetrical system of the early days. While the statute of the Valencian Community was approved within the framework prescribed by the Spanish Constitution of 1978, the Catalan statute of 2006 led to major changes, which will certainly lead to a new dynamics of regional competition. According to Roberto Blanco Valdés, there are three aspects of the statute that are innovative and will certainly affect the reform of other statutes. Firstly, the statute reduces to a minimum the presence of the Spanish state in the Catalan political system. Secondly, the creation of bilateral institutions such as the bilateral committee of Spanish government and Generalitat or the joint committee of the Spanish government and the Generalitat for economic and financial issues. Thirdly, there are several provisions that allow the Catalan government to be present in the institutions of the central state (Blanco Valdés, 2006: 201). This is also the reason why the People's Party decided to send an appeal to the Constitutional Court in order to check the constitutionality of this development.

In this sense, the Spanish state has already overcome the limited interpretation of the 'state of autonomies'. Several authors refer to Spain as a federal, or quasi-federal state. This expresses itself institutionally through its advanced multi-level political system, through the distribution of competences between centre and periphery, a process that started in the early 1980s and is still ongoing, and last, but not least, through the constitutional guarantees of such federalism, which is embodied in the constitution of 1978 and the seventeen autonomous statutes (Blanco Valdés, 2006b: 195–8; see also Aja, 2003: chapters 3 and 4; Requejo, 2007).

However, the issue of representation at central level continues to be a major problem. The Socialist government, under Prime Minister José Luis Zapatero, wanted to introduce a reform of the Senate, but, as in many attempts before, it has so far been delayed. Elisa Roller made aware of the impossible mission to reform the Senate due to the lack of consensus as to how to do it (Roller, 2002b).

Another formal issue that still needs to be resolved through a constitutional reform is the inclusion of the names of the seventeen autonomous communities in the constitution. Indeed, the whole constitutional process took place only after the constitution was ratified, and an update has become a necessity. Although the socialists are keen to introduce this update, PP are worried that this may lead to the end of the constitution, which worked so well for 30 years.

The Spanish constitution is also remarkable in another aspect. It lists a whole catalogue of personal, civil, political, economic and social rights. Although personal, civil and political rights are the most important ones in terms of the constitutional reality, economic and social rights represent the desire of the constituent assembly to write a modern constitution which would embody principles of the postwar welfare state. Moreover, it expressed the need to list all the rights of citizens in relation to the state authority after almost four decades of Francoism. The definition of the state as democratic and social, based on the rule of law clearly was designed to break with the previous regime (Gonzalez Marrero, 1995: 37). The model for this long catalogue which works juridically as interactive 'system of protection of rights and freedoms' (Blanco Valdés, 2006b: 228) is the German Basic Law (*Grundgesetz*). In this sense, the similarity of the experiences of both countries led the Spanish elite of transition to develop a strong catalogue of rights and catalogues in order to prevent such a situation from emerging again (Blanco Valdés, 2006b: 205).

One has here to emphasise the 'social dimension' of the constitution, one that wants to achieve a higher level of equality in society. This is expressed in the first paragraph, Article 1, of the constitution as follows:

> Spain constitutes itself into a social and democratic state of law which advocates liberty, justice, equality, and political pluralism as the superior values of its legal order.
>
> (Spanish Constitution, Art.1)

Since the Socialist Party came to power in 1982, the expansion of the welfare state has been an important aspect of policy-making. The governments of Prime Minister Felipe Gonzalez expanded considerably the education sector, particularly in Higher Education, and provided students with a generous grant system. They also created one of the most comprehensive health systems and considerably improved the social benefits system. Such policies were continued by the governments of Prime Minister José Maria Aznar. Prime Minister José Luis Zapatero has been also very keen to improve the quality of life of Spanish citizens. Some of the initiatives launched in 2007 include the one-off payment for families which have more new-borns (*cheque-bébé*) and free dental care for children. In spite of all these attempts, Spain continues to be one of the less egalitarian European societies along with Portugal, Greece, Italy, the United Kingdom and Estonia.

The relationship of the new state towards the Catholic Church was quite crucial. After centuries of a close relationship between state and the Church, with the exception of the Second Republic, this issue was quite relevant to the constitutional debate. The adopted formula ended the special relationship of the state with the Catholic Church, making the separation of state and Church definitive. The new formula clearly made it imperative for the state to have a neutral position in relation to all religious confessions (Gonzalez Marrero, 1995: 33). The recent disputes between the Socialist government and the Catholic Church over the role of religion in state schools, gay marriages and the state subsidies show that still today the latter wants a privileged position within the political system, something that the 'non-denominational state' cannot allow anymore.

The Spanish constitution introduces also a Constitutional Court of twelve judges appointed by the King upon a proposal of the Congress, Senate, Government and the Council of Judiciary Power. This is regarded as an important institution, which checks on the constitutionality of laws. The model is the Austrian constitution, which was influenced and designed by the constitutionalist Hans Kelsen. Due to high prerequisites to change the constitution, the constitution is quite rigid and the opinions of the Constitutional Court gain in special importance.

The Spanish constitution is clearly incomplete in many respects, meaning that it has an open-ended nature about it. The development of the state of autonomies is clearly the most visible example, but it also allowed for developments in other policy areas such as health and education. In this sense, it was able to accommodate all interests up until now. The consensualism of the transition process makes it difficult to repeat the experience. However, it was able to be a good framework for the Spanish political system for the past 30 years. This is one of the reasons why the PP do not want any change. It may in the end open a Pandora's box, leading to major changes which will lead potentially to a centre–periphery conflict. Although the Socialist Party wants a constitutional reform, it should be a light one, which just updates some of its aspects. Apart from the reform of the Senate, and the inclusion of the denominations of the seventeen autonomous communities, the Socialist government wants to lift the discriminatory regulations related to the female succession to the throne and adjust the constitution to the new developments in the European Union after 2004 (*El Pais*, 13 January 2006: 18).

The monarchy as the main pillar of Spanish democracy

One of the key personalities of the Spanish democratic transition is without doubt King Juan Carlos, who clearly steered the whole process up until 1981, when Colonel Antonio Tejero and General Milan del Bosch attempted a coup d'état on 23 February and to gain the support of the king for it. His firm commitment to democracy against these soldiers strengthened his position in Spanish politics and society. Since then, the monarchy has gained enormous prestige among the Spanish political elites and the population. Although the monarch only has formal powers, he is certainly an important symbol of political and territorial unity. He is the commander-in-chief of the Spanish armed forces, something that became quite evident in the 1981 coup attempt (Powell, 1996: 168–78).

Apart from this extraordinary situation, King Juan Carlos I remained more or less in the background of Spanish politics, fulfilling his formal duties with extreme competence. Among his powers are the ratification of laws adopted by the Spanish Cortes, the convention and dissolution of the Cortes, the call for new elections, the appointment of the prime minister and the members of cabinet after passing an investiture vote in the Cortes and eventual participation in the meetings of the cabinet, if so requested by the prime minister (Art. 62). After his father's renunciation of his claim to the throne on 14 May 1977[1], Juan Carlos was no longer dependent on the legitimacy coming from the Francoist dictatorship, and could claim to be the legitimate historical heir of the Bourbon dynasty (Art. 57). At the same time, the monarchy is regarded as a new dynasty breaking completely with the past. This is most visible in the definition of the state as a parliamentary democracy (Art. 1), meaning that parliament becomes the central legitimating source of the monarchy. In this sense, the monarchy acquires an almost republican flavour. It reflects the compromise achieved among the elites of the transition (Bernecker, 1998: 186–7). The symbolic role of the King as commander-in-chief of the armed forces was quite evident during the Aznar period. Former Prime Minister José Maria Aznar did not convene the advisory body in defence matters, the Junta of National Defence (*Junta de Defensa Nacional*) in questions such as the crisis with Morocco over the Perejil and the Iraq War. The Junta, with the presence of the King, was convened for the last time during the Aznar government in January 2002. This shows that the government is quite autonomous in its decisions to go to war. In November 2005, the Junta was replaced by the Council of National Defence (*Consejo Nacional de la Defensa*) with the same advisory powers. The first meeting of the new body took place only on 10 October 2007, in which both King Juan Carlos as well as Crown Prince Felipe were present (*El Pais*, 3 October 2007: 20).

The King is very charismatic and well liked by the population. In opinion polls since the 1970s, the King receives 70–80 per cent of support. He was even able to convince Spaniards who were against the monarchy. He received a greater degree of trust than any other political institution. This is regarded as a further source of legitimacy (*El Pais*, 22 November 2000: 4). In a survey in November 2006, undertaken by the Centre for Sociological Research (CIS), the monarchy came out as the institution with the highest score. In a scale from 0 to 10, it got 5.19 after the police with 5.76 and the army with 5.41 (*El Pais*, 2 October 2007: 19). In another survey conducted by Metroscopia on 4 and 5 October 2007, an overwhelming majority of 69 per cent supported the monarchy, only 22 per cent preferred a republic. The monarchy emerged as the most valued institution with 6.3 in a scale of 0 to 10. The most monarchic groups were those in the age over 55 years with 7.7, followed by the age group between 35 and 54 years with 6.1, and the age group between 18 and 34 with 5.8. The monarchy is particularly appreciated by the lower-middle classes which had a score of 7.1 above the average. The monarchy is particularly supported by PP voters with 7.6, and also by socialist ones with the lower score of 6.8. The monarchy is valued higher than local authorities (6);

autonomous communities (5.6); the media and entrepreneurs (5.5); parliament (5.3) and government (5.2) (*El Pais*, 12 October 2007: 22).

Although the role of the King is only formal, his diplomatic and political experience is quite invaluable for any prime minister. Meanwhile, King Juan Carlos has been able to advise five prime ministers. His knowledge of the political world and his network of contacts can be an asset to any prime minister. His authority does not flow from his weak powers, which are mostly of formal nature, but from his accumulated knowledge over decades in the political world. For example, he plays an important part in the Ibero-American summits which have been taking place since 1991, and he accompanies the Prime minister and the minister of foreign affairs. Among such events have been the Ibero-American summit of 16–17 November 2002 in Playa Bavaro, Mexico (*El Pais*, 17 November 2002: 2–3) and the one of 3–5 November 2006 in Montevideo, Uruguay (*Anuario, El Pais*, 2007: 102–3).

The recent intervention of King Juan Carlos during a speech of the populist president of Venezuela Hugo Chavez in the Ibero-American summit in San José, Costa Rica on 17–18 November 2007 was quite controversial. After a long speech by Chavez, in which he insulted José Maria Aznar as non-democratic and a fascist, Prime Minister Zapatero intervened and defended José Maria Aznar with whose opinions he may not agree, but whom he respected and who was democratically elected. After this intervention of Zapatero, Chavez started his attacks again, when King Juan Carlos intervened and asked him to literally 'shut up' (*calla-te!*). This intervention of the King was seen as inappropriate by most commentators, although many Spaniards liked this intervention. However, there were also many people who criticised this intervention of the King in politics. Many found that in recent times the King had stepped up their prominence in ongoing political debates, for example the speech of Oviedo in October 2007 (see below; *El Pais*, 17 November 2007; 18 November 2007). One has also to acknowledge, that president Hugo Chavez visited King Juan Carlos during his trip to Europe on 26 July 2008 and that both made up. The royal family is well liked among Spaniards and Prince Felipe is being prepared as the successor of Juan Carlos I. This will certainly be a challenge for the Spanish monarchy when the time comes.

Although the vast majority of population supports the monarchy as a symbol of national unity, and particularly King Juan Carlos I as an incumbent, the Republican tradition is still alive in Spain. Sometimes it emerges as a protest movement among smaller groups who want independence of certain regions, such as Catalonia, from Spain. The best example was an incident which led to major discussion in Spain. On 13 September 2007, King Juan Carlos visited the Catalan city of Girona in order to inaugurate the Scientific and Technological Park of the University. The King stayed overnight and a group of Republican supporters of Catalan independence burned a picture of the King and Queen Sofia and read a statement against the monarchy. Some politicians of the Catalan Republican Left regarded this as freedom of expression and no action should be taken against the perpetrators, but the People's Party regarded this as a major offence against the monarchy. After the arrest of one of the alleged perpetrators Jaume Roura, several hundred people joined a demonstration of solidarity in which slogans in Catalan such as 'I am also anti monarchistic' (*Jo també soc anti-monarquic/a*) were carried. On this occasion, further pictures of the royal family were burned. One week later further demonstrations took place across medium-sized towns in Catalonia. Most of these activists are young and belong to different ideological groups, in particular small Catalan independence movements (*El Pais*, 14 September 2007: 21; *El Pais*, 16 September 2007: 20; *El Pais*, 23 September 2007: 29).

In a speech at the University of Oviedo, the King Juan Carlos responded to these incidents by emphasising that the Monarchy had contributed to the longest period of stability and democracy in Spain. In spite of differences, all major political parties including representatives of the Catalan ERC and CiU supported the intervention of the King. The consequence was an isolation of minority radical groups of the Republican Left and the extreme Right (*El Pais*, 2 October 2007: 18–19). All this happened shortly before the national holiday (*Fiesta Nacional*), celebrated on 12 October. In spite of calls for national unity by the government, the PP campaigned against the former, by saying that it failed to defend the King and Spain. Even former Prime Minister José Maria Aznar intervened in the debate against Prime Minister Zapatero and his government (*El Pais*, 5 October 2007: 21; *El Pais*, 12 October 2007: 23).

In sum, the monarchy re-established itself after a very negative history in the nineteenth and twentieth centuries. The centrality of parliament as the source of legitimacy makes it closer and well integrated into the political system in comparison with the British or Dutch model. It is indeed a republican monarchy. However, the changing centre–periphery relations may have negative effects on the ongoing transition from King Juan Carlos to his heir Prince Felipe. It will be his ability to unite all these different nationalities as Spain that may neutralise the still radical independence movements across the country.

The presidentialisation of the government

A body called government in Spain emerged in the late eighteenth century shortly before the French Revolution. Charles III created the Supreme Board of Government (*Junta Suprema de Gobierno*) in 1787. However, the inclusion of government in the constitution took place only in the Real Statute of 1834. Since then, it has been an important part of Spanish constitutions (Montabes, 2001: 168). At the core of the government is the prime minister, who clearly has a very strong position in the Spanish political system.

The Spanish prime minister is actually called the president of the government (*el presidente del gobierno*). This is naturally important in many ways, because there is a tendency for Spanish prime ministers to be presidentialist. The so-called presidentialisation of the prime minister can naturally be found in most west European democracies, but in the Spanish constitutional context it acquires a similar status to that of chancellor of the Federal Republic of Germany. Indeed, the German model was used to strengthen the position of the prime minister vis-à-vis the ministers and parliament (Cascajo and Bustos, 2001: 111; van Biezen and

Hopkin, 2005: 109). The Spanish constitution decided for a strong prime minister in order to ensure a high level of stability. This decision of the drafters of the Spanish constitution, has to be understood against the historical background of the very unstable Second Republic. Moreover, some continuity to Franco's authoritarian political system and the idea of the leader(*caudillo*) was established by giving a strong position to the prime minister (van Biezen and Hopkin, 2005: 107–8).

Once invested with power, it is very difficult to oust the Spanish prime minister, because the opposition has to produce a constructive motion of censure, which has to contain the presentation of an alternative candidate and eventually an alternative programme. When there is an absolute majority or a strong majority it is really very difficult to challenge the Spanish prime minister. This became quite evident during the Gonzalez presidency between 1982 and 1996 and most recently during the second presidency of José Maria Aznar between 2000 and 2004. The procedure of the constructive motion of censure is presented against the governments by one-tenth of MPs, that is, thirty-five MPs, of the Congress. There is a 2-day period in which alternative motions can be presented. Afterwards, it is discussed in the plenary. Five days have to pass, before the Congress can vote on it. MPs vote not only on a motion of censure against the government, but also for an alternative motion which has an alternative candidate for prime minister. A successful motion of censure is approved by absolute majority. If the motion of censure is not successful, no other motion of censure can be presented in the same legislature period (Montabes, 2001: 181).

Until now, there have been only two motions of censure – one against Prime Minister Adolfo Suarez, proposed by the Socialist opposition under the leadership of Felipe Gonzalez at the end of May 1980, and one against Prime Minister Felipe Gonzalez proposed by the leader of the People's Alliance, Hernandez de la Mancha, but they were unsuccessful on both occasions (Montabes, 2001: 194). However, Enrique Guerrero Salom rightly asserts that actually the motion of censure does not affect the prime minister so much due to its high threshold, but actually affects the status of the challenger. According to him, Felipe Gonzalez profited and gained in political status from his motion of censure against Adolfo Suarez, who was presiding over a very fragmented and divided party and government. In contrast, Hernandez de la Mancha came out of the whole process quite damaged in terms of reputation. He was not able to present himself as a credible alternative (Guerrero Salom, 2004: 204).

Three principles guide the cabinet: the presidential principle, the principle of collective responsibility and the ministerial principle. Of all three the presidential principle is quite important in Spanish politics, thus leading to the already-mentioned presidentialisation of the prime minister. Even if the president is quite strong in constitutional terms, the principle of collective responsibility has become the practice of Spanish politics, leaving also a high level of autonomy to the individual ministries (Lopez Calvo, 1996: 48). The best example to show this fact is the case of how much Prime Minister Gonzalez knew about the Anti-Terrorist Groups of Liberation (*Grupos Anti-Terroristas de Liberación* – GAL) set up by the then Spanish secret services (CESID, called now National Central

Table 3.4 Spanish governments since 1975

Prime Minister	Date in	Date out	Party composition	Kind of government
Provisional governments (1975–79)				
Arias Navarro II	5 Dec 1975	1 Jul 1976	Provisional	Elites of authoritarian regime
Adolfo Suarez I	3 Jul 1976	5 Aug 1977	Provisional	Elites of authoritarian regime
Adolfo Suarez I	5 Aug 1977	4 Apr 1979	UCD	Minority government
Constitutional governments				
Adolfo Suarez III	6 Apr 1979	15 Feb 1981	UCD	Minority government
Leopoldo Calvo Sotelo	25 Feb 1981	2 Dec 1982	UCD	Minority government
Felipe Gonzalez I	2 Dec 1982	22 Jun 1986	PSOE	Absolute majority government
Felipe Gonzalez II	22 Jun 1986	29 Oct 1989	PSOE	Absolute majority government
Felipe Gonzalez III	29 Oct 1989	14 Jul 1993	PSOE	Absolute majority government
Felipe Gonzalez IV	14 Jul 1993	3 May 1993	PSOE	Minority government/agreement with CiU which collapsed in October 1995
José Maria Aznar I	4 May 1996	12 Mar 2000	PP	Minority government/ agreement with regionalist-nationalist parties
José Maria Aznar II	12 Mar 2000	16 Apr 2004	PP	Absolute majority government
José Luis Rodriguez Zapatero	17 Apr 2004	11 Apr 2008	PSOE	Minority government/ agreement with Catalan Republican Left and United Left

Intelligence – *Central Nacional de Inteligencia* – CNI) and other corruption scandals related to several of his ministries. According to Gonzalez's account, he was so preoccupied with coordinating his own ministry (*Ministerio de la Presidencia*) that he never controlled the activities of the other ministries, allowing for a high degree of autonomy. Although this sounds very surreal, there is some truth in this strong autonomy of ministerial work within the framework of the government (Prego, 2000: 281–2) (see Table 3.4).

The government structure consists of at least four levels. The first level is political and comprises the prime minister, deputy prime minister and the ministers. The highest formalised body is the Council of Ministers. Although Article 98.1. of the constitution is not specific about who should belong to the government, this was formalised in a Law of Government (*Ley de Gobierno*, law 50/1997 of 27 November) in 1997 by the Aznar government. According to Juan Montabes, the previous Socialist government had tried three times in vain to adopt such a law in 1992 and twice in 1995, but this was only possible during the Aznar government. One of the main reasons, is that these attempts were undertaken in the last Gonzalez governments, which was quite discredited due to the amounting corruption scandals (Montabes, 2001: 174–5). This is followed by a second political-administrative level which comprises politically appointed secretaries of state (junior ministers) and under-secretaries of state/general secretaries.

The third intermediate administrative level includes the main administrators of the general directorates and the technical general secretaries. Last, but not least, at the fourth level the government is complemented by a technical sub-general directorate and sections of it (Bar, 1988: 102–3). Although the Council of Ministers is the highest formalised body of the government, there are other delegated committee meetings (*comisiones delegadas del gobierno*), the under-secretaries' general committee and naturally several inter-ministerial committees. The delegated committees are a response to the growth in complexity of government. It was introduced in the 1950s by the Francoist regime and its main intention is to coordinate policies that belong are the competence of different ministries. These inter-ministerial committees include the relevant members of government and state secretaries. Moreover, relevant higher-ranking officials of public administration responsible for specific policies may be asked to take part (Montabes, 2001: 178–9). Each government is able to set up their own delegated committees. In 2004, the new Socialist government set up four delegated committees of the government for crisis situations, for economic affairs, for scientific investigation and technological innovation, and for policy related to the regional autonomies. The same decree abolished four of the previous delegated committees of government related to foreign policy, state security, cultural affairs and economic policy (Royal decree, 1194/2004, of 14 May).

Spanish governments are quite small in comparison with other southern European countries, particularly Italy and the United Kingdom (see Figure 3.4). José Maria Aznar was very keen to keep the number of ministers to an absolute minimum, in view of his commitment to make savings in public administration. (see Figure 3.3) Spanish governments have been also quite stable in terms of the life-span. Although the transition and post-transition governments did not complete their legislatures and were characterised by many reshuffles, this changed qualitatively during the Gonzalez and Aznar governments. Reshuffling was quite low in Gonzalez's first government, but it increased in Gonzalez's third after 1989. It showed the growing crisis of the Socialist governments. Three reshuffles in April 1990, March 1991 and January 1992 indicated that the government was losing its ability to retain cohesion. This became more evident in Gonzalez's last ministry

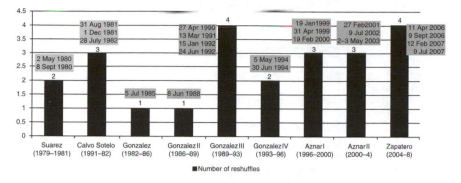

Figure 3.2 Number of reshuffles of Spanish governments, 1979–2008.

Source: Montabes, 2001: 210–213; Lopez-Nieto and Delgado, 2002: 1085; Lopez-Nieto and Delgado, 2003: 1088; Lopez-Nieto and Delgado, 2004: 1138.

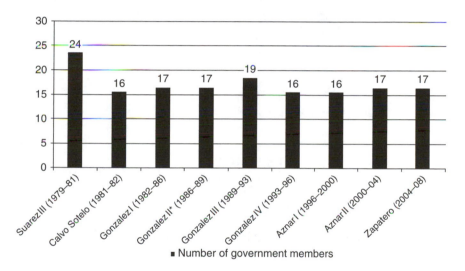

Figure 3.3 Size of government, 1977–2008.

Source: Ministry of Public Administration (MAP) www.map.es

after 1993 which led to three reshuffles as well in a very short period of time (Figure 3.2). In this respect, the successor Aznar government was able to show a much more cohesive image than its predecessor. In spite of being a minority government with parliamentary support from the regionalist parties, it led to three reshuffles in the very late phase of the first term. Particularly, the second on 31 April 1999 and the third one on 19 February 2000, shortly before the elections of 5 March 2000, each involved only one minister. This reduced major reshuffles to just one, which is a good sign of government cohesion. The second Aznar government had

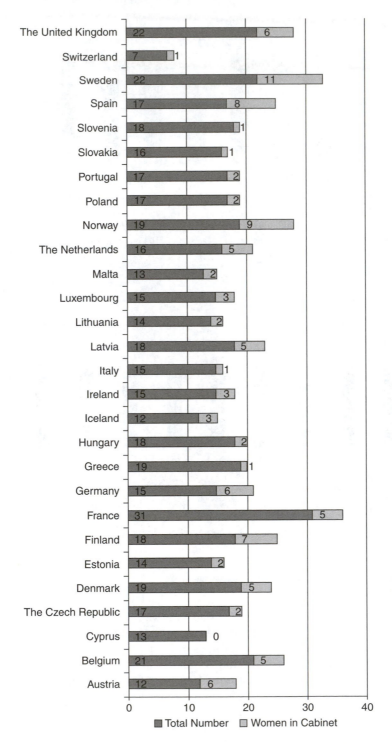

Figure 3.4 Cabinet size in comparative European perspective, 31 December 2005.

Source: Based on aggregated data provided by van Biezen and Katz, 2006: 1026.

a small reshuffling in 2001 and a large one in July 2002 (Montabes, 2001: 197–209, Roman Marugan, 2002: 256). However, the support for the war in Iraq led to a further resignation from the government after March 2003. In spite of this, one can speak of a high level of cohesion in the Aznar governments. The Zapatero government has had so far four reshufflings, two each in 2006 and 2007. However, only on 11 April 2006 and 9 July 2007 there were major reshuffles involving at least three ministers. The other two reshuffles involved only two ministers (Figure 3.2.).

The strong position of the president became only evident during the Gonzalez governments up to 1996. Before that, the Suarez and Calvo Sotelo governments were characterised by major problems of achieving a cohesive strong government, due to the factionalism inside the UCD. At one stage, Suarez lost complete support from the party leading to his resignation. This shows that the relationship between the party and the government is of absolute importance for a strong presidential government. During the Gonzalez majority governments up to 1993 the party clearly was controlled by the government, leading to strong party discipline in parliament. Such a situation did not exist any longer after 1993, when the party had to rely on the support of the Catalan regionalist-nationalist party Convergence and Union (*Convergencia i Unió* – CiU). The withdrawal of support by the CiU to the Gonzalez government in 1995 clearly announced the end of the ability of the PSOE to stay in power. The Aznar governments started first with parliamentary support of the main regionalist-nationalist parties, the CiU, PNV and BNG up until 2000. Party discipline and strong commitment to the leadership of José Maria Aznar then led to the achievement of an absolute majority which allowed for an even more presidential style of governmental leadership.

While Spanish governments have been supported by single-party absolute majorities and by parliamentary support from other political parties, there has never been a coalition government. Furthermore, this naturally reinforced the position of the president of the government, who had to strike a deal with other parties in parliament, but not within the government. This fact has led to astonishingly stable governments, due to the fact that up until now governments have been quite homogenous in their composition (Heywood, 1991: 111–12; Bar, 1988: 117–18; Roman Marugan, 2002: 251–6) (see Figure 3.5 and Figure 3.6).

The highest level of constraint for presidential governments was during the periods when the government relied on legislative support from other political parties. In 1993, PSOE had to rely on the support of the CiU to keep in power, while in 1996, it was the time for the PP to secure parliamentary support from the Catalans and the Basques. This allowed for the integration of moderate regionalist nationalism into central government, although regionalist-nationalist parties refused to become part of a coalition government, which, for example, the PSOE wanted them to. This naturally limited the level of co-responsibility of the moderate regionalist-nationalist parties. The experiments of the 1990s can be regarded as very positive to ensure macroeconomic and political stability. They were less successful in resolving aspects related to the state of autonomies, particularly financial issues. There were always conflicts, because of the central position of CiU in pacts with PSOE and then with PP. These were

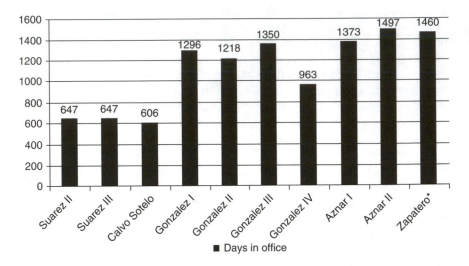

Figure 3.5 Life-span of governments 1977–2008 (Maximum 4 years = 1460 days).
*Based on date of 9 March 2008 General Elections.

Source: Own calculations based on the dates of incoming and outgoing governments.

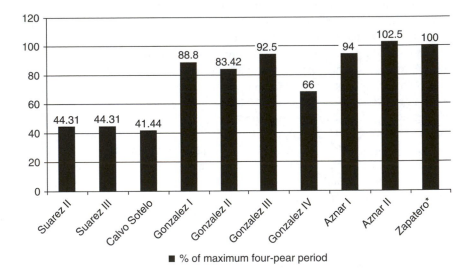

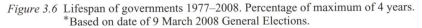

Figure 3.6 Lifespan of governments 1977–2008. Percentage of maximum of 4 years.
*Based on date of 9 March 2008 General Elections.

Source: Own calculations based on the dates of incoming and outgoing governments.

regarded as suspicious by the corresponding party in opposition and the other regionalist-nationalist parties. There was always suspicion about secret agreements parallel to the official one. It was difficult to create a climate of confidence in this context. Another aspect is that the ailing PSOE government after 1993 had a very bad image which with the support of CiU led to a major anti-Catalan feeling across Spain. This became less visible in the pact between the PP and the regionalist-nationalist parties. In sum, although integration of regionalist-nationalist parties led to a further normalisation of governmental politics in Spain, it was clearly only a last solution, if one of the main parties is not able to achieve an absolute majority (Aguilera de Prat, 2001; Reniu Vilamala, 2001).

An absolute government like the one led by José Maria Aznar between 2000 and 2004 clearly contributes to a very strong position for the president. The government can ignore many of the issues that they are not interested in tackling and concentrate on others. The Aznar government withdrew from negotiations with the regionalist-nationalist parties after achieving the absolute majority. The most evident aspect is the lack of progress in the reform of the Senate into a territorial chamber. Meanwhile, the list of conflicts with the opposition increased over the 4 years. The Quality in Higher Education bill (*Ley de Calidad*) presented by Education Minister Pilar del Castillo was put through without the support of the PSOE. The Aznar government tried to impose an unemployment benefit system reform (*decretazo*) without proper consultation with its social partners, leading to protests by the two main trade union confederations: CCOO and UGT. Both trade union confederations called for a general strike on 20 July 2002. The government wanted to make participation in the general strike illegal. It even used the police to get information on workers who would be on strike that day (*El Pais*, 5 June 2002: 23). It also led to a large demonstration in Madrid in October 2002. In the end, the government had to withdraw the highly disputed unemployment benefit reform (*El Pais*, 29 May 2002: 16; *El Pais*, 5 June 2002: 20; *El Pais*, 6 October 2002: 18). At the same time, it seeked support for a new law of political parties in order to outlaw the political arm of the Basque terrorist organisation, ETA. It was able to achieve such support from the PSOE during the summer of 2002, but this led to a stronger conflict between the central and the Basque regional government under Lehendekari Juan José Ibarretxe.

The main force of opposition against the Aznar government leading even to a decline of support in opinion polls was the unconditional support for the war in Iraq alongside US President George W. Bush and British Prime Minister Tony Blair. The opposition has been more intensive in Spain than in any other country including France, Germany and the United Kingdom. This complete intransigency of José Maria Aznar was regarded as a sign of arrogance by the vast majority of the population. The main opposition leader, José Luis Zapatero, opposed completely the approach of Aznar and asked for a UN resolution before going to war. Even the nongovernmental organisations such as *Medecins sans Frontiéres* and *Intermon* rejected money for postwar reconstruction of Iraq, as a protest against the war (*El Pais*, 3 March 2003: 22; *El Pais*, 12 March 2003: 18).

The Zapatero government after April 2004 achieved a strong majority, but was short of an absolute one. Therefore, it had to rely on support from the Catalan Republican Left (*Esquerra Republicana Catalana* – ERC) which reached an excellent result at national level, increasing their number of MPs from one to eight, and the communist-led coalition United Left, which in contrast continued to experience an erosion of its vote and a decrease of MPs from nine to five (Chari, 2004: 959–61).

The programme of the Zapatero government was quite progressive. Probably, the most important symbolic decision was the withdrawal of the troops from Iraq in the first week in office in April 2004. The withdrawal took place much earlier than expected at the end of April 2004 and during May. Zapatero fulfilled the main promise of his electoral campaign to the dismay of the Bush administration and former Prime Minister José Maria Aznar (see Chapter 10). He started with the adoption of a law allowing gay marriages and several pieces of legislation to improve the rights of women against domestic violence, including the fast-track divorce, in spite of a resistance of more right-wing groups and the Catholic Church. Conflict with the Church emerged also, when the Socialist government adopted a new Law of Education, in which religion was only an optional module. Moreover, a citizenship module was introduced, which the Church was against (see Chapters 7 and 8 for more information).

Prime Minister José Luis Zapatero was also very keen to push forward a law of historical memory which had at its prime aim to rehabilitate the victims of the authoritarian regime under Francisco Franco. The law of 'Reparation to the Victims of the Civil War and Francoism' also known as 'Law of Historical Memory, was quite important for a large older part of Spanish society, who had been involved in the anti-fascist resistance against the dictator. The grandfather of Prime Minister Zapatero, Captain Juan Rodriguez Lozano Puente de Castro fought on the side of the legitimate Republican government, before he was killed by Francoist troops on 18 August 1936 (Campillo, 2004: 16.47) This was a powerful motivating factor for Zapatero to support claims for such a law. However, a final consensus between mostly left-wing and regionalist parties such as IU-ICV and the PNV was difficult to achieve before the end of the legislature. The People's Party, which emerged out of the former regime and was originally dominated by many former members of the Francoist elite opposed vehemently such attempts to rehabilitate former victims of the authoritarian regime and introduce a more critical approach towards the achievements of Francoism. Zapatero was accused of trying to undermine the consensus established during democratic transition and create again divisions between Spaniards – the return of the 'Two Spains' (*El Pais*, 23 September 2007: 26).

The radical programme included also a review of the relationship between the centre and periphery. He created the conference of presidents which has met four times since 2004 to advance the development of the Spanish state of autonomies (*El Pais*, 10 September 2007: 29). Probably the most controversial measure of José Luis Zapatero was the support for the Catalan statute which led to a strong opposition of the People's Party under the leadership of Mariano Rajoy.

Although the statute was approved in the Cortes in Madrid in March 2006 and a referendum in June overwhelmingly endorsed the revised document, the PP sent an appeal to the Constitutional Court.

According to Andreas Baumer, many actions of the PP since the elections of 2004 are informed by a strategy of polarisation which denies the victory of the Socialist Party and ignores the evidence that there are no links between Al Qaeda and ETA in the perpetration of the 11 March bombings in Madrid. One of the leading politicians, sustaining the idea that victory was 'stolen' by the socialists and that they deserved to be the winners, was and is José Maria Aznar. This attitude of non-cooperation of the PP during the past 4 years damaged not the PSOE, but the country. The lack of qualitative consensual policy, allowed the Socialist Party to push a radical policy agenda without the necessary moderation, leaving a substantial part of the country unrepresented (Baumer, 2006: 145–6; 156). This became evident in basic institutional issues, such as the renewal and renegotiation of the Supreme Council of the Judiciary Power (*Consejo Supremo del Poder Judicial* – CSPJ) or even the Constitutional Court (*Tribunal Constitucional* – TC). This politicisation of the judiciary at its highest levels damaged the image of the political parties and the respective institutions (*El Pais*, 12 October 2007: 18). Moreover, the Zapatero government was not able to count on the support of the People's Party related to the revival of the Anti-Terrorist Pact established between the two main parties in 2000. Opposition's leader Mariano Rajoy tried to capitalise on being tough on terrorism, and in particular ETA. After ETA declared a ceasefire in early 2006, Zapatero wanted support from all main parties to start a process of negotiation. This move was originally supported by opposition leader Mariano Rajoy, but after 2 months he withdrew his support.

On 26 December 2006, a bombing in the car park of the Madrid airport Barajas, in which two Ecuatorian foreign workers were killed, damaged Zapatero's reputation considerably and PP leader Mariano Rajoy was able to capitalise on it, particularly in the regional and local elections. However, several successful strikes of the police against the logistics and the command centres of ETA in France and Spain during the summer 2007 strengthened again the position of Prime Minister Zapatero.

Last but not least, it is important to have a look at who are normally the ministers of the post-1978 parliamentary monarchy. An excellent study undertaken by Juan J. Linz, Miguel Jerez and Susana Corzo gives us some of the answers related to the socioeconomic background of the cabinets until 2002. In terms of gender, until 2002 only 10 per cent of ministers were women. It means that the figure of over 47 per cent of the Zapatero government may be regarded as a qualitative leap.

Geographically, almost one-third of ministers (30.8 per cent) come from Madrid, and 41.5 per cent from major provincial cities, while 26.1 per cent come from the rest of the country. During transition, half of all ministers came from Madrid (51.5 per cent), while 30.3 per cent came from major provincial cities and about one-fifth from the rest of the country (18.1 per cent). In terms of regions, after Madrid, the highest percentage of ministers came from Castille and León (13.1 per cent), the best example being Socialist Prime Minister José Luis Zapatero, and Andalusia (13.2 per cent), with the best example being former Socialist

Prime Minister Felipe Gonzalez and Vice-Prime Minister Alfonso Guerra. These are followed by Catalonia (8.5 per cent), Galicia (7.1 per cent) and the Basque Country (6.2 per cent). In terms of education, an overwhelming majority of ministers of 96.9 per cent have university degrees, only 1.5 per cent have a military graduation and 1.5 per cent reached only a non-university level. Most ministers have a degree in law (59.8 per cent), economics and management (28.3 per cent), engineering (8.7 per cent), social sciences (7.1 per cent) and maths and natural sciences (6.3 per cent). This means that lawyers predominate in the cabinet, which is certainly an excellent training for the job they are assigned too, due to its generalist nature. Almost two-thirds have studied in Madrid (60.3 per cent), while 10.3 per cent have done their studies in Barcelona and 7.1 per cent in Seville. A small minority undertook their studies in Deusto, a prestigious Catholic University in Bilbao in the Basque Country and 3.2 per cent in the oldest and quite prestigious University of Salamanca in Spain. A small minority also undertook studies in other countries such as France (12.3 per cent), the United Kingdom (8.4 per cent), United States (7.6 per cent), Italy (4.6 per cent) and Germany (3 per cent). In terms of occupational background, two groups dominate the successive cabinets of Spanish democracy: university professors (40 per cent) and lawyers (41.5 per cent). Sometimes both professions are not mutually exclusive, many lawyers are also university teachers. There are also about a quarter of higher civil servants (25.3 per cent), which shows the high level of politicisation of the civil service (particularly in highest ranks 28–30 of the civil service scale) and 15.3 per cent are economists. Once again, any of these professions may not be mutually exclusive. An overwhelming majority of 57.1 per cent worked in the public sector, before becoming a minister, while 24.2 per cent in the private sector. About 11.7 per cent worked in public–private partnership organisations. Over half of ministers were previously Members of Parliament (53.8 per cent), secretary or under-secretary of state (26.9 per cent), Mayors or local councillors (24.6 per cent), Director-General (18.5 per cent) and Senators (16.2 per cent). About two-fifths had no parliamentary experience (40.8 per cent), while 59.1 per cent had some kind of parliamentary experience. About 46.2 per cent were non-elected politicians, which shows the difference of the Spanish system from the British or Finnish systems, in which members of cabinet are drawn from the House of Commons or *Eduskunta*. Non-elected outsiders can always be appointed by the prime minister to be part of the cabinet. Naturally, the vast majority stays for about one term (53.8 per cent). Only one-quarter of ministers are able to stay for two terms (25.4 per cent) and a tiny minority for three terms (7.7 per cent). This means that the ministerial elite in Spain, is quite urban, academocratic, with legal university training, with some parliamentary experience and stays generally for one term, maybe two terms (Linz, Jerez and Corzo, 2003: 87–107).

In sum, the strong position of the prime minister within the government clearly leads to presidentialisation which, when backed by absolute majorities, may lead to problems for other institutions to control the government. Although governmental stability is achieved, it leads also in certain instances to a growing gap between the population and the government.

Executive–legislative relations: an asymmetrical partnership

Spanish parliamentarianism has quite a negative history, which did not change substantially when the new democratic order was established back in 1978. Indeed, it is probably accurate to say that the successful period of transition 1976–78 can be regarded as the single most important date in Spanish parliamentarianism. Afterwards parliament was not really able to become a strong controlling institution in relation to the government. This became evident during the absolute majority governments of Felipe Gonzalez between 1982 and 1993 and the government of José Maria Aznar. Several factors account for this asymmetrical relationship between the government and parliament, among them the tendency towards presidentialisation of the government structures and the existing constructive motion of censure, which requires the opposition to present an alternative candidate, if it wants to bring down a government. This central position of the government can be seen in the legislative process, where governments since 1982 were able to achieve approval between 80 and 90 per cent of all their bills, naturally sometimes after negotiations and amendments. This contrasts heavily to the success of private bills, of which only between 8 and 20 per cent are approved. This is quite normal across most west European countries, but explains the difficulty of parliament to play a major role in terms of legislation (Figure 3.5).

A factor that has been neglected so far is that the Spanish bicameral parliament, the so-called Cortes, is still unfinished in terms of final appearance. Although there is a lower chamber called the Congress of Deputies (*Congreso de Deputados*) with 350 MPs directly elected in 52 constituencies (the provinces plus Ceuta and Melilla) by the d'Hondt method of proportional representation and an upper chamber called the Senate (*Senado*) consisting on average of 256 senators partly directly elected (208) by a limited vote system at provincial level and partly indirectly elected (48) by the autonomous communities, their final relationship is still awaiting reform. There is a wish among the regionalist-nationalist parties, the PSOE and the IU to transform the Senate into a proper territorial chamber. Indeed, a General Commission of Autonomous Communities (*Comisión General de las Comunidades Autonomas*) was set up in the Senate to introduce reform of the Senate in 1994. The main task of the General Commission was to bring together and discuss proposals for the further development of the Senate. In fact, no approximation was achieved between the CiU approach which wants the acknowledgement of the so-called *hecho diferencial*, meaning the asymmetrical distribution of powers between the historical and the other regions, the PSOE approach of federalism and the 'more-or-less' PP approach of keeping the status quo.

By 1998, the General Commission ceased really to work, mainly because of the position of the PP. There is some fear that any reform of the constitution may lead to a general, wider reform than expected (Roller, 2002b: 80–84). This again fits into the already-mentioned ongoing discussion on the future of the state of autonomies (see Chapter 2). Due to this impasse in terms of reform, the Spanish parliamentary structure remains unfinished. The election of senators at provincial level still reflects the constitutional compromise, and not the reality of

Table 3.5 Presented and approved governmental and private bills, 1982–June 2007

	I (1979–82)		II (1982–86)		III (1986–89)		IV (1989–93)		V (1993–96)		VI (1996–2000)		VII (2000–04)		VIII (2004–June 2007)	
	N	A	N	A	N	A	N	A	N	A	N	A	N	A	N	A
Governmental Bills (*Proyectos de Ley*)	342	237	209	187	125	108	137	109	130	112	192	172	175	173	144	89
Private Bills (*Proposiciones de Ley*) of parliamentary groups	217	124	108	14	139	9	165	18	140	17	300	28	322	16	223	13
Other Private Bills (*Proposiciones de Ley*)			20	6	33	4	35	4	38	8	50	20	47	3	76	8

Source: Compiled from website of Congress of Deputies, http://www.congreso.es accessed on 18 October 2007.

Table 3.6 Use of control instruments in the Spanish parliament

	II (1982–86)		III (1986–89)		IV (1989–93)		V (1993–96)		VI (1996–2000)		VII (2000–2004)		VIII (2004–June 2007)	
	P	A	P	A	P	A	P	A	P	A	P	A	P	A
Written Questions	9,200		19,458		15,309		14,886		32,721		75,326		124,567	
Oral Questions	1,828		3,103		4,467		3,475		4,941		70,101		4,766	
Debated Interpellations	66		115		151		110		180		245		420	
Non-legislative Bills	224	41	501	102	786	145	953	108	2,240	175	3,245	242	2,655	173
Motions	37	10	74	23	120	40	304	50	799	59	623	69	806	73

Source: Website of the Congress of Deputies, http://www.congreso.es accessed on 18 October 2007.

Notes
P = Presented
A = Approved

the fully grown state of autonomies (Roller, 2002b: 77). This means that Spain is currently characterised by an asymmetrical bicameral system which is dominated by the lower house, the Congress of Deputies. The Senate is clearly important in territorial questions such as decisions related to the Interterritorial Compensation Fund (*Fondo Interterritorial de Compensación* –), the discipline of autonomous communities which may be acting against the general Spanish interest and sanction agreements of cooperation between the autonomous communities. Nevertheless, it is a subaltern chamber in the legislative process.

After a first reading which takes place in the Congress of Deputies, a bill is sent to the Senate which undertakes a second reading with the possibility of making amendments. This is then sent back to the Congress which may or may not accept the amendments with a single majority. Afterwards it is sent to the king for ratification. The Senate has a suspensive veto power of legislation, which after 2 months can be overturned by the Congress of Deputies with a single majority. All this gives a strong position to the Congress of Deputies in the parliamentary structure (Newton and Donaghy, 1997: 67). It means that the Senate adopted an important role as a reflective chamber, which concentrates on amending potential controversial laws. According to Lourdes Lopez Nieto the Senate is used to amend and improve the original text of the bill. After the heated discussions in the lower house, it takes a more impartial look at the bill in question in order to achieve a larger consensus for it. Almost half of all amended bills are so amended in the Senate: this was particularly so in the third and fourth legislatures (Lopez Nieto, 2001: 237). However, it can also be the case that, if a party has an absolute majority in the Senate, that it tries to push through controversial legislation. The best example is the government of José Maria Aznar in 1999, which tried to push through an amended tougher immigration law (*ley de extranjeria*) and used the absolute majority in the Senate to overcome a weaker version agreed in the lower House. In the end, the new tougher version of the bill was overturned by a majority in the Congress and the Aznar government, which had only a relative majority in the lower house and was dependent on support from other parliamentary parties, was defeated. However, in 2000, early in the next legislature period, the PP government, due to its absolute majority in the Congress, tabled again a revised tougher version of the law, which was passed without difficulties (Kreienbrink, 2007: 246–7).

As already mentioned, the dominance of the Congress of Deputies over the Senate does not extend in relation to the government. The imagery of the unicameral parliament of the Second Republic led to the creation of a strong powerful government vis-à-vis parliament, in order to prevent political instability. Actually, stability of government is a major desire among all political parties, leading them sometimes to give parliamentary support to minority governments for that reason (Guerrero Salom, 2000: 104–6; 2004: 193). The best example is the parliamentary support of the PSOE for the minority government of the UCD under Prime Minister Calvo Sotelo, even if the UCD was unwilling to do so to its own prime minister. In the 1990s, one can mention the support of regionalist parties for the fourth Gonzalez government and the first Aznar government. The Zapatero government had also to negotiate parliamentary pacts with mainly the United Left (IU-ICV) coalition and the Catalan Republican Left (ERC), but also with other regionalist parties. This will to preserve a high level of governmental stability, in spite of the danger of executive dominance, shows that the historical legacy still shapes the way main political actors behave in Spanish politics.

Such parliamentary support for minority governments allows opposition parties to improve their ability of governmental control. Indeed, according to a thorough study by Enrique Guerrero Salom, the instruments of governmental control were used more successfully in the period of PSOE minority government between 1993 and 1996 than during the three previous legislatures of absolute majority. The same can be said about the PP minority government between 1996 and 2000. There is a likelihood of a substantial number of motions, urgent interpellations and non-legislative proposals to be approved in parliament when the government is highly dependent on parliamentary support. This is also valid for private bills which are more likely to be taken into consideration by parliament (Guerrero Salom, 2000: 165–9). This does not mean that the quality of control is high. On the contrary, the frequent use of control initiatives may actually show weaknesses in relation to overall strategy and purpose. Naturally, one cannot underestimate the context in which this increase of importance of parliamentarianism is taking place. According to Enrique Guerrero Salom, there is a tendency of the parliamentary group of the main government party to use executive-friendly oral questions, interpolations and motions just to neutralise the control activity of the opposition. In this sense, he pleads for a reform of such control instruments, so that they are not misused by the already strong governments. Moreover, in the last three legislatures the number of written and oral questions has increased considerably, but the vast majority are of poor quality and just used for party-political purposes (Guerrero Salom, 2004: 229–32) (see Table 3.6).

The last two Gonzalez governments were really under constant pressure, because of the number of political scandals that emerged related to their government. The so-called Guardia Civil chief Luis Roldán affair, the Juan Guerra affair, the Mario Conde/Banesto affair and then in late 1994 and early 1995 the GAL affair as well as the CESID affair eroded completely the credibility of the government. The withdrawal of support by the Catalans in late 1995 further undermined the strength of the government. In spite of this, the Gonzalez government was able to bring through a successful presidency of the European Union leading up to the Barcelona Euro-Mediterranean partnership and the launch of the euro. One of the reasons is that establishment of any inquiry committee has to be supported by the government. This naturally makes the opposition highly dependent on the goodwill of the government. Very few committees of inquiry came into being during this period, in spite of the mounting scandals. During the three absolute majority governments of the PSOE only six committees of inquiry (three in the second legislature, one in the third legislature and two in the fourth legislature) were established. During the minority government of the PSOE there were three committees of inquiry related to the Roldán case, the Mariano Rubio affair concerning abuse of power between the Bank of Spain and insider trading as well as the Intelhorce case and two other inquiries connected to state intervention in Banesto and the financing of political parties (*El Pais*, 25 September 1995: 11–12; Guerrero Salom, 2000: 172–3; Heywood, 1995a). In the Senate, a committee of inquiry on political responsibilities in relation to GAL was established. The latter was achieved by only one vote, with the PSOE and the CiU voting against it and the opposition voting for it (*El Pais*, 23 October 1995: 12). Also during the absolute majority government of José Maria Aznar, committees of inquiry were restricted to an absolute minimum. The best example is the Gescartera scandal which led to collusion of interests between an investment firm and the responsible public regulatory body. In the end, the Aznar government was able to reject the continuation of any investigation in this matter (*El Pais*, 31 October 2001: 23; *El Pais*, 16 November 2001: 26). The Aznar government also prevented the establishment of a committee of inquiry about the oil spillage from the tanker *Prestige* in 2002, due to the fact that the government mismanaged the whole crisis. During the Aznar government there were three committees of inquiry, all three not dealing with these two important scandals (Balfour, 2007: 381).

During the term of the Zapatero government, the 11 March Madrid bombings remained the most important issue for parliamentary inquiry. Such a committee was established between June 2004 and December 2004, however the polarisation between the two parties led to disagreements over the findings, both parties accusing each other partisan bias towards the process.

The most important event in the parliamentary calendar, is the State of the Nation address (*Estado de la Nación*) of the prime minister. Similar to the State of the Union of the American president, the prime minister has to give a general account on the state of the country. This State of the Nation address is also an excellent opportunity for the opposition to criticise and sometimes embarrass the government. The prime minister has naturally an advantage, because he controls most of the facts. Prime Minister José Luis Zapatero has been quite successful in his State of the Nation addresses, always coming on top after surveys conducted afterwards. In a survey by the Centre for Sociological Research (CIS), after the 4 July 2007 State of the Nation address, Zapatero was declared the 'winner' by 43.9 per cent of respondents, while only 16.5 per cent thought it was Mariano Rajoy. About one-third (29.7 per cent) did not follow the debate. A vast majority of 63.5 per cent declared that terrorism was the most important topic discussed in the debate, but people were quite ignorant about other topics. The vast majority of the population regarded Zapatero more knowledgeable of the problems of the country, more moderate in his discourse and with a better capacity to respond to criticisms (*El Pais*, 7 July 2007: 25). Opposition leader Mariano Rajoy seems to lack the charisma of his predecessor José Maria Aznar who was also able to carry the support of the majority of the population.

The strength of the executive in relation to the legislative derives also from the strong dominance of the political parties over their MPs. The D'Hondt electoral system in plurinominal constituencies prevents a relationship between the MP and

Table 3.7 Committees in Spanish Congress, October 2007

Legislative standing committees

- Constitutional Committee
- Committee of Foreign Affairs
  - Subcommittee on the reform of the Diplomatic Service
- Justice Committee
- Home Affairs Committee
- Defence Committee
- Finance and Economy Committee
  - Subcommittee for the study of the social economy in Spain
- Budget Committee
- Development and Housing Committee
- Education and Science Committee
- Labour and Social Affairs Committee
  - Subcommittee for Immigration Policy
- Industry, Tourism and Trade Committee
  - Subcommittee on analysis of measures on de-location processes
  - Subcommittee on the Report of the Nuclear Security Council
- Agriculture, Fisheries and Food Committee
- Public Administrations Committee
- Culture Committee
- Health and Consumption Committee
- Environment Committee

Non-legislative standing committees

- Committee for the Standing Orders
  - Subcommittee for the reform of the Standing Orders
- Committee for the Statute of MPs
- Committee of Petitions
- Committee of International Development Cooperation
- Consultative Committee of Nominations (to public institutions – Constitutional Court, Audit Court, Spanish Television, etc.)
- Control Committee of credits related to reserved expenditure

Non-legislative committees

- Follow-up and evaluation of agreements of Pact of Toledo
- Road Security and Prevention of Traffic Accidents
- Integrative Policies for Disabled People

Standing joint committees congress-senate

- Relations with the Audit Court
- the European Union
  - Subcommittee on the Report on the Political Construction of Europe
- Relations with the Ombudsman (*Defensor del Pueblo*)
- Woman Rights and Equality of Opportunities
- Study of the drugs problem
  - Working Group on the Harming Effects of Drugs for the Health of Young People

Table 3.7 Continued

Joint committee congress-senate

- Parliamentary Control of RTVE and societies

Non-legislative committee

- Parliamentary Control of RTVE

---

the constituency. Indeed, the parties appoint the MPs without any consideration whether they are suitable for the respective constituencies. The main reason is that MPs are representatives of the whole of Spain and they are not accountable to their constituencies. They are only accountable to the parties which selected them for the position. In this sense, Spanish MPs are subject to a strong party discipline, particularly in the two main parties, the PSOE and the PP. There is a low level of defection within the Congress of Deputies and Senate, because the only option that MPs have is to join the powerless mixed group of all possible MPs that failed to achieve the minimum number of MPs to create a parliamentary group. Normally, a parliamentary group has to consist of fifteen MPs, but in the case of regionalist-nationalist parties that are only strong in certain regions this number has been lowered to a minimum of five MPs and at least 15 per cent of votes in the constituencies. Moreover, a parliamentary group needs to have fifteen members when it makes its application, afterwards it can decrease by up to eight MPs.

The strong party discipline makes it very difficult for MPs to vote against the government. This may lead to their replacement by a new MP, who would vote according to the wishes of party. Such strong discipline leads to a complete submission of the parliamentary groups to the direction of the party (Oñate, 2000: 110–23; Sanchez de Dios, 1995). Similarly, in committees, MPs may be replaced by others at any point in time, according to party wishes. This makes MPs quite weak in terms of developing their own position inside parliament. It is also the parliamentary group that receives any funding from the state. According to Enrique Guerrero Salom in 2004, parliamentary groups received overall €7.5 million (£5 million, $10 million) for running their offices, distributed according to the strength of each one (Guerrero Salom, 2004: 115). MPs get support from the parliamentary group and are therefore quite disadvantaged in relation to MPs in other countries such as Germany or the Netherlands, where each MP is well-provided for in terms of material and human resources by the state to fulfil their functions. In 2006, there were 109 assistants allocated to the parliamentary groups. Although the larger groups have more assistants, the ratio per MP is worse than for smaller parliamentary groups such as CiU, IU or EAJ-PNV (Table 3.8). In the past decades, the complex of buildings of the Congress and the Senate have expanded considerably to provide each MP with its own office space. Naturally, the MPs who act as presiding officers also have assistants allocated to them. The speaker can rely on the work of the speaker's office which consisted of eleven assistants in 2006. Such support is also provided for the Deputy-Speakers. The Presiding

Table 3.8 The distribution of assistants according to parliamentary groups (2006)

Parliamentary group	Number of MPs	Number of assistants	Ratio per MPs/assistants
Socialist Group	164	41	0.25
People's Party Group	148	44	0.30
Catalan Group (CiU)	10	6	0.60
Republican Left (ERC)	8	6	0.75
Basque (EAJ-PNV)	7	4	0.57
Green Left-IU-ICV	5	4	0.80
Canary Coalition–New Canaries	3	1	0.33
Mixed Group	5	3	0.60

Source: Congreso de Deputados (2007b). Many thanks to my student John Bruton for making me aware of this information.

Council officers (vice-presidents and secretaries) who organise the work of the house have two assistants each. Moreover, the chairmen or chairwomen of the committees have one assistant each allocated to them (Congreso de Diputados, 2006: 3).

In 2006, the amount provided for the parliamentary groups increased to €8.97 million (£6 million, $12 million) (see Figure 3.9). This is reinforced by a very low salary for an individual MP in comparison with other countries. In 2006, MPs received fourteen monthly salaries of €2,918.64 (£2,000, $4,000). Naturally, the speaker, deputy-speakers and chairmen of committees are able to receive additional income on top of this. The Speaker is entitled to a complementary payment of €3,365.66 per month as well as payment of representation expenses. The deputy speaker receives a complementary monthly payment €1,283.15 with similar expenses privileges. However, if we compare with other countries, the salary is quite low, particularly in comparison with parliaments in the larger countries of the United Kingdom, Germany and France (Jun, 2003: 178–9; Kreuzer and Stephan, 2003: 135; Borchert and Golsch, 2003: 156–7).

The low standing of MPs in the Spanish parliament can be deduced from the high level of rotation from legislature to legislature which decreased in the 1980s and 1990s, but it still reaches levels of between 45 and 60 per cent (see Figure 3.7). This naturally is not conducive to the professionalisation of parliament in Spain (Oñate, 2000: 131;Guerrero Salom, 2004: 75). On the contrary, Spanish parliamentarianism can be considered along with the Portuguese, Greek and probably some of the central and eastern European parliaments, such as Bulgaria and Romania, as the weakest of the European Union. This is also reflected in the committees. Renewal within and between legislatures may reach very high levels, which clearly prevent professionalisation of MPs along policy areas. According to Enrique Guerrero Salom about two-thirds of the presiding council of each house and the presiding MPs over the standing committees change from legislature to legislature.(Guerrero Salom, 2004: 75). This high level of renewal prevents the establishment of career patterns based on seniority and experience. This is

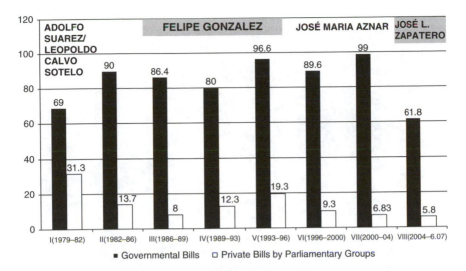

Figure 3.7 Survival rates of Governmental Bills and Private Bills of parliamentary groups, 1979–2007.

Source: Own calculations based on the data provided by the Congress of Deputies on its website http://www.congreso.es accessed on 18 October 2007, Figures for first legislature from Enrique Guerrero Salom, 2000: 156.

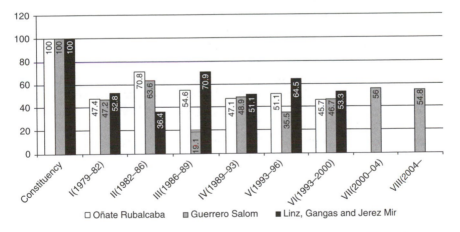

Figure 3.8 Renewal rate of Spanish MPs in the Congress of Deputies, 1977–2004.

Source: Oñate 2000: 131; Linz, Gangas, Jerez Mir, 2000; Guerrero Salom, 2004: 75. Two different results by Pablo Oñate and Enrique Guerrero Salom, probably right number lies somewhere in between, depending on your criteria of calculations.

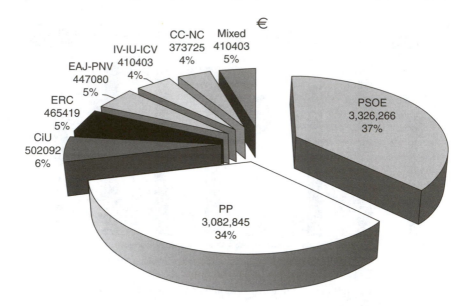

Figure 3.9 Annual state funding for parliamentary groups 2006–.

Source: Congreso de Deputados (2007b), Many thanks to my student John Bruton for making me aware of this information.

naturally a major problem for important committees such as for External Affairs, Economy and Finance, Justice and Home Affairs and above all the Budget. This is naturally not very conducive to a professionalisation and institutionalisation of the Congress and Senate. Moreover, The standing legislative committees can make final decisions on bills without going back to the plenary sessions.

Between 40 and 50 per cent of all bills are decided at committee level. The general assessment is that there is an imbalance between the work in the plenary sessions and in the committees, which is clearly complicated by the fact that MPs, information is often delayed. The discussion on the creation of a supporting office for MPs for scrutiny of the budget has been delayed, because no agreement was achieved on new parliamentary house rules (Guerrero Salom, 2000: 168–9). According to Lourdes Lopez-Nieto, based on analysis of the third and fourth legislature the concentration of the workload of the committees is essentially in four broad areas. About 50 per cent of the parliamentary work in committees is dedicated to budgetary and economic questions, 20 per cent to internal and external security policies, while about 15–22 per cent to distributive or regulatory questions such as agriculture, industry, public works, social policy and employment 10–15 per cent to value questions related to the constitution, education or culture (Lopez Nieto, 2001: 238–9).

As already mentioned in the previous chapter, the Spanish Cortes is not one of the institutions with the highest support among citizens. On the contrary, the perception of citizens of the Spanish parliament is split between those who say that they are satisfied with the work of parliament and those who are not. Among the MPs, satisfaction with their work is quite high and only a small number is less satisfied. It seems in some way that there is a growing gap between the Spanish political class and the population. In spite of this gap, the majority of the population agrees that parliament is important for the functioning of Spanish democracy and its work as such is important (Delgado Sotillos *et al.*, 1998: 33–4; Martinez and Mendez, 2000: 263). As already mentioned in the previous chapter, the Spanish Parliament has a similar standing as in other larger countries such as Germany, France, Italy and the United Kingdom (see previous chapter, Figure 2.8).

Last but not least, it is important to find out what is the gender and occupational background of these MPs. Probably, the most thorough study was undertaken by Juan J. Linz, Miguel Jerez Mir and Pilar Gangas. According to their study between 1977 and 1996 in the Congress there was a considerable increase of women from 5.9 per cent in 1977 to 21.6 per cent (Linz, Gangas and Jerez Mir, 2000: 440). According to an excellent comparative study by Irene Delgado and Miguel Jerez on the share of women in parliaments in Europe, Spain reached in 2005 36.2 per cent, only matched by the Scandinavian countries and the Benelux countries (Delgado and Jerez Mir, 2007: 13). Professionally, the larger groups are lawyers and university academics, similar to the ministerial elite, showing the importance of higher education degrees and positions as an important asset to achieve a parliamentary position. This is also confirmed by a study by Irene Delgado for the subsequent fifth, sixth and seventh legislatures between 1993 and 2004, in which about one-fifth of MPs are lawyers and university teachers. Moreover, functionaries are almost as large as these two groups (Delgado, 2007: 11).

In sum, parliamentarianism in Spain is still in the making. The unfinished parliamentary structure will certainly continue to be an important issue in years to come. Moreover, issues related to the dangers of longevity of the government and strong dominance of the executive in the overall political system may become part of discussions in the future, if constitutional reform ever materialises.

Governmental longevity and political corruption: from socialist patrimonialism to Aznarism

The longevity of the government of the Socialist Party between 1982 and 1996 led to the emergence of a string of highly publicised political corruption scandals, which found their way into the Spanish courts. Most of the cases were related directly or indirectly to the governing party, so that some questions about the effects of absolute majority government became quite visible. The strong connection of the Socialist political elite to the beautiful people, the *gente bonita* of the financial oligarchy, was regarded by James Petras as patrimonial socialism, meaning that after the PSOE repeated their absolute majority three times, they became complacent and began to use the state's resources as if they belonged to the party (Petras, 1990; 1993). Naturally, this is probably an overstated interpretation of what happened in the 1980s and 1990s, but certainly brings to the fore some features of the behaviour of the political elite. One of the first corruption scandals to erupt was the Filesa scandal. This involved a group of consulting firms, based in Barcelona, which advised the government on economic matters. The main accusation was that the consulting firms did not produce any reports and received funding which was redirected to the PSOE's own finances. A public contract was even awarded to Siemens after paying the PSOE through these consulting firms. On 28 October 1997, the Supreme Court found the PSOE guilty in this corruption case (*El Pais*, 29 October 1997: 15–17). According to Charles Powell, the PSOE government was involved in four kinds of corruption scandals, which came to the fore at almost the same time between 1989 and 1995 after a decade of economic boom: (1) the corruption of illicit party financing; (2) the exchange of influence between economic world and governmental institutions; (3) the abuse of power by state representatives for personal enrichment and (4) the abuse of power by state representatives for personal power enhancement within their field of work (Powell, 2001: 528–39). The first kind of corruption cases were related to the illicit financing of political parties.

Both main parties were involved in such cases. Apart from the Filesa scandal, the Naseiro scandal of 1990 involved the PP, but was less damaging than the cases involving the PSOE (Powell, 2001: 509–11). This second kind of case is related to the economy and the world of finance and their relationship to governmental institutions such as the Bank of Spain and the Stock Exchange. The lack of controls imposed by the new Spanish democracy allowed for speculative economic business to flourish. This so-called 'Casino Capitalism' led to major investments in the booming housing sector, but not so much in the industrial sector. It included personalities such as Mario Conde, who used personal connections to the Socialist Party to achieve an expansion of his bank, Banesto. Nevertheless, the number of accumulated non-retrievable debts increased to an extent that it led to its breakdown. Naturally, Conde was able to use some money-laundering mechanisms to hide some of his money in a secret account in Liechtenstein. Mario Conde went to prison in 1994 (*El Pais*, 10 November 1999: 72).

The third kind of corruption was related to people in public administration, who abused their powers for personal enrichment and sustained networks of abuses of power. The most famous case was the chief of the Civil Guard (*guardia civil*) who at some stage was even earmarked as a possible minister of the interior. Luis Roldán abused his power and misappropriated funding from ETA's extortion from business people in the Basque Country as well as the funding allocated to the payment of police informants for personal enrichment, which amounted to 5 million pesetas. In 1993, Roldán fled abroad to escape justice, but he was discovered in Laos and extradited to Spain 2 years later. He was sentenced to 31 years of imprisonment as well as a fine of 1.6 million pesetas.

After 8 years he was allowed conditional freedom for the rest of his sentence in 2002, although most of the money is still unaccounted for. His connection with powerful people helped him to improve his situation (*El Pais*, Domingo, 24 November 2002: 1–3). Other examples of abuse of power included the governor of the Bank of Spain, Mariano Rubio, and the director of the Spanish

Stock Exchange, Mariano de la Concha, who both used their position to get insider information and enrich themselves. This led to the resignation of the President of the Socialist parliamentary group, Carlos Solchaga, who had been finance minister back in the 1980s and the Agriculture Minister, Vicente Albero, who had made investments in Ibercorp, one of the scandals in which Rubio and Solchaga had acted illicitly. The fourth kind of scandals identified by Powell were abuse of power by representatives of the state in order to enhance their power within their field of action. The best example is the Anti-Terrorist Liberation Group (*Grupo Anti-terrorista de Liberación* – GAL) affair. This affair was discovered after the replacement of Interior Minister Antonio Asunción by Juan Alberto Belloch. He decided to undertake a general clean-up of his ministry and he uncovered networks of influences created over the years in the ministry. This included civil servants who had served under the former authoritarian regime and had strong connections with the anti-terrorist struggle in the Basque Country. The GAL was created by such networks within the ministry in order to destabilise and demoralise the ETA terrorists. It consisted of Portuguese and French mercenaries recruited by the Spanish secret services. The main field of action was to kill alleged terrorists and their family members. Such a policy happened in the 1980s, but it came out only under the leadership of Belloch at the ministry. This so-called dirty war (*guerra sucia*) was regarded as very negative in the press and among the population. The main reason was that the state resorted to terrorism to fight the terrorist organisation. This discredited the rule of law on which democracy in Spain was based. The GAL affair led to establishment of a committee of inquiry in the Senate, which was disbanded soon afterwards. Several people were held to account like the two policemen involved directly in the affair, José Amedo and Michel Dominguez. They clearly afterwards cooperated with the judiciary to bring former interior ministers José Barrionuevo and Luis Corcuera to justice.

They also found out that two ETA terrorists, José Antonio Lasa and José Ignacio Zabala, who had been kidnapped by Colonel Enrique Rodriguez Galindo in 1983, were buried in Bussot in Alicante under 50 kilograms of cement (Rubio and Cerdán, 1997; *El Pais*, 18 September 1995: 10; *El Pais*, 23 October 1995: 11; *El Pais*, 6 November 1995: 12; *El Pais*, 17 October 1997: 17–19). Another example was the telephone tapping by the Spanish secret services of politicians and civil servants at the Higher Council of Information for Defence (*Consejo Superior de Informacion dela Defensa* – CESID), part of the Ministry of Defence. It seems that Colonel Juan Alberto Perote, chief of CESID, had relations with Mario Conde, and that the latter was blackmailing the government and in the process of blackmailing the King. Moreover, it was found out that among the personalities under surveillance was Jordi Pujol, the president of Catalonia (*El Pais*, 25 September 1995: 11–12; *El Pais*, 13 November 1995: 1, 12–13). At some stage, connections between the GAL and CESID affair were discovered (*El Pais*, 25 September 1995: 13, 15). This clearly further undermined the position of Felipe Gonzalez, who denied any involvement or any knowledge of these scandals in other ministries. His main excuse was that he was so overwhelmed by his prime ministerial work and lacked information how the other ministries were being run. The last trials related to the GAL only ended in the summer of 2002 (*El Pais*, 7 June 2002: 19).

One of the main reasons for this proliferation of corruption scandals is the fact that the new Spanish democracy lacked the essential legislative controls and mechanisms to identify such acts of corrupt behaviour. Indeed, Spanish democracy in the 1980s and 1990s had to be characterised as being in transition from the previous legal order of authoritarianism and the new democratic order. In this sense, aspects of neo-patrimonial behaviour allowed for confusion between the private and public spheres. The transitional status of Spanish democracy was reinforced by the growing possibilities that the liberalisation of the markets and the privatisation of public firms were increasing opportunities for perpetrators. In this sense, many other countries reported cases of corruption in which politicians were involved like the Elf corruption scandal allegedly involving former French Foreign Minister Roland Dumas, acquitted after his appeal, the Helmut Kohl scandal in Germany related to party financing and naturally *tangentopoli* in Italy (Meny and Rhodes, 1997: 99–102; Jimenez and Cainzos, 2003: 15–17).

As a response to this neo-patrimonial legal situation the Gonzalez government introduced in 1995 several laws including an obligatory external audit of firms to control financial and economic transactions related to the illegality of insider trading and dishonest administration. Moreover, the telecommunications sector was regulated in 1994, after decades of patrimonial organisation. Also, the law of political parties was updated in relation to party financing (Powell, 2001: 559–64). Moreover, the new PP government introduced major reforms in the secret services, replacing the CESID by the National Council of Information (*Consejo Nacional de Información* – CNI) in 2002.

According to Transparency International, a major nongovernmental organisation specialising in the impact of corruption on governments, together with the perception of businessmen and women, corruption fell to a lower level between 1996 and 2000. Transparency International uses a 0 (very corrupt) to 10 (clean from corruption) spectrum to categorise countries around the world. Spain was regarded as quite corrupt with 4.31 in 1996, while it had improved to a score of 7 in 2000 (Jimenez and Cainzos, 2003: 9).

In spite of this changing perception, the second Aznar government after 2000 was already involved in several corruption scandals which may be compared with those of the PSOE. The best example is the Gescartera scandal. Gescartera was an investment firm managing several portfolios on behalf of their clients. It became such an investment firm with the blessing of the regulating public body, the National Commission of Market Values (*Comisión Nacional del Mercado de Valores* – CNMV), in 1997, in spite of the fact that the previous firm was always in the red. The lack of control by the CNMV led to the accumulation of a debt of 15.578 billion pesetas which affected 1,383 clients. Among the clients with the highest losses were the pension fund of the police and the fund for Guardia Civil orphans. Also several bishops invested Church funds in this firm, which they lost. The main part of the scandal was the improper control and the alleged connection of some people of CNMV with Gescartera. There were also allegations of involvement by the ministry of economy in approving the investment firm, in spite of the fact that they were falsifying the actual capital of the firm. This led to a general outcry by the opposition and to the establishment of a committee of inquiry which was abruptly ended without finding if there was any political responsibility to be taken by the government for the affair in November 2001 (*El Pais*, 12 December 2001: 23–35).

The trial on the responsibility for the Gescartera fraud started only in 2007, almost a decade after the scandal became known in the media. Several PP politicians are also charged of having been involved in the scandal. The main political issue is the suspicion of traffic of influences between the government representatives such as the former Secretary of State of Treasury Enrique Gomez-Reyna and his sister Pilar Gomez-Reyna, who was president of Gescartera. Fifteen people were indicted and the prosecution asked the Court to give them sentences of 8 years due to inappropriate taking of funds and for some of them further 3 years for inappropriate continuous falsification (*El Pais*, 18 September 2007: 18; *El Pais*, 24 September 2007: 22; *El Pais*, 2 October 2007: 24)

Similarly, the *Banco Bilbao y Vizcaya Argentaria* (BBVA) scandal of secret accounts in Jersey, Liechtenstein and Latin America came to the fore after an inspection by the Bank of Spain. Although the investigations and the judicial procedures are still going on, there was some connection to the government, involving allegedly Prime Minister José Maria Aznar and Economy Minister Rodrigo Rato. The main protagonist of this scandal of false accounting and personal enrichment was Emilio Ybarra who was able to consolidate a secret bank within a bank of 185 million euros (37 billion pesetas). The Socialist MPs alleged that Rodrigo Rato used privileged information to warn the BBVA about the investigation of the Bank of Spain, because he was a personal friend of the BBVA president, Francisco Gonzalez (*El Pais*, 11 April 2002: 46; *El Pais*, Domingo, 14 April 2002: 1–3).

Other scandals or irregularities related to the distribution of EU funding have become evident in recent years. In 2001, it was discovered that 21 billion pesetas of EU funding for the linen industry were misappropriated by persons connected to the Ministry of Agriculture and the autonomous communities. The former Agriculture Minister, Loyola de Palacio, clearly notified this to the anti-corruption authority in Spain. She was Commissioner for Transport at the European Commission under the presidency of Romano Prodi (1999–2004) and clearly helped the EU authorities in this affair, which she only discovered in 1999. Such fraudulent activities were going on between 1996 and 1999 with the knowledge of high-level officials in the Ministry of Agriculture. The Office for the Fight Against Fraud (OLAF) of the European Union took over the investigations. Minister of Agriculture, Miguel Arias Cañete, argued that Spain should pay a lower penalty of 6 billion pesetas for this fraud (*El Pais*, 28 October 2001: 23; *El Pais*, 16 November 2001; *El Pais*, 23 November 2001: 22; *El Pais*, 9 December 2001).

Other scandals revolved around selective allocation of funding to PP-controlled local authorities in the autonomous community of Castilla León. This naturally led to investigations by the European Union (*El Pais*, 21 May 2002: 55; *El Pais*, 23 May 2002: 16).

In spite of reforms related to party financing, the Audit Court in its report on party accounting in 1999 clearly brought to light the still existing lack of accountability in the actual funding of political parties. It highlights the fact that all parties make unaccountable transactions between the party and its attached enterprises. This means that the sources for potential corruption scandals are still in existence and very difficult for state institutions to control (*El Pais*, 20 August 2002: 14).

A further political scandal broke out in the autonomous community of Madrid. After the autonomous community elections results of 25 May 2003 were known, two PSOE MPs decided to defect, thus preventing the PSOE from forming the regional government with the support of the United Left regional parliament members. According to the PSOE version, these two MPs were corrupted by the construction sector lobby of Madrid, so that the PSOE would not be able to come to power. Allegedly there were strong financial interests connecting the construction sector with the PP, which before the elections was leading the regional government. Such a defection did lead to an impasse in the election of the new government and new elections were scheduled for 5 September 2003 (*El Pais*, 29 June 2003: 14; *El Pais*, 16 July 2003: 11). The PP won with an absolute majority and her candidate Esperanza Aguirre became the president of the autonomous community of Madrid and was able to repeat the victory in the regional and local elections of 28 May 2007. However, it became clear that soil and construction speculation did not exist only in Madrid, but it was a widespread phenomenon across Spain. Indeed, throughout recent years several scandals of municipal corruption have been discovered in Marbella, Valencia and other towns across Spain (*El Pais*, 2 October: 22–4). Probably, the most notorious one was in Marbella which had started already when the tycoon Jesus Gil, former owner of Atlético Madrid, became mayor with his party, the Independent Liberal Group (*Grupo Independiente Liberal* – GIL). His highly populist party was able to gain an absolute majority in the 1990s in Marbella and established a network of traffic of influences and corruption which led to arrest of several councillors and businessmen after the so-called 'operation Malaya' by the police had collected enough evidence against them.

This corruption network involving construction firms, businessmen, some members of the judiciary and local councillors was sustained over quite a long period of time. The trials of the responsible people are taking place at the time of writing, but one thing that has become evident is that there was no control of the activities of the Council. They could offer tenders for public works without competition and the works were either not completed or never came into being. Moreover, the accused were also involved in a permanent money-laundering system. At the centre of the huge network of illicit corrupt activities was the complex of firms of Fernando de la Valle, based in Marbella. He was able to manipulate the Council of Marbella in his construction speculation schemes. He had connections to the Italian and Russian mafia. Over twenty councillors and a further sixty-six persons are on trial for alleged corrupt activities since the 1990s

(*El Pais*, 18 Julio 2007: 18; *El Pais*, 19 July 2007: 24; *El Pais*, 24 July 2007: 22; *El Pais*, 12 October 2007: 26; see also Urquiza, 2005; Sands, 2007: 214).

Systemic municipal corruption can be found across Spain. Several local councillors from both parties have been involved in such alleged corruption scandals. Among the cases, are the local authority of Lorca in Murcia which re-valued land plots in exchange for €23 million from the interested estate firms. This case involved the Socialist mayor Miguel Navarro. This was stopped by the authorities as being a massive act of corruption. The land plots were to be assigned to the construction of 140,000 houses. Another case, involved the building of a luxury hotel in a environmentally protected area in Andratx, in Mallorca. This was stopped by the Consell de Mallorca. Eugenio Hidalgo, the former mayor of Andratx, had to go to prison for accepting a commission for such a building license (*El Pais*, 2 October 2007: 24). This systemic municipal corruption led to a re-evaluation by Transparency International about corruption in Spain. The Spanish problems with municipal corruption were highlighted in the 2005 Global Corruption Report and this was regarded as a major problem due to its systemic nature (Global Corruption Report, 2005). Major legislative bills for civil servants were introduced by the government of José Luis Zapatero, but according to Manuel Villoria, not all of them are well-designed in terms of sanctions (Villoria, 2006: 252). In the corruption perceptions index Spain declined slightly to 23 in 2006 with a score of 6.8, but better than other southern European countries, such as Portugal (6.6), Italy (4.9) and Greece (4.5) and most of the central and eastern European countries, such as the Czech Republic (4.8), Hungary (5.2) and Slovenia (6.4) (Transparency International, 2006: 326).

In sum, Spain is still very much affected by corruption scandals which involve members of the government. This naturally shows that some continuity of patrimonial behaviour can be found in the Socialist and PP governments.

The postponed reforms of the judiciary

One of the major problems of the Spanish political system is the inefficient and slow working of the judiciary system. For many years reform was postponed, creating a backlog of cases to be processed. One of the main reasons for this situation is the lack of sufficient resources to speed up trial processes (*El Pais*, 3 June 2001: 25). There are not enough judges for the amount of work that exists. In 1999 there were only 3,717 judges and magistrates across Spain were dealing with the growing number of cases. In 2006, the number of judges and magistrates across Spain increased to 4,576 supported by 3,536 court clerks, the ratio of judge to court clerks was 1.29. It means that there has been a slight improvement in the past 6 years, but still not enough. There are at the moment 10.24 judges for each 100,000 inhabitants (CGPJ, 2007: 11, 17). There are also 39,011 auxiliary personnel attached to the court system consisting of forensic doctors, legal management, processing and assistance personnel (CGPJ, 2007: 18). The budget for the court system has been modest, in spite of the growing workload. In 2006, about €2.72 billion were spent on the court system, 53.7 per cent is spent by the autonomous communities, 44 per cent in the Ministry of Justice and 2.4 per cent for the General Council of the Judicial Power (CGPJ, 2007: 22).

A further factor which complicates the deteriorating judiciary situation is naturally the exponential growth in criminal activity since the early 1990s. The crime figures suggest that domestic security is still a major problem for the Spanish government. It has been increasing in all possible categories since the transition to democracy. Since 1990 the average increase per year was 6.42 per cent. Indeed, in the year 2001 crime went up by 14.52 per cent in relation to the previous year and in the year 2002, it went up to 5.6 per cent. (*El Pais*, 17 September 2002: 22; *Anuario El Pais*, 2003: 201–2). However, since then the total number of crimes per year has been stabilising or even reducing. In 2005, the number of registered crimes was at 930,779 which was considerably fewer than at the beginning of the millennium. About 78.8 per cent were crimes related to robbery, fraud and extorsion, while only 0.12 per cent were murder (*Anuario El Pais*, 2007: 139).

The highest levels of criminality could be registered in centres of tourism. One of the factors leading to these alarming figures is organised crime in Spain, which clearly is not only perpetrated by Spaniards, but also by foreign organised criminal gangs. Strong centres of organised crime are concentrated on the coastal touristic centres and the main cities of the country. According to the Spanish police in 2001, 209 mafia groups were identified in Spain managing 5.711 billion euros. While the rest of the country has about 48 criminal acts per 1,000 inhabitants, it rose to 63 per 1,000 inhabitants along the Mediterranean coast. In 2005, there were on average 49.3 criminal acts perpetrated per 1,000 inhabitants, well below the EU average of 70. However, the province of Malaga had on average 64.1, Ceuta 72.2, Melilla 77.1, Alicante 71.6, Valencia 67.5, the Baleares 79.8 and Madrid 66.9.(*Anuario El Pais*, 2007: 138).

The highest number of mafia groups were in Madrid (seventy-six) and Barcelona (fifty-six) in the southern provinces of Malaga (forty-four), Valencia (thirty), Alicante (twenty-four) and Cadiz (twenty-four). The rest are distributed along the Galician and Mediterranean coastlines. Their main activities are drug trafficking, money-laundering, document falsification, robbery, illegal immigration and prostitution. Several foreigners are members or leaders of this mafia which consists of Colombians, Moroccans, Romanians, Russians, Lithuanians, Ukrainians and Italians. The centre of it all is the Costa del Sol in southern Andalusia around Marbella and Malaga. Due to the urbanisation explosion in these two cities, the police have been slow in updating records of the people who live in new houses. This shows also the linkage of organised crime and municipal corruption that existed in Marbella and Malaga and was recently targeted by the Spanish police. According to *El Pais*, allegedly about 8,000 British citizens are also part of the mafias and drug trafficking networks. They were allegedly employed by the state to fight against the IRA and became unemployed after the peace process and moved to Spain. There was also a growing concern about the relationship between drug trafficking and the financing of Islamic terrorism. The police became aware of such a link among some Moroccan individuals. The police force is naturally under-resourced and the court system overburdened, relying on temporary judges, because nobody wants to stay in Andalusia (*El Pais*, Domingo, 4 August 2002: 3; *El Pais*, Domingo, 12 December 2004: 1–3). This naturally contributes to a moderately insecure environment in Spain. According to previous police reports, 80 per cent of all groups include both Spaniards and foreigners, while a minority are merely Spanish or foreign. There are over 80 nationalities represented in these mafias (*El Pais*, Domingo, 12 December 2004: 2; Gomez, 2005). Moreover, the threat of Islamic terrorism has made the fight against drug trafficking a second priority. Madrid has become the capital of cocaine in Europe. Colombians, Ecuadorians and Galicians are highly active in this business. There is a growing air traffic from North Africa into Spain by the different drugs mafia. There has been also the use of old decommissioned submarines for this purpose. However, containers in ships are the most frequent route to bring drugs into the country. Spain is the main gateway for most of the cocaine coming from Latin America over West Africa. It is estimated that 100 tonnes of drugs are illegally imported to Europe per year. Europe has become the second largest market after the United States. Therefore, seven countries (France, Ireland, Italy, the Netherlands, Portugal, Spain and the United Kingdom) have created a new Centre for Analysis and Operations against Maritime Drugs Trafficking in Lisbon to share information and to help each other in the fight against the illegal drugs trafficking. However, the Spanish police are quite overburdened with the growing expanding drugs market (*El Pais*, 1 October 2007: 26).

Spain is also of the core countries for money-laundering, which becomes evident due to the high number of €500 and €100 banknotes in circulation. In 2007, such notes to the value of €88 billion, are being circulated in Spain, a doubling of the figure of 2002. About 113 million €500 bank notes are circulating in Spain, which is about 26 per cent of all notes. The crackdown against money-laundering and corruption led to the indictment of more than sixty lawyers and five notaries between the beginning of 2006 and mid-2007. All this is part of a major strategic fight of the government against corruption: due to the fact that Spain is part of the Group of Countries against Corruption (GRECO), the Spanish police force has reinforced considerably its human and material resources to fight this kind of crime. The already-mentioned operations Malaya and the White Whale (*Ballena Blanca*) could be regarded as successful actions within this reinforced fight against this kind of crime (*El Pais*, 15 July 2007: 22; Sands, 2007: 225).

According to an excellent study by Jennifer Sands, one of the main reasons for the expansion of organised crime in Spain is the fact that many of the institutions are still weak. Apart from the weak resources available to the police, also the overall judiciary sector was slow to response to the phenomenon of transnational organised crime. The corruption in Marbella was a major wake-up call. The construction and tourism sector offer ideal opportunities for organised criminal groups to launder money (Sands, 2007: 223–8).

Another source of dysfunctionality in the present Spanish judicial system is that the prison system, similar to that of the United Kingdom, has reached its capacity. In fact Spanish prisons are more than full, creating major problems for the prison authorities. Crime, particularly drug trafficking, is creating major problems inside Spanish prisons. In 2006, The prison population rose to 64,369, up by 5 per cent in relation to the previous year. Between 1999 and 2006, the prison population rose by 43 per cent. This is putting considerable pressure upon the prison system. The highest number of prisoners is in Andalusia (22 per cent), Catalonia (14 per cent), Madrid (13 per cent), Castilla-León (11 per cent) and the Valencian Community (10 per cent) (*El Pais*, Domingo, 11 August 2002: 5; *Anuario El Pais*, 2007: 136).

In 2001, this alarming situation led to a negotiated pact between the PP and PSOE with the backing of most parties. It took twenty-three meetings between these two main parties to achieve some agreement in relation to the reform of the judiciary. The pact for the reform of the judiciary (*pacto de justicia*) aimed to reform the Spanish judiciary in the mid to long term, so that it matched the quality of the European average. At the moment only 1 per cent of public expenditure is spent on the judiciary and the intention is to increase to 4.5 per cent within the next few years. It is estimated that 1 billion euros will be spent to implement the reform. The pact was agreed for a period of two legislatures. The main measures to be undertaken are related to the appropriate provision of the judiciary with financial and personnel resources, modernisation through the change of practices and the introduction of fast-track trials for minor criminal acts. One crucial aspect of the reform is to bring the judiciary system closer to the citizen and to simplify the highly bureaucratic procedures. At stake is also the modernisation of the highly corporatist nature of the judiciary system by placing the appointment of judges with the Supreme Council of Judiciary Power (*Consejo Supremo del Poder Judicial –* CSPJ). This body is in charge of the administration of justice and clearly tended to be quite conservative in appointing their own members. The CSPJ consists of twenty-one judges, of whom eight are elected by the Cortes (four by the Congress of Deputies and four by the Senate) and twelve by the judges themselves. These twenty judges are overseen by a president.

At the beginning of 2002, a crisis broke out between the PSOE and the PP in relation to the appointment of further conservative judges by the members of the CSPJ, which is creating an imbalance between the progressive and conservative groups of judges. In some way, a compromise was struck between both parties in relation to the future appointment of judges by making it more accountable and only indirectly involving the judges of the CSPJ. This case clearly showed that the CSPJ is sometimes a heavily politicised body, which affects negatively the proper running of the judiciary. These clientelistic practices of the judiciary were quite well established until recently. According to the Socialist Party, between 1982 and 1993, the period of Socialist majority government, of ninety-nine appointments made to the Supreme Court, only twenty-one were from the progressive sector (Ministerio de la Justicia, 2001; *El Pais*, 3 June 2001: 24–5; *El Pais*, 30 January 2002: 15; *El Pais*, 7 February 2002: 14; *El Pais*, 10 February 2002: 18).[2] There will be no major changes to the present structure of the judiciary, which comprises a Supreme Court as the highest court of the Spanish judiciary and the first instance courts across the country. In between, the seventeen higher courts of the autonomous communities clearly help to filter some of the judiciary cases, before they come to the Supreme Court. There is limited use of jury trials within the Spanish judiciary system (Sanchez de Dios, 2002: 264–74).

During the second term of the Aznar government, several meetings took place between the PP and the PSOE to come to an agreement on crucial aspects of the pact, but in many cases there were disagreements. The PSOE was rather disappointed with the slow progress in making available appropriate financial and personnel resources, without which it is very difficult to make a major change. In the state of the nation address of Prime Minister Aznar before the Congress of Deputies in July 2002, opposition leader José Zapatero clearly criticised the government for making so little progress towards implementing the pact (*El Pais*, 14 July 2002: 24).

The Zapatero government made efforts to provide the judiciary with more resources, however questions related to the justice became politicised throughout his term. At the centre was the attempt of Zapatero's government to negotiate a new more equitable composition of the CSPJ, in which some of the judges would be nominated by minority parliamentary groups (CiU, PNV, ERC and IU-ICV) inside parliament. However, no agreement was reached and during the second half of 2006, conservative judges inside the CSPJ refused to step down when their term finished. This crisis continued throughout 2007 which led to an intervention of the government in this matter in October 2007. However, the conservative judges held on to their jobs, hoping that the PP will win the next legislative elections and be able to impose its conservative majority upon these two highest bodies of the judiciary (*El Pais*, 18 July 2007: 14). Such politicisation of the highest bodies of the judiciary are quite damaging for democracy and certainly contribute to further political cynicism of the population.

In sum, the judiciary is presently undergoing a process of reform which still needs a stronger commitment of the executive in this respect. Only in a decade's time, will it be possible to assess if the agreed pact led to adequate reform.

Accountability and openness: the controlling institutions

Quite crucial for the smooth running of relations between the institutions is the Spanish Constitutional Court (*Tribunal Constitucional*). It is clearly very much influenced by the Austrian and German constitutional courts and attempts to be an important institution in solving inter-institutional disputes as well as constitutional issues. The Constitutional Court has a very good reputation among the Spanish political elites, because of its even-handedness in deciding disputes. It became particularly relevant in the 1980s, when the new autonomous communities were challenging the central government about certain powers. The Constitutional Court played a major role in resolving these particular disputes. In the early 1990s, such disputes over powers were more or less resolved after José Maria Aznar took over. In his first term, he was quite dependent on the vote of the regionalist parties and made major efforts to level the competences of all autonomous communities. Nevertheless, the ambitious progressive agenda of the Zapatero government after 2004 led to an increase of polarisation between the two main parties and consequently a politicisation of the Constitutional Court. Since the start of Zapatero's government until end of July 2007, PP sent twenty-three appeals against pieces of legislation initiated by the Socialists and approved in the Cortes. Out of the twenty-three, nineteen were appeals based on inconstitutionality of some of the aspects of the bill. Among the most prominent appeals were against the law of same-sex marriages, the reform of the Catalan Statute, change of the Organic Law of the Judicial Power, the reform of the Hidrological National Plan and the devolution of historical papers to the Generalitat that were archived in Salamanca(*El Pais*, 28 July 2007: 21). Moreover, PP obstructed also the renewal of the Constitutional Court which is due in December 2007. PP-friendly judges were involved in party-political disputes inside the Constitutional Court, which contributed to considerable damage of the image of the Constitutional Court as being above party politics. The upcoming legislative elections in 2008 further paralysed the work inside the Constitutional Court. This policy of obstruction of the PP was contraproductive in view of the number of appeals that they had lodged against the Socialist government (*El Pais*, 22 July 2007: 14; *El Pais*, 28 July 2007: 21; *El Pais*, 12 October 2007: 18).

The Audit Court (*Tribunal de Cuentas*) was able to gain in some influence due to the continuing lack of openness and weak accountability of Spanish public administration. Several scandals connected with the misappropriation of structural funds led to a connection of the Audit Court with EU institutions. Indeed, the Spanish Audit Court can rely on anti-corruption mechanisms created by the Office for the Fight Against Fraud (OLAF) at EU level. The Audit Court has also been critical of how political parties are financed.

Quite an important office modelled along the lines of the Scandinavian ombudsman is the People's Prosecutor (*Defensor del Pueblo*). This institution is quite important for Spanish citizens, because it is designed to help and advise them about how to proceed against irregularities or abuses in public administration. This institution is decentralised according to the autonomous regions and clearly plays a role in creating more openness and accountability in the political system. Between 1989 and 1999 there were on average 20,966 complaints. Since 2000, figures of complaints have been between 12,000 and 40,000 depending on the year. There were 28,454 and 39,256 complaints in 2004 and 2005 respectively. In 2005 64.52 per cent were by individuals, 35.12 per cent by collective actors and 0.35 from public institutions. In 2005, The overwhelming share of complaints is concentrated in Madrid with 61.37 per cent. Distant centres of complaints are Extremadura (8.86 per cent), the Valencian Community (7.28 per cent), Catalonia (4.3 per cent) and Andalusia (4.26 per cent). (Defensor del Pueblo, 2003; *Anuario El Pais* 2007: 135).

In sum, the controlling institutions are crucial to achieve a higher level of accountability and openness. Their integration in trans-European networks within the European Union strengthens their case in Spain. It is expected that they will become even more important in the future with a growing professionalisation of these bodies.

Public administration: democratisation and decentralisation

A modern Spanish public administration is essential for further democratisation of the country. The authoritarian legacy of Francoism clearly still influences the way the civil service is structured and organised. The transition and consolidation to democracy had other priorities than transform Spanish public administration. Indeed the early governments up to Prime Minister Gonzalez's governments were not able to prevent the continuity of the former administrative elites in the new democratic structures. This naturally was a major problem for the democratisation of the state machinery. Between 1975 and 1982, 996 appointments to high-ranking positions within the public administration were made, of which 57.6 per cent included civil servants who had served under the Francoist regime. Almost half of these Francoist civil servants held high-ranking positions at the time of new appointments. It shows clearly that similar to the Italian case, there was almost no change in the civil service during the transition from authoritarianism to democracy. This is reinforced by the fact that actually the Spanish Cortes during the authoritarian regime was dominated by civil servants. It was a method used by Franco to control the institutions of the regime and prevent dissent (Villoria Mendieta, 1999: 108). One of the characteristics of Spanish public administration is that it was dominated by so-called specialised corps (*cuerpos*). This meant that the different categories of civil servants formed groups according to the task assigned within the administration (engineers, inspectors of taxes) and subject to the same selection process, legislation and line of work. These *cuerpos* are almost military-style, self-disciplined organisations and respond to a command hierarchical structure. This model was introduced in the late phase of the Canovist constitutional monarchy under Prime Minister Antonio Maura in 1918. Most of the *cuerpos* were specialised and extremely protective of their position inside the administration. Some attempt was made to introduce corps of generalists during the late phase of Francoism in the 1960s (Molina Alvarez de Cienfuegos, 1999: 36; Ballart and Ramió, 2000: 62).

During the long period of Socialist government some reform was undertaken, which did not directly attack the *cuerpos*, due to the fact that they were quite embedded and strong in public administration. The whole problem of *cuerpos* was circumvented by creating a parallel system of progression based on the working place. There was also the attempt to introduce more competitive and meritocratic elements into careers in public administration, but this was blocked by the Constitutional Court in its ruling of 99/1987 introduced by the PP. In spite of that, there were some attempts to make public administration better equipped to fulfil more efficiently the tasks of a democratic decentralised state. The resistance of the *cuerpos* cannot be underestimated. Indeed, the PP can be regarded as a party that has drawn many high-ranking officials from the *cuerpos*. The best example is Prime Minister Jose Maria Aznar, who was a tax inspector belonging to a *cuerpo* before he became the party leader. According to Ignacio Molina this strong linkage between the PP and the *cuerpos* of public administration may contribute to a strengthening of the latter and provide a field for party-political patronage.

Somehow both parties can combine practices of political patronage without looking for candidates to fill high-ranking political positions outside the *cuerpos* (Molina, 2000: 50–1).

The PP governments between 1996 and 2004 were very keen to make changes in order to modernise public administration. Within 1 year, the PP government changed 3,000 high-ranking offices in the public administration. In the political-administrative structure (secretaries of state, sub-secretaries and directors-general) it changed 91 per cent of all positions, in absolute numbers 294 out of 322. Moreover, 554 out of 1,185 of the high-ranking administrative structure (subdirector-general and equivalent) were substituted by new persons. At provincial and regional levels a further 2,200 positions changed hands. This naturally shows the magnitude of possibilities for political patronage, when there is a change of government (*El Pais*, 6 April 1997: 16). Another measure that the PP government undertook was to abolish the so-called civil governors in the provinces and appoint instead high-ranking civil servants at the subdirector-general level. All this has to be regarded as positive in terms of renewal of the high-ranking positions in public administration, a process started under the Socialist government and continued by the PP governments. There is always the danger of political corruption, patronage and clientelism emerging in certain cases, but clearly there are signs that public administration is actually counteracting such practices by achieving a more mobile and rotating leadership (Beltrán, 2002: 74).

The democratisation of public administration was accompanied by a party-political consensus to decentralise public administration from the centre to the periphery. The creation of seventeen autonomous communities between 1978 and 1983 clearly opened up a process towards redistribution of human and financial resources from the centre to the autonomous communities and local government. Such a process was started in the 1980s, but gained in momentum and speed in the 1990s. The allocation of human resources was accompanied by a transfer of powers and financial support. Since all these administrative processes took place simultaneously in the past decade, it is naturally too early to make an assessment, but one can at least assert that Spain has become one of the most decentralised countries of the world along with Germany, the United States, Sweden, Denmark and Switzerland. Although there is still a long way to go, decentralisation has become a reality in Spain. Out of the 2,512,038 million civil servants slightly half of them were allocated to the autonomous communities in 2001. Within a decade, the proportion of civil servants in central administration was almost halved (see Figure 3.10 and Figure 3.11).

In 1992 the two main parties agreed to achieve a more even distribution of public administration across the autonomous communities. The main intention was to upgrade the position of the autonomous communities with weaker powers in relation to that of the historical regions. Each main party was doing it for different reasons. The PSOE intended to move towards an agenda of fully fledged federalism, while the PP wanted to neutralise the demands of the historical regions by making the autonomous communities more equal to each other (Ferri Durá, 2002: 297). In December 2001, the PP government

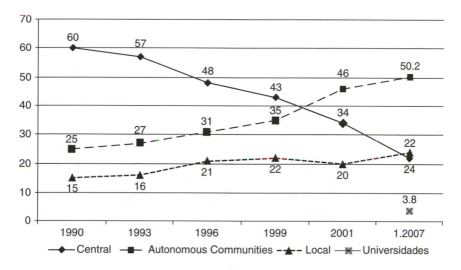

Figure 3.10 Distribution of public administration according to central, regional and local level, 1990–2007.

Source: Based on data from Beltrán, 2002: 75; Registro Central de Personal, 2007: 12.

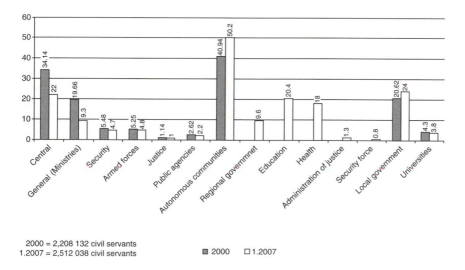

2000 = 2,208 132 civil servants
1.2007 = 2,512 038 civil servants

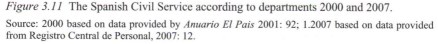

■ 2000   □ 1.2007

Figure 3.11 The Spanish Civil Service according to departments 2000 and 2007.

Source: 2000 based on data provided by *Anuario El Pais* 2001: 92; 1.2007 based on data provided from Registro Central de Personal, 2007: 12.

finalised the transfer of powers related to the health sector to the ten outstanding autonomous communities of Aragon, Asturias, the Balearics, Cantabria, Castilla La Mancha, Castilla León, Extremadura, La Rioja, Madrid and Murcia. The hasty way in which this transfer was undertaken led to some transitional problems (*El Pais*, 17 February 2002: 24). In terms of funding, a proportional income tax (*Impuesto sobre la renta de las personas físicas* – IRPF) can be retained by the autonomous communities. Such a proportion was 15 per cent when the Socialist government left office and was doubled to 30 per cent when the PP came to power. There is a general intention to raise this share to 50 per cent of income tax. Since 1985, there is also a Inter-Territorial Compensation Fund (*Fundo de Compensación Interterritorial* – FCI), which was designed to tip the balance of public investment from the richer to the poorer regions (Ferri Durá, 2002: 304–5) (see Chapter 5). The reform of the Catalan Statute led to some changes in terms of the distribution of funding, due to the fact that Catalonia has been contributing more to national GDP than receiving in terms of central transfers. Some negotiated adjustments were undertaken to compensate for the growing deficit. However, the system of financing remains the same (Nagel and Requejo, 2007: 285).

At the moment, the PP and PSOE are trying to find common ground to reform the local authorities, which still are underfunded in spite of adjustments made in the 1990s. The basic problem is that while there was decentralisation from central to regional government, there is also the impression of a renewed centralisation of public administration at regional level in detriment to local government. Aznar's government offered a proposal which was limited to the transfer of some powers of the autonomous communities to the local authorities. It excluded a review of the funding system and the direct election of the mayor, as envisaged by the Socialist government. In this sense, the Socialists rejected such an offer (*El Pais*, 7 February 2002: 22). One basic problem of the local authorities is that many of them are in debt and are clearly caught in a growing gap between the allocation of an increasing number of powers which is shared with the autonomous communities without being accompanied by the appropriate allocation of financial and human resources. A more differentiated perspective shows that there are now different patterns of relations between autonomous communities and the local authorities. For example, one may find tendencies of centralisation in Catalonia, but less so in the Basque Country. Indeed, the latter has kept a programme of decentralisation from regional government to the local authorities. Additionally, there is a growing cooperation between different municipalities, the so-called inter-municipal consortia (*mancomunidades*) which help to share the burden. There is also a need for the rationalisation of the 8,000 local authorities. The reform of local government is, after the regionalisation process and reform of public administration, the next challenge for any government in the future (Carrillo, 2002). This situation of underfunding was certainly a major factor leading to municipal corruption across Spain. Many councils tried to offset the chronic underfunding with paid commissions or licences to use municipal land for construction complexes.

Like all European Union member-states and candidates for accession Spanish public administration is embedded in the European networks connected with the establishment of a single market in the public administrative sector. The so-called European administrative space, comprising the public administrations of the member-states and the European Commission, is clearly contributing to reform of the previous practices of the Spanish administration. In 2000, the PP government presented its White Paper on improvement of public services which is the blueprint for the further modernisation of public administration. The blueprint is influenced naturally by the proposals of the Organisation for Economic Cooperation and Development (OECD) to introduce more flexibility, accountability and openness in national public administrations. The doctrine of new public management which wants a cross-fertilisation between the public and private economic sectors in terms of practices is being implemented in Spanish public administration. Aspects of quality control and a better relationship with the citizens as the main customers are part of this modernisation. Moreover, the Spanish public administration is very keen to be moving towards the information society, so that several training programmes are designed to improve knowledge of new technologies among staff. Spain took part in the overall EU plan e-Europe which wants to bring together the national public administrations and the supranational administrations through the new information technologies. In this sense, Spain has been increasing its spending on new information technologies in public administration. In 2002, such spending increased by 17.8 per cent at national level and 10 per cent at subnational level (*El Pais*, Domingo, Negocios, 17 August 2003: 5–6). There is also a general wish to improve the link between the regional administrations of the autonomous communities and the national administration by strengthening the already existing sectorial conferences bringing together representatives of all these different units (MAP, 2000; Beltrán, 2002: 73–5).

In sum, the 1990s saw a general impetus by both the Socialist as well as the PP governments to democratise, decentralise and modernise, Spanish administration and make the final move from an authoritarian resilient culture to a modern democratic open one, in order to become a motor of quality enhancement of Spanish democracy. The Zapatero government just continued this long commitment of Spanish governments towards decentralisation and democratisation of public administration.

Conclusions

After two and a half decades of development, Spanish core institutions are still evolving. Major changes happened since 1978, which are still far from complete. The most important transformation has been the decentralisation of public administration from the centre towards the autonomous communities.

The core political institutions need still to address this shift of emphasis by giving a new role to the Senate. Up until now reform of the Senate remains unfinished. Probably, the devolution processes will put pressure on the central political elites to address this question sooner rather than later.

The strengthening of the controlling institutions, the Constitutional Court, the Audit Court and People's Prosecutor has been very positive for Spanish democracy. They constitute an important instrument for accountability, openness and enhancement of the quality of democracy. This is quite important, because there are still many cases of corruption, patronage and clientelism today. The cases of municipal corruption in Marbella and other local authorities have damaged considerably the reputation of the country. Moreover, aspects of politicisation have been emerging in the past 5 years that are damaging their neutral impartial role. Quite problematic is the internal struggle within the Constitutional Court which is induced by the main political parties.

The next area of reform will be most certainly local government. Neglected in the past two and a half decades, it is the unit of government which matters most in terms of strengthening democracy, of positive performance evaluation and of grassroots participation.

In sum, Spanish core institutions are clearly well equipped to cope with the challenges of the future. The coordinates of such endeavour are already laid, and it now remains to move towards new horizons of institutional transformation.

4   Political parties and elections

The rules of the game: the centrality of governmentability and stability

One of the main characteristics of the Spanish party system and consequently the political system is the high degree of political stability. This was naturally a conscious choice by the political elites of transition led by the main architect of Spanish democracy, former Prime Minister Adolfo Suarez. Stability and governability of the new political system were high on the agenda, when the different parties of political transition decided upon the electoral system to which they were willing to submit themselves in the transition and after the constitutional settlement. Indeed, the decision for a proportional representation system moderated by small constituencies was certainly influenced by the negative experiences of former electoral systems up until the Civil War, but in particular the Second Republic between 1931 and 1936, which was an electoral system leading to political instability, fragmentation of the vote and simultaneously polarisation along a left–right spectrum.

The designers of the electoral system of the new Spanish democracy after 1978 clearly wanted to prevent the repeat of the negative experiences of the Second Republic which culminated in one of the bloodiest civil wars in the European continent. No mobilisation of the electorate was undertaken and the whole process towards the design and acceptance of the new rules of the game was essentially controlled by the political elites of the transition. Somehow the Spanish political elites were influenced by the same concerns as the German political elites when they devised their own electoral system after the Second World War to prevent repeat of the interwar democratic experience. In the case of Germany, it was the highly volatile, fragmented and polarised Weimar Republic. In the case of Spain it was the similar situation during the Second Republic. Clearly, the greatest achievements of the political elite of transition was to reconcile and lay the seeds of a new political culture which would put at the forefront the peaceful alternation and respect for the opposition.

Even today, the Civil War plays a major role in the definition of Spanish political culture. Indeed, the Iraq War of March–April 2003, which was supported by Prime Minister José Maria Aznar, was opposed by 90 per cent of the population. In spite of a successful campaign by the American, British and Australian forces, the population just continued their protest in many forms. In my assessment such behaviour has to do with the deep opposition of the Spanish people to war as a form of conflict resolution. This is the reason why the withdrawal of troops from Iraq was one the first actions of the Zapatero government and welcomed by the vast majority of the population (*El Pais*, 20 March 2004: 27; *El Pais*, 19 April 2004: 16; *El Pais*, 15 May 2004: 28). In a country where transition to democracy was achieved peacefully, without interference from abroad, this counts even more.

The Spanish electoral system is based on proportional representation. It chose the d'Hondt electoral formula which allows for a division of the votes collected by the largest parties by 1, 2, 3 and so forth, allowing for a representation of other parties. The main difference from most d'Hondt electoral formula systems across Europe is that legislative, autonomous community and municipal elections in Spain are characterised by very small electoral districts. The d'Hondt system becomes more proportional the larger the constituency. The best example for a highly proportional system is naturally the Netherlands, which allows a party to enter the second chamber with 0.67 per cent of the vote, because there is only one large national constituency. In this sense the Dutch system is quite fragmented, with, on average, more than ten parties in parliament and forcing the main parties, which do not reach as a rule of thumb more than 25 per cent of the vote, to share power with other parties. In contrast, the Spanish party system is among the most disproportional systems in spite of the proportional representation electoral system. This is achieved by very small electoral constituencies based on the fifty provinces of Spain and the additional North African enclaves of Ceuta and Melilla. This is also reinforced by the fact that the number of MPs in the lower chamber, the Congress of Deputies, is 350, which is quite small in comparison with other countries such as Italy (630), the United Kingdom (659) or Germany (656). For each of these fifty-two constituencies, there is also a 3 per cent threshold which parties have to surpass to be represented in the party system.

Each province is apportioned a minimum of two MPs. Additional MPs are allocated according to population. Only Ceuta and Melilla are uninominal constituencies. In this sense 202 out of 350 MPs are allocated automatically, while the remaining 148 may vary from election to election. In spite of changes since the decree of 1977 and the Organic Law on the General Electoral Regime (*Ley Organica del Regime Electoral General* – LOREG, 5/1985) of 19 June 1985, the core of the electoral system has not changed substantially since then and it is extremely difficult to achieve consensus among political parties to introduce widespread reform. Such an electoral system is quite favourable to the larger parties like the PSOE and the PP, but less so to the smaller parties such as the communist coalition United Left. The regionalist-nationalist parties are better off, because they are quite strong in some concentrated constituencies. CiU is quite strong in the constituencies of Catalonia, while the Basque National Party (PNV) is strongest in the Basque provinces.

Another factor plays a major role in contributing to disproportionality in the distribution of seats across Spain. It stems from the unequal distribution of seats across the country (malapportionment). It means that some provinces are over-represented in seats where the population has fallen and others have fewer seats in spite of population increases. Such problems have been only partially tackled by the political elites. This uneven distribution continues to be a major problem for representation. Some examples may make the case more explicit. In the 2000 elections the province of Soria in Castilla León elected three MPs, two went to the PP and one to the PSOE. The total of registered voters was 79,525, which gives a ratio of one MP to 28,508 voters. In contrast, the province of Seville has 1.4 million registered voters and thirteen allocated seats, but the ratio is 107,814 voters per MP, three times more than an MP needs in Soria. Similar calculations can be made across the country for all the provinces and the less populated provinces are over-represented in the Spanish parliament.

Table 4.1 clearly shows that almost two-thirds of the constituencies are allocated between four and nine seats, while only a minority has over ten seats. The largest constituencies are naturally Madrid with 34 seats for 4.3 million registered voters and Barcelona with 31 seats for 4 million registered voters. In these constituencies. This naturally leads to distortions in electoral results, where some parties get more seats than their actual share of the vote. If a party is strong in these small provinces, which are predominantly conservative, it can beat parties that are stronger in the urban centres, which are predominantly left-wing. This is the case of the Catalan Socialist Party, a regional branch of the Socialist Party, in relation to nationalist-regionalist Convergence and Union. This is the reason why Jordi Pujol won the Catalan elections in 1999, in spite of the PSC having the highest share of the vote (see Crespo and Garcia, 2001: 333). According to Jordi Capo Giol, the electoral system favours right-wing parties against the left. This is due to the large number of seats which are malapportioned in most provinces. If the PP and the PSOE would receive the same share of the vote, the former would be able to have nine more seats than the later. The electoral system actually punishes all parties with exception of PP (Capo Giol, 2000: 77).

The largest constituencies are naturally Madrid with 34 seats for 4.3 million registered voters and Barcelona with 31 seats for 4 million registered voters. In these constituencies with a higher number of voters and seats, one can expect a higher level of proportionality, while enclaves of Ceuta and Melilla, which together have 55,848 registered voters, have the one seat allocated to each. This leads to a mere first-past-the-post system with a low level of proportionality.

This electoral system is mimetically translated to the other arenas of domestic electoral competition, namely the elections to the autonomous communities and the local elections. All of them also copy closely the model of government introduced at national level, namely presidentialisation of the government and a strong position of the executive, particularly through the constructive motion of censure, in relation to the legislative. The exception to the rule is the elections to the European Parliament which are fought in one large national constituency, thus penalising the smaller regionalist-nationalist parties. Normally, these parties which represent less than 3 per cent of the voters at national level join strategic coalitions with other regionalist-nationalist parties in order to achieve representation in the European Parliament.

Table 4.1 Elections to the constituent assembly and the legislative elections, 1977–2008

| | 1977 | | 1979 | | 1982 | | 1986 | | 1989 | | 1993 | |
| | UCD minority governments | | | | PSOE absolute majority governments | | | | PSOE minority government | | | |
	%	Seats	%	Seats	%	Seats	%	Seats	%	Seats	%	Seats
UCD	34.6	166	35	168	6.5	12	–	–	–	–	–	–
PSOE	29.3	118	30.5	121	48.4	202	44.1	184	39.9	175	38.7	175
AP/CD/PP	8.8	16	6.1	9	26.5	106	26	105	25.9	107	34.8	157
PCE/IU/IU-ICV	9.4	20	10.8	23	4	4	4.61	7	9.1	17	9.57	18
CDS	–		–	–	2.9	2	9.2	19	7.9	14	–	
CiU	2.8	11	2.7	8	3.7	12	5	18	5	18	4.95	17
PNV	1.7	8	1.5	7	1.9	8	1.53	6	1.2	5	1.24	5
HB/EH	–		1	3	1	2	1.15	5	1.1	1	0.88	2
ERC	0.79	1	0.7	1	0.7	1	0.42	1	–	–	0.80	1
EE	0.3	1	0.5	1	0.5	1	0.53	2	0.5	2	0.54	–
EA	–		–		–		0.4	1	0.7	1	0.55	1
PAR	–		0.2	1	–		0.3	1	0.3	1	0.8	1
Pa	–		–		–		–		1	2	0.61	–
UV	–		–		–		–		0.7	2	0.48	1
CC	–		–		–		–		0.32	1	0.88	4
BNG	–		–		–		–		–		0.54	–
CHA	–		–		–		–		–		–	
Other	12.3	7	11	7	3.9	–	6.76	2	6.7	0	5.46	–
TOTAL	100	348	100	350	100	350	100	350	100	350	100	350

Table 4.1—Continued

| | 1996 | | 2000 | | 2004 | | 2008 | |
| | PP minority government | | PP absolute majority government | | PSOE minority government | | | |
	%	Seats	%	Seats	%	Seats	%	Seats
PSOE	37.5	141	34.1	125	42.64	164	43.46	159
AP/CD/PP	38.9	157	44.6	183	37.64	148	40.11	153
PCE/IU/IU-ICV	10.6	21	5.5	8	4.96	5	3.80	2
CiU	4.64	16	4.2	15	3.24	10	3.05	11
PNV	1.28	5	1.5	7	1.63	7	1.2	6
HB/EH	0.7	2	–	–	–	–	–	–
ERC	0.7	1	0.8	1	2.54	8	1.17	3
EE	–	–	–	–	–	–	–	–
EA	0.46	1	0.4	1	0.32	1	0.20	–
PAR	–	–	–	–	–	–	0.16	–
Pand	–	–	–	–	–	–	–	–
UV	–	–	0.89	1	0.71	–	–	–
CC-PNC	0.88	4	1.07	4	0.86	3	0.65	2
BNG	0.9	2	1.3	3	0.8	2	0.82	2
CHA	0.2	–	0.3	1	0.37	1	0.15	–
NA-BAI	–	–	–	–	0.24	1	0.24	1
UPyD	–	–	–	–	–	–	1.2	1
Other	3.24	–	5.34	1	4.05	–	3.61	–
TOTAL	100	350	100	350	100	350	100	350

The consequence of the Spanish electoral system for the Congress of Deputies and the other subnational electoral arenas is that it is one of the less proportional systems in Europe. One can place the consequences of the Spanish electoral system closer to the British simple plurality system, the French two-ballot majoritarian system and the Greek Bischoff–Hagenbach reinforced proportional representation system. As already mentioned, it is a contrast to the proportional representation electoral systems in the Nordic countries (Sweden, Denmark, Finland and Norway), Portugal, the Benelux countries (particularly the Netherlands), Austria and Switzerland. This also contrasts heavily with the German-mixed electoral system which clearly is aimed at reducing fragmentation, but at the same time

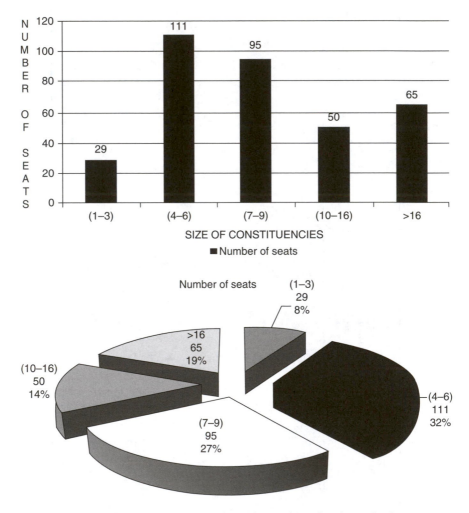

Figure 4.1 Size of constituencies, number of constituencies in each size category and aggregate amount competed in the particular constituencies, legislative elections of 2000.

allowing for a moderation of the simple plurality system by topping up seats in the proportional representation part (Ramirez *et al.*, 1998: 104–5).

In sum, in spite of the d'Hondt system, the Spanish electoral system has majoritarian characteristics and it was devised by the fathers of the Spanish constitution in order to avoid fragmentation and political instability.

Indeed, the Spanish party system, in spite of strong volatility between the two main parties between 1993 and 2004, is quite stable. Moreover, the governmentability aspect of the electoral system has been a success so far. There were some criticisms that the elections of 1993 and 1996 did not create straightforward absolute majorities leading to legislature agreements of these two main parties with the regionalist-nationalist parties, but the elections of 2000 showed that such situations may be regarded as important signs towards alternation in power as well as allowing for the integration of the smaller parties.

The high level of responsibility of political leaders both in the national political parties as well as in the regionalist-nationalist parties has strengthened the political culture embedded in the consequences of the electoral system. One has to mention particularly the contribution made by Jordi Pujol's CiU to the strengthening of the party and political system, which allowed both the PSOE and PP to govern in the 1990s without an absolute majority, only with CiU support. In sum, one has to agree with Pilar del Castillo, when she comes to the conclusion, that many of the ideas to reform the electoral system in the end are driven by the wish to improve other things such as the relationship between the parties and the electorate or enhance the quality of democracy. In this sense, what is an issue of long-term political cultural patterns cannot be reduced to the reform of the electoral system. The tendency to blame the electoral system for negative aspects of Spanish democracy is probably not the best way to achieve a higher level of quality of democracy (Castillo, 1998b: 75–6). A more straightforward way is to democratise even more the selection process within Spanish political parties, which until now have remained a little bit distant from the population, reinforcing the already existing gap (Hopkin, 2001).

The lack of constituency links between MP and voter certainly is an aspect that can be explored, but one has to realise that such links cannot be established overnight. Also the idea to introduce open lists, where voters can rank their candidates, has met with mixed feelings, particularly after the abuse of preference voting in the former proportional representation system in Italy up until 1992. There is also some apprehension about changing the electoral system, because it may lead in the end to constitutional reform. Indeed, there were some calls for the introduction of the German electoral system, but this could only be achieved by changing the constitution which clearly declares that proportional representation is the way the Congress of Deputies is elected. To my mind, the only minor flaw, if at all, of the present electoral system is that it is too successful in providing a high degree of political, party and governmental stability. The cost of this stability was the inability of new nationwide parties to challenge the major parties. In the end, this was certainly an impoverishment of the rich political culture of Spain. However, in contrast to the instability of the Second Republic, the present system seems to guarantee stability and reduction of fragmentation among statewide parties (see Oñate, 2006: 427–9).

In July 2007, leader of the PP, Mariano Rajoy proposed a reform of the electoral law, which would reinforce even more the majoritarian bias. He was proposing that only parties with over 30 per cent of the vote were entitled to government at national and subnational level. Should no party reach the 30 per cent threshold, then a second round of the two most voted parties should be undertaken. This proposals comes close to the French system. Although he was prepared to negotiate his proposals, all major parties in the Congress rejected outright this proposal. The main reason was that in spite of the majoritarian bias, all parties still adhere to the principle of proportional representation enshrined in Article 68.3 of the constitution (*El Pais*, 14 July 2007: 25; *El Pais*, 19 July 2007: 14).

The asymmetrical nature of bicameralism in the Spanish political system makes the electoral system of the Congress of Deputies centre stage to the detriment of the electoral system of the Senate. Article 69 of the Spanish constitution defines the Senate as a chamber of territorial representation. Similar to the Congress of Deputies the province is the basic electoral constituency, but the electoral process is quite different. The 257 senators are elected in two parts. The first part consists of 208 directly elected senators at provincial level. Each province, apart from the insular provinces and Ceuta and Melilla, elect four senators by a limited vote. Each voter can cast up to three votes out of a list of candidates. The candidates with the highest numbers win the election. In the islands, there are only three seats per constituency, so that the voter has only two votes, while in Ceuta and Melilla, with two seats each, the voter has only one vote. The direct elections to the Senate take place at the same time as the elections to the Congress of Deputies. The second part of the elections is undertaken indirectly by the parliaments of the autonomous communities which are allocated seats according to the population living in each autonomous community. One Senate seat is allocated to each of the autonomous communities and then for each million further seats are added. This may change from election to election. The distribution among the parties in each autonomous community is related to the distribution of seats in the last regional elections of each of the autonomous communities. In total, forty-nine senators are elected indirectly by the autonomous communities. This naturally causes changes in the composition of the Senate during a legislature period, because regional elections take place at different times for the autonomous communities. The electoral system continues to be a major issue for eventual reform of the Senate (see Chapter 3). On one hand, the subaltern role of the Senate in the parliamentary system leads also to a low level of interest for the direct election of this chamber. On the other hand, the limited vote employed is probably the only opportunity for voters to cast a preferential voting. However, according to an excellent study by Juan Montabes Pereira and Carmen Ortega Villodres, voters rarely use their preferential voting and tend to vote en bloc for the candidates of one particular party. The strategies of parties concentrate on reducing the choice of voters by offering the equal number of candidates as there are seats to be allocated. This was reinforced by the Electoral Law of 1985, which ranked candidates alphabetically and according to political parties. This led to an advantage to candidates first on the list. Another factor that leads to this lack of use of preferential voting, is that candidates are almost unknown to the voters. Most of the candidates are party-nominated and have a weak linkage to the constituency (Montabes Pereira and Ortega Villodres, 2002: 113–4, 128).

In spite of all the criticisms and calls for reform, the Spanish electoral system has been quite successful in creating stable governments and provides the conditions for long-term institutionalisation and professionalisation of national, regional and local political elites. The main problem has been so far the necessary democratisation of the political parties in view of improving the quality of democracy in Spain.

The political parties in Spain

Legislation and public party financing

One of the big achievements of Adolfo Suarez was to put his personal reputation on the line when his government legalised the Communist Party by decree during the early transition period to democracy, in spite of strong opposition from the Francoist establishment. This important event made his efforts credible to the Spanish opposition. Indeed, the first elections to democracy experienced the emergence of new parties, some of them even called 'taxi parties', because they consisted of not more than two people.

According to José Ramón Montero about 579 parties declared intention to take part in the founding elections of 1977. Such high figures continued to be quite common. In 1986, there were 681 declared parties, while in 1993 the number had risen to 805 parties. Similar figures can be reported for the Senate (Montero, 1998a: 54–6). In the 2000 elections ninety-seven parties registered some kind of vote. In spite of a high level of concentration of the vote, small constituencies and a threshold of 3 per cent, there is still a strong engagement by many parties that remain outside the parliamentary arena (*El Pais*, 2001: 94–5). In spite of this diversity of political parties which are spread along two main axes, the ideological and the regionalist-nationalist one, only a few parties are able to achieve representation in the different arenas of electoral competition.

One of the most important factors in modern election politics is the role of party financing in the corresponding political system. The Spanish political system adopted a straightforward public subsidy system which allocates yearly funding to each of the parties according to the votes and seats obtained in the last elections. This naturally makes parties highly dependent on state subsidies. This dependence becomes even more salient, when one takes into account that membership of political parties is quite low. This means that parties tend to use other ways of fund-raising, and this may involve irregular party financing as in several cases such as Filesa for the Socialist Party and the Naseiro case for the People's Party. Indeed, in the early days of transition to democracy the PSOE was supported logistically and financially by the German Friedrich Ebert foundation. Other German foundations such as the Konrad Adenauer Foundation of the Christian Democratic Union, the

Hans Seidel Foundation of the Christian Social Union and the Friedrich Naumann Foundation of the German Liberal Party were also subsidising political parties in Spain. It is estimated that 27 million German marks (€13 million) were distributed among Spanish parties between 1976 and 1980 and 38 million German marks (€19 million) between 1983 and 1988 (Powell, 2001: 413). The main reason for this blossoming of illicit financing is the fact that electoral campaigns are quite expensive and lead to high debts by the main parties. Today, all Spanish political parties are massively in debt. The loss of elections leads automatically to loss of income. Indeed, the PSOE lost forty-four seats in the Spanish Cortes in the legislative elections of 2000 and lost automatically €3.5 million. The catastrophic result of the United Left in the same elections, in which their share of the vote declined from about 10 to 5 per cent, had a serious effect on the organisation. They had to deal with a cut of €4.52 million in 1999 to 2.41 million in 2001. United Left had to lay off 75 per cent of their party employees and make substantial savings in order to survive as the third largest party (*El Pais*, 5 June 2000: 6).

Until the end of 2007, party financing was regulated by the Organic Law for the Financing of Political Parties (*Ley Organica de Financiación a los Partidos Politicos* – LOFPP 3/1987). Moreover, the LOFPP regulates party financing during electoral campaigns. Parties had free access to public media according to their electoral strength. Furthermore, any posting of electoral leaflets and material was covered by the state. According to LOFPP, no individual private contribution to campaigns was exceed the value of €5000. Moreover, donors that gave contributions exceeding more than €3,005 had to be declared by the political parties. (*El Pais*, 18 April 2005:17). The strong dependence of Spanish political parties on generous state subsidies for electoral campaigning, party structures and parliamentary groups make them oriented towards seeking the highest possible number of public offices at national, regional and local levels. In this sense, Spanish parties can be characterised as cartel parties, meaning that they are interested in keeping a strong stake in state subsidies, because they are the main source of income (Katz and Mair, 1995). In 2004, political parties at all levels of the political system received €175.6 million in annual state funding which excludes additional funding for electoral campaigns. In 2004, the subsidy for electoral campaigns was €94 million. All in all, between 73 and 80 per cent of all funding goes to the two main parties, the PP and the PSOE, the rest is distributed among all the other parties (Tribunal de Cuentas, 2007: 20–21; see also Table 4.2. and Table 4.3.) This gives a great advantage to the two main parties on top of the already-mentioned majoritarian tendencies of the electoral system. Therefore, Jonathan Hopkin speaks of an 'adulterated' two-party system. In spite of a high number of non-state parties being represented in parliament, the party system is dominated by the two large parties, the PP and the PSOE (Hopkin, 2005: 13).

Political parties are also entitled to receive funding for their political foundations. According to *El Pais* in 2007, €7,018,587.41 of state funding was distributed to political foundations. Again the two main parties received 81 per cent of all the funding (*El Pais*, 8 August 2007; see Table 4.4).

Table 4.2 Distribution of annual party financing in 2004

	State subsidy		Autonomous governments		Cortes Generales (Parliament)		Legislative autonomous assemblies and autonomous cities		Local authorities		TOTAL	
	Amount	Share	Amount	Share	Amount	Share	Amount	Share	Amount	Share	Amount	Share
BNG	512,788.9	0.85			137,095.21	1.05	466,315.08	0.9	407,562	0.9	1,523,761.29	0.86
CHA	208,271.4	0.34			62,848.52	0.48	347,829.14	0.66	155,588.27	0.34	774,537.29	0.44
CC	582,990.1	0.97			572,861.7	4.4	436,022.64	0.8	792,706.62	1.7	2,384,581.05	1.4
CiU	2,083,243	3.45			722,516.57	5.5	4,386,401.98	8.4	2,029,870	4.4	9,222,031.33	5.3
EA	200,408.6	0.33			62,848.52	0.48	589,080	1.1	926,613.84	2	1,778,850.99	1.01
ERC	1,279,788	2.1			331,414.75	2.5	2,403,306.39	4.5	1,199,292.99	2.6	5,213,802.07	3
IC-V	437,943.7	0.7			11,398.05	0.09	1,177,975.86	2.25	1,275,098.71	2.8	2,902,416.27	16.5
IU	1,921,665	3.2	200,333	5.6	385,578	3	2,770,067.47	5.3	3,568,541.38	7.7	8,846,184.37	5
NA-BAI	125,511.2	0.2			51,450.47	0.4					176,961.64	0.1
Pand	86,505.26	0.14			11,398.05	0.09	528,758.85	1	1,005,752.14	2.2	1,632,414.30	0.93
PNV	1,079,718	1.8	1,710,714	48.1	651,297.15	5	1,051,794.5	2	2,027,220.14	4.4	6,520,742.98	3.7
PP	25,126,249	44	945,723	26.6	5,118,579	39.2	16,627,693.33	31.7	13,320,092.77	28.8	61,459,222.08	35
PSOE-PSC	26,270,024	42	702,319	19.8	4,316,555.56	33.1	18,989,259.5	36.2	16,065,150.67	34.7	66,343,309.05	37.8
UPN	349,184.7	0.6					826,687.05	1.6	54,764.48	0.12	1,230,636.21	0.7
Other Parties					617,042.48	4.7	1,861,646.99	3.6	3,451,979.54	7.5	5,614,884.03	3.2
TOTAL	60,264,290	100	3,559,089	100	13,052,884.03	100	52,462,838.78	100	46,280,233.55	100	175,624,335.56	100

Source: Tribunal de Cuentas, 2007: 20.

Table 4.3 State funding for electoral campaigns, 2003–2004

IN €	State subsidies General elections 2004		European elections 2004		Local elections 2003		Regional elections 2003 and 2004		Elections to local government 2003		TOTAL	
	Amount	Share	Amount	Share	Amount	Share	Amount	Share	Amount	Share	Amount	Share
BNG	130,825.15	0.28									130,825.15	0.14
CHA	60,295.96	0.13					27,752.57	0.13			88,048.53	0.09
CC	457,540.57	0.99									457,540.57	0.49
CiU	1,831,995.98	3.98					1,417,196.14	6.4			3,249,192.57	3.5
EA	38,951.93	0.08									38,951.93	0.04
ERC	1,737,233.19	3.8					1,136,011.85	5.2			2,873,245.04	3.1
IC-V	23,752.44	0.05	1,562,142.96	6.2			792,326.54	3.6			816,078.98	0.9
IU	5,971,440.45	12.98					1,494,192.83	6.8	99,249.64	36.7	9,127,025.88	9.7
NA-BAI	49,053.68	0.11									49,053.68	0.05
PAnd							208,975.51	0.95			208,975.51	0.22
PNV	778,463.50	1.7							50,954.32	18.9	829,417.82	0.9
PP	16,185,352.73	35.2	10,198,535.57	40.7			8,519,420.8	38.7	34,172.48	12.6	34,937,481.58	37.2
PSOE-PSC	16,264,321.2	35.4	10,101,197.8	40.3			8,017,980.46	36.4	22,050.24	8.2	34,405,549.7	36.6
UPN	215,420.96	0.46			47,285.71	6.9					262,706.67	0.28
Others	2,246,180.04	4.9	3,190,637.45	12.7	640,684.08	93.1	411,535.52	1.8	63,844.37	23.6	6,552,881.46	7
TOTAL	45,990,827.78	100	25,052,513.78	100	687,969.79	100	22,025,392.22	100	270,271.05	100	94,026,974.62	100

Source: Tribunal de Cuentas, 2007: 21.

Table 4.4 State funding for political foundations in Spain in 2007

Foundation	Party	Funding
Foundation for Analysis and Social Studies (FAES)	People's Party (PP)	2,890,086.25
Foundation Pablo Iglesias	Spanish Socialist Workers' Party (PSOE)	2,820,000.00
Foundation Rafael Campalans	Catalan Socialist Party	470,000
Foundation Trias Fargas	Democratic Convergence of Catalonia-CDC (Part of Convergence and Union-CiU)	187,944
Institute for Humanistic Studies Coll i Alentorn	Democratic Union of Catalonia-UDC (Part of Convergence and Union-CiU)	62,418
Foundation for a Europe of Citizens	United Left (IU)	201,000
Foundation Our Horizon	Initiative for Catalonia-Greens (IC-V)	58,690
Foundation the Alternative	United Left (EUiA-Catalan Branch)	11,732
Foundation Luis Bello	Republican Left (ER)	30,000
Foundation President Josep Irla i Bosch	Catalan Republican Left	195,620
Foundation Galiza Forever	Galician Nationalist Bloque (BNG)	62,594
Foundation Gaspar Torrente	Aragonese Junta (CHA)	28,270
Foundation Sabino Arana	Basque Nationalist Party (PNV)	No figures
TOTAL		7,018,587.41

Source: *El Pais*, 8 August 2007; Boletin Oficial del Estado, 7 August 2007.

In contrast, the funding from membership fees is quite negligible, inconsistently endeavoured and depends on whether the party is in government. A party in government may attract many fellow supporters which may leave when the party falls from power again. This can be confirmed by the rise of PSOE membership in the 1980s and 1990s and its subsequent decrease after 1996, or the rise of membership of the PP between 1989 and 2004 (van Biezen, 2001; Castillo, 1985).

The main controlling body is the Audit Court which is naturally dependent on the accurate accounts of the political parties. The present practice has shown that the Audit Court is several years behind in scrutinising the finances of the political parties. In August 2002, it issued the annual report for 1999 and it found several irregularities of financing among all parties. The main reason for concern was the use of political foundations or other societies to disaggregate funds or debts of the political parties. These late reports and the lack of appropriate measures to penalise the parties just perpetuates a situation of illicit party financing and potential political corruption as has happened during the 1990s (Holgado Gonzalez, 2002: 133–8; *El Pais*, 20 August 2002: 14). The situation has not changed in the new millennium. On the contrary, in the last report of the Audit Court on the accounts

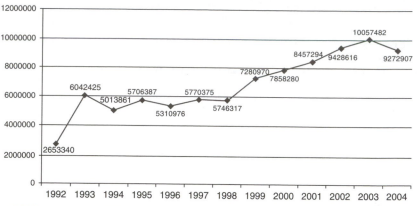

TOTAL = € **89,619,230**   ──◆── Yearly aggregated amount of private donations in €

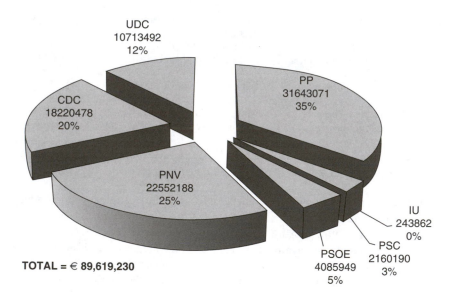

UDC
10713492
12%

CDC
18220478
20%

PP
31643071
35%

PNV
22552188
25%

IU
243862
0%

PSC
2160190
3%

PSOE
4085949
5%

TOTAL = € **89,619,230**

Figure 4.2 Total aggregated amount of private donations and distribution among political
parties 1992–2004.

Source: José Maria Irujo, La caja negra de los partidos. In: *El Pais*,18 April 2005:17.

of the political parties in 2004, published on 27 June 2007 the shortcomings of
accounting among the political parties were reiterated (Tribunal de Cuentas, 2007:
239–43). It is very difficult to get a clear picture of the accounts of the political
parties. The legislation in force until end of 2007 had many loopholes that political
parties were able to use to finance the party. According to *El Pais* between 1992
and 2004, political parties received €89,619,230 in private donations: the vast
majority went to the Basque PNV, the Catalan CiU and the People's Party.

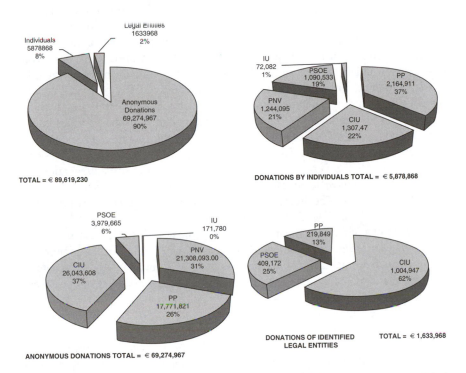

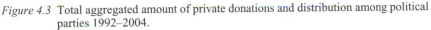

Figure 4.3 Total aggregated amount of private donations and distribution among political parties 1992–2004.

Source: José Maria Irujo, La caja negra de los partidos. In: *El Pais*,18 April 2005: 18.

There is a strong linkage between high levels of private donations and a party that is in power. Indeed, PNV has been in power in the Basque autonomous government since its creation in the late 1970s. This applies also for the CiU that was in power in the autonomous community of Catalonia between 1979 and 2003. Last but not least, the access of the PP to power between 1996 and 2003 led to a considerable increase of private donations. The main problem of private donations has been the considerable amount donated by anonymous donors. Anonymous funding remains intransparent and suspicions of economic clientelistic trade-offs, particularly at the regional level in the Basque Country and Catalonia have emerged, although very difficult to prove (*El Pais*,18 April 2007: 17–18).

In 2007, after an initiative of the Catalan Republican Left, a new bill on party funding was agreed among all political parties with exception of the PP. The new law 8/2007 entered into force on 4 July 2007. The new law wants to give more transparency to donations by abolishing the possibility to do it anonymously. According to the new law, persons or private entities can give donations up to €100,000, but the donor has to identify itself. It is forbidden to accept anonymous donations. Moreover, a procedure of payment of this donation which can be follow-up by the Audit Court was agreed. It was agreed that political foundations can get up to €150,000 by a person or private entity. Public institutions and private firms with contracts with the different national and regional public administrations are not allowed to make donations. Should a party be found out to be receiving anonymous donations, it has to pay a penalty of double the amount that it received as a donation and this is imposed by the Audit Court. Should the party not comply, any state funding will be frozen, until the penalty is paid. Any party that may be illegalised, because it is contravening against the law of political parties, loses its right to get state funding. The tightening of the loopholes of the previous law of party financing of 1987 is also followed by a considerable increase of basic funding from €65 million in 2007 to €78 million in 2008, a 20 per cent increase. It is very difficult to assess if this new law will reduce the opacity of private donations, in any case this is a quite belated response to what the Audit Court has been calling for since the early 1990s. The three parties that will be penalised by the new legislation will be PP, PNV and CiU (*El Pais*, 6 April 2007).

After months of negotiation and controversy, the new Organic Law of Political Parties (*Ley Organica de Partidos Politicos* 6/2002 of 27 June 2002) was approved by an overwhelming majority in the Congress of Deputies and the Senate. It replaced the outdated previous organic law 54/1978 and added several new elements into it related to the difficult situation which Spain is facing towards dealing with Basque terrorism. The new law explicitly forbids parties which promote or support racism, xenophobia and violence. The new law was a joint endeavour of the PP and the Socialist Party. It allowed for the subsequent illegalisation of Peoples's Union (*Herri Batasuna* – HB) which changed the name in 2001 to Basque Nation (*Eusko Herritarrok* – EH). The main reason for this illegalisation was that according to the PP *Herri Batasuna* used its formal status as a political party to create a vast network of formal Basque firms which were designed to finance Basque terrorism. The new law, which was naturally influenced and supported by the global war on terrorism, became an important weapon to deal with the networks of Basque terrorism. The new law was rejected by the PNV, IU, *Eusko Askartasuna* (EA) and the Nationalist Galician Block (*Bloque Nacionalista Galego* – BNG) (*El Pais*, 9 May 2002: 22; *El Pais*, 15 May 2002: 15; *El Pais*, 26 June 2002: 14).[1] *Herri Batasuna* has been able to circumvent the law by presenting new political groups to regional and local elections. For example, in the Basque regional elections of 26 September 2005, the new political formation the Communist Party of the Basque Country (PCTV–EHAK) took part in elections and won the same amount of votes (9.9 per cent and two seats) that normally *Herri Batasuna* would get. Moreover, many *Batasuna* politicians were also taking part in this new formation. However, it was allowed to take part in elections, in spite of strong protests of the PP.

Similarly, before the regional and municipal elections of 2007, *Batasuna* presented again a new list, which was referred to the Supreme Court to be forbidden, but delays and appeals led to the formation being able to take part in elections. This again led to protests of PP against the inability of the government to outlaw a political organisation connected to Basque terrorist organisation ETA. However, the Zapatero government stepped up the investigations and arrests against prominent leaders of the new political formations the Basque Nationalist

Action (*Acción Nacionalista Vasca* – ANV) and the Basque Communist Party (*Partido Comunista de las Tierras Vascas*), who were allegedly involved in the illegalised *Herri Batasuna*. Judge Baltasar Garzón, one of the most prominent figures in the fight against Basque terrorism, was able to arrest nineteen of thirty-eight leaders of the leadership between the summer 2007 and early February 2008. The Zapatero government was under considerable pressure from the PP and the Association of Victims of Terrorism to take action against *Herri Batasuna* and its proxy organisations (*El Pais*, 5 February 2008: 18).

In sum, the Spanish political parties are generously supported by the political system, if they are able to get representation in these highly difficult electoral arenas.

Although in the past 25 years several parties achieved representation, today there are only three national parties and over ten regionalist-nationalist parties. While the vote of the national parties is quite concentrated among the two main parties, the remaining 10–12 per cent of the vote is shared among several regionalist-nationalist parties that are strong and highly concentrated in regional strongholds. Among them the Catalan CiU and the Basque PNV are by far the most important. In the past there were other national parties, but they collapsed, disappeared or lost public support. The Union of Democratic Centre (*Unión del Centro Democratico* – UCD) was the pivotal party of transition. It was chaired by Prime Minister Adolfo Suarez. It was a coalition of fourteen parties, which was never able to transform itself into a new party. After the democratic transition was successfully achieved, the quarrels and factionalism inside the party increased substantially, leading to the resignation of Adolfo Suarez in early 1981 and his replacement by Leopoldo Calvo Sotelo. Before the elections of 1982, the UCD collapsed and most of the vote went to the People's Party and the new party of Adolfo Suarez, the Democratic Social Centre (*Centro Democratico y Social* – CDS) (Hopkin, 1993; Huneeus, 1985; Caciagli, 1993). The CDS was able to achieve some representation in the Cortes and in the other electoral arenas up until 1993. It was able to attract the liberal and centre-right vote. The highest vote was 9.2 per cent in elections of 1986, achieving about nineteen MPs. The transformation of the People's Party into a centrist party after 1989 led to the final demise of the CDS. The evolution of political parties in Spain can only partially be compared to those in more established continuous democracies such as the United Kingdom, Sweden, France, Denmark and the Netherlands. The new Spanish parties emerged after a long period of an authoritarian dictatorship and in a context of a growing importance of the media. As such they have to be considered as political parties in a new democracy. The seminal study by Ingrid van Biezen shows that they are all cartel parties, which are very dependent on public funding and therefore office-seeking. They have become electoral machines which are in a permanent electoral campaign. Ingrid van Biezen asserts as follows:

(The) path of party formation and development in new democracies is in fact best understood as a process sui generis, by which parties in new democracies generally start out as 'parties in state' which subsequently expand their organizations beyond the confines of state institutions and reach out, albeit only minimallly, towards society.

(van Biezen, 2003:9)

Hence, while parties in the old democracies generally started out as organizations of society demanding participation, parties in new democracies are faced with the challenge of enticing citizens who already have rights of participation to actually exercise those rights. The sequence of organization building is of importance, because the emergence of the party in public office before or concurrent with the opportunities for the development of the extra-parliamentary party diverts attention from the development of organizational linkages between parties and society.

(van Biezen, 2003:32–3)

Her study compares Spanish parties to Portuguese, Hungarian and Czech ones and she is able to show similarities in the relationship between party in office and extra-parliamentary party. The dependency of extra-parliamentary party from party in office has become a major characteristic of these political parties in southern and central and eastern Europe. They are all cartel parties, membership has been so far a secondary concern. The role of state funding and therefore winning elections is the primary aim of such parties (van Biezen, 2003).

The People's Party (PP): the long road towards the centre

In spite of all the transformations of the People's Party since its foundation in 1977, it symbolises the conservative subculture that exists in Spain. The transformation of the party into a catch-all centrist party after 1989 does not change the legacy of this most Spanish of all political parties. It is Spanish in the sense that it is instinctively a party that advocates a unitary conception of Spain, which goes back to the origins of the formation of the Spanish national state. *España una y catolica* (united and Catholic) are two elements that still characterise the political culture of the PP, but no longer in a rigid authoritarian way. The PP is a democratic, centrist and Christian democratic party well integrated into the structures of the European People's Party in the European Parliament. It clearly adopted a more flexible attitude towards Spanish politics, becoming a crucial key to the moderation and transformation of the Spanish political system. However, according to Sebastian Balfour there is a strong Francoist legacy. Many of the leading politicians of the PP are sons, daughters or grandchildren of leading members of the former Francoist political elites (Balfour, 2005: 147).

The development of the party can be divided into two main historical periods. The first can be characterised as the period of the old generation under Manuel Fraga Iribarne, the former Minister of Information of Franco's authoritarian regime in the 1960s and until the last elections of 20 June 2005, the president of the Xunta de Galicia, the regional government of the autonomous community. The second period can be characterised as a generation change under the leadership of José Maria Aznar, a former tax inspector and a protegé of Manuel Fraga.

The first period is characterised by a very insecure period in terms of finding a way to relate to the electorate. Indeed, the PP was able to capture most of the extreme and moderate right-wing vote, but had extreme difficulties to make inroads into the centrist and naturally left-wing vote. Between 1979 and 1989, on average 66.75 per cent of voters were close to a right-wing position when voting for the PP, while only 31 per cent had a centrist position. This was quite disadvantageous for the party in an environment in which 72.7 per cent of the electorate on average after the long dictatorship adopted a centre-left or centre position from election to election.[2] The party was perceived by the population as being the representative of the former authoritarian regime and this was not helped by the fact that many members of the former Francoist regime were its leading politicians. Manuel Fraga was also not the most charismatic leader. He conveyed the feeling of being a politician of the past and this was rejected by the majority of the population. In the first elections of 1977 and 1979, the party received merely 8.8 per cent and 9 per cent of the vote respectively. The fortunes of the party changed in the historical elections of 1982 when it was able to attract a large part of the collapsed UCD vote. It instantly became the second largest party. It tried hard to change the image of being a party connected with the former authoritarian regime by changing its name in elections. The original name was People's Alliance (*Alianza Popular* – AP). In 1979, it changed its name to Democratic Coalition (*Coalición Democrática* – CD) so that it could challenge the UCD, but it was not very successful (López Nieto, 1986). In the 1982 elections, it coalesced with the People's Democratic Party (*Partido Popular Democratico* – PDP) and in 1986, it called itself People's Coalition (*Coalición Popular* – CP). It was only in January 1989, with the rise of new leader José Maria Aznar that it stabilised to the PP.

One of the main problems of this first period is that after 1982, the PP just stagnated in subsequent elections to 25 to 26 per cent. The PP was the second largest party, but remained throughout the 1980s ten points behind the largest party, the PSOE. This so-called electoral ceiling of the PP was called the ceiling of Fraga (*techo de Fraga*), because he was not able to achieve more than this share of the vote (Hopkin, 1999:222). After continually failing to break the electoral ceiling, Fraga clearly decided to step down and a new leader was appointed in 1987. In the eighth party congress in February 1987, Antonio Hernández de la Mancha became the new leader who was in charge of reforming the party, particularly in view of bringing it into the mainstream of Spanish and European politics. He was particularly supported by the strong youth organisation New Generations (*Nuevas Generaciones* – NG). Nevertheless, Antonio Hernández de la Mancha was not successful in changing the fortunes of the party. Throughout 1987 and 1988, he lost the support of most sectors of the party. Since 1986, the party was facing major economic problems due to the fact that most industrial groups and the main employers' organisations were not willing to support the party and tended to work with the Socialists (Gilmour, 2005: 423).

After informal talks with Marcelino Oreja and other politicians Fraga decided to become again the leader of the party. In the negotiations with Marcelino Oreja he had to agree to streamline the party, change the name to People's Party (PP) and play only an interim role as leader to be replaced later by a younger post-Francoist politician. This was the only way to be integrated in the European People's Party. Any other parties within the coalition were to be merged into the PP (Gilmour, 2005: 424). In January 1989, Hernandez Mancha was replaced by Manuel Fraga in the ninth 'refounding' party congress. This was a crucial party congress, because Fraga forced all different regional barons to accept the change from People's Alliance to People's Party. This party congress also reduced internal democracy and established more cohesion and hierarchical structures (Garcia-Guereta Rodriguez, 2001:146–69). In August 1989, after a meeting with several young notables of the PP in Perbes, Fraga designated José Maria Aznar as his successor. For the legislative elections of October 1989, the PP moderated its programme by including a more generous welfare programme and respected the de-penalisation of abortion. All this helped to improve the image of the PP and get a better result than in previous elections. After Fraga became the new regional president in Galicia, Aznar was officially crowned the new president of the PP in the tenth party congress which took place between 31 March and 2 April 1990 (Garcia-Guereta Rodriguez, 2001: 168–69).

The second period of party development can be regarded as more successful. The rise of José Maria Aznar as the new leader of the party clearly introduced a period of major reforms inside the party. Manuel Fraga was made honorary president. From then on, Fraga concentrated on being president of the Xunta de Galicia. The rise of José Maria Aznar was accompanied by the growing deterioration of the Socialist government of Felipe Gonzalez. Already in 1989, the PSOE did not manage to achieve an absolute majority by one seat, but the distance between it and the PP allowed for a continuing dominance of the party system.

Nevertheless, between 1990 and 1996, José Maria Aznar was able to lead the party towards replacing the discredited Socialist government. Cases of corruption and trafficking of influences, which could also be found among the PP regional and local governments, had a devastating effect on the government. Finally in 1993, Aznar was able to break the techo de Fraga and become a credible challenger to the PSOE. The elections of 1993 are regarded as a turning point in the party system of Spain, because for the first time the two main parties were only separated by four percentage points. In the 1996 legislative elections, after victories in the European elections of June 1994 and the local and autonomous communities of May 1995, the PP became the largest party. In this period, the party had moved considerably to the centre as well as attracting right-wing and extreme right-wing elements into the electorate. In spite of winning the legislative elections of 1996, the PP was not able to achieve an absolute majority (Garcia-Guereta Rodriguez, 2001: 170–200). It forced José Maria Aznar to further moderate the positions of the party in relation to the state of autonomies and other issues. This was very much supported by the éminence grise Manuel Fraga, who as president of the Xunta de Galicia contributed to a pact of legislature of Catalan CiU the Basque PNV , the fourth largest party, and Canary Coalition with the PP. This led to the overall support of other regionalist-nationalist parties, so that Jordi Pujol's party would not have a special position in relation to the PP (Tusell, 2004: 68–70; Gilmour, 2005. 427, Balfour, 1996).

The period between 1996 and 2000 was an important learning curve for the PP which had for the first time achieved government responsibility. The positive management of the economy, the restoration of the social dialogue and the further development of the state of autonomies by achieving a high degree of devolution gave credibility to PP as a party which had moved from the right to the centre. The highly centralistic state ideology of the origins of PP was replaced by a more modern version in which the state of autonomies is fully supported and further developed, but the party remains sceptical about changing the constitution towards federalism.

The moderation of the party and the good management of the economy, which was growing by 4 per cent in 2000, contributed to a historical victory on 12 March 2000. Aznar had achieved an absolute majority for the party, in spite of all the difficulties during the previous parliament. Between 1993 and 2000, the party moved ideologically to the centre, taking with it the continuing voters on the right. This big achievement cannot be underestimated. (Tusell, 2004: 81–2). It was brought about by major transformations of party organisation strategy, particularly in the way campaigns were fought and the media were used, which clearly took the losing Socialist Party by surprise (Mendez Lago, 2000: 299–301). Between 1993 and 2000, the party moved clearly to the centre. On average 46.9 per cent of voters positioned themselves on the right, with 48.9 per cent in the centre. In the 2000 elections, the corresponding figures were 37.7 per cent on the right and 58.4 in the centre. (Torcal and Medina, 2002: 65).

Within a decade, the PP was transformed into a credible catch-all party, which had left behind the rigid conservative ideology of the former generation. It was a party able to attract young new voters, which agreed with the short assessment of José Maria Aznar that *España va bien!* (Spain is doing well!) (Roller, 2001: 220). Aznar also was able to bring discipline into the party and show constructive leadership which strengthened his position.

According to John Gilmour, José Maria Aznar had a pragmatic reformist-centrist ideology which included Christian values, but was framed in the Anglo-Saxon model of economic liberalism. This is the reason why Aznar was closer to pragmatic politicians of the Third Way such as Tony Blair and Gerhard Schröder. He became a major leader in the EPP and also in the Christian Democratic International, which incidentally was renamed into Centrist Democratic International after a proposal by Aznar himself. However, it became also clear that this international role was used and abused to marginalise the PNV, which in the 1980s had been one of the main opponents to the integration of AP/PP into the European People's Party due to its Francoist legacy.

Such behaviour by Aznar was condemned by the Democratic Union of Catalonia's (one of the parties of CiU) leader Duran Lleida (Gilmour, 2005: 428). Quite innovative for Spanish politics was the fact that he intended to be prime minister for only two terms. He reconfirmed it after the elections of 2000, so that he could step down after completion of the seventh legislature. This naturally led to frantic discussions within the party about who would replace him, when he was gone. At the twenty-fourth party conference on 26 and 27 January 2002 Aznar set up the process of succession by delaying it until September 2003 after the municipal elections. The three deputy secretaries of the party, Rodrigo Rato, Mariano Rajoy and Jaime Mayor Oreja, were considered to be potential successors. Before and after the local autonomous communities elections of May 2003, the present mayor of Madrid, Alberto Ruiz Gallardón, was also named as a potential successor. Jaime Mayor Oreja who is quite popular in the Basque Country for being so uncompromising with the political violence of ETA was regarded as the strongest candidate. Rodrigo Rato was the chief architect of the economic boom during the first PP legislature, while Mariano Rajoy was identified as the main architect of the shift in the ideological foundations of the PP from the right to the moderate centre and was in charge of managing the effects of ecological catastrophe caused by the sinking of the oil tanker Prestige off the Galician coast (*El Pais*, 30 April 2000: 22; *El Pais*, Domingo, 1 September 2002: 1–3; *El Pais*, 17 November 2002: 22; *El Pais*, 8 December 2002: 31; *El Pais*, 5 January 2002: 10–11).

The greatest rival to all of them was naturally the new leader of the PSOE, who in opinion polls before the municipal elections was preferred by the electorate in relation to Aznar and any of his potential successors (*El Pais*, 30 March 2003: 25). There was naturally also an attempt by the old guard of the PP under the leadership of Francisco Alvarez Cascos and Juan José Lucas to ask José Maria Aznar to be the candidate for the presidency of the government for the third time. Aznar clearly rejected this choice by the old guard (*El Pais*, 12 November 2001: 30). In Autumn 2003, Mariano Rajoy became the official candidate to succeed Aznar. Mariano Rajoy was selected, because he was regarded as the one most loyal to José Maria Aznar. Some of the potential candidates such as the charismatic Rodrigo Rato lost support from Aznar, after they declared themselves against the Iraq War. Rato knew that his anti-War position would in the end cost him the leadership of the party. Instead, Rajoy was a supporter of the war and followed most of the positions taken by José Maria Aznar (Garcia-Abadillo, 2005: 207–8).

Since he took over the party in 2004, Mariano Rajoy was not able to achieve the same successes as José Maria Aznar, in spite of his aggressive polarisation strategy. The defeat in the general elections of 14 March 2004, 3 days after the 11 March bombings in Madrid and the abysmal mismanagement of information to the public between these 3 days, remained a major blow for the PP. All opinion polls were predicting up until 7 March 2004 a victory for the PP, but between 11 March and 14 March there was an increase of mobilisation of electorate by nine points that led to a victory of the Socialists. Such bitter defeat was not overcome by Mariano Rajoy who seemed to be extremely dependent on José Maria Aznar who regularly intervened in the press to discredit the Zapatero government. Therefore, the PP lost in the Galician and Basque elections of 2005, and was not able to make progress in the Catalan elections of 2006 and the regional and municipal elections of 2007. There was a general feeling that the PP did not want to accept the results of the investigations conducted by Judge del Olmo, which showed that there was no link between Al Qaeda and ETA, as Rajoy and other PP politicians such as Manuel Acebes continued to propagate. According to Andreas Baumer, a kind of 'conspiracy theory' of Islamists, Socialists and Etarras began to emerge among the PP politicians, led by José Maria Aznar, which propagated that the party had been 'robbed' of the 14 March elections (Baumer, 2007: 153). In late March 2005, the Foundation for Analysis and Social Studies (*Fundación de Analisis y Estudios Sociales* – FAES) chaired by José Maria Aznar and close to the PP presented a video called 'After the Massacre' (*Tras la massacre*) on the 11 March bombings and clearly emphasised this thesis of complicity of the left in the incidents. Members of the parliamentary 11 March investigation committee felt that their work was being not valued by the PP. Members of PNV and the Mixed Group asked Rajoy to distance himself from the video, something that Rajoy did do. There is a general feeling among parts of PP that Mariano Rajoy has had so many difficulties, because of the prominence of Aznar through the think tank, FAES. Some of its actions can lead to embarrassment of PP, because they adhere extremely to neoconservative ideology, in spite of the fact that they advocate being committed to be a think tank of the reformist centre and working only for Rajoy (*El Pais*, 1 April 2005: 20; *El Pais*, Domingo, 22 May 2005: 1–3). Moreover, inside the party there was growing concern about his poor leadership skills. He was accused of lack of vitality and visibility. Criticisms came particularly from Josep Piqué, who decided to quit as leader of the Catalan PP. One of his criticisms was that the party should open more and change to a more embracing and conciliatory style of opposition. (*El Pais*, 3 April 2005: 34; *El Pais*, 6 July 2005: 17; *El Pais*, 9 July 2005: 23). The fear of internal conflict is one of the reasons why PP tries always to present a united front. The spectre of ending up like the UCD is one of the reasons for the support for Mariano Rajoy. The inconclusive outcome of the regional and municipal elections of 28 May 2007 has clearly helped Mariano Rajoy to remain in power. The defeat of PP in the legislative elections of 2008 showed that electoralist polarization strategy did not lead to success.

The structure of the party organisation of the PP is dominated by the regularly held party conference. Meanwhile twenty-six party conferences have been held since December 1976. The high number of party conferences shows that the party was characterised by a high level of instability up to 1989. This is due to the high level of personalism, the dominance of powerful party notables and difficulties in surpassing the techo de Fraga. After 1989, Aznar was able to control the centrifugal forces inside the party, particularly the regional and other potential critics. The party became more disciplined with a strong image of unity on the exterior. One positive element was that José Maria Aznar separated the position of president of the party, of which he was incumbent, and the position of secretary general held by Javier Arenas. In this respect, he could concentrate his energy on governmental work.

The party conference elects the National Directing Board (*Junta Directiva Nacional* – JDN) which elects a smaller National Executive Committee (*Comité Executivo Nacional* – CEN). While the former consists of representatives from the subnational levels, the CEN is a smaller executive board which deals with

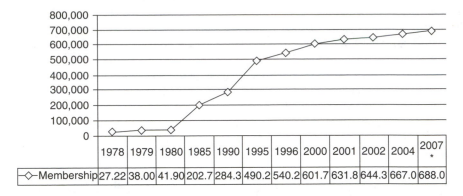

	1978	1979	1980	1985	1990	1995	1996	2000	2001	2002	2004	2007 *
◇—Membership	27.22	38.00	41.90	202.7	284.3	490.2	540.2	601.7	631.8	644.3	667.0	688.0

Figure 4.4 Evolution of membership of the People's Party (1978–2007).

Source: Mendez and Ramiro Fernandez, 2004 quoted in Ramiro Fernandez, 2005: 212; 2007, own estimates based on figure of 1.6 per cent of overall party membership.

the daily running of party business. An even smaller standing committee (*comité permanente* – CP) clearly centralises further decision-making in the hands of the secretary general and the president of the party (Lopez Nieto, 1986; Garcia-Guereta Rodriguez, 2001: 390–421). According to Luis Ramiro Fernandez, the party is dominated by the president and his inner circle. The 'presidentialisation' of the party is something that was genetically imprinted by founding leader Manuel Fraga Iribarne and continued very successfully by José Maria Aznar. Normally, the successor is selected by a inner circle. This was the way Aznar was selected. Rajoy was selected by Aznar personally. Only Antonio Hernandez de la Mancha had to compete with Miguel Herrero Miñon. One of the factors was that the youth organisation New Generations (*Nuevas Generaciones*) supported the young Extremaduran Hernandez de la Mancha (Ramiro Fernandez, 2005: 218; Garcia-Guereta Rodriguez, 2001: 145).

This structure is more or less copied at regional, provincial and local levels. The regional party conferences take part normally in the year before the municipal and autonomous communities elections. In 2002, fifteen of these regional party conferences (Galicia, Ceuta and Melilla took place earlier in the year) were held in September and October and they selected their candidates for the corresponding autonomous community elections. President José Maria Aznar was very keen to push the whole party to support the campaigning efforts of the subnational branches of the party. Indeed, the seventeen autonomous communities bring together a total of 16,711 delegates (*compromisarios*) representing 632,000 members.

Thus the party can be regarded as having a well-organised campaigning machinery which clearly is mobilised during election periods (*El Pais*, 22 September 2002: 20). The candidate selection and coordination is strongly done by the central office. The regional branches are strongly controlled by the centre, so that cohesion of the party can be maintained (Ramiro Fernandez, 2005: 217). For example, the Valencian PP, one of the strongest branches of the party with 45,000 members (2.6 per cent of the population of the Valencian community) started preparations towards the legislative elections in August 2007 and Rajoy started his campaign there, all in an effort to strengthen the unity of the party throughout the electoral process (*El Pais*, 26 August 2007). If we do not count private donations, in 2004 about 28.1 per cent of funding (€9.4 million) came from membership fees, which is higher than the PSOE (Tribunal de Cuentas, 2007: 139).

There is quite a loose relationship with civil associations and interest groups. It is more used for electoralist mobilisation effects, than a real penetration of society. Probably, the strongest organised part of PP is the youth organisation, New Generations (*Nuevas Generaciones* – NG), while the women's organisations has only recently gained more importance within the PP due to the inclusion of gender issues in the programme of the PP (Ramiro Fernandez, 2005: 216).

In sum, under José Maria Aznar's leadership the PP became a modern mainstream party which clearly adopted some of the innovative elements of social democratic parties such as New Labour under Tony Blair in the United Kingdom by modernising the party and adopting a third way (*tercera via*) catch-all strategy. However, some reflexes from its Francoist legacy still emerge from time to time. To date, his successor, Mariano Rajoy, has been unable to show an independent protagonism from that of éminence grise José Maria Aznar. The polarisation strategy which had at its core the discrediting of the PSOE government has not been endorsed by all parts of the party.

The Spanish Socialist Workers' Party (PSOE): reinventing the left

The PSOE is the oldest national party in Spain. It was founded in 1879 and became the main representative of the working-class since the late nineteenth century. Organisationally, the party evolved slowly founding a trade union confederation, the General Workers' Union (*Unión General de Trabajadores* – UGT) in 1888. The founding father of the party was Pablo Iglesias, who was able to maintain his leadership up until 1925, when he died. The foundation of the party carries a motto which is still quite important today: protection of the party organisation at all costs, due to the fact that this is the main vehicle to achieve political representation. This so-called *Pablismo*, after the first name of founding father Pablo Iglesias, led to the establishment of a strong organisation which would avoid political revolutionary adventures at all costs. Ideology based on Marxism was only of secondary importance for the main leaders. *Pablismo* was referred by Paul Heywood as decaffeinated socialism (*socialismo decafeinado*), so that the more realistic aims of the party could be achieved in the parliamentary arena (Heywood, 1990). Representation at the Cortes during the period of canovismo was only achieved in 1910 and remained quite small due to the fact that the majority of the population lived in the countryside and the electoral system was extremely restrictive.

During the Miguel Primo de Rivera dictatorship such pablismo became quite evident, when the PSOE agreed to participate in the corporatist *comités paritarios*, in order to be the central representative of the working-class and destroy its main rival the anarchosyndicalist National Confederation of Labour (*Confederación Nacional del Trabajo* – CNT). Such collaboration with the Primo de Rivera dictatorship was abruptly ended when the Socialist leadership realised that the dictatorship was on the verge of collapse in the late 1920s.

The Socialist Party became the largest party and played a central role during the Second Republic. It supported the Republican governments and contributed to the radicalisation of the overall climate of the Second Republic. Apart from the anarchosyndicalists, the PSOE had also to deal with the small Communist Party, which was formed in 1921 from a splinter group of the PSOE and was member of the Third Communist International. During the Civil War, the PSOE fought on the side of the Republicans. It was targeted by the Stalinist Communist Party similar to the Social Democratic Party (SPD) in Germany, so that it was substantially weakened during this period. After the Civil War, the PSOE leadership left the country and went into exile in France.

Throughout the Francoist period, the PSOE organisation was absent from Spain. The main anti-fascist party was the Spanish Communist Party. A restoration of activity by the PSOE in Spain started in the late 1960s and early 1970s. The main leaders of this organisation inside the country were the Andalusians Felipe Gonzalez and Alfonso Guerra. They believed that the Francoist regime was on the verge of moving towards democracy, in the eventuality of the death of the dictator. Between 1970 and 1972, the young leaders challenged successfully the leadership of the party in exile, which was then called *PSOE-histórico*. With support and acknowledgement of the Socialist International, the new PSOE leadership started the establishment of a basic party infrastructure.

The new leader, Felipe Gonzalez, was clearly moderate during the transition to democracy. In spite of that, the PSOE was far more radical than the Communist Party in their demands. While the Communist Party accepted the monarchy in order to achieve democracy, the PSOE were more supportive of republicanism. In the end, the PSOE accepted the constitutional monarchy, but it was a major sacrifice for many of the leaders. Before the 1977 elections, the PSOE leadership believed that they would not be able to compete with the Communist Party, because the latter had a stronger party organisation. The results of the elections were a pleasant surprise for the leadership, because in spite of its weak party organisation the PSOE became the main party of the left and the second largest party in the country. While the PCE received only 9.4 per cent of the votes and twenty seats, the PSOE attained 29.3 per cent and 123 seats. This was an extremely positive result on which the PSOE could build a successful party for the future. Between 1977 and 1979, the party was characterised by some internal factionalism between the *sector critico*, who were supporters of an ideological Marxist working-class mass party, and the modernisers under the leadership of Felipe Gonzalez, who saw a need for the party to drop the references to Marxism altogether and move to the centre, so that it could challenge its main rival the Union of the Democratic Centre (*Unión del Centro*

Democrático – UCD). The lack of electoral progress in the legislative elections of 1979 led to major decisions to move towards the centre. Probably, a crucial factor was the fact that UCD leader Adolfo Suarez used the Marxist definition of the PSOE in order to gain more voters in the centre, who were not prepared to vote for such a party (Mendez-Lago, 2005: 174).

The crucial decision came at the twenty-ninth extraordinary party conference in September 1979, when Felipe Gonzalez was able to impose the modernisation agenda and reduce Marxism as an instrument of inspiration and guidance, but not of rigid ideology. Felipe Gonzalez had stepped down at the previous party conference, because he did not agree with the strategy of the PSOE left, supported by Francisco Bustelo, Pablo Castellano and Luis Gomez Llorente. After the September party conference, Felipe Gonzalez became the uncontested leader (Nash, 1983: 40–50). One of the most important lessons learned from the party conference is that the party ought to act united, otherwise the electorate may choose alternatives. Gonzalez's leadership style supported by Alfonso Guerra, who was in charge of party organisation, was to lead to the historical victory of 1982, in which it inherited part of the vote of the UCD and attracted a large part of the PCE vote. It led to a successful period for Spanish socialism which lasted until the elections of 3 March 1996, when the PP was able to defeat the PSOE by 1 per cent. Between 1982 and 1996, the PSOE introduced several reforms in the health, education and social sectors. In terms of economic policy, the PSOE followed closely neoliberal policies in order to open up the Spanish market and make it more competitive in relation to other economies. In some way, Socialist policies were regarded as being very close to the policies of the British Conservatives under Margaret Thatcher (Boix, 1996; Merkel, 1993).

The inability to create new jobs, the growing dissent between the UGT, the main Socialist trade union confederation, and the government and the austerity measures in the public sector industries clearly led to disappointment among supporters of the PSOE. Moreover, at the end of the 1980s and the early 1990s, the party was involved in so many corruption scandals related to trafficking of influences, illicit party financing and abuse of power, that it came to be regarded as patrimonial socialism by some commentators, meaning that it tended to use the resources of the state for its own profit (Petras, 1990; 1993). In the end, this led to the break-up of the close relationship between the UGT and the PSOE, due to the neoliberal economic policies of the government. The general strike of 1988 was the crucial turning point in the deterioration of the relationship (Gillespie, 1990; Royo, 2001; Astudillo Ruiz, 2001).

In this period, one can also speak of the centralisation of the party organisation at the hands of Gonzalez and Guerra. The lack of renewal of leadership, the limited level of internal party democracy and the failure to build up a committed membership contributed to the decline of the party as the leading party of the country. The better organisation of PP was able to challenge the complacent organisation of the PSOE (Mendez Lago, 2000: 132, 230).

After the resignation of Alfonso Guerra from the vice-presidency of the government in 1992, due to the involvement of his brother Juan Guerra in the use of public offices to make private business transactions, factionalism became quite virulent in the party. While Felipe Gonzalez represented the *renovadores* (renewers) of the party, who wanted a renewal of the party, Alfonso Guerra and his supporters, the so-called *Guerristas*, opposed these plans of reform. This division inside the party did not go well with the electorate, which in 1993 began to move towards the PP. Finally, in the thirty-third party conference the *renovadores* were able to impose themselves on the *Guerristas* and modify the structures of the party (Gillespie, 1994). In spite of that, the PSOE lost the elections in March 1996 and went into opposition. One of the problems that the party encountered was a lack of coordination between party in office and the party organisation once Alfonso Guerra was no longer vice-president of government (Mendez-Lago, 2005: 184).

Between 1996 and 2000, the party was more or less in turmoil. After just over a year, Felipe Gonzalez resigned from his post as secretary general and the party had to search for a new candidate. Indeed, the leadership vacancy was quite a surprise for everyone, because he had resigned only shortly before the scheduled party conference (Mendez-Lago, 2005: 186–7).

Joaquin Almunia became new leader at the thirty-fourth party conference in June 1997, but it was a compromise choice. Almunia was not regarded as a very charismatic politician.[3] He tried to strengthen his position by organising primaries inside the party to select the candidate for the presidency of government in the 2000 elections. Indeed, such primaries were organised, but to his embarrassment, the members of the PSOE voted for the more charismatic Catalan Josep Borrell. Nevertheless, in May 1999 Borrell had to resign, because of a financial scandal involving his wife and some of his closest collaborators while he was minister (Roller, 2001: 223). Again, Joaquin Almunia became the official candidate of the PSOE for the March 2000 elections. In the March 2000 elections the PSOE suffered a major defeat. It lost more votes than in the 1996 elections and the PP was able to achieve an absolute majority. Apart from the uncharismatic appeal of the PSOE leader, one major factor that may have contributed to the defeat was the electoral alliance which Almunia formed with the United Left under the leadership of the also uncharismatic Francisco Frutos. They defined it as a coalition of the left to bring down the PP government. It showed that one element of the centrist vote of the PSOE moved to the PP, because it did not accept the alliance of the Socialist Party with the Communist coalition.

After the resignation of Almunia after the elections results were declared, the PSOE leadership left it until the summer to select a new secretary general. The senior leaders of the party, particularly Manuel Chaves, the president of the regional government of Andalusia, were in charge of overseeing the process which culminated in the thirty-fifth party conference of 22 and 23 July 2000. Out of the 995 delegates' votes, José Luis Zapatero achieved 41.79 per cent and his main contender José Bono, the president of the autonomous community Castilla La Mancha, 40.69 per cent. Zapatero had achieved the leadership of the party with nine votes more than Bono. José Luis Zapatero was at that time 40 years of age and since 1986 has been an MP for the province of León. The election of Zapatero was regarded as a sign that the party could renew itself (*El Pais*, 23 July 2000: 16).[4] Since then, Zapatero has been spearheading the renewal of the party. He was able to gain credibility as a responsible leader of the opposition by supporting the government in several issues such as reform of the judiciary through a pact on the reform of the judiciary (*Pacto de la Justicia*) and supporting the new law of political parties (*Ley de Partidos Politicos*) which criminalises *Herri Batasuna/Eusko Herritarok*, the political arm of ETA.

Inside the party, he introduced a new document called 'The Necessary Party for the Spain of the Twenty-First Century' (*El Partido Necesario para la España del Seculo XXI* –), which wanted to revive internal democracy by limiting the incumbency of public offices and party offices (*El Pais*, 16 May 2001: 22). Moreover, ideologically the party moved again to the centre offering the concept of a social liberalism in Spanish politics (*El Pais*, 1 July 2001: 22). The climax of this repositioning of the party was the political conference of 20–21 July 2001, in which the new ideological foundations of the 'smooth change' (*cambio tranquilo*) was presented. It was agreed to extend the principles of 'freedom, equality and solidarity' to new social groups and to adjust it to new social realities. The role of enhanced qualitative citizenship became central to the new Socialist project (Bernecker, 2006: 124).

The stand of Zapatero and PSOE against the war in Iraq during March and April 2003, thus opposing José Maria Aznar's support for the American-led invasion, won him a high level of popularity among the population. Indeed, the Spanish population was overwhelmingly against the war before and after (*El Pais*, 26 March 2003: 24, 25, 27; *El Pais*, 30 March 2000: 24, 26, 30; *El Pais*, Domingo, 20 April 2003: 14). The victory of the party in the legislative elections of 14 March 2004 strengthened the position of leader José Luis Zapatero. His party was able to form a minority government with the parliamentary support of the Catalan Republican Left (ERC), United Left (IU), Canary Coalition (CC), Galician Nationalist Block (BNG) and Aragonese Junta (CHA). Overall he won the investiture battle with 183 votes, against 148 (PP) and 19 abstentions.

On 2–4 July 2004, the thirty-sixth party congress took place in Madrid. The victory on 14 March 2004 gave an enormous boost to the party. The party congress was used to reiterate the commitment of the electoral programme. In his address, Prime Minister Zapatero outlined to the audience that the party 'wants a modern, lay, tolerant and solidarous Spain, which is a plural Spain' (*El Socialista*, August 2004: 3). The resolutions of the congress clearly indicate the wish to have a strategic alliance with civil society groups in order to mobilise the citizens. In terms of strategy, they also want to target the group of abstentionists in order to create a 'social majority' for the Socialist project (*El Socialista*, August 2004:14–17). There were 972 delegates representing all federations of the party in Spain and abroad (*El Socialista*, August 2004: 28).

The Socialist government of José Luis Zapatero introduced major controversial laws during the legislature period. Apart from the controversial law allowing gay marriages and a new education law, both opposed vehemently by the Catholic Church and the People's Party, the Socialist government introduced also a whole package of social policy and equality laws which were designed to protect workers in Spain. Probably, the most important test for Zapatero was the Catalan Statute, which in the end was approved without the votes of the PP and confirmed in a referendum. Critical voices began to emerge during the negotiations of the Catalan Stature in the Cortes. Prime Minister Zapatero was able to keep the party united, and was able to change course, when there was criticism coming from the senior notables of the party like Manuel Chaves or José Ibarra. In the party conference on 15–17 September 2006 titled 'New times, new politics' , the 'project of values' was again reiterated by leader José Luis Rodriguez Zapatero (*El Socialista*, 2006: 7–8).

The conclusions of the party conference were quite progressive and intended to concede new rights to marginalised groups and strengthen gender equality. It clearly, takes into account the technological revolution and wants to use it for the benefit of society. Policies on terrorism and immigration are less divisive, and the diversity of society is embraced. The PSOE was able to combine a progressive agenda with the package of 'New Labour'. Interestingly, it was Howard Dean, the former candidate for the US presidency of 2004 and presently president of the Democratic Party, that was invited to speak to the conference via videolink. There is a will in the leadership of the party to be seen as cooperating with the political establishment in the United States, particularly in view of the 2008 US presidential elections (*El Socialista*, September 2006: 8). This is quite important for the Zapatero government after the decision of George W. Bush not to meet him, because he withdrew the troops from Iraq in May 2004. It shows, that the PSOE was able to combine the traditions of the past with a pragmatic flexible policy forum. In the conference, José Blanco in charge of party organisation, presented the new Internet-interactive channel 'psoetv', showing that the battleground between political parties has expanded to the virtual world (*El Socialista*, September 2006: 26). José Blanco has been instrumental in reorganising the party towards a post-modern progressive agenda and overcome the organisational inertia of the 1980s and 1990s.

The PSOE has a federal party organisation structure. There are regional party organisations adjusted to the needs of each autonomous community. It is naturally steered by the national party organisation. The highest body of the party is the regular party conference which takes place every 3 years. As already mentioned, 995 delegates took part in the thirty-fifth party conference in 2000 and 972 in the thirty-sixth party conference in 2004. It is clearly a major event for the party. The delegates are selected by the provincial congresses, which consist of members of the local groups (*agrupaciones locales*). Between elections, the federal executive committee (*comisión ejecutiva federal* - CEF) is the main decision-making body, which is supported by an advisory federal committee (*comité federal*). In the 1990s, the federal committee became much less important (Mendez Lago, 2000: 121–6). There was some renewal of importance at the thirty-fifth party conference. Zapatero had a committee of forty-nine, including several of the losers in the leadership elections. It was chaired by the Mayor of Barcelona, Pascual Maragall. The CEF is where the power lies. The members of the CEF are chosen according to strength of the different groups inside the party. One group consists of senior party leaders, who are the presidents of the regional governments or secretaries general of the regional parties. They are normally represented in the CEF. Moreover, there are also factions such as the Guerristas in elections to the CEF.

The CEF had thirty-three members at the thirty-fourth party conference. Zapatero reduced the CEF to twenty-five members and there was a total renewal and rejuvenation of the leadership. It was quite a young group with an average age of 42 years (*El Pais*, 24 July 2000: 18). The national structure is rigorously copied at regional and provincial level. According to Monica Mendez-Lago, members have only a very limited power of influence. In the end, the party has become more or less a cartel party similar to the PP. In early 2002, the PSOE has 210,000 active members (*militantes*). The rest were sympathisers (*simpatizantes*) of the party, who have no right to vote in primaries and do not need to pay subscriptions. This puts the total supporters of the PSOE at a 400,000 ceiling. There was no really proper survey of membership undertaken in the past 20 years, so that this exercise was important to gain control over the abuses of several local groups which tended to manipulate membership recruitment to get reelected and prevent other candidates being elected or just to have an inflated representation in the provincial congresses. The most prominent case was the manipulation by the party of Jesus Gil, former mayor of Marbella, who attempted to manipulate the membership of the Socialist Party groups, so that Isabella Garcia Marcos could be prevented from victory. Many of these cases went to court. The survey was also important to sort out the financial problems resulting from increases in the membership fee. In 2002, one-fifth of all the party's income was raised from membership fees, while 80 per cent came from state subsidies equalling €12 million (*El Pais*, 28 April 2002: 18), in 2004: the share of membership fees has only slightly improved to 23 per cent equalling €7.7 million (author's calculations based on Tribunal de Cuentas, 2007: 147).

There are also some issues of centre–periphery tensions. This became evident during the discussion over the Catalan Statute. Several regional barons such as Manuel Chaves, regional president of Andalusia, and José Ibarra, regional president of Extremadura were very critical of the original version of the Catalan Statute proposed by PSC, ERC, IU-ICV and CiU. Prime Minister Zapatero had to calm down the barons inside the party, so that he could negotiate a statute that it is compatible with the constitution. Marathon negotiations took place between Zapatero and Artur Mas, the leader of Convergence and Union in early January, thus allowing for an approval of the Statute against the votes of the PP and also the Catalan Republican Left, which was not happy about these changes and to be kept outside the negotiations (Nagel and Requejo, 2007; 281–8). Another case where the central office had to intervene against the will of the regional branch was the veto against the formation of a coalition between the Navarran Socialist Party, the nationalist-regionalist *Nafarroa-Bai* and United Left. The Navarran Socialist Party had to break the deal with the other parties due to this veto from central office in Madrid. The main reason for this decision seems to be the fact that such an electoral coalition would harm the electoral chances of the PSOE in the forthcoming regional and municipal elections (*El Pais*, 2 August 2007: 15; *El Pais*, 3 August 2007: 15).

In sum, the PSOE is clearly one of the two most important parties of Spanish politics. It moved from a mass party in the 1970s to a cartel party today. Ideologically, it adopted a more pragmatic and flexible approach towards electoral politics.

The United Left (IU): the inevitable decline

The United Left was founded in 1986 as an electoral coalition of the Spanish Communist Party (*Partido Comunista Español* – PCE) and several left-wing smaller parties. It is regarded as the successor of the PCE which was one of the main parties in the peaceful transition to democracy. Former leader, Santiago Carrillo, played a major role in moderating the discourse of the PCE during the transition to democracy, and allowed for a systemic integration of this party. Then, the PCE wanted to move towards the Italian way which was to change from a revolutionary anti-systemic party to a parliamentary systemic one and work from within the democratic political system to achieve a hegemonic cultural position of the left. When the PCE was legalised shortly before the elections of 1977 by the government of Adolfo Suarez, the Italian Communist Party (*Partito Comunista Italiano* – PCI) was the most successful communist party in the western hemisphere. It proposed a Eurocommunist position independent of Moscow, in contrast to most other communist parties. Santiago Carrillo hoped that he could achieve a similar transformation of the PCE.

The PCE was founded in 1921 as a splinter group of the PSOE and was quite prominent during the Civil War, when it was dominated by Stalin's Soviet Union and attempted to destroy all left-wing alternatives in the Republican zone. This negative image of the PCE was never to go away among the cadres of the Socialist Party. During Franco's dictatorship it was the most important anti-fascist opposition. It infiltrated the official vertical trade unions with a very flexibly designed trade union confederation called Workers'Commissions (*Comisiones Obreras* – CCOO). The latter was to become one of the largest trade union confederations in the new democratic political system. (Mujal-León, 1983: 14–24; 54–75).

After the death of the dictator, all political forces assumed that the PCE would have a strong advantage in relation to the other parties, because it had a strong organisation already in place during the dictatorship. The election results of 1977 and 1979 were quite a surprise for most parties, because the PCE was not able to achieve more than 10.5 per cent. Instead, the PSOE became the most important party on the left, probably aided by the historical memory of part of the Spanish population (Maravall, 1982; Mujal-León, 1983: 132–55). The strategy of Santiago Carrillo, which included ideological moderation and rejection of Marxist jargon such as the dictatorship of the proletariat and democratic centralism, led to dissent and infighting in the PCE between 1979 and 1982. Expulsions at the end of this period clearly gave way to a very negative image of the party and a halving of their electorate in the 1982 elections. Most of the voters decided to vote for the PSOE instead. The collapse of the vote, the decline of the party due to splinter groups spearheaded by Santiago Carrillo and Ignacio Gallego led to a period of reflection (Bosco, 2000: 131–2). Between 1982 and 1986, the new secretary general Gerardo Iglesias started to rebuild the party. It decided to form an electoral coalition with several other smaller left-wing parties in the spring of 1986 called United Left (*Izquierda Unida* – IU). The founding members were the PCE, the Communist Party of the Peoples of Spain (*Partido Comunista de los Pueblos de España* – PCPE) of Ignacio Gallego, the Party of Socialist Action (*Partido de Acción Socialista* – PASOC) which comprised members of the former *PSOE-historico* founded in 1983, the Republican Left (*Izquierda Republicana* – IR) founded in 1931, Progressive Federation (*Federación Progresista* – FP), Humanist Party (*Partido Humanista* – PH) and Carlist Party (*Partido Carlista* – PC). At some stage the IU also included Green parties from Andalusia and the Basque Country, but they left the party after a while. Both the Carlist and the Humanist Party were also excluded from the party at an early stage. Today, the three main parties of IU are the PCE, PASOC and IR (Colomé *et al.*, 1998; Ramiro Fernandez, 2000: 247). In the 1986 elections, the IU was able to achieve a slightly better election result than the previous PCE. A modest return of former voters came from the PSOE. The breakthrough of the party came at the 1989 elections, when the IU was able to double the share of the vote from 4.5 to 9.1 per cent. This was achieved by a growing restructuring of the loose electoral coalition into an operating political party. In the 1993 elections, the party was even able to improve on this figure. One of the factors leading to this success was the replacement of Gerardo Iglesias, by the former mayor of Cordoba, Julio Anguita, who was a respected figure on the left. Indeed, Anguita took the leadership both of PCE and IU. From 1989 onwards, the IU celebrated their assemblies which were to lead to a more structured party organisation, in spite of some opposition from members. The dominance of the PCE clearly tended to lead to tensions inside the party. The first federal assembly (*asamblea federal*) took place in 1989 and it clearly was an important step towards establishing the basic rules within the party. This was followed by further assemblies in 1990, 1992, 1994, 1997 and 2000.

The decline of the PSOE led to a slight improvement by the IU in the 1996 elections, in which it received 10.54 per cent of the vote. Nevertheless, the deteriorating health of the leader, Julio Anguita, made a change of leadership inevitable. The new leader Francisco Frutos was less charismatic and appealing than Anguita. He was successful in achieving an electoral coalition shortly before the March 2000 elections with the PSOE under the leadership of Joaquin Almunia. The massive victory of the PP led to huge losses for the two left-wing parties. The IU's loss of half of the vote from 10.54 to 5.46 per cent threatened the very survival of the organisation. The loss of votes and seats automatically meant the loss of state subsidies, which would clearly affect the organisation drastically, due to the fact that 95 per cent of the income of IU comes from state subsidies and only 5 per cent from the 67,812 members (half of them in the PCE) (Ramiro Fernandez, 2000: 262).

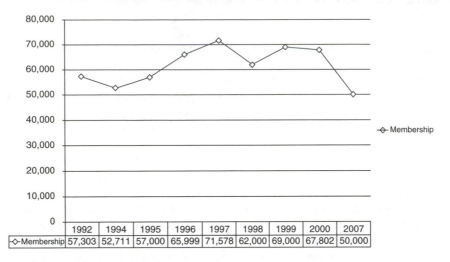

	1992	1994	1995	1996	1997	1998	1999	2000	2007
◇ Membership	57,303	52,711	57,000	65,999	71,578	62,000	69,000	67,802	50,000

Figure 4.5 Evolution of membership of IU (1992–2007).

Source: Ramiro Fernandez, 2004: 59; 2007 figure from *El Pais*, 2 October 2007: 27.

In 2000, the party's debt amounted to 8.5 million. It had to lay off forty-seven of its sixty-two employees and reduce costs by two-thirds (*El Pais*, 2 April 2000: 22).

In the sixth federal assembly which took place on 28–29 October 2000 a new IU coordinator was elected. Gaspar Llamazares won 42.59 per cent of the vote, while Francisco Frutos got only 39.38 per cent. This showed how divided the coalition was. Francisco Frutos is now the secretary general of the PCE (*El Pais*, 18 October 2000: 32; *El Pais*, 31 October 2000: 31; *El Pais*, Anuario, 2001: 89). Llamazares advocated an opening up of the coalition towards new social movements such as the environmental movement, improvement of living conditions movements and naturally the recent anti-Iraq War movement. The IU has been in the frontline in opposing the PP government, in most cases with PSOE support. One can witness this joint support for social movements against government in the student demonstrations against university reform proposed by Education Minister Pilar del Castillo in December 2001, the general strike of 20 July 2002 against the so-called government decree allowing for cuts in unemployment benefit and naturally the anti-Iraq War demonstrations during March and April 2003.

The poor results in the 14 March 2004 legislative elections, in which IU fell to 4.96 per cent and won only five seats confirmed the declining trend of the coalition. The ideological modernisation of the PSOE has taken over large part of the progressive agenda of the IU. Many potential voters of IU decided to vote for PSOE in order to maximise a left-wing victory against the People's Party. In spite of the bad results, IU leader Gaspar Llamazares was able to hang just on to his position in the seventh federal assembly in November 2005. He got a majority below 50 per cent and the number of people contesting his leadership has increased. One of the major criticisms was that Llamazares was too supportive of the Socialist government and unable to present a left-wing alternative.

In early 2006, Felipe Alcaraz, the president of PCE; Antonio Romero, Andalucian parliamentarian; and the MP, Angel Perez criticised the lack of amendments of the IU parliamentary group to the Catalan Statute during its discussion in the Spanish Parliament (*El Pais*, 3 January 2006: 19). Tensions between the different federations also became evident in relation to the leadership of Gaspar Llamazares. On 1 October 2007, the Communist Party, the largest party in the IU coalition announced that it would propose its secretary general Marga Sanz to contest the leadership of Llamazares. If approved by 25 per cent of the Federal Political Council or by 10 per cent of signatures of the 50,000 members, than primaries had to take place among its members. The enemies of Llamazares control the more important federations of the party which are in Andalucia, Valencian Community and Madrid. Llamazares was still able to count on about 55–60 per cent in the Political Council. The main criticism continued to be the lack of opposition to the PSOE government (*El Pais*, 2 October 2007: 27). On 13 November 2004, the results of the party primaries became known. Out of the 21,909 party member voters 62.5 per cent supported Llamazares, while only 37.5 per cent cast their vote for Marga Sanz. These were the first primaries of the IU coalition in its 21 years of history. They were part of a general strategy of party regeneration.

As already mentioned, the IU organisation is still very loose in nature. The individual parties are certainly still intact. The structure is naturally dominated by the federal assembly where all major decisions are taken. The position of the leader of the IU is of a coordinating nature. He is called the general coordinator (*coordinador general*). He chairs the federal political council (*consejo federal politico*), the federal presidency (*presidencia federal*) and the federal executive committee (*comisión federal executiva*). The federal political council acts between elections and is chaired by the joint presidency of several IU leaders. Day-to-day running of affairs is undertaken by the smaller federal executive committee. The whole structure is meticulously reproduced at regional level. The grassroots structures of the IU are the *asambleas*, which are the grassroots structures of the individual parties.

In sum, the IU is presently one of the four most important Spanish parties, being the third national party. However, while the regionalist-nationalist CiU and PNV have a stronghold in their particular regions, IU is becoming more and more a victim of the 'adulterated party system', meaning that potential IU voters vote usefully in the PSOE against the PP. The electoral fortunes of IU have stagnated at around 5–6 per cent. It declined even to 3.8 per cent and 2 seats, unable to form its own parliamentary group, after the legislative elections of 2008.

Convergence and Union (CiU): a regionalist party in transition

Convergence and Union (*Convergencia i Unió* – CiU) is a coalition of two parties, the Democratic Convergence of Catalonia (*Convergencia Democratica de Catalunya* – CDC) and the Democratic Union of Catalonia (*Unió Democratica de*

Catalunya – UDC), founded in September 1978 to run for the legislative elections of 1979. The larger party is the CDC, which was chaired from its beginning up until 2003 by the charismatic leader, Jordi Pujol. Since then it has been and continues to be chaired by his successor Artur Mas. It was founded in 1974 and wanted to attract most nationalist vote on the centre-left. It clearly had a nationalist mission from the beginning which was defined in Pujol's words of *fer pais* (nation-building of Catalonia). The CDC was able to become one of the largest parties on the Catalan scene. The party was up until 2003 dominated by Jordi Pujol who became the president of the Generalitat , the regional government of Catalonia since the first elections of 1980. The party has around 30,000 members (Baras and Dalmases, 1998: 162–7).

The smaller partner in the coalition is the UDC, founded in November 1931. It is essentially a Christian democratic party looking for centre-right votes. The current leader is Josep Duran Lleida, who clearly has a more moderate view about Catalan nationalism. He has often criticised Jordi Pujol for adopting positions related to the sovereignty of Catalonia within Spain and he has preferred to speak of political Catalanism, than nationalism (*El Pais*, Cataluña, 26 October 2000: 4). The positions within the party, the Catalan government and national institutions such as the Cortes are allocated on a quota of 75:25 adopted in the 1978 coalition agreement (Baras and Dalmases, 1998: 169).

In spite of tensions within the coalition, the CiU has been quite successful, both regionally as well as nationally. The incumbency of the Generalitat from 1980 to 2003 clearly strengthened the position of the previous leader, Jordi Pujol. However since 1995, the party was in decline in terms of votes and being challenged by the Catalan Socialist Party, the quite autonomous regional federation of the PSOE. In 1995 and 1999, the CiU fell short of absolute majorities and was dependent on support from other parties. After the elections in 1999 it had to form a pact of legislature with the PP. Finally, in 2003 new leader, Artur Mas, was unable to achieve an absolute majority, and to his surprise the left-wing Catalan Republican Left increased its vote considerably and negotiated a coalition agreement with the PSC and the Catalan branch of United Left, EUiA. Such coalition agreement was reconfirmed after the Catalan elections of 2006, which became necessary after ERC decided to leave the previous coalition under president of Generalitat Pascual Maragall. This means that the CiU has been in the opposition since 2003. Such a transition from governmental to opposition party has been difficult.

One of the most delicate issues was the succession of Jordi Pujol. In 1999, he appointed Artur Mas as *conseller en cap* (main councillor, First Minister) to the Generalitat of Catalonia. Mas became the successor of Pujol, when the latter decided to leave the political stage. Pujol and Mas increased their demands for a plurinational Spanish state acknowledging the different peoples of Galicia, the Basque Country, Catalonia and naturally the rest of Spain.

At national level, the CiU became a pivotal party in ensuring the viability of both a PSOE and a PP minority government between 1993 and 2000. Clearly, it played a major contribution to the stability of the political system. In spite of being offered a full coalition agreement, the CiU chose against participation in the national government and preferred the less compromising formula of a pact of legislature. CiU was willing to influence the political processes at central level, but not to decide upon policy-making which could be detrimental to its standing in their main electoral arena Catalonia (Matas Dalmases and Reniu Vilalala, 2003: 108–9). During 2002 and 2003, there were growing tensions between the PP and CiU in relation to different issues such as the general strike on 20 July 2002, and the law of zero deficit. The main point of divergence has naturally been the differences in the conception of the Spanish state (*El Pais*, 31 January 2002: 15; *El Pais*, Domingo, 10 February 2002: 8; *El Pais*, 27 June 2002: 18). The Catalan government under Jordi Pujol was weakened in 2001 when the European Commission decided to freeze funds destined for vocational training, because they were being diverted to finance the UDC. The Pallerols affair, which concerned the Andorran entrepreneur Fidel Pallerols, who owned several vocational training schools for the unemployed, is based on allegations that students never took part in courses and that their signatures were falsified, with some of the money ending up illicitly financing the UDC (*El Pais*, Cataluña, 18 October 2000: 4; *El Pais*, Cataluña, 24 October 2001: 5).

Artur Mas has been slowly gaining in reputation as the leader of CiU. The decision of Prime Minister José Luis Zapatero to negotiate the final draft of the Catalan Statute just with CiU and excluding ERC in early 2006 alienated particularly the coalition partner of the Catalan Socialist Party, ERC. However, on 21 January 2006, after a 7-hour marathon session Zapatero and Mas were able to achieve an agreement about all outstanding points. This bilateral negotiations between the two leaders of political parties enhanced the reputation of Mas as a pragmatic politician able to keep nationalist-regionalist demands within the constitutional framework. At the same time he was able to expand the level of autonomy for Catalonia. For the Catalan Republican Left (ERC) was more of a humiliation and they, who originally were one of the drafters of the Catalan Statute, voted against in parliament and campaigned for the 'no' vote in the referendum in Catalonia (Nagel and Requejo, 2007: 285).

Tensions between the CDC and the UDC resurfaced in mid-September 2007 which almost led to a split between the two parties. The reasons for these main tensions is related to the lack of coordination in announcing policies between the two parties. The coalition is dominated by two heads, Artur Mas for CDC and Josep Antoni Duran LLeida for UDC. Many of the policies of CDC are more radical than UDC. The announcing of policies by CDC without consulting the other half of the coalition is the main difficulty in the relationship between the two main parties. Several disagreements between the main leaders of the coalition led to considerable tensions, which threatened to lead to a split. One crucial catalyst of the crisis was the rejection of UDC in May 2004 to merge with CDC after the coalition lost the elections in 2003. This was reinforced by disagreements in relation to the referendum on the Constitutional Treaty in June 2004 on the issue of gay marriages in January 2006 and issues of political corruption which were blamed on UDC by CDC in April 2006. However, central to all these disagreements was the radical Catalan sovereignty project of CDC which was rejected by UDC in November 2004 and the negotiation of the Catalan statute excluding UDC in January 2006. The tensions exacerbated when Artur Mas presented the new plan to refound political Catalanism without consulting UDC in September 2007. Last but not least, there were also disagreements about the nomination of Duran Lleida as the leading candidate for the general elections of March 2008 and his support for a potential support and participation in a PSOE-led government. The fundamental difference is that UDC wants to achieve the highest level of autonomy within Spain, while CDC hopes to achieve independence in long-term perspective. These two views are difficult to reconcile, so that further tensions and conflicts may continue to undermine the cohesion of the party (*El Pais*, 18 September 2007: 19; *El Pais*, 2 October 2007: 27).

In sum, in spite of recent problems the CiU is an important pivot in the Spanish party system. It was the third largest party before due to is concentration of vote in Catalonia IU. However, lack of party political cohesion and coordination within the coalition has become a major issue which may reduce the pivotal position of this political formation in the Spanish party system.

The Basque Nationalist Party (PNV): the politics of moderate nationalism

One of the most important regionalist parties of the Spanish party system is the Basque Nationalist Party (*Eusko Alderdi Jeltzalea–Partido Nacionalista Vasco –* EAJ–PNV) which is one of the oldest Spanish parties along with the PSOE. It was founded in 1895 by Sabino Arana. Originally the ideology was quite racist and extremely anti-Spanish. It was an active party during the Second Republic. During Francoism, there was a splinter group which decided to follow the path of terrorism. The so-called terrorist organisation Basque Country and Freedom (*Euskadi ta Askatasuma –* ETA) began to operate in 1958 and became a major problem for the PNV, which wanted to follow a peaceful route. A splinter group from ETA created a party in 1977 called Basque Left (*Euskadiko Ezquerra –* EE) which further undermined the position of the PNV as the only regionalist-nationalist party. In 1986, Carlos Garaikoetchea, the former president of the Government of the Basque Country (1980–85), the so-called *lehendakari*, decided to form a splinter party called Basque Solidarity (*Eusko Askartasuna –* EA) with a strong base in Navarre against controversial leader, Xabier Arzalluz. Since then, the PNV has become more compact in spite of factionalism which may support more radical or more moderate forms of politics. The PNV remained the central party in the Basque Country in the 1990s. Indeed, the PNV was instrumental in creating the conditions along with the two main national parties, the PP and the PSOE, in solving the terrorism problem in the Basque Country. An anti-terrorist front called the *Mesa de Ajuria Enea* was established in 1988. It also played an important role in persuading all nationalist parties to endorse the Basque Declaration in Lizarra on 12 September 1998 which included the political arm of ETA, *Herri Batasuna*. The declaration committed all the parties to an inclusive peace dialogue and also the Basque right for self-determination (Gillespie, 1999a: 125). ETA declared a ceasefire which lasted for over a year. The return of ETA terrorism after December 1999 led to a growing polarisation between the government of José Maria Aznar and the PNV. In the Basque elections of 13 March 2001, the PNV-EA profited from this polarisation induced by a hardening of the position of the Spanish government in relation to the terrorist question. It led to a strong majority for the moderate nationalists, while the political arm of ETA HB/EH lost half of the vote. After the elections, the *Lehendakari* and leader of the PNV, Juan José Ibarretxe, presented a plan to allow Basque self-determination which would involve the development towards an association in the first instance, leading up to full independence. This so-called 'Ibarretxe plan' has been rejected by the PP government under José Maria Aznar. Instead, Aznar was able to achieve consensus with the PSOE and CiU to reinforce the law of political parties in relation to parties using or supporting violence and terrorism to achieve their aims. It led to the illegalisation of HB/EH during the summer of 2002. The PNV voted against the law of political parties.

Although the 'Ibarretxe' plan was approved by the Basque regional assembly in December 2004, the national parliament in Madrid rejected it outright in February 2005. At the end of September 2007, Regional President Ibarretxe presented a new plan leading up to self-determination, which was immediately rejected by the main parties in Madrid. Moreover, it became evident that the PNV had split into at least two main factions. The more radical faction, of which the main representative is Juan José Ibarretxe, wants to achieve independence through peaceful means, meaning mainly the conduct of a referendum. The more moderate faction, of which former presidents, Josu Jan Imaz and Xabier Arzalluz are the main representatives, wants to achieve it consensually through negotiations with other political parties. The moderate faction wants to keep any change of the negotiated Statute of Gernika of 1978 within the constitutional-legal framework. At the end of September, President Josu Jon Imaz resigned, when he found out that *Lehendakari* Ibarretxe would go ahead for the second time with a project that had no chance of being approved by Madrid, because of its lack of constitutionality (*El Pais*, 1 October 2007: 18, 20; *El Pais*, 2 October 2007: 20; *El Pais*, 3 October 2007: 17).

In electoral terms, the party achieved about 1.2–1.5 per cent of the vote nationally. The polarisation strategy of the PP strengthened considerably the position of the coalition PNV-EA, which gained votes from HB in the 13 March 2001 regional elections. In the Basque elections of 2005, the pre-electoral coalition PNV-EA lost the absolute majority, while the PSOE was able to make substantial gains. Moreover, a new party called Communist Party of the Basque Country (PCTV–EHAK), which included many members of the forbidden *Herri Batasuna* was able to gain almost 10 per cent of the votes. In the local elections of 2007, PNV had to deal with Basque Nationalist Action (*Acción Nacionalista Vasca* – ANV), another proxy political formation of *Herri Batasuna*, which has done well in the heartland of the Basque Country (see Chapter 5). Both PCTV–EHAK and ANV are being investigated by the courts, if they are not proxy parties of *Herri Batasuna*, which is regarded as the political arm of the ETA terrorist organisation and was illegalised after the adoption of the 2002 Law of Political Parties.

Other regionalist-nationalist parties

In the 2000 and 2004 elections four more parties achieved more than 0.8 per cent of the national vote. All the rest are below the 0.8 per cent ceiling. The *Unió Valenciana* failed to get representation in the 2004 elections, while BNG and CC declined to below 1 per cent. The big surprise at the legislative elections of 2004 was the steep rise of the Catalan Republican Left which was able to increase the national vote from 0.8 per cent to 2.54 per cent and the number of seats from one to eight (see Table 4.1.).

The National Galician Bloc (*Bloque Nacional Galego* – BNG) is a left-wing regionalist-nationalist party. It is the third largest party in Galicia and was founded in 1983 as a coalition of several parties, but within a decade it transformed itself into a major party. The party normally holds an anti-Maastricht Treaty Eurosceptic position. The rise of the BNG was consolidated in 1997 and 2001, when the other left-wing parties, the PSOE and IU, lost votes to this party. In the 2000 elections it achieved 1.32 per cent of the vote, becoming the sixth largest party in Spanish politics (*El Pais*, Domingo, 26 October 1997: 1–4; Atta, 2003). However, after factional struggles due to differences in the strategy to be pursued in view of a future participation in the regional government, the charismatic Xosé Maria Beiras was replaced by Anxo Quintana (*El Pais*, 17 April 2005: 28). Although the party lost votes and four seats in the last regional elections of 19 June 2005, it entered in a coalition with the PSOE as a junior partner (*El Pais*, 20 June 2005: 30; *El Pais*, 11 July 2005: 20; *Neue Zürcher Zeitung*, 21 June 2005: 5). The government was invested in the Galician parliament in Santiago de Compostela on 18 July 2005. The BNG was able to get four out of the twelve regional ministries. Moreover, Anxo Quintana became the only vice-president of the regional government which was chaired by leader of the Galician Socialist Party, Emilio Pérez Touriño. (Blanco Valdés, 2006b: 414–6). BNG has been also a loyal supporter of the minority government of Zapatero. The BNG intends to pursue an extension of autonomy, but within the constitutional framework. The development towards federalism in long-term perspective is part of the programme of the party. Moreover, Galicia is defined as a nationality within a plurinational Spain.

The Canary Islands Coalition (*Coalición Canaria* – CC) which achieved 1.06 per cent of the vote is a coalition of small centre-left parties. Each of the parties is strong in different parts of the Archipelago, so that only together can they achieve national representation. After the last regional elections on 28 May 2007, CC formed a coalition with the Socialist Party. This means that CC is quite a pragmatic formation able to change coalition partners according to the results after each election.

The small Republican Catalan Left (*Esquerra Republicana de Catalunya* – ERC) was founded in 1931 and was quite an important opposition force within the Catalan parliament. It was able to improve in terms of votes and seats both in the Catalan and national parliaments in the regional elections of 2003 and in the legislative elections of 2004. At regional level it is now one of the junior partners with the PSOE. The charismatic leader, Josep Carod i Rovira, was able to improve the standing of the party in relation to the right-centre nationalist-regionalist CiU. ERC became an important supporter of the PSOE minority government in the Cortes in Madrid. However, some tensions emerged between ERC and the PSOE, when Prime Minister Zapatero decided to complete negotiations on the Statute just with CiU leader Artur Mas and excluded ERC. It led to the collapse of the regional government of Pascual Maragall in 2006 and after the positive referendum on the Catalan Statute new early elections took place, in which new Catalan Socialist Party leader, José Montilla, renegotiated a new coalition agreement with ERC and EUiA. Josep Carod i Rovira returned to the government.

Similarly, the left-wing Initiative for Catalonia (*Iniciativa per Catalunya* – IC) is a coalition of parties, of which the most important is the former Socialist Unified Party of Catalonia (*Partit Socialista Unificat de Catalunya* – PSUC). It worked closely with the IU until the early 1990s, but then it became more independent. It has representation both in the Catalan parliament and in the Cortes.

The Andalusian Party (*Partido Andalucista* – PA) is a small left-wing party founded after 1976. It clearly has a regionalist-nationalist agenda. It has not been able to achieve representation in the Cortes since 1989. It may play a pivotal role in regional politics. It is the natural coalition partner of the PSOE in Andalusia.

The Aragonese Junta (*Chunta Aragonesista* – CHA) is a regionalist party from the autonomous community of Aragón. It competes the regionalist vote with the Aragonese Party (*Partido Aragonês* – PAR). The CHA achieved between 8–14 per cent of the vote in regional elections (Oñate Rubalcaba, 1998: 66–7). However, in 2003 regional elections CHA was able to get just one seat more than PAR in the regional parliament and form a coalition government with the PSOE in the autonomous community. The party was able to get one seat in the Cortes in the legislative elections of 2004. In the last regional elections, CHA's share of the vote decreased from 14 to 8.1 per cent and in terms of seats from nine to four seats, while PAR increased slightly from 11.1 per cent to 12.4 per cent and one more seat.

Nafarroa Bai is a coalition of regionalist-nationalist Navarran parties, including the Basque Nationalist Party, ARALAR, *Eusko Askatarsuna* (EA) and the left-wing group *Batzerre*. They formed the coalition to improve their electoral chances in Navarre. In the 2007 regional elections in Navarra they got 23.5 per cent and twelve seats. The leader of the party Patxi Zabaleta hoped to form a coalition with the Navarran Socialist Party. A coalition agreement was agreed in early August 2007, but the prospective coalition government was vetoed by the PSOE in Madrid, mainly because it could jeopardise the electoral chances of the PSOE in the forthcoming legislative elections. The PSOE gave the support to the main party of the region the Union of the People of Navarre (UPN). NA-Bai was quite disappointed, because they reiterated they had no ambitions towards independence. NA-Bai is also represented in the Congress with one seat.

All these parties were represented in one or both legislatures after the elections of 2000 and 2004. Together they got 10–11 per cent of the vote and 13.2 per cent of the seats.

The transformation of the party system

Since the founding elections of 1977, the Spanish party system has changed substantially. One can split the development of the Spanish party system into at least three main periods:

1   The party system of democratic transition (1977–1982);
2   The period of 'patrimonial socialism' based on an imperfect bipolarism (1982–1993);
3   The period of quasi-perfect bipolarism also called 'adulterated two-party system' (1993–).

The party system of democratic transition (1977–1982)

The founding elections of 1977 produced a moderate pluralist party system in which the Union of Democratic Centre (UCD) and the Socialist Party (PSOE) were the strongest parties. On the left, there was also the Communist Party (PCE) and on the right, the neo-Francoist People's Alliance (AP). Other parties were also represented in the Congress, but they were all small parties. There were also nationalist-regionalist parties from the Basque Country such as the Basque Nationalist Party (PNV) and the Democratic Pact of Catalonia (PDC) and the Democratic Centre and Christian Democracy of Catalonia (UDC–IDCC). The pivotal formation was the UCD under the leadership of Adolfo Suarez, who became an important honest broker in terms of negotiating and drafting the constitution of 1978. However, the political formation was a coalition of different social-democratic, Christian-democratic and liberal parties and therefore characterised by major tensions. The early incumbency in government prevented also the development of an organisation that would include all the other parties.

After the constitutional settlement was achieved at the end of December 1978, consensus was replaced by a polarised party system. (Although, the party won the legislature elections of 1979, the different factional tensions between the different parties within the coalition became unmanageable (Gunther and Hopkin, 2002; Gunther, Sani and Shabad, 1988: 127–58). The party broke up before and after the October legislature elections due to the fact that parties and personalities left the UCD and created their own formations. Most of the vote of the UCD was split between the PSOE and the AP.

The period of 'patrimonial party system' based on an imperfect bipolarism (1982–1993)

The second period started after the 1982 legislature elections when the PSOE moved to the centre and was able to win an absolute majority under the slogan of 'change' (*cambio*). The victory of the PSOE was achieved due to the collapse of the UCD in electoral terms. At the same time, A part of the UCD voters went to the People's Alliance. Between 1982 and 1996 the PSOE remained in power with an absolute majority and in the last two legislatures as a minority government dependent on the support of the regionalist-nationalist parties. Between 1982 and 1993, People's Alliance/People's Party was not able to overcome the ceiling of party leader Manuel Fraga (*techo de Fraga*) of about 26–27 per cent. This meant that the PSOE dominated the political system and party system. Longevity in power led to the emergence of accumulating cases of political corruption. This close relationship of the PSOE to the centres of economic influence led to the characterisation as 'patrimonial socialism' by James Petras, meaning that the party used and abused its control of government to keep in power. Among the corruption scandals are the Filesa party financing scandal, the GAL affair and the Luis Roldán affair (Petras,1990; 1993). Moreover, the Socialist leaders also had a close relationship with the wealthy banking and financial industry, which shifted its allegiance after 1986 to the Socialist Party, because it was disappointed with the progress made by Manuel Fraga (Gilmour, 2005: 423). Between 1988 and 1990, the AP was transformed into a more cohesive united party by Manuel Fraga and later by José Maria Aznar.

The period of quasi-perfect bipolarism also called 'adulterated two-party system' (1993–)

The revamped PP under the leadership of José Maria Aznar changed the fortunes of the party. In the 1993, legislature elections, the PP was able to challenge the PSOE and lost the elections only by 4 percentage points. The PSOE had to use a negative campaign against the PP based on their Francoist past. However, the electorate perceived the PP now as a more centrist catch-all party which was almost undistinguishable from the PSOE. The corruption affairs further eroded the trust of the population in the PSOE. The new socialist government under Prime Minister Felipe Gonzalez was able to get support from regionalist-nationalist CiU and other non-statal parties to hang on to power as a minority government. CiU ended its support in the autumn 1995 and Gonzalez had to call for early elections. In the 1996 legislature elections, the PSOE lost by one point to the PP. This result confirmed that the PP was now a challenger at equal level. The PP had moved to the centre and the volatile new middle classes shifted the vote to the revamped right centre party. Further mistakes by the PSOE in the 2000 elections, particularly the pre-electoral coalition with IU led to an absolute majority of PP. However, in the 2004 and 2008 legislature elections the party lost to the PSOE, consolidating so what Jonathan Hopkin characterises as an 'adulterated two-party system' in which the two main parties are able to concentrate most of the vote among themselves, while non-statal parties are very divided and unable to challenge them. Moreover, the vote of third statal party, United Left, is eroding in this dynamics between concentration of the vote and dispersion of territorial representation (Hopkin, 2005: 13).

Multi-level electoral arenas

Spanish political parties compete in different electoral arenas, which in some way are extremely intertwined. The best example is the fact that all national parties had to develop national federalised versions of themselves at regional level, using dominant symbols of politics in these autonomous communities (Oñate Rubalcaba, 2006: 419; Magone, 1997).

This means, for example, that in Catalonia the two main parties are called Socialist Party of Catalonia and People's Party of Catalonia respectively. The same is valid for all the other autonomous communities. Normally their names are also translated into the language of the respective region. Results in the local elections and in the European Parliament elections are quite similar to legislative elections, suggesting a close relationship.

Indeed, in some cases the results of local and European Parliament elections may indicate significant changes in the forthcoming legislature elections. This could be witnessed in the 1994 European elections and in the 1995 local and autonomous communities elections in which the PP was able to win against the PSOE. In the March 1996 legislature elections the trend was confirmed with a narrow victory for the PP. This intertwinedness gives us naturally some hints about the relationship between national and regional levels. The elections of 13 March 2001 in the Basque Country clearly showed that the indiscriminate polarisation of the PP against Basque nationalism led to a strengthening Basque nationalism, despite the PP gains. In sum, although there are peculiarities in each electoral arena, there is a fluid inter-systemic influence among them. The victory of the PSOE in the legislature elections of 2004, led also to changes at regional level. In Galicia, the PP lost its absolute majority and it opened the way for a coalition government between PSOE and BNG. Moreover, in the 2007 regional elections in the Canary islands, CC decided to coalesce with the largest party, the PSOE, instead of its ideological coalition partner, the PP.

The legislature elections: the growing concentration of the vote

One clue to the importance of one kind of election over others is the level of participation. Normally, legislature elections have quite high levels of participation when we compare them with other kinds of elections and with similar elections in other countries.

If we look closely there is a tendency for the electorate to participate in greater numbers, when they want to achieve alternation of parties in government. Apart from the historical founding elections of 1977, which led to the formation of the new party system, one has to look at the elections of 1982, 1993 and 1996 as historical turning points. The 1982 elections allowed the PSOE to come to power and establish a new party system. It was an imperfect two-party system, in which the PSOE was able to achieve absolute majorities or strong majorities, while the second largest party, the PP, was not able to pass the *techo de Fraga* at around 25–27 per cent. In the elections of 1993 and 1996, the deteriorating image of the PSOE in government which was reinforced by multiple corruption scandals clearly led to a mobilisation of the electorate to achieve an alternative government. The PP under José Maria Aznar became a credible alternative to the PSOE. The high levels of participation in 1993 and 1996 were still below the 1982 and 1977 participation

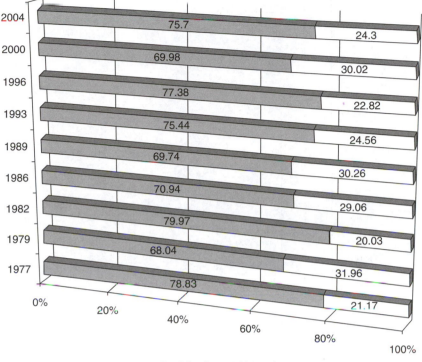

Figure 4.6 Participation and abstention in Spanish legislature elections, 1977–2004.

Source: Ministry of interior, http://www.elecciones.mir.es, accessed on 11 February 2008.

rates, but they were important enough to induce a change. After achieving it, the high levels of participation normalised to around 70 per cent. In the elections of 2000, José Maria Aznar was able to gain an absolute majority which was partly related to his own achievements during his first term in office, but partly due to the strategy of the PSOE to form a pre-electoral coalition with IU. Both parties lost heavily in this election. Some regular centrist voters of the PSOE just decided to vote to the PP due to their move towards centrist moderate policies. Many PSOE voters decided not to vote, which also harmed the party.

The transformation of the PSOE towards the moderate centre introduced by leader Zapatero were instrumental in changing the electoral fortunes of the party in the 2004 elections. Both parties were neck and neck before the elections and some polling suggests that the PSOE may have surpassed PP by a couple of percentage points a couple of days before the elections. Even today, claims and counterclaims of opinion pollsters show that the election could have gone either way. There was a 'technical tie' between the two main parties (Lago and Montero, 2006: 9; 23; Campmany, 2005: 259). The only thing that pollsters could be sure about was that the PP would have lost the absolute majority. However, unexpectedly the tragic

Table 4.5 The elected and appointed members of the Senate, 1979–2008

	1979		1982		1986		1989		1993		1996		2000		2004		2008	
	E	A	E	A	E	A	E	A	E	A	E	A	E	A	E	A	E	A
PP	3	–	55	13	63	13	78	13	93	13	112	21	127	23	102	21	101	23
PSOE	71	4	133	24	124	25	107	21	96	21	81	15	61	19	81	10	86	18
PNV	8	2	7	2	7	2	4	2	3	3	4	2	6	1	6	1	2	2
CiU	1	2	7	2	8	3	10	2	10	4	8	3	8	3	4	2	4	3
Entesa Catalan (PSC-ERC-ICV)	–	–	–	–	–	–	–	–	–	–	–	–	–	–	12	4	12	4
CC	–	–	–	–	–	–	–	–	5	1	1	2	5	1	3	1	–	–
Mixed	7	1	2	5	3	3	8	4	1	6	2	7	1	4	–	4	3	5
UCD	118	1	4	–	–	–	–	–	–	–	–	–	–	–	–	–	–	–
CDS	–	–	–	–	3	–	1	6	–	–	–	–	–	–	–	–	–	–
TOTAL	208	10	208	46	208	46	208	48	208	50	208	50	208	51	208	51*	208	55*

Source: Roller, 2002b:76; Delgado, Lopez-Nieto, 2003:1191 and database on website of the Senate, http://www.senado.es accessed on 14 February 2008. Entesa Catalana=parliamentary groups consisting of three Catalan parties: Socialist Catalan Party (PSC), Catalan Republican Left (ERC) and United Left. *Not all appointed members allocated.

Table 4.6 Allocation of appointed senators according to autonomous communities

	Allocation of appointed senators according to autonomous communities	
	2004–2008	*2008*
Andalusia	8	9
Aragon	2	2
Asturias	2	2
Balearics	1	2
Canary Islands	2	3
Cantabria	1	1
Castilla-La-Mancha	2	2
Castilla-León	3	3
Catalonia	7	8
Valencian Community	5	5
Extremadura	2	2
Galicia	3	3
Madrid	6	7
Murcia	2	2
Navarre	1	1
Basque Country	3	3
La Rioja	1	8
TOTAL	51	56

Source: Website of the Senate, http://www.senado.es, accessed on 14 February 2008.

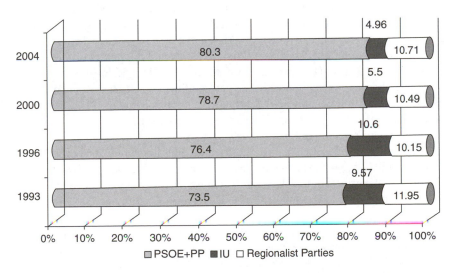

Figure 4.7 Concentration of the vote in Spanish Legislature Elections, 1993–2004.

Madrid bombings in commuter trains in the early morning of 11 March 2004 by Al Qaeda became a decisive factor for the shift of undecided and former abstentionists to vote for the PSOE against the PP government. The main reason for the ultimate victory for the PSOE were not the Madrid bombings, but actually the way the absolute majority government of José Maria Aznar handled the crisis. Very early on in the day, Basque *lehendakari* Juan José Ibarretxe blamed ETA for the bombings. Intelligence seemed to suggest that ETA was planning a big terrorist attack in the months before. Probably, the main mistake was to use the political channels such as the United Nations Security Council to condemn the attack of ETA, in order to make a political gain. In the end, the perception of the population was that government was not telling the truth, and therefore as Ignacio Lago and José Ramón Montero conclude, the population voted out the government, because in the end politicians are accountable to the voters (Lago and Montero, 2006: 9). According to their analysis, about 6 per cent of voters were mobilised after the bombing attacks and 65 per cent of those decided to vote for the PSOE. Moreover, Lago and Montero found out that 5 per cent voted as a direct consequence of the attacks, in normal electoral circumstances they would have abstained. Again, 65 per cent of those voted for the PSOE, and 45 per cent of those that changed their vote voted for the PSOE. Only 11 per cent and 3 per cent voted for the PP and the IU. The PSOE profited also most from protest voters against the Iraq War and the handling of information by the government after the Madrid bombings after 11 March (Lago and Montero, 2006: 9–10).

A survey conducted soon after the elections, showed that the majority of the population regarded the behaviour of the PP government between 11 and 14 March 2004 as manipulative or believed the government to have been withholding information. The majority was satisfied with the outcome of the elections (*El Pais*, 4 April 2004 quoted from van Biezen, 2005: 104). In a major study conducted by the public Centre for Sociological Research after the Madrid bombings of 11 March 2004 and the subsequent elections on 14 March, the majority named the war in Iraq (26.8 per cent), religious fanaticism (20.4 per cent) and the policy of the United States (18.7 per cent) as the main causes of the attack (Llera, Retortillo, 2005: 85).

As already mentioned previously, the nature of the constituencies, the d'Hondt electoral system and the threshold clearly give a strong advantage to the two main parties in relation to all other smaller parties. The concentration of the vote is one of the characteristics of the Spanish party system.

The dominance of the two main parties is overwhelming. Over 70 per cent of the vote is shared between the PP and PSOE. The main party will also profit in terms of seats due to the effects of the electoral system which gives advantage to the larger parties in detriment to the smaller ones. The share of the regionalist-nationalist parties has been remarkably stable at around 10–15 per cent. The electorate of the IU is probably quite volatile at certain times. In spite of a 9–10 per cent potential, the IU's electorate may be reduced to the core party loyalists as in the legislature elections of 2000 and 2004. One factor affecting the electoral prospects of IU is that so far they have been unable to find a strong charismatic leader who would challenge critically the PSOE. Moreover, Zapatero's transformation of the PSOE has led also to a growing influence upon left-wing progressive social movements, thus reducing the appeal of IU for these constituencies.

In the 2000 elections, both the PSOE and the IU were punished for not bringing to the fore credible alternative programmes to the PP and above all an alternative leader. The turbulence in the two parties strengthened the PP. The electoral coalition between the PSOE and IU also contributed to the fact that the Catholic vote, which was quite dormant among PSOE voters, shifted to the PP in these elections. Although it is a hidden dimension of Spanish politics, it became quite evident in these elections. The more conservative voters of PSOE, who did not like the electoral coalition between the PSOE and the IU and in the past did not vote for the PP, because of its authoritarian legacy, felt able to do so then (Calvo and Montero, 2002: 23, 41). After 2000, Zapatero moved the party back to the centre, and was able to create a credible alternative to the PP.

The ideological vote ceased to be important in elections. Similar to other countries, the decline of the main divisions around religion and ideology led to all-embracing main parties. The centre is where most voters can be found and both parties compete for it. Any sign of radicalisation towards the left or the right may harm chances in the forthcoming elections. Broadly speaking, the PP is regarded as a more catch-all pluralistic party with tendencies towards more conservative neo-liberal policies, while the PSOE is identified as the party of the working-class, which is now understood as much broader and inclusive than the original working-class concept (Torcal and Chhiber, 1995).

As already mentioned, one important feature of the Spanish party system is that the ideology of parties is becoming less important, while pragmatism, electoral marketing and leadership have become essential for doing well in elections. The choices are much broader allowing the voters to shift more easily from one party to another. The growing individualisation of voters, the decline of the family, the appearance of new forms of family are trends which are contributing to the emergence of a US-style electoral arena which uses electoral marketing, focus groups, the media and personalisation of politics as strategies to win the votes at elections (Montero and Torcal, 1995; Gunther, Montero and Botella, 2004: 148–51). This is confirmed by the levels of volatility despite the strong stability of the party system.

According to Richard Gunther and José Ramón Montero, voting swung between left and right in all legislature elections between 1977 and 2000, giving an average inter-bloc volatility of 2.7 per cent, but between the elections of 1996 and 2000 it reached 7.6 per cent. In contrast, between 1993 and 2000 inter-bloc volatility has been 2.7 per cent in contrast to a mean of 11.9 per cent. Between 1996 and 2000, total volatility was 10.1 per cent which is lower than the mean of 14.6 per cent. Nevertheless, inter-bloc volatility has been responsible for 38.6 per cent between 1993 and 1996, and 52.9 per cent between 1996 and 2000 of total volatility. This clearly is significant in comparison to the average share of 22 per cent (Gunther and Montero, 2001: 90). According to the post-electoral survey after the 2004 legislature elections, the overwhelming majority is in the centre and centre-left. Both parties compete for the votes in the centre.

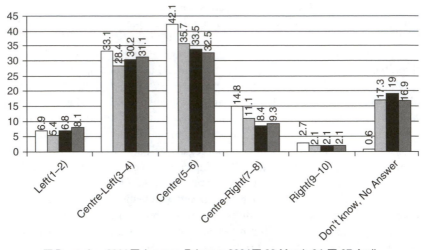

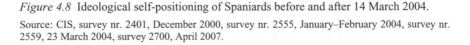

☐ December 2000 ▨ January–February 2004 ■ 23-March-04 ■ 07-April

Figure 4.8 Ideological self-positioning of Spaniards before and after 14 March 2004.

Source: CIS, survey nr. 2401, December 2000, survey nr. 2555, January–February 2004, survey nr. 2559, 23 March 2004, survey 2700, April 2007.

This naturally helps us to understand the position of the electorate of the two main parties in the elections of 2000 and 2004.

As one can see the PP moved clearly from a right to a centre-right position and even made some gains in the centre-left. It shows that in the last elections of the older generation of AP in 1989, there was an inability to pass the *techo de Fraga* which was restricted to the centre-right and right vote. One has to acknowledge that up until 1989 the PP was challenged by the CDS, which was a small centrist party. In the 1993 elections, it inherited this vote and also transformed itself into a centrist catch-all party (Castillo and Delgado Sotillos, 1998: 129–38).

In the case of PSOE, we see that Almunia pushed the PSOE electorate towards the left and centre-left. The presence on the centre-right and right almost disappears. Most of these voters had already changed throughout the 1990s to the PP, as they felt more comfortable with the new image of the PP. Abstention also affected the PSOE considerably, more so than other parties in the 2000 elections (Barreiro, 2002). However, Zapatero was able to move the party back to the centre by taking many of the issues presented by the new middle classes and post-materialist social movements. It is a modernisation of the left-wing social-democratic project taking into account the emergence of a wealthier Spanish society oriented towards the centre. At the same time, aspects of solidarity, equality and liberty summarised under a package of 'new rights' retain the progressive nature of the social-democratic project. Moreover, organisational change undertaken under the leadership of José Blanco after decades of inertia helped to turn around the fortunes of the party in the 2004 elections.

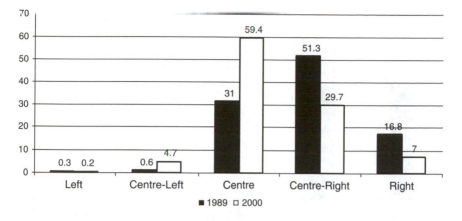

Figure 4.9 Distribution of People's Party voters, 1989 and 2000.
Source: Based on data provided by Torcal and Medina, 2002: 65.

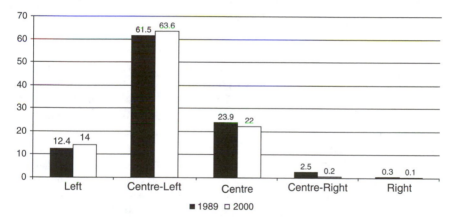

Figure 4.10 Profile of the Socialist Party vote, 1982 and 2000.
Source: Based on data provided by Torcal and Medina, 2002: 66.

The profile of IU voters changed considerably over the past decade. There was a moderation of the voters since the left-wing voters were dwindling due to erosion of communist ideology in post-modern society. They are moving slowly towards the centre-left and centre, but this is already occupied by the PSOE and the PP. The 2000 general elections show that any electoral alliance with the PSOE will damage considerably the strongholds of the party on the left. As already mentioned, the catastrophic results of 2000, in which the IU lost half of the vote, will remain an important lesson for the future (Figure 4.9). In the 2004 elections, the PSOE was able to reduce the electorate of IU, because most voters cast a useful vote for the left, in order to vote the PP out of office.

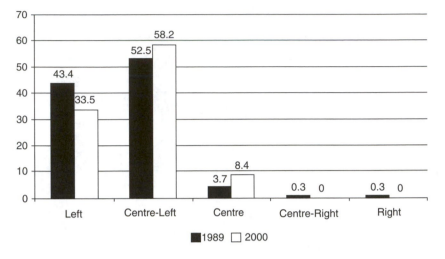

Figure 4.11 Profile of United Left voters, 1989 and 2000.

Source: Based on data provided by Torcal and Medina, 2002: 67.

The most important division in present Spanish politics is now the polarisation between regionalist-nationalist and the state-wide parties (*españolismo*). This is quite salient in the three autonomous communities with the highest regional consciousness: Catalonia, the Basque Country and Galicia. This became an important issue in the autonomous communities' elections. However, the dynamics has become quite important in the Canary Islands and Navarre as well (Llera, 2006: 242–9) (see next section and Chapter 5).

In sum, the legislature elections have produced an Americanised electoral arena with moderate parties aiming towards the centre and an electorate which is keen to undertake change of parties in government, when necessary, by increasing their participation (Gunther and Montero, 1998: 542–5; 2001: 144–7).

The 9 March 2008 general elections

One of the major fears of the incumbent Socialist government was the possibility of another terrorist act shortly before the elections. Since the beginning of the year the security alert was increased in order to prevent a repeat of a 11 March or similar terrorist act. Throughout the pre-campaign the Socialist Party was slightly ahead in the polls. However, there was some nervousness in the Socialist headquarters about the narrow lead of the party in relation to the PP in the pre-electoral survey conducted by the prestigious Madrid-based public Centre for Sociological Studies (CIS) on 21 January 2008. In spite of the narrowing difference between the two parties, the survey showed that the population was content with the political and governmental performance of the Zapatero government (CIS, 2008). One characteristic of the pre-campaign and campaign period was the polarisation between the two political parties. The challenging PP used all possible arguments, including the immigration card to reduce the lead of the Socialist Party. Other parties had difficulties in bringing their message across. The third largest national party, the Communist coalition United Left (IU) under leader Gaspar Llamazares complained about this bipolarisation of the campaign, because it reduced the electoral chances of the smaller parties (*El Pais*, 22 February 2008: 17).

One crucial turning point of the campaign was the appointment of Manuel Pizarro, a former executive of the Spanish energy transnational corporation Endesa, who, on 22 February 2008 had his television debate with the Socialist minister of economy, Pedro Solbes, who was a former European Commissioner responsible for economic matters. The debate was a clear victory for Pedro Solbes and a catastrophe for Manuel Pizarro. Solbes was able to present a very well-prepared and self-confident image, while Pizarro stumbled over simple economic and finance issues. In spite of the success in the pre-campaign, the performance of Manuel Pizarro damaged the changes of PP to close the gap to the PSOE (*El Pais*, 23 February 2008: 11–12).

After months of negotiations, both candidates agreed to two debates in the Academy of Television in Madrid, which should be transmitted by all relevant television channels. One of the reasons for the negotiations, was that Mariano Rajoy was afraid that the debates on the public television (TVE) channel would help the Socialists. The first debate took place on 26 November and was watched by 13 million people. Although there was no clear winner, Prime Minister Zapatero was more successful in transmitting a positive image than Mariano Rajoy, who used a strategy of polarisation to bring its message across (*El Pais*, 27 February 2008: 13; 17–20).

In the second debate on 3 March 2008, the audience level declined considerably. The polarisation between the two leaders did not lead to a substantial change in the perception of the population. In spite of a very aggressive style of Mariano Rajoy, who was supported by former Prime Minister José Maria Aznar in the last days of the campaign, PP was not able to catch up with the PSOE. There was also some frustration in the PP about the campaign strategy adopted by Mariano Rajoy, which was aimed at discrediting the policies of the Zapatero government. Three topics were dominant in this polarising strategy of Mariano Rajoy, – the anti-terrorism policy of the government; the immigration policy; and the economy. The anti-terrorism policy in relation to the Basque separatist ETA became central to his strategy of polarisation. The support of Prime Minister Zapatero in 2005 for negotiations with ETA was assessed by Mariano Rajoy as weakness. According to Rajoy, the tough approach of former Prime Minister José Maria Aznar in relation to Basque terrorism was the right policy and was confirmed after the bombing of a car park in which two Ecuadorians died. Rajoy's message in a nutshell was that one cannot trust ETA. He instrumentalised also the terrorism victim associations against Prime Minister Zapatero. Again the policies of former Prime Minister Aznar were used as a counter-example.

The Zapatero government started a considerable crackdown on surrogate organisations of ETA in the autumn of 2007 and at the beginning of the year. One of the reasons for the delay in arresting leaders of ANV and PCTV was the fact, that it had to be preceded by a judiciary process based on a proper collection of proof by the police. In the last phase of the campaign, Rajoy used the immigration card to discredit the Socialist government. Again the policies of former Prime Minister Aznar were used as a positive counter-example. The third issue was the economy, which was doing well, although since January unemployment was rising due to the after-effects of the international recession caused primarily by the subprime crisis in the USA. The third issue was the most difficult to use against the government, because Minister of Economy, Pedro Solbes, could look back at an impressive record of growth, budgetary surplus and also increase in employment.

In spite of the tight security measures and crackdown on ETA, on 5 March 2008 the Basque terrorist group killed Isaias Carrasco a former Socialist councillor of the Basque town of Mondragón, which was governed by ANV, a surrogate of ETA. Although all parties condemned ETA violence, including PNV, ANV did not. Both Zapatero and Rajoy visited jointly the family to express their condolences. The family asked the people to vote massively in the forthcoming elections of 9 March as a message against Basque terrorism, only ANV asked for abstention. Sandra, the oldest daughter of Isaias Carrasco pleaded that none of the parties use her father's death for electoral purposes (*El Pais*, 9 March 2008). On election day, 75.32 per cent of voters cast their vote. This was almost as high as in the previous elections of 14 March. A high level of participation tends to help the PSOE against PP.

The elections led to a victory for the PSOE, although the party was not able to achieve the absolute majority. It got 43.64 per cent and 169 seats, six seats short of the absolute majority. The PP was able to improve from 37.64 to 40.11 per cent and won 153 seats. The smaller parties suffered considerably under the bipolarised campaign. Most of them lost votes. The polarisation strategy of the PSOE led to the further erosion of the vote for IU which got 3.8 per cent and two seats: this was a decline of 1.16 per cent and three seats in relation to 2004. It meant that IU was not able to form a parliamentary group in the Congress. The two Catalan parties CiU and ERC lost votes, but the former was able to improve the number of seats from ten to eleven, while the latter lost five seats and 1.37 per cent of vote. Apart from the BNG and Na-Bai, all other smaller parties lost votes and some of them their seats, like the Aragonese regionalist party, CHA. The big surprise was the success of a new national party, which was led by former Socialist Rosa Diez. Union Progress and Democracy (*Unión Progreso y Democracia* – UPyD) was able to get one MP elected in Madrid with 1.2 per cent of the vote. This was a great achievement, when we take into account the almost majoritarian nature of the Spanish PR system. The UPyD is against the devolution process in education and health, because it creates inequalities across the territory. The party advocates a centralising unitary concept of the Spanish nation. Moreover, it wants a reform of the electoral law which distorts the representation of national in relation to regionalist parties. The UPyD is basically a citizens' movement which wants to contribute to a reform of the Spanish institutions (UPyD, 2008).

In the PP, there was a general debate discussing the succession to Mariano Rajoy. A party conference was scheduled for June. The main rival for his position was Esperanza Aguirre, the president of the autonomous community of Madrid.

Due to the loss of 300,000 votes and three seats, IU lost considerable party funding. However, negotiations were undertaken to form a parliamentary group with the Catalan ERC, which would reduce partly the financial downturn. IU had also debts of about €12 millions with the banks. Last but not least, in the PNV the opposition to *Lehendekari* Juan José Ibarretxe and his intention to conduct a referendum on Basque independence in autumn increased considerably (*El Pais*, 28 April 2008: 16). In sum, the 9 March elections strengthened the position of the Zapatero government and weakened both national and regional oppositions.

Local elections and autonomous community elections: second-order elections

Local and autonomous community elections have taken place regularly at the same time since 1983. The first local elections took place in 1979. Normally, local elections have the same effect as legislature elections. The only big difference is the lower level of participation, which is still high in comparison with other west European countries.

Figure 4.12 shows that in local elections roughly 66–69 per cent of the voters take part. It is about 10 per cent lower than the participation at legislature elections. In this sense, local elections can be called second-order elections. Although the participation level is a little higher in autonomous community elections,

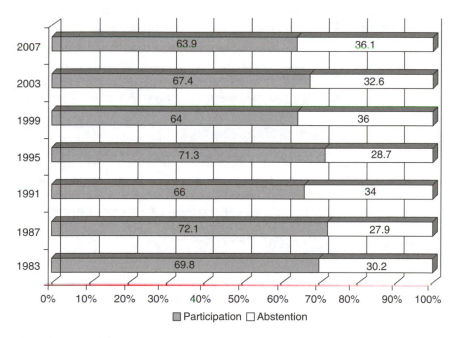

Figure 4.12 Participation in local elections, 1983–2007.

Source: Ministry of the Interior, http://www.mir.es and *El Pais*, 28 May 2007: 21.

particularly in the historical regions, they also have to be considered second-order elections (see Figure 4.13).

In recent years, abstention has been quite strong in Catalonia, the Canary Islands, the Basque Country and the Balearics. Galicia is also among the autonomous communities with the highest abstention rates, although this improved considerably in the 1990s.

The electoral results clearly show the dominance of the two larger parties, the PP and the PSOE. The electoral results in local elections tend to confirm trends that are happening at national level. This nationalisation of local politics can only be exceptionally superseded by local issues.

Indeed, in the 1999 elections the independents won 5.95 per cent of the vote. They were able to get 4,706 council seats, which is quite good in comparison to the CiU which obtained 4,089 and the IU with 2,295 seats. Overall thirty different political parties got some representation in the 1999 elections. In 1991 and 1995, the number of competing political parties was far larger than in 1999. In 1995, there were 171 different political parties taking part in local elections which shows that a certain rationalisation and integration of political groups is taking place, so that they stand a better chance of achieving representation (Delgado Sotillos, 1997; Vallés and Picanyol, 1998). The local elections of 27 May 2007 confirmed the trend towards concentration of the vote between the two main parties, PP and PSOE, IU has been losing votes since the 1999 elections. Last but not least, about 23.9 per cent of the vote went to the regionalist-nationalist, regionalist parties and independent citizen's groups. Local and regional elections, if we exclude the Catalan, Basque, Galician and Andalusian elections, are an important indicator

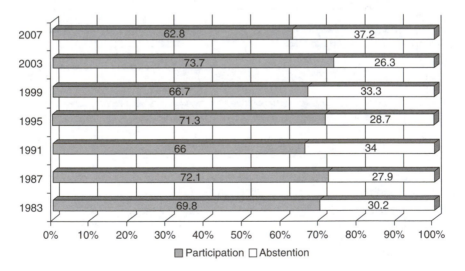

Figure 4.13 Participation in regional elections, 1983–2007.

Source: http://www.mir.es, accessed on 28 October 2007 and *El País*, 28 May 2007: 21. Also included are the Catalan, Andalusian, Basque and Galician elections that take place at different times in the electoral cycle.

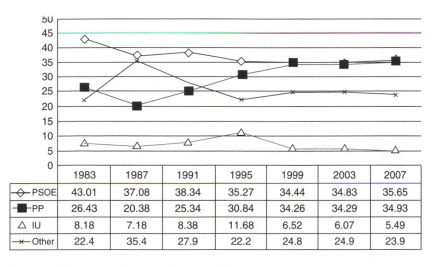

	1983	1987	1991	1995	1999	2003	2007
◇ PSOE	43.01	37.08	38.34	35.27	34.44	34.83	35.65
■ PP	26.43	20.38	25.34	30.84	34.26	34.29	34.93
△ IU	8.18	7.18	8.38	11.68	6.52	6.07	5.49
✕ Other	22.4	35.4	27.9	22.2	24.8	24.9	23.9

Figure 4.14 Results of local elections, 1983–2007.

Source: Based on data from Ministry of the Interior, http://www.elecciones2003.mir.es, accessed on 27 May 2003 and *El Pais*, 28 May 2007: 21.

for the strength of both political parties, before the legislature elections the year afterwards. In 2007, Mariano Rajoy was able to hold on the leadership of PP due to the fact that the party won the local elections and was able to hold on the Madrid community and city. Although, the PSOE made major gains in regions such as Canary Islands, Aragón, Basque Country, Asturias and Andalucia, the inability to win the capital city and the community of Madrid is always perceived by the political establishment as a defeat. One of the reasons for the success of the PP in the capital city is the fact that the party has an excellent charismatic figure as mayor in Madrid, who has been tipped as one of the potential leaders of the party in the future. Alberto Ruiz Gallardón is a well-liked figure in Madrid and has contributed to the improvement of living conditions in the capital.

In sum, local elections reflect very much the pattern of representation at national level. The main representative forces obtained the vast majority of councillors, although there is a great variety of other parties that were not able to achieve national representation, but still exist at local level, including parties related to the former authoritarian regime such as the Spanish Falange (*Falange Española* – FE), which is a successor organisation to the Francoist organisation.

In the next chapter there will be a more detailed account of the autonomous community elections. It is sufficient to say at this stage that autonomous community elections are also dominated by the two main parties. Only in a few historical regions are they superseded by regionalist-nationalist parties such as the PNV-EA in the Basque Country and CiU in Catalonia. In Galicia, the BNG was the second largest party after the PP under the leadership of Manuel Fraga until the last elections of June 2005. In other regions, the PP and the PSOE are the strongest

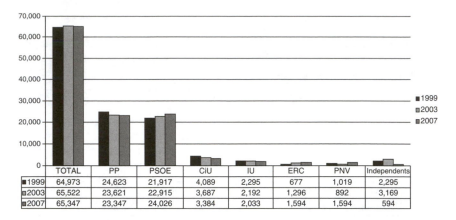

	TOTAL	PP	PSOE	CiU	IU	ERC	PNV	Independents
1999	64,973	24,623	21,917	4,089	2,295	677	1,019	2,295
2003	65,522	23,621	22,915	3,687	2,192	1,296	892	3,169
2007	65,347	23,347	24,026	3,384	2,033	1,594	1,594	594

Figure 4.15 Elected councillors for main political groups after the local elections of 1999, 2003 and 2007.

Source: Based on data from Ministry of the Interior, http://www.elecciones 2003.mir.es, accessed on 27 May 2003 and *El Pais*, 28 May 2007.

parties even if they need sometimes to establish legislature pacts or form coalitions with other parties. In the 1999 elections the PP was able to achieve government responsibility in eight autonomous communities, namely Galicia, Castilla León, La Rioja, Madrid, Cantabria, Navarre, Murcia and the Valencian Community, while the PSOE was able to win six, namely Andalusia, Extremadura, Castilla La Mancha, Aragón, Asturias and the Balearics. In three autonomous communities the regionalist-nationalist parties are strong. Apart from the Basque Country and Catalonia, one has to include the Canary Islands, where the Canarian Coalition is quite strong (Pallarés, 1998; Wert, 1998). In 2007, the PSOE was able to improve its standing in the Canary islands, Aragón and Navarre. The pragmatic approach after the 2005 Galician and 2006 Catalan elections led to coalition governments with nationalist-regionalist parties. It means that the PSOE now is in government in eight autonomous communities, and could have secured Navarre, if the central office of the party had not vetoed the coalition government of the regional branch with the regionalist-nationalist *Nafarroa Bai*. The PP controls eight autonomous communities, of which the Valencian Community is the most important. The Basque Country is governed by PNV-EA and the statewide parties decided not to take part in any government of *Lehendekari* Juan José Ibarretxe due to his plans for independence for the Basque Country.

In sum, despite an extensive programme of devolution, the two main national parties are dominating most of the governments of the autonomous communities. This certainly shows the limitations of any regionalist-nationalist aspirations.

The European Parliament elections: third-order elections?

As already mentioned, Spaniards elect their MEPs in one large national con-stituency which clearly strengthens the two main parties, but actually is quite

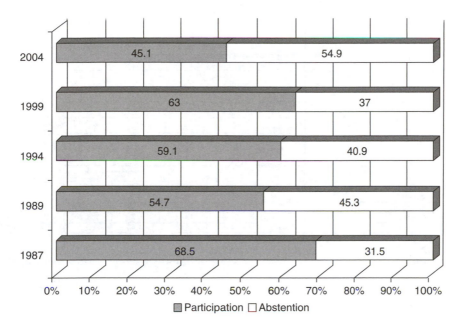

2004	45.1	54.9
1999	63	37
1994	59.1	40.9
1989	54.7	45.3
1987	68.5	31.5

0% 10% 20% 30% 40% 50% 60% 70% 80% 90% 100%

■ Participation □ Abstention

Figure 4.16 Participation in European elections, 1987–2004.

detrimental to the opportunities of the small regionalist-nationalist parties. Regionalist-nationalist parties normally form electoral alliances to fight elections, so that they are able to achieve representation in the European Parliament. In some cases, like in the 1994 elections, the regionalist-nationalist representation was limited to the strongest parties, such as the CiU and PNV. In the 2004 elections, regionalist-nationalist parties formed two coalitions. Galeusca included the three main regionalist-nationalist parties of Galicia, Basque Country and Catalonia, the BNG, CiU and PNV respectively. The second group was Peoples's Europe (*Europa de los Pueblos*), which consisted of the smaller regionalist-nationalist parties. There were six parties in the electoral coalition which were the Basque EA, the Catalan ERC, Catalan Action, Nationalist and Ecologist Coalition, Common Land and the Nationalist Castilian Party. In the 1999 elections, People's Europe formed a coalition with Nationalist Coalition which consisted of the Basque PNV, the Canary Coalition (CC) and Valencian Union (UV) (Delgado and Lopez-Nieto, 2003: 1192). The results show that it is quite difficult for these non-statewide coalitions to achieve representation in the European Parliament.

One of the characteristics of European parliamentary elections is that the turnout is even lower than that of local and autonomous community elections. Therefore, one has probably to correct Karl Heinz Reif's assessment that these are second-order elections (Reif and Schmidt, 1980). In reality, they even seem to be third-order elections. Although Spain is among the countries with the highest election participation rates in the European Union, participation in European Parliament elections is low when compared with all internal Spanish elections. In the 2004

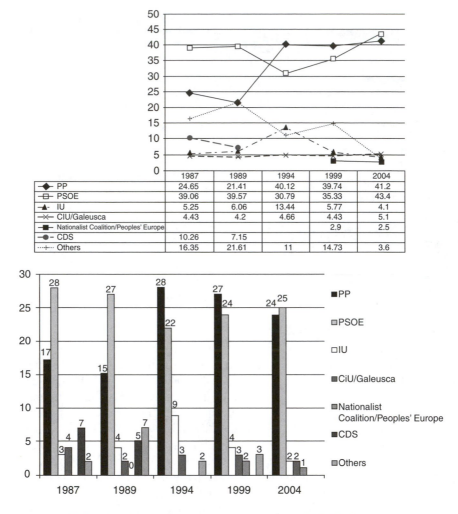

	1987	1989	1994	1999	2004
◆ PP	24.65	21.41	40.12	39.74	41.2
⊟ PSOE	39.06	39.57	30.79	35.33	43.4
▲ IU	5.25	6.06	13.44	5.77	4.1
✕ CIU/Galeusca	4.43	4.2	4.66	4.43	5.1
■ Nationalist Coalition/Peoples' Europe				2.9	2.5
● CDS	10.26	7.15			
┼ Others	16.35	21.61	11	14.73	3.6

Figure 4.17 Results of the European Parliament elections, 1987–2004.

elections, only 45.1 per cent cast their vote and 54.9 per cent abstained. This was lowest figure of participation and the highest of abstention since the first elections in 1987. It shows really that these elections are of third order for Spanish voters. (see Figure 4.16)

Spanish European elections are also dominated by national issues and fail to become European affairs. In the 1999 elections, there was some attempt by the major parties to articulate their political campaigns with those of the European transnational federations, so that the electorate was able to perceive the distinctiveness of these elections (Gibbons, 2001: 191–4). In the 2004 elections, the PSOE was able to repeat its victory of 14 March 2004, but the margin became narrower. However, the party became the largest Spanish group in the European Parliament. It used a campaign based on the slogan 'We return to Europe' (*Volvemos a Europa*) in order to show the more constructive position of the Zapatero government in relation to the European Union in comparison to the previous Aznar government (Campmany, 2005: 274–7). (see Figure 4.17)

In spite of all attempts to mobilise the electorate, European elections certainly have the lowest priority for Spanish voters and this is quite in line with voting behaviour in other countries. The difficulties of small parties to get representation also strengthen the position of the two main parties. The electoral system clearly rewards the larger parties with disproportionately more seats, while smaller parties are under-represented. In sum, European elections are not very different from national elections. Similar to local elections, European elections are basically influenced by the discourse of the main parties, which use them as a barometer for their electoral fortunes at national level. (Castillo, 1998a).

Conclusions: the moderation and Americanisation of Spanish politics

Any conclusions about the Spanish party system and electoral politics cannot ignore the fact that Spain is following the same trend towards the Americanisation of electoral politics and similar party strategies as in other European countries. Americanisation means that the former electoral market which was divided along ideological and religious lines is being transformed into an electoral market of individuals. Individualisation, diversity of living forms, decline of religious observance and modernisation of living styles has been happening in Spain since the 1960s. Parties cannot rely on labels such as working-class or conservative classes and anti-clerical Republicanism. Instead, the whole electoral market is quite fluid. Parties cannot build on membership to achieve electoral success. They have to resort to expensive media, focus groups and political marketing to reach the voter. Spanish parties have become cartel parties, highly dependent on state subsidies. They are office-seeking. Any major loss of voters at elections may lead to financial ruin, or at least to difficulty. This naturally has transformed political parties into electoral machines. The PP is clearly the best example of this transformation. Other parties have had to learn from it.

Another influence that is shaping Spanish politics is the growing importance of charismatic personalities to mobilise the electorate. The best example was Felipe Gonzalez during the 1980s and early 1990s. The former PP leader José Maria Aznar obtained his charismatic position, because of his hard work in transforming the PP into a modern party. However, the PP leader Mariano Rajoy has difficulties in becoming detached from the personality of José Maria Aznar. Present Prime Minister José Luis Rodriguez Zapatero has gained charismatic status through his left-wing progressive policies and moderate style. In sum, Spanish electoral politics is becoming more Americanised and political parties are more interested in the cartelisation of the state, so that they can survive in the twenty-first century.

5 The dynamics of regional politics

The process of regionalisation since 1978

The development of the state of autonomies

A central aspect of the success of present Spanish democracy is its territorial definition as a state of autonomies (*estado de autonomias*). This compromise formula of the architects of the constitution remained the most important issue to achieve a lasting constitutional settlement in Spain. Indeed, the constitutional formula was so open-ended, that today there are growing calls for a further revision of the constitution to acknowledge the present reality of seventeen autonomous communities. The danger of such open-endedness spilling over into an unstable unresolved settlement is quite real (Villacorta Mancebo, 2000: 88–102; Colomer, 1999: 41; Nagel and Requejo, 2007: 278–81; Nuñez Seixas, 2007). Indeed, the compromise formula envisaged only a restricted autonomy to the historical regions of the Basque Country and Catalonia. Article 151 allowed these historical regions to become autonomous communities with greater powers through a fast-track route.

The main instrument to achieve such an autonomous community statute was a positive referendum on this issue. The constitutional architects also allowed for other regions, which were not historical nations per se, to achieve autonomy. Article 143 allowed for a slow route to autonomy with lesser powers. The dynamics of regionalisation fed by regionalism led to a somewhat chaotic emergence of seventeen autonomous communities between 1979 and 1983. Therefore, there is basically a two-tier system of autonomous communities ruled by either Article 143 or Article 151. After the Basque Country and Catalonia, a further five – Andalusia, Galicia, the Canary Islands, Navarre and the Valencian Community – were able to obtain the same status as the two most prominent historical regions. Among the five newcomers only Galicia can really be considered as a historical region due to language and culture. The other ten autonomous communities – Aragón, Asturias, the Balearics, Cantabria, Castilla León, Castilla La Mancha, Extremadura, Madrid, Murcia and La Rioja – are still governed by Article 143 and have lesser powers than the other seven communities (Table 5.1).

Table 5.1 The autonomous statutes, 1979–2007

Autonomous communities	Legal basis and date of statute		Revision of statute
Andalusia	Organic Law 6/1981,	30 Dec 1981	2002, 2007
Aragón	Organic Law 8/1982,	10 Aug 1982	1994, 1996, 2007
Asturias	Organic Law 7/1981,	30 Dec 1981	1991, 1994, 1999
Balearics	Organic Law 2/1983,	25 Feb 1983	1994, 1999, 2007
Basque Country	Organic Law 3/1979,	18 Dec 1979	
Canaries	Organic Law 10/1982,	10 Aug1982	1996, 1997, 2002
Cantabria	Organic Law 8/1981,	30 Dec 1981	1991, 1994, 1998
Castilla La Mancha	Organic Law 9/1982,	10 Aug 1982	1991, 1994, 1997
Castilla León	Organic Law 4/1983,	25 Feb 1983	1994, 1999, 2007
Catalonia	Organic Law 4/1979,	22 Dec1979	2006
Extremadura	Organic Law 1/1983,	25 Feb 1983	1991, 1994, 1999
Galicia	Organic Law 1/1981,	28 April 1981	1997, 2002
La Rioja	Organic Law 3/1982,	9 June 1982	1994, 1999
Madrid	Organic Law 3/1983,	25 Feb 1983	1991, 1994, 1998
Murcia	Organic Law 4/1982,	9 June 1982	1991, 1994, 1998
Navarre	Organic Law 13/1982,	10 Aug 1982	2001
Valencian Community	Organic Law 5/1982,	1 Jul 1982	1991, 1994, 2006
Ceuta	Organic Law 1/1995,	13 Mar 1995	
Melilla	Organic Law 2/1995,	14 Mar1995	

Source: *Anuario El Pais*, 2007: 94.

In the past 25 years, central government, dominated either by the UCD, the PSOE or the PP, tried to bring some structure and organisation into this dynamics of regionalisation (for an overview see Figure 5.1 and Table 5.2). The first big attempt was undertaken by the UCD government with the support of the PSOE in July 1981. Both signed an autonomous communities agreement (*acuerdos autonómicos*). Included in this agreement was the so-called Organic Law for the Harmonisation of the Autonomous Process (*Ley Organica para la Armonización del Proceso Autonómico* – LOAPA) which was presented by the UCD government in order to prevent the non-historical regions (all except the Basque Country, Catalonia and Galicia) from upgrading their autonomy by the route envisaged in Article 151. This attempt was a reaction to what had happened the year before in terms of the dynamics of regionalisation. The positive referendum in Andalusia on 28 February 1980 in which 55.8 per cent of the population approved the autonomous statute based on Article 151 clearly undermined the position of the government. The condition for the granting of autonomy based on Article 151 was conditional on achieving an absolute majority in all provinces of the autonomous community. Andalusia achieved this in seven out of the eight provinces, but failed in Almeria by merely 20,000 votes. Nevertheless, the government had to grant Andalusia autonomy according to Article 151.

The referendum in Galicia on 21 December 1980 also granted this historical region an autonomous statute with greater powers. Similarly, Valencia, Navarre and the Canary Islands were granted special statutes which were between Article 151 and Article 143. Between 1981 and 1983, we see the emergence of

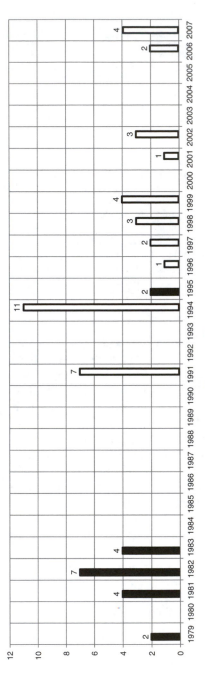

Figure 5.1 The development of statutes and revisions of statutes (1970–2007).

Table 5.2 Development of statutes and revisions of statutes

Year	Autonomous statutes	Revisions
	Founding statutes	
1979	Catalonia, Basque Country	
1980		
1981	Andalusia, Asturias, Cantabria, Galicia	
1982	Aragón, Canaries, Castilla-La Mancha, La Rioja, Murcia, Navarre, Valencian Community	
1983	Balearics, Castilla-León, Extremadura, Madrid	
	First wave of revision of statutes	
1991		Asturias, Cantabria, Castilla-La Mancha, Extremadura, Madrid, Murcia, Valencian Community
1994		Aragón, Asturias, Balearics, Cantabria, Castilla-La-Mancha, Extemadura, Castilla-Leon, Extremadura, La Rioja, Madrid, Murcia, Valencian Community
	Statutes for enclaves in northern Africa	
1995	Ceuta, Melilla	
	Second wave of revision of statutes	
1996		Aragón, Canaries
1997		Canaries, Castilla-La-Mancha, Galicia
1998		Cantabria, Madrid, Murcia
1999		Asturias, Balearics, Castilla-León, Extremadura
2001		Navarre
2002		Andalusia, Canaries, Galicia
	Third wave of revision of statutes	
2006		Catalonia, Valencian Community
2007		Andalusia, Aragón, Balearics, Castille-León

other autonomous communities with lesser powers (Hildenbrand, 1998: 106–8). The LOAPA was rejected by the autonomous communities. They submitted a complaint on constitutional grounds to the Constitutional Court (*Tribunal Constitucional*). The Constitutional Court supported partly the position of the autonomous communities which allowed for a more flexible interpretation of both Articles 143 and 151.

The 1980s have to be regarded as a decade of building the structures of the new autonomous communities and their relationship with the national and local government. One of the most important aspects of this institution-building process was the establishment of intergovernmental mechanisms to deal with power conflicts and public policy implementation. In this phase of uncertainty, the Constitutional Court was overwhelmed with complaints coming from the autonomous communities against the central state due to power disputes on unconstitutionality grounds. The climax of this intense activity of the autonomous communities was between 1982 and 1989.

The dynamics of regionalisation reached new levels in the 1990s, when many of the autonomous communities – Asturias, Cantabria, La Rioja, Murcia, the Valencian Community, Aragon, Castilla La Mancha, the Canary Islands, Extremadura, the Balearics, the Community of Madrid, Castilla León – began to reform and upgrade their statute of autonomy. In 1992, the two main parties, the PSOE and the PP, came to a new autonomies agreement (*acuerdos autonómicos*) in order to create a level-playing field in terms of powers for all autonomous communities. This levelling out of powers across the autonomous communities has been going on throughout the 1990s. The last two major powers to be transferred to the autonomous communities were education and health. Indeed, the latter was completed by the PP and PSOE governments in the new millennium. In November 1994, a further agreement between the main parties allowed for greater participation by the autonomous communities in both policy decision-making and policy-implementation processes. The new position of an autonomous communities adviser (*consejero*) was created at the Spanish permanent representation in Brussels. This was still quite distant from calls by the autonomous governments to allow for participation of autonomous community representatives in the Council of European Union as was granted to the German Länder and to the Belgian regions. However, after 19 years of demands in the meeting of 9 December 2004 an agreement was signed between the central government and the autonomous communities, which ensures that representatives of the regions can take part in four formations out of nine of the Council of Ministers of the European Union. These formations are environment, agriculture and rural development, cohesion and social policy, youth and consumers' rights. Each autonomous community representative takes part according to a rotation system. Harmonisation mechanisms were created to coordinate positions between the government and the autonomous regions (Morata, 2007: 307).

The present discussion of the decentralisation process is no longer about outstanding powers. The disputes between regional governments and the central government over powers declined completely in the 1990s. The present issue is about the open-ended nature of the process. As already mentioned in Chapter 3, there are three different views of how to finalise the whole devolution process.

For the PP the full implementation of the autonomous agreements is also the end of the devolution process. It wants to keep the constitution unchanged, because constitutional change may lead either to the end of consensus democracy that the constitution has provided for and/or change to Chapter 8 of the constitution may acquire dynamics of its own and affect other parts of the constitution. For the PSOE and the IU a constitutional change to fully fledged federalism has been part of the agenda since the 1990s. This means that the present highly unstable situation would become enshrined in a revised constitution. Last but not least, Catalans, Basques and Galicians are demanding recognition of their national status within the Spanish constitution. They demand that Spain should be declared a plurinational country with four nations: the Basque Country, Galicia, Catalonia and the rest of Spain. They are willing to reform their autonomy statutes despite some resistance from the government. The third wave of revision of statutes has highlighted the importance of this formula for most of the autonomous communities, particularly Catalonia, Galicia, Andalusia and the Basque Country. A compromise formula has been so far that all these autonomous communities can call themselves as nationalities within the Spanish nation. However, future revisions of the statutes may lead to definition of Spain as plurinational (Nagel and Requejo, 2007: 289–90).

Moreover, the Basque regional president, the so-called *lehendekari*, Juan José Ibarretxe, is willing to push forward the independence agenda by developing the concept of association as an intermediary form of relationship with the Spanish state, before full independence. This has been clearly rejected by both the PP as well as the PSOE as being against the Spanish constitution. Juan José Ibarretxe has presented a new slightly revised plan at end of September 2007, but the main political parties the PSOE and the PP have rejected it as being unconstitutional. Due to this intransigence position of Ibarretxe, the Basque Country remains the only autonomous community, which has not revised its statute, due to the lack of support in the national parliament. This is creating tensions in Ibarretxe's party, the Basque nationalist party, because the more moderate pragmatic factions want to achieve a revision of the statute within the constitutional boundaries. The successful negotiation of an enhanced Catalan Statute became an important model for parts of the PNV (*El Pais*, 1 October 2007: 18).

Although the Aznar government period has to be regarded as one of devolution to the autonomous communities, the Zapatero government introduced quite an ambitious agenda in the policy towards the autonomous communities. Among the achievements of the Zapatero government was probably the successful negotiation of the Catalan Statute within the constitutional framework in spite of opposition from the People's Party. Moreover, it was able to achieve a smooth revision of the Valencian Community statute and to initiate the processes of revision of the Galician, Aragonese and Andalusian statutes. One important innovative structure, which is emulating similar structures in federal countries such as Switzerland, Austria and Germany, is the regular conference of presidents initiated in November 2004, which brings together Prime Minister José Luis Zapatero with the seventeen regional presidents. Moreover, the role of the autonomous communities in shaping the European integration process has been enhanced through participation of the regions in the Council of Ministers. A growing complex network of intergovernmental relations between central government and the autonomous communities has emerged and is becoming similar to what we are accustomed to in Switzerland, Austria and Germany.

The institutionalisation of intergovernmental relations between the central government and the regions

We can differentiate at least three phases in the development of intergovernmental relations in Spain. The first phase ran from 1981 to 1991 and established the first structures of intergovernmental relations. The main legal framework was the Law for the Harmonisation of the Autonomous Process (*Ley Organica para la Armonización del Proceso Autonómico* – LOAPA) adopted in 1983. It gave a basic framework for intergovernmental relations. The second phase started in 1992 after the two main parties signed the agreements on the autonomous communities on 28 February of the same year. This led to the Legal Framework for the Public Administrations and the Common Administrative Process (*Regimen Juridico para las Administraciones Publicas y el Proceso Administrativo Comun* – RJAPPAC). The third phase began in 1999, after the Legal Framework for Public Administrations and the Common Administrative Process was revised to adjust to the growing complexity of the system of intergovernmental relations (Gonzalez Gomez, 2006: 99–100).

There was clearly a period of considerable instability in the relations between the government and the autonomous communities which allowed for the emergence of a system of intergovernmental sectorial conferences (*conferencias sectoriales*) related to all policy areas. The first sectorial conference was established in 1982 between the finance ministry and the corresponding counterparts in the autonomous communities. The Council for Fiscal and Financial Policy of the Autonomous Communities (*Consejo de Politica Fiscal y Financiera de las CCAA*), which deals mainly with the process of distributing budgetary powers among the regions as well as allocation of funding, was somewhat hyperactive up until 1992, but thereafter its activity decreased considerably. In the past 25 years, these sectorial conferences became important fora of institutional courtesy, used foremost for information exchange or policy coordination between the different levels of government. In spite of their diminished position as mere administrative structures, they are relevant to keep the state of autonomies together (Maiz, Beramendi and Grau, 2002: 395–401). A general assessment of the ability of the regional governments to affect policy-making and formulation seems to suggest that they are subordinate to the will of the minister of the respective central government ministries. In some cases, ministers are heavily engaged in a dialogue with the regions. In others, ministers tend to regard intergovernmental sectorial conferences as of low priority (Agranoff and Ramos Gallarin, 1998; Bañon and Tamayo, 1998; Saracibar, 2002: 30–2).

Naturally, certain areas such as health, education and finance display a high level of activity, while others less so. The CCAA is quite asymmetrical in its efficiency. In some areas, it gives the impression of meeting regularly (meaning twice or more a year), in other cases meetings take place less than once a year. One factor that seems to affect the role of the sectorial conference considerably is what Tanja Börzel called the Europeanisation of the Spanish political system and policy process since 1986. The sectorial conferences are quite important decentralisation and coordination structures, so that public policy implementation can be made more efficient. The more important sectorial conferences are related to policies that the European Union, in particular the European Commission, is monitoring more closely. While agriculture, finance, health and education as well as European affairs are important, labour and social affairs, fisheries and the environment have been less salient in terms of meetings (Börzel, 2000: 27–31; Maiz *et al.*, 2002: 399 400). This process of Europeanisation in the second half of the 1980s led to a growing demand from the regions to be integrated into the European policy-making process. This formalised network of intergovernmental relations comprise of three levels. The highest ministerial level are the twenty-nine sectorial conferences (2005). About sixty meetings take place every year, in which more general issues are decided. At a second level there are forty-five sectorial committees (*comisiones sectoriales*), which consist of directors-general and tend to deal with more specialised issues. About 150 meetings take place at this level. At third level are the technical working groups (*grupos de trabajo*) and subcommittees (*ponencias*). According to the 2005 report on the sectorial conferences, it is impossible to quantify the number of meetings at this level due to the fact that many of these meetings are informal and non-institutionalised (Ministerio de Administraciones Publicas, 2007a: 4).

In 1988, the sectorial conference of European Affairs (*Conferencia para Asuntos Relacionados con la Comunidad Europea* – CARCE) was established: this really became the most important coordinating conference. The number of sectorial areas has been growing steadily since 1982. In 1982 there was only one sectorial area. By 1989 the number had increased to seventeen, reaching twenty-four in 1995. In 2003, there were fifty-five sectorial areas with first and second-level sectorial conferences and in 2005, this had increased to twenty-nine sectorial conferences and forty-five sectorial committees, totalling seventy first- and second-level meetings (Ministerio de Administraciones Publicas, 2007a: 3–4). This shows the high level of complexity that the relationship between the central and the regional governments is acquiring. (see Figure 5.2 and Figure 5.3) Among the areas that are dealt with witnin the sectorial conference are the following:

- Information about forthcoming legislation initiated by the central government which the autonomous communities will have to implement when approved. There is a possibility to consult the autonomous communities about the proposed legislation. For example, the Draft Bill on Education (Sectorial Conference on Education).
- Information to the autonomous communities by the central government on proposed legislation by the European Union. It serves also to consult the autonomous communities about it.
- Debate about co-financing of budgetary actions established by the budget, such as subsidies decided by the government.
- Adoption of common plans and programmes which have a common objective, For example, restructuring of the milk sector (sectorial conference for agriculture), or revision of the plan for research and development (sectorial conference for science and technology).
- Information about policy activities of the central government, but that may affect interests of the autonomous communities, for example, the strategic plan for infrastructure and transport(sectorial conference infrastructures and territorial planning) (Ministerio de Administraciones Publicas, 2007a: 5–11).

Although the sectorial conferences are the most important instrument of coordination between the central government and the periphery, one has also to mention other important instruments that contribute to homogeneisation and integration of policy-making across the country.

The Bilateral Committees of Cooperation (*Comisiones Bilaterales de Cooperación* – CBC) are probably the most important after the sectorial conferences. They contribute to a homogeneisation of policy-making across Spain. There are nineteen CBCs, seventeen with the autonomous communities and two with the cities of Ceuta and Melilla. Most of the issues discussed are related to transfer of powers from the centre to the autonomous communities. Between 1984 and 2004, there were 109 meetings. However, the distribution is quite asymmetrical between autonomous communities. For example, there were twenty-six meetings between the central government and Navarre of which seventeen of these meetings were during the Aznar governments between 1996 and 2004. In contrast, Castilla-León, Extremadura, Ceuta, Madrid and the Valencian Community had only one meeting (Ramos Gallarin, 2006: 124). Among the most important topics discussed were public administrative issues (25.7 per cent), economy and finance (14.3 per cent) and immigration (11.4 per cent). Almost half of all meetings deal with disagreements about legislation (45.7 per cent) (Ramos Gallarin, 2006: 128). In contrast to the sectorial conferences, there is a lower level of intensity and continuity of meetings within the framework of CBCs. The highest level of continuity and intensity can be found in the relationship between the central government and the ultraperipheral archipelago of the Canaries (Ramos Gallarin, 2006: 126). Meetings have increased in the past 15 years due to the growing problem of illegal immigration coming from the African coast.

A further important instrument of coordination and cooperation between the central government and the autonomous communities are the common plans and programmes (*Planes y programas communes*). They are instruments of multilateral cooperation. According to Alda Mercedes, between 1997 and 2003 most of these plans and programmes were in the policy areas of labour and social affairs (53.5 per cent) economy, finance, industry and energy (18.2 per cent) and environment (18 per cent) (Mercedes Fernandez, 2006: 140). After 1999, there has been a growing takeover of the common plans and programmes by the sectorial conferences. Moreover, their number per year has been diminishing if compared with the period 1989–95 (Mercedes and Fernandez, 2006: 138–9).

Another important instrument are the agreements of cooperation(*Convenios de Colaboración*) which in May 2007 reached the figure of 10,098. On average, 600 cooperation and 300 development agreements are signed every year (Ministerio de Administraciones Publicas, 2007b: 3; see Figure 5.4.). Between 1984 and 2006, 28.5 per cent of all cooperation agreements were related to labour and social affairs,13.9 per cent to education and science, 10.1 per cent to agriculture, fisheries and food, 9 per cent to industry, tourism and trade and 8.3 per cent to health and consumption (Ministerio de Administraciones Publicas, 2006). In an excellent study on the cooperation agreements, Lourdes Lopez Nieto found out that in 2002 that there are different relationships in terms of financing the agreements.

In her study, in the overall costs of €5.5 billion the central government financed 65 per cent and the autonomous communities 29 per cent of autonomous communities. The rest is split between the local authorities, the European Union and the private sector (Lopez-Nieto, 2006: 166–7) (see Figure 5.4 and Figure 5.4).

The reform of the upper chamber of parliament, the Senate, is one of the major issues that has to be addressed in an eventual constitutional reform. Until now, the promised reform of the Senate in 1994 has come to a halt. There are different views about how the Senate should be reformed, but the basic idea is to transform it into a territorial chamber, where the autonomous communities would be represented similar to the German Bundesrat or the Indian Council of the States. After a very enthusiastic phase between 1994 and 2000, the whole process came to a halt, because the PP government had clearly shifted the agenda (Roller, 2002b). Although the Zapatero government wanted to reform the Senate through a minimalist revision of the Constitution. However, the intransigent position of PP during the eighth legislature period blocked this intention (Chapter 3). The General Committee of Autonomous Communities in the Senate has gained some more profile in 2004 and 2005. A debate of the autonomous communities took place in 2004 and 2005 and the Zapatero government was quite engaged in this process as part of their overall project of renewal of Spanish politics. However, after February 2005 the government reduced its presence in the General Committee of Autonomous Communities. According to *El Pais*, 22 requests for debates were not responded about the government between February 2005 and September 2007. Most of these requests came from the People's Party and certainly used for party political gain. However, it certainly showed that the initial thrust of the PSOE to restructure the relations between centre and periphery had reached a low point during this period (*El Pais*, 23 September 2007: 24).

There was also the call for the establishment of a conference of the regional governments similar to Austria, which would allow for more horizontal concerted action among the autonomous communities. Some government promises were made in this respect. Finally, the Zapatero government introduced the first conference of presidents (*Conferencia de presidentes*) on 28 October 2004. Meanwhile further conferences took place in 2005 and early 2007. While both the conferences of 2004 and 2005 have to be regarded as a success, the meeting of 11 January 2007 was used by PP to start a bipolarisation strategy towards the regional and local elections on 27 May 2007. It was also overshadowed by the bombing of a car park by the Basque terrorist organisation at the end of December. Therefore, it ended in failure due to the intransigence of the PP to sign any agreements (*El Pais*, 24 October 2004: 20, 22; *El Pais*, 2 October 2007: 29) (see Table 5.3).

The transfer of powers from central government to the autonomous communities

As already mentioned in Chapter 3, such processes of decentralisation and reorganisation of policy-making and implementation have been accompanied by a decentralisation of the civil service and naturally of financial resources.

Table 5.3 Conferences of presidents, 2004–2007

Conference	Day	Place	Topics discussed
First conference	28 October 2004	Madrid, Senate	• Institutionalisation of the conference • Participation of autonomous communities in EU Council until end of the year
Second conference	10 September 2005	Barcelona	• Financing of health systems • Increase of financing of health systems by €1.6 billion
Third conference	11 January 2007	Madrid, Senate	• Hijacked by PP-dominated regional government to issue a declaration against terrorism • Agreements on immigration and water were not accepted by PP-dominated governments

Source: *El Pais*, 2 October 2007: 29.

In the past 25 years, the central government has transferred 1,888 powers to the autonomous communities. The whole process is more or less coming to an end. Health and education were transferred to all autonomous communities and this was also followed by a more generous re-negotiated financial settlement. It seems that these transfers in 2002 caused some problems of adjustment for the autonomous communities. Nevertheless, the whole process has strengthened the position of the autonomous communities vis-á-vis the central government (*El Pais*, 17 February 2002: 24). In the 2005 conference of presidents, Zapatero government announced a further financial increase of €1.6 billions to manage the decentralised health systems (*El Pais*, 2 October 2007: 29). One can recognise at least two main waves of transfer of powers. As Figure 5.6 shows the first wave was during the late phase of the UCD governments under Adolfo Suarez and Leopoldo Calvo Sotelo and reached its climax in the mid-1980s during the first absolute majority governments of the socialist government of Felipe Gonzalez. The wave ended in 1988 and for a couple of years the number of transfer of powers was negligible. The second wave took off after the 1992 agreements on the autonomous communities between the two main parties and reached its climax in the late phase of the last Socialist minority government under Felipe Gonzalez. This second wave continued well into the two Aznar governments, but the numbers of transfers of powers continued to decline with the exception of 1999. In the new millennium, the last transfer of powers has been undertaken, affecting mainly the health sector. Transfer of powers during the Zapatero government period has been so far negligible (see also Figure 5.7).

As already mentioned in Chapter 3, in early 2007, 50.2 per cent of all civil servants were employed in the administrations of the autonomous communities, comprising more than 1 million persons. In 1990, this figure was 25 per cent. The increase of powers and civil servants has been difficult to absorb. In some

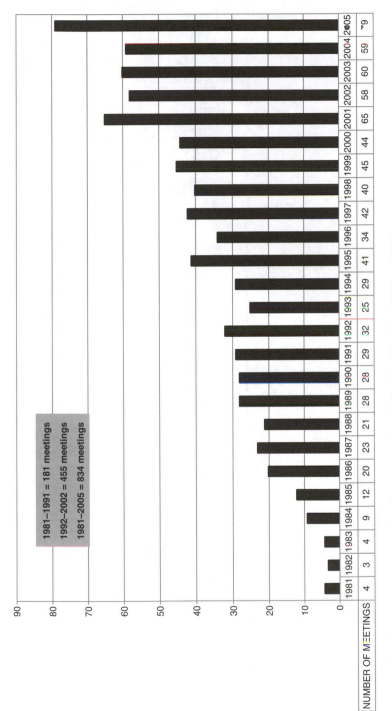

NUMBER OF MEETINGS	4	3	4	9	12	20	23	21	28	28	29	32	25	29	41	34	42	40	45	44	65	58	60	59	79
	1981	1982	1983	1984	1985	1986	1987	1988	1989	1990	1991	1992	1993	1994	1995	1996	1997	1998	1999	2000	2001	2002	2003	2004	2005

1981–1991 = 181 meetings

1992–2002 = 455 meetings

1981–2005 = 834 meetings

Figure 5.2 The development of sectorial conferences meetings (at first level) between 1981 and 2005.

Source: Own graph based on data from Ministério de Administraciones Publicas, 2007a: 19.

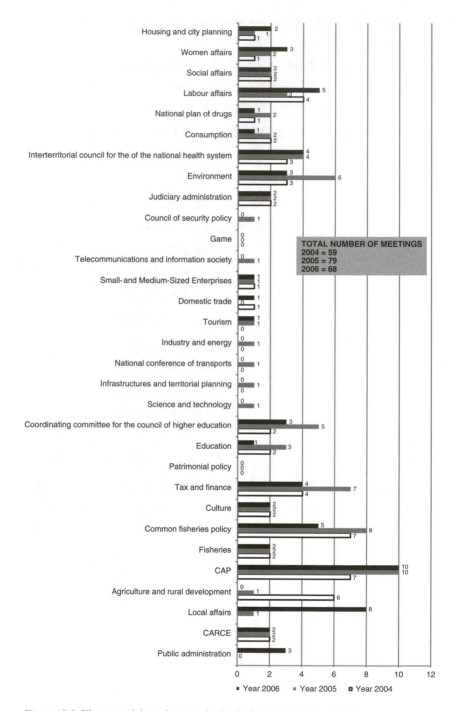

Figure 5.3 The sectorial conferences in Spain, in 2004, 2005 and 2006.

Source: own graph based on data from Ministério de Administraciones Publicas, 2007a: 18.

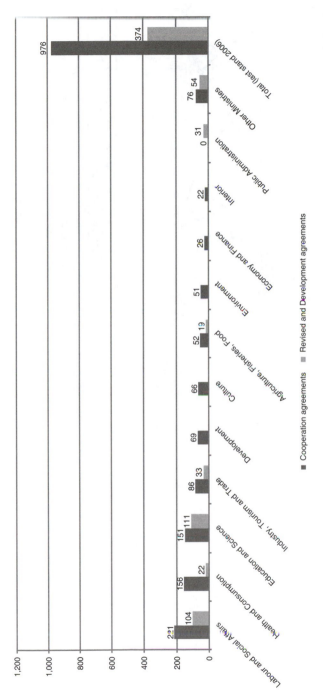

Figure 5.4 Cooperation agreements (*Convenios de Colaboracion/Desarollo*) between autonomous communities and central government in 2005.

Source: Ministerio of Administraciones Publicas, 2007b: 6–7.

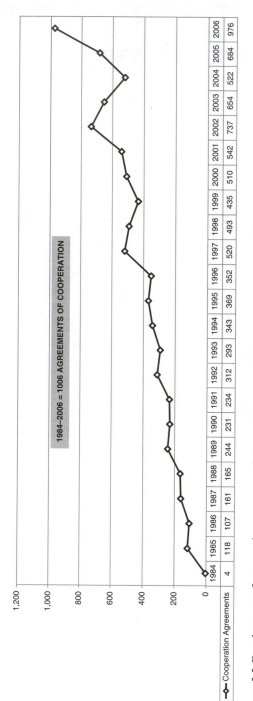

Cooperation Agreements	1984	1985	1986	1987	1988	1989	1990	1991	1992	1993	1994	1995	1996	1997	1998	1999	2000	2001	2002	2003	2004	2005	2006
	4	118	107	161	165	244	231	234	312	293	343	369	352	520	493	435	510	542	737	654	522	684	976

1984–2006 = 1006 AGREEMENTS OF COOPERATION

Figure 5.5 Development of cooperation agreements between the state and the autonomous communities, 1984–2006.

Source: Ministerio de Administraciones Publicas, 2007b: 6.

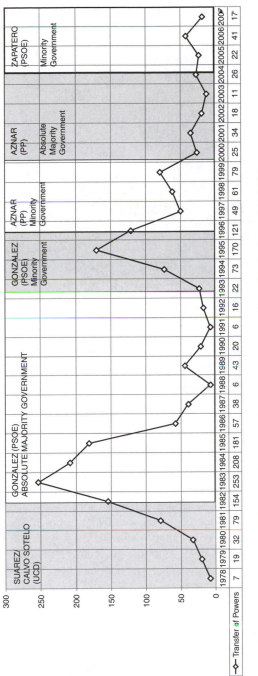

	1978	1979	1980	1981	1982	1983	1984	1985	1986	1987	1988	1989	1990	1991	1992	1993	1994	1995	1996	1997	1998	1999	2000	2001	2002	2003	2004	2005	2006	2007
Transfer of Powers	7	19	32	79	154	253	208	181	57	38	6	43	20	6	16	22	73	170	121	49	61	79	25	34	18	11	26	22	41	17

Figure 5.6 Development of transfer of powers from central government to the regions (1978–September 2007).

Source: Ministério de Administraciones Publicas, 2007c, last accessed on 14 September 2007.

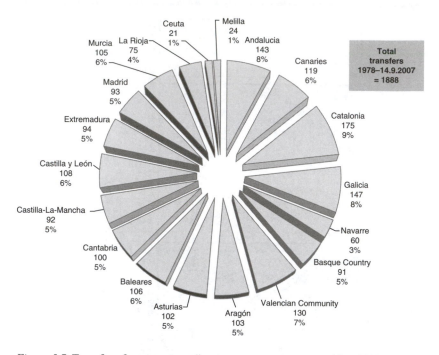

Figure 5.7 Transfer of powers according to autonomous communities, 1978–2007.
Source: Ministerio de Administraciones Publicas, 2007c, 14 September 2007.

autonomous communities, the process of adjustment is still going on (see Figure 3.10).

While the transfer of competences has been achieved over the past three decades – education and health being the last ones – financially there is still a long way to go. Spain fares well in relation to other countries such as Belgium, but still lags behind Germany and Switzerland in terms of decentralisation of public expenditure (Cicuendez Santamaria and Ramos Gallarin, 2006: 197–8).

In terms of financial transactions the central government has been steadily increasing transfers to the autonomous communities in view of an incremental transfer of powers. Indeed, since 1985 the government has been increasing the income tax contribution of the autonomous communities. There was an increase from 15 per cent to 30 per cent in the 1990s. It is expected that it will rise to 50 per cent in the next few years. In 1979, only 0.1 per cent was spent by the autonomous communities and 91 per cent was controlled by the central government. The rest was allocated to local government authorities. In 1989, the share of the autonomous communities rose to 13.2 per cent (Agranoff and Ramos Gallarin, 1998: 78). In 2002, the figure reached the 30 per cent threshold. The former PP government wanted to achieve a formula of approximately 40 per cent of public expenditure would be distributed by central government, 40 per cent by autonomous communities and 20 per cent by local government authorities in 2004 (*El Mundo*, 15 May 2001: 15).

The whole process of financing of the autonomous regions is coordinated by Council of Fiscal and Finance Policy (*Consejo de Politica Fiscal e Financiera –* CPFF). This is the highest intergovernmental coordinating unit and is enshrined in the Law of Financing of the Autonomous Communities (*Ley Organica de Financiación de las Comunidades Autonomas –* LOFCA). Several specialised working groups are attached to this highly institutionalised structure in which many decisions are taken before the budget is drawn. These informal structures are quite relevant, because until now the Senate was not able to take over the role of a territorial chamber. The continuing 'impossible mission' of reform (Roller, 2002b) has allowed the development of a huge network of structures dealing with financial issues between the central governments and the autonomous communities. Apart from this multilateral framework institution, in which decisions are taken by a two-thirds majority in the first round and an absolute majority in the second round, there are also bilateral joint committees between the central government and each of the autonomous communities. Moreover, each autonomous community has more specialised Joint Committee of Coordination of Fiscal Management (*Comisión Mixta de Coordinación para la Gestión Tributaria –*) and further specialised structures. However, the special budgetary rights of Navarre and the Basque Country have led to deviating more complex structures in relation to all other autonomous communities (Cicuendez Santamaria and Ramos Gallarin, 2006: 182).

The financing of the autonomous communities consists of different parts. The autonomous communities can recur to own resources based on taxes and other income, although they are very limited and did not represent more than 7 per cent. Furthermore, it can recur to credit and other sources. Most of the resources are the unconditional and conditional block grants of the central government. While the unconditional block grants allow the autonomous communities to spend as they see fit with certain minor limitations, the conditional grants are related to specific services or purposes that the autonomous communities have to provide for its citizens. The block grant for health and education are such conditional grants. One can also include the Interterritorial Compensation Fund as being a conditional grant which is linked to investment in the particular autonomous community. Navarre and the Basque Community have historical special rights (*fueros*) in budgetary policy and can therefore control their own fiscal policies. As we can see from Figure 5.8, the most important source of income are the conditional and unconditional central governments grants which make up almost 90 per cent of the budget of the autonomous communities (Cicuendez Santamaria and Ramos Gallarin, 2006: 190–2) (see also Figure 5.9 and Figure 5.10).

In spite of these transfers, there are major economic and social disparities between the autonomous communities. Therefore, the central government established the already-mentioned Interterritorial Compensation Fund (*Fondo de Compensación Inter-territorial –* FCI). The FCI makes annual transfers to the poorest regions. The Basque Country, Catalonia, Madrid and the Balearics are not

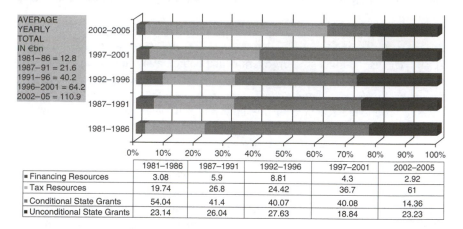

AVERAGE YEARLY TOTAL IN €bn
1981–86 = 12.8
1987–91 = 21.6
1991–96 = 40.2
1996–2001 = 64.2
2002–05 = 110.9

	1981–1986	1987–1991	1992–1996	1997–2001	2002–2005
■ Financing Resources	3.08	5.9	8.81	4.3	2.92
▨ Tax Resources	19.74	26.8	24.42	36.7	61
■ Conditional State Grants	54.04	41.4	40.07	40.08	14.36
■ Unconditional State Grants	23.14	26.04	27.63	18.84	23.23

Figure 5.8 Sources of finance of the autonomous communities, 1981–2001.

Source: Circuendez Santamaria and Ramos Gallarin, 2006: 191, for the transitional period 1981–86; own calculations from BADESPE, Database on economic facts of the Spanish Public Sector, compiled by Institute of Fiscal Studies of the Spanish Ministry of the Economy, website: http://www.estadief. meh.es/ accessed on 6 August 2008.

eligible for funding due to the fact that they have a higher GDP per capita than the Spanish average. There is a major development and income divide in Spain. Indeed, there are eight regions above the Spanish average in terms of GDP per capita. Their unemployment rates are, with exception of the Basque Country, lower than the other nine regions and Ceuta and Melilla. Basically, there is a growing south-west/north-east divide going through Madrid (see Figure 5.9).

If we look more closely, there are two subgroups within the regions with a GDP per capita below the Spanish average. On one hand, there are the southern regions of Andalusia and Extremadura, Castilla La Mancha and Murcia and the northern regions of Galicia and Asturias which have a GDP per capita below 90 per cent of the Spanish average and high figures of unemployment. On the other hand, there is a group close to the Spanish average comprising Castilla León, the Canary Islands and Cantabria (see Table 5.4 and Figure 5.11). In this sense, there are still certain disparities of economic and social development in Spain, which central government tries to moderate by reallocating additional funds to the poorest regions through the FCI. In Figure 5.14 one can see clearly that Extremadura and Galicia are eligible for most of the funding from the FCI. This inter-regional solidarity has been a strong foundation of the Spanish state of autonomies. In spite of the financial distribution, the autonomous communities of Extremadura, Andalusia and Galicia are trailing behind most of the other regions. One of the major problems is the fact that all these three regions have large agricultural sectors which lead to seasonal unemployment. Moreover, the industrial base and services industries are weaker than in the north-eastern regions. However, the annual amount available for the FCI has been decreasing over the years as a share of all grants and resources.

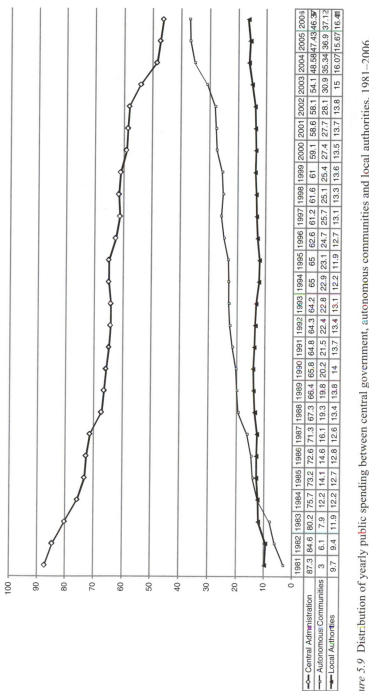

	1981	1982	1983	1984	1985	1986	1987	1988	1989	1990	1991	1992	1993	1994	1995	1996	1997	1998	1999	2000	2001	2002	2003	2004	2005	2006
Central Administration	87.3	84.6	80.2	75.7	73.2	72.6	71.3	67.3	66.4	65.8	64.8	64.3	64.2	65	65	62.6	61.2	61.6	61	59.1	58.6	58.1	54.1	48.58	47.43	46.37
Autonomous Communities	3	6.1	7.9	12.2	14.1	14.6	16.1	19.3	19.8	20.2	21.5	22.4	22.8	22.9	23.1	24.7	25.7	25.1	25.4	27.4	27.7	28.1	30.9	35.34	36.9	37.12
Local Authorities	9.7	9.4	11.9	12.2	12.7	12.8	12.6	13.4	13.8	14	13.7	13.4	13.1	12.2	11.9	12.7	13.1	13.3	13.6	13.5	13.7	13.8	15	16.07	15.67	16.4

Figure 5.9 Distribution of yearly public spending between central government, autonomous communities and local authorities, 1981–2006.

Source: : Ministerio de Administraciones Publicas, Informe Economico-Financiero de las Administraciones Territoriales 2006 posted on website http://www.map.es/documentacion/politica_autonomica/info_ecofin/2anaeco/iefaatt.html accessed on 6 August 2008.

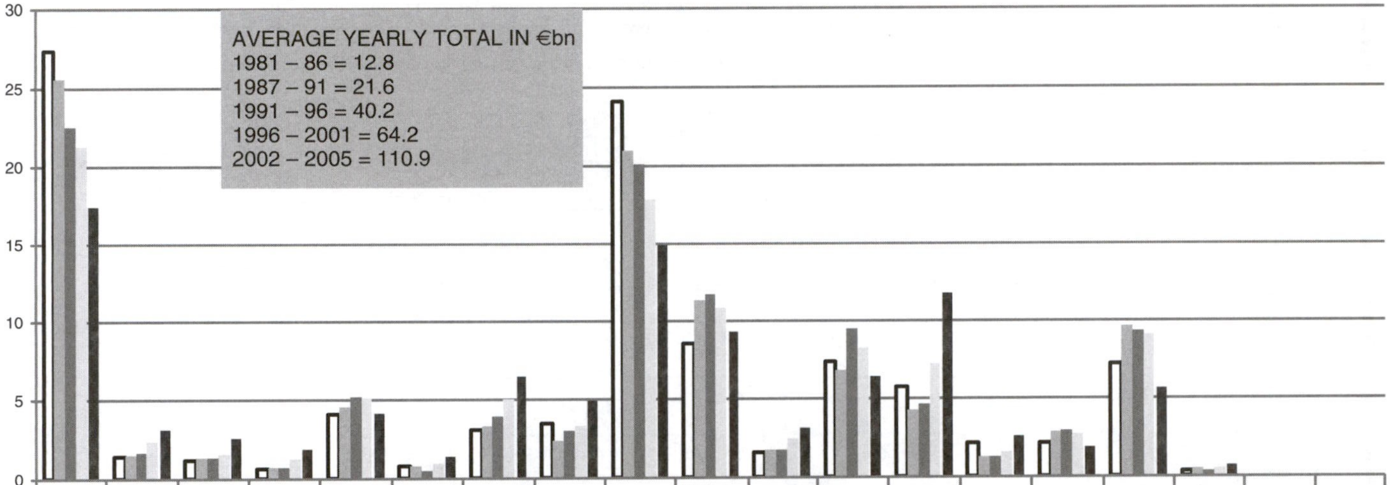

Figure 5.10 Development of distribution of funding according to autonomous communities, 1981–2005.

Source: Cicuendez, 2006: 194 for the transitional period 1981–86; own calculations from BADESPE, Database on economic facts of the Spanish Public Sector, compiled by Institute of Fiscal Studies of the Spanish Ministry of the Economy, website: http://www.estadief.meh.es/ accessed on 6 August 2008

AVERAGE YEARLY TOTAL IN €bn
1981 – 86 = 12.8
1987 – 91 = 21.6
1991 – 96 = 40.2
1996 – 2001 = 64.2
2002 – 2005 = 110.9

	Andalucia	Aragón	Asturias	Balearics	Canary Islands	Cantabria	Castilla y León	Castilla La Mancha	Catalonia	Valencian Community	Extremadura	Galicia	Madrid	Murcia	Navarre	Basque Country	Rioja	Ceuta	Melilla
1981–86	27.38	1.41	1.21	0.64	4.05	0.78	3.08	3.48	24.14	8.55	1.59	7.33	5.72	2.14	2.14	7.19	0.33		
1987–1991	25.6	1.49	1.3	0.73	4.54	0.76	3.3	2.33	21	11.33	1.7	6.85	4.23	1.24	2.84	9.6	0.49		
1992–1996	22.57	1.7	1.36	0.69	5.15	0.48	3.92	3.01	20.1	11.8	1.74	9.48	4.64	1.3	2.89	9.3	0.35	0.02	0.02
1997–2001	21.32	2.35	1.6	1.31	5.07	0.97	5.02	3.34	17.9	10.9	2.43	8.2	7.2	1.6	2.66	9.1	0.51	0.02	0.02
2002–05	17.57	3.22	2.68	1.98	4.22	1.48	6.6	5	15.02	9.37	3.2	6.5	11.87	2.7	1.96	5.7	0.75	0.05	0.038

Table 5.4 GDP per capita (National and EU15 average) and unemployment according to autonomous communities, 2005

Autonomous communities (CCAAS)	GDP per capita in purchasing power parity in 2005 Spain = 100	EU convergence index 2005 EU 15 = 100	Unemployment Spain = 8.3 % in 2006
CCAAs with GDP above Spanish and EU = 15 convergence index			
Community of Madrid	130.97	126.37	6.5
Basque Country	126.53	120.87	6.7
Navarre	126.17	121.69	4.6
Catalonia	118.75	110.76	6.7
Balearics	111.63	105.15	6.2
La Rioja	107.01	104.94	7
Aragón	106.78	109.13	5
CCAAs with GDP below Spanish and EU = 15 convergence index			
Cantabria	98.11	99.24	6
Castilla y León	94.56	99.46	7.5
Valencian Community	91.85	88.9	8.5
Ceuta	91.08	96.36	12
Canary Islands	90.82	94.57	11.5
Melilla	89.85	95.93	12
Asturias	88.23	80.06	9.2
Murcia	83.56	81.92	7.9
Galicia	81.36	83.26	8.1
Castilla La Mancha	78.36	84.23	8
Andalucia	77.63	77.5	12.2
Extremadura	67.6	77.07	12.9

Source: *Anuario El Pais*, 2007: 310–11, 319.

While in 1986 it was 7.6 per cent, by 2001 it was just over 1.1 per cent of total resources (see Figures 5.13. and 5.14.). In sum, it is difficult to change this stagnant position in relation to the centres of dynamic economies (Barcelona and Madrid), in spite of many attempts such as the Expo 92 in Seville, which was designed to attract investment towards this peripheral region.

The inter-territorial solidarity has also to take into account the financial necessities of the wealthier regions, due to the fact that they contribute over proportionally to the GDP. This is the reason why during the negotiations of the Catalan Statute the central government agreed to increase the package of investments in Catalonia to the level of Andalusia. Such a move has been controversial, but in the long term it was necessary to keep the political cohesion of the country. For the past three decades, Catalonia had been contributing more to the GDP than receiving in terms of state grants and investments, creating therefore a major deficit in this respect. The renegotiated settlement was a recognition of this fact and only partly covered this deficit (Nagel and Requejo, 2007: 285–6) (see Figure 5.12). A new financing agreement between the central government and the autonomous communities is being drafted during the Zapatero government, which may rebalance some of these deficits. Depending on how you measure the fiscal

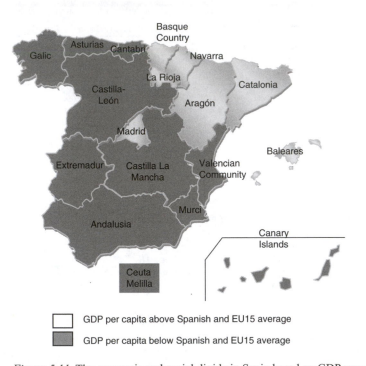

GDP per capita above Spanish and EU15 average

GDP per capita below Spanish and EU15 average

Figure 5.11 The economic and social divide in Spain based on GDP per capita 2005.

Source: Own graph and calculations based on figures from the Spanish National Institute of Statistics (INE) quoted in Anuario *El Pais* 2007: 319.

deficit between autonomous communities, Catalonia and the Balearics are the two regions which pay more than they receive from the central government. The Community of Madrid, the Community of Valencia and Navarre are also among the net payers. Depending on the methodology, the Basque Country, Aragón and La Rioja may also be net payers. In contrast, the largest net receivers are Extremadura, the enclaves of Ceuta and Melilla, Asturias, Andalucia and Galicia. All the others, depending on the methodology, are net receivers to a lesser extent than those previously mentioned (Espasa, 2005: 245–6).

In sum, the Spanish state of autonomies clearly has become model of territorial organisation. It is highly decentralised and with the ambition of going even further. This makes it necessary to look closely at the new regional political systems which emerged after 1979 in Spain.

The regional political systems

The regional political systems of the autonomous communities had no model of a political system apart from the national one. The consequence was a close imitation of the national political system by these regions. Although simplified and adjusted to the regional level, all seventeen autonomous communities have a

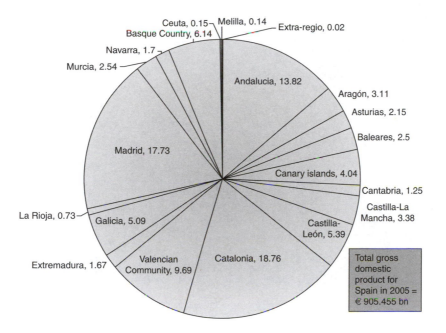

Figure 5.12 Share of gross domestic product in Spain according to autonomous communities 2005.

Source: Own graph based on data in *Anuario El Pais*, 2007: 319.

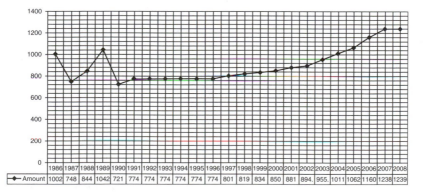

Figure 5.13 The development of the Inter-territorial Compensation Fund, 1986–2008.

Source: Ministerio de Administraciones Publicas, 2008 posted on website http://www.map.es/documentacion/politica_autonomica/info_ecofin/3inverpub/fci/fci_distrib.html accessed on 6 August 2008

regional government chaired by a president and a parliament. The electoral system is based on a proportional representation system which, tends to strengthen the two major parties of the corresponding political system. Each autonomous government is supported by a regional administration, which liaises and coordinates policies

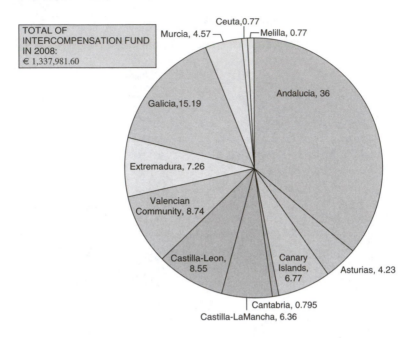

TOTAL OF
INTERCOMPENSATION FUND
IN 2008:
€ 1,337,981.60

Figure 5.14 Share of the Inter-territorial Compensation Fund by autonomous community
2008. (in thousand €).

Source: Ministerio de Administraciones Publicas, 2008: 8

with the central administration through a network of policy-makers. In this sense, the past two and a half decades have led to the institutionalisation and inter-relationships of eighteen (autonomous community systems and the national system) political systems. In the next few pages, a brief account is given of the working of the seventeen regional systems in comparative perspective. We will discuss the government, public administration and parliament before we come to an overall assessment.

Regional governments

The presidentialisation of the regional governments is one of the characteristics in which we can find parallels to the national system. The different regional presidents, particularly if they have been in power for a long time, such as Jordi Pujol in Catalonia between 1980 and 2003, Manuel Chaves in Andalusia and Manuel Fraga in Galicia between 1989 and 2005, play a major role in shaping the climate of politics in the particular region. Another factor affecting the position of the regional president is naturally the question of the region where he/she was able to get elected. Extremadura, Murcia or even the Valencian Community are not very prominent in the national news. The presidents of Catalonia, the Basque Country and Andalusia tend to be the dominant players among the different

Table 5.5 Types of government in the autonomous communities, 1979–2007

Autonomous communities	Single party absolute majority	Single party minority	Majority coalition	Minority coalition
Andalusia	4(PSOE)	1(PSOE)	2(PSOE+PA)	
Aragón		1(PSOE) 1(PAR)	1(PAR+PP) 1(PP+PAR) 2(PSOE+PAR)	
Asturias	2(PSOE)	3(PSOE) 1(PP)	1(PSOE+?)	
Balearics	2(PP)	1(PP)	2(PSOE+) 1(PP+)	1 (PP+) 1(PSOE+)
Basque Country		2(PNV)	1(PNV+PSOE) 1(PNV+EA+IU)	3(PNV+PSOE) 1(PNV+EA+IU)
Canaries	2(PP)	1(PSOE)	2(PSOE+AIC/CC) 1(PP+AIC/CC)	1(PP+AIC/CC)
Cantabria	1(PP)	1(PP)	2(PP+PRC) 1(UPC+) 1(PRC+PP)	1(PP+PRC)
Castilla La Mancha	7(PSOE)			
Castilla León	5(PP)	1(PSOE) 1(PP)		
Catalonia	2(CiU)	3(CiU)	1(CiU+ERC) 2(PSC+ERC+IC-V)	
Extremadura	6(PSOE)	1(PSOE)		
Galicia	4(PP)	2(PP)	1(PSOE+BNG)	
La Rioja	1(PS) 4(PP)	1(PP)	1(PS)	
Madrid	1(PSOE) 5(PP)	2(PSOE)		
Murcia	3(PSOE) 4(PP)			
Navarre		2(PSOE) 3(PP/UPN)	1(UPN+CDN) 1(UCD+PSOE+HB)	1 (PSOE+CDN+EA)
Valencian Community	2(PSOE) 3(PP)	1(PSOE)	1(PP+)	
TOTAL	58(47.5%)	29(23.8%)	26(21.3%)	9(7.3%)

Source: Calculations based on the detailed data of Revenga Sanchez and Sanchez Manzano, 2002: 330–31, Alda Fernandéz, and Lopéz Nieto, 2006: 64–66 and after the autonomous elections of 27 May 2007.

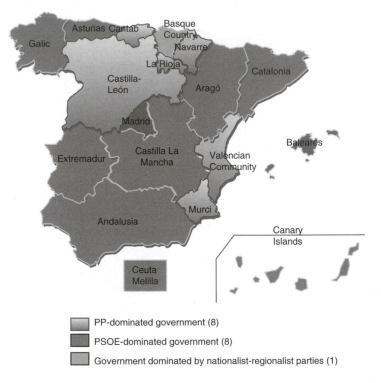

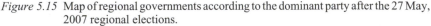

Figure 5.15 Map of regional governments according to the dominant party after the 27 May, 2007 regional elections.

Source: Own graph based after the regional elections of 27 May 2007.

regional autonomous governments. Most governments tend to follow the national pattern by creating single-party governments. Coalition government was and is quite rare. Most governments, if they do not achieve an absolute majority, may become minority governments with parliamentary support through a so-called pact of legislature, similar to what happened to the PSOE and the PP between 1993 and 1996 at national level. Indeed, a study of all ninety-four governments formed between 1979 and 2001 in all autonomous communities shows that an overwhelming 74.46 per cent were single-party homogenous governments and only 25.54 per cent were coalition governments. Similarly, 79.78 per cent of all these governments were majority or quasi-majority governments while only 20.21 per cent were minority governments (Revenga Sanchez and Sanchez Manzano, 2002: 328). However, after the 27 May 2007 elections the figure of single majority governments declined to 71.8 per cent, while coalition governments increased to 28.2 per cent. This shows that the main parties and the nationalist-regionalist parties are more flexible in their choices to form more stable governments. Among the best examples of a flexible cooperation can be mentioned the Canary Coalition which may coalesce either with PSOE or PP. The same can be said about the coalition between the Catalan Socialist Party (PSC), the regional branch of the PSOE, and the Catalan Republican Left (ERC) and IU, in spite of concerns coming from the central party office in Madrid. Another example is also the coalition between PSOE and the Galician Nationalist Block (BNG) after the defeat of the PP under former president Manuel Fraga Iribarne after the June elections of 2005. However, in some cases such as the intention of the Navarran branch of the PSOE to form a coalition with NA-Bai was blocked by the central office in Madrid. One of the main reasons was that NA-Bai is a coalition of parties which includes also the PNV and an eventual coalition would harm in the long term the electoral chances of the PSOE in the legislative elections of 9 March 2008.

The autonomous governments are dominated overwhelmingly by the two main national parties, the PSOE and the PP. Exceptions to this rule occur in the autonomous communities with strong regionalist parties such as Catalonia with the CiU and ERC, the Basque Country with the PNV and the Canary Islands with the Canary Coalition. However, the 2003 and 2005 regional elections in Catalonia allowed for the PSOE to become the senior partner in a coalition with ERC and IU. It means that after the 2007 May elections 16 regional governments are governed by one of the two main parties. Only the Basque Country has a nationalist-regionalist government consisting of PNV–EA and IU. In all other autonomous communities, the two main parties are dominant even if in some cases they have to form coalitions with some of the regionalist parties. The regional governments are much smaller than the national one, although some of them have grown substantially. On average, each government has seven to eight members, although the Basque Country, Catalonia, Extremadura and Castilla La Mancha are above this average. According to Adela Mesa del Olmo, the rapid incrementalism in the establishment of the new public administrations in the autonomous communities led to politicisation of the high levels of the public service. Indeed, both Catalonia and the Basque Country are in this respect regarded as highly politicised administrations (Mesa del Olmo, 2000: 211–35). As already mentioned in the previous chapter on political parties, the longevity of power of PNV in the Basque Country and CiU in the Catalonia until 2003 led to a high level of anonymous donations being channelled to these two parties. Although there are no studies indicating a direct relationship between anonymous donations and traffic of influences, it is suspected that some important donors may have gained special treating in the awarding of major contracts. However, these are only allegations and to date they have not been proved (*El Pais*, 18 April 2005: 17).

In terms of public administration it is clear that the autonomous communities with a greater number of powers also have a more stable and professionalised civil service, while the public administrations in the autonomous communities with a lower level of powers have to resort more often to temporary staff. Also there are more civil servants per person in the autonomous communities with greater powers than those with the lesser powers. The Basque Country, Navarre, Murcia, La Rioja, Galicia, Catalonia, the Balearics and Andalusia are among the autonomous communities with the higher level of professionalised civil servants, while Madrid, Andalusia, Asturias and the Canaries have a lower

Table 5.6 Government and administration of autonomous communities after 27 May 2007 regional elections

Autonomous community	Official name	President	No. of ministries – Consejerías	Number of civil servants (Jan. 2007)	Type of government 2007
Andalucia	Junta de Andalucia	Manuel Chavez Gonzalez	14	251,160	Absolute majority PSOE
Aragón	Diputación General	Marcelino Iglesias Ricou	11	39,277	Coalition PSOE-
Asturias	Principado de Asturias	Vicente Alberto Alvarez Areces	10	33,007	Coalition PSOE-IU
Balearics	Gobierno balear	Francesc Antich i Oliver	13	22,469	Coalition PSOE-UM
Basque Country	Gobierno vasco	Juan José Ibarretxe Markuartu	12	60,245	Coalition PNV-EA-IU
Canary Islands	Gobierno canario	Paulino Rivero Baute	10	56,855	Coalition PSOE-CC
Cantabria	Diputación regional	Miguel Angel Rovilla Ruiz	10	18,652	Coalition PSOE-PRC
Castilla La Mancha	Junta de Comunidades	José Maria Barreda Fontes	15	66,102	Absolute Majority PSOE
Castilla León	Junta de Castilla León	Juan Vincente Herrera Campo	12	85,853	Absolute Majority PP
Catalonia	Generalitat de Catalunya	José Motilla	14	147,793	Coalition PSOE-ERC-EUiA
Extremadura	Junta de Extremadura	Guillermo Fernandez Vara	10	45,234	Absolute Majority PSOE
Galicia	Xunta de Galicia	Emilio Perez Touriño	13	82,381	Coalition PSOE-BNG
La Rioja	Consejo de Gobierno	Pedro Sanz Alonso	9	9,713	Absolute Majority PP
Madrid	Gobierno de la Comunidad	Esperanza Aguirre	13	148,789	Absolute Majority PP
Murcia	Consejo de Gobierno	Román Luis Valcarcel Siso	9	45,950	Absolute Majority PP
Navarre	Gobierno de Navarra	Miguel Sanz Sesma	11	19,978	Minority single party PP
Valencian Community	Generalitat Valenciana	Francisco Camps Ortiz	13	124,360	Absolute majority PP

Source: Websites of regional governments; Registro Central de Personal, 2007: 14.

level of professionalised ones (Ramio and Salvador, 2002: 118–20). Similar to the political system, most of the autonomous public administrations, apart from the Basque Country and Navarre, followed the national public administration model, due to the fact that when they were constructing new political structures, there was no other model available. The Basque Country and Navarre were able to introduce specific regional administrative aspects which were related to previous historical experiences of limited autonomy in former political regimes (Ramio and Salvador, 2002: 127). This development of the autonomous communities public administrations underwent a process of learning and institutional engineering, before it attained stabilisation and consolidation. In sum, the regional political systems and public administrations have more or less reached a high level of institutionalisation after more than two decades of incrementalism in terms of powers assigned to them.

Such a process of institution building was assigned also to the new regional parliaments. They can be considered as important fora of representative democracy. Parliamentarianism at regional level is quite limited by the powers assigned to them by the national political system, though nevertheless they play a role in designing and shaping the new regional political systems. In terms of institutionalisation, one can find similarities to the problems encountered by the national parliament.

Although the parliament is more or less institutionalised in interinstitutional terms, internal organisation and parliamentary group organisation, the renewal of MPs from legislature to legislature is extremely high and far from consolidated. The average rotation for all autonomous community parliaments from the second legislature up to 2000 is 54.6 per cent. It means that more than half of MPs change from legislature to legislature. Castilla La Mancha is the parliament with the highest turnover ratio with a 69.2 per cent average, while Extremadura has the lowest turnover with an average of 39.3 per cent. All the other autonomous communities are in between, but most of them are close to the averages of Castilla La Mancha. This is quite negative for the establishment of a stable regional political class within parliament, which would accumulate knowledge to be passed on to the new members of parliaments (Collier, 2002: 78).

The legislative activity of the new regional parliaments can be divided into two phases. The first phase can be considered as the phase of institution building, in which most legislation for the regulation of the new institutions was adopted. Such a phase ran from 1980 to 1989 and was replaced by a second phase, which was more oriented towards adopting legislation for policy-making powers. Between 1980 and 2000, the autonomous communities produced in total 3,330 laws.

One interesting finding is that while between 1980 and 1989 the number of laws approved by the autonomous communities with greater powers amounted to 63.8 per cent of all laws, this share has been decreasing steadily in the 1990s with 61.3 per cent in 1993 and 56.93 in 2000. This may indicate a convergence in the level of legislative activity between the different parliaments. Most of the autonomous communities produce ten laws per year but only Catalonia and Navarre may reach fifteen to eighteen laws per year. Most of the laws are related to the economy and finance (38 per cent), while institution-building laws were

Table 5.7 The legislative output according to autonomous communities, 1989–2005 (accumulated values)

	1989	%	1993	%	2000	%	2005	%
Andalucia	68	5.3	89	4.6	149	4.6	222	5
Aragón	55	4.3	105	5.5	197	5.9	316	7
Asturias	75	5.9	96	5	148	4.4	197	4.4
Balearics	60	4.7	103	5.4	183	5.5	246	5.5
Basque Country	122	9.6	159	8.3	240	7.2	273	6.1
Canary Islands	66	5.2	105	5.4	180	5.4	226	5.1
Cantabria	55	4.3	90	4.7	161	4.8	200	4.5
Castilla La Mancha	39	3.1	56	2.9	124	3.8	209	4.7
Castilla León	50	2.4	53	2.8	112	3.4	184	4.1
Catalonia	177	13.9	259	13.5	377	11.4	495	11.1
Extremadura	30	2.4	53	2.8	112	3.4	170	3.8
Galicia	82	6.5	127	6.6	190	5.7	243	5.5
Madrid	61	4.8	106	5.5	254	7.6	312	7
Murcia	74	5.8	101	5.3	179	5.4	238	5.4
Navarre	163	12.8	235	12.8	388	11.7	525	11.8
La Rioja	21	1.7	37	1.9	97	2.9	148	3.3
Valencian Community	74	5.8	100	5.2	176	5.33	245	5.5
TOTAL	1,272	100	1,918	100	3,330	100	4,449	100

Source: Based on data provided by Subirats, 1998: 166; Porras, *et al.*, 2002: 169; Instituto de Derecho Publico, 2002–2006.

18 per cent of the total in 2000. Education and health have become more important sectors in which legislation is needed, each representing 10 per cent of the laws in total (Porras, et alia, 2002: 170) (see Table 5.7 and Figure 5.16).

The already-mentioned high level of turnover prevents continuous control of the regional governments. Executive–legislative relations are still in the process of institutionalisation. There is no salient pattern emerging from the relationships in the seventeen autonomous communities systems. Most regional parliaments are still too weak in using their controlling functions in relation to the regional government. According to a study Aragón, Asturias, Cantabria, Castilla La Mancha, Castilla León, Extremadura and La Rioja have the weakest level of parliamentarianism, while the Valencian Community, Galicia and the Balearics have improved considerably over the years. All the other parliaments are between these two extremes (Lopez Nieto *et al.*, 2002: 59–65). Political stability has been so far one of the criteria for the limitation of the instruments of control available to the opposition. According to a study by Alfredo Allué Buiza, the number of MPs necessary to present a motion of censure against the government is quite high in some regional parliaments. In the Basque Country is one-sixth, in Andalucia a quarter and in Navarre one-fifth of MPs, although the agreements on the autonomous communities of 1981 set a desirable figure of 15 per cent of MPs, or the constitutional regulation of a tenth of MPs.

This naturally is quite a high threshold to initiate such a parliamentary process (Alluó Buiza, 2006: 212).

The regional party systems

Along with the regional political systems, the autonomy process has created seventeen regional party systems which are more and more intertwined with the national and regional party system. Since 1980, elections to the autonomous communities have taken place which have created seventeen party systems. As already mentioned in Chapter 4, the level of participation in these elections is lower than in national elections, but in some sense higher than in local or European elections. They have to be considered second-order elections, although in some circumstances regional elections may reach the participation levels of national elections. The best example was the 13 May 2001 regional elections in the Basque Country, in which there was the extraordinary participation of over 80 per cent of the Basque voters. This was naturally due to the high level of polarisation between the regional nationalist parties such as PNV, EH and EA and the national parties such as the PP and the PSOE. The elections also reproduced the division between Basque nationalism and *Españolismo* (supporters of the state of autonomies as it is).

The whole dynamics of electoral politics in the seventeen autonomous communities were first mentioned by Josep M. Vallés who spoke of the so-called *Españas electorales*, meaning that all seventeen autonomous communities had created seventeen party systems, each of them with its own dynamics (Vallés, 1991). In this sense, Spain has now eighteen party systems if we add the national electoral arena.

As already mentioned, Spanish regional party systems can be subdivided mainly in two groups. The main group are the autonomous communities, in which both main parties are able to achieve an absolute majority or at least a working majority. This can be found in thirteen of the autonomous communities. The second group consists of the other four autonomous communities, consisting of Catalonia, the Basque Country, the Canary Islands and the Balearics. The latter two are naturally related to the fact that no party or coalition is able to achieve a working majority, so that the main parties have to work with the highly fragmented regionalist party system. If one wants to be more accurate, it is sensible to use the typology of party systems used by Pablo Oñate and Francisco Ocaña who distinguish between three groups: A common model, in which the two statewide parties dominate, an excentric model in four autonomous communities with strong regionalist-nationalist parties (the Basque Country, Catalonia, the Canary Islands and Navarre) and a third group which lies in between (Aragón, Galicia) (Oñate and Ocaña, 2005: 178).

In an extreme case, one could say that the second group is only restricted to Catalonia and the Basque Country. In Navarre, the PP is allied to the UPN, which is a regionalist party. However since 2003, the new regionalist-nationalist coalition, *Nafarroa Bai*, has been changing the political landscape. After the 27 May elections, there were serious talks between the Navarran Socialists and NA-Bai to form a government and replace the UPN government of Miguel Sanz Sesma.

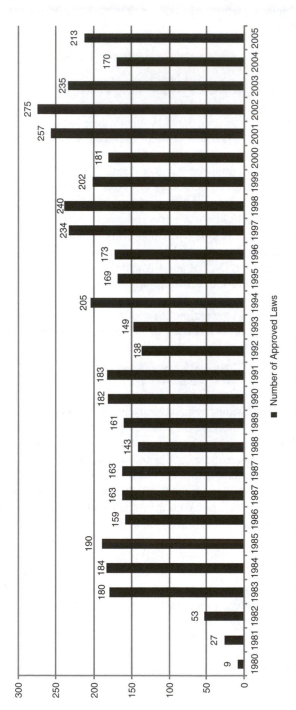

Figure 5.16 Laws produced each year by autonomous communities, 1980–2007.

Source: Porras *et al.*, 2002: 170; Instituto de Derecho, 2002–2006.

The coalition negotiations led to a successful agreement at the beginning of August, but the deal was vetoed by the central office of Socialist Party in Madrid which was afraid this would affect their chances in the legislative elections on 9 March 2008, due to the tense relationship of both main statewide parties with the regionalist-nationalist PNV-EA (*El Pais*, 24 July 2007: p17; *El Pais*, 3 August 2007: 15; 4 August 2007).

Another important factor is that thirteen of the autonomous communities share the same electoral cycle. It comprises all the autonomous communities that achieved their autonomous community statute later than the four first autonomous communities, namely Catalonia, the Basque Country, Andalusia and Galicia. The latter four each have different electoral cycles, so that they are less subject to the intertwined nature of the major electoral cycle. However, in some of these autonomous communities, the main parties were able to form coalition with some of the regionalist-nationalist parties. For example,after the 2005 Galician elections, the PSOE formed a coalition with the regionalist-nationalist BNG, in spite of the fact that the PP was the largest party in Parliament, however without an absolute majority. Last but not least, after the Catalan elections of 2003 and 2006, the CiU was the strongest party, but without an absolute majority, so that the Catalan Socialist Party, the regionalist branch of the PSOE formed a coalition with the regionalist-nationalist ERC and the IU. This shows that now only in the Basque Country has there been an interrupted dominance of regionalist-nationalist party. They are able to focus more on the regionalist issues and be less dominated by national politics or national party campaigning. The stronger nationalisation of elections in the main electoral cycle is reinforced by the fact that at the same time local elections are taking place.

Before we study more deeply the regional politics of Catalonia, the Basque Country Galicia and Andalucia, the historical nationalities of Spain, it is important to compare the other fourteen party systems. Indeed, the d'Hondt proportional representation system creates a similar outcome at regional and at national level. The largest party achieves a disproportionate higher share of the seats, while the smaller parties have to content themselves with a lower share of seats in relation to their share of the vote.

Over the past two decades, regionalist parties have also emerged in these fourteen regions. In some cases, they were able to achieve representation and play a role in regional politics. In other cases, such as in Castilla La Mancha, Murcia or Madrid they do not exist or are very weak. This naturally strengthens the position of the main parties which are able to reproduce the same kind of contest as is common at national level. Strong regionalist-nationalist parties which are able to influence the outcome of government in the respective regional autonomies can be found in Aragón, the Balearics, the Canaries, Cantabria, La Rioja, Asturias and the Valencian Community.

Where there is no absolute majority regionalist parties can play a pivotal role in contributing to the formation of stable governments. In 1999 and 2003, the Aragonese Party (*Partido Aragones* – PAR) formed a coalition with the PSOE, although the PP was the party with the largest share of the vote and seats. In the Balearics, In 2003 and 2007 *Unión Mallorquina* formed a government with the

PSOE as well as having previously formed one with the PP. In Cantabria, the Regionalist Party of Cantabria (*Partido Regionalista de Cantabria* – PRC) led by Miguel Angel Rovilla formed a government with the largest party, the PP. In the Canary Islands, Canary Coalition formed a coalition government with the PSOE after the 1995 elections and changed to the PP after the 1999 elections. This shows that despite the fact that in most autonomous communities regionalist parties are only the third or fourth largest party in the regional parliament, they may have a pivotal role in forming stable governments (*El Pais*, 13 May 2003: 21; *El Pais*, 28 May 2007: 20–46).

Indeed, many of these regionalist parties are reactions to the nationalist-regionalist emergence after 1979. Parties such as the UPN (Navarre), the PRC (Cantabria), the UM (the Balearics), the PR (La Rioja) and the PAR (Aragon) are quite conservative in their outlook. Nevertheless they are pragmatic as well, so that they can influence government formation in the region. The UPN in Navarre and the Alavian Union (*Unión Alava* – UA) in the Basque province of Alava were established to resist against the threat of the PNV expanding in their regions. Similarly, the UM in the Balearics and the UV in the Valencian Community were founded to fight off claims of Greater Catalonia, due to the fact that Valencian and Mallorcan are dialects of Catalan (Seixas, 1999: 152–7). All this shows that the dynamics of the state of autonomies led to the creation of at least four kinds of party systems. First, there are the mere regionalist-nationalist party systems with a hegemonic position of regionalist-nationalist parties (the Basque Country and Catalonia). Second, there are party systems where regionalist-nationalist parties are strong, but are still in a minority position in relation to the national main parties (Galicia). Third, there are party systems with strong regionalist parties which are in pivotal position in terms of government formation (Navarre, Aragon, the Balearics, Cantabria, the Canaries). Fourth, there are all the others where the national parties are quite dominant and regionalist parties have only a very small or no percentage of the vote (La Rioja, Asturias, Castilla León, Castilla La Mancha, Andalusia, the Valencian Community, Murcia, Extremadura, Madrid) (see Hamann, 1999: 118–21; Molas and Bartolomeus, 2003).

In sum, autonomous community elections created seventeen different party systems which have led to the emergence of more or less strong regionalist parties. This naturally enhances the importance of the state of autonomies. Regionalist parties have acquired different meanings in each autonomous community. The closer to the centres of the two Castiles, one can find conservative regionalist parties reacting against the centrifugal forces in the regions with higher levels of national-regional consciousness: Catalonia, the Basque Country and Galicia.

Political developments in Catalonia: from Jordi Pujol to the tripartite governments of Pascual Maragall and José Motilla

The starting point of modern political Catalanism can be found in the second half of the nineteenth century, when a cultural *Renaixenca* (Renaissance) pushed forward the agenda of cultural revival. In this sense, political Catalanism has been moderate

Table 5.8 Regionalist parties in the autonomous communities after 27 May 2007 elections

Autonomous communities	Parties	Significance	Party system
Andalucia	• Andalusian Party/(Partido Andaluz – PA)	Small party, can be pivotal if PSOE does not achieve absolute majority	PSOE dominant
Aragon	• Aragonian Regionalist Party (Partido Regionalista Aragonés – PRA) • Aragonese Junta (Chunta Aragonexista – CHA)	Both parties are almost equal in electoral strength, since 2007 PAR was able to be stronger than CHA	PSOE dominant
Asturias	• Asturian Regional Union (Unión Regional Asturiana – URAS)	Not able to achieve representation in 2003 and 2007 regional elections	PSOE dominant, support from IU
Balearics	• Mallorcan Union (Unión Mallorquina – UM) • Mallorcan Socialist Party – (Partido Socialista Mallorquino – PSM)	Small parties, between 9 and 6 per cent, able to form coalition with major parties	PSOE dominant
Basque Country	• Nationalist Basque Country (Partido Nacionalista Vasco – PNV) • Herri Batasuna (HB) • Eusko Askartasuna (EA)	• Largest party is regionalist-nationalist (PNV) and in coalition with EA, dependent on support of IU • Political arm of ETA is illegal due to being associated to terrorist organisation	PNV-EA dominant, support from IU
Canaries	• Canarian Coalition (Coalición Canaria – CC)	After 2003 regional elections it was first party, after 2007 elections third party, important coalition party for PP and PSOE	PSOE strongest party, CC in coalition
Cantabria	• Regionalist Party of Cantabria (Partido Regionalista de Cantabria – PRC)	Strong growing third party in 2007 elections, can coalesce with PP and PSOE, leader is president of the autonomous community	PRC in coalition with PP

Continued

Table 5.8 Continued

Autonomous communities	Parties	Significance	Party system
Castilla-Leon	• People's Union of León (*Union Popular de León* – UPL)	Third largest party between 2–4 per cent and 2–3 seats, IU has no representation	PP dominant
Castilla La Mancha	• None		PSOE dominant
Catalonia	• Convergence and Union (*Convergencia i Unió* – CiU) • Republican Left of Catalonia (*Esquerra Republicana de Catalunya* – ERC)	• CiU: Strongest party in terms of share of vote and seats, however since 1999 without absolute majority (30–32 per cent of vote) • ERC: Improved considerably, third strongest political force after CiU and PSOE (between 14–16 per cent of vote)	Coalition between PSOE-ERC-IU, CiU largest party, but without absolute majority
Extremadura	• United Extremadura (*Extremadura Unida* – EU)	No parliamentary representation	PSOE dominant
Galicia	• National Galician Bloc (*Bloque Nacional Gallego* – BNG)	BNG was second largest party in 2001 elections with 23.1 per cent, but third largest party in 2005 elections with 19.9 per cent	PSOE-BNG coalition PP strongest party, but without absolute majority
Madrid	• None		PP dominant
Murcia	• None		PP dominant
Navarre	• Union of Navarrese People (*Unión del Pueblo de Navarra* – UPN) • *Nafarroa Bai* (NA-Bai)	• UPN: Strongest party, regionalist, united with PP • Coalition of all regionalist-nationalist parties (PNV, Aralar and others), second largest party	UPN/PP dominant, but NA-Bai is becoming a major player, second largest party in 2007 elections
La Rioja	• *Party of Rioja* (Partido de Rioja – PR)	PR: Small regionalist party with about 6–7 per cent and two seats in 2003 and 2007 elections	PP dominant
Valencian Community	• *Entesa* • *Compromis*		

Source: Compiled from individual chapters of Alcántara and Martínez, 1998; updated from *El País*, 13 May 2003: 21; *El País*, 28 May 2007: 21; political parties' websites.

Table 5.9 Results of autonomous community elections, 1983–2007

Autonomous communities	Parties	1983 %	1983 Seats	1987 %	1987 Seats	1991 %	1991 Seats	1995 %	1995 Seats	1999 %	1999 Seats	2003 %	2003 Seats	2007 %	2007 Seats
Aragon	PP	22.6	18	15.5	13	20.7	17	37.5	19	39	28	30.9	22	31	23
	PSOE	46.8	33	35.7	27	40.3	30	25.7	27	31.4	23	37.9	27	41	30
	PAR	20.5	13	28.1	19	24.7	17	20.4	14	13.5	10	11.2	8	12.1	9
	CHA	–	–	–	–	2.3	–	4.8	2	11.2	5	13.6	9	8.1	4
	IU	4	1	4.9	2	6.7	3	9.2	5	3.92	1	3.04	1	4.1	1
	CDS	3.3	1	10.2	6	3.1	–	–	–	–	–	–	–	–	–
Asturias	PSOE	52.1	26	39.3	20	41.5	21	34.2	17	46.7	24	40.3	22	41.6	21
	PP	30.3	14	25.5	13	30.7	15	42.4	21	32.8	15	39.3	19	41.8	20
	IU	10.7	5	12.2	4	15.1	6	16.6	6	9.1	3	11.2	4	9.8	4
	PAS/URAS	–	–	1.2	–	2.7	1	3.2	1	7.2	3	1.8	–	2.3	–
	CDS	3.8	–	18.7	8	6.8	2	1.8	–	–	–	–	–	–	–
Balearics	PP	35.6	22	36.6	25	47.3	32	44.7	31	44.8	28	44.7	29	46	28
	PSOE	34.7	21	32.4	21	30.1	21	23.9	16	22.4	13	24.6	15	27.1	16
	PSM-Bloc*	6.6	4	6.2	4	6.6	5	12.2	6	11.9	5	11.9	5	9	4
	UM	15.2	7	9	4	–	–	5.3	2	7.4	2	7.5	2	6.7	3
	IU*	–	–	2.6	–	2.3	–	6.6	3	4.8	3	4.9	3	–	–
	Other	5.4	–	13.5	5	13.7	1	7.3	1	–	8	4	6	5.7	8
Canaries	AIC/CC	–	–	20.16	11	22.87	16	32.82	22	36.54	25	33.3	23	23.3	19
	PP	29	17	11.26	6	12.83	6	31.08	18	26.85	14	30.82	17	24.3	15
	PSOE	41.45	27	28.02	21	33.03	23	23.03	16	23.77	19	25.8	17	34.7	26
	IU	4.41	1	6.14	–	–	–	5.1	–	2.71	–	1.32	–	0.4	–
	CDS	7.19	6	19.63	13	14.41	7	–	–	–	–	–	–	–	–
	Other	–	7	–	7	–	7	–	4	–	–	4.9	3	1	–

Continued

Table 5.9 Continued

Autonomous communities	Parties	1983 %	1983 Seats	1987 %	1987 Seats	1991 %	1991 Seats	1995 %	1995 Seats	1999 %	1999 Seats	2003 %	2003 Seats	2007 %	2007 Seats
Cantabria	PP	43.9	18	41.3	18	14.4	6	32.5	13	43.5	19	43.3	18	41.5	17
	PSOE	38.4	15	29.6	13	34.8	16	25.1	10	33.9	14	29.9	13	24.3	10
	PRC	6.7	2	12.9	5	6.3	2	14.5	6	13.8	6	19.47	8	28.8	12
	UPCA	–	–	–	–	33.5	15	16.6	7	–	–	–	–	–	–
	IU	3.9	–	3.6	–	4.4	–	7.4	3	–	–	–	–	–	–
	CDS	2.6	–	6.6	3	2.7	–	4	–	–	–	–	–	–	–
Castilla-León	PP	40	39	34.9	33	44.2	43	53.2	50	51.9	48	49.6	48	49.4	48
	PSOE	44.8	42	34.5	32	37	35	30.1	27	33.8	31	37.6	32	37.4	33
	PDL/UPL	2.7	1	0.6	–	0.83	–	2.6	2	3.8	3	3.8	1	2.7	2
	IU	3.2	–	3.8	–	5.44	1	9.7	5	4.1	1	3	–	2.7	–
	CDS	6	2	19.6	17	8.2	5	–	–	–	–	–	–	–	–
Castilla-La Mancha	PSOE	47.01	23	46.75	25	52.7	27	46.18	24	54.2	26	58.6	29	51.9	26
	PP	41.19	21	34.38	18	26.27	19	44.77	22	41	21	37.1	18	42.4	21
	IU	6.9	–	5.41	–	6.22	1	7.68	1	3.5	–	3.04	–	3.4	–
	CDS	3.04	–	10.66	4	3.53	–	0.41	–	–	–	–	–	–	–
Extremadura	PSOE	53.01	35	49.17	34	54.15	39	44.01	31	48.42	34	51.62	36	52.9	38
	PP	30.1	20	24.19	17	26.78	19	39.75	27	40.12	28	38.74	26	38.7	27
	PCE/IU	6.48	4	5.45	2	7.11	4	10.6	6	6.07	3	6.27	3	4.5	–
	EU	8.48	6	5.85	4	–	–	3.82	1	1.64	–	–	–	–	–
	CDS	3.04	–	10.66	4	3.53	–	0.41	–	–	–	1.8	–	–	–
Murcia	PP	35.42	16	31.5	16	33.51	17	52.23	26	52.84	26	57.5	28	58.4	29
	PSOE	52.22	26	43.71	25	45.47	24	31.87	15	35.91	18	34.04	16	31.8	15
	IU	7.02	1	7.45	1	10.21	4	12.46	4	7	1	5.66	1	6.2	1
	CDS	1.15	–	11.93	3	5.01	–	0.69	–	–	–	–	–	–	–

Region	Party	%	S	%	S	%	S	%	S	%	S	%	S	%	S
Navarre	PSOE	35.8	20	28	15	33.8	19	20.8	11	20.76	11	21.14	11	22.4	12
	UPN	23.5	13	24.8	14	35.4	20	31.3	17	42.42	22	41.43	23	42.2	22
	AP/PDP	14.2	8	–	–	–	–	–	–	–	–	–	–	–	–
	HB	10.6	6	13.6	7	11.3	6	9.2	5	15.9	8	–	–	–	–
	PNV	6.8	3	0.9	–	1.1	–	0.9	–	5.5	3	7.43	4	–	–
	EA	–	–	7.1	4	5.5	3	4.5	2	–	–	–	–	–	–
	IU	–	–	1.3	–	4.1	2	9.3	5	7	3	8.77	4	4.4	2
	CDN	–	–	–	–	–	–	18.5	10	7	3	7.6	4	4.4	2
	NA-BAI	–	–	–	–	–	–	–	–	–	–	–	–	23.7	12
	Other	–	–	–	6	–	–	–	–	–	–	–	–	–	4
La Rioja	PP	39.98	15	34.78	13	41.7	15	49.53	17	52.4	18	48.6	17	48.7	17
	PSOE	47.17	18	39.64	14	42.37	16	34.03	12	36.1	13	38.1	14	40.4	14
	PR	7.46	2	6.39	2	5.38	2	6.67	2	5.9	2	6.84	2	5.9	2
	PCE/IU	2.17	–	2.41	–	4.53	–	7.23	2	–	–	2.7	–	3	–
	CDS	2.41	–	10.84	4	4.37	–	–	–	–	–	–	–	–	–
Valencian Community	PSOE	31.89	32	23.7	25	27.81	31	42.83	42	34.4	35	36.5	36	34.2	38
	PP	51.41	51	41.27	42	42.81	45	33.98	32	48.6	49	47.9	48	52.2	55
	PCE/IU / Compromis (EU-Bloc)	7.46	6	7.94	6	7.54	6	11.53	10	6.1	3	6.64	6	7.9	7
	UV	–	–	9.14	6	10.36	7	7.01	5	–	–	–	–	–	–
	BNV	–	–	–	–	–	–	–	–	–	–	–	–	–	–
	CDS	–	–	11.24	10	–	–	–	–	–	–	–	–	–	–

Source: Compiled from individual chapters of Alcantara and Martinez, 1998; Generalitat of Valencia website http://www.pre.gva.es/pls/argos, accessed on 22 Jul 2003 and 23 November 2007) and Ministry of Interior website http://www.elecciones2003.mir.es/autonomicas, accessed on 27 May 2003 and 23 November 2007; E Pais, 29 May 2007: 26.

Table 5.10 Results of autonomous community elections in Madrid, 1983–2007

	1983		1987		1991		1995		1999		2003		2003		2007	
	%	*Seats*	*%*	*Seats*	*%*	*Seats*	*%*	*Seats*	*%*	*Seats*	*%*	*Seats*	*%*	*Seats*	*%*	*Seats*
PP	34.3	34	31.9	32	43.2	47	50.9	54	52.1	55	48.48	57	49.34	57	53.3	67
PSOE	50.8	51	39.1	40	37.1	41	29.7	32	37.2	47	39	45	39.69	45	33.4	42
IU	8.9	9	7.6	7	12.2	13	16.5	17	7.8	8	8.5	9	8.65	9	8.8	11
CDS	3.1	–	16.9	17	3.4	–	–	–	–	–	–	–	–	–	–	–

Source: Generalitat of Valencia website http://www.pre.gva.es/pls/argos (accessed on 22 July 2003 and 23 November 2007) and Ministry of Interior website http://www.elecciones.mir.es/autonomicas (accessed on 27 May 2003 and 23 November 2007); *El País*, 29 May 2007: 26.

and based on a more evolutionary approach towards the rebirth of a nation, which had tried since the sixteenth century to regain independence from the Spanish composite monarchy. Political Catalanism was quite conservative and elitist in the nineteenth century. It gained political expression in the beginning of the twentieth century with the creation of new political parties attempting to strengthen the position of Catalonia within the Spanish monarchy. The first political party was the *Lliga de Catalunya* and later on the *Unió Catalanista*, but they were weak movements with a very small number of supporters. The foundation of the *Lliga Regionalista* was to change this situation and create the first strong Catalan party, which was supported by the Catalan bourgeoisie. Four MPs of the Lliga were elected in 1901. The *Lliga* began to be challenged by left-wing Catalan parties in the late phase of the Restoration system. It was able to achieve some limited autonomy by the creation of the Mancomunitat with a low level of powers in 1913. This led the *Lliga* to support the dictatorship of Primo de Rivera, in spite of the fact that in the end, it forbade political Catalanism. In the Second Republic, Catalonia was dominated by left-wing Republican Catalanism, which was centred around the Republican Left of Catalonia (*Esquerra Republicana de Catalunya –* ERC) founded in 1931. The *Lliga* lost importance in this period. The granting of autonomy to Catalonia in 1932 allowed for the emergence of a Generalitat, last constituted in the middle ages. This became an important landmark in the quest of the ERC for further autonomy. In 1934, the uprising against the right-wing central government led to the suspension of the statute of autonomy. Between 1934 and 1936, Catalonia became one of the centres of Republicanism, which opposed the policies of the right-wing government.

During the Franco period most Catalan politicians went into exile. A return of political Catalanism came only about in the 1960s. Quite an important figure in this respect is Jordi Pujol, who along with others helped to revive some form of political Catalanism based around the hierarchy of the Catholic Church in Catalonia. The cultural movement was also political in character. Again political Catalanism was quite evolutionary and peaceful in outlook. It was also inclusionist and moderate (Conversi, 1997).

During the transition, it was Adolfo Suarez who facilitated the reconciliation process with Catalonia by allowing the return of Josep Tarradellas, the last president of the Generalitat before the Civil War broke out. Some provisional pre-autonomy structures were established which led to an engagement of Catalans in the drafting of the new constitution. This constructive approach towards the state of autonomies may be regarded as an example of Catalan pragmatism. The Catalan Statute of autonomy was approved by a referendum with 59.6 per cent of the vote in 1979.

The Catalan political system established after 1979 was dominated until 2003 by Jordi Pujol, the leader of the Democratic Union of Catalonia (*Unió Democratica de Catalunya –* UDC). The formation of an electoral coalition between the UDC and the CDC (*Convergencia Democratica de Catalunya –* CDC) led to a hegemonic position within the Catalan party system. The ERC became a smaller party within the Catalan party system. The second largest party remained the PSOE under the leadership of the charismatic Pascual Maragall, who was the mayor of Barcelona. The PP was able to improve its position since the first autonomous communities elections and supported CiU through a pact of legislature in 1999 (*El Pais*, Cataluña, 30 November 2000: 4; *El Pais*, Cataluña, 22 May 2001: 4).

The main Catalan slogan for Jordi Pujol was *fer pais* ('to build a country'). This slogan was quite important, because it included the evolutionary building of the Catalan nation, which in the past had so many difficulties in asserting itself. This policy of Jordi Pujol and CiU has been at the forefront of the project of political Catalanism (Ballart, 2000: 174–6). This so-called Pujolism calls for a recognition of the Catalan nation alongside the Basques, the Galicians and the rest of Spain. The plurinational character of Spain would ultimately recognise four nations. The last Catalan government under Jordi Pujol prepared a draft for a reform of the statute which included proposals for enhanced sovereignty of Catalonia. Similar to the demands of the PNV and the ERC, the CiU presented as well the possibility to redesign the relationship of Catalonia with Spain as an association arrangement (*El Pais*, 24 March 2003: 35). Such a model was rejected so far by the two main parties, particularly the PP.

Jordi Pujol was the president of Generalitat since the first autonomous community elections in 1980 until 2003. As he was six times president of the Generalitat he shaped considerably the nature of Catalan politics. Jordi Pujol's charismatic personality strengthened political Catalanism considerably through his presence in national and international politics. In national politics, Pujol was able to gain some leverage for continuing decentralisation and extended autonomy through supporting PSOE and PP minority governments in the 1990s. This also contributed to an upgrading of the autonomy statutes of the other autonomous communities.

Internationally, Pujol was a major player in what has become known as 'Europe of the Regions'. He was a salient figure in the first legislature of the newly founded Committee of the Regions and Local Authorities in Brussels back in 1994. Indeed, Pujol officially travelled abroad sixty-seven times to promote Catalonia. This so-called paradiplomacy is a major characteristic of the Spanish autonomous communities. Catalonia has fifty trade and cultural offices around the world, two embassies, two Catalan centres and one centre for labour information. It plans to open four civic consulates in Mexico, Chile, Argentina and Paraguay and two embassies in New York and Singapore (*El Pais*, Domingo, 20 July 2003: 5; Davis, 2004: 138). Other autonomous communities are following the Catalan example.

Jordi Pujol declared after the 1999 autonomous community elections that he would be retiring from office after the end of the legislature. Simultaneously, he prepared Artur Mas, who became the newly created *conseller en cap* (regional first minister) of the Generalitat, as his successor (*El Pais*, Domingo, 10 February 2002: 8–10). In spite of this arrangement, it has been difficult for CiU to find someone of the stature of Pujol.

Pascual Maragall was able to break the hegemony of CiU in the November 2003 elections and became the new president of Generalitat. Indeed, the last Pujol government was a minority government and was successfully challenged by the

Table 5.11 Autonomous governments in Catalonia

Legislature	President	Parties	Type of government	Support in Parliament	Reason for end of government
1980–84	Jordi Pujol	CiU(CDC-UDC)	Minority/pre-electoral coalition	31.85% (43 CMPs)	End of legislature
1984–87	Jordi Pujol	CiU(CDC-UDC) and ERC	Coalition government	57.04% (77 CMPs)	Crisis of government
1987–88	Jordi Pujol	CiU(CDC-UDC)	Absolute majority/ pre-electoral coalition	53.33% (72 CMPs)	End of legislature
1988–92	Jordi Pujol	CiU(CDC-UDC)	Absolute majority/pre-electoral coalition	51.11% (69 CMPs)	Early elections
1992–95	Jordi Pujol	CiU(CDC-UDC)	Absolute majority/pre-electoral coalition	51.85% (70 CMPs)	Early elections
1995–99	Jordi Pujol	CiU(CDC-UDC)	Minority/pre-electoral coalition	44.44% (60 CMPs)	End of legislature
1999–2003	Jordi Pujol	CiU(CDC-UDC)	Minority/pre-electoral	41.48% (56 CMPs)	End of legislature
2003–2006	Pascual Maragall	PSC/ERC/IC-V/EUiA	Coalition government	54.81% (74 CMPs)	Crisis of government
2006–	José Montilla	PSC/ERC/IC-V-EUiA	Coalition government	52.9% (70 CMPs)	

Source: Matas Dalmases, and Vilalala Reniu, 2003: 89, own updating after 2006 Catalan election.

Table 5.12 Autonomous elections in Catalonia, 1980–2007

	1980		1984		1988		1991		1995		1999		2003		2006	
	%	Seats	%	Seats	%	Seats	%	Seats	%	Seats	%	Seats	%	Seats	%	Seats
CiU	27.7	43	46.6	72	45.4	69	45.9	70	40.8	60	38.1	56	30.9	46	31.52	48
PSC	22.3	33	29.9	41	29.6	42	27.4	40	24.8	34	38.2	52	31.2	42	26.81	37
ERC	8.89	14	4.39	5	4.12	6	7.94	11	9.46	11	8.8	12	16.4	23	14.06	21
AP/PPC	2.35	–	7.66	11	5.28	6	5.94	7	13.1	17	9.6	12	11.9	15	10.64	14
PSUC/IC-V-EUiA	18.7	25	5.5	6	7.7	9	6.5	7	9.7	13	2.53	3	7.3	9	9.56	12
C-Pc	–	–	–	–	–	–	–	–	–	–	–	–	–	–	3.4	3
CDS	–	–	–	–	3.81	3	0.91	–	–	–	–	–	–	–	–	–
UCD	10.6	18	–	–	–	–	–	–	–	–	–	–	–	–	–	–

Source: http://www.pre.gva.es/pls/argos, accessed on 23 November 2007 and Ministry of Interior website http://www.elecciones2003.mir.es/autonomicas, accessed on 23 November 2007.

PSOE under Maragall in the autonomous community elections of 1999. Quite a climax of this legislature was the motion of censure presented by the PSOE and IC-V (*Iniciativa per Catalunya-Ver*) against the government in October 2001. Although Pujol won the vote, Maragall used the opportunity to present himself as the potential successor of the current president of the Generalitat (*El Pais*, 18 October 2000: 5; *El Pais*, Cataluña, 16 January 2001: 5; *El Pais*, Cataluña, 23 February 2001: 5; *El Pais*, Cataluña, 7 April 2001: 4; *El Pais*, 31 October 2001: 31). Apart from nominating Artur Mas as his successor, Pujol has been quite keen to strengthen the link between the UDC and the CiU. In December 2001, the two parties decided to become a federation, so overcoming the mere electoral coalition character (*El Pais*, 2 December 2001: 25). The relationship between the CiU and the PP was a pragmatic one, not one based on affinity. Indeed, the CiU resisted in taking part in any PP government due to their position in wanting to finalise the whole decentralisation process and not being willing to revise the constitution. At the same time, the PP clearly warned Pujol that they would end their support in the Catalan parliament, if he continued to make comments on the sovereignty of Catalonia (*El Pais*, Cataluña, 16 November 2000: 4).

During 2002, tensions between the CiU and the PP became more evident, particularly concerning the Law for Budgetary Stability, also popularly called the Zero Deficit Law (*Ley de Estabilidad presupuestaria* or *Ley de Deficit zero*) which forced all autonomous community governments and the central government to end their yearly budget without deficit. This was related to the Growth and Stability Pact that Spain signed within the context of Economic and Monetary Union. Such a law was passed in October 2001 in the Cortes by the government with the support of Canary Coalition. All the other parties were against the law, because it restricted the spending of the autonomous communities unnecessarily, due to the fact that the Maastricht criteria allowed for a 3 per cent deficit. This was regarded as a financial LOAPA by the CiU and the PNV. The CiU decided to take the matter to the Constitutional Court with the argument that the law takes powers away from the autonomous communities (*El Pais*, 31 January 2002: 15). Further motive for conflict was the CiU support of the 20 July 2002 general strike called by the trade union confederations against changes in the unemployment benefit system. Such conflicts led to growing divisions in the Catalan parliament between the PP and the CiU. The PP voted against several Catalan government bills (*El Pais*, Domingo, 30 June 2002: 8; *Avui*, 3 May 2001: 16).

Longevity in government led to the emergence of political abuse scandals attributed to elements in the party or even in government. As already mentioned in Chapter 3, the Pallarols affair, which involved the misuse of EU funding for vocational training, in which the junior partner of the CiU, the UDC, was implicated, was quite damaging for the government (*El Pais*, Cataluña, 18 October 2000: 4; *El Pais*, Cataluña, 24 October 2000: 10; *El Pais*, Cataluña, 26 October 2000: 5; *El Pais*, Cataluña, 1 February 2001: 5).

Pujol's Generalitat was also involved in the manipulation of opinion polls, in order to present a better image of the CiU, which has been characterised by a high level of weariness and governmental inefficiency. The main person involved in this affair was *conseller en cap* Artur Mas, the appointed successor of Jordi Pujol for the successive autonomous community elections in 2003. Indeed it is alleged the data of the opinion polls were not only changed for benefit of the government party, but were actually invented. Jordi Pujol had, in the end, to take responsibility for this political scandal, so that Artur Mas could be cleared of any wrong doing. The opposition regarded this as a further example of abuse of power by the CiU (*El Pais*, 4 February 2003: 22; *El Pais*, 2 March 2003: 27; *El Pais*, 13 March 2003: 32).

After Pujol's retirement, Artur Mas became the main leader of CiU. His youth and inexperience led to the re-emergence of factionalism and different positions between the two parties of the coalition in relation to political catalanism. The main leader of UDC Josep Antoni Duran i Lleida is more moderate and wants to avoid any discourse related to the independence of Catalonia from Spain. In contrast, Artur Mas, as main protagonist of CDC, is continuing the life work of Jordi Pujol, meaning mainly a peaceful development towards greater autonomy, and eventually independence. Such tensions have become more exacerbated during the negotiations of all Catalan parties over the Catalan Statute in 2005 and 2006. During September 2007, tensions between Josep Antoni Durán Lleida leadership and Artur Mas erupted because of long-standing disagreements and lack of coordination between the two half of the party. Various CDC leaders, including Oriol Pujol Ferrusola, son of former President Jordi Pujol, came out in support of Artur Mas against Duran Lleida. However, growing criticism of Mas' leadership style came also from within his own party. In the end the crisis could be overcome this time, although the coalition in opposition had difficulties in sustaining its cohesion (*La Vanguardia*, 21 September 2007: 15). A 4-hour meeting between the two leaders led to a compromise. While both parts of the party agreed that Duran Lleida should be the official main candidate in the main legislative elections, UDC would respect the political Catalanism approach of Mas. One of the main concerns of Duran Lleida and UDC was that Mas was pushing the coalition towards an independence position, which the former did not agree (*El Pais*, 22 September 2007: 19).

One of the reasons for the tensions inside the CiU coalition is the fact, that Artur Mas was not able to achieve an absolute majority neither in the regional elections of 2003 nor in the ones of 2006. Although CiU won the elections in terms of share of the vote in both occasions, it was not enough to form government on its own. Due to the right-centre bourgeois background of the party, the more left-wing regionalist-nationalist party, the ERC, preferred in both occasions to form a coalition government with the Catalan Socialists (PSC) and the communist-dominated United Left. This naturally led to a strengthening of the PSC which was able to present a more political Catalanist and centrist image in order to win over part of the CiU electorate (Dowling, 2005: 241). The change of image was an important factor leading to the success of the PSC in being a more suitable coalition partner to the more extreme nationalist tendencies of ERC.

The new tripartite coalition government consisting of Catalan Socialist Party (*Partit Socialista de Catalunya* – PSC), the regionalist-nationalist Catalan Republican Left (*Esquerra Republicana de Catalunya* – ERC) and the communist dominated Initiative for Catalonia-United Left and Alternative (*Iniciativa per Catalunya-Verts-Esquerra Unida i Alternativa* – IC-V-EUiA) under the Socialist leader Pascual Maragall had at its main objective the reform of the Catalan Statute. As coalition model it was not new. Such left-coalition blocks are quite common in local councils, particularly in those smaller than 10,000 inhabitants (Ridao, 2007: 9). Moreover, between 1999 and 2003 the left-wing parties worked together against the last Pujol government. In terms of coordination, the coalition created a commission for the follow-up of the pact which guaranteed the implementation of the agreed policies (Ridao, 2007: 16). Moreover, a unit of coordination consisting of the three parties without any executive powers worked in the regional president office in order to coordinate policies, emulating many of the coalition governments that exist in Europe. Common positions were also coordinated in the national and Catalan parliaments (Ridao, 2007: 31–2).

Already in early January 2004, 2 months before the legislative elections, newspapers reported that the leader of ERC, Josep Lluis Carod i Rovira, who was also the *conseller en cap* (regional first minister) or number two in the government, had met secretly with Mikel Albizu and José Antonio Urrutikoetxea, leaders of the Basque terrorist organisation, ETA, near Perpignan in France to negotiate that ETA would not commit acts in Catalonia in exchange for a declaration of self-determination of peoples. Carod i Rovira confirmed the meeting, but denied any allegations of negotiations with ETA. Nevertheless, he was forced by Pascual Maragall to resign from his position. Maragall himself was under pressure from Zapatero to fire Carod i Rovira, because the scandal was damaging the chances of the PSOE in the forthcoming legislative elections. On 18 February 2004, ETA announced the suspension of a campaign of all armed actions against Catalonia. This naturally seemed to confirm the story presented by the newspaper (Campmany, 2005: 230–1). According to Casimiro Garcia-Abadillo, the Aznar government intentionally allowed this secret information gathered by the secret services to be leaked to the press, in order to gain political advantage in relation to the PSOE in the legislative elections. According to him, this is also one of the reasons why there were tensions and an atmosphere of distrust between the PP government, led by José Maria Aznar and Jorge Dezcallar, the head of the Council of National Intelligence (*Consejo Nacional de Inteligencia* – CNI), which contributed to the disarray in intelligence information flow in relation to the 11 March bombings (Garcia-Abadillo, 2005: 169–73).

After the legislative elections of 14 March 2004, Maragall was able to rely on the support of the Socialist government in Madrid to achieve a radical change of the Catalan Statute. Throughout 2004 and 2005, the statute was negotiated. CiU was also included in this process. The final draft of the Catalan Statute was quite radical and represented the maximal programme. PP was the only party that remained outside this negotiation process. Growing tensions between Josep Piqué, the leader of PP in Catalonia, and Mariano Rajoy's polarisation strategy led to the resignation of the former (*El Pais*, 3 April 2005: 34; *El Pais*, 6 July 2005: 17; *El Pais*, 9 July 2005: 23). One of the most contested issues was the wish of the coalition parties and CiU to characterise Catalonia as a nation. This was rejected by the PP and the PSOE was split over this (*El Pais*, 12 June 2005: 28; *El Pais*, 9 July 2005: 21). It was quite important for all parties that any radical reform of the Catalan Statute had to remain within the constitutional framework, otherwise it would be impossible to get approval in the national parliament. In mid-July 2005, the PSC and the CiU were able to achieve an agreement about the Catalan Statute.

Artur Mas had seven conditions for supporting the Catalan Statute, but he was flexible and pragmatic enough to negotiate a final text. The seven conditions were: (1) the protection of exclusive competences, giving the statute a proper name thus making it irreversible; (2) no negotiation of the level of achieved self-government and those proposed by the committee in charge of the drafting of the statute; (3) a new negotiated financing framework; (4) the local authorities to be transferred to the autonomous communities and no longer be dependent on the central government; (5) rejection of a change of the electoral system towards a higher level of proportional representation; (6) unity in action of all parties in the national parliament and (7) opposition against the expression in the original text that education should be public and lay (*El Pais*, 10 July 2005: 25). The tripartite was able to present an initiative with one-fifth of Catalan members of parliament, but it needed the support of the CiU to get it approved. For an approval a two-thirds majority was necessary (*El Pais*, 9 July 2005: 20). The tripartite had only 74 (54.8 per cent) out of 135 seats. They needed the 46 (34.1 per cent) votes, or at least some of them, to get it approved in the Catalan parliament.

After the summer, a radical draft of the Catalan Statute was approved by the Catalan parliament with 88.9 per cent of the votes (PSC, ERC, IC-V-EUiA, CiU). Only the PP rejected it. This was then sent to the Congress, the lower house of national parliament for approval in early November 2005. This led to further negotiations in order to adjust the statute to the constitution. Due to the existing unconstitutional aspects, there was continuing opposition from the PP and some important barons of the PSOE, such as Defence Minister, José Bono Andalusian; Regional President, Manuel Chaves; President of the Parliamentary Constitutional Committee, Alfonso Guerra; and Extremadura Regional President, Juan José Rodriguez Ibarra. One particular issue was the financing model, which was regarded as an upgrading for those of the Basque Country and Navarre (Nagel and Requejo, 2007: 284). Therefore, Prime Minister José Luis Zapatero and CiU leader Artur Mas negotiated, in a marathon session on 21 January 2006, an alternative way of compensating the deficit in GDP contribution that Catalonia had been incurring so far. Indeed, Zapatero and Mas were able to agree on a financial settlement, which allows Catalonia to keep 50 per cent of the IRPF (until then 33 per cent), 50 per cent of the VAT (until then 35 per cent), 58 per cent of special taxes such as those on alcohol and tobacco (until then 40 per cent) and the increase of investments from 11–12 per cent to 18.5 per cent, matching the same amount as those destined to Andalusia.

In exchange, Catalonia remained in the common model of financing of the autonomous communities which is regulated by LOFCA and subject to the decisions of the Council of Fiscal and Finance Policy (see above). Moreover, the need to know two languages was watered down to merit, than a condition to be member of the Catalan judiciary power. The negotiations also allowed an increase presence of Catalan representatives in state and international institutions, including UNESCO (Nagel and Requejo, 2007: 285–7). The Catalan Statute was finally approved on 30 March 2006 in the Congress of Deputies and on 10 May 2006 in the Senate. However, Zapatero's negotiations with Artur Mas led to an alienation of ERC within the tripartite government. The party voted against the negotiated Catalan Statute with the PP and the Basque EA. ERC campaigned against the Catalan Statute in the referendum of 18 July 2006. In spite of the opposition of ERC, the vast majority of the population approved the Catalan Statute to the delight of PSC, IC-V-EUiA and CiU. The overwhelming endorsement of the Catalan Statute by the population disguises the fact that almost 50 per cent did not bother to cast their vote. This strong abstentionism shows that there was a lukewarm public interest for the whole process towards the revision of the Catalan Statute (see Figure 5.17).

The whole process of negotiations was paralleled by actions against the Catalan Statute by PP, the main party of the opposition. The PP collected 2 million signatures until February to organise a parallel nationwide referendum on the Catalan Statute. Less connected to the PP, but supported by the Catholic-conservative media group COPE, an action of boycott of Catalan products and enterprises led to a substantial reduction of sales of Catalan Cava, in Spain. Moreover, anti-Catalanist propaganda spread the rumour that Spanish was being suppressed and people were forced to learn Catalan in Catalonia (Nagel and Requejo, 2007: 283).

After the referendum, the relationship of ERC to the other parties of the tripartite deteriorated substantially leading after the summer to the collapse of the coalition after the withdrawal of its members from the government by

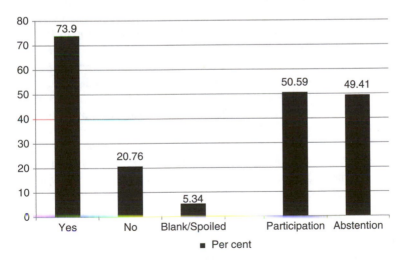

Figure 5.17 Results of the referendum on Catalan Statute in Catalonia on 18 July 2006.

Source: Anuario *El Pais*, 2007: 9.

the regionalist-nationalist party. New elections had to be called 1 year earlier on 1 November 2006. In spite of the early break-up of the coalition, the tripartite government was quite successful in bringing through the process of the revision of the Catalan Statute. Although in terms of coalition government it survived only 29 months, according to Joan Ridao it is above the EU average (Ridao, 2007: 35).

President Pascual Maragall decided not to stand for another term as secretary general of the PSC and José Montilla became the new candidate for the presidency. The elections led again to a victory for the CiU, which improved slightly the share of the vote to 31.52 per cent and 48 seats. However, the party failed again to win an absolute majority. The PSC under José Montilla lost more than 4 percentage points reaching 26.81 per cent and 37 seats. The share of the vote of ERC decreased by 1.25 per cent of the vote to 14.06 per cent and the regionalist-nationalists lost two seats. IC-V-United Left (ICV-EUiA) was able to win three seats and improve from 7.28 per cent in 2003 to 9.56 per cent in 2006. This is quite significant, because the Catalan branch reversed the trend of decline. Last but not least, a Citizens' list called *Ciutadans-Partido de la Ciudadania* (Citizens-Party of Citizenship – Cs) achieved also representation. New PSC leader José Montilla was able to form again a new tripartite government, in which Josep Luis Carod i Rovira became again *conseller en cap* (see Table 5.12).

President José Montilla was able to control better the different political parties within the tripartite government. However, several incidents related to public services damaged the image of the government. Among them was the lighting blackout (*apagón*) in Barcelona in July 2007, the second largest Spanish city. Montilla was quite fast in resolving the crisis by demanding successfully from the electric company Endesa an immediate extra-legal compensation of €60 to (€300 euros until the investigation on who is to blame was completed (*El Pais*, 28 July 2007: 17). In October, a report of the regulatory body, National Commission of Energy (*Comisión Nacional de Energia* – CNE), found out that both Endesa as well Rede Electrica were the main companies responsible for the blackout in Barcelona and they were forced to pay compensation to customers (*El Pais*, 5 October 2007: 22). Furthermore, the delay in building the high-speed train between Barcelona and Madrid which was expected to be finished in December 2007, remained a major theme of criticism of the main opposition party CiU (*La Vanguardia*, 21 September 2007: 15).

The nationalist tendencies of the tripartite government continued to cause tensions between the centre and the periphery. This also led to a growing distance between ERC and the central office of the PSOE, which was still a consequence of the final negotiation of the Catalan Statute in January 2006 only with CiU. There was an extreme possibility that Duran Lleida could become a member of the government, if the PSOE won the elections on 9 March 2008 (*El Pais*, 23 July 2007: 26).

There were also growing worries about the intolerance of some parts of the population against anti-Catanists. Indeed, Albert Rivera, the leader of the Citizens' group *Ciutadans*, received death threats against his person by unknown Catalan nationalists. The main reason is that he criticised the coalition government and some of its more nationalist positions. Police protection had to be allocated to him (*El Pais*, 22 September 2007: 19). The burning of photographs of the royal family by Republican nationalists in Catalonia led also to several solidarity gatherings and repetition of the act during September 2007. Such acts are punishable under Spanish law, because they are offences against the head of state. Last but not least, there were demands of the nationalist-regionalist parties represented in the Congress to allow national teams of the other Spanish nationalities – Basque Country, Galicia and Catalonia – to take part in international competitions. This was rejected by the two main statewide parties PP and PSOE (*El Pais*, 19 September 2007: 21).

Moderation vs radicalism in the Basque Country: the continuing threat of Basque terrorism

One of the big differences between Catalan and Basque nationalism according to Daniele Conversi is that the former is inclusionist, while the latter has strong tendencies towards exclusionism. It means that it is possible for outsiders to become part of the Catalan identity or even have a dual identity, but among the most radical Basque nationalists outsiders are not able to become part of the Basque nation (Conversi, 1997). In the Basque Country, the formation of Basque identity was very much shaped by a political religion created by nineteenth-century political theorist and writer Sabino Arana Goiri. It is clearly an exclusionist nationalism, because it not only emphasises culture and language as important attributes of the identity, but race as well. It was a reaction against the abolition of the fueros, medieval privileges of the Basque region in relation to central government, in 1876. The erosion of the fueros and the special status of the Basque Country and Navarre had already started in 1833, but it became more evident when the Restoration monarchy was installed. Sabino Arana Goiri used the image of an idealised free Basque Country against the centralising tendencies of the modern Spanish state. Spaniards were regarded as foreign, immigrants, called *maketos* in Basque (Beriain, 1997).

Naturally, *Aranismo* is the extreme form of Basque nationalism but there are other more moderate inclusionist forms which found their representation in Basque society. Indeed, the success of the Basque Nationalist Party (*Partido Nacionalista Vasco* – PNV), founded in 1897 by Sabino Arana Goiri, was a product of a compromise between the radical *Aranistas* and the moderate nationalists. It is this moderation of Basque nationalism which led to success and the creation of an inter-classist nationalist party in the early twentieth century. The PNV was also able to survive the dictatorship of Primo de Rivera and became an important regionalist party in the Second Republic. Aranismo was always present, but it did not create any alternative to the parliamentary route in order to attain more autonomy for the Basque regions in Spain (Seixas, 1999: 65–75, 98).

The establishment of Franco's dictatorship forced the PNV leadership into exile. A revival of *Aranismo*, also influenced by the book by German industrialist

Federico Krutwig entitled *Vasconia* and the liberation movements of the Third World, emerged in 1959 when students attached to the PNV decided to create a revolutionary organisation called *Euskadi ta Askatasuma* – ETA. Throughout the 1960s and 1970s, ETA became a major destabilising factor against the authoritarian regime. The climax was the assassination of Admiral Luis Carrero Blanco, number two in the regime, by a car bomb in December 1973 in Madrid (Carr and Fusi, 1979; Conversi, 1997).

During democratic transition, the Basque elites were quite sceptical about the new constitution of 1978. While most Spaniards endorsed the constitution, in the Basque Country it was characterised by a very high level of abstention and 'no' votes. The re-emergence of the PNV as the major party of the Basque Country allowed for the return of moderate nationalism, but at the same time ETA continued its terrorist campaign up to the time of writing.

ETA can be regarded as an extreme interpretation of *Aranismo* based on racist exclusion. In this sense, it is certainly a major problem for all moderate nationalist parties such as the PNV and EA which are representatives of a more moderate inclusionist peaceful nationalism. We can recognise, at least, three main subcultures in the Basque Country, that clearly characterise the fragmented nature of Basque society. On the one hand, there are the moderate nationalists of PNV and EA, which clearly want an end to the terrorist violence, because they want to achieve autonomy, and even independence, through peaceful means. The moderate nationalists are not exclusionists, but tend to emphasise the need to cultivate and speak *Euskera*, the Basque language, in all Basque institutions and society. The second group are the non-nationalists living in the Basque Country. They are content with the state of autonomies and the present status quo. It is quite a large group and quite moderate. It supports the two main parties, the PP and the PSOE, and is categorically against the terrorist violence of ETA. The third group of radical nationalists has a strong Basque identity, which may assume racist tendencies in some cases. Politically, they are close to then People's Unity/Basque Citizens (*Herri Batasuna/Eusko Herritarrok* – HB/EH), the political arm of ETA. If there is a moderation of the discourse, this radical nationalism may represent one-fifth to one-quarter of the Basque population. The hard core of supporters is about 10–15 per cent of the population (Moreno del Rio, 2000; Mata, 1998; Martinez-Herrera, 2002: 436–8).

In the past 25 years, the Spanish government was not able to find a way to eradicate terrorism in Spain. During the 1980s, the Socialist government, allegedly without the knowledge of the Spanish Prime Minister Felipe Gonzalez, engaged in a dirty war campaign against ETA. The Anti-Terrorist Groups of Liberation (*Grupos Anti-Terroristas de Liberación* – GAL), consisting of French and Portuguese mercenaries, killed family members of alleged terrorists in order to demoralise ETA. The GAL affair led to a major political scandal in Spain. It seemed that civil servants and secret service operatives which were taken over from the former authoritarian administrative structure were still using their old contacts and network and acting in the same manner as during the authoritarian regime. The public was outraged, because the Spanish state had sunk to the same level of ETA by using terrorist methods. The former Minister of the Interior José Barrionuevo was convicted (Rubio and Cerdan, 1997; see also Chapter 3). GAL killed twenty-seven people, including ten with no links at all to ETA (Roller, 2002a: 116).

Throughout the 1980s and 1990s, the PNV tried to integrate HB/EH into the political process and isolate ETA. In 1988, the so-called *Mesa de Ajuria Enea* constrained the PNV to isolate HB/EH from the political process, but in 1998 under the leadership of the former president, the *Lehendekari*, of the Basque government, José Antonio Ardanza, an attempt was made to bring together all the Basque nationalist parties. On 12 September 1998 the Declaration of Lizarra was issued which committed all parties to present an inclusive approach to a peace process. The main objective was to achieve self-determination for the Basque Country (Gillespie, 1999a: 125). They were very much influenced by the Northern Irish peace process and wanted to achieve the same for the Basque Country. According to José Mata, twenty-three groups, associations, trade unions and political parties signed the agreement, among them were eight organisations close to ETA. However, none of the main constitutionalist parties signed the agreement. IU signed the agreement initially, but withdrew later on. The Lizarra agreement clearly wanted to achieve a political solution to the conflict between the Basque nationalists and the Spanish state. However, the lack of participation of the main political parties weakened considerably the agreement (Mata, 2005: 89). ETA kept a ceasefire from early 1998 to December 1999. Afterwards it commenced a renewed terrorist campaign, killing mainly PSOE and PP local councillors which lasted until early 2006. In this sense, the whole Lizarra peace process came to a halt. Instead, the central government under Aznar reinforced its position against ETA terrorism. First of all, it signed a pact with the PSOE against terrorism (*Pacto por las Libertades y contra el Terrorismo*). Second, it reinforced the struggle against terrorism by working more closely with the French police and taking a hardline position against institutions related to ETA. Third, in 2002, it changed the law of political parties by introducing constraints to political organisations which support terrorism and violence. This led to the subsequent outlawing of HB/EH. Fourth, Prime Minister Aznar used the international climate against terrorism after the 11 September 2001 events in New York to step up the pressure against ETA. Fifth, it began a judiciary process against the vast legal institutional network that was supporting the organisation. Indeed, ETA is supported by a vast network of enterprises and support organisations. The criminalisation of HB/EH was a major blow to this organisation. The well-known judge Baltazar Garzón, also known popularly as '*Super-Garzón*', who led the investigations on the vast financial empire of ETA discovered the connections between ETA and the huge network of supporting legal organisations (*El Pais*, Domingo, 21 October 2001: 1–5; *El Pais*, Domingo, 6 May 2002: 20; *El Pais*, 18 August 2002: 1–4; Mata, 2005: 98).

The Madrid bombings on 11 March 2004 were initially blamed on ETA by Basque President Juan José Ibarretxe and later on by the Aznar government, particularly by Interior Minister Manuel Acebes. Such allocation of blame was done in a rushed way before all the evidence had been gathered. Later on this was denied by Arnaldo Otegui, leader of the political arm of ETA, *Herri Batasuna*. However, the government stuck to this version of events until the 14 March 2004 elections. Probably, the most embarrassing aspect was the unanimous condemning of ETA for allegedly having perpetrated these atrocious acts by the Security Council of the United Nations on 11 March 2004. On 27 March 2004, the Spanish ambassador had to apologise for this (Alonso, 2007: 124). In the end, the police and secret service investigation found out that actually a north African cell of Al Qaeda led by Imad Eddin Barakat Yarkas, alias Abu Dahdah based in Spain perpetrated the Madrid bombings (Alonso, 2007: 125).

The new evidence already began to emerge during 11 March 2004, but this new line of enquiry became the main one in the following days before the election. One of the reasons for the government to advocate the theory of ETA being involved is that intelligence had indicated that the terrorist organisation was preparing a massive terrorist attack in Madrid. Due to Aznar's strong stance against ETA terrorism, the involvement of the ETA organisation would have boosted its chances in the forthcoming legislative elections. However, an attack by Al Qaeda would remind people that the Spain was involved in the Iraq War, although 90 per cent of the population was against it. This abuse of the ETA version by the Aznar government during the 3 days before the elections was an important additional factor that led to the mobilisation of the population to vote against the government. The Aznar government was held accountable in the 2004 legislative elections for being economic with the truth, and by sticking to a discredited version of events (Lago and Montero, 2006: 24).

The new Zapatero government was very keen to keep the anti-terrorist pact with the PP. However, PP under the leadership of Mariano Rajoy resented still the defeat in the legislative elections after months of being predicted a victory. Party leader Mariano Rajoy and former Prime Minister José Maria Aznar stuck to a thesis of an allegedly ETA involvement in the Madrid bombings and refused to work with the new Socialist government. PP regarded itself as the only party fighting against terrorism, while perceived the PSOE as being weak in this matter. Indeed, during 2005 statements of politicians close to the political arm of ETA, HB/EH began to give signs that a political dialogue and ceasing of all military activities by ETA was possible. In May 2005, Prime Minister José Luis Zapatero was able to get the support of all political parties against ETA terrorism, with exception of PP. The main reason according to PP, is that the party was not previously informed about the intentions of the government. Although Prime Minister Zapatero reiterated the fight against Basque terrorism, continuing so the policies of the former PP government, it left also a door open for political dialogue. However such political dialogue could only take place, if ETA would declare a ceasefire. PP was adamant that this was too easy to meet, it wanted instead a complete disbanding of the terrorist organisation (Alonso, 2007:132).

Finally, ETA declared a ceasefire on 22 March 2006. Although this was welcomed by the Socialist government under Prime Minister José Zapatero, only in June 2006 did Zapatero agree to start a dialogue. However, already in the beginning, the government kept changing the conditions for development of such dialogue. In particular, there was a growing concern about the street violence (*kale borroka*) in the Basque Country, which exacerbated particularly in the autumn (Alonso, 2007:136). Initially, Mariano Rajoy declared that it would support the government, but soon after distanced itself from the government. It also mobilised and instrumentalised the Association of Terrorism Victims (*Asociación de Victimas del Terrorismo* – AVT) against the government on 25 November 2006, because the latter was engaged in a political dialogue with a terrorist organisation. The 'accummulation of conflicts' and tension increased through street violence in the Basque Country.

In the city of San Sebastian over 30 violent incidents took place on 21 December 2006, among them the burning of a public autobus (*Anuario El Pais*, 2007:82). The end of the ceasefire came about when ETA bombed a car park at the Barajas airport on 30 December 2006. Two Ecuadorian nationals who were working in Spain were killed by this bomb, leading to national wide indignation. The bombing in the airport was a major blow for Prime Minister José Luis Zapatero's policy of political dialogue. Opposition leader Mariano Rajoy used the situation to gain political capital, particularly in view of the forthcoming regional and local elections. This became evident, when the main parties had to agree on a common banner for an anti-ETA demonstration on 13 January 2007. In spite of long negotiations, PP decided not to take part in the demonstrations across the country. About 170,000 and 80,000 marched respectively in Madrid and Bilbao, in spite of the lack of support from PP (*El Pais*, 14 January 2007: 26–36). On 15 January 2007, the government asked for the support of all political parties, including PP. It also wanted to change the terrorist pact to broaden the anti-terrorist pact to all parties in the national parliament. Instead, Opposition leader Mariano Rajoy requested first an apology from Prime Minister Zapatero for the mistaken policy of political dialogue with ETA (*El Pais*, 15 January 2007: 1, 18–19).

Since the Zapatero government started its incumbency in July 2007, it has never ceased to strike against the infrastructure of ETA in Spain and France. Indeed, the cooperation between the Spanish and French police has been quite extensive and well coordinated. Since the end of the ceasefire on 30 December 2006, they dismantled several of ETA's key logistics centres. The Franco-Spanish police cooperation was particularly successful during the summer and the autumn of 2007. According to figures from the French police, seventeen *Etarras* were arrested between 30 December 2006 and July 2007. Moreover, a very important logistics headquarters in Aveyron was also seized by the police (*El Pais*, 27 July 2007: 14; *El Pais*, 28 July 2007: 14). However, a bombing of the headquarters of the *Guardia Civil,* a decentralised police force, in Durango near to Bilbao, took place in late August. A further attempt was foiled by the police 2 days later (*El Pais*, 25 August 2007: 17; 28 August 2007: 16–17). The disruption of operations in France and Spain seems to have led to a growing organisational network in Portugal which facilitates operations in Spain. In view of this possibility, the Spanish government has already signed an agreement with the Portuguese government to create similar joint investigation teams of the two countries to prevent such logistics network to establish itself in Portugal. It follows very much the model of the Franco-Spanish police cooperation which has so far created eleven joint investigation teams (*El Pais*, 2 October 2007: 28).

Although the government allowed the Communist Party of Basque Country (PCTV-EHAK) to take part in the 2005 Basque elections, it has been more determined to achieve the illegalisation of the Basque Nationalist Action (*Acción Nacionalista Vasca* – ANV) for the local elections of May 2007. In spite of major efforts of the government, some lists of ANV were able to take part in the local elections of 27 May 2007. Violence of the '*izquierda abertzale*'(Nationalist Left belonging to the successor organisation of HB called *Abertazle Sozialisten Batasuna* – ASB) against PSOE and PNV candidates became a major feature of the local elections in the Basque Country (*El Pais*, 17 May 2007: 20; *El Pais*, 19 May 2007: 26). ANV was successful in gaining twenty-five local councils in the Basque Country, in seventeen of which they gained an absolute majority. They were quite strong in the northern provinces of Vizcaya and Guypuzcoa, but less so in the province of Alava. However, they also won in nine local councils in Navarre, in eight of which with an absolute majority (*El Pais*, 29 May 2007: 20).

However, in the summer, Judge Baltasar Garzón arrested several members of ANV, because of alleged links to *Herri Batasuna* and thus indirectly to ETA. This was possible under the law of political parties adopted in 2002, which stated that legal parties should not have any links to terrorist organisations, nor support or propagate violent actions and organisations (*El Pais*, 5 October 2007: 18–19). Further arrests and dismantling of HB, PCTV and ANV were undertaken during the autumn and the 2 months preceding the 9 March 2008 elections (*El Pais*, 5 February 2008: 18). There has been a growing pressure coming from the Association of Victims of Terrorism (AVT) particularly under the leadership of Francisco Alcaraz, the head of the organisation to ban both the PCTV and the ANV. Since 2004, AVT has undertaken seven demonstrations against terrorism and their proxy organisations, of which three were in 2007. There was a general dwindling of numbers over time. Quite problematic was tendency of some members of PP to use and abuse the AVT for political electoral purposes was quite problematic (*El Pais*, 25 November 2007: 16–17; Baumer, 2007: 156–7).

Since 1968 ETA has killed over 815 persons, among them over 339 civilians and 476 members of the armed forces and police forces. The terrorist campaign in the summer 2003 has increased the number of ETA victims (Ministerio del Interior, 2003). In this sense, the quality of life in the Basque Country has deteriorated considerably. Many young people want to move to other parts of the country in order to have a more peaceful life. Aznar was able to include HB/EH in the list of forbidden terrorist organisations of the European Union and also of the United States. By making it an illegal organisation HB/EH, the political arm of ETA, lost sixty-three mayors and 873 councillors in the Basque provinces of Vizcaya, Alava and Guipuzcoa and in Navarre. It also lost seats in both the Basque and Navarrean parliaments. It also meant that about 10.12 per cent of voters in the Basque elections of 2001 and 15.96 per cent in the Navarran elections lost their representatives over night (*El Pais*, Domingo, 18 August 2002: 4). However, as already mentioned, in the 2005 regional elections PCTV and in the 27 May local elections the new ANV formation was able to capture local councils in the northern provinces of the Basque Country and in Navarre.

ETA also relies very much on its youth movement the *Jarrai*, which clearly are the main protagonists in the street violence (*kale borroka*) in the Basque Country. The terror climate in the Basque Country is reinforced by the fact that enterprises have to pay a so-called revolutionary tax for the cause. If they do not pay, they may be faced with consequences such as kidnapping or other forms of violence. There are also other forms of daily intimidation and threatening behaviour(including death threats) that occur against non-nationalists, which clearly undermine a secure quality of life (Mata, 2005: 100).

Outlawing HB/EH has been rejected by present *Lehendakari* Juan José Ibarretxe, who pushed the debate on Basque autonomy/independence to a new level by calling for a reform of the autonomy statute towards an association. He proposed a roadmap towards independence of the Basque Country with the possibility to achieve integration of the Basque territories in France and Navarre. This has led to a growing polarisation between the Basque government and the central government. The so-called Ibarretxe plan was supported by ETA as a platform for discussion (*El Pais*, 12 May 2003: 15). The plan was approved on 30 December 2004 in the Basque parliament with the votes of the nine *Batasuna* MPs, who, in spite of the illegalisation of the party, were able to keep their seats.

Nevertheless, the two main parties, the PP and the PSOE, were against the Ibarretxe plan as it was against the constitution. Ibarretxe found allies throughout the confrontation in the major regionalist-nationalist parties in Catalonia and Galicia, the CiU and the BNG respectively. The so-called Barcelona conference established in 1998 was revitalised in 2002 and was a sign of a growing polarisation between the centre and the main historical regions. However, the changing political situation in Galicia and Catalonia weakened this regionalist-nationalist block. In February 2005, the Ibarretxe plan was rejected with an overwhelming majority of the Socialist and PP MPs.

At the end of September 2007, Ibarretxe pushed forward anew his plan towards independence. He wanted to organise a referendum in the Basque Country based on his revised plan. Nevertheless, Prime Minister José Luis Zapatero regarded such a plan as being already unconstitutional. Therefore, Zapatero rejected his plan. Ibarretxe also faces opposition from inside the PNV. In particular, the Secretary-General Josu Jon Imaz resigned from his position, because he wanted to achieve a reform of the Basque statute, but still within the constitutional framework. Imaz could find support among other members of the party (*El Pais*, 1 October 2007: 21).

In the past two and a half decades, PNV has been the dominant party in the region. Nevertheless, they were never able to have the same hegemonic position as the CiU in Catalonia. In 1986, PNV had to deal with a splinter party under former *Lehendekari* Carlos Garaikatchoa which advocated a more evolutionary and peaceful approach towards Basque self-determination. Basque Freedom (*Eusko Askatasuna* – EA) is now part of the coalition with PNV and was able to do quite well in the elections of 13 May 2001, but lost votes in the 2005 regional elections. In 2001, together they polled for the first time almost 600,000 votes (42.7 per cent),

Table 5.13 Autonomous elections in the Basque Country, 1980–2005

	1980		1984		1986		1990		1994		1998		2001		2005	
	%	Seats	%	Seats	%	Seats	%	Seats	%	Seats	%	Seats	%	Seats	%	Seats
PNV	38.1	25	42	32	23.7	17	28.4	22	29.8	22	28	21	–	–	–	–
PNV-EA	–	–	–	–	–	–	–	–	–	–	–	–	42.7	33	38.67	29
PSOE	14.2	9	23	19	22	19	19.9	6	14.2	11	17.6	14	17.9	13	22.68	18
EA	–	–	–	–	15.8	13	11.4	9	10.1	8	8.7	6	–	–	–	–
HB	16.5	11	14.7	11	17.4	13	18.3	13	16	11	17.9	14	10.7	7	17.4	15
PP	4.8	2	9.4	7	4.8	2	8.2	6	14.2	11	20.1	16	23.1	19	5.37	3
IU	4	1	1.4	–	1	–	1.4	–	9	6	5.68	2	5.6	3	12.44	9
EHAK-PCTV	–	–	–	–	–	–	–	–	–	–	–	–	–	–	2.33	1
ARALAR	–	–	–	–	–	–	–	–	–	–	–	–	–	–	–	–
EU	–	–	–	–	–	–	–	–	–	–	–	–	–	–	–	–
UA	–	–	–	–	–	–	1.4	3	2.7	5	1.26	2	–	–	0.38	–
CDS	–	–	–	–	3.5	2	–	–	–	–	–	–	–	–	–	–
UCD	8.5	6	–	–	–	–	–	–	–	–	–	–	–	–	–	–

Source: Generalitat of Valencia, http://www.pre.gva.es/pls/argos, accessed on 22 July 2003 and 22 November 2007 and Ministry of Interior website http://www.elecciones2003.mir.es/autonomicas, accessed on 27 May 2003 and 22 November 2007 Note: S = Seats.

Table 5.14 Autonomous governments in the Basque Country since 1980

Legislature	President	Parties	Type of government
1980–84	Carlos Garaikoetxea	PNV	Strong minority government
1984–86	Carlos Garaikoetxea	PNV	Strong minority government
1986–90	José Antonio Ardanza	PNV+PSOE	Coalition government
1990–94	José Antonio Ardanza	PNV+EA+EE, later PNV+PSE	Coalition government
1994–98	José Antonio Ardanza	PNV+PSE+EA	Coalition government
1998–2001	Juan José Ibarretxe	PNV+EA	Coalition government
2001–2005	Juan José Ibarretxe	PNV+EA	Coalition government
2005–	Juan José Ibarretxe	PNV+EA+IU	Coalition government

while HB/EH lost more than two-thirds of the votes, mainly due to ETA's cruel terror campaign. Their share of the vote was reduced from 17.9 per cent in 1998 to 10.1 per cent in 2001 (see Table 5.13).

Francisco Llera Ramo characterises the Basque party system as polarised pluralism. It means that the high level of fragmentation in the different subcultures of the Basque Country leads to polarisation (Llera Ramo, 1998: 430; 1999: 23). Although in the Basque elections of 2005, PNV-EA won the elections, it lost votes and seats. The big winner was the Socialist Party which made substantial gains and contributed to the strengthening of the non-nationalist block. However, a new party called the Communist Party of the Basque Country (*Euskal Herrialdeetako Alberdi Kommunistak/Partido Comunista de las Tierras Vascas* – EHAK/PCTV) which allegedly is strongly linked to ETA obtained 12.44 per cent of the votes and nine seats. PCTV-EHAK has got almost the same amount of votes as Batasuna. As already mentioned, PP and ANV put pressure upon the PSOE to illegalise the new party, which the latter rejected (Baumer, 2007: 151–2).

Growing polarisation between the regionalist-nationalist and the non-nationalist block could be witnessed during the 13 May elections of 2001 and to some extent in the 2005 elections, when the PP tried to use a strategy of polarisation to achieve hegemony in the Basque Country over the nationalist vote. Such an attempt failed, because it led to a strengthening of moderate nationalism under the leadership of the coalition of PNV-EA. Indeed, PNV-EA got the best result ever in the two Basque countries. Such a recovery of the PNV became evident when compared with the previous 1998 elections. In the 2001 elections, moderate nationalism made major inroads into the radical nationalist vote of HB/EH (*El Mundo*, 15 May 2001: 8; Roller, 2002a). In the 2005 regional elections, the coalition government was able to hold on to power, although without an absolute majority. This has consequences for the Basque government. The fragmentation of the party system tends to create minority governments. The PNV has the role of the hegemonic pivotal party in terms of government. It may form a coalition with the PSOE or the PP, but until now it has only had coalitions with the PSOE (see Table 5.14).

In sum, the outlawing of HB/EH has contributed to a further polarisation of the political climate in the Basque Country. Indeed, in the municipal elections of 25 May 2003 the moderate nationalists were able to make further gains, and in the municipal elections of 27 May 2007 keep the losses to a minimum, so that they remain the most important political force in the Basque Country. There is also a general opposition among PNV supporters to the outlawing of HB. The recent demands for further autonomy from the PNV leadership has not been conducive to a rapprochement between the Basque and the central governments.

Emerging nationalism in Galicia: from the dominance of PP to the Socialist-BNG coalition government

In comparison to Catalan and Basque nationalism, Galician nationalism is a late starter. Nevertheless, like these nationalisms, it can be traced back to the nineteenth century. A similar renaissance of Galician culture, the so-called *rexurdimento*, carried out by writers and intellectuals became the first visible signs of a Galician cultural movement. Although there were some political organisations in the early twentieth century, it was only during the Second Republic that political Galicism began to take off. The foundation of the Galician Party (*Partido Galleguista* – PG) in 1931 was an important stepping stone which put the Republican government under pressure to grant an autonomy statute. By the end of the Second Republic the PG had become a strong force in the region. A statute of autonomy was granted shortly before the Civil War in 1936, because the PG supported the Popular Front (*Frente Popular*) consisting of several left-wing parties (Seixas, 1999: 107). During the Francoist period, Galician nationalism had almost disappeared from the region. Some revolutionary groups based on Galician nationalism and influenced by Third World movements appeared in the 1960s, but without major success.

In comparison to Catalonia and the Basque Country the resurgence of Galician nationalism during and after the transition to democracy was a slow process. The fragmentation and in some cases the radicalisation of nationalist parties prevented a strong presence in the Galician party system. Since 1982, Galician nationalism under the leadership of the Nationalist Galician Bloc (*Bloque Nacionalista Galego* – BNG) re-emerged successfully in the regional party system. Its leader was the left-wing intellectual Xosé Manuel Beiras. The main reason for the improvement of the BNG in electoral terms was the fact that the once very radical left-wing nationalist movements joined together and their discourse was moderated. Moreover, the BNG became more inclusionist and tolerant of different currents within the party. Although the party was small in the 1980s, it became the second largest party today. The BNG is ideologically a left-wing nationalist party with strong reservations about European integration. Nevertheless, it clearly supports the state of autonomies and the evolutionary process towards a more federal structure.

There are no ambitions for full independence of the region (Atta, 2003). In 1997 and 2001, the party was able to surpass the PSOE and become the second largest party in the autonomous community. However the losses in the regional elections of 2001 and the municipal elections of 2003 led to a growing call for the resignation of long standing leader Xosé Manuel Beiras. On 22 and 23 November

Table 5.15 Autonomous elections in Galicia, 1981–2005

	1981		1985		1989		1993		1997		2001		2005	
	%	Seats	%	Seats	%	Seats	%	Seats	%	Seats	%	Seats	%	Seats
PP	30.5	26	41.2	34	44.1	38	52.9	43	52.9	42	52.5	41	45.8	37
BNG	6.2	3	4.2	1	8	5	18.7	13	25.1	18	22.9	17	18.9	13
PSOE	19.6	16	28.9	22	32.5	28	25.5	19	19.7	15	22.2	17	33.6	25
IU	2.9	1	5.7	3	5.3	2	3.1	–	0.9	–	–	–	0.75	–
CG	–	–	13.3	11	3.7	2	0.4	–	–	–	–	–	–	–

Source: Generalitat of Valencia http://www.pre.gva.es/pls/argos (accessed on 23 November 2007) and Ministry of Interior website http://www.elecciones2003.mir.es/autonomicas (accessed on 23 November 2007).

meeting of the National Assembly of the BNG he was relieved from his functions by a majority of 75 per cent of the members present. New leader became Senator Anxo Quintana who was more moderate than Beiras and very keen to enter a coalition government with the PSOE after the next Galician elections (Blanco Valdés, 2004: 26). In July of 2004, there was again a challenge of Beiras against the new leadership of the party under Anxo Quintana, but it remained unsuccessful. Quintana was able to consolidate his position until end of the year and become the candidate for presidency for the 2005 elections (Blanco Valdés, 2005: 24) (see Table 5.15).

Galicia was for a long time dominated by the PP. Francisco Franco was born in El Ferrol in Galicia and Galician society is quite conservative due to their socioeconomic agricultural structure. This naturally was an ideal condition for the hegemonic position that the PP had been able to enjoy since the first autonomous elections of 1982. The former President of the Xunta de Galicia was Manuel Fraga, a former information minister of the Franco regime and former leader of PP in the 1980s. He is quite a charismatic figure in Galicia. This autonomous community is one of the poorest of the country, and therefore the decentralisation process contributed to a more focused regional development strategy. This meant a need to modernise the more or less predominantly rural economy (Maiz and Losada, 2000: 67–86). Manuel Fraga was quite successful in promoting the modernisation agenda between 1989 and 2005 (see Table 5.16).

Nevertheless, the sinking of the oil tanker *Prestige* close to the Galician coast on 13 November 2002 led to a change of opinion in Galicia about the regional and central PP governments. The main reason is that oil from the tanker began to leak out and moved towards the Galician coast, destroying the fishing industry and several animal habitats. The environmental catastrophe could have been prevented or alleviated if central and regional government had been faster in responding to it. Instead, there was a delay in preventing the oil spillage from reaching the coast, supporting the clean-up operation afterwards and compensating the people who had lost their income (*El Pais*, 5 January 2003: 16–21; *El Pais*, 25 February 2003: 22–3).

Table 5.16 Autonomous governments in Galicia since 1981

Legislature	President	Parties	Type of government
1981–1985	G. Fernandez Albor	PP	Strong minority government
1985–1989	G. Fernandez Albor	PP	Strong minority government
1989–1993	Manuel Fraga Iribarne	PP	Strong minority government
1993–1997	Manuel Fraga Iribarne	PP	Absolute majority government
1997–2001	Manuel Fraga Iribarne	PP	Absolute majority government
2001–2005	Manuel Fraga Iribarne	PP	Absolute majority government
2005–	Emilio Perez Touriño	PSOE-BNG	Coalition government

This led to a general outrage in Galicia which was directed against former president Manuel Fraga and José Maria Aznar (*El Pais*, Domingo, 19 January 2003: 6–7; *El Pais*, 25 February 2003: 20). An investigation began into the whole process (*El Pais*, 21 January 2003: 19; *El Pais*, 17 February 2003: 23). One basic problem is that the search for the people responsible for the oil tanker catastrophe became an extremely difficult exercise to locate (*El Pais*, 8 December 2002: 28–9). The central government approved an emergency package of 12,459 million euros for a period of 5 years from end of January 2003 to ease the environmental, economic and social problems in Galicia. This was regarded by the Socialist opposition as a mere re-packaging exercise of projects already existing for Galicia (*El Pais*, 25 January 2003: 18). The prestige oil spillage crisis led to the emergence of a major social movement called *Nunca Mais* (Never Again) in Galicia. It included 285 different civil society associations and supported by many parties including BNG, PSOE and IU and trade union confederations. The movement soon became involved also in the anti-Iraq war movement. It organised major demonstrations in Galicia and Madrid and became an important pressure group against the national and regional governments (Aguilar Fernandez and Ballesteros Peña, 2004: 3).

The ecological catastrophe led also to a reshuffling of the Galician government, which was regarded as a sign of factional infighting between Xosé Cuina, accused of conflict of interests due to the participation of his family's firm in the clean-up operation after the catastrophe and Jesus Palmou, loyal to Mariano Rajoy, who at that time was deputy prime minister in the central government. At the last, minute, Jesus Palmou was excluded from the reshuffle (*El Pais*, 19 January 2003: 24). All these developments certainly strengthened the position of the BNG and the PSOE. They were at the forefront in criticising the regional government.

In the regional elections of 28 June 2005, the PP under their president Manuel Fraga Iribarne won the elections, but lost the absolute majority. In contrast, the Socialists were able to improve considerably and become the second largest party in the region. The regionalist-nationalist BNG declined in terms of seats and votes. Throughout July PSG and BNG conducted negotiations towards a coalition government. In the end, a coalition government was formed on 28 July 2007 in which the Socialist leader Emilio Perez Touriño became the president of the Xunta and BNG leader Anxo Quintana its vice-president. Eight of the twelve ministries (*consejerias*) were allocated to the PSG, and four to the BNG. The coalition was also very keen to keep a fifty-fifty balance in terms of gender. Among the main priorities were employment creation through innovation in the regional economy and the re-negotiation of the autonomous statute, particularly in view of including issues such as the definition of Galicia as a nation/nationality and the financial settlement (Blanco Valdés, 2006a: 17–20). In the national parliament, the PSOE could rely on the loyal support of the BNG for his government agenda.

In sum, Galicia is clearly an interesting alternative example of regional nationalism, due to the fact that the main regional nationalist party is not hegemonic, but has gained substantially in electoral terms in the past two decades. The end of the Manuel Fraga period government and the growing credibility of a regional nationalist alternative will make this part of Spain an interesting research topic. One positive thing is that abstention in Galicia has been declining steadily over the years, which is quite important for the political process.

The dominance of the Socialist Party in Andalusia: the problem of underdevelopment

The most stable and large stronghold of the PSOE is the autonomous community of Andalusia. It was also the first autonomous community which tried to achieve a similar status as Catalonia, Basque Country, Navarre and Galicia through the fast-track route defined in Article 151. Although a regionalist sentiment was restricted to a minority before the transition to democracy, during the 1970s it became a social movement. Vast part of the Andalusian population wanted to achieve an equal level of autonomy as the 'historical regions'. The original plan of the UCD was only to grant autonomy to the historical regions, and transform all other regions into administrative units. However, the dynamics of regionalisation led to a growing demand for equal rights in Andalusia. Most of this regionalist sentiment came out of the general feeling that Andalusia was an underdeveloped region within the Spanish economy and wanted therefore to achieve more autonomy to deal with their own internal economic development. A referendum initiative supported by the main political parties took place in 1979, in which 97 per cent of local and provincial authorities supported the referendum. The referendum on 28 February 1980 led to an overwhelming victory of 55.7 per cent of the 'yes' camp, however they failed to achieve the prescribed absolute majority in the two provinces of Jaen and Almeria. In the end, only Almeria remained as a major obstacle for Andalucia to go through the fast-track route of autonomy prescribed by Article 151 of the constitution. After difficult and long negotiations the two main parties, UCD and PSOE, found a way of granting equal rights to Andalusia (Montabes Pereira and Torres Vela, 1997: 10–17; Porras Nadales, 1980).

Andalucia has remained an important stronghold of the Socialist party. The PSOE has been able to keep in power since 1982. Manuel Chaves, the president of the regional government, is one of the most important leaders of the national PSOE. Chaves played a major role in shaping the policies of the Socialist party with main leader José Luis Zapatero. In Andalucia, the party can rely on the left-wing

Table 5.17 Results of autonomous community elections in Andalusia, 1982–2004

	1982		1986		1990		1994		1996		2000		2004	
	%	Seats	%	Seats	%	Seats	%	Seats	%	Seats	%	Seats	%	Seats
PSOE	52.5	66	47	60	49.6	62	38.6	45	43.8	52	44.9	52	51.07	61
PP	17.1	17	22.2	28	22.2	26	34.5	41	34.5	41	38.1	46	32.23	37
PCE/IU	8.6	8	17.8	19	12.7	11	19.2	20	13.9	13	8.1	6	7.61	6
PSA/PA	3	5.4	5.9	2	10.7	10	5.8	3	6.6	4	7.5	5	6.25	5
UCD/CDS	13	15	3.3	0	1.2	0	0.3	0	–	–	–	–	–	–

Source: Generalitat of Valencia website http://www.pre.gva.es/pls/argos (accessed on 23 November 2007) and Ministry of Interior website http://www.elecciones2003.mir.es/autonomicas (accessed on 23 November 2007).

Table 5.18 Governments in Andalusia since 1982

Legislature	President of government	Parties of government	Type of government
1982–1986	R. Escuredo	PSOE	Absolute majority government
1986–1990	J.R. Borbolla	PSOE	Absolute majority government
1990–1994	Manuel Chaves	PSOE	Absolute majority government
1994–1996	Manuel Chaves	PSOE	Minority single party government
1996–2000	Manuel Chaves	PSOE-PA	Coalition government
2000–2004	Manuel Chaves	PSOE-PA	Coalition government
2004–	Manuel Chaves	PSOE	Absolute majority government

vote of the vast majority of the population which is economically disadvantaged in relation to the northeastern regions. During the 1990s, PSOE was involved in several corruption scandals. One of them related to the brother of Alfonso Guerra, Juan Guerra showed tendencies of neopatrimonial behaviour, clientelism and even political corruption. Allegedly, Juan Guerra used official PSOE sites in Seville for private dealings (Heywood, 2005: 42) (see Table 5.17).

In the mid-1990s, the PSOE lost its absolute majority and was dependent on support from the other left-wing groups. Between 1994 and 2004, the PP was able to improve considerably its electoral share, however in the 14 March 2004 regional elections the PSOE was able to regain its absolute majority. Between 1996 and 2004, the PSOE formed a coalition with the small regionalist Andalucian Party (*Partido Andalucista* – PA). This did not have very much effect on the dominance of the PSOE in government. Cases of clientelism and patronage related to the employment programme were highlighted by the opposition in 2001 (Menudo, 2002: 4). The restructuring of the management structure of employment in Andalucia has caused concerns among PP members of Parliament (see Table 5.18).

After the regional elections of 14 March 2004, the PSOE under the leadership of Manuel Chaves emerged as the strongest party. It was able to achieve an absolute majority and therefore did not need the parliamentary support of the PA. During 2004 and 2005, a debate between the political parties about a revision of the autonomous statute took place, in which also the concept of the 'nation' and the financial settlement were included. Finally, a draft of the reform statute negotiated between the PSOE and than IU came to fruition. After being discussed in the Congreso and Senate it was approved during early 2007. Here again compromises were made to include the concept 'nationality' to characterise Andalusia. However, the Andalusian reform of the statute was achieved without any major problems.

In sum, Andalusia is characterised by a high level of stability due to the continuous rule of the PSOE since the founding elections in the region in 1982. It is the main stronghold of the PSOE along with Castilla-La Mancha and Extremadura. Longevity in power has created networks of clientelism and patronage, and political corruption. Probably, the most concrete cases, admittedly not related to the PSOE, were the municipal corruption scandals in Marbella and other towns in the region.

Conclusions: the future of regionalism

After twenty-five years since the approval of the Spanish constitution, it is the state of autonomies that still arouses passions across the country. The three historic nationalities Galicia, Catalonia and the Basque Country are very keen to keep the so-called *hecho diferencial* in relation to the other regions of Spain. This means that there is also a demand for an extension of the autonomies. The Catalan Statute and the controversial 'Ibarretxe plan' for an independent Basque Country created major centre-periphery tensions. The PSOE government under José Luis Zapatero was quite successful in framing and controlling the Catalan Statute within the constitutional framework. However, he was less successful in dealing with the demands of Juan José Ibarretxe for the Basque Country.

This is creating new areas of conflict with the main opposition party, the PP, which is interested in keeping the status quo and cooling off the autonomy process. The PP and the PSOE are very keen to achieve some form of symmetrical autonomy for all regions. While the PP is keen to keep the constitution unchanged and preserve the status quo, the PSOE wants constitutional change and transform the country into a fully fledged federal structure. It means that the PSOE wants not only to positively contribute to the reform of the statutes, but also to achieve a minimalist revision of the constitution. The Basque Country and Catalonia want an asymmetrical position within the Spanish state, which acknowledges their nationalities and Galician nationality at the same level as the rest of Spain. The strong position of the PP at national and regional level makes it very difficult to move towards any change at the moment. Nevertheless, the pressure upon the regional and national elites is rising, due to the fact that the whole process of autonomy is still incomplete and many institutional aspects such as the reform of the Senate into a genuine chamber have still to be solved.

6   Media and politics

The transformation of the media landscape in Spain

In the past 30 years the Spanish media landscape has become very rich and diverse. The growing importance of the media for political campaigns and image management of political parties transformed this aspect essential to understand contemporary Spanish politics. In the development of the modern Spanish media market since the Civil War of 1939 one has to differentiate at least between five main phases.

The first phase comprises the early period of the Francoist regime up until 1965 which was characterised by complete control of the media. The media were controlled by pro-Franco groups, any dissent was censored and prevented. There was no pluralism in the media landscape. Regime propaganda streamlined publications towards the overall message of Francoism, which was directed against the defeated Republican opposition (Cal, 1999; Fadiño, 2003; Eiroa San Francisco, 2007: 27–31).

The second phase started after 1965, when Minister Manuel Fraga Iribarne introduced a law of the press, which liberalised considerably the media landscape. Although there was some control of information, a proper competitive media market was able to emerge. The opening up of the media market was paralleled by major reforms of the authoritarian regime in the economic sector. The new middle classes that emerged in the 1960s clearly represented new markets for the expanding media landscape.

The third phase comprises the transition to democracy between 1975 and 1982. The new democratic structures allowed finally for a new free press to emerge, which should shape substantially the overall process. A major symbol of such democratisation of the media landscape was the daily newspaper *El Pais*, which was supported by politicians from different party affiliations.

The fourth phase can be defined as a consolidation of the new democratic media market. It started in 1982 when the Socialist Party came to power and ended in 1989, when the monopoly of the national television TVE was replaced by a more competitive environment in which three new private channels got licenses to broadcast. After 1995, one could see also the rise of regional televisions in the autonomous communities.

Table 6.1 Distribution of share in media diet (2006)

	Daily newspapers	Magazines	Radio	TV	Internet	Total
Audience (% of population)	41.8	30	56.1	88.6	32.3	
Consumption by user (minutes and seconds)	30	9	199	250	60	
Consumption per capita (minutes and seconds)	125	2.7	112	222	19.4	368,6
Share of Daily Media	3.4	0.7		30.4	60.2	5.3	100

Source: Diaz Nosty, 2007: 29.

The fifth phase started after 1989 and is one of growing competition and concentration of media. It is also a phase where political parties have to develop strategies to bring their messages across in different TV channels, radios and newspapers. From early on, *El Mundo*, founded in 1989 became an important critical voice against the corruption scandals of the Socialist government at end of the 1980s and early 1990s.

One of the major features of this transformation is the role that media is playing in contemporary Spain. As already mentioned in Figure 2.24, in April 2007 65 per cent of Spaniards are informed through the news on television or radio, while only 17 per cent are informed through newspaper reading (see Chapter 2). These figures show that Spaniards are basically informed about politics through the succinct daily television bulletins. The importance of television in the multimedia 'diet', meaning, the share in the total consumption of an individual of all media, cannot be emphasised strongly enough. Bernardo Diaz Nosty calculated based on time of exposition to the individual media, the average multimedia diet of Spaniards. Table 6.1. shows that television by far the most important medium, followed by radio and the Internet – this particularly among young people. In contrast, the printed daily, weekly and monthly press are less relevant in the overall consumption. In 2005 and 2006, Spaniards spent about one-third of their time (excluding sleeping time of 7 hours) consuming multimedia. In total, an average individual spent 369 minutes, equivalent to 6 hours and 9 minutes of their time reading news, listening to the radio or watching television or doing all of them. In 2005, 9 out of 10 minutes was spent listening to the radio and television (Diaz Nosty, 2006: 20). Quite interesting is the growing importance of the Internet, which is used mainly by the younger generations. It bypasses the printed press, but many of these cybernauts may be reading the printed versions on the Internet. Out of the 369 minutes, Spaniards spend about 56.43 minutes reading, listening or watching news. About 51.7 per cent is consumed watching television, 28.4 per cent listening to the radio and 16.1 per cent reading newspapers. Only 4.4 per cent is consumed via the Internet. However between 1995 and 2004 the number of people watching news on television has declined by 3.7 million viewers, the audience shrinked from 57.7 per cent to 48.9 per cent (Diaz Nosty, 2006: 22). Moreover, the quality of

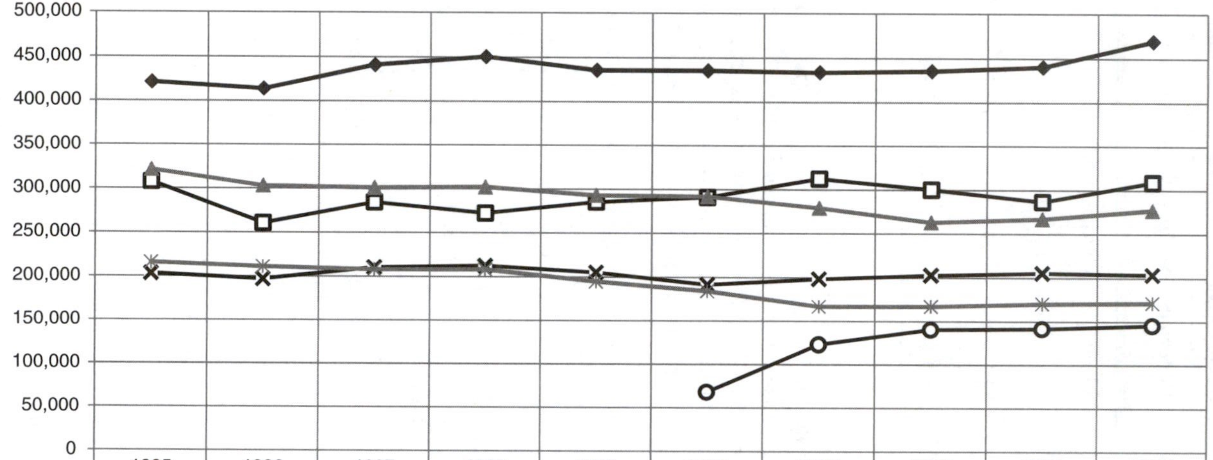

	1995	1996	1997	1998	1999	2000	2001	2002	2003	2004
El Pais	420,924	413,543	440,628	450,176	435,433	435,302	433,617	435,298	440,226	469,183
El Mundo	307,618	260,616	284,519	272,299	285,303	291,063	312,366	300,297	286,685	308,618
ABC	321,573	303,019	301,054	302,013	293,053	291,950	279,050	262,874	266,818	276,915
La Vanguardia	203,026	196,807	210,012	212,202	205,126	191,673	198,337	202,794	205,330	203,703
El Periodicode Catalunya	215,581	210,793	207,772	208,070	194,920	184,251	166,590	166,951	170,170	171,211
La Razon						68,123	122,896	140,096	141,207	145,165

Figure 6.1 Diffusion of six main daily newspapers (1995–2004).

Source: Fundación Telefonica, 2006: 84.

television news bulletins have declined towards a 'tabloidisation' in which scandals and information about celebrities have increased over time (Diaz Nosty, 2006: 23). Last but not least, similar to the north–south gap in the European Union in terms of balanced multimedia diet, the same can be asserted for Spain. People in the northern regions of the Basque Country, Navarra and Asturias read more newspapers and watch less television, in contrast in Extremadura, Castilla La Mancha, Andalucia and Murcia the consumption of television news is much higher and the readership of newspapers lower (Diaz Nosty, 2006: 24).

Political parties and politicians therefore target television and radio increasingly in order to make their message heard. As Richard Gunther, José Ramon Montero and Ignacio Wert have found out, Spanish politics has become considerably Americanised after 1993, when for the first time political parties had to deal with a competitive market consisting of the main public television channels and three further private channels at national level (Gunther, Montero and Wert, 1999). In a study by Javier Alcalde Villacampa on the electoral campaigns during the general elections of 1993, the first time political parties were faced with private television channels, it was found out that viewers that watch the public Channel 1 and Telecinco tended to vote for the PSOE, while those who watched Antena 3 voted for the PP. This was a crucial election, because it led to a considerable rise of the PP in relation to the PSOE (Alcalde, 2003: 159). This means that television plays a major role in reinforcing polarisation in the electoral campaign. As such, it has gained more importance in the past 30 years, but particularly after 1990.

Moreover, one has also increasingly to take into account the regional public channels. Inspite of considerable public funding for electoral campaigns and free time on public television during electoral campaigns, the overall costs have increased considerably. Here suffice to mention that political parties have to work closely with a marketing firm in order to create original campaigns. The Socialist campaign for the 2004 general elections started more than 2 years earlier and comprised a global approach by taking account of regional and local elections (Campmany, 2005).

The printed press: shaping politics and civil society

There is a rich variety in the Spanish press from daily newspapers to weekly and monthly magazines. Probably the most influential newspaper is *El Pais* which reaches almost the half million mark of copies sold every day. This is quite a small number in a country of over 40 million, but it fares well if we take into account that the readership is quite small in comparison with other countries. The readership is also quite fragmented according to regions and provinces. According to the database of the OJD in January 2008, there were ninety-four daily newspapers, of which 90 per cent covered just the regional and provincial level. However, in 2005 in terms of diffusion, regional and provincial papers represented only 40.6 per cent of the market, while national daily newspapers based in Madrid had a share of 27.7 per cent and the two main Catalan daily papers Periodico de Catalunya and

Vanguardia represented 9.7 per cent. Last but not least, daily newspapers of general information have a share of 78 per cent, while daily newspapers that specialise in Sport such as Marca, As and Sport and those that specialise in economic matters represent 19.6 and 2.4 per cent respectively of overall diffusion (Fundación Telefonica, 2006: 84).

Nationally, two main newspapers compete for hegemony, *El Pais* and *El Mundo*. As already mentioned, *El Pais* was founded by the PRISA group under former tycoon Jesus de Polanco. It started as a platform for the liberal opposition against the Francoist regime, but in the 1980s and 1990s was perceived as being to close to the policies of the Socialist Party. This became quite problematic when the PSOE governments were engulfed in several corruption scandals. In 1989 this led to the emergence of a new newspaper, *El Mundo* under the talented chief editor Pedro J. Ramirez. This reported critically and extensively on the corruption scandals of the Socialist governments. Before that, Ramirez was in charge of *Diario 16* but was fired after editorial disagreement (Trenzado and Nuñez, 2001: 517–18). Apart from these two main newspapers, there is also the traditional *ABC* which is quite conservative and is supported by the Catholic media empire. Another major newspaper is *La Razón*, which emerged only in the new millennium. Overall, these newspapers tend also to produce regional editions in order to gain a national readership. The model is naturally *El Pais* which is also well established in the autonomous communities (see Figure 6.1).

Two important aspects allows us to differentiate from other national print press. First, in Spain there is no yellow press such as *The Sun* or *News of the World* in the United Kingdom or *Bild* in Germany. All daily newspapers belong to the serious kind. There have been attempts to open up such a market by German media groups, but without success. Most of the these newspapers survived only a very few weeks or months. According to Manuel Trenzado and Juan Nuñez this has to do with the fact, that this niche is already occupied by so-called '*prensa del corazón*', which are magazines that specialise in gossip and the world of celebrities (Trenzado and Nuñez, 2001: 515). Second Spaniards, like Italians and Portuguese, read specialised papers on sport. In Spain there is *Marca, As, Sport* and *Mundo Desportivo* and they have a large, sometimes a larger audience than the serious press. Therefore, the serious press has also to have a large section on sport in the back pages (Trenzado and Nuñez, 2001: 514).

The three main daily newspapers *El Pais*, *El Mundo* and *ABC* are all based in Madrid. The regional papers target specifically the autonomous community in which they are published. The most influential and prestigious daily newspapers with some national reach are *El Periodico de Catalunya* and *Vanguardia* both based in Barcelona. Both sell over 160,000 copies. In other autonomous communities, regional papers are smaller. In Galicia, *Voz de Galicia* sells over 100,000 newspapers daily, but, for example, *Diario Vasco* sells just under 90,000. In spite of these figures, regional papers are well liked and it shows that Spaniards have a strong affinity to what is happening in their regions and provinces (see Table 6.2).

Table 6.2 Main daily newspapers in Spain and circulation (2007)

Newspaper	Place of publication	Number of newspapers sold (June–August 2007)
El Pais	Madrid	425,000–435,000
El Mundo	Madrid	320,000–337,000
ABC	Madrid	320,000–330,000
La Razón	Madrid	142,000–150,000
La Vanguardia	Barcelona	207,000–210,000
Periodico de Catalunya	Barcelona	162,000–178,000
La Voz de Galicia	La Coruña	103,000–104,000
Diario Vasco	San Sebastián	84,000–88,000

Source: OJD, database on website http://www.ojd.es accessed on 29 January 2008.

Bernardo Diaz Nosty shows in an excellent study that Spain belongs to a southern pattern of low readership of newspapers. According to his figures, in 2004 based on World Association of News figures, circulation per thousand inhabitants was 102.2 newspapers, slightly above that of Italy (101.2), Greece (56.7) and Portugal (56.5). This contrasts heavily with the Nordic countries and the Netherlands with values above 250 newspapers. At the top one can find Sweden with 430.8 and 413.2 newspapers per thousand inhabitants respectively. They are followed by the United Kingdom with 299.2, Austria 292.2, Germany with 260.3 and the Netherlands with 257.5. He comes to the conclusion that overall the Northern countries with a more evolved democracy, social capital and spending ability, have a more balanced expenditure on cultural goods factored into their household budgets (Diaz Nosty, 2006: 18–19). In spite of this north–south gap, Spanish readership of newspapers has been increasing steadily. It reached about 40 per cent of the population in 2005 (Tendencias, 2006: 467). However, the diffusion is quite asymmetrical. As already mentioned Asturias, Cantabria, the Basque Country and Navarra have the highest index of diffusion, while Andalusia, Castilla La Mancha, Extremadura and Murcia have the lowest (Fundación Telefonica, 2006: 88,91). This fact, combined with the studies on the asymmetrical distribution of social capital and associationism further confirms this major north–eastern–southwestern political–cultural division in Spain (see Chapters 2 and 7). In relation to magazines, the readership is even lower and again part of the southern European pattern of cultural habits (Diaz-Nosty, 2006: 19) (see Figure 6.3).

In spite of this low level of readership, one has to acknowledge that Spanish national press is of high quality. *El Pais* has become one of the most important international newspapers around the world and is available globally. The international section and the national news section are excellent and of high quality. The reports are very detailed and well researched. *El Mundo* has also gained quite an important place in Spain, but in many ways remains second to *El Pais* due to its late arrival and emulation of the basic design (León Gross, 2006).

In many ways the free daily press of newspapers such as *Qué!*, *Veinte Minutos*, *Metro* have larger circulations and have now gained a place in the public space.

Table 6.3 Diffusion of regional press in Spain 2004–2005

Ranking consumption/ Diffusion	Autonomous communities	Number of local/ Provincial/ Regional newspapers	Most important local/ Provincial/ Regional newspapers (ranking in terms of diffusion)	
1	Basque Country	4	El Correo (1)	112,588
			Diario Vasco (2)	85,514
2	Asturias	3	La Nueva España (1)	58,150
			El Comércio (2)	27,843
			La Voz de Asturias (3)	9,510
3	Navarre	2	Diario de Navarra (1)	58,208
			Diario de Noticias (2)	16,752
4	Cantabria	2	El Diario Montañez (1)	39,490
			El Correo (3)	4,993
5	Madrid	10	El Pais	171,180
			ABC	117,152
			El Mundo	107,579
6	Catalonia	13	La Vanguardia (1)	180,794
			El Periodico de Catalunya (2)	161,514
			El Punt (3)	27,640
			Avui (4)	25,951
7	Galicia	12	La Voz de Galicia (1)	103,376
			Faro de Vigo (2)	41,430
8	Aragón	4	Heraldo de Aragón	51,080
			Periodico de Aragón	13,469
			Diário de Altoaragón	7,079
9	La Rioja		La Rioja	16,337
			El Correo	2,745
10	Balearics	6	Ultima Hora (1)	33,852
			Diario de Mallorca (2)	22,252
			Diario de Ibiza (5)	7,110
11	Castilla León	16	El Norte de Castilla (1)	38,056
			Diario de León (4)	15,855
			La Gaceta Regional (5)	14,671
12	Canary Islands	7	La Provincia (1)	35,528
			Canarias7(2)	34,453
			Diario de Avisos (5)	10,971
13	Valencian Community	13	Levante/EMV (1)	47,446
			Las Provincias (2)	42,421
			Información (4)	33,513
14	Murcia	5	La Verdad (1)	31,417
			La Opinión de Murcia (2)	10,876
15	Andalucia	25	Sur (3)	37,263
			Ideal (4)	34,403
			Diario de Cadiz	29,004
16	Extremadura	2	Hoy (1)	25,212
			El Periodico de Extremadura (2)	6,899
17	Castilla La Mancha	13	La Tribuna de la Ciudad Real (5)	3,957
			La Verdad (6)	2,657

Source: Own table based on data compiled by Fundación Telefónica, 2006: 45–65.

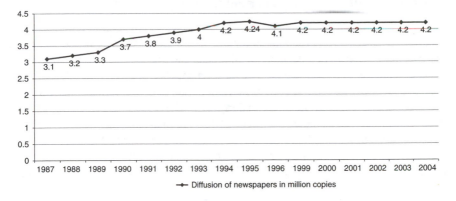

Figure 6.2 Diffusion of newspapers in million copies 1987–2004.

Source: Fundación Telefónica, 2006: 78.

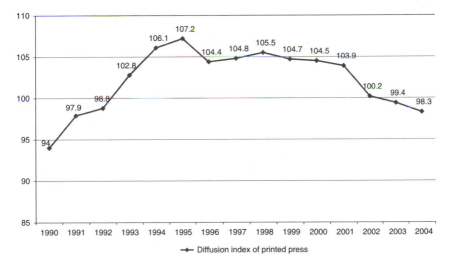

Figure 6.3 Diffusion index of daily printed press in Spain 1990–2004 (daily newspapers per 1,000 inhabitants).

Source: Fundación Telefónica, 2006: 78.

It is estimated that about 7 per cent of the population reads free daily newspapers, corresponding to 800,000 readers. Overall, it is estimated that the readership of the daily papers is about 4.2 million (Gomez Calderón, 2006: 71) (see Figure 6.2).

In terms of ownership, there is a growing concentration of the sector both nationally and regionally. About 60 per cent of income from sale of newspapers was shared between five main corporations Vocento, Prisa, Godó, Zeta and Prensa Ibérica (Gomez Calderón, 2006: 69).

The broadcasting sector: from monopoly to pluralism

For decades the RTVE (*Radio Television Española*) dominated the broadcasting sector. This public broadcasting company had a monopoly until 1989 when the Socialist government decided to liberalise the sector and give licenses to private broadcasting companies. The new channels Antena3, TeleCinco and Canal+ created more competition in relation to audiences. In 2002 further three channels received licenses making now the broadcasting sector quite diverse. This excludes naturally many of the regional and international channels. The Spanish broadcasting market is moving towards the digital age. Spain is committed to the European Union deadline of shutting down the analogue signal by 2012. However, the national deadline is even earlier, on 3 April 2010.

In 2006, RTVE completed 50 years of existence, but its record of the past 30 years has been quite mixed. In spite of major changes in the audiovisual market, it was not able to move with the times. Many experts speak of the high level of governmentalisation of RTVE and the use and abuse for partisan prospects (Herreros, 2007).

All this is considerable pressure upon the national public broadcaster RTVE which has accumulated a deficit of €7.5 billion over the years and still continues to receive considerable subsidies from the government and top ups to cover the yearly deficits. In 2007, RTVE received €435 million in subsidies and had to raise the rest through advertising. The private channels are putting the government under pressure to limit the advertising time of RTVE from 12 to 9 minutes per hour due to the fact that it receives so many state subsidies (*El Pais*, 23 March 2007).

Therefore, the Zapatero government appointed a new president in order to cut costs and create a more virtuous circle in financial and cultural terms. Up until the end of 2008, 4,150 television employees have to leave the corporation, out of which already 3,100 have done so during 2007. Financially, the new administration under Luis Fernandez has created already a superavit. The new regime also forbids the public broadcaster to be in debt at the end of the year. Moreover, RTVE has already reduced advertising from 12 to 11 minutes and there is a possibility of moving fully towards the British system of complete suppression of advertising (*El Pais*, 16 January 2008).

Similar to other national public broadcasters, there is a Council of Administration of RTVE (*Consejo de Administración de RTVE*) in which all main parties are represented. The appointment of the president is no longer done by the government but by the members of the Council of Administration in order to avoid governmentalisation and politicisation of the main public broadcaster. The profile of the appointee, should be based on professional competence in the audiovisual sector.

Luis Fernandez presents himself as a reformer. Among his major projects is the construction of a new RTVE state of the art building, which in the long term will allow to make major savings in different sectors of the company. The basic idea is to sell all RTVE's buildings scattered across Madrid and other places and concentrate all of them in one place, thus creating major savings. There is a follow-up committee on the construction of the RTVE building which integrates the major parties. Some criticisms about the appointment of Pedro Pablo Mansilla, who is allegedly close to the Socialist party to oversee the project were expressed by the opposition. Moreover, he had shares in over twenty estate firms which were incompatible with the position. However Luis Fernandez was very keen to point out that the new appointment was based on its merits and there were no incompatibilities. The appointment also created some unease because Luis Fernandez considered Pedro Pablo Mansilla to be a friend (*El Pais*,13 December 2007; *El Pais*, 21 December 2007). This naturally may lead to substantiated or unsubstantiated rumours and speculations about '*amiguismo*', clientelism and possibly political corruption. This sector has been central to many municipal corruption scandals in past years.

Another major project is to upgrade the position of RTVE in the Internet market. The development of a new more interactive portal has become central to the renewal strategy of Luis Fernandez. The growing importance of television on the Internet is being regarded as an important strategic instrument to compete against other channels. This is something that other Spanish channels are experimenting and developing similar strategies (*El Pais*, 11 January 2008). For RTVE, there has been a transformation of the news sector on the Internet in order to stimulate the national debate about politics (*El Pais*, 9 January 2008). Another innovation will be the use of the co-official languages of the country in the website, achieving so an adjustment to the Spanish plurinational reality. This has been worked out and decided by the parliamentary Joint Committee on the RTVE (*El Pais*, 5 December 2007).

As Figure 6.4, shows the hegemony of RTVE declined since liberalisation of the audiovisual sector. Today, it has a share of 20–25 per cent in the share of the TV audience. The public channels of the autonomous communities kept a stable share of 17–18 per cent, while the private channels captured 45.5 per cent of viewers. This is quite important, because it affects the income from advertising. This becomes even evident, when we take into account that Telecinco (Mediaset + Vocento) and Antena 3 (Planeta + Bertelsmann) are able to challenge its hegemony with similar or higher shares of the audience (Figure 6.5).

In political terms, the private channels have gained importance politically, because opposition leaders refuse to take part in television debates with the government in the public RTVE. A good example is the negotiation between Mariano Rajoy and José Luis Zapatero to have such debates in the private channels Telecinco and Antena3 for the 9 March 2007 elections. Zapatero wanted the national broadcaster to carry out the debates, but it should be broadcast simultaneously by Telecinco and Antena3. Mariano Rajoy, the leader of the main opposition party, rejected this proposal and wanted only Telecinco and Antena3 to carry out the debates. This naturally contributes to the decline of the national provider, it is not trusted to be independent from government.

Economically, in 2005 the market was worth €6.025 billion, of which 72.73 per cent was generated through advertising. The three big channels which are able

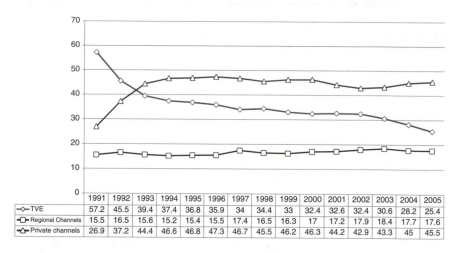

Figure 6.4 Share of television channels (1991–2005).

Source: Ecotel/TNSofres quoted in Fundación Telefónica, 2006: 244.

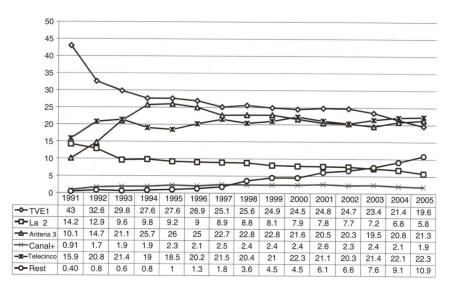

Figure 6.5 Share of television channels at national level (1991–2005).

Source: Ecotel/TNSofres quoted in Fundación Telefónica 2006: 244.

to attract most advertising are TVE1 (16.64 per cent), Antena3 (15.05 per cent) and Telecinco (14.67 per cent) (Fernandez Beaumont, 2006: 223).

   Although public and private channels agreed to self-imposed self-regulation, of which particularly the protection of young people in the prime time period is the most important aspect, there is a lack of adherence to such a code of practice.

On the contrary, Spanish television has deteriorated considerably particularly due to the increased number of reality shows, such as 'Big Brother' The Socialist government introduced the first legislative proposals towards a reform of the audiovisual sector which consists of

- making RTVE more accountable by creating professional criteria for the appointment of the director general;
- streamlining of the financial settlement of the public corporation by not allowing the accumulation of debt;
- creating the conditions for the transition to Terrestial Digital Television (TDT) which implies the switch off of the analogue sign by April 2010;
- approving of a General Law of Audiovisuals, which ensures pluralism and is extremely linked to the transition to TDT;
- introducing a State Council for Audiovisual Media (*Consejo Estatal de Medios Audiovisuales*), but this is still being discussed among experts.

A Law of Public Radio and Television was approved on 11 May 2006; however, apart from this reform of the RTVE all other proposals were not fulfilled. It means that Spain remains without a regulatory body, a unique situation in the European Union. The lack of a watchdog allows the sector to remain unregulated and in some way allows the quality of television to sink even further (Fernandez Beaumont, 2006: 241). Spaniards are quite concerned with what they call 'telebasura'(telegarbage) meaning the flood of low quality programmes on television. The number of reality shows has increased considerably in the past decade. Most of them are imported programmes of low quality appealing to the basic instincts of the population. The main concern is naturally that many of these programmes are broadcasted on prime time television. This means that children may be able to watch such programmes (*El Pais*, 16 November 2007; Parés i Maicas, 2006). One of the reasons for lack of the regulatory agency in the audiovisual sector has been also the wish of parties of government to keep the sector unregulated in order to use and/or abuse the public broadcaster for partisan political purposes (Palacio, 2006; Bustamante, 2006).

Although there is consensus about the transition to digital television, the implementation of the timeline towards switch-off of the analogue signal by April 2010, much earlier than the EU's 1 January 2012, is already delayed. It was scheduled that on 1 January 2008 all local televisions would switch to the digital platform, however the competitions in the autonomous communities are quite delayed or were not even prepared. For example, Andalucia and Extremadura are still to prepare such competitions. Although Spain regards itself as part of the vanguard of countries in the European Union which are implementing TDT, only 9 per cent of households are tuned to it. The highest percentage is in Madrid (16.6 per cent) and the lowest is in Castilla La Mancha (3.8 per cent) (*El Pais*, 9 January 2008; Banegas Nuñez, 2003).

The importance of regional broadcasting

It is also important to make reference to the press and audiovisual markets in the seventeen autonomous communities with their regional newspapers and public television channels. Most of them have no difficulty in exchanging programmes among themselves, similar to what happens in Germany and the United Kingdom. The big differences are the regional press and public channels in the Basque Country and Catalonia with a higher level of regional consciousness.

Programmes in Basque and Catalan are quite expensive to make, because they are confined to the regional market and cannot be exported to other regions. It means that some of the regional public televisions are a major luxury, but they are politically endorsed by the political parties, because it helps to strengthen the regional consciousness. Public television channels in the autonomous communities are instruments of consensual political agendas, particularly in Catalonia and the Basque Country. This means all these public channels receive large state subsidies, due to the fact that their ability to attract advertising is quite low. Dependency on the public purse is high in all public television channels in the autonomous communities but is considerable in Andalusia and Castilla-La Mancha. The Basque, Catalan and Valencian public are somehow in-between, while Madrid, being the capital, has the best record to attract funding from advertising (see Table 6.4).

Similar processes of reform of the audiovisual sector are happening at the regional level. One example is the new Law of the Catalan Audiovisual Corporation which regulates both public radio and television. The new law approved in early

Table 6.4 Budget of public television in autonomous communities (2004)

	Annual budget 2004	Subsidies (Share in percentage)	Advertising (Share in percentage)	Other (Share in percentage)
Radio Televisión de Andalucia (RTVA)	469.5	82.8	11.1	6.1
Radio Television Castilla-La Mancha (CMTV)	55.8	91.9	8.1	
Corporació Catalana de Rádio-Televisió (CCRTV)	481.6	62.5	25.6	11.9
Radio Televisió Valenciana (RTVV)	251.1	70.9	16.4	12.7
Compañia de Radio Televisión de Galicia (CRTVG)	122.6	71.7	13.6	14.7
Radio Television Madrid (RTVM)	150.3	50.4	42.6	7
Euskal Irratia Telebista (EITB)	146.4	75.3	19.7	5

Source: Fundación Telefónica, 2006: 265.

October 2007 created a new council of government which was directly elected by the Catalan Parliament with two thirds majority. This reform seeks, similar to the national one, to reduce the influence of the government in the running of public television. However, PP and the new citizen's group *Ciutadans* voted against it, because the Law defines Catalan as the institutional language of the corporation. The Law was approved with the votes of PSC, CiU, ERC and IC-V (*El Pais*, 6 October 2007). However, the proposed twelve members nominated by the main parties of the Catalan parliament, of the first oversight committee were regarded as too close to partisan politics to act independently on behalf of the general interest. The Catalan Audiovisual Council (CAC) criticised the Catalan parliament for nominating people very close to the Catalan political parties. Before the twelve members are ratified, there will be also committee hearings in the Catalan parliament. Among the nominated prospective members are Albert Saez (ERC) who is Secretary of Communication of the Catalan Government, Roger Loppacher (CiU) the former General-Secretary of the Interior and Angela Vinent (PSC) Chief of the Press Cabinet of President Pascual Maragall (*El Pais*, 17 January 2008). This naturally further undermines the original reform intentions in the eyes of the population. Partisan interest remains a major problem in the governance of the public audiovisual sector, both at national and subnational levels.

The growing importance of the Internet

Spain is lagging behind in terms of use of the Internet by the population. However, use of the Internet has been growing steadily. The sector of Technologies of Information and Communication (TIC) have been increasing annually on average by 8 per cent and in 2005 the industries generated €15.5 billions. It is particularly the younger people who use the Internet. However, mobile phones and other technologies such as TDT may help increase the number of people connected to the world wide web. As Figure 6.6. based on data from the Association for the Research of Communication Media there has been a steep increase of people using the Internet, which is just slightly below 40 per cent. However, regularly use (using the Internet yesterday) is only done by 8.838 million people or 23.4 per cent (AIMC, 2007: 5) (see Figure 6.7).

As Figure 6.8 shows Spain is still lagging behind in comparison to the Nordic countries, the Benelux and the British isles. It is also lagging behind in relation to the EU-15 and EU-25 average. However, Spain is doing better than France, Poland and Italy (see Figure 6.8).

In spite of these small numbers, the role of the Internet as a media of information and communication has increased considerably. A large number of Spanish cybernauts use the Internet for information purposes (see Figure 6.9). Spain is also characterised by gender inequalities in access to the Internet. There are more male cybernauts, than female ones. However, this inequality has been decreasing since 2001 (see Figure 6.10). As already mentioned the vast majority of cybernauts are young, in the ages between 15 and 44, while the older population is quite excluded.

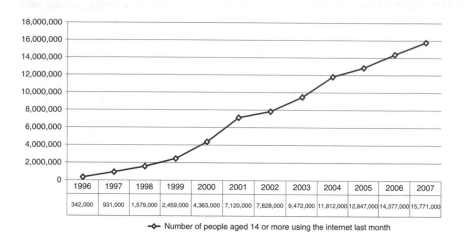

	1996	1997	1998	1999	2000	2001	2002	2003	2004	2005	2006	2007
	342,000	931,000	1,579,000	2,459,000	4,363,000	7,120,000	7,828,000	9,472,000	11,812,000	12,847,000	14,377,000	15,771,000

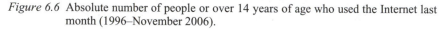
—◇— Number of people aged 14 or more using the internet last month

Figure 6.6 Absolute number of people or over 14 years of age who used the Internet last month (1996–November 2006).

Source: Associacion para la Investigación de los Medios de Comunicación, 2007: 5.

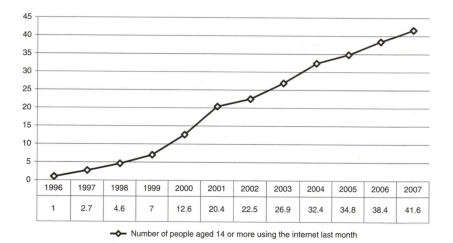

	1996	1997	1998	1999	2000	2001	2002	2003	2004	2005	2006	2007
	1	2.7	4.6	7	12.6	20.4	22.5	26.9	32.4	34.8	38.4	41.6

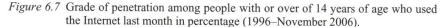
—◇— Number of people aged 14 or more using the internet last month

Figure 6.7 Grade of penetration among people with or over of 14 years of age who used the Internet last month in percentage (1996–November 2006).

Source: Associacion para la Investigación de los Medios de Comunicación, 2007: 5

Particularly, the age groups after 65 are excluded from the new technologies (see Figure 6.11).

Moreover, the vast majority of cybernauts belong to the wealthier classes. There is considerable social inequality in the access to the Internet in Spain. Over 75 per cent of cybernauts are students, which shows that education plays a major role in facilitating access to the Internet (Fundación Telefónica, 2007: 20) (see Figure 6.12).

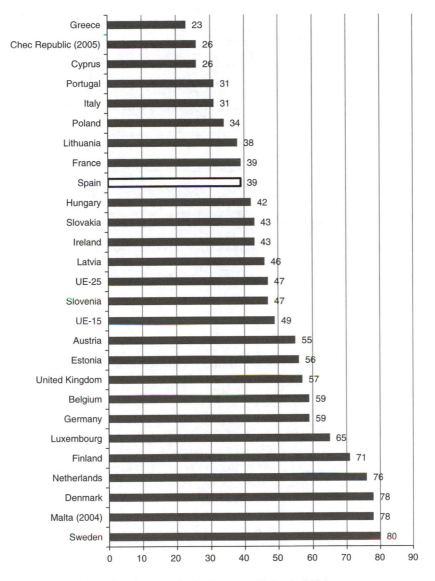

Figure 6.8 Penetration of Internet in the European Union in 2006.

Source: Eurostat, quoted from Fundación Telefónica, 2007: 7.

In sum, Spain is still lagging behind in terms of access to the Internet. Newspapers, television and radio channels have increased their attention to their Internet websites. For example, *El Pais* has a link to the Spanish version of CNN. Moreover, it has also established links to other European newspapers such as *Le Monde*.

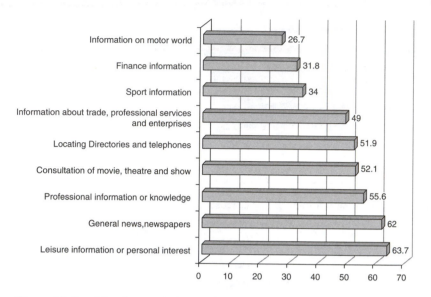

Figure 6.9 Spanish cybernauts who use the Internet for different information purposes in 2006.

Source: Fundación Telefónica, 2007: XXIII.

The political economy of the multimedia landscape in Spain

One of the reasons for the decline of quality of television has been the fierce competition between the different media groups in Spain. Since the transition of democracy there has been a steady concentration of all the media among few groups. The growing importance of TDT and Internet has led to multimedia platforms of the major groups. The media landscape is constantly changing due to the buying and selling of some of the companies between the media groups in order to increase the market share or its yearly profit. One can speak of a political economy in the multimedia sector, of which main objective is to increase profit through attracting more advertising revenue. There are seven main groups which are engaged in a competition for market share in all media sectors. These are VOCENTO, PRISA, Unidad Editorial (Unidesa), Recoletos, Godó, Zeta and Planeta.

In 2004, in the printing market VOCENTO had slightly the largest share of market with 18.7 per cent. It publishes *ABC* and many provincial and local papers such as *El Correo Español* (Bilbao), *Diario Vasco* (Santander), *Diario Sur* (Malaga), *Ideal* (Granada) and *Hoy* (Badajoz). In total it publishes fourteen newspapers. VOCENTO has a share in Telecinco of 13 per cent, but has concentrated on regional and local television markets. Its dominance in the printed press market, is less evident in other media.

PRISA is a close second with the first newspaper of the country, *El Pais* and the second Sport newspaper As, all other newspapers are quite small. However, it

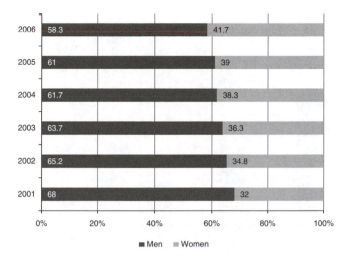

Figure 6.10 Gender inequality in access to Internet in 2006.
Source: AIMC, EGM quoted in Fundación Telefónica, 2007: 17.

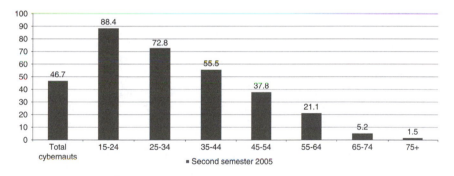

Figure 6.11 The cybernauts according to age in second semester of 2005.
Source: Redes, quoted from Fundación Telefónica, 2007: 19.

is probably the largest market group with stakes in all media sections. In total it has seven newspapers. It controls the private channel Canal+. The PRISA group is also quite engaged in the TDT market and is very keen to expand to the Latin American markets, in particular to Argentina. In terms of income it is the strongest of the three main private channels. Moreover, PRISA has also a strong presence in the radio sector with cadena SER.

Although in the printed press the Planeta group is not very important, in terms of a multimedia platform it is the second-largest group. It controls the popular private channel Antena3. The fourth group is Recoletos with 10.1 per cent market share, among the three newspapers that it publishes one has to highlight the main Sports newspaper Marca. In terms of market share, Grupo Zeta consists of nine

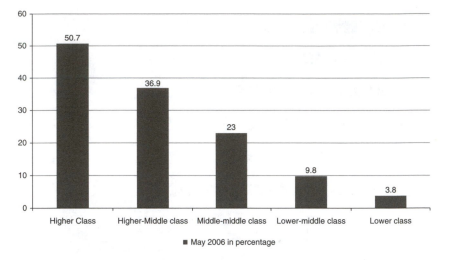

Figure 6.12 The social class of Spanish cybernauts in May 2006.

Source: AIMC, quoted in Fundación Telefónica, 2007:20.

newspapers and has 8.3 per cent of the market share. The most important newspaper is *Periodico de Catalunya*. The ZETA group is also more interested in the regional TV and radio market. Moreover, it has been engaged in having a share in the free newspaper market, which is a growing phenomenon in the major cities of Madrid, Barcelona and Seville.

The sixth group is Prensa Ibérica, which publishes fifteen regional newspapers and is not as strong as the other main media groups. It has a market share of the printed press of 7.3 per cent. The family enterprise Godó controls two newspaper, among them La Vanguardia and achieves therefore a market share of 7.2 per cent. It concentrates its main activity in Catalonia. It is engaged in regional and local television in Catalonia. The group Recoletos is also involved in VEO TV together with Unedisa.

Planeta controls the Barcelona-based newspaper *Avui*. Moreover, It has a stake in the radio market through the popular *Onda Cero* with about 1.3 million listeners everyday, the third largest audience after PRISA's SER and the Catholic Church owned COPE. This contributes to the strong position of the group in the market.

Unedisa in which Italian tycoon Silvio Berlusconi has a large share, controls *El Mundo*, the second largest national newspaper. Unedisa has not been very successful with the new VeoTV, because of the delays in TDT. The group Recoletos is also involved in VEO TV together with Unedisa (Palacio, 2006: 425–38).

Other smaller groups in terms of the printed press are the Voz group which publishes two newspapers, among them *Voz de Galicia*, and the Joly group which controls many of the regional papers in Andalucia. Each have 2.8 and 2.3 market share respectively (Fundación Telefónica, 2006: 108–9).

In sum, in the past three decades there has been a growing concentration of the multimedia market. Although there are about seven groups dominating the market, PRISA is gaining a considerable advantage in all sectors, particularly in the multimedia sector. However, VOCENTO remains the strongest in the printed press market. All other groups have areas of strength, but overall remain weaker than these two main groups.

Conclusions: the marketisation of the media landscape

In the past 30 years, the Spanish media have changed considerably. After decades of censorship and control of the media by the authoritarian regime, Spain experienced a boom in publications, television and radio channels. In spite of the diversity, there is a growing concentration of multimedia taking place. Similar to other European countries, the large media groups are interested in creating multimedia platforms. The race for TDT and Internet-based services will determine the future of some of the larger groups. In terms of politics, political parties and interest, groups have to use the new media to spread their message. Such multimedia strategy are quite expensive, even with the generous state funding of political parties. This means that the media and their control have become a battleground for political parties. The recent reforms of the RTVE and public television in the autonomous communities have to be regarded in this context. The politicisation of the mass media and the mediatisation of politics will continue to be a major issue in contemporary Spanish politics.

7   Interest groups and civil society

The growing importance of interest groups in Spain

One of the main indicators about the quality of democracy is the strength and involvement of interest groups and civil society in a particular political system. Most new democracies need a long period of at least three decades to develop new democratic patterns of interest intermediation. As already mentioned in Chapter 2, Spain has still one of the lowest levels of associativism in the European Union. It contrasts heavily with countries in Northern Europe such as Norway, Sweden, Denmark, Finland, Germany and the Netherlands. However, apart from the exception of Slovenia, Spanish civil society is stronger than most countries in central and eastern Europe, which had to dismantle previous state organisations in order to create a pluralist society. The Spanish authoritarian regime under Franco allowed for some associativism, however it was biased towards associations with ideological affinity. Interest groups and associations of civil society are here understood as private organisations which are independent from state and are committed to influencing public policy within a democratic context. Although this chapter stands on its own, it is advisable to read it in conjunction with Chapter 2 which has much additional information.

After three decades, Spanish economic, social and political interest groups have gained an indispensable place in society, however their material and human resources are still weaker than in most countries. Among the youth, nongovernmental organisations are very popular, particularly if they deal with aspects of global justice such as poverty, trade imbalances and development. The Zapatero government made a commitment to increase the Spanish contribution to the elusive 0.7 per cent of GDP for international development requested from the United Nations. In this chapter, we want to give a brief overview of the main traditional interest groups and then speak of the new social movements in Spain, since the women's, gay, environmental and other movements that have contributed to a more diverse, richer and tolerant society in the past three decades.

Business organisations: the quest for unification

The main social partners are the employers' organisation, the Spanish Confederation of Business Enterprises (*Confederación Española de Organizaciones Empresariales* – CEOE) and the Spanish Confederation of Small and Medium Sized Enterprises (*Confederación Española de Pequeñas y Medias Empresas* – CEPYME) on the one hand, and the main Employees' organisations on the other, which were the Workers' Commissions (*Comisiones Obreras* – CCOO) and the General Workers' Union (*Unión General de Trabajadores* – UGT). CEPYME is actually part of the CEOE (see further for more detail).

After the creation of several local business organisations, the CEOE was founded in June 1977 to defend the interest of employers vis-à-vis a very militant trade union movement. It was an organisation that reacted to the dynamics of the emerging democratic order. The main policy of CEOE was to become the dominant, hegemonic organisation in Spain. After negotiating with CEPYME by offering additional services which the latter could not afford it was able to gain a foothold in small- and medium-sized enterprises, which are quite numerous in Spain. CEOE was always active in lobbying for a liberalisation of the economy. During the 1980s, it supported the People's Party politically, in the hope that Manuel Fraga would come to power. However, after 1986 CEOE became more neutral in relation to the different political parties. The social liberal policies of the PSOE under Prime Minister Felipe Gonzalez were compatible with many demands of the main Spanish organisation.

The growing importance of the social partners after the Treaty of the European Union signed in 1993, strengthened the position of the main business organisation. The convergence process initiated by Economic and Monetary Union (EMU) required growth and stability pacts in which the social partners were important to achieve its implementation. During the Aznar period, CEOE was a strong partner of the government. Soon after the general elections of 1996, several agreements were signed and implemented which allowed for the improvement of the labour market situation. Among them was the Agreement on the Extrajudicial Solution of Labour Conflicts (*Acuerdo de Solución Extrajudicial de Conflictos Laborales* – ASEC), Agreement on Social Protection and Pensions, Basic Agreement on Vocational Training Policy. The climax of such activity by Minister Javier Arenas were agreements related to the liberalisation of the labour market on 28 April 1997. This was an important breakthrough, because the late Gonzalez governments after the general strike of 1988 were not able to achieve any major progress in this respect (Molins and Casademunt, 2001: 483). The present leader José Maria Cuevas, re-elected to the general assembly in February 2002 for a sixth term, has been so far a supporter of social dialogue. This became apparent when CEOE, in spite of change of government, continued to support the process towards reform of the labour market. This became evident when the 'Law of Improvement of Growth and Employment' was endorsed by the CEOE and the trade union confederations (Martin Artiles, 2005a; 2007). This cooperation has led to a considerable expansion of the Spanish economy, a considerable reduction of strike activity and a high level of social peace, preconditions to make the Spain an attractive investment place.

CEOE's ambition to become the main business organisation led to the integration of the National Confederation of Farmers and Cattle-Breeders (*Confederación Nacional Agricultores y Ganaderos* – CNAG) which comprises the larger land owners in Andalusia and Extremadura. CNAG originated from the former vertical corporatist organisations of the former regime and was transformed into a democratic interest group. The weak level of associationism in the agricultural sector led to this strategic choice of CNAG (Molins and Casademunt, 2001: 476, 485). Also the Agrarian Association of Young Farmers (*Associación Agraria de Jovenes Agricultores* – ASAJA) is part of the CEOE. It comprises small landowners, their family members and tenants. It consists of small- and medium-sized enterprises which are organised in the CEPYME within CEOE. It has a membership of about 200,000 members and comprises about 230,000 full-time employees. It has a coverage of about 50 per cent of the type of companies in the agricultural sector, and about 8 per cent overall. The ASAJA covers about 25 per cent of all employees in the agricultural sector (Gangas, 2007).

It is difficult to estimate how many enterprises are part of the CEOE. In the mid-1990s it claimed to represent 1.3 million firms or approximately 90 per cent of trade and industry, which were organised in 165 regional and branch organisations (Meer, 1996: 321; Schmitter, 1995: 299; Molins and Casademunt, 2001: 476; Campo, 2002: 169–71). Organisationally, CEOE has to deal with conflicts with the territorial organisations which sometimes have other priorities than the central leadership of the confederation. There is also the issue of representativeness. There is some asymmetrical representativeness of enterprises and a continuing problematic relationship with Chambers of Commerce.

Trade union confederations: problems of unionisation

The trade union confederations UGT and CCOO were founded before 1974. The UGT was the trade union branch of the PSOE and was founded in 1888. It was quite an important trade union movement up until the end of the Civil War along with the anarchosyndicalist National Confederation of Labour (*Confederación Nacional del Trabajo* – CNT). During Francoism, it was unable to act inside Spain. It re-emerged in the 1970s, before the death of the dictator. It had considerable support from the German Trade Union Confederation (*Deutscher Gewerkschaftsbund* – DGB) and the Friedrich Ebert Foundation (*Friedrich Ebert Stiftung* – FES) (Führer, 1996: 190–1). It is presently the largest trade union confederation along with the Workers' Commissions (*Comisiones Obreras* – CCOO). The CCOO was founded in the early 1960s as a loose confederation of several workers' commissions. It consisted of communist and christian trade unionists. It was able to penetrate the Francoist vertical corporatist structure and play a major role in destabilising the regime.

Outlawed in 1967, it continued to play a major role in establishing an alternative trade union movement. During and after transition, CCOO became the largest trade union confederation, only to be matched at a later stage by the UGT. Although initially both trade union confederations were competing against each other, disappointment with the policies of the Socialist party after 1982 led to a major split of the so-called 'Socialist family' and subsequently a growing cooperation between the two main trade union confederations. The crucial turning point was in 1988, when the two trade union confederations organised a general strike against the government due to its intentions to liberalise the highly rigid labour market. The split of the 'Socialist family' should lead to a growing conflict between the two trade union confederations and the government (Gillespie, 1990). This meant that between 1988 and 1996, the Socialist government was unable to undertake major labour market reforms. There was a stronger inclination to support the demands of the business organisation CEOE, than those of the trade union confederations (Royo, 2001). One of the major factors affecting the decision-making process towards liberalisation of the labour market was the growing importance of EU-level policies. This 'Europeanisation of labour market policies' has to be understood within the framework of the growth and stability pacts which sustained the convergence processes of the Spanish government towards EMU (Chari, 2001: 66). According to Raj Chari financial support from members of the Spanish Banking Association (*Associación Española de Bancos –* AEB) such as Banco Bilbao Vizcaya, Santander and Central Hispano Americano in the value of 4.5 billion pesetas in interest-free loans for electoral purposes moderated also the discourse of the '*guerristas*' in the first half of the 1990s. Allegedly, these loans were never repaid (Chari, 2001: 63). In the 1990s, the UGT and CCOO slowly abandoned their ideological linkages to the PSOE and PCE respectively and became more up to date. As already mentioned, since the general strike of 1988, there has been a transformation of trade unionism towards a more professional approach. This led also to internal restructuring of the confederations in the 1990s in order to strengthen the leadership of both confederations. In this context, leaders Antoni Gutierrez of the CCOO and Candido Mendez of the UGT have to be singled out for their moderate and professional approach towards trade unionism. In 2000, Antoni Gutierrez was replaced by Hidalgo, who pursued a similar moderate constructive approach towards social partnership and social dialogue. Both confederations decided to have a more neutral position in relation to the political parties. Therefore, the Aznar government was able to achieve agreement on many areas related to the labour market and social welfare (Magone, 2001).

However, in 2002 the Aznar government tried to introduce more labour market reforms including a lowering of the dismissal financial compensation and of the umemployment benefit without the support of parliament by introducing a governmental decree and this led to considerable protest of the trade union confederations and the opposition parties. In the end, the government had to give in and negotiations with the social partners led to a compromise.

The Zapatero government emulated many of the policies of the Third Way by keeping at equidistance both trade union confederations and business organisations. This policy allowed for the conclusion of several agreements, which are accompanied by new social legislation. The social market economy model of the Zapatero government finds strong support among trade unionists. Moderation and consultation are two aspects of the social dialogue which attempts to work alongside long-term policies of strengthening the Spanish economy, in order to achieve better employment, employability and quality of life. So far, the government avoided major confrontations with the two trade union confederations, which allowed to preserve a climate of social peace in the country.

Spain has the lowest level of trade union membership in the European Union, although in recent times it has been rising again. In the 1990s, membership was around 11–16 per cent, while figures of the Ministry of Labour and Social Affairs suggest that it has risen to 18.1 per cent in 2001 (Simón, 2003: 72). According to Pere Beneyto, quoted by Antonio Martin Ardiles, in 2003 trade union affiliation was at 17 per cent (Figure 7.2.), however one has to take into account that the overall occupational rate among the working population has increased considerably as Figure 7.1. shows. The strongholds of Spanish trade unionism are Madrid, Catalonia, Asturias, Valencia and the Basque Country. The main source of tensions is between the grass-roots organisations and the central leadership in Madrid. In the 1990s, there were also conflicts within certain sectors due to the fight between the more ideological left-wing sector and the new professionally oriented emerging group. In particular, Candido Mendez of UGT had to deal with opponents of the left. Similarly, Antoni Gutierrez of CCOO was an important reformer within the organisation, in spite of considerable resistance of a large ideologically sector close to the Communist Party (Molins and Casademunt, 2001: 481; Magone, 2001). Nevertheless a comparison with other west European countries shows how weak trade union membership is in Spain (see Figure 7.3).

Trade unionism in Spain is not only measured by membership rates. More important are the regular trade union elections which take place every 5 years. From

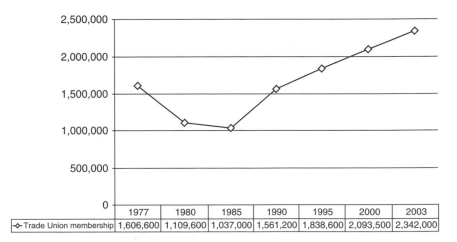

Figure 7.1 Trade Union Membership 1977–2003.

Source: Beneyto, 2004 quoted in: Martin Ardiles, 2005.

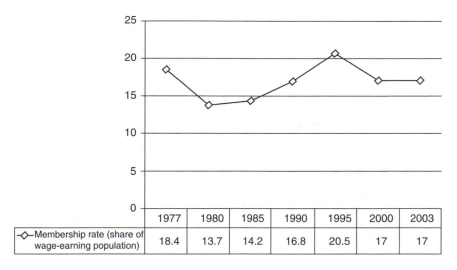

	1977	1980	1985	1990	1995	2000	2003
Membership rate (share of wage-earning population)	18.4	13.7	14.2	16.8	20.5	17	17

Figure 7.2 Trade Union Membership 1977–2003.

Source: Beneyto, 2004 quoted from: Martin Ardiles, 2005b.

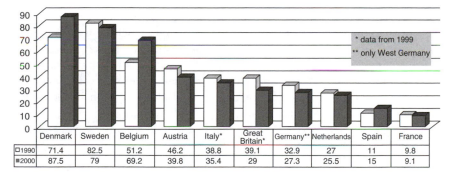

	Denmark	Sweden	Belgium	Austria	Italy*	Great Britain*	Germany**	Netherlands	Spain	France
□1990	71.4	82.5	51.2	46.2	38.8	39.1	32.9	27	11	9.8
■2000	87.5	79	69.2	39.8	35.4	29	27.3	25.5	15	9.1

* data from 1999
** only West Germany

Figure 7.3 Trade Union Membership in selected European countries 1990–2003.

Source: Institute for German Economy,Cologne, quoted from Fischer Weltalmanach 2004: 299.

there one can see that both main trade union confederations are almost equal in terms of electoral support. According to unofficial results provided by the Ministry of Labour and Social Affairs in the elections of 2000, the UGT is supported by 37.86 per cent of voting workers, CCOO by 38.15 per cent, while other trade union confederations at national and regional level are supported by 15.51 per cent (EIRO, 2001: ES0107150N). However in 2003, the slight advantage of one confederation over the other inverted from 39 per cent for the UGT and 37 per cent for the CCOO (see Figure 7.4.). According to Antonio Martin Ardiles, over 50 per cent of workers in enterprises take part in these elections, although enterprises with less than six employees do not (Martin Ardiles, 2005b) (Figure 7.4 and Figure 7.5).

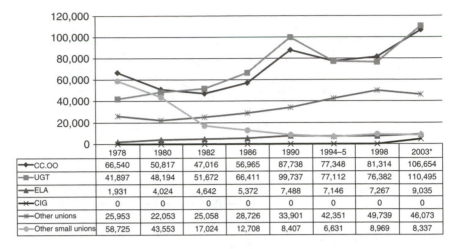

	1978	1980	1982	1986	1990	1994–5	1998	2003*
—♦—CC.OO	66,540	50,817	47,016	56,965	87,738	77,348	81,314	106,654
—■—UGT	41,897	48,194	51,672	66,411	99,737	77,112	76,382	110,495
—▲—ELA	1,931	4,024	4,642	5,372	7,488	7,146	7,267	9,035
—✕—CIG	0	0	0	0	0	0	0	0
—✳—Other unions	25,953	22,053	25,058	28,726	33,901	42,351	49,739	46,073
—●—Other small unions	58,725	43,553	17,024	12,708	8,407	6,631	8,969	8,337

Figure 7.4 Trade Union Elections 1978–2003.

Source: Beneyto, 2004 quoted in : Martin Ardiles, 2005.

In sum, Spanish trade unionism has evolved from a highly ideological fragmented movement, which was attached to different political parties such as the CCOO to the Communist Party and the UGT to the PSOE to a more professionalised one, in which workers and employees are offered a package of services, including protection of their rights. This transformation has led on one hand to a close relationship of cooperation between the two main trade union confederations, but on the other hand the emergence of new sectoral and occupational trade unions which also adhere to the professional approach of delivery of services. In regional terms, only in Galicia and the Basque Country did trade unionism emerge, which are closely linked to the BNG and the PNV respectively.

The farmers' organisations

The Spanish agricultural sector is quite fragmented in terms of representation both on the employers' as the well as the workers' sides. This naturally weakens the position of the agricultural lobby in relation to the government. The use of unconventional protest actions is common among the strategies of farmers. In spite of the large funding coming from the Common Agricultural Policy (CAP), most Spanish farmers and land labourers struggle to make ends meet.

According to a study by Pilar Gangas there are about 2.3 million people (5.07 per cent of overall employment) working in the agricultural sector, of whom about 1.3 million (3.2 per cent of overall employment) are employees. They work in 1.14 million agricultural enterprises. All this shows that the agricultural sector is still very fragmented depending on the region. There are huge differences between Galician, where small-and medium-sized enterprises predominate, and Andalusia

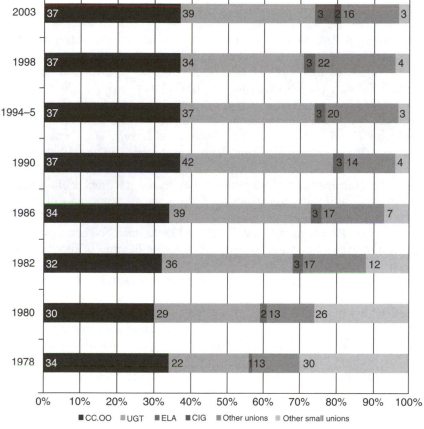

Figure 7.5 Results in Trade Union Elections 1978–2003 in percentage.

Source: Beneyto, 2004 quoted in : Martin Ardiles, 2005.

were large landowners contract seasonal land labourers. In terms of coverage by representative organisations, there is a considerable asymmetry (Pilar Gangas, 2007).

In the same study, Pilar Gangas identifies several agrarian trade union and employers organisations. The two main trade union federations are part of the CCOO and the UGT respectively. The Agri-food federations (*Comisiones Obreras-Federación de Agricultura* – CCOO-FA; *Unión General de los Trabajadores-Federación de Trabajadores en Agricultura* – UGT-FTA) are not able to give any estimates for its membership. Both confederations stress that the density of membership is low, dominated predominantly by male members, although about 30 per cent in the CCOO-FA and 20 per cent in the UGT-FTA are female workers (Gangas, 2007).

On the employers' side, Pilar Gangas identified four main confederations excluding CNAG. It seems that these organisations were more forthcoming with information on their membership. The four confederations are the already-mentioned ASAJA which is also a member of the CEOE, the Coordinating Organisation of Farmers (*Coordinadora de Organizaciones de Agricultores y Ganaderos* – COAG), the Confederation of Spanish Agricultural Cooperatives (*Confederación de Cooperativas Agrarias de España* – CCAE) and the Union of Small Farmers (*Unión de Pequeños Agricultores* – UPA) (Pilar Gangas, 2007). COAG is really an extremely decentralised organisation comprising three main territorial federations in Catalonia (*Unió de Pagesos*), Valencian Community (*Unió de Llauradors i Ramaders*) and Navarre (*Unión de Agricultores and Ganaderos de Navarra*). UPA was founded in the 1980s and is historically related to the Federation of Land Workers (*Federación de Trabajadores de Tierra*) of the 1930s which followed the tradition of the socialist agrarian syndicalism. Its strongholds are Galicia and Extremadura (Molins and Casademunt, 2001: 485).

According to Pilar Gangas, COAG has about 125,000 members and covers about 4 per cent of the enterprises in the agricultural sector. In terms of specific sector, it reaches an organisational density of 30 per cent. The CCAE has a membership of 2,815 cooperatives and cover about 5,000 full-time workers. It covers about 67 per cent of the particular sector, but represents only 1 per cent of companies in the sector. UPA is part of the UGT, because most of the members are self-employed small farmers. There are 80,000 member companies which comprises 125,000 workers. It covers about 8 per cent of firms in the particular sector, and covers about 12 per cent of workers (Gangas, 2007). From these numbers, it becomes evident that organisational density on both employee and employer sides is quite low. This naturally leads to major questions related to the representativeness of these organisations and ability to influence government policy.

The institutions and practice of interest intermediation

Interest intermediation in Spain has changed considerably since the 1970s. Although Francoism was based on a corporatist system which forced both employers and employees to work together in vertical syndicates, its architecture remained half done. In terms of phases of nationally practised interest intermediation between the main economic actors, one has to differentiate between four main phases: democratic transition (1975–82), The early period of the Socialist governments (1982–88), the crisis of interest intermediation (1988–96) and the relaunching of the social dialogue in the context of the EMU since 1996.

Democratic transition (1975–1982)

During transition to democracy the UCD governments were dependent on the moderation of the social partners in order to undertake the democratisation of the political system and liberalisation of the economy. Democratic transition took place in a period of recession, which required support from the emerging social partners. The Moncloa pacts in 1977 and 1978 were designed to curb inflation and introduce major reforms in the economy. The continuing difficult economic situation undermined the capacity of the government to continue on the path of austerity. Moreover, the UCD government was on the verge of collapse.

The early period of the Socialist governments (1982–1988)

After transition to democracy, there was an attempt to institutionalise some kind of neo-corporatist structures from above. The Moncloa pacts are a good evidence of this attempt. Throughout the 1980s, the Socialist government used neocorporatist agreements between the social partners, in order to undertake reforms in the labour market. Wage moderation was one of the key elements of this strategy. Interest intermediation in Spain entered crisis at the end of the 1980s. The high level of unemployment and the introduction of short-term temporary contracts in order to integrate young people into the labour market, led to the already-mentioned rift between the Socialist government and the trade union confederations in December 1988 (Oliet Palà, 2004: 264–90).

The crisis of interest intermediation (1988–1996)

Between 1988 and 1996, the pattern of interest intermediation of Spain is one of crisis. Tripartite agreements were only able to gain half-hearted or no support from trade union confederations. In 1992, the Economic and Social Council (*Consejo Economico y Social* – CES) was founded which integrated all relevant economic and social interest groups . The CES is a consultative institution, which has no decision-making powers. Tripartite agreements are concluded outside the CES. The establishment of CES was linked to the growing integration of Spain into the European Union. After the ratification of the Treaty of the European Union Spain became more dependent on agreements with the social partners. Spain was engaged in the process towards Economic and Monetary Union (EMU) which required the establishment and implementation of growth and stability pacts with the social partners. Without the social partners, it was impossible for the country to fulfil the convergence criteria. The relationship with the trade union confederations was quite tense. Their support could not be taken for granted (Molina, 2006: 646–7; Chari, 2001: 68–9).

The relaunching of the social dialogue in the context of EMU (1996–)

The crisis-laden late period of the Gonzalez government was replaced by the People's Party government of José Maria Aznar who relaunched a tripartite regulatory neocorporatism. As already mentioned on 28 April 1997, the Aznar government was able to achieve agreement on important aspects of the labour market. Indeed, flexibility of the labour market became the major issue of tripartite agreements. In spite of these national long-term agreements, the Spanish system of intermediation is quite fragmented with many collective agreements being concluded at sectorial or company level. This naturally undermines partly efforts of centralisation.

The Zapatero government emphasised continuity of this approach. As already mentioned the Agreement on Improvement of Growth and Employment signed in 2006 reflects the move towards a comprehensive interconnected reform approach. The integration of the social partners has been a major factor leading to a stable economy, which is growing faster than other countries in the European Union.

There is some dispute about the level of change that has actually taken place. Although inter-associational macroeconomic coordination within the context of EMU has increased considerably, the high level of fragmentation of collective bargaining and the continuing economic structural problems related to low level of investment in research and development are major factors undermining a change. According to Oscar Molina, industrial relations are still in the transition from a state-led neocorporatism to new soft methods of governance in which the state is only one part of it complemented by the private interest groups. In spite of innovation in the way interest intermediation is undertaken in Spain, the weak mandate of the social partners due to the high level fragmentation undermines any considerable change in patterns of behaviour (Molina, 2007: 471–3).

The Catholic Church: adjusting to the aconfessional state

One of the most important institutions in Spain is the Catholic Church. It played an important role in shaping the national consciousness of the Spanish population. The *Reconquista* against the Islamic rulers of southern Spain was supported by a religious ideology which would shape the history of Spain until the transition of democracy in 1975. The Spanish Catholic Church is and was known for being more conservative and ultramontane than the Vatican itself, to be more papist than the pope itself.

Dictator Franco was able to rely on the support of the Catholic Church, which was an important representative of conservative Spain. One of the strongest supporters of conservative Spain were the large landowners and other richer echelons of society. The other Spain was left-wing and anti-clerical. It comprised mainly the working-class, land labourers and other lower classes. The Second Republic would lead to the entrenchment of the two Spains. Francoism created a political religion around the myths of the *Reconquista* and the danger of regional nationalisms for the democracy of Spain. The new enemy was the undifferentiated left, which was eliminated through partisan killings and persecution. The main slogan was that Spain should be '*Católica y una*' 'Catholic and united' (Saz, 2007: 51–5). Even after the Vatican II Council (1963–65) reforms introduced between 1962 and 1965, Spanish Catholicism resisted considerably against it. However, in the 1960s other modern currents coming mainly from Latin America led to the growth of a considerable grassroots movements. The modernisation of grassroots movements was also supported by some archbishops who dared to criticise the

Francoist regime and demand a return to democracy (Brassloff, 1998). Among the personalities who represented this critical approach to the Francoist national Catholicism one has to name Archbishops Vicente Enrique y Tarancón and Gonzalo Ruiz y Aranguren. Such critical currents existed from the 1950s onwards, but they became more vociferous in the second half of the 1960s. The critical view slowly became dominant in the 1970s, when a majority in the Archbishops' Conference rejected the closeness of the Spanish Church to the Francoist regime (Montero, 2007: 153–62). Carlos Collado Seidel and Antonio Duato emphasised also the fact that the Archbishops' Conference under the leadership of Enrique y Tarancón apologised with a simple majority for the acting of the Catholic Church during the Civil War (Collado Seidel and Duato, 2007: 41).

Economically, the Church also provided the Francoist regime with important leaders. One particular Catholic organisation, the Opus Dei (The Work of God), founded by the priest, José Maria Escrivá de Balaguer y Albas in 1928 and recognised by the Vatican in 1950, was instrumental in providing Francoism with talented leaders. Opus Dei economists introduced major liberal reforms in the early 1960s. Such modernising currents inside the broad Catholic Church led also to the emergence of new young leaders who wanted to achieve a transition to democracy. Probably, the most important was the '*Tacito*' group of young members of the regime which dared to contact members of the semi-legal opposition in order to achieve a compromise towards democratic transition. The '*Tacito*' group was a crucial factor in order to achieve a smooth bargained transition to democracy (Powell, 1990).

Apart from this Catholic elite engagement, Pamela Radcliff makes us aware of the importance of many so-called 'labour priests' or at least priests who took part in social movements. Neighbourhood associations which were formed around the Church communities of the 1960s and 1970s influenced indirectly the grassroots movements of democratic transition. One important factor was also the influence of socialist ideas coming from the trade union movements and also from liberation theology (Radcliff, 2007).

During and soon after transition, the Church hierarchy dealt with the new emerging democratic regime in a moderate way. Quite important was to preserve some kind of spiritual hegemony in the new democratic system. In the constitution of 1978, the Catholic Church is singled out among other creeds, but a strict separation of state and Church is enshrined as well. Article 16 does not grant any special rights to the Catholic Church, but becomes one among many other creeds. Article 16 runs as follows:

Article 16 [Religion, Belief, No State Church]

(1) Freedom of ideology, religion, and cult of individuals and communities is guaranteed without any limitation in their demonstrations other than that which is necessary for the maintenance of public order protected by law.
(2) No one may be obliged to make a declaration on his ideology, religion, or beliefs.

(3) No religion shall have a state character. The public powers shall take
into account the religious beliefs of Spanish society and maintain the
appropriate relations of cooperation, with the Catholic Church and other
denominations.

This means that the Catholic Church has to deal with an aconfessional state, which
has to treat all creeds the same way.

This became evident during the Gonzalez governments between 1982 and
1996. Throughout the 1980s, the Catholic Church was unhappy about the reforms
in the school system that the Socialist government were introducing. There
were also issues related to the financing of the Catholic private schools. In the
end, the Socialist government was able to achieve some kind of compromise
with the Catholic Church. One positive aspect was that the Church refrained
from interfering in the political process. It remained neutral in relation to the
two main parties PSOE and PP, although the latter was more supportive of its
policies.

It would be the policies of the Aznar government, particularly after the second
term (2000–04) that would lead to a revival of the polarisation between the two
Spains. This became clear when the Aznar government made a major reform of the
school system in which religion became a compulsory discipline (see Chapter 8).
However, the Aznar government refrained from changing several laws introduced
during the Socialist government, such as the divorce law and the abortion law, in
spite of pressure from the Church to do so.

The Zapatero government led to a renewed polarisation with the Catholic
Church. As already mentioned in Chapter 2, this has to do with the policy agenda of
the Socialist government which included the legalisation of same-sex marriages,
the fast-track divorce for married persons who are suffering under matrimonial
violence, and the downgrading of religion as part of the school curriculum.
Some archbishops took to the streets to protest against these policies of the
Zapatero government, but without any success. Some high-ranking politicians
of the People's Party supported the Catholic Church against the policies of the
Aznar government such as, for example, former Minister of Education, Pilar del
Castillo (*El Pais*, 11 November 2005: 19; *El Pais*, 12 November 2005: 21; *El Pais*,
13 November 2005: 21; 23–4). The Catholic Church also opposed the introduction
of a new module in the school curriculum, called citizenship education, because of
some of the potential topics, such as tolerance towards same-sex couples (*El Pais*,
23 April 2007: 22; *El Pais*, 13 July 2007: 36).

The most important interest group allied to the Catholic Church in this respect
is the National Catholic Confederation of Family Parents and Parents of Pupils
(*Confederación Católica Nacional de Padres de Familia y Padres de Alumnos –*
CONCAPA). The organisation was founded in 1929 and became an important
association in the context of school education. According to CONCAPA's
figures it consists of 51 federations which comprises about 3 million parents.
CONCAPA resists against the new module of citizenship introduced by the
Socialist government. It organised several demonstrations against the new Law

of Education in November 2005, which downgrades the religion module in the Spanish school curriculum (CONCAPA, 2008)

According to Carlos Collado Seidel and Antonio Duato the present militant and fighting approach of the Church is due to a strengthening of strong conservative groups such as the Opus Dei and the Legionnaires of Christ. José Maria Escrivá de Balaguer y Albas was beatified in 1992 and canonised in 2002, all this in record time. Legionnaires of Christ, is an organisation founded by Marcial Maciel in Mexico and quite active in Spain since 1946 (Collado Seidel and Duato, 2007: 344). Cardenal Antonio Cañizares is quite an important conservative figure, who advocates a more fundamentalist approach, which also implies a return to a pre-Vatican II Catholic Church. The fierce opposition of the Church against the policies of the Zapatero government is reinforced by its media network COPE, in which archbishops and prominent leaders of the Catholic Church bring their position across (Collado Seidel and Duato, 2007: 347). The overall conflictive strategy of the Church was condemned by some high-ranking Catholic politicians, such as Josep Antoni Durán Lleida, the leader of the Democratic Union of Catalonia, who asked the Catholic Church to moderate its discourse and refrain from transmitting so much hate through its media empire (*El Pais*, 3 November 2005: 13). The bishops of Andalucia also dared to intervene in the discussion about the reform of the Andalucian statute, due to allegedly undermining some important fundamental rights. This naturally seemed to be part of an overall strategy of the Church against change (*El Pais*, 24 May 2006: 25).

Some representatives of the People's Party such as former Prime Minister José Maria Aznar and the MP Maria Salom were vociferous supporters of the position of the Catholic Church creating divisions inside the party. It is also generating a discussion about the vision of society of the two parties (*El Pais*, 9 January 2008: 20). The growing tensions between the Spanish Catholic Church and the government is creating also a crisis in the relations between the Vatican and Spain. The former regard the policies of the Zapatero government as an assault on the integrity of the family and as such it is extremely opposed to it.

A climax of the tensions between the Vatican and the Spanish government was when Prime Minister José Luis Zapatero refused to meet Pope Benedict XVI when he came to Valencia in June 2006. He justified himself by saying that since May 1996 he was no longer Catholic (Collado Seidel and Duato, 2007: 346). In the end, Prime Minister Zapatero wanted to make the point that Spain was an aconfessional state, therefore presence at the religious gatherings would be inappropriate in his position.

Another major event was the beatification of 498 persons referred to as 'martyrs' in the Vatican on 28 October 2007 because they were persecuted during the Second Spanish Republic. This was a record in terms of beatification and very controversial in view of the ongoing discussion on the historical memory in Spain (*El Pais*, 29 October 2007). Many victims of Francoism feel that the Church is taking sides and opening old wounds between the two Spains. According to the prominent sociologist Vicenç Navarro, there were many left-wing Catholics who fought against Francoism, but they were never recognised as martyrs by the Church. In the end, all these actions are understood as a general campaign of the Church against the policies of the Zapatero government, the main protagonist of the aconfessional state. It is the re-emergence of the two Spains, in which the Catholic Church played also a pivotal role (Navarro, 2007: 189–92). This action also has to be understood in the context of the attempt of the left-wing parties in the Spanish Cortes to come to an agreement about the law on historical memory, which wants to honour all those that were persecuted during the Franco regime, a kind of belated Truth and Reconciliation process similar to those in South Africa and currently in Morocco.

Shortly before the general elections on 9 March 2008, the Catholic Church restarted its campaign against the policies of the Zapatero government, particularly those that were allegedly undermining the family. Mariano Rajoy, leader of the PP, was very keen to keep distance to this new offensive due to the fact that this may jeopardise his chances in the forthcoming elections. In the end PP relies on a *Volkspartei* appeal and cannot afford to side too strongly with the conservative Church. However, inside the party there are strong supporters of the position of the Church. One of them is Esperanza Aguirre who attended the beatification ceremony in the Vatican (*El Pais*, 2 January 2008).

One major issue was the reform of the financing of the Church. Throughout 2005 and 2006, the Zapatero government negotiated with the Church about a new formula. In spite of the fact, that Church faithfuls could give a voluntary contribution of about 0.52 per cent of their income, the reality was that the number of people doing so has dwindled over the years. Therefore, the State subsidised the gap in the funding of the Church. Originally, the formula was just a transitional solution agreed between the former Socialist government under Felipe Gonzalez and the Catholic Church in 1987. However, the transitional formula became a permanent one. Both parties agreed on a new formula of 0.7 per cent of the income of persons who are willing to contribute to the Church. Originally the Church asked for 0.8 per cent. This increase in the contribution ends the extraordinary state subsidies to close the deficit of the budget of the Church. This formula applies only to the normal running of the Church and does not affect other social services. Moreover, the Catholic Church must now submit an annual report of how it spends the funding. Furthermore, commercial operations are no longer exempted from Value Added Tax (VAT) (*Conferencia Episcopal Española*, 2006: 3).

According to the Archbishops' Conference in 2007 it was estimated that the state had to transfer to the Church about €12.5 million per month, €150 million per year. According to *El Pais*, in 2002 the Church received €133 million (€105 million of the voluntary contribution out of income, and €27 million to fill the deficit). The reason for this gap is that every year fewer and fewer people ticked the box for voluntary contribution to the Church. According to *El Pais*, in 1993 42.73 per cent did so, but in 2002 this declined to 34.32 per cent and in 2004 to 33.46 per cent (*El Pais*, 23 September 2006: 33). All this shows the growing secularisation of Spanish society and the difficulties to finance a huge institution. According to another report of *El Pais*, apart from the €150 million, the Catholic Church receives €5.057 billion funding from central, regional and municipal administrations in order to fulfil social welfare and education tasks. Just for the Catholic education sector alone, the state grants a subsidy of €3.2 billion This sector comprises 2,376 centres (80 per cent of all subsidised private schools), 1.4 million pupils and 80,959 teachers. The Church also has a vast higher education sector of which the Deusto University in Bilbao run by the Jesuits, and the pontifices of Comillas and Salamanca are the most famous (*El Pais*, 30 September 2006: 31).

In sum, the Spanish Catholic Church has become a major actor in the political life of the country. After decades of neutrality, the Church has become quite partisan, partly because of the policies of the Zapatero government related to same-sex marriages, fast-track divorce and the law of education, and partly because Spanish Catholicism was always more papist than the pope itself. There is always the danger that the continuing partisan activity of the Church may lead to the return of negative aspects of the two Spains. One positive aspect is that many Catholic politicians are keeping a distance to the radicalisation of the discourse of the Church hierarchy.

Nongovernmental organisations: the emergence of the third sector

As already mentioned in Chapter 2, associativism in Spain is still quite weak. Most associations have very few human and material resources. They are extremely dependent on donations and in many cases funding from the state. In spite of these constraints, nongovernmental organisations are quite popular in Spain. They are an important check and balance to government policy and therefore worth supporting. Although the international organisations such as Greenpeace and Medécins sans Frontiéres have their Spanish branches in the country, there are many NGOs that are national organisations and which fulfil important work in different social areas. According to the directory of Spanish NGOs there are about 889 such organisations working across all possible fields (see Figure 7.6).

Here is not the place to make a thorough study of the nongovernmental organisations in Spain. Suffice to say, that there is an asymmetrical evolution of the sector. Many Spanish NGOs are engaged in the field of international cooperation and development education. This was also an important area for successive Spanish governments. The Zapatero government upgraded international cooperation in the government by including it in the title of the Ministry of Foreign Affairs. Cooperation was also given its own state secretariat. In spite of these changes, the contribution of Spain towards international development has been below the 0.7 per cent. There was a pledge of the government to achieve this by the end of the legislature period in 2008.

The main confederation of the NGOs dedicated to development is the Coordinating Organisation of NGOs of Development (*Coordinadora de ONGs de Desarollo* – CONGDE), which conducts annual surveys about the activities of its members. In the 2006 report, it was revealed that these NGOs received €538 million in 2005, of which 69 per cent was spent on development projects, 14 per cent in humanitarian aid, 6 per cent in awareness and education work and

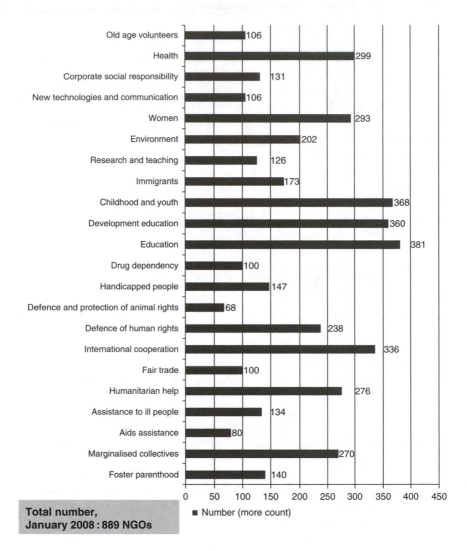

Figure 7.6 Nongovernmental organisations in Spain (2008).

Source: website Guia ONGs, http://www.guiaongs.org accessed on 27 January 2008.

11 per cent on administration (CONGDE, 2006: 23). Taking into account the 2004 and 2005 report, between 1995 and 2005 central government support declined from 20 per cent of funding to 16 per cent. Similarly, the EU reduced the support to Spanish NGOs by €20 million in the same period between 1995 and 2005, a decline from 19 to 9 per cent. In contrast, there is a stronger engagement of the autonomous communities (so-called decentralised cooperation), which provided 24 per cent of funding in 2005. Moreover, the NGOs had difficulties in raising

funds from their members. Between 1995 and 2005 funding from membership fees declined from 36 to 17 per cent. In total, NGOs received 57 per cent from the private sector and 43 per cent from the public sector (*El Pais*, 6 June 2005: 35; CONGDE, 2006: 15–16).

In 2005, among CONGDE's 85 NGOs which comprise 400 members and 15 autonomous coordinating organisations, it was found out that most of the NGOs are small- (43 per cent) and medium-sized (38 per cent). The larger ones comprise only 4 per cent and large- and medium-sized 15 per cent. In 2005, almost 1.5 million persons engaged for a short period in the NGOs, further 400,000 volunteered to work for the NGOs for one or another event. About 17,000 persons worked for the sector, while 241,000 were permanent volunteers (CONGDE, 2006: 12).

Another factor is that the vast majority of NGOs are engaged in projects for Latin America (51 per cent), a priority area for the Spanish government. Nevertheless, Spanish NGOs of development are also engaged in other regions such as Africa (28 per cent of projects), Asia and the Pacific region (16 per cent), the Middle East (3 per cent) and eastern Europe (2 per cent) (CONGDE, 2006: 25). The decentralisation of funding has also led to a less coherent development policy, although Latin America remains the main area of engagement (Gonzalez Sanchez, 2007).

In spite of the difficulties, one can recognise a trend towards professionalisation and an ability to raise funds from the private sector. There is also a growing concern about transparency and accountability in order to prevent funds to be diverted from its actual purposes. It is a long-term process which is influenced by developments in the international arena.

New issues in Spanish society and social movements

Another interesting development is the emergence of new social movements which are contributing to change of Spanish society.

Probably the most important social movement of contemporary Spain is the women's movement. The Francoist regime endorsed a paternalist family, which, in its more conservative way, would prevent women from going out to work. Democratic transition was an important liberating moment for women in Spain. Already in the 1960s, there was a considerable increase of women in the labour market, but it was considerably less than for men. This is also still one of the reasons for the continuing asymmetrical rates of employment along gender lines. The new Socialist government under Felipe Gonzalez was instrumental in introducing policies which would improve the role of women in Spanish society. In 1983, the Institute for Women was founded which today has about 170 persons working for it and has a budget of over €26 million. The Institute for Women is attached to the Ministry of Labour and Social Affairs (Valiente, 2007: 317–18). It became an important catalyst for many laws and measures to achieve gender equality. Among the most important measures was the abortion law of 1985, which was liberalised by the Royal Decree of 1986. The Institute for Women allied with women's movements to achieve an increase in the proportion of women in the main political institutions (Valiente, 2007: 321–2). Other sectors in which protective legislation for women was introduced were in the prostitution and immigration sector (Valiente, 2007: 322–4). The fast-track divorce legislation introduced by the Zapatero government was designed to protect women from marital violence, which continues to be a major problem in Spain.

According to Celia Valiente, the leading Spanish scholar in this field, the Institute for Women is more an institution directed at changing the political culture of the country by raising the awareness of gender inequalities. This means that there is a kind of state feminism which slowly penetrates the political and social institutions and influences indirectly public policies. In this sense, the so-called 'state feminists' (*femocratas*) of the Institute for Women are important agents in change in Spanish society (Valiente Fernandez, 2000: 142–4). A major ally of the women's movement has been the European Union. The policies of gender equality and gender mainstreaming had considerable impact in Spain. Although most legislation is related to economic aspects of gender equality, such as equal pay or parental leave, the pressure has allowed for some Europeanisation of gender issues. According to Emanuela Lombardo the *femocratas* regard the impact of Europeanisation as positive, because it allows gender issues to remain on the agenda even if conservative governments come to power (Lombardo, 2003: 73–6). Moreover, there is still considerable resistance from an entrenched patriarchal culture to achieve an expansion of gender mainstreaming to other areas than the economic (Lombardo, 2004: 153–254). However, one important aspect is the growing transnationalisation of the Spanish women's movement. The exchange of good practice in gender mainstreaming allows the movement to grow and overcome many of the obstacles that exist still in Spanish society. The informal nature of many of these networks and gatherings create a cultural change momentum for the movement (Lombardo, 2004: 158–60). In sum, the women's movement has made major progress, but there is still a long way to go. The patriarchal society exists still in Spain, although democracy has allowed for a slow process of gender mainstreaming to take place.

The legalisation of same-sex marriages has strengthened the gay and lesbian movement, which clearly was persecuted during the Francoist regime. As already mentioned in Chapter 2, the tolerance of otherness is an important indicator of the quality of democracy. In this sense, the legislation on the legalisation of same-sex marriages (Law 13/2005 of 1 July) introduced by the Zapatero government gave a boost to this social movement. The social movement emerged already in the 1970s. One of the main first attempts was to achieve the repeal of the Social Menaces and Rehabilitation Act, which was directed also against homosexuals (Monferrer Tomás, 2004). According to Kerman Calvo, the movement evolved through the 1970s and 1980s creating two main currents, one reformist and the other revolutionary. It was only in the 1990s, that the reformist current gained the upper hand and was able to develop a rights-based campaign around the issue of same-sex marriages. It targeted the Socialist Party, particularly after 1996, which was sympathetic to new post-materialist rights, but also as an opportunity to differentiate itself from the People's Party, which made great efforts to be neutral in relation to the Catholic Church, but with only limited success. This alliance of the gay and lesbian movement with the Socialist party led to the submission of private bills by the Socialist party in 2001 and 2003, but these were defeated by the absolute majorities of the People's Party (Calvo, 2007: 304). When the new Zapatero government came to power, the same sex legislation was an important aspect of the new socialist agenda, which tried to build on the Gonzalez legacy by broadening rights of new groups. As Kerman Calvo asserts, the strategy of the gay and lesbian social movement was to open up new channels in order to achieve political incorporation of their rights. In order to achieve a focused strategy, this social movement decided to concentrate on demanding legalisation of same-sex marriages in detriment of other rights (Calvo, 2007: 309). This political incorporation serves us away to change the culture of the country, from a survival society towards a more self-expressive society in the sense of the already-mentioned model of Ronald Inglehart and Christian Welzel (see Chapter 2).

The autonomous scene in Spain is less coherent and consistent. Urban social movements emerge and disappear within a very short period. However, the diversity of small groups that exist dealing with all possible issues shows that there is a vibrant subculture. Many of these autonomous groups create networks, but the impact has been so far quite weak. The Autonomous scene represents the first signs of a 'post-materialist self-expressive' society. This would include sympathy for the Zapatista movement in Mexico, anti-globalisation groups and civil disobedience groups (Fominaya, 2007).

All these examples show that Spanish civil society is growing, but it remains weaker than in more developed democracies. This can be asserted both for nongovernmental organisations as well as key social movements.

National interest group representation in the European Union

Spanish interest groups act now in a multi-level governance system. The European integration process has created many opportunities for interest groups to create transnational networks and influence policy at different levels of the emerging EU political system. Since 1986, the different autonomous communities recognised the importance of being present at the European level. Their growing importance in EU policy-making has been recognised by the Spanish state. Representatives of the regional governments are allowed to participate in some meetings of the Council of Ministers. The coordination between national government and the autonomous communities was upgraded in December 2004. In spite of this attention of the autonomous communities for what happens at supranational level, one has to acknowledge that some are stronger than others. A study by Gary Marks and his team shows that regions with more human and material resources can not only network and create alliances with other regions, but also influence policy. The Brussels offices of Catalonia and the Basque Country are stronger in pushing forward their interests than Murcia or La Rioja, due to their human and material resources (Marks, Haesly and Mbaye, 2002: 12). Spanish autonomous communities are able to influence EU policy through cooperative work with other regional and local representatives in the Committee of the Regions. This institution was founded in 1993, and allows regional and local representatives to shape European Commission proposals by stating opinions. It became an important channel through which the regions could bring forward their concerns.

Other national interest groups are not as well represented than the autonomous communities. The main trade union confederations as well as the smaller ones are integrated in the European Trade Union Confederation (ETUC). Although larger countries tend to have their own independent office, this is not the case for UGT and CCOO. All this is related to lack of resources and also lack of interest to play an influential role in European politics. The CEOE is integrated in UNICE, which is more fragmented and less supranationally organised than ETUC. CEOE has an office since 1980.

Overall Spanish interest groups have increased their representation at supranational level, however their presence is lower than other big countries such as France, Germany and the United Kingdom. This became quite evident in the number of national interest groups which sent contributions to the European Convention of 2002–03 (Magone, 2006).

Conclusions: the accommodation of diversity in Spain

After 36 years of authoritarian rule, Spanish civil society had to rebuild itself in a democratic setting. Spain is still characterised by a low level of associationism. However, in the past three decades Europeanisation processes have led to the establishment of a more stable, less conflictive system of interest intermediation. Both employers' as well as employees' organisations have become more professional and integrated in the overall policies of the European Union. The growth and stability pacts in the context of Economic and Monetary Union were important instruments to streamline and moderate demands from both sides. The continuing growth of the Spanish economy and the budget surplus in recent years strengthens confidence in the Spanish system of interest intermediation, leading to more agreements at different levels. The macroeconomic settlements achieved both by the Aznar and the Zapatero governments were not accompanied by a centralisation of decision-making. On the contrary, collective bargaining is still quite decentralised and fragmented. Different levels of collective bargaining undermine sometimes achievements at national level.

One important feature of Spanish civil society is the growing number of NGOs. Among them the NGOs dedicated to international development issues have gained an important place in Spanish civil society. According to the reports of the largest coordinating organisation the number of occasional volunteers has been growing steadily year by year. Spanish civil society has also to consider new social movements. Probably, the most prominent and successful social movements were the women's and the gay and lesbian movements. In spite of many successes such as the legalisation and liberalisation of abortion (1985/1986) and the legalisation of same sex marriages (2005), there is still a lot to be done. Spanish society is still quite patriarchal and social movements therefore remain essential to raise awareness about inequalities of certain groups in society. Last but not least, one can observe an increase in presence of interest groups at supranational level. However, this presence is still below those of other larger countries such as Germany, France and the United Kingdom.

In sum, Spanish civil society has been evolving slowly and still falls behind the more developed democracies of the Nordic countries, Germany, the Benelux, Austria and Switzerland in terms of its strength and influence. However, it is more developed than many civil societies in central and eastern European countries.

8   A semi-peripheral economy in the European Union

The development of the Spanish economy

In 2006, Spain was ranked as the eighth-largest economy of the world based on GDP, although it is still characterised by levels of asymmetrical dependency on the developments in the global economy and other major economies of the world. One of the reasons is that Spain has still a very inefficient agricultural and industrial sector, and the services sector is still lagging behind that of most other developed countries. It belongs to a category of countries that neither belong to the periphery, nor to the centre of the global economy. They are semi-peripheral, because they have still many peripheral forms of production and struggle to keep up technologically with the more advanced economies. In spite of being a member of the European Union, Spain continues to suffer from chronic under-investment and a low capacity of research and development.

The factors contributing to this state of affairs are manifold. Nevertheless, one major factor is cultural. The Spanish economy is extremely adversarial to a business enterprise culture. In spite of major improvements in the 1990s, the productivity of the Spanish economy is still one of the lowest of the European Union in all sectors. In the past two and a half decades, Spanish governments tried to improve the economy by flexibilising the labour market, while they tended to neglect the necessary structural transformation of the agricultural, industrial and services sector. Spain is also lagging behind in pushing forward the new information technologies. This chapter intends to give a general overview of the problems of the Spanish economy, which in the end are linked to any political ambitions that the country may have domestically or internationally.

From Francoism to the Maastricht treaty

As already mentioned in Chapter 1, the roots of the semi-peripherality of the Spanish economy go back to the sixteeenth and seventeenth centuries, when Spain's decline as a great power became quite clear. The Spanish economy progressed slowly and was always behind that of the most advanced European economies such as Germany, France, the United Kingdom and Italy up to the 1950s. After the Spanish Civil War, Franco adopted an autarkic economic policy, which clearly contributed to even more impoverishment of the Spanish population. The turning point came about, when a new group of economic technocrats close to the Catholic elitist organisation, Opus Dei, became part of Franco's government and decided to implement measures towards a liberalisation of the Spanish economy. This so-called developmentalism (*desarollismo*) was designed to achieve a faster pace of economic development with the ultimate end of catching up with the other more advanced European countries. The liberalisation of the economy was naturally constrained by political authoritarianism, which clearly established corporatist laws for the protection of the workers.

These new technocrats transformed the country within a decade. This led to the emergence of the new middle classes which clearly pushed towards the full completion of the Spanish market. Between 1960 and 1970 the Spanish GDP increased on average by 7.5 per cent annually. This was naturally possible, because Spanish economy after the Civil War and the autarkic period was in a very bad way. In spite of that, one has to recognise that the so-called 'Spanish miracle' resembles in many ways the Italian and German ones which had happened one decade earlier. The authoritarian regime used development plans to stimulate demand in the country.

Between 1964 and 1975 there were three plans, modelled on the French planning system (Carr and Fusi, 1979: 83; OECD, 1964: 29–37; 1970: 6). In this period, Spain experienced a growing internal migration from the rural areas to the urban centres (Bradshaw, 1972). One major instrument of this planning system was the huge public sector created since 1941 and under the control of the National Institute of Industry (*Instituto Nacional de Industria* – INI). The INI became an inefficient holding in the 1970s and 1980s, when privatisation and liberalisation of markets became essential to achieve a higher level of competitiveness with European markets. Massive emigration also took place to the more industrialised countries such as France, Germany, the United Kingdom, Belgium and Switzerland. One basic problem of the Spanish government was the inability to create a more stable macroeconomic policy to sustain the exponential growth of the GDP. Policies of stop-and-go clearly played a major role in undermining the stability of the economy. It showed how vulnerable the Spanish economy was to external global economic issues. The oil crisis of 1973 led to major problems for the Francoist regime. Stagflation, meaning that a stagnating economy was experiencing high levels of inflation, became a negative feature throughout the 1970s. This was further reinforced by the fact that many Spanish emigrants returned to Spain, due to the fact that unemployment in more advanced countries was growing too. After a decade of rapid economic development, the Spanish economy stagnated.

Franco's death in 1975 and the subsequent transition to democracy did not help to improve the conditions of the Spanish economy. Rising inflation, rising unemployment and stagnation of productivity clearly created major problems of instability and imbalance in the Spanish economy. The Moncloa Pacts established in 1977, which imposed austerity measures on the public services and the workers, were designed to get the macroeconomic stability needed to introduce major

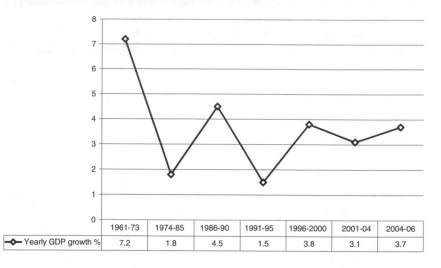

Figure 8.1 Yearly growth of Gross Domestic Product on average, 1961–2006.
Source: European Commission, 2002h: 210; *El Pais*, 25 March 2007: 64.

reforms. Nevertheless, the weak governments, under Adolfo Suarez and later under Calvo Sotelo, which were regularly destabilised by their own fragmenting party, could not prevent the rise of further unemployment and inflation (Tamames, 1995: 141–62).

The necessary structural reforms were undertaken by the PSOE when it came to power in 1982. The overall economic policy of the PSOE was to overcome the highly protectionist nature of the Spanish economy, a legacy of the authoritarian regime, and move towards a liberalised open economy.

The main aim was to achieve a more competitive economy in order to compete at global level. The Spanish Socialists hoped that this economic policy would open markets, particularly in Latin America. Most countries of Central and South America were engaging in processes of democratic transition throughout the 1980s and this was regarded as an opportunity for Spanish investors to gain a privileged position due to language and historical legacy. One problem of this strategy was that central and southern American markets were facing huge problems in their transitions to democracy and fully fledged liberal economies. The Spanish Socialists were also able to learn from the French Socialists who were in government from 1981. The nationalisation policy created problems for the French economy through 1982 and in 1983 they had to abandon these policies and move towards Thatcherite policies of liberalisation (Sassoon, 1996: 552; Merkel, 1993; Boix, 1996). One of the crucial points of the Spanish socialist strategy was to reduce the huge public sector, which had been established during Francoism. Loss-making firms were restructured or even closed to reduce the financial burden on the state. The industrial re-conversion was quite necessary to achieve more productive competitive industries. The increase in unemployment throughout the 1980s and 1990s became a characteristic of these policies of the Gonzalez government. So-called Zones of Urgent Reindustrialisation (*Zonas de Urgente Reindustrialización* – ZUR) were identified and investment plans prepared to make these industries interesting for potential buyers. The Gonzalez government just kept control of the most strategic sectors of the economy. Over the years, the restructuring of the ailing Spanish public sector was opposed vehemently by the main trade union confederations UGT and CCOO. In spite of that, the government continued the liberalisation and privatisation processes. By 1992, the public sector contributed only 10 per cent to the Spanish GDP. After 1986, the Spanish economy improved considerably.

The measures of the government clearly made the Spanish market more attractive for direct foreign investment (Caloghirou, Valgouris and Zambarloukous 2000: 84–8; Chari, 1998). Indeed, between 1986 and 1992 the Spanish economy was able to experience a boom and a considerable reduction of unemployment. Moreover, accession to the European Union and the structural funds helped to develop strategically economic projects which contributed to an increase in direct foreign investment. Two major projects symbolised this new-found confidence of the Spanish policy-makers: the Olympic Games in Barcelona and the World Exhibition in Seville both scheduled for 1992. Both were catalysts for increase of foreign capital in Spain. The main problem was that most of the investment did not go into upgrading the technology basis of Spanish firms, but to take advantage of the low labour costs. Most of the investment went into labour-intensive industries or towards the speculative sector such as the booming construction industry. The necessary structural changes towards upgrading the technological basis of the Spanish firms were not undertaken. After the so-called Fiesta finished, direct foreign investment declined considerably, leading to a major recession of the Spanish economy (Maxwell and Spiegel, 1994: 72). The period between 1986 and 1992 has been characterised as a period of casino capitalism, because of the high levels of speculative capital circulating in Spain (Petras, 1993; Vergopoulos, 1990). The Spanish government was also under pressure from the European Commission to liberalise further in accordance to the directives of the Single European Market, due to commence in the beginning of 1993. In sum, in spite of widespread reforms introduced by the Socialist government with the view of making the Spanish economy more competitive, it clearly also made it more vulnerable to the trends in the global economy.

Economic and monetary union: macroeconomic policy and growth and stability pacts

The adoption of the Maastricht Treaty setting up the calendar for the establishment of an Economic and Monetary Union was an opportunity for the Spanish government to demand a further increase of structural funds and the establishment of a new cohesion fund, designed to increase the pace of the politics of catching up with the rest of the European Union. The Socialist government made efforts to re-establish the social dialogue with the trade union confederations and the employers' organisations in order to achieve a pact for competitiveness in 1994. Such an effort was frustrated by the trade union confederations due to the fact that they were sceptical about the guarantees of the government. Nevertheless, the Spanish government established a convergence plan which clearly helped to restructure the macroeconomic policies of the government and adjust to the growing hollowing out of the state by the increase in importance of the supranational institutions. It had to revise the plan in 1994 and abandon the policy of the strong peseta after having to devalue it twice, due to problems in the European and Spanish economies in 1992. The Spanish economy improved slightly in 1995 and 1996 which allowed for a better fulfilment of the convergence criteria related to low inflation, low interest rates, a budget deficit below the 3 per cent of GDP threshold and public debt below 60 per cent of GDP (Perez-Alcalá, 1998: 257–62). When Prime Minister José Maria Aznar came to power he increased the macroeconomic policy discipline to which the previous governments were forced to, so that Spain would be able to qualify automatically for membership in the third stage of EMU. One of the factors that brought down the Socialist government was the lack of legitimacy and credibility after the emergence of so many political and economic scandals. Although the Socialists started the convergence plan towards integration into EMU, it was the PP government that was able to achieve better conditions for the Spanish economy. Indeed, Aznar, a former tax inspector, was very keen to introduce the major reforms needed to achieve a more competitive economy. One of his priorities was the control of public expenditure towards levels that were sustainable by the economy (Murphy, 1999; Alberola Ila, 2002).

A bolder privatisation policy led to the additional income to finance the transition to EMU. Among the privatised companies were Repsol (petrochemical industry), Telefonica (telecommunications), Argentaria (the fourth-largest Bank) and Endesa (electrical goods). Such a privatisation programme was linked to the growing Europeanisation of the Spanish economy in terms of competition policy and the single European market (Molina, 2002). In October 2002, the Spanish public sector had been considerably reduced and the Aznar government was in the process of privatising the remaining state enterprises, all integrated into the State Holding of Industrial Participations (*Sociedad Estatal de Participaciones Industriales* – SEPI) created as a successor to the Francoist INI in 1995. The government was able to reduce considerably the debt inherited from the INI. Further public sector firms as Alicesa (food oil), Cetarsa (tobacco), Expasa (agriculture) and ENA (national motorway enterprises) were sold subsequently. In 2002, fourteen companies were still 100 per cent in public ownership. One major problem continued to be the Spanish state television service (RTVE) which accumulated a huge deficit and needed to be restructured. RTVE cannot be privatised, because it is a company of national interest (*El Pais*, 6 October 2002: 57).

Aznar also initiated a promising reform of the labour market by achieving a social dialogue between trade union confederations and employers' organisations in 1996 and 1997. This led to a major agreement related to the flexibilisation of the labour market and pensions system reform. Although interrupted between 2000 and 2002, such a social dialogue restarted in early 2003 in view of achieving a new more extensive agreement (see next section).

During and after the discussion of the introduction of EMU, there was a general assessment that it would lead to a two-tier or multi-speed Europe, where there would be core states, such as Germany and France and the Benelux countries, and the southern European countries which would have difficulties in becoming part of it in the early stages. Such a scenario created by most northern political scientists and economists never took place.

Indeed, the Southern European governments regarded early entry to the EMU as a prestige issue. All Southern European countries, including Greece, were able to join the third stage of EMU and introduce the euro by early 2002. This is a big achievement for those countries, which in the past used to solve their problems by devaluation of the currency or stop-and-go policies. Spain became a leader in this respect. Aznar's macroeconomic policy management, in spite of all criticisms, was very successful. This naturally made the Spanish economy more stable and attractive for foreign investors. In 2001, Aznar introduced legislation to force central and regional government to maintain a zero deficit at the end of each year, in spite of protests from the autonomous communities and the opposition. One of Aznar's big achievements was that Spain was able to reduce unemployment from 17 to 20 per cent to a figure below 10 per cent in 2004.

This was accomplished by the continuing growth of the GDP, in spite of recession in most countries, and the labour market reforms introduced after 1997. One has naturally to be aware, that the working conditions have deteriorated over the past three decades. Most new jobs are not permanent, but temporary, fixed-term or part-time. Prime Minister Aznar also intended to reduce unemployment benefits further in 2002, leading to a general strike backed by the opposition on 20 July. Some of the leaders of the strike were almost criminalised by the government. EMU institutionalised a stability regime which clearly constrains any of the governments of the member-states. Macroeconomic policy is shared across the European Union in order to create a single European market. Although today most member-states think in national terms, the long-term outcome is a single market, in which there are no boundaries between the national economic systems (Dyson, 2000: 65–7).

After a decade of liberalisation in the 1980s and early 1990s, the European integration process has led to the re-emergence of social pacts across Europe. The Economic and Monetary Union demands that each member-state government acts in a constructive way to involve the social partners in the reforms needed to make their economies more competitive within the context of the Lisbon strategy agreed in 2000, which wants to transform the European Union into the strongest knowledge-based economy by 2010. Although the target will be missed, the ambition remains. However, as Kerstin Hammann and John Kelly argue, social pacts include also party political calculations. When the PP government under José Maria Aznar came to power in 1986, social pacts not only responded to the EU demands, but were also an important device to show the democratic legitimacy of the party, which before then had been associated with the former regime. It showed that it was able to include the social partners in long-term policies, which would contribute to the improvement of the Spanish economy. In this sense, Spain was not very different from other countries, such as Ireland, Austria, Netherlands and Finland, in which party-political calculations were important to reduce the costs of unpopular policies (Hamann and Kelly, 2007: 988–9). The Spanish economy has become part of this larger whole, which clearly is creating further rules of the game such as the upgrading of budgetary statistics (in order to prevent false accounting by governments in relation to budget deficits) or the actual coordination of budgetary policies. This means that Spain is fully committed to a project which is both nationally but mainly transnationally defined. Such macroeconomic policies are gradually being determined at the supranational level.

The main institutions coordinating and monitoring the economies of the member-states towards the creation of EMU are the European Central Bank, which sets the interest rates and controls the monetary policies of the Eurozone to which Spain belongs, the Economic Policy Committee (EPC) of the Council of Ministers which monitors and advises the national economies and naturally the European Commission which provides most of the information to the Council. The European Commission also deals with aspects of competition rules infringement which are all now European Union law and naturally introduces excessive budgetary procedures if a country exceeds the 3 per cent threshold set up in 1997. Moreover, participation in EMU entails also long-term structural reforms which are being monitored closely by the supranational institutions (Issing, 2002).

Like any other country, Spain is now fully integrated in this regime of stability which is structuring more and more the limits of national macroeconomic policy. Indeed, Spain has to observe the broad economic policy guidelines (BEPG) set up each year by the Economic Policy Committee (EPC) of the Council. The EPC consists of senior officials appointed by the member-states, the European Commission and the European Central Bank who are of outstanding competence in the field of economic and structural policy formulation. It also produces yearly reports monitoring the structural reforms of the member-states in view of achieving the goals related to the BEPG. The EPC liaises with the new Economic and Financial Committee (EFC) which consists of members from the member-states, the European Commission and the European Central Bank. Most of the recommendations of the EPC to the Spanish government up until now have been related to competition policy aspects as well as to labour market reform.

The 2001 report clearly emphasised the positive developments in the competition policy area by introducing mechanisms to reduce state aid, but pointed to problems in achieving a more competitive labour market, so that the regional disparities in unemployment can be reduced (Economic Policy Committee, 2001: 51, 54–5). More problematic is investment in the new technologies related to the information society, one of the central pillars of the Lisbon strategy. In 2000, only 15.7 per cent of the population had access to the Internet, while more than half had access in Sweden, the Netherlands and Denmark (Economic Policy Committee, 2001: 14). In the long-term perspective financial and employment policies will also be interconnected more strongly and shaped by supranational policies. After the Lisbon Extraordinary Council of March 2000, employment is also being monitored by an employment committee in the Council. The so-called open method of coordination (OMC) was designed to create a European employment market through a European Employment Strategy (EES).

The Zapatero government emphasised continuity to the sound policies of the previous Aznar government. The good governance of the macroeconomic policies became central to the policies of continuing growth. Unemployment was reduced to about 8 per cent which was a considerable improvement to the figures of over 20 per cent of the early 1990s, although in 2007 due to the deteriorating global economic conjuncture it has been rising again. The growth in the economy has allowed for the creation of over half a million jobs every year since 1997. In 2005 and 2006 the number of jobs created was 1 million and 687,000 respectively. However, there is still a major gender gap. Women have more difficulties in finding jobs and in 2006 their unemployment was at 11 per cent, while men enjoyed almost full employment with a rate of just 6 per cent in the same year (Figure 8.2). It was quite important to keep a balanced budget, but at the same time to use the growth in the economy to further invest in infrastructures, research and development and improvement of living conditions. Indeed, in 2005 and 2006 the Spanish government ended with a 1 per cent and 1.8 per cent of GDP budgetary surplus which helped to finance further reforms in the economy and some redistributive social policies. Moreover, public debt was 39.8 per cent of GDP in 2006 (*El Pais*, 25 March 2007: 64). The Ministry of the Economy was headed by Pedro Solbes, the experienced former European Union Commissioner for the Economy, who has been one of the strongest allies of José Luis Zapatero. Moreover, the Prime Minister Zapatero had also his own economy unit in order to be well-informed about the progress of the economy. Pedro Solbes was supportive of the economy unit attached to the office of the

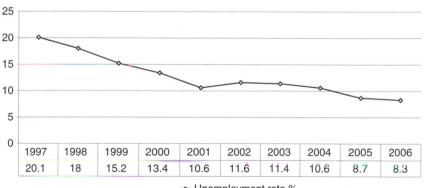

	1997	1998	1999	2000	2001	2002	2003	2004	2005	2006
	20.1	18	15.2	13.4	10.6	11.6	11.4	10.6	8.7	8.3

-◆- Unemployment rate %

Figure 8.2 The development of the unemployment rate.

Source: *El Pais*, 25 March 2007: 64.

prime minister as long as it did not interfere with his own ministry (*El Pais*, 28 November 2007: 25).

Like any other European Union government Spain is engaged in improving the competitiveness of its economy within the framework of the Lisbon strategy agreed in the Lisbon European Council of March 2000. The Spanish government has to draw up a yearly national plan of reforms. All this makes Spanish economic policy very much part of a larger whole which is still in the making (see next section).

In macroeconomic terms, Spain has improved considerably in the past two and a half decades. It is now one of the largest economies of the world. In 2006, Spain was the eighth-largest economy of the world in terms of GDP with a share of 2.39 per cent of the overall world GDP. Indeed, in comparison with Germany (6.16 per cent), the United Kingdom (4.89 per cent) and France (4.71 per cent) this is still quite low. Spain is also behind the United States (28.03 per cent), Japan (10.78 per cent), China (4.89 per cent) and Italy (3.73 per cent). In terms of the GDP per capita, Spain is only twentieth in global terms with US$ 25,800 purchasing power adjustment (*El Pais, Anuario*, 2007).

Spanish economic policies are now fully integrated into the long-term policies of the European Union, which are known as the Lisbon strategy. The Lisbon strategy was agreed in the European Council in Lisbon in 2000 and is designed to achieve the most competitive knowledge-based economy by 2010. Most indicators show a lagging behind to achieve this aim. A major review took place in 2005–6, which led to a revamping of the monitoring process of national achievements. All member-states of the EU including Spain have to draw a medium- to long-term programme of national reforms which is reviewed annually and reported to the supranational monitoring bodies attached to the Council of Ministers in Brussels. Such a programme of national reforms (PNR) is also integrated with the Broad Economic Policy Guidelines drafted by the European Commission and approved by the European Council. The European Council of 16–17 June 2005 approved the relaunching of the Lisbon strategy by 'refocusing on growth and unemployment in Europe'. It consists of broad macroeconomic, microeconomic and employment guidelines for the period 2005 until 2008 (European Commission, 2005: 9). The PNR runs from 2005 until 2010 and is coordinated by the Lisbon permanent unit (*Unidad permanente de Lisboa*) attached to the new Economic Bureau of the Prime Minister (*Oficina Economica del Presidente*). It consists of the Economic Bureau of the President and the Ministries of economy; labour and social affairs; industry; trade and tourism; and environment. It works closely with the Delegated Committee for Economic affairs, which comprises all the relevant ministries related to economic affairs. The Lisbon permanent unit relies on a flexible network of eleven representatives from the relevant ministries. Moreover, the Lisbon permanent unit has established a network with the governments of the autonomous communities, which are engaged in implementing regional programmes of reforms. There is also an overall effort made to consult the social partners in relation to the adoption of policies. Moreover, the national coordinator works closely with the Portuguese counterpart in order to maximise the economic benefits for the Iberian peninsula (PNR, 2006: 1–2). The PNR is structured around seven axes which are interrelated and together form part of an ambitious programme of economic reform in order to make the Spanish economy more competitive in the Single European market, and above all achieve convergence of GDP per capita and of technological development. The seven axes are:

1   Reinforcement of the macroeconomic and budgetary stability: This has been so far one of the success stories of the Spanish economy, which as already mentioned has been able to run surpluses due to the growth of the economy.
2   Infrastructures: There is a concentration of investment in the transport system which includes among other things the expansion of high-speed trains. The Strategic Plan for Infrastructures and Transport (*Plano Estrategico para Infrastructuras y Transporte* – PEIT) is integrated in the overall Transeuropean networks. Among further investments features the high-speed train between Madrid and Lisbon. The second strategic area is the management and use of water resources. Spain has big asymmetries between north and south in relation to water availability. The AGUA programme is financing several projects across the country to achieve this sustainability in the use of water resources.
3   Increase and improvement of human resources: Spain has probably one of the worst structures of qualifications. The educational attainment levels are lower than in other advanced democracies (see Chapter 9). Several programmes and laws were introduced by the Zapatero government to improve the quality of education. Spain has still one of the worst of drop-outs rates from secondary education. Only time can tell if these programmes at all levels of the education system, including lifelong learning and vocational training, will lead to the desirable results.
4   The Strategy of Research & Development & Innovation(R+D+i): This is the most ambitious part of the PNR. A considerable increase of governmental investment in Research & Development and innovation of 27 per cent in 2005 and 32 per cent in 2006 is trying to strategically attract private funding in order to overcome the deficit in relation to the technologically stronger countries in the EU. Spain was also able to negotiate €2 billion of an EU-sponsored technology fund in order to finance this ambitious plan. The overall programme is called Ingenio 2010 and is subdivided in three other specialised programmes (CENIT, Consolider and Avanza).
5   More competence, better efficient regulation in public administration and competitiveness: The Spanish public administration is committed to the Single European market and regards the modernisation of public administration as an important factor to achieve more competitiveness in the Spanish economy. Several plans are designed to improve regulatory frameworks and their monitoring by the responsible authorities.
6   Labour market and social dialogue: The liberalisation of the labour market is an important aspect of the Zapatero government. In this sense, it emphasises

continuity with the previous Aznar government. In order to increase the level of employment, subsequent governments have been reforming the law of dismissal and allow the introduction of more flexible, temporary and new working forms contracts. One major problem is that temporary contracts increased to 30 per cent, the highest figure in the European Union. However, British-style reforms have allowed to overcome the stagnation of the employment level around 12–13 million in the mid-1990s to more than 20 million in 2006. The negotiation and consultation of the social partners is essential for such labour market reforms.

7   Plan for the Development of Business Enterprises: A package of measures were introduced in order to strengthen the business enterprises in Spain. Most of the measures wanted to promote new enterprises and thus foster a more dynamic business culture in Spain. Several financial instruments are used in order to support the development of new projects by business enterprises. Among them is also a micro-credit financial instruments with a funding of €6 million. The measures are designed to internationalise the Spanish economy (PNR, 2005: 53–140; 2006: 5–50; 2007: 9–53).

It is too early to assess, if the PNR will contribute to an improvement of the weaknesses of the Spanish economy such as the low level of qualifications of the population and naturally low investment in R+D+i. However, one cannot discard the major efforts that both the Aznar and Zapatero governments are and have been making to strengthen the competitiveness of the Spanish economy. In spite of all the rhetoric among the two main parties, the economy has been so far something where ideological differences were replaced by a pragmatic nationally oriented long-term strategy.

One strategic factor that has supported the positive growth rates of the Spanish economy is that of the structural funds. According to the report of the Economic Bureau of the Prime Minister in the period 2000–2006 Spain received the largest share of structural funds which comprised €61.890 billion and equalled to 1.3 per cent of GDP annually. It is expected that Spain will reach the GDP average of the EU25 in 2008. However, the asymmetries between the less developed regions and more developed regions still remain a major problem for the Spanish economy. Even so, according to the report, between 2000 and 2006 the highest growth rates which are above the average of 3.3 per cent of GDP were registered in the less developed regions of southern Spain such as Andalusia (3.7 per cent), Extremadura (3.5 per cent), Castilla-La Mancha (3.5 per cent), Murcia (3.9 per cent) and Madrid. The regions slightly below the average Spanish GDP growth rate were in the northeast, for example Galicia (3.1 per cent), Asturias (2.8 per cent), the Basque Country (3.1 per cent) and La Rioja (2.9 per cent) (Economic Bureau of the President, 2007: 32).

In sum, Spain was able to become part of the EU macroeconomic stability regime which certainly contributed to a more stable environment for the economy. Many of the structural reforms which are being undertaken related to the SEM are very much induced by this stability regime. They have only partially solved the core problems of the Spanish economy which are related to the culture and structure of business enterprises in Spain. Only in the next decade we will see, if Spain will be able to change the structures towards a knowledge-based economy.

The centrality of labour market policy and the social partners

The main strategy of alternating Spanish governments to improve the competitiveness of the Spanish economy has been so far oriented towards a reform of the labour market. Indeed, during Francoism a package of labour laws protected workers from dismissal and guaranteed them rights (Martinez Lucio and Blyton, 1995: 345–8). The *Ordenanzas Laborales* (Labour Laws) became a target for reform both for the Socialist and the PP governments. The liberalisation of the labour market has been the main strategy to open up the economy and make it more competitive. This naturally led to major conflicts with the trade union confederations.

The main problem of the strategy is that it was not accompanied by a sustainable long-term plan to improve the quality of the labour market force and upgrade the technological basis of firms. The process of flexibilisation led considerably to a fragmentation of the labour market by reducing substantially permanent jobs and replacing them with temporary, part-time or fixed-term positions (*El Pais*, Domingo, 17 November 2002: 1–3). In 2006, although 20 million people were in employment, 34 per cent of the labour market consisted of temporary contracts. This is naturally detrimental to productivity, because there is a reluctance to invest in human capital. Moreover, it creates problems for collective bargaining due to the under-representativeness of this group. Last, but not least, it allows for social inequalities, because any cutbacks affects primarily temporary workers (Economic Bureau of the President, 2007: 54). In spite of a flexibilisation of the dismissal laws, still many firms are reluctant to transform temporary work into permanent positions. Most of the new employment is in temporary jobs, which due to immigration, are filled without problems. Although temporary work has increased substantially and it is the highest rate in the European Union, the number of permanent contracts has been increasing in absolute numbers. In 2005, on average the EU25 had 14.3 per cent of people working on temporary contracts, the lowest could be found in Estonia with 3.2 per cent, because it is a new phenomenon, and the highest is Spain with 33.3 per cent, followed by Poland with 25.5 per cent, Portugal with 19.5 per cent and Finland with 18.1 per cent (Broughton, 2007) (see Figure 8.3).

This is negatively reinforced by the fact that Spain is one of the labour markets with the highest number of industrial accidents. In 1999, 1,570 people died because of accidents at work. This was 25 per cent of all work-related accidents in the European Union (*El Pais*, 30 April 2000: 59; *El Pais*, 2 April 2000: 30).

In many ways, the different governments tried to win social partners for this strategy of opening up the market, which was very much influenced by the British model when the Labour government came to power in 1997. When the Socialist government came to power, the trade union confederations were willing to support

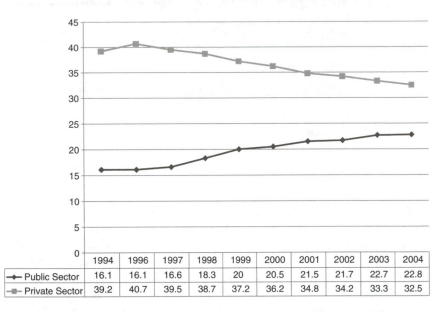

Figure 8.3 Temporary contracts in the public and private sector 1994–2004.
Source: Martin, 2007.

the structural reforms, but by 1988 they realised that there was no other long-term strategy accompanying these labour reforms. After a fall in unemployment between 1989 and 1992, it increased again after this period (Gillespie, 1990; Astudillo Ruiz, 2001; Martinez Lucio and Blyton, 1995: 352–7).

Such a course of policy reached its climax under José Maria Aznar. He was able to call upon the social partners to achieve agreement about reform of the labour market. In many ways, Aznar continued the work already started by the Socialists in trying to integrate the social partners for the necessary austerity measures for the implementation of EMU. The growth and stability pact became a major element of policy making in all member-states. Aznar was very keen to achieve the reforms with the broadest possible consensus, in order that macroeconomic stability would be implemented in a climate of social calm.

The main social partners were the employers' organisation, the Spanish Confederation of Business Enterprises (*Confederación Española de Organizaciones Empresariales* – CEOE) and the Spanish Confederation of Small- and Medium-Sized Enterprises (*Confederación Española de Pequeñas y Medias Empresas* – CEPYME) on the one hand, and the main employees' organisations on the other, which were Workers' Commissions (*Comisiones Obreras* – CCOO) and the General Workers' Union (*Unión General de Trabajadores* – UGT). CEPYME is actually part of the CEOE (see Chapter 7 for more detail).

In 1997, three inter-sectoral agreements were signed by the social partners. The agreements covered (1) the issue of employment stability by making permanent employment cheaper to employers; (2) collective bargaining in order to bring some structure into what has been regarded as a very chaotic system inherited from Francoism and (3) filling the gaps in regulation related to the replacement of the abolished labour ordinances on 31 December 1995 by the Socialist government through new collective agreements.

In spite of the agreements, Spain had still the highest unemployment rate in the European Union. According to 2002 figures, 30.9 per cent (1997: 34 per cent) of all contracts were temporary in contrast to the European Union average of 13 per cent. This meant that the agreements did not have a substantial impact on changing the ratio between permanent and temporary employment. In the summer of 2000, the social partners were very keen to renegotiate the agreements which were due to expire in May 2001. While the trade union confederations wanted to raise the costs of temporary employment mainly through employers' social security contributions and dismissal payments, the employers' organisations were more interested in making permanent contracts even cheaper than in the previous agreement.

According to their proposals they wanted to reduce the number of unfair dismissal payments from 45 to 33 days per year of seniority. All this, naturally, further contributed to tensions between the social partners. Moreover, the government was very keen to introduce a labour market reform which would decentralise collective bargaining to the company level, while sectoral level collective bargaining should be more related to general structural issues. The trade union confederations wanted a more coordinated collective bargaining between the different levels. Furthermore, company level agreements represent only a minimal part of the overall collective bargaining system. The best level was the provincial level where most agreements were signed (EIRO, 2001: ES103237FES.DOC; 2003: ES301110F; see Figure 8.4). An interconfederal agreement on collective bargaining (*Acuerdo Interconfederal para la Negociación Colectiva* – ANC 2002) was signed in December 2001.

The attempt of the government to impose a reform of the unemployment benefit system against the social partners led to major protest demonstrations. A general strike on 20 July 2002 was organised against the so-called *decretazo*. The government had to withdraw all proposals and continue to consult with the trade union confederations. This led to a further ANC interconfederal agreement on collective bargaining for the year 2003, which would clearly contribute to stability of the macroeconomic policies of José Maria Aznar (ANC, 2003). The trend towards collective bargaining agreements has been stable, if not slightly stagnant, since 2000 and there was a sharp decline in 2006 (EIRO, 2003: ES0301110F) (see Figure 8.4).

Similar to the macroeconomic policies, the social dialogue at national level is more and more integrated into an overall European multi-level system of industrial relations. Although still very loose and incomplete, a social dialogue is taking place at supranational level which is slowly having a strong impact on the member-states, particularly in Spain. Even more important, since the Lisbon Extraordinary European Council of 2000, Spain's employment policies are being monitored in

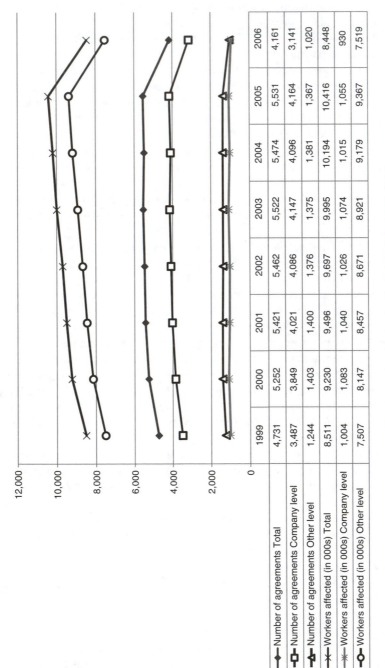

	1999	2000	2001	2002	2003	2004	2005	2006
Number of agreements Total	4,731	5,252	5,421	5,462	5,522	5,474	5,531	4,161
Number of agreements Company level	3,487	3,849	4,021	4,086	4,147	4,096	4,164	3,141
Number of agreements Other level	1,244	1,403	1,400	1,376	1,375	1,381	1,367	1,020
Workers affected (in 000s) Total	8,511	9,230	9,496	9,697	9,995	10,194	10,416	8,448
Workers affected (in 000s) Company level	1,004	1,083	1,040	1,026	1,074	1,015	1,055	930
Workers affected (in 000s) Other level	7,507	8,147	8,457	8,671	8,921	9,179	9,367	7,519

Figure 8.4 Coverage of collective agreements in terms of company level, other levels and workers 1997–2006.

Source: Ministry of Labour and Social Affairs quoted from Martin Ardiles, 2007 and EIRO, 2001, ES0107150N.

view of the objectives set in Lisbon in 2000, Stockholm in 2001 and Barcelona in 2002. All member-states are now integrated into a monitoring system which is undertaken annually by the advisory Employment Committee in the Council. This so-called open method coordination (OMC) is regarded as a new method of integration with a more long-term perspective. The ultimate aim is to create a single employment market by integrating the individual national markets. Indeed, European Services of Employment (EURES) are being set up across the European Union to facilitate mobility of employment and naturally the level of employability. Between 1998 and 2005, Spain like any other country had to submit annual employment plans to the Employment Committee from which the latter draws policy recommendations for the respective country. A report on developments in the European Union is issued annually presenting examples of best practice or innovation.

An overall assessment of the national action plans for employment since 1998 has to be a positive one. This has clearly forced the government to address the problem of long-term and youth unemployment. Within 5 years, unemployment has been reduced substantially. According to government figures, there was a substantial increase of funding for the national action plan from €7.5 million in 1998 to €13.2 million in 2002. In total, additionally €54.1 million was spent. A big emphasis has been the need to shift from passive to active policies in targeting unemployment. More than one-third of funding went towards these active employment policies accumulating in the past 5 years to a total of €18.1 million. One cannot deny that the Spanish strategy has been quite successful so far. According to the government figures between 1997 and 2002, 1.9 million jobs were created, half of them for women. In 2001, there were 17 million persons active in the labour market, a considerable increase since the early 1990s, when the labour market was stagnating. The overall national action plans were able to reduce unemployment by one million between 1996 and 2001 (MTAS, 2002; Magone, 2001: 244–6; Tobes Portillo, 2002). In spite of these successes, there is still a long way to go to make the Spanish labour market sustainable.

After 2005, the Lisbon strategy and all its instruments including the European Employment Strategy (EES) and a more integrated approach was developed which is identical to the already discussed National Programme of Reforms (PNR), which is reviewed each year. Axis 6 of the PNR targets the labour market and social dialogue. The Zapatero government emphasised continuity than break with the previous Aznar government. Since coming into office, Prime Minister Zapatero is very keen to have all social partners on board in order to improve the competitiveness of the Spanish economy and the quality of the labour market. In this respect, a declaration in favour of the social dialogue named 'Competitiveness, Stable Employment and Social Cohesion' (*Competitividad, Empleo Estable y Cohesion Social, Declaración para el Dialogo Social* 2004) was signed by the government and the representatives of the CEOE, CEPYME, UGT and CCOO on 8 July 2004. The agreement reiterates the importance of the social partners in order to improve the quality of employment and the competitiveness of the Spanish economy. The document makes references to the previous agreements achieved by the late Gonzalez governments such as the Toledo agreements on pensions and sustainability of the social security systems and the Aznar government such as the 1997 Interconfederal Agreement for Stability and Employment (*Acuerdo Interconfederal para Estabilidad y Empleo*).

Zapatero is interested in continuing the sound policies of the Aznar government, but also emphasises the social dimension of such reforms. The Agreement highlights the two main problems of the Spanish labour market: the insufficient level of employment in comparison to other European countries and the high level of temporary work. Four main areas are addressed as strategically important in order to change this situation in the long term:

1   the quest to improve considerably the quality of education and vocational training in order to have a better workforce in the labour market;
2   a continuation in public investment and the expansion of infrastructures;
3   increased investment in research and development, in order to foster innovation in the Spanish economy;
4   a balanced industrial policy which takes into account the environment (*Declaración para el Dialogo Social*, 2004:3).

This declaration on the social dialogue is framed in the growth and stability pacts that all national governments have to sign with the social partners in the context of the Economic Monetary Union (EMU) and the objectives of the Lisbon Strategy, which wants to make the European Union the most competitive knowledge-based economy of the world.

An important basis for the continuing reform of the labour market was the report commissioned by the government and the social partners prepared by the commission of experts for the social dialogue named 'More and Better Employment in a new Socio-Economic Scenario: For Effective Flexibility and Work Security' issued on 31 January 2005. The report highlighted the deficiencies of the Spanish labour market related to its precariousness and the lack of progress in increasing the number of permanent contracts. The very detailed report ends with some recommendations which basically advise policy-makers to assume a global approach to reform the labour market.

One major problem identified is that the Spanish economy is creating new, mostly temporary, precarious jobs, but is losing competitiveness internationally. The main indicator for the loss of competitiveness is the trade balance deficit which has been a persistent feature until now. The report highlights the importance of active employment policies, something that successive Spanish governments have neglected and created problems for the employability of people who become unemployed. Moreover, the report emphasises the importance of flexibility for firms in a fast changing world economy, but it needs to be accompanied by a stronger protection of workers and not so much of workplaces (*Comisión de Expertos para el Dialogo Social*, 2005: 147–50). The author assumes that the report is asking policy-makers to follow a moderate Danish system, in which the flexibility of the labour market is accompanied by strong welfare and active labour market policies should anybody lose their job.

During 2006, several pieces of legislation, which were designed to restructure the labour market were adopted. The most important was the agreement between the government and the social partners on 'Improvement of Growth and Employment' which comprised a package of subsidies to make employment more stable up to a period of 4 years and to transform temporary employment into permanent positions. This was approved by parliament and became Royal Decree Law 5/2006 of 9 June. According to Antonio Martin, the new measures had an immediate effect. Over 2.1 million temporary jobs were made permanent an overall increase of 41 per cent. Further important accompanying legislation passed by Parliament included the Personal Autonomy and Dependent Care Law passed by parliament and the Equal Opportunities Law (Martin Ardiles, 2007).

There are still islands and pockets of discrimination in pay and working conditions. One of the problems that the Spanish government is trying to address is that of inequality between men and women. There are still disparities in pay and also in the equality of opportunities area. The employment rate of women is much lower than men, and women are among the groups that have the highest level of unemployment. It is the female population that takes up most of the part-time, fixed-term and temporary jobs, grouped as atypical working forms. This is reinforced by the motherhood effect, which, in comparison with other European countries, makes Spanish women more vulnerable (Cousins, 2000: 112–17). This was included in the interconfederal agreements of 2002 and 2003. Moreover, unemployment is higher among women and young people. Furthermore, the Spanish unemployment rate of the active population stagnated up until 1997. The Lisbon European Council set as intermediary employment rate targets for 2005 67 per cent generally and 57 per cent for female employment. The main problem is the imbalance between women and men. Since 2004, the Zapatero government has emphasised the aspect of equal opportunities and gender mainstreaming, in order to redress the imbalance. According to government figures, in 2005 the expanding labour market exceeded the targets set for Spain in the context of the European Employment Strategy. Figure 8.5 shows the imbalance between men and women and also between young and old segments of the population in the age group between 25–64 years.

This slow and steady improvement of the employment rates is accompanied by a slow sustainable change of the overall educational system, which is being upgraded year after year to produce a higher-qualified working force. Naturally, the system still falls below the quality of more developed economies such as the United Kingdom, France, Germany, Benelux and the Nordic countries. The Zapatero government has reformed school and university legislation in order to improve the quality of education in Spain. More funding was made available for the restructuring of the education system. One important aspect is the growing decentralisation of education policy. Investment in human capital is regarded as one of the axis of the PNR.

As already mentioned in the previous chapter Spain has the highest level of school leavers along with Portugal in the secondary sector. The share of school leavers in secondary education is 30 per cent, only Portugal has a higher figure.

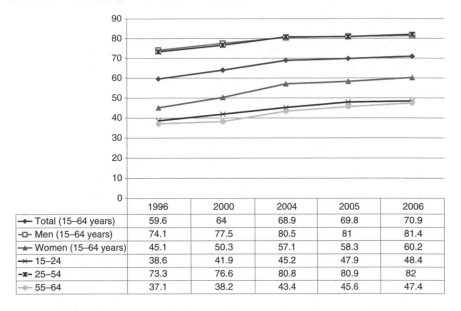

	1996	2000	2004	2005	2006
Total (15–64 years)	59.6	64	68.9	69.8	70.9
Men (15–64 years)	74.1	77.5	80.5	81	81.4
Women (15–64 years)	45.1	50.3	57.1	58.3	60.2
15–24	38.6	41.9	45.2	47.9	48.4
25–54	73.3	76.6	80.8	80.9	82
55–64	37.1	38.2	43.4	45.6	47.4

Figure 8.5 Employment rate in Spain according to gender and age groups (1996–2006).
Source: Economic Bureau of the President, 2007: 55.

Spain is not below the EU average, but contrasts heavily with the 100 per cent figure of some countries such as Denmark, the United Kingdom and the Czech Republic (Economic Bureau of the President, 2007: 89). Moreover, there is a major crisis in the vocational training system due to the fact that many young people fail to complete the programmes successfully. This is creating major imbalances between the academic and vocational training routes (Economic Bureau of the President, 2007: 90). Furthermore, the university system has still major problems related to access of students from lower social background, also issues of quality. This is reflected in the high student drop-out rates. The Bologna process which envisages the harmonisation of higher education system across the European Union is regarded as an opportunity to redress the problems (Economic Bureau of the President, 2007: 91–2).

The slow convergence with Europe can be also observed in the changing labour market structure. The CAP (Common Agricultural Policy) has contributed substantially to reducing the number of people working in agriculture and making that sector more efficient. The industrial sector is declining as in many other countries, while the services sector is increasing. Due to the infrastructure programmes boosted by the European Union structural funds, the construction sector has been quite constant.

The services sector is clearly dominated by the very important tourism industry. Spain is the second most important tourist destination after France. In 2005, it had a share of 7.25 per cent of all tourists globally and 7.02 per cent of all income.

In total, there were 75.7 million tourists in Spain in 2001, 78.9 million in 2002, but it declined to 55.7 million in 2005. Most tourists come from Germany, France, Italy and the United Kingdom. There was some concern that Spain may have lost some attraction in 2002, but in spite of 11 September 2001 and the 11 March 2004 Madrid bombings the country was able to increase the number of tourists. Spain is facing growing competition coming from all Mediterranean countries, particularly Turkey, Greece, Italy and Portugal. The tourism industry has to take into account a more environmental friendly approach to satisfy customers coming from northern Europe. In many ways, the boom in the tourist industry led to considerable damage of the Spanish coast. Nevertheless, Spain continues to be one of the favourite holiday destinations in the European Union, generating important income for the overall performance of the economy (Valenzuela, 1996; *El Pais, Anuario*, 2003: 393; *El Pais*, 4 August 2002: 35; *El Pais, Anuario* 2007).

In sum, integration into the European Employment Strategy (EES) established since the early 1990s has contributed to major improvement of the labour market. It became more flexible and diverse. In spite of the gains made, the major problems are related to the need to upgrade the qualification structure of the labour market as well as the technological basis of the industrial and services sector. These structural problems have still to be solved before the Spanish economy can become more sustainable in the pursuit of job creation and in order to achieve full employment by 2010 as was set out in the Lisbon strategy.

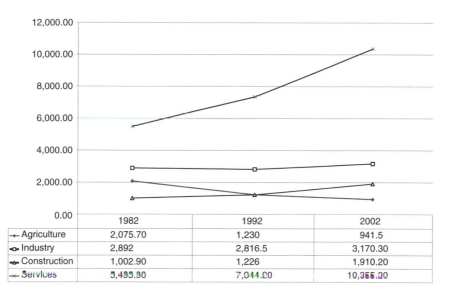

	1982	1992	2002
Agriculture	2,075.70	1,230	941.5
Industry	2,892	2,816.5	3,170.30
Construction	1,002.90	1,226	1,910.20
Services	5,495.90	7,044.20	10,355.20

Figure 8.6 Distribution of employment according to sectors (1982–2002) in absolute numbers.

Source: Instituto Nacional de Estadistica, Encuesta de Población Activa quoted from Piedrafita, Steinberg and Torreblanca, 2006: 79.

The challenges for the Spanish economy

Although there is not enough space here to discuss thoroughly the challenges for the Spanish economy, it is still imperative to create awareness of them. Apart from the labour market reforms which were set out in the European employment strategy, there are other structural aspects that are intertwined and contributed to the semi-peripherality of the Spanish economy. One can, at least, identify four main aspects, described in the following sections, which different governments were still not able to improve in the past two and a half decades, which makes any change appear only superficial up until now. They are all of a structural nature and therefore, if tackled, would certainly contribute positively to an overcoming of the semi-peripheral nature of the Spanish economy.

Capital-weak small- and medium-sized enterprises

Spanish firms are in general capital-weak and small and medium in size. The family business structure of the Spanish industry and services sector clearly prevents a change of culture towards economies of scale. About 90 per cent of all Spanish firms have fewer than 250 employees. Most of them have between none and six employees. Most firms are characterised by a low level of investment in capital goods and are not very competitive, using mostly labour-intensive methods of production. It clearly is widespread among the food, drink and tobacco industries, in the textiles and clothing industries and in the wood, cork and furniture industries. Most of the firms are not very concerned about the global and European dimension of trade, because they tend to produce for the domestic market. Most of the Spanish industrial firms are located in a triangle between Madrid, Barcelona and Bilbao in the Basque Country. The largest Spanish firms are located in this triangle (Salmon, 1995: 164–9). Only two Spanish firms have become international players. They were previously part of the state public sector. Repsol has been quite successful in the European market, while Telefonica was able to gain a foothold in Latin America. In spite of the problems caused mainly by the Argentinian crisis, Telefonica is still a strong player in most Latin American markets.

Nevertheless, it shows that the Spanish economy is still too weak to produce more multinationals. In global terms, Spain is among the twelve countries with the largest number of enterprises. While the United States is heading globally with 37 per cent of all enterprises, Spain has only 1 per cent. In comparison, Germany has 10 per cent, France 7 per cent, the United Kingdom 3 per cent and Italy 3 per cent (*El Pais, Anuario*, 2003: 405).

In sum, Spain is still characterised by a weak enterprise structure which is clearly under-invested and is characterised by a business culture of short-term thinking. Although several governments including the Zapatero government have identified this weakness of the Spanish economy, their programmes had only a modest effect, due to the fact other countries are also using similar programmes to boost their national entrepreneurial cultures.

Low research and development investment

The culture of Spanish enterprises is inimical to investment on research and development. In contrast, in the past decade this has been a strategy for peripheral economies such as Ireland and the Nordic countries, in particular Finland. The re-confirmed Lisbon strategy in the European Council of Stockholm in 2001 and Barcelona in 2002 was set out to make the European economy more competitive by 2010. One of the pillars of the strategy is investment in the new information and communications technologies. The Aznar government tried to address the problem by introducing the Info XXI plan, nevertheless Spain failed to improve its position in terms of use and dissemination of the new technologies. Spain is still at the bottom of the EU countries in terms of investment in information technologies or readiness for the information society. It is estimated that 20 per cent of small and medium enterprises do not use any information technology. The main reason is that these firms cannot afford it, due to their subsistence status. It is also estimated that Spain is still 30 per cent behind if judged according to its economic indicators.

The government plan Info XXI period between 1999 and end of 2003 was designed to promote the use of the new technologies, but it failed completely. Although it envisaged 300 measures and had a budget of €30.1 million, it only spent 25 per cent of the total. After this failure, former Prime Minister Aznar decided to take over the commission in charge of improving the position of Spain in the information society. The biggest success was and has been so far in the Basque Country where the government subsidised the whole process of connecting the population to the Internet. The Basque Plan for the Society of Information financed training programmes and opened 136 centres in 121 municipalities. It also subsidised the purchase of computers between November 2000 and July 2002. This success story is clearly a good sign that a proper strategy may push the Spanish population towards the information society. One of the aspects that the Aznar government tended to emphasise was the growing importance of e-government, strengthening a direct linkage between government institutions and the citizens (*El Pais*, Negocios, 20 April 2003: 5–6).

In 2005, 23.1 per cent of Spaniards used the Internet in comparison with 50.8 per cent in Germany, 55.1 per cent in the United Kingdom, 60.6 per cent in the Netherlands, 44 per cent in Italy, 69 per cent in Denmark, 47.3 per cent in Belgium, 56.8 per cent in Austria, 42.3 per cent in France, 68.9 per cent in Sweden and 26.9 per cent in Poland. It shows that Spain is still far behind in terms of embracing these new technologies (Figure 8.8). These reflects also in the low number of websites with the Spanish '.es' address. Germany and the United Kingdom have been so far the most dynamic countries in producing websites with the '.de' and '.uk' addresses. However, even smaller countries such as the Netherlands, Denmark, Belgium and Austria have been more dynamic in producing websites with their national addresses (see Table 8.1).

The main obstacles to this access to the Internet is the fact, that only a small number of all sites in the Internet are in Spanish. Moreover, access to the Internet

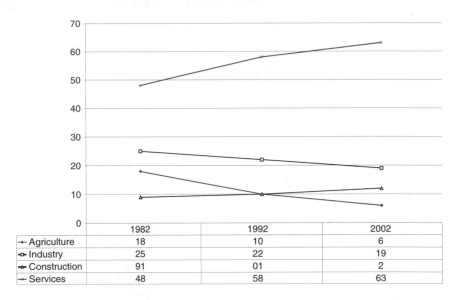

	1982	1992	2002
Agriculture	18	10	6
Industry	25	22	19
Construction	91	01	2
Services	48	58	63

Figure 8.7 Share of employment in the occupational sectors of the economy (1982–2002) in percentage.

Source: Own calculations based on Instituto Nacional de Estadistica, Encuesta de Población Activa quoted from Piedrafita, Steinberg and Torreblanca, 2006: 7.

in Spain is far more expensive than in the Nordic countries or Germany, reflecting the fact that Internet services are more expensive in southern Europe. Clearly, this is detrimental to access, due to the fact that these two countries have the lowest average wages in the European Union (*El Pais*, 17 June 2002: 33).

Research and development expenditure, which will change in the long term the overall structure of the Spanish economy, is well below the EU average and most larger European countries. Spain continues to be well below the 1 per cent point, while Finland, France, Germany and Sweden are well above the 2 percentage point threshold. This further exacerbates the dependence on technology transfer from other countries. Figure 8.9 shows the gap between the EU15 and Spain.

The Zapatero government used the PNR 2005–2010 to accelerate public funding for research and development. It devised the INGENIO 2010 programme which consists of several sub-programmes. The sub-programme CENIT wants to improve public–private cooperation in terms of research and development. The critical mass of the researchers is supported by the CONSOLIDER sub-programme. In order to close the gap to the EU25 average in terms of the knowledge-based society the sub-programme AVANZA was devised. Last but not least, sub-programme EUROINGENIO is dedicated to projects integrated in the European Research Space. Moreover, the policy-makers emphasise a change in cultural behaviour in terms of following-up the implementation and the results of the programme. The total funding available for 2007 was €6.4 billlion, a doubling of the 2004 budget.

Table 8.1 Registered sites in the countries of the EU in absolute numbers and share of
total in 2005

Country	Registered sites	Share of total sites in the European Union
Germany	8,669,000	46.6
United Kingdom	4,108,000	22.1
Netherlands	1,332,000	7.2
Italy	1,258,000	6.8
Denmark	596,000	3.2
Belgium	413,000	2.2
Austria	392,000	2.1
France	361,000	1.9
Sweden	285,000	1.5
Poland	284,000	1.5
Czech Republic	186,000	1
Hungary	165,000	0.89
Finland	95,000	0.51
Spain	88,000	0.48
Greece	80,000	0.44
Slovakia	65,000	0.4
Ireland	44,000	0.25
Portugal	43,000	0.24
Lithuania	30,000	0.17
Estonia	25,000	0.15
Slovenia	22,000	0.13
Latvia	20,000	0.11
Luxembourg	18,000	0.1
Cyprus	4,000	0.02
Malta	2,000	0.01
TOTAL	18,585,000	100

Source: *El Pais*, Domingo, 15 May 2005: 8.

The main objective is to reach an annual rate of 2 per cent of GDP by 2010.
According to government figures funding for research and development increased
by 27 per cent in 2005, 32 per cent in 2006 and 34.5 per cent in 2007. In 2005, the
research and development increased to 1.13 per cent. Another major objective is
to change the relationship between public and private funding. Until now research
and development is dominated by the public sector, however the INGENIO
programme intends to promote an increase of the share of the private sector to
55 per cent by 2010. In the negotiations of the financial perspectives 2007–2013,
Zapatero was able to secure a special technology fund of €2 billion to boost
the research and development of Spanish enterprises. This is also accompanied
by a fiscal reform reducing tax and social security payments in exchange for
more investment in research and technologies. Particularly, small- and medium-
sized enterprises are targeted, so that they are able to increase their expenditure
in research and development (*Oficina Economica del Presidente del Gobierno*,
2007).

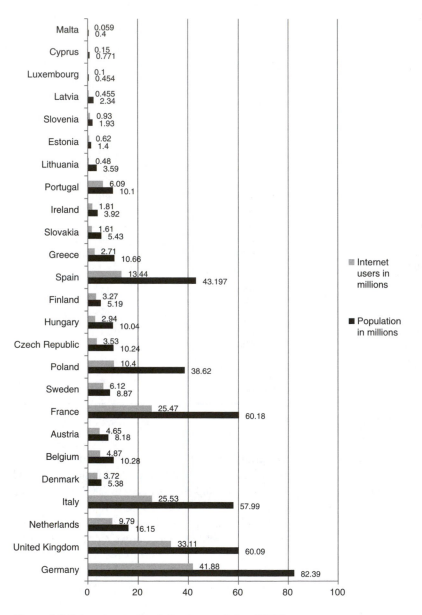

Figure 8.8 Internet users in relation to population (2005).

Source: *El Pais*, Domingo, 15 May 2005: 8.

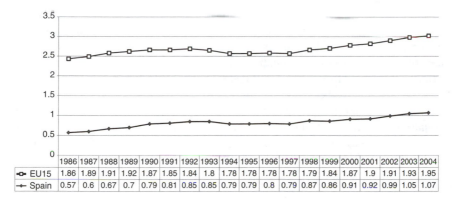

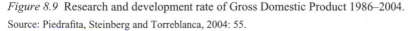

	1986	1987	1988	1989	1990	1991	1992	1993	1994	1995	1996	1997	1998	1999	2000	2001	2002	2003	2004
EU15	1.86	1.89	1.91	1.92	1.87	1.85	1.84	1.8	1.78	1.78	1.78	1.78	1.79	1.84	1.87	1.9	1.91	1.93	1.95
Spain	0.57	0.6	0.67	0.7	0.79	0.81	0.85	0.85	0.79	0.79	0.8	0.79	0.87	0.86	0.91	0.92	0.99	1.05	1.07

Figure 8.9 Research and development rate of Gross Domestic Product 1986–2004.
Source: Piedrafita, Steinberg and Torreblanca, 2004: 55.

From Figure 8.9, it is evident that Spanish firms are less involved in research and development than in other industrialised countries. The most successful countries have a high share of research and development carried out by private firms. This naturally shows that Spain has still a long way to go, if it wants to become part of the group of core countries of the global economy.

Between 1990 and 1998, the annual growth rate of employment in high-and low-technology industries decreased by 3 per cent. In contrast Ireland had an annual increase of over 10 per cent in the same period (Eurostat, 2002: 275). This continues to reinforce the position of the Spanish economy as semi-peripheral. This is particularly evident when one compares the number of patents produced by Spain with that of other countries. Spain is far behind most European countries, apart from Portugal and Greece, which have even lower innovative rates. The larger countries, the United Kingdom, France and Germany, are clearly well above in terms of high-technology than Spain. The case of Finland is quite interesting, being characterised by a high level of unemployment and an economic crisis after the collapse of the Soviet Union, but then achieving a remarkable reversal of fortunes by strengthening its high-technology base.

In sum, past and present policies of research and development did not lead to major successes in Spain. On the contrary, the Spanish economy is lagging behind and is also still characterised by the same negative structural problems which prevented a transition from a semi-peripheral to a core position in the modern world economy.

The dependency on foreign direct investment

The Spanish economy is extremely dependent on foreign direct investment (FDI). Decline in FDI affects considerably the prospects of the Spanish economy. A large part of this FDI goes to the automotive industry which clearly is the main export product. All major international car manufacturers are among the most important Spanish firms. One can find Renault, Volkswagen, Opel, Peugeot, Ford, Nissan and Mercedes among the hundred largest firms in Spain. Most of the production is earmarked for export. Spain is an attractive place, because the labour costs are still lower than in other countries of the European Union. Moreover, Prime Minister Aznar and Prime Minister Zapatero were able to create a climate of social peace which clearly helps to keep these multinationals in Spain. The problem of this flow of foreign direct investment is that Spain is regarded as an ideal country for intermediary industries of major automobile manufacturers, but not so much as a centre of research and development. This means that Spain is highly vulnerable to the decisions of multinational companies when they want to change their production location (Salmon, 1995: 192–202; *El Pais, Anuario*, 2003: 409).

Whilst in 1980, FDI amounted to €513.4 million, in 2001 it increased to €48.2 billion (almost half of the total EU budget). Although there was an estimated decline in 2002 to €24.3 billion due to recession and the 11 September 2001 incidents, it is clearly a considerable amount compared with the 1980s (*El Pais Anuario*, 2003: 385). In 2005, €13.7 billions of FDI went to Spain, however by September 2006 only €6.3 billions FDI came into the country, which may suggest a slowdown of this long period of international investment in the country. At the top, in September 2006 were Luxembourg (30.35 per cent), Netherlands (27.47 per cent), the United Kingdom (11.61 per cent), United States (6.06 per cent), Germany (4.64 per cent) and France (3.73 per cent) (*El Pais Anuario*, 2007).

In a study by the Instituto Real Elcano, four major economies are fundamental for the Spanish economy due to its investment in the country: Germany, UK, France and USA. This is called the 'European Union A' (The USA is included to simplify the ranking of countries). The United Kindom, France and Germany represent 54.12 per cent of all trade relations of Spain in 2004. In a second tier, one can find Portugal, Italy, the Netherlands and Luxembourg, which are characterised as 'European Union B', however the level of density of economic relations is much lower than with the first group. The third main group is 'European Union C' which comprises Belgium, Ireland, Sweden, Denmark, Austria and Finland. The level of the density of economic relations is lower than in the other groups, but still of considerable relevance. The Spanish economy is extremely well integrated in the European Union, in spite of its interest in new risky emerging markets in Latin America and Asia (Isbell and Arahuetes, 2005: 26; 34–7).

In spite of this dependence, Spanish investment has gained momentum since the mid-1990s. In the past 2 years, Brazil has become an important market for Spanish investors, but also other countries in Latin America. Telefónica has been extremely successful in establishing itself in several south American countries. Moreover, Spanish enterprises have increased their interest in gaining access to the Central and Eastern European markets. According to William Chislett, Argentina, Brazil, Chile and Mexico have been the main destinations of Spanish FDI. Between 1992 and

2001 they absorbed 85 per cent of all Spanish FDI. The rest is distributed between Columbia, Peru, Venezuela, Bolivia, Cuba, Ecuador, El Salvador, Guatemala, Honduras and Nicaragua (Chislett, 2003: 39). Apart from the language and cultural aspects, the main reason for a considerable increase of investment since the 1990s, is the fact that these are growing emerging markets are privatising and liberalising their public utilities.

Apart from Telefonica in the telecommunications market, the main investors are the oil company Repsol, the Santander Central Hispano and the Bilbao Vizcaya Argentaria Bank. Moreover, the energy company Endesa has also been an important investor in the region. (Chislett, 2003: 35–6). These investments are quite risky, because most of these new democracies and emerging markets are unstable and still quite protected. Populist leaders like Hugo Chavez in Venezuela and Evo Morales in Bolivia may threaten previous investments. Overall, Spanish investment in Latin America is only second to the United States. All other EU members have penetrated, to a lesser extent, these new emerging markets (Figure 8.10). In Europe, efforts have been made to increase the presence of Spanish firms in Poland (*El Pais*, 12 June 2000: 80).

In sum, the Spanish economy is clearly attractive for FDI because of low labour costs and better conditions for enterprises. Nevertheless, at the same time, these favourable conditions make the Spanish economy extremely vulnerable to trends in the global economy and decision-making processes in the main multinational companies.

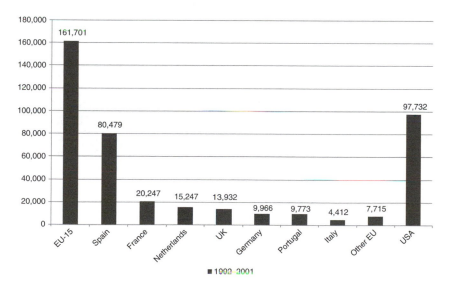

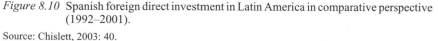

Figure 8.10 Spanish foreign direct investment in Latin America in comparative perspective (1992–2001).

Source: Chislett, 2003: 40.

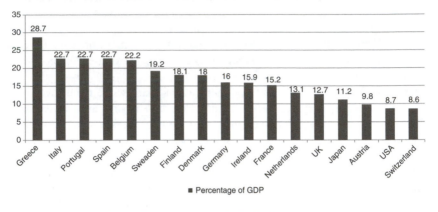

Figure 8.11 Size of the informal economy, 1999–2000.
Source: Die Zeit, 10 March 2001: 25.

The informal economy, invisible factories and tax evasion

Another obstacle to the development of a strong formal economy is the fact that in Spain this is paralleled by an informal market which is quite large when compared to other European countries. Estimates of the informal economy are quite difficult to make. According to a study by Friedrich Schneider from the University of Linz in Austria, Spain is at the top of a list of countries along with Greece, Italy, Portugal and Belgium in terms of percentage of GDP generated by the informal economy (Figure 8.11).

The *Ordenanzas Laborales* (Labour Laws) of the Francoist regime were regarded as quite rigid. They forced employers overburdened by high social costs and a legislation protecting workers to change to informal forms of production. Many of these employers did not pay taxes and had small sweatshops where there were no social rights and guarantees for workers. These 'invisible factories', as Lauren Benton calls them, are exploitative in nature. They can be found across the country. In Madrid, the electronics sector has a lot of informal factories, while in Valencia, one can find clandestine work in the footwear, textiles and toy manufacturing industries. Invisible factories are also widespread in Catalonia. It is estimated that one-fifth of the working population works in this so-called *economia submergida*. Nevertheless, the flexibilisation of the labour market may have contributed to a more blurred division between the official and clandestine labour market, due to the rise of less secure work arrangements. Therefore, the informal economy may be larger than the official estimates. There is also the widespread phenomenon of moonlighting between the formal and the informal sector and official unemployment status and informal jobs (Benton, 1989; Salmon, 1995).

All this shows that there is still a long way to go to have a more accurate picture of the Spanish informal market.

In sum, the Spanish economy is still characterised by many obstacles which prevent it from becoming one of the core economies of the world.

Conclusions: the continuing problems of a semi-peripheral economy

In spite of three decades of democracy, the Spanish economy is still characterised by many semi-peripheral features which have been inherent since the nineteenth century. One positive aspect is that it is today an open economy with ambition to gain a global role. This ambition cannot be fulfilled overnight. The chronic main problems of the Spanish economy need to be tackled. First, the qualification structures of the labour market have to be upgraded. This can only be accomplished in the long-term perspective. The growth of the economy contributed to a substantial decline of unemployment and the creation of new jobs. Measures introduced by the Aznar and Zapatero governments made it possible to increase the employment rate and even probably meet the national targets set by the Lisbon Strategy. The new PNR (2005–2010) has a global approach and a better integration of funding and evaluation of progress which may contribute to a qualitative transformation of policy-making in this respect. Second, small- and medium-sized enterprises have to accept wholeheartedly the challenges coming from the new technologies. Innovation will be a keyword, so that a coordinated research and development strategy has to be a strategy linking up to other aspects of innovation. The INGENIO research and development programme is certainly a step in the right direction. However, such accelerated increased public investment needs to be maintained for a number of decades, before it spills over into private investment. This also involves attracting foreign direct investment for high-technology industries. Third, the Spanish government has to transform the informal market into part of the formal market, where there is a change of mentality from the short-term temporary nature to long-term sustainable gain. All this takes time to attain, but it is essential in order to make the Spanish economy more competitive and closer to the core European economies.

9   The policy-making process
The impact of the European Union

Policy style and European integration

One of the most seminal articles on the transformation of the public policy process in Spain was written by Richard Gunther. There, he clearly sees a relationship between the quality of public policy and regime change from authoritarian dictatorship to democracy. Gunther's assessment is that the democratisation of the public policy process made the outcomes of implementation accountable to the population which is able to show support or disappointment every four years. A major aspect of public policy is that the share of the budget related to the redistribution of social policies and education has increased considerably in the 1980s and 1990s. The policies of the Socialist government of the 1980s were important redistributive ones, in order to create a more democratic society. Another aspect that Gunther mentions is the fact that the new public policies were better integrated into global trends set up by the OECD than the previous Francoist regime. Another feature of the new democratic political system was the growing inclusion of interest groups in the policy process. Although civil society was and is still quite anaemic in comparison to other west European countries, democratic conditions allowed for the emergence of interest groups which are more or less successfully influencing the policy process.

> The overall impact of regime change on public policy has been to transform Spain from a society whose policy processes and outputs bore unfortunate similarities to those of some Third World countries into one that fits well within the mainstream of affluent Western Democracies. In short, we can unequivocally conclude that politics does, indeed, matter.
>
> (Gunther, 1996: 198)

This transformation of the policy-making process does not mean that everything changed overnight. In fact, in many cases the policy process is still hampered by past forms of behaviour. Aspects of protectionism, clientelism, patrimonialism and corruption may play a role to prevent the public policy process from becoming fully democratic. Indeed, one characteristic of the Spanish public policy process is that it is moving from a highly protectionist closed process dominated completely by the state to one which is pluralist, open and integrated into the national, European and global networks. Such transformation is quite complex and asymmetrical. In some areas such liberalisation and democratisation is very advanced, but in other cases it is lagging behind. In this respect, the role of the European Union cannot be underestimated. The integration process clearly contributed to a speeding up of this transformation.

This can be observed particularly in the telecommunications sectors. The European integration process broke previous patterns of behaviour is the telecommunications sector. Indeed, in Spain the main provider of telecommunications was Telefónica, a monopoly established during the Francoist period. It clearly attempted to delay the process of liberalisation and privatisation as long as possible. Indeed, this policy area was very much characterised by a patrimonial policy style, meaning that one major monopoly was able to set the pace of reform towards liberalisation and privatisation (Briole *et al.*, 1993). After negotiations between the Socialist government and the European Commission a date for full liberalisation of the sector was set for 1998. Since then, Spanish telecommunications have been in the process of being completely liberalised and privatised. Telefónica, naturally, was able to keep a dominant position in the Spanish market and expand into the Latin American market. Parallel to this, the liberalisation of the television sector was agreed, leading to the establishment of Retevision, a network of television signal posts, which needed some delay after 1998 to achieve a liberalisation of the television sector. This was opposed by Telefonica which had the advantage of starting earlier with the process of liberalisation and privatisation and wanted to prevent rivals to profit from more time. The compromise reached at the end of 1998. In June 1996, the PP government created the regulatory agency Commission of the Communications Market (*Comisión del Mercado de Telecomunicaciones*) to supervise and monitor the whole process of liberalisation and privatisation and assume regulatory functions in case there were problems emerging from the process. The government also established an Advisory Council on Telecommunications (*Consejo Asesor de Telecomunicaciones*), integrating the main actors of this sector. It is merely an advisory council to the government, nevertheless a sign of a changing policy style, making it more congruent to the single European market and the European public policy pattern. An association of users of telecommunications (*Asociación de Usuarios de Telecomunicaciones –* AUTEL) founded in 1987, which takes a position in favour of liberalisation, further strengthens this policy style transformation (Jordana, 1998; 2001; Gil, 2002).

This change in the Spanish public policy process from a narrow-minded interventionist to an open-minded regulatory framework is due to a large extent to the European Union. Europeanisation was always regarded as modernisation of the Spanish infrastructures and naturally policy behaviour. In this sense, the European Union is regarded as an external link to overcome the cycle of patrimonial public policy behaviour similar to what is happening in other southern European countries such as Italy, Portugal and Greece. There have been intensive learning processes going on ever since Spain joined the European Union in 1986 (Dyson and Featherstone, 1996). They are related to the fact that the ambition of Spanish governments is to transform the country into a central country of the European Union. The improvement, democratisation and Europeanisation of the policy-making processes in the past three decades made the country more similar to most other west European countries. There are still problems, but they are being solved steadily by alternating governments. These two and a half decades have to be regarded as a long cultural transition from authoritarian to democratic public policy-making.

The Spanish contribution to European integration since the early 1990s

Spain's main interest has been mainly in the area of regional and cohesion policy as well as CAP and the Common Fisheries Policy. Throughout the 1990s, the Spanish position has been the toughest in these issues, leading to increased structural funds for the country. Moreover, Prime Minister José Maria Aznar Spain intended to maintain a strong position in relation to the larger countries, particularly in terms of votes in the council. In the Nice Treaty of 2000, Spain accepted a reduction of its representation in the European Parliament from sixty-four to fifty, in order to achieve almost equal number of votes to the larger countries, in spite of a smaller population. Proposed changes to this agreed formula during the European Convention chaired by former French President Valery Giscard D'Estaing met strong opposition from Spanish representatives. Although Spain had to settle for a bad outcome of negotiations in the agricultural and fisheries sector when it joined the European Union in 1986, mainly due to French concerns that the newcomer would become a major competitor for their farmers and fishermen, it was able to protect their interests very efficiently since then. In any of the crucial meetings concerning financial settlements during 1988, 1991–92 and 1999 Spain was able to maintain or even increase its share of the structural funds. The creation of a cohesion fund dedicated to reducing the disparities of the countries with less than 90 per cent of the EU GDP average per capita was a major achievement of Spanish diplomacy. Indeed, Spain found allies in the southern European countries of Portugal and Greece as well as Ireland (Jones, 2000: 88–95; Hooghe and Marks, 2001; Ross, 1995: 182). This became quite evident during the budget negotiations in the Berlin summit of 1999 during the German presidency. According to Francesc Morata, Spain found allies in the other cohesion countries Greece, Portugal and to a lesser extent Ireland, while Germany coalesced with Austria, the Netherlands and Sweden, all net payers and called informally 'the gang of four'. The in-between group was formed by France, Italy, Denmark, Belgium and Luxembourg which opposed the cohesion policies, in case they would encroach on the CAP. The United Kingdom was a free-floating agent interested in keeping its compensation for the agricultural sector intact. In this sense, the Berlin summit of 1999, was not able to make major changes to the allocation of structural funds, leading to a delay of important decisions.

   Although all countries came out from the negotiations as winners, according to Morata, Europe was the big loser. The weak bargaining position of the European

Commission was related to the fact that it had to resign after a vote of no confidence in the European Parliament. This was related to a very negative report revealing certain cases of corruption, trafficking of influences and nepotism in certain departments of the European Commission (Morata, 2000: 172–3; Powell, 2001: 583). This clearly contradicts suggestions that Spain is a peripheral player in the European Union along with the other southern European countries (Beyers and Dierickx, 1998: 305–6). In reality, it has been an effective player in crucial political discussions, during the governments of Felipe Gonzalez, José Maria Aznar and José Luis Zapatero. In the European Convention of 2002–03 under the leadership of Giscard d'Estaing, Aznar found an ally in Prime Minister Tony Blair, by presenting an alternative to what was then called the Franco-German proposals of institutional reform. In spite of this alliance, Spanish foreign policy is very keen to push forward the European integration process. However, there are differences in emphasis between the two main parties, the PP and the PSOE. Former Prime Minister Aznar was very keen to emphasise the national interest by negotiating hard on policies important to the country such as the structural funds, fisheries and the institutional settlement negotiated in Intergovernmental Conferences, while Zapatero, also before him Gonzalez, is interested in defending the national interest in the context of further European integration. It means, that European integration is regarded as a positive aspect for the Spanish Socialists, which may lead to short term national sacrifices, but long term collective gains. A good example of the differences in approach of the two political parties could be seen in the negotiations of the Constitutional Treaty in 2003 and 2004.

The voting system agreed in the Nice Treaty was regarded by Aznar as a major victory for the country. He therefore opposed, along with Poland, the proposed changes to the Constitutional Treaty. This was one of the reasons why the Italian presidency was not able to break the deadlock. British Prime Minister Tony Blair tried to act as honest broker and achieve a settlement, but Aznar would not give in. The Intergovernmental Conference (IGC) during the Italian presidency was scheduled to finish on the 18–19 December 2003 summit in Brussels, but in the end it did not lead to an agreement. The positions of Spain and Poland in this respect were quite crucial in blocking any compromise. The main reason was that the new proposals would lead to a reduction of the share of power among countries. The main issue was to achieve a compromise in the share of the votes in the Council according to the principle of the double majority (50 per cent of member-states and at least three fifths – 60 per cent – of the population of the European Union) agreed in the European Convention. Prime Minister Aznar and the Polish Prime Minister Leszek Miller opposed any change of the Nice Treaty compromise. During the summit Italian Prime Minister Silvio Berlusconi met several times both with Aznar and Miller, but without any result. The larger problem was Poland, which felt that the Germans were not flexible enough in the negotiations. Therefore, they themselves also adopted a very intransigent position. Aznar was quite isolated in the summit. He tried to convince the smaller countries to join him in the opposition what he perceived as a model which would strengthen the larger countries against the smaller countries. He was not able to gain any support from most countries. Although the population weighting was accepted by most countries, the main issue became the way countries could block a majority. Aznar preferred a solution of 50 per cent of states and 66 per cent of the population. He had some occasional support in terms of intermediation from British Prime Minister Tony Blair, but it did not lead to any change.

In sum, the summit ended in failure. Although most of the blame was thrown at Poland, the Spanish position as well contributed to the general breakdown of negotiations. The whole approach of Prime Minister Aznar was quite personal, giving a low level of manoeuvre to his foreign minister Ana Palacio and the secretary for European affairs Alfonso Dastis (*El Pais*, 7 December 2003: 3–4; *El Pais*, 14 December 2003: 3–5). Giscard d' Estaing, the president of the European Convention, gave a press conference after this failed IGC and said that actually the Spanish proposal was presented by him at the beginning of the European Convention and was then watered down by Michel Barnier and Antonio Vitorino in a meeting of the presidium in Brussels. Nevertheless, Spanish delegates were instructed to reject the double majority and negotiate in order to keep the Nice settlement (*El Pais*, 19 December 2003: 2).

Spanish diplomacy's lack of constructive negotiation skills led to quite negative reactions in the Spanish Cortes. The opposition felt that Prime Minister José Maria Aznar had given a bad name to Spain by not engaging properly with the other European leaders. Socialist opposition leader José Luis Zapatero, the Chairman of the Parliamentary Joint Committee for European Union, Josep Borrell, as well as the leader of the United Left coalition, Gaspar Llamazares, heavily criticised the approach of Aznar, which was regarded as a major break with the overall pro-European integration policies in which Spain had been engaged since 1985. According to them, Spain was never before so isolated in Europe. Aznar blamed France for joining Germany in changing the system agreed at Nice. Aznar did not understand why there should be a change to the double majority and repeated this in his declarations in Spain (*El Pais*, 18 December 2003: 15–16). In early January 2004, president of the European Commission Romano Prodi warned that a continuing failure in approving the Constitutional Treaty would lead eventually to a two-speed Europe, in which some countries would advance faster than others towards integration. Commissioner for enlargement Gunther Verheugen expressed also support for the importance of the Franco-German alliance in pushing forward the European integration process. They set the mood for a continuation of the negotiation process (*El Pais*, 7 January 2004: 2).

The March 14, 2004 general elections led to a change of government in Spain. Against all expectations, the Socialist party won the elections. Although a general dissatisfaction with the People's Party existed in Spain, it was the March 11 Al Qaeda bombings in the Atocha station and the mishandling of the crisis by the government that contributed to the alternation in power (Chari, 2004).

Newly appointed Prime Minister José Luis Zapatero was unable to achieve the absolute majority. It had to rely on the parliamentary support of the United Left coalition which continued to lose votes and the Catalan Republican Left (*Ezquerra Republicana Catalana* – ERC), a left-wing regionalist party. The Zapatero government was committed to European integration like the previous governments under Felipe Gonzalez. Although Zapatero was committed to protect Spanish national interests, he was also very keen to overcome the isolation of Spain which had been created by former Prime Minister Aznar. He was very keen to emphasise that the interest of Spain is to be at the centre of Europe. In this sense, Zapatero regarded the role of Spain to be one of an important bridge between the smaller and larger member-states. The overall strategy of Zapatero is to be an active member of the big six (France, Germany, UK, Italy, Poland, Spain). There is also a strong support for the Franco-German alliance.

Such a change of atmosphere was further strengthened by the fact that the Polish Prime Minister Leszek Miller had to resign due to pressure coming from public opinion and his own party, the Alliance of the Democratic Left (SLD). The new Prime Minister, Marek Belka, was instructed by President Aleksander Kwasniewski to be more compromising. One of the main problems of the Polish position was the opposition to a strong Franco-German alliance, due to the negative experiences of Poland with Germany during World War II. A conciliatory rapprochement between Germany and Poland contributed to a better atmosphere.

Throughout the period of the Irish presidency in the first half of 2004, the member-states committed themselves to overcome their differences. A marathon meeting on 23–24 May led to a final compromise. In the Brussels European Council of the Irish presidency on 18 June 2004 a final agreement was reached. Spain was able to shift the original proposal made at the European Convention from the 50–60 to a 55–65 double majority voting. It was able to receive three more seats in European Parliament out of the fourteen that Spain lost in the negotiations of the Treaty of Nice. The blocking minority rose from ninety-one votes (26.4 per cent) to thirteen states or 351 votes (35 per cent). On this occasion, it were the smaller states that bargained quite hard on their behalf. Zapatero was quite satisfied with the outcome. It was quite close to the Spanish bargaining position of 50–66. (*El Pais*, 27 January 2004: 5; *El Pais*, 27 April 2004: 4; *El Pais*, 22 May 2004: 7; *El Pais*, 23 May 2004: 11; *El Pais*, 19 June 2004: 2). Overall, according to calculations made by Wolfgang Wessels and his colleagues, Spain lost about 0.2 per cent of its power in relation to the previous arrangement, while Germany (4.9 per cent), France (1.1 per cent), the UK (1.1 per cent) and Italy (0.9 per cent) are the winners from these changes (Wessels, 2004: 171).

At the end of June 2004, the new State Secretary for European Affairs, Alberto Navarro, defended the achievements of Spanish diplomacy in the Parliamentary Joint Committee of the European Union. Nevertheless, the People's Party representatives were very keen to present it as a negative result in comparison with the situation reached at Nice. It showed that there is a continuing animosity between the two main parties after the legislative and the European elections (Diario de Sesiones de las Cortes Generales, 2004: 5–7).

Zapatero remained a loyal supporter of the Franco-German axis throughout his term. The first test after the negotiations of the constitutional treaty was to achieve a positive vote in the national referendum scheduled for 20 February 2005. In spite of the sacrifice by the Zapatero government of some of the 'red lines' set out by Aznar in the previous government, the People's Party supported the 'yes' camp. The population approved the European Constitutional Treaty with an overwhelming majority of 76.96 per cent, in spite of a 41.8 per cent turnout (Delgado and Lopez Nieto, 2006: 1266). Zapatero was also engaged in the European campaign of the 'yes' vote in France and the Netherlands, but there the referendum ended with a victory of the 'no' vote and slowly to the end of the Constitutional Treaty (*El Pais*, 28 May 2005: 2; *El Pais*, 2 June 2005: 2–4; *El Pais*, 3 June 2005: 3–5).

After a long period of reflection, German Chancellor Angela Merkel revived the idea of a revision of the Constitutional Treaty during the German Presidency of the Council of the European Union in the first half of 2007. On 12 May 2007, in the Portuguese town of Sintra, Chancellor Merkel met with a core group of politicians, including the Portuguese Prime Minister José Socrates and the Slovenian Prime Minister Janez Jansa, who were chairing their respective EU presidencies in the second half of 2007 and first half of 2008 respectively. President of the European Commission, Manuel Durão Barroso and President of the European Parliament, Gerd Pöttering were also present in the meeting. Merkel could count on the support of twenty-two countries, of which a core group included Spain, Italy, Belgium, Luxembourg and Greece. However, five countries had major difficulties in advocating a revival of the actual Constitutional Treaty. These were France, the Netherlands, the United Kingdom, the Czech Republic and Poland. The Spanish support for the initiative of Angela Merkel showed the wish of the Zapatero government to be at centre of the European integration process (*El Pais*, 13 May 2007: 9; *El Pais*, 16 May 2007: 7).

Although changes have to be made to it, the new Lisbon Treaty still has many elements of the previous document that failed to be ratified. Among the innovative aspects are the introduction of an EU president who can be elected for a renewable term of 2.5 years, an EU foreign minister for the external relations of the European Union and the replacement of the Nice Treaty voting system by the one agreed in the Constitutional Treaty. Considerable opposition came from Poland, backed by the United Kingdom. However, after the legislative Polish elections on November 2007, the change of government from the conservative and nationally inclined Law and Party-led coalition government by Jaroslaw Kaczynsky to Donald Tusk's pro-European liberal citizen's platform led to a more positive constructive engagement of Poland. Spain remained one of the most important allies of Angela Merkel and Germany's efforts to save a revised constitutional Treaty, without calling it that in name. It belonged to the countries that openly supported a revision of the Constitutional Treaty in order to make it work. The final result became the Lisbon Treaty which became approved in the Lisbon summit of November 2007.

Zapatero's government was also important in the bargaining that took place to agree on the financial perspectives for the period 2007–2013. In spite of major difficulties, a deal was struck on the summit in Brussels during the British presidency on 17-18 December 2005. This was again achieved through a positive engagement of Chancellor Angela Merkel which increased the contribution of Germany to the budget in order to close the gap in funding that emerged, because the United Kingdom was not prepared to give up completely on the rebate which had been gained by Prime Minister Margaret Thatcher in the 1980s. In this regard, Spain was one of the losers in terms of structural funds. One of the reasons is that Spain has become richer since joining the European Union and by 2013 the national GDP average would match or even surpass the EU27 average. This means that between 2007 and 2013 Spain will receive substantially less funding yearly, so that at the end the country will become a net payer. On one hand, this has to be regarded as very positive, because the Spanish economy has been performing very well since 1996, but on the other hand it means that now investment has to come from within the country or attraction of foreign direct investment (FDI). One of the aspects that Prime Minister Zapatero emphasised at the press conference of this marathon session on 17–18 December 2005 in Brussels, was that part of the funds will be ring-fenced in order to improve the weak research and development expenditure of the country.

National coordination of European public policy in a multi-level governance system: the growing importance of the autonomous communities

Originally, the policy process was controlled by the central government, a legacy of the authoritarian regime, but steadily, in particular after joining the European Union, it became a multi-level coordination process. The growing importance of the autonomous communities in the past three decades changed the outlook of policy-making coordination. As in most other EU countries, the centre of national coordination of European public policy is located in the Ministry of Foreign Affairs (*Ministério de Asuntos Exteriores* – MAE). The main reason for allocating the MAE this coordinating role is that it is the traditional location for communication systems with the external world. The main body within the ministry coordinating the decision-making process related to EU policy is the State Secretariat for European Affairs (*Secretaria de Estado para Asuntos Europeos* – SEAE).

At the heart of the SEAE is the Interministerial Committee for Community Affairs (*Comisión Interministerial para Asuntos Comunitarios* – CIAC). It brings together weekly, generally on Thursday mornings, representatives of the ministries, which discuss pending positions and decisions of the Spanish government in the working committees and the committee of permanent representatives integrated in the Council of the European Union in Brussels. This formalised structure can be found in all EU member states. The representatives of the individual ministries come normally from the Technical General Secretariats (*Secretariados-Generales Técnicos*). The CIAC reports to the Delegated Government Committee for Economic Affairs (Ministry of the Economy), which is also the deputy chair of the CIAC. In total there are seventeen to twenty members in the CIAC, according to the size of the government. According to Ignacio Molina, the CIAC has been downgraded to a junior minister level since 1995. Moreover, the high level of fragmentation and sectorialisation because of the power of the Spanish *cuerpos* in the administration has led to more informal approaches of individual ministries to the permanent representation, by-passing the CIAC. This fragmented administrative pattern clearly applies mainly to low politics, and is less visible at political level, where the centralised executive in the hands of the prime minister is able to present the Spanish political position with one voice (Molina, 2000b: 126–36). There are other interministerial committees dealing with the trial processes related to the European Court of Justice which is also attached to the Ministry of Foreign Affairs, and the Delegated Committee on Economic Affairs, which meets weekly and hierarchically above the CIAE. The role of the Super-ministry of Economy has to be emphasised here, due to the fact that the deputy chair of the CIAC is also the junior minister of the economy ministry (Molina, 2001: 172–3) (see Figure 9.1).

The participation of the autonomous communities in the European public policy decision-making process has improved considerably since the end of the 1980s. The establishment of the Conference for European Affairs (*Conferencia para Asuntos Relacionados con las Comunidades Europeas* – CARCE), which comprises representatives of the autonomous communities and the central government, has gained in importance over time. It was founded in 1988 and gained more importance in the 1990s. It is linked to the growing system of sectorial committees related to different policy areas (see Chapter 5). The whole system of involvement of the regions is still too new to produce substantial gains of influence for the autonomous communities; nevertheless it is certainly contributing to a multi-level governance system in Spain. Europeanisation, as already mentioned, has contributed substantially to a more cooperative federalism, although the regions are still weak in shaping the decision-making process. Law 2 of 1997 has further institutionalised and strengthened the position of the CARCE. It is located in the Ministry of Public Administrations and it has created a second-level committee of coordinators which may improve considerably the coordination efforts between the regions and the central government (Colino, 2001: 245–6). The Aznar government introduced a representative of the autonomous communities in the permanent representation in Brussels to facilitate the exchange of information. In December 2004 this was upgraded by José Luis Zapatero's government to two representatives and the right to take part in four of the nine formations of the Council. These formations were environment, agriculture and rural development, cohesion and social policy and youth and consumers' rights (Morata, 2007: 307).

This is reinforced by the fact that parliament and civil society only have quite a weak influence on policy. In spite of all the developments, the autonomous communities are still very much lagging behind in terms of influence when compared to similar political systems such as Germany, Belgium and Austria.

The interface of the Spanish government with the European Union is the permanent representation in Brussels consisting of over fifty civil servants seconded from the individual ministries to work in the different working groups of the council. These official fifty civil servants are supported by a staff of some 200 persons and this clearly represent the fragmented nature of Spanish public administration at supranational level. Informal networks which link directly the REPER with the individual ministries make it more difficult for the SEAE to

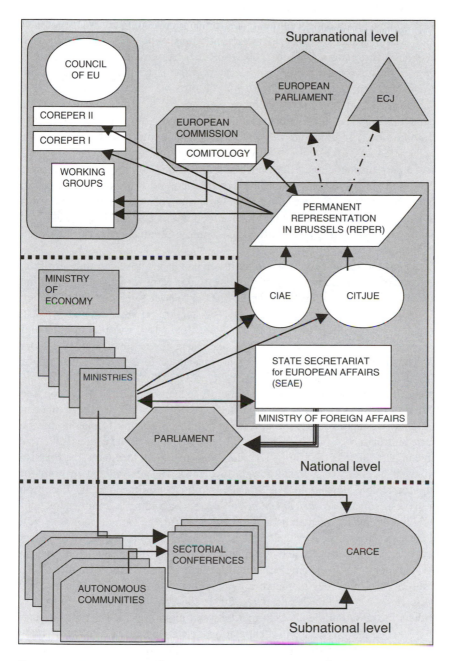

Figure 9.1 The national coordination of European policy-making in Spain.

Source: CIAE: Interministerial Committee for European Affairs (Comisión Interministerial para Asuntos Europeus).

dominate and oversee the whole process. The distant position of the REPER from the decision-making centre Madrid gives also a unique strong position to the civil servants involved in the negotiations, who are in general terms experienced negotiators (Molina, 2001: 168–70). As already mentioned, since 1996, the PP government after an agreement with the Catalan CiU created the position of a representative of the regions (*consejero autonomico*) in REPER which informs regularly the autonomous community. In 2004, it was upgraded to two representatives and as already mentioned the possibility to take part in four of the nine Council formations, related to policy developments that may fall under the competences of the regions. In this sense, both the Aznar and the Zapatero governments responded to calls from the autonomous communities to upgrade the position of the regions within the decision-making process of the council, by allowing representatives of the regional governments to take part in meetings related to topics falling under their remit. Autonomous communities are allowed to take part in over thirty committees of comitology attached to the European Commission.

Although the regions are demanding involvement in more committees, these developments can already be regarded as positive in terms of enhancement of the position of the autonomous communities in the overall European public policy decision-making process (Ortuzar, 1998; Fernandez, 1998; Saracibar, 2002). The main work of the REPER is to represent Spain in the 250 committees of the council. Most of the decisions are taken at a lower level; only the more important political and technical issues are discussed further at the Committee of Permanent Representatives (COREPER). COREPER I is for the deputy permanent representatives and is related mainly to technical problems in proposed directives from the European Commission. COREPER II consists of the permanent representatives themselves and is devoted to political problems. Decisions may be deferred ultimately to the Council of Ministers, which has to take a decision.

In comparison with the United Kingdom, Germany and Denmark, the Spanish parliament is quite weak in its powers to control the government in terms of European Union legislation. The so-called Joint Committee for the European Union (*Comision Mixta para la Unión Europea*) is a standing committee, but non-legislative. It consists of members of the lower house, the Congress of Deputies, and the upper house, the Senate. It increased considerably the number of members since 1985 when it was created. Originally, there were fifteen members back in 1985, but membership was increased to forty-six in the seventh legislature which started in 2000, in order to secure a better representation of all parliamentary groups (Basabe and Gonzalez Escudero, 2001: 206). In 2006, there were forty-six members in the committee, which met between eight and twelve times a year. A major exception was during the deliberations related to the Constitutional Treaty in 2002 during which time the committee met thirty-one times. In the eighth legislature (2004–08) the number of meetings declined to just seven to eight times a year (Magone, 2007a: 124).

It is one of the weakest committees of the so-called Committee of Bodies Specialised in Community Affairs (*Comité des Organs Specialisés en Affaires*

Communautaires – COSAC) which brings together twice a year the committees of European Affairs of all member countries. While the United Kingdom, Germany, Denmark, Sweden and Finland receive legislation in due time to propose changes to the final draft agreed in the Council of Ministers, the Spanish Joint Committee has only *ex post facto* competences, meaning that it reviews the work done by the government after a national law has been passed. Attempts to change the role of the Joint Committee succeeded only sporadically. Most of the work of the committee is dedicated to hearings of officials and specialists as well as oral questions in the committee. Non-legislative proposals were quite rare in the fourth (1989–93) and fifth (1993–96) legislatures, but increased considerably during the sixth (1996–2000), seventh (2000–04) and eighth legislatures (2004–08) from three and five respectively to over twenty-seven (Basabe and Gonzalez Escudero, 2001: 208; Magone, 2007a: 126) (see Figure 9.2).

One of the reasons for the weakness of the Spanish parliament in terms of EU legislation scrutiny, is that from the outset EU affairs was regarded as foreign policy and therefore a competence of the government. The government should consult parliament, but it had autonomy to shape it without being constrained by parliament. In spite of the substantial transformations of the European Union since 1985 and 1993, there has been no desire to change the role of parliament in the shaping of European affairs. This is reinforced by the fact that the Spanish population is probably one of the most pro-European along with Belgium, Italy, Ireland and Luxembourg (see Figure 9.3) In this sense, there was an all-party agreement about the strategic importance of the European Union for the standing of Spain in the world. Although there is some moderate critical euroscepticism

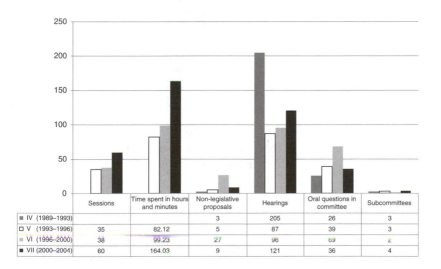

	Sessions	Time spent in hours and minutes	Non-legislative proposals	Hearings	Oral questions in committee	Subcommittees
■ IV (1989–1993)			3	205	26	3
□ V (1993–1996)	35	82.12	5	87	39	3
▨ VI (1996–2000)	38	99.23	27	96	69	2
■ VII (2000–2004)	60	164.03	9	121	36	4

Figure 9.2 Activity of the Joint Committee for the European Union (1993–2004).

Source: Adjusted and update from Basabe Llorens, Gonzalez Escudero, 2001: 208; Congreso de los Diputados, 2005: 169–76.

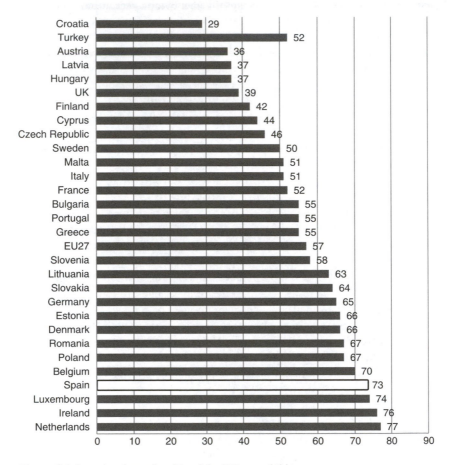

Figure 9.3 Is national membership of the EU a good thing.
Source: EB67, June 2007; fieldwork April–May 2007:16.

among the United Left and the BNG, the vast majority of parliamentarians supports European integration, even if they may have differences in relation to certain processes. Prime Minister José Maria Aznar was quite an exception to a general tendency of Spanish politicians and diplomats to be constructively at the fore of the European integration process. All this limits the role of the Spanish parliament in shaping the European integration process and scrutinising legislation. Spain belongs to a pattern of EU scrutiny legislation that can be labelled as southern European. It shows similarities to Greece, Portugal and Italy which are countries that traditionally support European integration (Magone, 2007b: 245).

Like parliament, interest groups are marginalised from the European public policy process. The late emergence of democratic interest groups and their weak establishment across the territory prevent a more active role in this process.

Some interest groups have created offices at the supranational level such as the Spanish Confederation of Business Enterprises (*Confederación Española de Organizaciones Empresariales* – CEOE), but in general terms Spanish organised civil society is still too weak to influence policy. This can be said for most policy areas, although improvements in certain areas such as environmental policy can be found. The increase in the number of environmental associations at local, regional and national levels makes the whole policy process more open. Most of these associations are linked to European networks which reinforce the pressure exerted upon the Spanish government in a multi-level governance style. This is accompanied by a fast change of attitudes from a materialist to a post-materialist culture, in which the protection of the environment becomes an essential part of the quality of life (Gomez Benito *et al.*, 1999; Aguinaga Roustan, 1997).

In 1999, there were twenty interest group representations at supranational level. They corresponded to 5.5 per cent of all 361 national interest group representations. Seventeeen were representations of the regional governments, while the other three were related to the Chambers of Trade, Industry and Agriculture or Employers' and Employees' Associations. In this sense, Spain is certainly not among the countries with the highest level of representation, which indicates a weakness of organised civil society at national level. The largest share of national interest group representations came from Germany (23.5 per cent), France (23.2 per cent) and the United Kingdom (11.6 per cent). Even Sweden (6.5 per cent), Denmark (6.5 per cent) and Austria (5.8 per cent) had a larger share of national interest group representations (Magone, 2003: 204). The most important economic interest groups, CEOE and the trade union confederations Workers' Commissions (*Comisiones Obreras* – CCOO) and General Workers' Union (*Unión General de Trabajadores* – UGT), are integrated in the supranational European-wide respective confederations. The CEOE is integrated in the Union of Business and Employers' Confederations in Europe (*Union des Confederations de Industrie et des Employeurs* – UNICE), while the UGT and CCOO are members of the European Trade Union Confederation (ETUC). Both are the main social partners involved in the social dialogue and contribute indirectly to any social agreement achieved at supranational level. CEOE, UGT, CCOO and other associations are also represented in the merely advisory European Economic and Social Committee (Magone, 2003: 203–5). This shows that interest groups have multiple points of access, which they are able to use or not. Nevertheless, as far as the Spanish case is concerned the weak position of interest groups at national and regional level, due to lack of a culture of consultation, is not compensated by more influence at supranational level. On the contrary, the weak position at national level repeats itself at supranational level both in the decision-making process of the supranational organisations as well as the supranational institutions (Campo, 2001; Magone, 2001).

In spite of this assessment, one could witness a high level of dynamic participation of Spanish national interest groups in the European Convention. From all 266 national organisations (public and private authorities, socioeconomic groups, academic think tanks and other) 26 (9.8 per cent) were Spanish. Stronger presence could be found only from Germany with 66 organisations (24.8 per cent), France with 47 (17.7 per cent), Italy 40 (15 per cent) and the United Kingdom with 29 (11 per cent) (Magone, 2006: 180).

In sum, the Spanish national European policy coordination is very much dominated by the central government, in spite of the fact that in the past two and a half decades other domestic actors were able to improve their capabilities of influence in the Spanish political system. Particularly, the regions are moving slowly but steadily towards a similar place as in countries such as Germany, Belgium and Austria. Similarly, interest groups are gaining more importance in certain policy areas, while in others such an involvement is lagging behind. The most problematic aspect of the Spanish political system is the lack of a serious and consistent parliamentary input from the Joint Committee for the European Union. This may change in the future, but for this a reform of the Senate and a higher level of professionalisation of MPs will be essential (see also Chapter 4).

The structural funds and Spanish public policy

A central European policy for Spain are the structural funds destined for the upgrading of the economic and public infrastructures of the country. As already mentioned in the previous chapter, Spain was the champion of upgrading the role of the structural funds as a compensation mechanism for the emerging Single European Market. Spain has been a recipient of structural funds since 1985. The whole process was originally controlled very much by the central government. Only gradually did the central government allow stronger involvement of the regional governments in the whole formulation and decision-making process. In the past 18 years a learning process has taken place, which has certainly contributed to a better management and implementation of the structural funds. According to Gary Marks and Ivan Llamazares, the emerging EU multi-level governance system was an important reinforcing factor and structure of opportunities to allow Spanish regions, particularly Catalonia and the Basque Country, to bypass the central government and have direct links to other regional and supranational actors (Marks and Llamazares, 2006: 256).

In the first Common Support Framework (CSF I) (1988–93) financed by the Delors I Package, the central Spanish government did not involve the regions efficiently in the whole process. One of the main reasons was the lack of experience in dealing with the European policy-making process. Moreover, the time frame of formulation and decision making was too short to achieve a better integration of the regions. This changed for the better in the process towards the formulation and decision-making leading up to CSF II (1994–99). A better coordination and allocation of the funds clearly was related to lessons learned from CSF I. In spite of the stronger involvement of the regions, the overall picture was still characterised by the strong dominance of the central government in the whole process, mainly because the regional administrations were not equipped to deal with all aspects related to the structural funds. CSF III (2000–06) allowed for further adjustments in terms of subsidiarity and partnership to take place. Spain was eligible for 22 per cent of all structural funds (see Figures 9.5) They represented an important strategic tool for economic development. Spain was able to come closer to the EU GDP average in the past decade. While it had only 74 per cent of the EU average GDP per capita in 1988, in 1998 this had risen to 81.4 per cent and in 2005 to 103 per cent. The main problem in Spain, as already mentioned in Chapter 5, is the asymmetrical distribution of this GDP per capita. While Madrid, the north-east (the Basque Country, Navarre and La Rioja) and the east (Catalonia, the Balearics and Valencia) come close to or surpass the EU average, the north-west (Galicia, Asturias and Cantabria), the South (Andalusia and Murcia) and the Centre (Castilla León, Castilla La Mancha and Extremadura) are still lagging considerably behind (see Figure 9.4). Although Spain was able to improve its GDP per capita towards the EU average, the internal disparities, in spite of structural funds, continue to be salient. This can be observed particularly in the southern regions of Andalusia and Murcia which were not able to make substantial improvements in relation to the richest regions of Madrid, Catalonia, the Basque Country and Navarre.

The structural funds have been directed primarily to the upgrading of the Spanish infrastructure. Both telecommunications and transport infrastructures have been important target areas in the first Common Support Framework. The Barcelona Olympic Games and the Seville Expo'92 are clear examples of this heavy investment in infrastructures. The Seville project was quite comprehensive, because it improved considerably the city's links to other parts of the country. The high speed train (AVE) from Seville to Madrid was regarded as important to overcome the peripheral status of the region and make it more interesting for potential investors. A technology park was created, which had difficulties establishing itself after the Expo '92 came to an end. Other examples were the modernisation of the airport of Lanzarote in the Canary Islands, the expansion of the metro of Valencia and the improvement of water management in the city of León. Moreover, a technology park was established in Malaga in Andalusia.

This emphasis on infrastructures was quite important, so that Spain would attain a better integration into the single European Market. In CSF II, the infrastructures programme was still relevant, but it was balanced by a growing concern for investment in the small- and medium-sized enterprises as well as human resources. In spite of huge efforts, the Spanish government had difficulties in mobilising enterprises to present research and development (R&D) projects for the available funds. CSF I had found out that the emphasis on infrastructures was not very sensible, if it was not accompanied by stronger investment in a weak industrial sector. According to the ninth report on the structural funds for the year 1997, the aim of involving 80 per cent of all small- and medium-sized enterprises in the programmes, in order to upgrade their capabilities was not achieved. Instead only 50 per cent of small- and medium-sized enterprises were involved in projects financed or to be financed by the structural funds (European Commission, 1999: 69).

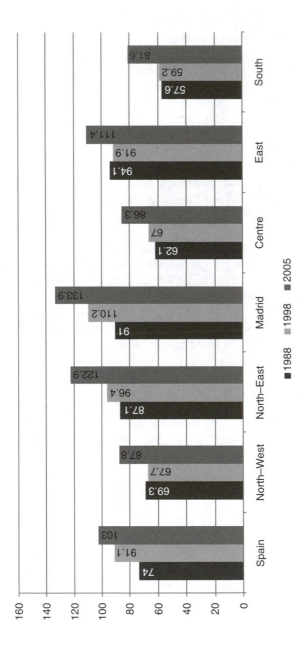

Figure 9.4 GDP per capita in Spain, 1988, 1998 (EU15) and 2005 (EU27).

Source: European Commission, 2001d: 68 = 100; Eurostat news release,19/08, 12 February 2008.

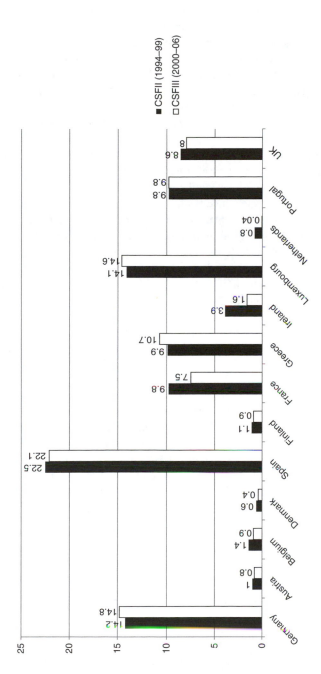

Figure 9.5 Distribution of structural funds in CSF II, 1994–99 and CSF III, 2000–06 for EU15 (without additional enlargement funding 2004–06).

Source: European Commission, 2001a:11.

One of the characteristics of the implementation of structural funds is that since 1986 both the European Commission, the national governments and the regional authorities are learning lessons from this quite innovative way of dealing with regional development. For example, after the reform of the structural funds of 1988 six objectives were formulated, which helped to target better the fund for the specific problems of each region. The most important, objective 1, was directed at regions lagging behind and constituted 70 per cent of all the funding in CSF II. The other objectives were dedicated respectively to regions in industrial decline (objective 2, 10 per cent), the long-term unemployed (objective 3, 5 per cent), workers whose employment situation is threatened by changes in industry and production (objective 4, 5 per cent), farmers and restructuring of the employment situation in rural areas (objectives 5a and 5b, 9 per cent) and areas with an extremely low population density (objective 6, 4.5 per cent). The last objective was created specifically for northern regions of Sweden and Finland after 1995. The enlargement to central and eastern Europe initiated a process of reform of the structural funds proposed by the Agenda 2000 document of the European Commission. This allowed for a reduction of these objectives from six to three. Objective 1, which targets regions lagging behind, which applies only to regions with a GDP per capita less than 75 per cent of the EU average, remained unchanged. Almost 70 per cent of the available €195 billion was allocated to this objective. The other objectives were regrouped into two objectives. Objective 2 is related to economic and social restructuring of declining regions and comprises 11.5 per cent of the structural funds, while objective 3 is now assigned to improving human resources with 12.3 per cent allocation of the total.[1] Part of the funds are allocated to EU, Community initiatives which target certain industries or other particular problems. There was a decline of funds and programmes for Community initiatives and CSF III was halved to 5 per cent of the total funds. The ten different programmes of CSF II were reduced to four programmes – Interreg, Leader, Equal and Urban(2) – for the period 2000–06. Spain was eligible for 18.75 per cent of the €10.4 billion. Forty-six per cent is allocated to Interreg, while the rest is split among the other Community initiatives. As already mentioned, a cohesion fund was created in 1993 to support countries that had a national GDP per capita below 90 per cent of the EU average. This extra fund is allocated to finance large projects in the environmental and transport sector. The total allocated in 1994–99 was €15.5 billion, which was increased to €18 billion for the period 2000–06. Spain received €11.16 billion or 63.5 per cent of the total fund (European Commission, 2001a: 11–13).

The reduction of the objectives, the growing simplification of procedures, the decentralisation of decision making and openness are elements of the revamped strategy of the structural funds (Morata, 2000: 178–81). This put the Spanish public administration further under pressure. According to the twelfth annual report of the European Union for the year 2000, the balance of implementation of ERDF was quite positive in terms of implementation of funds and respect for the guidelines and principles of European regional policy. A more negative aspect has been related to the highly complex system which is in some way hampered by problems of coordination between the institutions. Moreover, interventions are too traditional, not innovative enough, and still lack sensitivity in addressing problems of inequality between men and women (European Commission, 2001b: 34). The last aspect is quite important, because Spain still has a very low involvement of women in the labour market. Unemployment is highest among women and new jobseekers. (Cousins, 2000; Threlfall, 1997; European Commission, 2002a: 78–9).

For the period 2000–06 Spain prepared three CSFs, one for each objective. The most important one was naturally objective 1 concerning regions lagging behind. Eleven regions were covered by objective 1 funding: Andalusia, Asturias, the Canary Islands, Cantabria, Castilla León, Castilla La Mancha, Extremadura, Galicia, Murcia, the Valencian Community and the North African enclaves of Ceuta and Melilla.

In terms of priorities, CSFIII (2000–06) clearly concentrated more on enhancing the competitiveness of the Spanish enterprises. It wanted (1) to improve competitiveness and development of the productive tissue; (2) to innovate through R&D towards an information society; (3) improve the environment, nature and water resources; (4) to develop human resources, employment and equality of opportunities; (5) to emphasise local and urban development; (6) to strengthen transport and energy networks; (7) to focus on agriculture and rural development; and (8) to improve the structures of fisheries and aquaculture. In general terms, the new CSF envisaged an improvement of partnership as one of the major aims of the structural funds, in order to create a system of co-responsibility between central, regional and local authorities. There is at least the desire to improve the relationship to interest groups which may be relevant to a particular project. Another feature of this CSF is that it reduced substantially the number of operational programmes from seventy-three to twenty-three, in order to prevent a fragmentation of the implementation of structural funds. This reduction of forms and interventions and the growing co-responsibility of the different levels of governance is strengthened by a growing decentralisation of the structural funds to the regional level. The monitoring and evaluation mechanisms were also reinforced in order to identify problems at an early stage (European Commission, 2001b: 35–6). In total, it was expected that the CSF III for objective 1 regions would spend €80.4 billion, of which 68.24 per cent will be public funding (48.8 per cent from EU funding, 19.4 per cent from Spanish public funding and 31.76 per cent from private funding) (European Commission, 2000a: 14).

Objectives 2 and 3 were also designed to follow the same logic of strengthening the technological basis of Spanish enterprises. They also were organised along common support frameworks. Objective 3 included measures to integrate less disadvantaged groups and ensure equality of opportunities between men and women in the labour market (European Commission, 2001b: 37).

This shift of focus is quite important, because in the past the emphasis on infrastructures has certainly led to the neglect of the industrial sector (Held, Sanchez-Velasco, 2001: 236–46). The transformation of the technological basis of

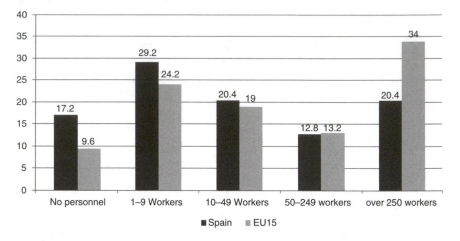

Figure 9.6 The structure of industrial enterprises in Spain, 1997.
Source: Eurostat, 1999.

the industrial sector is a pre-condition to improve the overall quality of the Spanish economy.

In spite of major efforts, Spain is still lagging behind in terms of R&D investment. In 2003, Spain spent 1.05 per cent of GDP, still well below the EU25 average of 1.82 per cent. However, this has been a considerable improvement from the figure of 0.72 per cent of 1998 (European Commission, 2006a: 2–3). Several reports commissioned by the European Commission in the process of drafting the Spanish CSFIV (2007–2013), advised Spanish policy makers now to shift from investment in infrastructures such as the High-Speed train between Madrid and Barcelona to investment in R&D and innovation. This referred also to the asymmetrical distribution of R&D+i in the autonomous community of Madrid, Catalonia, Basque Country and Navarre. About two-thirds of all spending takes place in these regions. Moreover, there is still a lot to do in inverting the relationship between public and private funding. In comparison to more advanced economies, Spanish R&D+i is disproportionately financed by public institutions and less by private enterprises. The reports urged Spain to invert the relationship towards private funding (European Commission, 2006c: 3–8; see also European Commission, 2005b: 22–5).

The structure of business enterprises is dominated by small- and medium-sized enterprises with a very low R&D base. Their spending on R&D is very low or almost non-existent in comparison to the larger, mainly foreign firms. According to Esther del Campo, small- and medium-sized enterprises generate most of the employment in Spain. Indeed, 74 per cent of all employment is in small enterprises with fewer than 100 employees. Most of the employment is temporary, unstable, part-time, low-paid and carried out by a female workforce. Fifty to 60 per cent of the larger firms carry out research and development activities, but only 20 per cent of medium-sized enterprises and 1 per cent of small enterprises (Campo, 2001: 75).

The cohesion funds were so far being spent on environmental projects, related to urban waste management and water supply to the more arid regions of Spain (European Commission, 2001c). The cohesion fund has been used to finance transeuropean networks. The high-speed train link between Madrid and Barcelona was a major priority. This will bring Spain closer to the French system (*El Pais*, 17 February 2003: 26; *El Pais*, 12 March 2003: 25). On 27 November 2007, due to delays in the construction of the Madrid–Barcelona high-speed train, Minister of Development Magda Alvarez was subject to a vote of no confidence, which she won only by three votes (*El Pais*, 28 November 2007: 10). The AVE (high-speed train) Madrid–Barcelona was scheduled to be ready by end of December, but faced difficulties in achieving this deadline. There is now also the major project of linking Lisbon and Madrid via a high speed train in order to achieve the completion of the planned transeuropean networks (see Figure 9.7).

CSFIV (2007–2013) focuses much more on issues of R&D. The Spanish government envisages that the share of the GDP will increase to 2 per cent by 2010. Due to the enlargement after 2004, many regions are now above 75 per cent of the EU average. This so-called 'statistical effect' created regions that are in transition, labelled as 'phasing in' and 'phasing out' regions. In spite of a

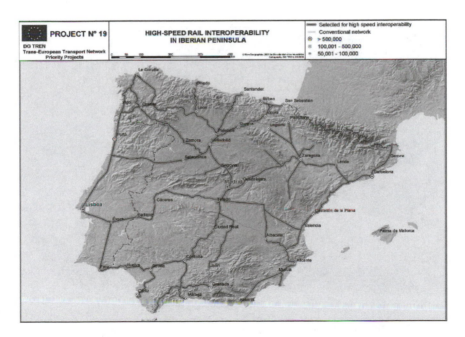

Figure 9.7 The long-term plan to create a the high-speed train network in the Iberian Peninsula.

Source: European Commission, 2005b: 33.

considerable loss of the share of the structural funds, which were now diverted to central and eastern European countries, many Spanish regions still qualify for funding. While Spain received €54.671 billion in the 2000–2006 period the sum has decreased to €31.457 billion for the 2007–2013 period. This corresponded to 9.05 per cent of the total sum of €347 410 billions. The new period also redesigned the objectives of the structural funds. There are three main objectives. Objective 1 is for convergence for regions below 75 per cent of EU average GDP. Objective 2 regional competitiveness and employment, particularly in more advanced regions. Objective 3 is for European territorial cooperation which includes the three dimensions of inter-regional cooperation (cross-border cooperation, transnational cooperation and inter-regional cooperation) (Figures 9.8 and 9.9).

The fact that Spain is engaged in several projects of cross-border cooperation which are financed by the Interreg programme is quite important. Such cross-border Interreg programmes can be found along the Spanish–Portuguese border (Galicia–Norte de Portugal, Andalusia and the Algarve, Extremadura–Alentejo and Castilla León–Beiras), the Spanish-French border (C-6 Project and the Euroregion project) and between Spain and Morocco. All these projects have been important to improve the economic and social situation of border regions (Magone, 2001; Morata, 1995, 1997). Moreover, the new transregional and transnational aspects of Interreg (B and C) are linking Spanish regional development to the EU policies

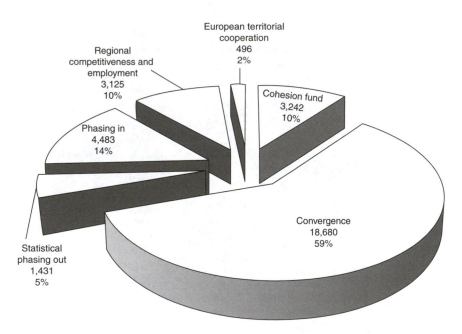

Total: 2007–2013 = € 31 457 billions

Figure 9.8 The Structural Funds allocated to Spain for CSFIV (2007–2013).

Source: Inforegio, factsheet, Cohesion policy 2007–2013 – Spain, October 2006.

Convergence regions (Andalusia, Extremadura, Castilla La Mancha, Galicia)

Statistically Phasing out regions (Murcia, Asturias, Ceuta and Melilla)

Phasing in regions (Castilla-León, Valencian Community, Canary islands)

Competitiveness and Employment regions (Cantabria, Basque Country, Naarre, L a Rioja, Aragón, Catalonia, Baleares)

Figure 9.9 Allocation of structural funds (2007–2013) according to objectives.

Source: Inforegio, factsheet, October 2006, Cohesion Policy 2007–2013, Spain.

of inter-territorial cohesion. One of the best examples is the *Arco Latino* which links the local councils of Italy, France and Spain.

In sum, the structural funds are an important strategic tool to increase the pace of development of the Spanish economy. Nevertheless, the main problem remaining is a need to change the structure of the industry and the underlying business culture based very much on low-technology products. The recent priorities related to R&D, the information society and vocational training are welcome, but they need to be reinforced by a stronger effort by the government.

Reform of the agricultural and fisheries sector

Spain and the common agricultural policy

In both the agricultural and fisheries sector, Spain was a big loser in the negotiations of accession to the European Community between 1977 and 1985. The opposition of the French to allow the Spaniards to get a share of the CAP and CFP led to an entry of Spain into the European Union under very disfavourable conditions. It is to the credit of the Spanish diplomacy and negotiation skills which contributed to a major change in this situation.

Today Spain is one of the largest net receivers of funds from the CAP and the CFP. A look at the evolution of the Spanish share of the funds shows that it evolved from just 1.2 per cent of the overall EAGGF of 22.2 billion ecus in 1986 to 14.7 per cent of 42.1 billion in 2001. Along with France, Italy, Germany and the United Kingdom, Spain is the largest recipient of CAP funds. Any attempts of radical reform of the CAP have been watered down mainly by the Spaniards and the French. The CAP came into force in 1962 and the main purpose was to stabilise prices in the European Community, protect European agriculture from worldwide competition through the establishment of import tariffs and subsidising of European production. This made sense in the 1960s, when a large part of the population was still employed in agriculture. In 2001 only 4.2 per cent of the employed population was working in the agricultural sector. In total there are 6.7 million people working in the agricultural sector in the EU15. After the 2004 enlarged of the European Union to twenty-five member-states the share went up to 6.86 per cent or 10.5 million of a total population of 453.1 million. In this context, Spain is slightly below the EU average with about 5 per cent. This figures are without including the increase of the agricultural population after the 2007 enlargement to Romania and Bulgaria. The CAP has become a problem for the European Union as a whole, because it really it is not radical enough in terms of preparing European agriculture for complete abolition of protectionist measures. The World Trade Organisation (WTO) clearly became a battlefield between the United States and the European Union in relation to this issue. In the European Commission Agenda 2000, a major reform of the CAP due to the Central and Eastern European enlargement was envisaged. In 2001, the European Commission issued a Green Paper on the reform of CAP which led to major consultations across the European Union.

The outcome was a mid-term review of the CAP with major reform proposals by European Commissioner Franz Fischler. The main aim is to make European agriculture more competitive by 2013. Flexibility in production decisions combined with income stability for farmers is one of the aspects of the new reform. There is also a demand for environment-friendly incentives (a growing concern), so that farming practices become more sustainable. There will also be a decline of subsidies for larger farmers, so that new funding can be freed for rural development and create savings for further reforms. Single farm payments will be now undertaken independently from production. Instead growing links to environment-friendly measures, food safety, animal welfare, health and occupational safety standards, as well as keeping all farmland in good condition, will become part of the new package. As already mentioned Germany and France achieved a compromise in Brussels in January 2003, to stagger the transition of payments from 2005 to 2013 (European Commission, 2002c).

The reform introduced by Franz Fischler and negotiated in January 2003 among member-states led to a compromise in relation to the share of subsidies for central and eastern European countries. The biggest problems remain Poland

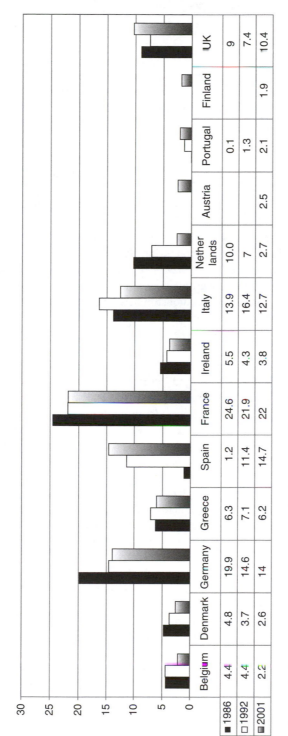

	Belgium	Denmark	Germany	Greece	Spain	France	Ireland	Italy	Netherlands	Austria	Portugal	Finland	UK
■ 1986	4.4	4.8	19.9	6.3	1.2	24.6	5.5	13.9	10.0		0.1		9
□ 1992	4.4	3.7	14.6	7.1	11.4	21.9	4.3	16.4	7		1.3		7.4
▨ 2001	2.2	2.6	14	6.2	14.7	22	3.8	12.7	2.7	2.5	2.1	1.9	10.4

Figure 9.10 Distribution of CAP funds to EU member-states, 1986–2001.

Source: European Commission, 2002e: Annex 10.

and Romania with almost one-fifth and one-third respectively of the working population employed in the agricultural sector. This consists of 2.7 million people and it will be the largest proportion of agricultural workers in an individual country. Spanish interests are being fought in Brussels to keep the present regime intact as long as possible. The compromise now allows for the status quo for still some years to come coupled with a transitional period where most of the funding will be shifted to central and eastern Europe. This will further exacerbate the relationship between so-called net payers and net receivers. Indeed, Germany, the United Kingdom, the Netherlands, Belgium, Denmark and Sweden are net payers into the EAGGF, while Spain, France, Greece and Ireland are among the largest recipients (see Figure 9.11).

For the period 2007–2013, the EU will spend €862.4 billion on CAP. In 2007, €126.5 billion were allocated to CAP funding, 9.8 per cent is being invested in rural tourism, 33.8 per cent is used for direct payments to farmers, while the rest is for other purposes (European Commission, 2006b: 3).

Spanish opposition to the reform has been quite strong. Many of the sectoral interest groups lobbied the government to water down the proposed reforms. According to John Gibbons, the relationship between agricultural interest groups and central government was not very harmonious up until 1988. This changed steadily in the 1990s. Interest groups such as the National Confederation of Arable and Livestock Farmers (*Confederación Nacional de Agricultores y Ganaderos* – CNAG), the National Confederation of Young Farmers (*Confederación Nacional de Jovenes Agricultores* – CNJA) and the more regionally bound Coordinating Body for Organisations of Agricultural and Livestock Farmers of the Spanish State (*Coordinadora de Organizaciones de Agricultores y Ganaderos del Estado Español* – COAG) are now better integrated into the consultation mechanisms of the government. Interest groups are always an important element of European policy making, so that central government had to modify their past patterns of behaviour towards the European pattern (Gibbons, 1999: 126–9).

Although Spain was only partly affected by the reforms due to the fact that most farms are small- or medium-sized, interest groups were quite virulent in pushing the government to protect their interests. The decline of farmers income has been also a major cause for demonstrations against the Spanish government (*El Pais*, 4 March 2002: 72; *El Pais*, 7 July 2002: 47) (see Figure 9.12).

In comparison to France, Germany and the United Kingdom, Spain is still far behind in terms of creating a more competitive agricultural sector. The structure of farming is still dominated by small- and medium-sized enterprises. In terms of final product, Spain with a larger population working in the agricultural sector produces only 12.4 per cent of all agricultural products in the European Union in comparison with France which produces 21.7 per cent with 5 per cent of people working in the agricultural sector. Nevertheless, it is among the largest producers along with France, Germany and Italy. Ninety-five per cent of all Spanish agricultural production is subsidised in terms of price support to farmers. Most of the subsidies go to olive oil and wine production sectors (Magone, 2003: 261).

Among the structural reforms, Spain is engaged in increasing the production of organic farming, which is clearly finding a market in a segment of the population

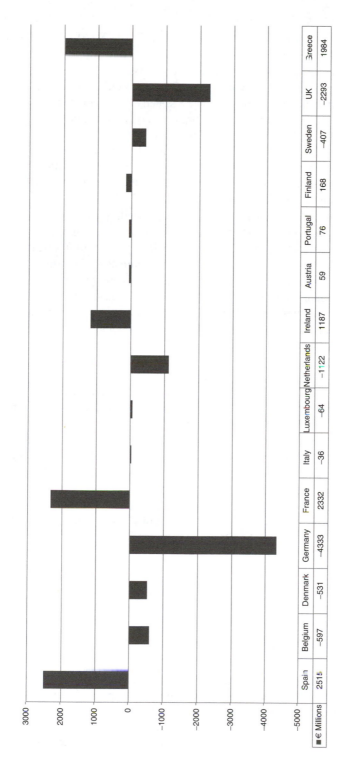

	Spain	Belgium	Denmark	Germany	France	Italy	Luxembourg	Netherlands	Ireland	Austria	Portugal	Finland	Sweden	UK	Greece
■ € Millions	2515	−597	−531	−4333	2332	−36	−64	−1122	1187	59	76	168	−407	−2293	1984

Figure 9.11 Net payers and receivers in CAP fund, 2000.

Source: *Die Zeit*, 18 July 2002: 19.

across the European Union, which is adopting a post-materialist lifestyle away from Máss production of food. According to data from the European Commission, Spain is not among the leaders of organic food production, although it is quite difficult to get exact data. Organic food production is quite widespread in Italy, Austria, Germany, Finland, Denmark and Sweden. These countries allocate the largest share of land in national terms to organic food production. Looking at this in a different way, in EU terms Spain comprises 7.4 per cent of all organic food enterprises of the EU, in comparison to Italy with 41.36 per cent and Austria with 18.93 per cent. It means that Spain has still a long way to go to exploit this more environmental friendly form of agricultural production (European Commission, 2000b: 22; European Commission, 2001e: 4–5.

In terms of rural development, Spain's policy style has changed considerably. It clearly is willing to decentralise the whole process of decision-making to the regional and even local levels. Quite important is that multiple measures are being applied to improve the quality of the environment in the rural areas. The re-forestation of sites devastated by forest fires which are quite common during the summer in Spain is one of these measures. There are also measures to ease the transition to retirement of older farmers, so that the number of people employed in the agricultural sector can be reduced. Agro-environmental projects are also financed by CAP. More relevant is the fact that funding is also provided for the modernisation of farms, which belong to young farmers. Regional programmes and the horizontal Community Initiative Leader+ contributed to a decentralisation of the whole process. Indeed, local action groups were established which act as a network to promote modernisation of the rural areas. Although the input of interest groups has been weak so far and everything was very much set up by central and regional governments, some slow change of attitude is taking place. In the end, it is the mobilisation of rural actors that will bring success to any of the long-term measures (European Commission, 2002d; Morata and Barua, 2001; 3–4; Morata, 2004:182–4).

In sum, CAP is a major restructuring device for the Spanish agricultural sector. The next period up until 2013 will certainly put pressure on Spanish farmers to further rationalise their large agricultural sector towards structures similar to Germany, France and the United Kingdom.

Common fisheries policy (CFP) and Spain

The CFP was created in 1983 to transform the European fisheries industry into a more efficient sustainable one. Since 1983, four multi-annual guidance programmes (MAGP) were implemented to achieve a reduction of the European fishing fleet and restructuring of the sector. In spite of a European monitoring system which improved over time, only modest progress was made. Similarly to agriculture, the European Commission represents the EU member-states in international fora such as the World Trade Organisation. The main policy of the European Union is to achieve a sustainable fisheries industry worldwide. One of the main problems of the fisheries industry is the depletion of certain

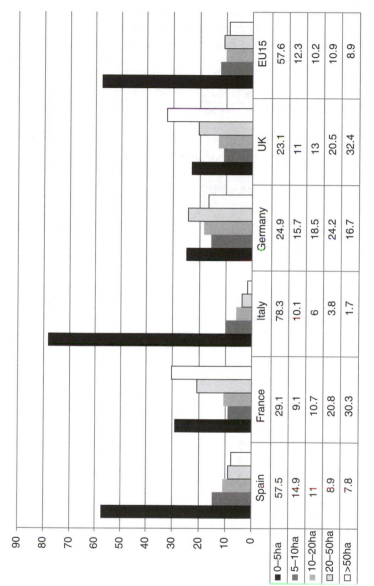

	Spain	France	Italy	Germany	UK	EU15
■ 0–5ha	57.5	29.1	78.3	24.9	23.1	57.6
■ 5–10ha	14.9	9.1	10.1	15.7	11	12.3
■ 10–20ha	11	10.7	6	18.5	13	10.2
☐ 20–50ha	8.9	20.8	3.8	24.2	20.5	10.9
☐ >50ha	7.8	30.3	1.7	16.7	32.4	8.9

Figure 9.12 Structure of farms, 2000.

Source: European Commission (2003), Agriculture website http://www.europa.eu.int/agriculture (accessed on 10 June 2003).

fish species such as cod, whiting and the Nordic hake. Total Admissible Catches (TAC) constrain the national fisheries sector of all countries. The role of the TACs is to prevent overfishing of certain species and allow for a certain sustainability of fishing grounds. In spite of a reform in 1993, the overall fishing sector was not able to improve substantially in terms of efficiency. Therefore, in 2001 former European Commissioner Franz Fischler, who was also responsible for Fisheries, prepared a consultation paper for the public in order to introduce a reform of the fisheries industry. The Green Paper on the Common Fisheries Policy clearly acknowledges the failure of the Common Fisheries Policy as it stands. The main aim was to scrap up to 8,500 vessels between 2003 and 2006. This is to be financed by the structural funds and by additional funding provided by the European Commission that amounts to €272 million (European Commission, 2001f; Magone, 2003: 264–5). Moreover, the new fisheries policy that came into force on 1 January 2003 shifted fisheries management from an annual decision-making system to a more long-term one.

Furthermore, more involvement of the stakeholders in decentralised Regional Advisory Councils (RACs) consisting of fishermen and scientists became part of the new fisheries policy. These RACs are assigned to find ways of keeping the fisheries policy at sustainable levels. Furthermore, the role of EU fisheries inspectors will be reinforced, so that the rules are better applied and a level playing field is created. Other measures such as openness of processes, a code of conduct for the fisheries industry, an action plan to improve stock evaluation in non-Community waters are also being prepared for a better fisheries policy (European Commission, 2001f).

This reform affects all countries with a large fishing industry, but in particular Spain, because it has the largest fishing fleet of the European Union. A general overview shows that Spain's coastline is still characterised by a complex fisheries industry which includes industrial transformation of fish, aquaculture and repairs and manufacturing of vessels. This makes it quite difficult to achieve any short-term reform (European Commission, 2000c: 18–31).[3]

Spain has the largest share of people working in the fisheries sector of the European Union. In 1997, the overall figure was 132,631 persons, which represented 25.2 per cent of all the persons working in the fisheries sector of the European Union. An estimated 50 per cent were fishermen, while the rest was distributed between aquaculture, the processing industry and other ancillary industries (European Commission, 2001g: 7–8). This declined to overall 91,000 in 2005, of whom 57 per cent were fishermen. In 2004, 38.5 per cent of fishermen were concentrated in Galicia with a high level of dependency ratio for the region, followed by Andalucia with 18.3 per cent, Catalonia with 9.8 per cent and the Valencian Community with 7.8 per cent. The rest of employment of 25.6 per cent is split between Asturias, Basque Country, Balearics, Murcia,Ceuta, Melilla and the Canary Islands (Salz *et al.*, 2006: 168) (Figure 9.13, Figure 9.14, Table 9.1, Table 9.15). The new common fisheries policy will allow for a more decentralised approach. The member-states will be in charge of managing their capacities within limits imposed by the European Commission.

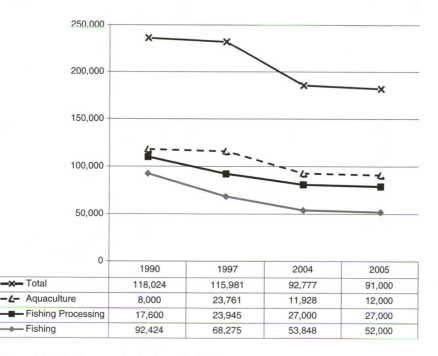

	1990	1997	2004	2005
━✕━ Total	118,024	115,981	92,777	91,000
━∠━ Aquaculture	8,000	23,761	11,928	12,000
━■━ Fishing Processing	17,600	23,945	27,000	27,000
━◆━ Fishing	92,424	68,275	53,848	52,000

Figure 9.13 Employment in the Spanish fisheries sector 1990–2005.
Source: Salz *et al.*, 2006: 168.

According to Rachel Jones, the fishing industry is quite well organised in defending its interests. In a case study related to the renewal fishing agreement of the European Union with Morocco in 1995 which allows for Spanish fishermen to fish in Moroccan waters, the fishing industry rallied around the government and used multiple strategies, including walkouts, demonstrations and violent actions to achieve their objectives. She referred to the case of Andalusia, where there was a working together between regional government and the representative interest groups at regional level (Jones, 2000: 159–76). Before and after the Green Paper was published, Spanish officials were very keen to influence the European Commission to make the proposals more lenient. This was supported by most Spanish interest groups during 2002.

Overall the EU accounts only for 5 per cent of the world's fisheries production. A more important region and under even more pressure in terms of its environmental damage to the fisheries stock is the Asian-Pacific rim. China is the most important fisheries producer of the world and this is felt across the region (*Le Monde*, 13 September 2006: 20–1). Nevertheless, Spain within the EU can gain from this transition and create a sustainable fisheries industry. It is an opportunity to transform an ailing industry into an environmentally friendly one. It will at least one decade to achieve a complete overhaul, however restructuring

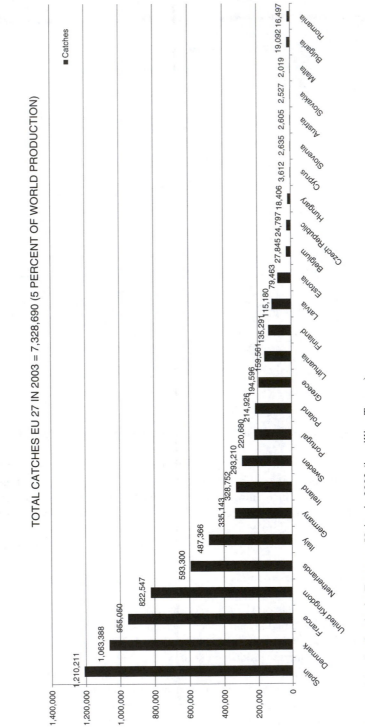

Figure 9.14 Catches in the European Union in 2003 (in million Tonnes).

Source: European Commission, 2006c: 1–2.

Table 9.1 Number of vessels, tonnage and engine power of fishing nations in the European Union in 2003

Country	Number of vessels	% Number of vessels	Tonnage (GT*)	% Tonnage	Engine power (kW)	%Engine power (kW)
Belgium	106	0.12	20 003	1.03	60 632	0.86
Bulgaria	1 261	1.43	5 806	0.30	33 052	0.47
Cyprus	868	0.99	4 992	0.26	38 852	0.55
Denmark	3 041	3.46	81 722	4.21	293 122	4.16
Germany	1 951	2.22	68 243	3.52	159 847	2.27
SPAIN	13 148	14.94	476 640	24.56	1 076 964	15.27
Estonia	991	1.13	20 568	1.06	52 369	0.74
France	7 636	8.68	209 402	10.79	1 060 531	15.04
Finland	3 169	3.60	16 220	0.84	168 800	2.39
United Kingdom	6 834	7.77	216 197	11.14	872 920	12.38
Greece	17 969	20.42	92 392	4.76	528 687	7.50
Ireland	1 865	2.12	71 152	3.67	203 953	2.89
Italy	13 999	15.91	200 065	10.31	1 171 977	16.62
Lithuania	260	0.30	60 080	3.10	68 929	0.98
Latvia	883	1	33 994	1.75	56 630	0.80
Malta	1 407	1.60	15 199	0.78	98 459	1.40
The Netherlands	832	0.95	163 167	8.41	392 128	5.56
Poland	892	1.01	31 688	1.63	100 850	1.43
Portugal	8 684	9.87	106 488	5.49	378 327	5.36
Romania	436	0.50	2 491	0.13	8 229	0.12
Slovenia	174	0.20	1 073	0.06	11 179	0.16
Sweden	1 574	1.79	43 146	2.22	215 992	3.06
TOTAL	87 980	100	1 940 728	100	7 052 429	100

Source: Website of DG agriculture and fisheries, European Commission, http://www.europa.eu accessed on 7 December 2007.

may create new opportunities in the regions that are particularly dependent on fishing.

Investment in the sector of aquiculture is probably the most viable form to reduce the dependency on fishing. This would have also to be accompanied by a change of lifestyles in order to increase the market of the fish species that can be cultivated. In 2003, Spain was still at bottom of EU15 fishing nations in terms of share of aquiculture in the overall fisheries production (see Figure 9.15).

In sum, Spain still has a long way to go to achieve a proper reform of the fisheries industry. Compared to Denmark, France and the United Kingdom their structure is still very inefficient. The modernisation of the fishing sector will become even more of a priority after enlargement, because some countries such as Poland, the Czech Republic and Hungary have strong aquaculture sectors, not to speak of the competition that the eventual membership of Turkey within the next decade may represent (European Commission, 2001g: 12; 2006: 2) (see Figure 9.15).

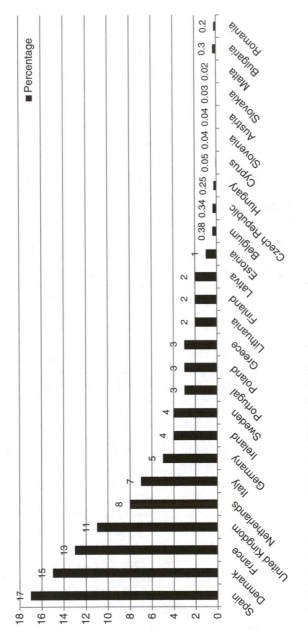

Figure 9.15 Catches in the European Union in 2003 (national share in percentage).

Source: European Commission, 2006: 1–2.

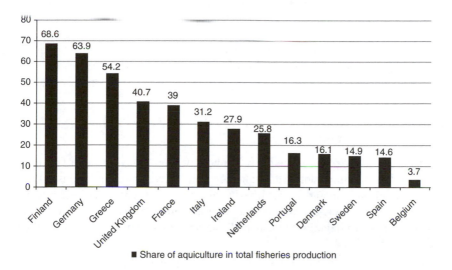

■ Share of aquiculture in total fisheries production

Figure 9.16 Aquaculture in the EU15 in 2003.

Source: European Commission, 2006c: 19. And Website of DG agriculture and fisheries, European Commission, http://www.europa.eu accessed on 7 December 2007.

Welfare state policies: education, health and social policy

One of the most important factors leading up to democratisation of Spanish society was the expansion of welfare policies throughout the 1980s and 1990s. A kind of very selective and particularistic welfare system had been established during the late phase of the Franco regime in the 1960s and early 1970s. Nevertheless, it never became as large and all-comprising as the welfare systems in most other west European countries. The policies of education, health and social policy became important policy areas for the Socialist governments between 1982 and 1996. The PP's governments continued these policies, although they emphasised the need for reform and sustainability. Although democratic Spanish governments made considerable efforts to increase public expenditure in order to match the welfare systems in western Europe, their capacities remained weaker than their west European counterparts. There is a general feeling that Spain belongs to a southern European welfare system model which is distinctive from the Scandinavian, Anglo-Saxon and the continental model of welfare. This was recognised in a report which served as a preparation for the Lisbon strategy established during the Portuguese presidency of the European Union in 2000. Compared with other models this southern European model is characterised by a low level of welfare benefits, the still important role of family networks and negative aspects related to clientelism, institutional inertia and a late development of the welfare state (Ferrera, Hemerijck and Rhodes, 2000: 54–60). Although education, health and social policy are still powers of the member-states and most EU social policy legislation is soft, meaning that it does not cost very much to implement, there is a growing dynamics towards integration of education, health and social policy across the European Union. This will naturally take decades, but there are signs of policy integration. This is leading to major pressures for reform in Spain, particularly in the education and social policy sector. This is not the place to make a thorough study of the three policy areas and it suffices to give a short overview of them in the next few pages.

Education policy: the policy reforms of the People's Party and the Socialist governments

The democratisation of the education sector became one of the priorities of the new political elites after transition. Although there were different interpretations as how this democratisation should happen, the overall trend was a considerable expansion of the education sector. During the authoritarian regime education was regarded very much as a privilege for the better-off classes, entry to higher education was selective and elitist.

Democratic transition and the constitutional settlement made education a priority of the new democratic regime in order to achieve more equality of opportunities. This became the most important objective of the Socialist government when it came to power in 1982. Within a decade, the annual amount freed to finance the expansion of the education sector had increased by almost 300 per cent in primary education and almost 500 per cent in secondary education by 1990 (Bonal, 1998: 165). The Socialist government also expanded the higher education sector. One of the most prestigious political scientists, José Maria Maravall, became associated as Minister of Education with the reforms which allowed for free access to universities for all Spaniards. At first, this opening up of the universities created problems to accommodate existing structures to this demand, but over two decades more universities were created in the larger cities and in the regional capitals thus easing the pressure of demand substantially. The policies of quantitative expansion were also accompanied by growing concern for the quality of education. This led to the creation of a National Institute for Quality and Evaluation (*Instituto Nacional de Calidad y Evaluación* – INCE). The Socialist government introduced scholarships for less well-off students, in order to sustain this access to higher education. The number of scholarship holders increased from 162,269 in 1982 to 927,586 in 1996. Between 1982 and 1996 the scholarship scheme had increased by more than 1,000 per cent, spending a total amount of €615.5 million (Bonal, 1998: 165). In the academic year 2006, the number of scholarship holders was 540,616 persons and in terms of funding a total of €855,900 million. According to Education minister Mercedes Cabrera this was increased to over one billion € in the 2007–08 session (*El Pais*, Anuario, 2007: 122).

The Spanish education system is dual. There is a very strong private sector, where the Catholic Church is strongly involved. The private sector is entitled to be subsidised by the state, in order to preserve freedom of choice for citizens. The Socialist reforms of the 1980s clearly strengthened the position of the state vis-à-vis the Catholic Church,[4] though different interpretations between right and left have clearly led to this compromise solution of dual education. Such a compromise solution was necessary to avoid a similar situation as during the Spanish Second Republic where education became a major ideological conflict area between left and right.

This ideological conflict came to the fore, when after 2000 the PP introduced a reform of the education system, which clearly undermined equality of opportunity at a very early age. Education minister Pilar del Castillo, who is also one of the most prestigious political scientists of the country, put through a reform of the education system in December 2001, which was opposed by all relevant interest groups in the sector as well as the opposition parties. Throughout November and December 2001, there were huge demonstrations of students and teachers protesting against the intended reform. In spite of suggested amendments and severe criticisms, Pilar del Castillo pushed through the Quality Law (*Ley de Calidad*). The Organic Law of Quality of Education (*Ley Organica de Calidad de Educación* – LOCE) abolished the unified secondary sector and introduced several routes including the vocational training route. It envisaged that weak students will be taken out of the academic stream and moved to the vocational training stream. This was suppose to happen as early as the age of 12 years. The policy would also target to weak students in the secondary sector. This system was criticised for being in some way discriminatory and undermining equality of opportunities (*El Pais*, 12 March 2002: 24, 27; *El Pais*, Anuario, 2003: 194). Similarly, a new structure of the university system was approved in December 2001, restructuring the whole system towards what had been decided in the declaration of Bologna, which envisaged a convergence of European university systems. It reduced the first degree courses (*licenciaturas*) from 5 to 4 years and exceptionally 3 years. Moreover, possession of a Master's degree was made compulsory before one could begin doctoral studies. The new law also wanted to strengthen the efficiency of Spanish universities in terms of research (*El Pais*, 4 June 2003: 30). The approval of both the general education system bill and the universities were revoked by the Socialist government under José Luis Zapatero when it came to power. It showed that the ideological struggle between left and right concerning the education sector has made a dangerous comeback which was haunting the political class. On 7 April 2006, the new Law of Education (*Ley Organica de Educación* – LOE) replaced the Quality Law introduced by the PP government. The new law increases the level of decentralisation of education by devolving it to the autonomous communities, however with some common curricular units which represent 55 per cent in the historical regions and 65 per cent in the others. The LOE included many of the provisions of the Quality Law of the former conservative government and also reinstated some aspects of the Law for the General Organisation of the Educational System (*Ley de Ordenación General del Sistema Educativo* – LOGSE) approved in 1990 under the previous Gonzalez Socialist government. One important difference to the Quality Law, is that students can, but do not have to take part in religion modules. There is also no alternative offered instead of the religion module; pupils can just go home if they like. This again was important for the Zapatero government, because they wanted to ensure this secular choice for the pupils. (Bernecker, 2006: 362–3). The PP voted against LOE whilst CiU, BNG and Cha abstained (*El Pais*, Anuario 2007: 122).

Between 2004 and 2006, the Zapatero government had to deal with a fierce opposition of several conservative organisations linked to the Catholic Church. The most fierce opposition came from the Catholic Church and the Catholic Confederation of Family Parents and Pupils' Parents (*Confederación Católica de Padres de Familia y Padres de Alumnos* – CONCAPA). On 12 November 2005, there was a major demonstration of CONCAPA in Madrid, in which according to the official figures of the police there were 407,000 persons, among them six archbishops and some prominent PP politicians (13 November 2005, pp. 20–1).

Another controversial measure of the PSOE was the introduction of a Citizenship Education module, in which the different family forms such as single parent and gay families are included in the curriculum. Moreover, it also intends to combat homophobic prejudices in order to contribute to a more tolerant society. All this led to a fierce opposition of the Catholic Church and linked organisations, which included even a call for a boycott of the new module which started in the school year 2007–2008 (*El Pais*, Anuario, 2007: 124).

Last but not least, despite the increase in spending over the past two decades reaching 5.6 per cent in 1998 and spending about €30.9 billion of public money (the percentage is related to both public and private sectors which increased the amount spent to €38.6 billion) (*El Pais*, Anuario, 2003: 195), Spain is spending well below the OECD average on education compared with other countries. This is the reason why the Zapatero government decided to increase investment in education by including in the law €7 billion in order to finance the reform. Moreover, the Zapatero government wanted to adjust public spending in education to the level of the OECD average (Bernecker, 2006: 363).

The Spanish population is lagging behind in relation to other advanced OECD democracies in terms of the level of qualifications. In particular, Spain has a major problem among the older population and the levels of attainment in the second phase of secondary education (see Figure 9.17.)

The secondary sector continues to be the major worry for policy makers in Spain. It has one of the highest drop-out rates in the European Union. Thirty per cent of all pupils dropped out in the academic year 2003–04. (*El Pais*, 14 September 2006: 47). Spain is part of the southern European group of underperforming countries, which includes Portugal and Italy. Moreover, there are fewer people with higher qualifications compared with the rest of the European Union. The OECD average of number of persons with upper-secondary education aged between 25 and 34 reached 77 per cent in 2005, while in Spain it was only 64 per cent. In Europe only Portugal (43 per cent) had lower education attainment rates. This becomes even more evident among the older generation. In the age group 50 to 64 years the percentage was 26 per cent well below the 54 per cent EU average. Only Portugal has a lower rate of 11 per cent.

This will be quite problematic, if Spain has ambitions to join the stronger economies of the OECD (European Commission, 2002a: 69, 2007a: 120–1;

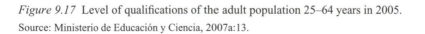

Figure 9.17 Level of qualifications of the adult population 25–64 years in 2005.
Source: Ministerio de Educación y Ciencia, 2007a:13.

Ministerio de Educación y Ciencia, 2007a: 14; see Figure 9.17 and Figure 9.18).
In spite of this negative aspect of the Spanish education system, one has to
acknowledge that within the past 25 years many efforts have been made to
reverse the disadvantages created by the Francoist authoritarian regime. The transfer of education responsibilities to the autonomous communities will be also an

important element in allowing for a very diverse education system. All this will depend how the funding will be allocated and organised. Spain is also torn between those who want a more centralised Spanish school curriculum and those who want to achieve more decentralisation. The Zapatero government is very keen to find a middle way in order to keep the autonomy process and independence wishes under control.

Like other more advanced European democracies, the Spanish education system has experienced a considerable growth of the foreign pupil population. In the school year 2006–2007, the share of foreign pupils was 8.4 per cent. In the public education sector this share rises to 10.4 per cent and in the private sector it is 4.6 per cent. (Ministerio de Educacion y Ciencia, 2007b: 8) The main problem for the Spanish education system is not so much the increasing numbers of foreign pupils, most of them children of inmigrants, but the concentration in certain autonomous communities such as Madrid, Valencian Community, Catalonia and the Basque Country, which are the main industrial centres of the country. In some schools 70 per cent are already foreign students, creating so the possibility of educational ghettos which may later on lead to similar problems as in France (*El Pais*, 14 September 2006: 49; Fundación Encuentro, 2006: 29). In 2004–2005 Almost 50 per cent of foreign students were from South America, particularly from Ecuador, Bolivia and Argentina. This is followed by African students coming mainly from Morocco. The third major group are Bulgarians and Romanians, nationals of two countries which today are members of the EU, but at that time were still outside. The number of students of the EU member-states was smaller than the three previously mentioned groups (*El Pais*, 14 September 2006: 49). All this shows that Spain is moving towards a multicultural society and that integration of the migrant community will become more relevant and central to the success of the country. Spain, like other west European country such as the United Kingdom, France, Germany and Italy, is struggling with this increase of the immigrant community and the pressure on public services to accommodate the new demand. So far, the approach of integration has been traditional, basically assimilationist, without trying new innovative ways which would include a more qualitative intercultural approach. The migrant community, continues to be therefore, disadvantaged in terms of being able to progress beyond the compulsory education system, reinforcing so the social divisions within society and the labour market (Fundación Encuentro, 2006: 33–7) (see Figure 9.19).

The university sector also became a focus point of reform. One of the reasons is that after the expansion of higher education in the 1980s and 1990s, the number of students decreased, so that some courses were not able to recruit. Apart from a review of courses, the university sector needs also to implement the Bologna process reforms, which envisages a better integration of the European education system. It means that the five-year licenciaturas and the three-year diplomaduras will be replaced by a four-year Bachelor degree (*grado*), which is followed by a professionally oriented master's degree and later on an academically oriented doctorate. Such implementation is already taking place, but it is uneven across

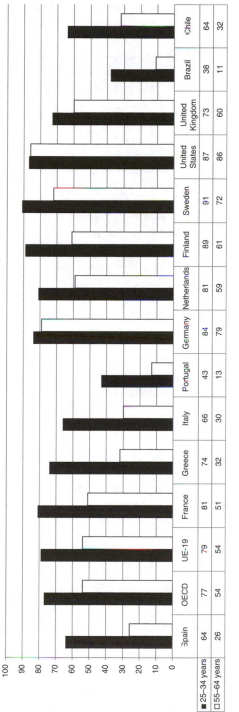

	Spain	OECD	UE-19	France	Greece	Italy	Portugal	Germany	Netherlands	Finland	Sweden	United States	United Kingdom	Brazil	Chile
25–34 years	64	77	79	81	74	66	43	84	81	89	91	87	73	38	64
55–64 years	26	54	54	51	32	30	13	79	59	61	72	86	60	11	32

Figure 9.18 Level of attainment of the second phase of secondary education for age groups 25–34 and 55–64 in 2005.

Source: Ministerio de Educacion y Ciencia, 2007a: 14.

the country as in other EU member-states. The controversial law of universities of the previous conservative government was replaced by a new one on 14 December 2006 in the Congress. The new Organic Law of Universities (*Ley Organica de Universidades* – LODE) enhances the autonomy of universities and creates the conditions for a better relationship between the academic world and the private sector. All this is part of the wider plan of increasing the level of investment in R&D+i (*El Pais*, Anuario, 2007: 123).

The universalisation of the health system

At the end of the authoritarian dictatorship a large part of the working population was paying contributions into the Spanish social security system. At the end of the transition period 84.5 per cent of the population was integrated in the social security system. This was an ideal condition to move towards a universal system of healthcare. Such a project was part of the Socialist government programme when they came to power in 1982. After several consultations with the relevant interest groups a General Law on Health (*Ley General de Sanidad* – LGS) was approved by parliament in 1986. It really created the conditions to move from a national system of health to a national health service. Such a transformation was slow and long term. The main reason is that economic conditions in the early 1980s were such that the budget could not be put under further strain. Nevertheless, at the end of the decade, taxation was used to finance the emerging national health service. Royal Decree 1088 of 1989 universalises national health cover for all the Spanish population (Guillén and Cabiedes, 1998: 177–80). This was accompanied by a growing decentralisation and transfer from Insalud, the main institute managing the emerging national health service, to the autonomous communities. Such a process was continued and completed under the Aznar government in the year 2002.

The last transfers were made to the regional governments of Asturias, Aragón, the Balearics, Cantabria, Castilla La Mancha, Castilla León, Extremadura, La Rioja, Madrid and Murcia. This meant that the Spanish national health system (*Servicio Nacional de Sanidad* – SNS) consists now of seventeen regional health services. There were many criticisms about the hasty transfer of powers without proper coordination. A framework law called the Law of Quality and Cohesion of the National Health System (*Ley de Calidad y Cohesión del Sistema Nacional de Salud*) was approved on 6 October 2002, one year after completion of the transfer of powers (Rico, Gonzalez and Fraile, 1998; *El Pais*, Anuario, 2003: 209–10). Among the problems of the Spanish national health system are the consequences of decentralisation. The richer autonomous communities such as the Basque Country and Navarre with their financial autonomony have higher spending per capita, than other regions such as Ceuta and Melilla. Moreover, the higher the social class and income the less the system is used, so that autonomous communities with a low structure of qualifications is quite under pressure in relation to the richer regions with a more qualified workforce. In the second conference of presidents on 10 September 2005, Prime Minister José Luis Zapatero announced that a further €1.677 billion were allocated to the regionalised health system. In spite of initial resistance of the autonomous communities led by PP politicians, in the end it was accepted by all parts. Such allocation was dependent on signing the agreement which in some cases was delayed (*El Pais*, 2 October 2007: 29).

The Spanish health service is quite modern in nature and has expanded considerably in the past two decades. The quality of service is also extremely good, particularly in new hospitals. There is a surplus of doctors and nurses who are finding work in the United Kingdom, Portugal and other countries. In spite of problems of coordination or asymmetrical differences between the autonomous communities (*El Pais*, Anuario, 2007:142), the Spanish health service can be regarded as a success story. According to an excellent study by Ana Rico and Joan Costa-Font, decentralisation has led to a coalition between regional governments, trade unions and citizens against cost-minded tendencies of the Central State which allowed to keep the high levels of funding across the country. Moreover, competition and cooperation between institutions are balanced by processes of interregional policy transfer processes and regionally tailored policy innovation processes. This means that in spite of the inequalities, the Spanish national health system has created mechanisms of keeping these at a low level (Costa-Font and Rico, 2005: 243–4; 249–50).

Social policy: still catching up with Europe

The social protection system in Spain is among the weakest in the European Union. It clearly fits into what has been called the southern model of welfare state. Spain is well below the EU average along with Greece, Portugal and Ireland (Ferrera, Hemerijk and Rhodes, 2000; and 9.20). This affects the level of pensions and other benefits that Spaniards may receive. Luxembourg spends 2.5 times more in social benefits than Spain does. Moreover, it seems that Spain has so far been spending at below or exactly the same rate as the EU-15, so that the gap may increase in relation to some countries. In Figure 9.21 the United Kingdom, Luxembourg, Italy and France spent more and increased their expenditure yearly more than Spain. Germany spent more, but due to the economic recession had to moderate its yearly increase remaining slightly below the EU-15 average and naturally Spain. It means that the southern European welfare state will remain a reality in Spain for the near future. The distribution of expenditure on welfare policies shows that Spain spends more than the EU-15 average on unemployment benefit and significantly less on housing and social protection (see Figure 9.22).

In 2002, there was an attempt by the PP government to further reform and reduce the number of people eligible for unemployment benefit. It wanted to impose the new reform, in spite of the fact that the social partners and a large part of the population were opposing it. The so-called little decree (*decretazo*) led to a general strike on 20 July 2002 (*El Pais*, Anuario, 2003: 411; see also Chapter 7). The government had to withdraw the measure and re-establish the social dialogue. Major pensions reform will be necessary for the ageing Spanish

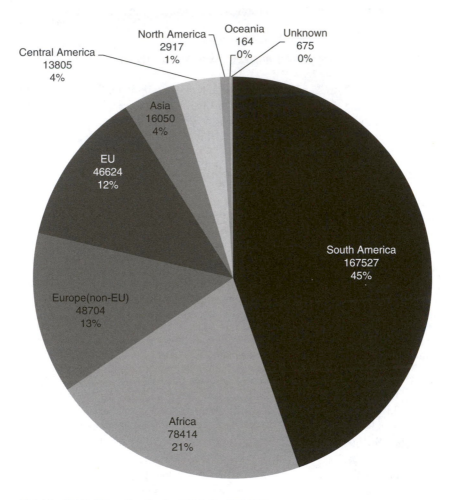

Total for Public Education Sector 2004–5 = 374,880

Figure 9.19 Foreign pupils in the public educational sector 2004–05.
Source: *El Pais*, 14 September 2006, p. 49.

population. Such reforms are taking place in several countries, including Germany and France.

The Zapatero government was very keen to improve the welfare system by introducing new laws. Among the most prominent ones, which fits in a general EU-wide strategy to increase the number of children across the European Union and so counteract the trend of the decrease of national populations, was the allocation of a one-off payment of €2,500 for each new born child announced and approved in 2007. Such measure was originally criticised by the opposition, however soon gained the support of all parliamentary parties. Negotiations at

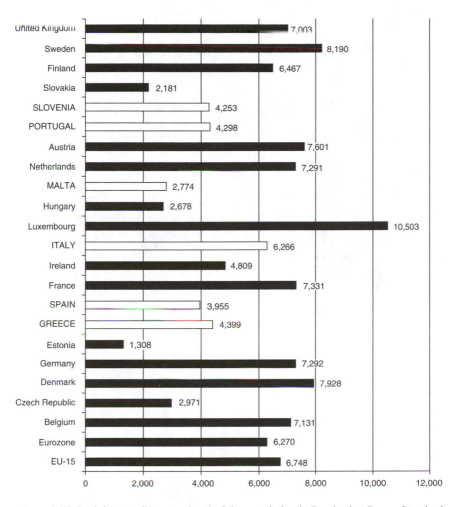

Figure 9.20 Social expenditure per head of the population in Purchasing Power Standard in Spain and selected countries of the European Union in the year 2002.

Source: European Commission, 2007a: 156.

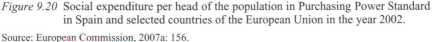

the end of legislature sought for a compromise about the date from which such payments should be undertaken (*El Pais*, 20 September 2007: 18). Moreover, in the housing sector further measures were approved through the plan of Minister Carmen Chacón which has to be regarded as complementary to the plan of the previous PP government developed by former minister, Maria Antonia Trujillo. The essence of both plans was to facilitate the access to rent accommodation for young people, socially excluded families, handicapped people and mono-parental families. The differences were mainly in terms of the age groups and the time span of support (*El Pais*, 20 September 2007: 19).

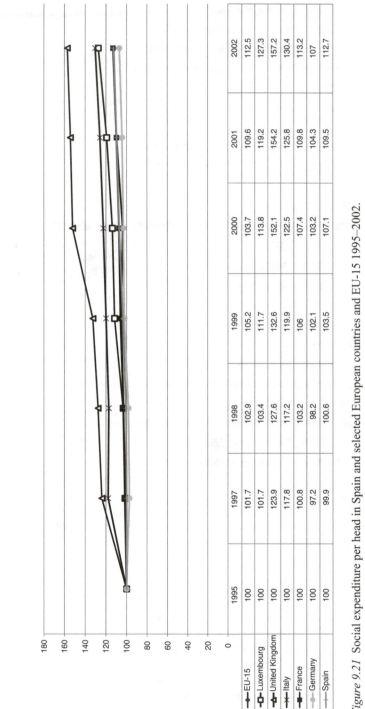

	1995	1997	1998	1999	2000	2001	2002
EU-15	100	101.7	102.9	105.2	103.7	109.6	112.5
Luxembourg	100	101.7	103.4	111.7	113.8	119.2	127.3
United Kingdom	100	123.9	127.6	132.6	152.1	154.2	157.2
Italy	100	117.8	117.2	119.9	122.5	125.8	130.4
France	100	100.8	103.2	106	107.4	109.8	113.2
Germany	100	97.2	98.2	102.1	103.2	104.3	107
Spain	100	99.9	100.6	103.5	107.1	109.5	112.7

Figure 9.21 Social expenditure per head in Spain and selected European countries and EU-15 1995–2002.

Source: European Commission, 2007a: 156.

Since 1996, both the PP and the PSOE governments have been successful in considerably reducing unemployment, which stands today at 8–9 per cent; quite a considerable decline in comparison to the early 1990s of between 18–22 per cent. However, unemployment is quite uneven distributed. In the more complex, urbanised and industrialised autonomous communities of the north-east (Catalonia, Aragón, Basque Country, Navarre, Madrid) unemployment is below this average, while the highest levels of unemployment can be found in the predominantly agricultural regions of Andalusia and Extremadura. According to an excellent study by Simon Pedro Izcara Palacios, these two autonomous communities have large agricultural sectors, but work is normally seasonal, so that local land labourers are unemployed for large parts of the year. If they work a minimum of days per year, they are entitled to unemployment benefit which is 75 per cent of the minimum wage. However, in the past decade there is growing number of migrant workers coming from Morocco, Bulgaria and Romania who are able to work for less money than the local land labourers. This naturally leads to competition and even less possibilities to work for such local land labourers. The consequence is an increase in social exclusion and a perpetuation of the high levels of unemployment (Palacios, 2007: 178–9) (see Figure 9.22).

In spite of advancements in the social protection of the Spanish population, in 2004, 20 per cent of Spaniards were at risk from poverty compared to 16 per cent of the EU25. Moreover, this figure rose to 29 per cent for older people aged more than 65 years compared to the EU average of 19 per cent. The Socialist government adopted a plan to raise pensions by 26 per cent between 2004 and 2008, in order to reduce the gap to other western European democracies. Moreover, measures to tackle dependency problems such as enshrined in the Law on the Promotion of Personal Autonomy and Care for People in a Situation of Dependency (2007–2015) are design to deal with the growing ageing population. Spain is assessed as being a medium-risk country in terms of financial sustainability due to the growing high of an ageing population. Spain has still a very high level of income inequality. In 2004, the income difference between the highest 20 per cent and lowest 20 per cent was 5.4 times (European Commission 2007b: 238–46).

In sum, the Spanish welfare system continues to be one of the weakest in the European Union. The necessary reforms within Economic and Monetary Union will not allow for an improvement in this area. Somehow the Spanish welfare system development was caught between a late start at the outset and the change of the state rationale across the European Union and the OECD countries in the 1980s and 1990s, which emphasised macroeconomic stability, flexibility of labour markets and limited government as the way to more competitive economies.

The European Union and environmental policy

Spain was, and is, still lagging behind in terms of implementation of environmental policy. Although some kind of environmental policy existed during later Francoism, it was uncoordinated and sporadic. The European integration process, particularly since the Single European Act, put Spain under pressure to comply

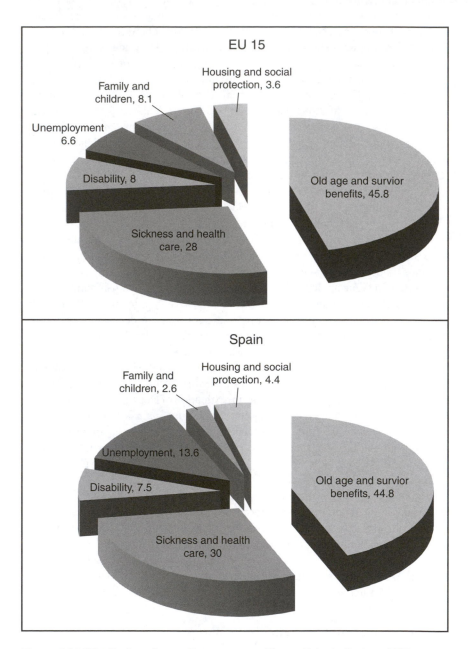

Figure 9.22 Distribution of expenditure among welfare policies in Spain and EU.
Source: European Commission, 2007a: 156.

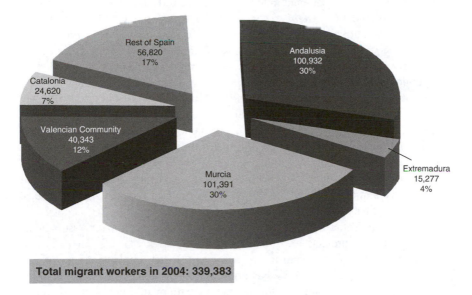

Total migrant workers in 2004: 339,383

Figure 9.23 Distribution of migrant workers among the autonomous communities in 2004.

Source: Own graph based on figures from Ministerio de Trabajo y Asuntos Sociales (MTAS), Anuario de Estatisticas laborales and asuntos sociales quoted from: Izcarate Palacios, 2007: 179.

with the directives of the European Union, not only legally, but also in real terms. With support of the European Union, environmental policy slowly became an important element in developing new projects. In some sense, Spain had to abandon the exponential growth model, which caused so much damage to the environment, and introduce a more balanced sustainable growth model. This is naturally still asymmetrically implemented, but several factors are strengthening the environmental agenda in Spain. First, there was a strong improvement in terms of coordination of policy making between the different levels, European, national and regional. The sectoral conference on the environment established in 1987 brought together on a regular basis regional and central government representatives to discuss and coordinate environmental policy measures. Second, this was reinforced by regular coordinating meetings in the Secretariat for Foreign Policy and the European Union between the European Commission, the central government and the autonomous communities in 1995, in order to solve any problems related to infringements of environmental directives. Third, in 1998, again by initiative of the European Commission, a network of environmental authorities was created to coordinate both regional and environmental policies. This dense establishment of networks is integrating Spain into an overall European policy style and creating the effect of an ecological modernisation (Font, 2001: 393–7). Fourth, in 1996, a Ministry of Environment (*Ministerio de Medio Ambiente* – MMA) was created by the PP government, in order to strengthen the position of the environment in the policy process. Fifth, an Advisory Council on the Environment (*Consejo Asesor de Medio Ambiente* – CAMA) comprising several representatives of interest groups, of the central government and regional governments was established. It has been so far an important forum for discussion, but clearly without major influence. The policy process tends to be controlled by the public administrations (Aguilar, 1998: 266–8; Font, 2001: 398).

In spite of the fact that Spain is still far behind all countries in terms of waste management, air pollution and disposal of toxic waste, overall the picture has improved considerably, leading to the assessment by Tanja Börzel that actually Spain is no longer among the laggards of environmental policy directives both in legal and real terms (Börzel, 2000b). Nevertheless there are still many problems related to the real implementation. Although there was an increase in environmental policy powers at regional and local levels over the past two and a half decades, there are still many problems of coordination.

According to Tanja Börzel, many of the Environmental Impact Assessments (EIAs) related to projects are done insufficiently or not at all. There is still a lack of monitoring mechanisms to achieve a better implementation of EU directives (Börzel, 2002:180–8). Nevertheless, in the second half of the 1990s one can recognise a change in the behaviour pattern in environmental policy in Spain. Indeed, the increased number of EU directives, which are expensive to implement, led to a different relationship between central and the regional governments from a bilateral competitive pattern to a multilateral cooperative one. The sectorial conference of environment, which was very inactive up until 1994, regained a central role in coordinating multilateral long-term efforts such as Joint Plans and Programmes (for example, the implementation of the Urban Waste Treatment directive). Börzel comes to the conclusion that actually the Europeanisation process is transforming the Spanish policy process from one of competitive to one of cooperative federalism. The process seems to be slow and steady, but is contributing to an overall change of mentalities in Spain (Börzel, 2002: 192–208).

Apart from the growing integration of environmental policy at global level, the multilevel governance system of the European Union is playing a major role in raising environmental awareness. In December 2007, there were 389 environmental associations registered with the Ministry of Environment showing that Spanish civil society is becoming more important in shaping national and naturally European Union policy. According to an excellent study by Manuel Jimenez, the Spanish environmental associations began to emerge in the 1970s during and after democratic transition at local level. This bottom-up emergence of the Spanish environmental movement is still one the major characteristics. The network like structures of many of the environmental movements shows this local roots origins. Another more interesting feature, is that these movements were able to transform themselves into efficient actors due to their horizontal cooperation, but also by framing their local issues into a global frame. This 'glocalism' is one of the main characteristics of today's postmodern flexible so-called movements. One indicator of the strengthening of the environmental movement is for example the increase of membership of Greenpeace from 16,000 members in 1984 to 85,000 members in 2004 (Jimenez, 2007: 364).

The main environmental problem for Spain are the consequences of unplanned growth of tourism around the coast of Spain. The case of Marbella also shows that the construction of new housing and tourist sites has been partly achieved through networks of political corruption. Municipal corruption around the Spanish coasts is widespread and was exposed throughout the past 4 years. Particularly, Andalusia in the provinces of Malaga, Sevilla, Granada and Cadiz there are lots of illegal urban complexes which are used for money laundry for the narcotraffic (*El Pais*, 24 September 2007:18) This may be an opportunity to change the rules of the game and become more environmentally conscious about building tourism sites. Probably, the greatest pressure in this regard can be found in the Balearics and in the Canary Islands. The latter archipelago is under considerable environmental pressure in the main islands of Gran Canary and Santa Cruz de Teneriffe. One of the main problems is the scarcity of water resources to sustain such a continuing urbanisation of the islands. There are plans to demolish some of the tourist sites in order to increase the level of sustainability.

According to the figures of the European Environment Agency, Spain is the country which is farthest away from complying with the target of reduction of emissions of CO_2 by 2012 as agreed in the Kyoto protocol. The European Union as whole is on target to achieve the agreed 8 per cent reduction of CO_2 emissions by 2012. One of the reasons is that the Spanish economy has been growing much more than other national European economies. Therefore, the Zapatero government had to introduce urgent measures to at least reduce the deficit. Overall, the Spanish government is part of the overall effort of the European Union to reduce the CO_2 emissions by 20 per cent in 2020. The consequences of global climate change for Spain are not very positive. Spain will lose land to the sea due to the increase of the water levels by 15 centimetres by 2050. Moreover, Spain will become more like Africa, because large part of the territory will become a desert. Already today one third of the Spanish territory is in risk of desertification. The consequences are the erosion and salinisation of the land. Moreover, the increase in temperature will increase the number of diseases which are produced by the atmospheric contamination. This will affect particularly the quality of the air. The desertification and increase in temperature will also lead to scarcity of water resources. Last but not least, the biodiversity in Spain will also decrease substantially, because many species will not be able to survive the new climatic conditions. It means that Spain is at the forefront of the consequences of climatic changes and called to take drastic actions in order at least to delay such a process (*El Pais*, 28 November 2007: 34–6).

In spite of major improvements in the past three decades, Spain has still a lot to do to achieve a sustainable environment. According to the OECD Environmental Report of 2004, Spain continues to have major problems in dealing with several air pollution aspects and ensure that the water quality of certain rivers is of high standards. Moreover, the fisheries industry puts an enormous strain on the sustainability of the fishing stocks. Moreover, the report highlights the problems related to the tourism industry along the coastal areas and islands, where 60 per cent of the population lives. During the summer over 77 per cent of people may be living in the coastal areas. According to the report, environmental policy is too dependent on state funding and applies inconsistently the 'polluter pays' principle. Also the use of fiscal means such as the ecotax or rubbish collection taxes have been used sparingly. The coordination between the central and the autonomous communities' governments has improved, but is still in the early stages. The network of environmental authorities is regarded as a positive development in this respect. Last but not least, the involvement and consultation of environmental associations and the public in public policy making has been so far not used widely (OECD, 2004: 17–32).

Spain belongs to a southern European pattern which includes Portugal, Spain, Greece and Italy, possibly many other countries on the northern Mediterranean. The late development of environmental policies shows that Spain is a laggard in many policies, however it was able to improve over time and achieve a better record over time than, for example, Greece or Italy. There is also a growing post-materialist public which takes quality of life and the new global environment issues more seriously. In this sense, Spain has made progress, but has still a long way to go (Pridham and Magone, 2006).

Conclusions

After decades of authoritarianism, the Spanish policy style had to become more democratic. A democratic policy style which allows for openness and accountability of decision-making cannot be created overnight as the Spanish example clearly shows. It is a long process that may take decades.

In some policy areas, this transformation of policy style may achieve democratic standards sooner, but later in others. This asymmetrical expansion of new patterns of behaviour is facilitated by the fact that the central Spanish state is engaged in a major programme of decentralisation.

This affected particularly crucial areas of the welfare system such as health and education, but it is also contributing to better policy implementation in environmental, regional, agricultural and fisheries policy. The role of the European Union in overcoming the cycle of patrimonial policy making cannot be emphasised enough. Indeed, Europeanisation since the early 1990s has been crucial to improving the quality of environmental policy and regional policy. The European public policy process introduced modernising elements into the Spanish policy process. This clearly fits into the overall understanding of the Spanish population about integration into the European Union, which is equalled with the modernisation of the Spanish political system and public policy process.

10 Spanish foreign and defence policy within the European Union

The imperative of the European Union for Spanish foreign policy

In spite of all the opening moves on the part of the Franco regime, Spanish foreign policy was not very influential. It was very dependent on the bipolar Cold War division between the Western powers and the Soviet Bloc. Franco presented himself as the prototype of an anti-communist ally, making it possible for Spain to be part of the Western alliance, despite being a dictatorship. The nature of the regime was the major obstacle to a sustainable open foreign policy (Fossati, 2000). The death of the dictator in 1975 allowed for a rethinking of Spanish foreign policy. Between 1975 and 1979, Spanish foreign policy remained undefined because the domestic agenda was more important than the international stage. There were only two issues that were of prominent importance in Spanish foreign policy. First, there was the unanimous consensus of the political elite who wanted to achieve accession to the European Community at the earliest possible point in time which led to the application for EU membership in July 1977 by Prime Minister Adolfo Suarez, who was still engaged in the constitutional settlement process. Second, a more controversial issue was to join the North Atlantic Treaty Organisation (NATO) with which Spain had cooperated during the Francoist regime. The authoritarian government had a defence agreement in place, which was up for renewal by the Francoist dictatorship shortly before it collapsed. The new treaty signed in January 1976 lasted for 5 years and was up for renewal in 1981.

Pressure from the United States upon Calvo Sotelo's government led to the renewal of the defence agreement and simultaneous accession to NATO. This was reinforced by pressures from other countries of the European Community which belonged to NATO and saw European Community membership intrinsically linked to membership of NATO. After discussions in parliament, Prime Minister Calvo Sotelo was able to obtain a majority in favour of accession to NATO. The protocol of accession was signed on 10 December 1981 (Rodrigo, 1995: 54–8). Calvo Sotelo's approach was regarded by the opposition as quite negative, due to the fact that it broke with the culture of consensualism established during transition. When the PSOE came to power in 1982, a referendum on NATO membership became an important item in the Party manifesto. Prime Minister Felipe Gonzalez was known to be against membership, but shortly before the referendum, he made a case in support of NATO membership.

The referendum took place in 1986 and led to an overwhelming victory for the supporters of NATO; 52.2 per cent of the voters supported membership, while 39.8 per cent were against (Rodrigo, 1995: 63). It meant also that a re-negotiated defence agreement in 1988 led to the withdrawal of American troops and a change in the relationship between the United States and Spain. It moved from a bilateral asymmetrical relationship to a multilateral one inside NATO (Cotarelo, 2002: 375). Moreover, Spain joined the European arm of NATO, the west European Union (WEU), in 1988. The WEU was a mere nominal organisation which was fully integrated into the European Union after the negative passive role played during the Kosovo war of 1999. Gonzalez clearly began to develop a coherent Spanish foreign policy based on EU membership and in which the Atlantic alliance continued to be crucial, although always balanced towards Spanish interests.

Between 1982 and 1995, Felipe Gonzalez laid the foundations for a very active ambitious Spanish foreign policy, in spite of the meagre resources at its disposal. Its main priority was to play a central role in the European integration process, because this was in Spanish interests. The second priority was related to the countries of the Maghreb, in particular Morocco.

There was a need to improve the relationship with these countries so that security in the Mediterranean could be enhanced, and ultimately new potential markets opened up for the Spanish economy. A third priority was to play a leading role in Southern and Central America. A more coherent Latin American policy began to be developed in the late 1980s leading up to the Ibero-American summits of the 1990s. Gonzalez's energetic commitment to global issues made him an important actor in international relations enhancing considerably the position of Spain in the world. According to Fabio Fossatti, the foreign policy of the authoritarian regime was low profile and of small power until 1975. This meant that it had very scarce capabilities to mobilise multilateral intermediation processes. It is the integration into the European Union that has helped Spain to move to a medium-sized power position, in particular the policies of the Socialist governments under Felipe Gonzalez (Fossatti, 2000: 4–5).

As already-mentioned, Spain was fully committed to all the projects that would lead to a stronger Common Foreign and Security Policy (CFSP) established in the Treaty of Maastricht and replacing the former European Political Cooperation (EPC) agreement. In November 1996, the Spanish parliament eventually decided to join, 10 years after the referendum, the military structure of NATO (Kennedy, 2000: 110). In 1995, Javier Solana became Secretary-General of NATO, playing a major role in the whole process leading up to the Kosovo war. After the ratification of the Amsterdam Treaty in 1999, he combined the positions of High Representative of Common Foreign and Security Policy, a position he shared with the Commissioner for External Relations Chris Patten, and Secretary General of the Council of Ministers. The policies of the Socialist government were continued by Prime Minister Aznar. In spite of the continuity of Spanish European policy, Aznar was very interested in strengthening the special relationship with the United States.

During the first Gulf War in 1991, Felipe Gonzalez's government supported the coalition forces (Kennedy, 2000: 117–18). It showed that the American dominance of NATO conditioned completely the foreign policy of Spain. Aznar just reinforced this Atlanticist dimension of Spanish foreign policy. In the European field, Aznar found allies in the British Prime Minister Tony Blair from 1997 onwards and the Italian Prime Minister Silvio Berlusconi from 2001 onwards. They represented a group of countries along with Portugal after the election of a centre-right government under Manuel Durão Barroso in 2002 that had a strong Atlanticist orientation. This special relationship with the United States strengthened by Aznar could go against the European project in certain circumstances. The best example was the privatisation of the public defence firm Santa Barbara, which was well integrated with a German consortium Krauss Maffei und Reihnmetall. It was building a Leopard tank for the Spanish forces. In April 2000, there was interest from the German consortium to buy the enterprise, but Aznar decided to sell it to General Dynamics, an American consortium. The German consortium protested vehemently, because they were the main contract suppliers to Santa Barbara. Moreover, it clearly contradicted the policy of the government to take part in the establishment of a European armaments industry (*El Pais*, Anuario, 2003: 170).

Despite this aspect, Spain has been involved in several projects towards a European armaments industry. One example is the participation of Spain in the Eurofighter project along with the United Kingdom and Italy as well as the European aircraft which is designed to compete with the American C-130J and C-17. The latter project allowed Spain to become part of the Joint Cooperation Organisation in the Field of Armament (OCCAR) along with the United Kingdom, France, Italy and Sweden. Moreover, in June 2003 Spain decided to buy European helicopters from Eurocopter and thus support the European armaments industry.

Table 10.1 The European Rapid Reaction Force

Country	Number of troops
Germany	13,500
United Kingdom	12,500
France	12,000
Italy	6,000
Spain	6,000
Netherlands	5,000
Greece	3,500
Austria	2,000
Finland	2,000
Sweden	1,500
Belgium	1,000
Ireland	1,000
Portugal	1,000
Luxembourg	100
Denmark	Committed to Nordic troops
Central and eastern European countries	32,500

Twenty-four Tiger helicopters were bought for the Spanish army with a value of €1.3 billion. Eurocopter, which is part of the European armaments consortium, EADS, was able to win the contract against the American Apache helicopter from Boeing (*El Pais*, 16 June 2003: 29). Indeed, in 2000 one-third of all Spanish research and development expenditure was undertaken in the defence sector, amounting to €1.3 billion. In comparison, the United States spent 54.1 per cent of all R&D and €46.2 billion and the United Kingdom 32.8 per cent and €3.3 billion. In contrast, Germany spent only 8 per cent of R&D equivalent to €1.3 billion and France 22.6 per cent and €2.96 billion. After 11 September 2001, the government restricted arms sales licences to several countries (*El Pais*, 18 March 2003: 36; *El Pais*, Domingo, 29 June 2003: 8–9).

The CFSP is still very much in the making. There is the big ambition to move towards a Common European Defence and Security Policy (CEDSP), but this is hindered by national reservations related to the loss over their own defence policies. The so-called European Security and Defence Identity (ESDI) still has a long way to go before fulfilment. The commitment to such a long-term project has been made by most countries including Spain, but in substance national interest still prevails. Since early 2000, there are structures in the Council of Ministers such as the military-political committee and a military planning committee which want to make further developments towards a CEDSP. Central to this is the creation of a European intervention force of 60,000 to 100,000 which can be deployed within 60 days for up to 1 year what have been defined as Petersberg Tasks, such as peacekeeping missions, catastrophe rescue operations and humanitarian interventions. It has been operative since 2003 (Barbé, 2000b; *El Pais*, Anuario, 2003: 170) (see Table 10.1). At present, Spain is part of the second phase of this increase in capabilities of the European Union, called Headline Goal 2010, which aims at improving the interoperability between the different battlegroups. Spain does not only contribute with a national battlegroup, but is also integrated in a southern European one with Portugal, Spain, Italy and Greece. In 2006, there were thirteen battlegroups in which twenty member-states are taking place. The European Capabilities Action Plan (ECAP) plans to have eighteen battlegroups ready for action in 2010. By 2007, it was planned that European Union should have the capability of two battlegroup based rapid reaction forces which were ready for action for two different missions (Permanent Representation of France to the European Union, 2006: 38). (see Table 10.2.) Overall, Spain has been an important supporter of the newly formulated European Security Strategy.

This is accompanied by a similar programme to strengthen civilian capabilities, in which Spain is also an important contributor.

Spanish involvement and withdrawal from the Iraq War (2003–2004): torn between Atlanticist and Europeanist loyalties

There was a major rift among the European countries before the second Gulf War in March–April 2003. The United States wanted the allies to support a war against Iraq

Table 10.2 ESDP battlegroups in 2006

Kind of battlegroup	Member-states involved
National	
	• France
	• Italy
	• *Spain*
	• United Kingdom
Transnational	
	• France, Germany, Belgium, Luxembourg and potentially Spain
	• France and Belgium
	• Germany, the Netherlands and Finland
	• Germany, Austria and Czech Republic
	• Italy, Hungary and Slovenia
	• *Italy, Spain, Greece and Portugal*
	• Poland, Germany, Slovakia, Latvia and Lithuania
	• Sweden, Finland and including Norway as a third State
	• United Kingdom and the Netherlands
Niche bataillons	
	• Cyprus (Medical group)
	• Lithuania (water purification unit)
	• Greece (the Athens Sealift Co-ordination Centre)
	• France (structure of a multinational and deployable Force Headquarters

Source: Military Capability Commitment Conference, 2004.

for allegedly not complying with the UN Resolutions in getting rid of their weapons of mass destruction. French President Jacques Chirac and German Chancellor Gerhard Schröder were vehemently opposed against the war and wanted the UN inspectors to finish their job before any decision would be taken by the Security Council to use military means to disarm Iraq. The Iraqi leadership assured that they had disposed of all weapons of mass destruction, in particular biological and chemical arsenals. Prime Minister José Maria Aznar along with Prime Minister Blair and six other European countries, supported the American position, in spite of the fact that most European populations were against the war.

In Spain, 90 per cent of the population was against the war and this was expressed in several demonstrations across the country. Banners with ¡No a la guerra! (No to war!) could be seen everywhere, particularly in many windows of Gran Via, one of the main streets of Madrid. The opposition under the leadership of Socialist secretary general José Luis Zapatero and the United Left coordinator Gaspar Llamazares joined the population in protesting against the war in Iraq. During this period Spain was a member of the Security Council and seconded the initiatives led by the United States and the United Kingdom, although the overwhelming majority of the population was against it. In the last days of the war, the Spanish public was outraged about the killing of two Spanish journalists José Couso from Antena 5 and Julio Anguita Parrado from *El Mundo* by American forces. Julio Anguita Parrado was the son of former IU coordinator Julio Anguita.

This further exacerbated the anti-war climate in Spain. Throughout the conflict PP lost members of government (*El Pais*, 12 March 2003: 2–3; *El Pais*, 30 March 2003: 28, 30; *El Pais*, 9 April 2003: 21). The American military was not forthcoming with a plausible explanation of the killing of the journalists. Still in 2007, friends of José Couso and Julio Anguita Parrado were demanding an independent inquiry by the American authorities on the deaths of the two journalists.

The Aznar–Blair alliance was not only restricted to their common Atlanticist position, but also related to other areas such as economic issues. In many ways, both leaders found common ground in the 'Third Way' of reform that they both were trying to achieve for their respective countries, in spite of being representatives of different party traditions. Such a position led to continuing rifts between the Franco-German alliance and the British-Spanish-Italian position. At the end of April, four countries, France, Germany, Belgium and Luxembourg, decided to establish a closer Defence Union and invite other countries to join. It was naturally opposed by Washington and London, in spite of the fact that the four countries explicitly denied allegations that this was to undermine NATO. They emphasised that the new defence alliance was designed to complement the NATO structure and push forward the European integration process in the defence sector (*Die Zeit*, 24 April 2003: 9; *El Pais*, 26 March 2003: 18; *El Pais*, 29 April 2003: 5; *El Pais*, 30 April 2003: 6). This fits in with the provisions in the Treaty of Nice and the new European constitution arising from the European Convention, where a small number of countries could advance faster than others in certain policy areas. This so-called reinforced cooperation allowed for this inner circle of countries to develop more integrated structures in the field of defence. Indeed, the Iraq crisis has strengthened the union between France and Germany, which clearly led to conflict with the more Atlanticist countries such as Spain, Italy and the United Kingdom (*El Pais*, Domingo, 15 June 2003: 2, 6–7).

In spite of achieving a good result in the local and autonomous community elections of 25 May 2003, similar to what was happening in Washington and in London, the opposition demanded a full enquiry into the reasons for going to war in Iraq, due to the lack of evidence on weapons of mass destruction.

In particular, IU coordinator Gaspar Llamazares made the point that Prime Minister Aznar did not analyse any information coming from the United Kingdom or the United States. He just took it for granted, including the alleged plagiarised dodgy dossier, which contained unsourced 10-year-old information on Iraq compiled by the British government (*El Pais*, 9 June 2003: 19). A survey conducted by the Real Elcano Instituto showed that Spaniards perceive the country to have more power after the Iraq war, but still lagged behind the United States, the United Kingdom, China, France, Russia and Italy. Seventy-seven per cent were against preventive strikes as practised in Iraq. Eighty-two per cent considered it illegal to remove a dictatorship by external force and replace it with a democracy. Sixty-two per cent found that the image of Spain had deteriorated, while only 16 per cent thought that it had improved. Nevertheless, 70 per cent regarded as positive the fact that Spain would have an active role in reconstructing the country, while only 21 per cent found it negative (*El Pais*, Domingo, 15 June 2003: 8).

One of the first actions of the newly elected Socialist government under José Luis Zapatero on 14 March 2004 was to withdraw the very small number of Spanish troops from Iraq, in spite of representations by president George W. Bush and British Prime Minister Tony Blair. The withdrawal was even more sudden than expected. The withdrawal was expected for 30 June 2004, but first troops were already withdrawn at the end of March 2004. Overall, about 2,000 soldiers were deployed to Iraq and the Defence Ministry spent about €350 million. Already in May 2004 the first troops began to return to Spain. In this sense, Zapatero kept his promise given before the elections. He was supported by the overwhelming majority of the population, which had been constant in its general attitude towards the war (*El Pais*, 19 April 2004: 16; *El Pais* 20 March 2004: 26–7; *El Pais*, 19 March 2004: 25). Shortly afterwards, Zapatero realigned Spanish foreign policy towards the Franco-German alliance, represented then by president Jacques Chirac and German chancellor Gerhard Schröder. Spanish foreign policy became more constructive in relation to the European integration process. While former Prime Minister José Maria Aznar vetoed the revised voting system of the Constitutional Treaty, Prime Minister José Luis Zapatero was pragmatic and willing to negotiate a solution. Zapatero followed very much the approach taken by the Gonzalez governments, which saw Spain as an influential player at the centre of the European Union. He was also successful in achieving a ratification of the Constitutional Treaty after a national referendum in Spain in February 2005. Moreover, he also tried to contribute to the 'yes' campaign in France in order to achieve a positive result.

Zapatero was also very important in the negotiations of the financial perspectives of the European Union 2007–13 negotiated under the auspices of the British presidency in mid-December 2005, when Spain had to accept a substantial cut of structural funds, because Spain was slowly becoming a rich country close to the EU average. It is expected that Spain will be a net payer to the EU budget by 2013. Last, but not least, Zapatero has been a supporter of Angela Merkel's bid to revive the Constitutional Treaty, even under the new name of Lisbon Treaty. Spain was one of the most loyal supporters of the process towards the Lisbon Treaty (for more detail see Chapter 8). Zapatero represents a complete shift from the pro-American policies of José Maria Aznar. In someway, the policies are regarded as part of the quest of the Zapatero government to return to Europe, after the highly conflictive period during the premiership of José Maria Aznar. However, Zapatero had to pay a price for this shift of policy. President George W. Bush refused to restore cordial relations with the new government. In spite of the attempts of Foreign Minister Miguel Moratinos and Prince Felipe since 2004, President Bush did not allow an official meeting between the two leaders to take place. The withdrawal of troops from Iraq led to an alienation between the government of the United States and Spain. In spite of this, the diplomatic and other channels continue to be open and work smoothly, only the official cordial relations between the two leaders is still forthcoming.

In sum, the European integration process continues to be a priority for the Spanish government, but they have a very realistic notion of the superpower status of the United States. In a transitional process towards the creation of a CEDSP, Spain is caught between the two. On the one hand, it clearly is very pro-European, but worried about the growing union between France and Germany. This led to counter-alliances with Italy and the United Kingdom during the Aznar governments. On the other hand, Aznar wanted to have a strong position in Washington, and therefore continued to nurture the special relationship with the United States, which for the latter is one among many, in order to keep a hegemonic position in the world. The withdrawal of troops from Iraq in May 2004 by the Zapatero government led to a deterioration of relations between the two governments. Prime Minister Zapatero reiterated the commitment to the European project and became an important ally of the Franco-German alliance.

Spanish foreign policy: a tale of two worlds?

Spanish actors in the European arena are well conscious of the size of the country. They are pragmatic and flexible in their approach. They are very keen to preserve their influence and credibility in the decision-making processes of the European Union. They are not interested in being the dominant country in the EU, but they want to place Spain among the leaders. The Franco-German axis is important for Spanish interests. In spite of the Atlanticist policies of the second term of the José Maria Aznar, successive Spanish governments want the European project to be successful and they regard the Franco-German alliance as essential. The question is not one of long-term strategy, but of tactics. While socialist governments under Felipe Gonzalez and now under José Luis Zapatero support unconditionally such leadership and pursue policies to become part of it, the right-centre government under Aznar was very keen to find allies that felt left out from this core Franco-German alliance. Spanish governments perceive themselves as being a crucial country tipping the balance between the five main countries in the European Union.

According to the regular surveys of the public by the Elcano Real Institute, the vast majority of the population is not so keen that Spain becomes a superpower. It is more interested in the way power is used in the international stage. The Spanish population is highly internationalist and very keen to improve the quality of life in the world. In this sense, they rate quite highly priorities such as humanitarian aid to third world countries and international cooperation in order to improve the quality of life in developing countries. Power in the European Union and presence in international organisations is very important for Spaniards, due to the fact that the population hopes that such power or presence may be instrumental to improve the overall living quality of the planet. This also applies to the long-term desire of successive Spanish governments, in particular the former Aznar government, to become a G8 member and even to get a permanent seat in the Security Council of the United Nations. This international presence is regarded as more important than pursuing the national interest or aiming to be a superpower (see Figure 10.1).

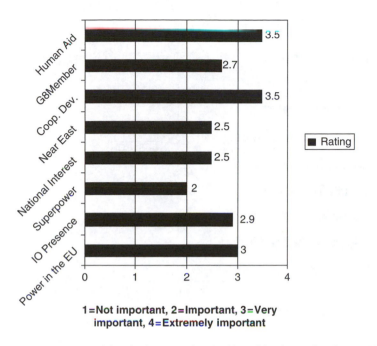

1=Not important, 2=Important, 3=Very
important, 4=Extremely important

Figure 10.1 Spanish attitudes towards priorities of foreign policy (June 2004).

Source: Barometro Real Instituto Elcano, June 2004, 6th survey (Madrid: Real Instituto Elcano
de Estudios Internacionales y Estrategicos 2004), p. 38 http://www.realinstitutoelcano.org accessed,
17.9.2004.

This is backed by the general perception of the influence of Spain in the
world in relation to other superpowers. Indeed, the perception of the power
of Spain improves considerably the stronger it follows the policies of the
Franco-German alliance. Surveys undertaken before and after the withdrawal of
the Spanish troops from Iraq in 2004 show an improvement of the perception
of power of the country. The position of Spain in the world is greatly enhanced
when governments are able to show autonomy, independence and decision-making
ability. The ranking in a scale from 1 to 10 shows the realist perception of the
population of Spain in relation to other countries which is of 5.9, behind the UK,
Germany and France (see Figure 10.2).

The Real Instituto Elcano describes this tendency of the population as disinterested internationalism (*internacionalismo desinteresado*) in which 51 per cent
of respondents to the already-mentioned survey believe that Spain should play an
important role in advancing the European Integration process, even if it loses some
power and some of the existing benefits. Nevertheless, the survey also shows that
41 per cent think that the most fundamental task of Spain in Europe is to defend its
national interests, even if it has conflicts with other countries. This shows that the
dominant perception of the population in Spain is one of cooperation with other

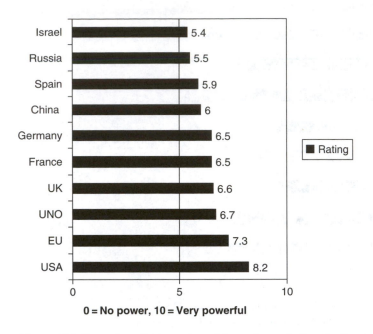

Figure 10.2 Perception of power of countries and organisations by Spaniards (June 2004).

Source: Barometro Real Instituto Elcano, June 2004, 6th survey. (Madrid: Real Instituto Elcano de Estudios Internacionales y Estrategicos 2004). p. 42 http://www.realinstitutoelcano.org, accessed, on 17/09/2004.

member-states and the outside world, nevertheless a strong minority presents also a nationalist position (Real Instituto Elcano, 2004: 38–9).

This may explain the division in electoral terms between the PSOE, which follows policies along disinterested internationalism, and the PP, which is very keen to defend the national interest. The same survey shows that Spaniards changed their perception of friends of the country during 2003 and 2004, in particular after withdrawal of the troops from Iraq. France was topping the ranking of best friends of Spain with 28 per cent, while the USA declined from 42 to 16 per cent. Germany was able to improve from 5 to 15 per cent. The perception of the United Kingdom as a friend declined from 7.1 to 5.7 per cent. This low perception of the UK as a friend may have been reinforced by the continuing dispute over Gibraltar. Last but not least, the perception of Poland as a friend has improved slightly from 4.5 to 6.5 per cent (Real Instituto Elcano, 2004: 13).

The reform of the Spanish foreign service

Basically, during the Aznar governments the Ministry of Foreign Affairs (*Ministerio de Asuntos Exteriores* – MAE) was structured along three main state secretariats responsible for international cooperation, aid and Latin America, external affairs and last but not least European affairs. All three were subdivided into general directorates for different policy areas. A sub-secretariat of state of European affairs was responsible for the Spanish diplomatic service. The main two regions where the Spanish diplomatic service was well equipped and well represented are Latin America and Europe. There is a smaller number of personnel operating in other regions. In spite of more than doubling the diplomatic personnel from 290 in 1943 to 643 in 1990, the three main areas where they were posted were still Latin America (12 per cent), Europe (29.1 per cent) and Madrid (35.9 per cent). The ministry has also a small staff of civil servants in comparison to other ministries. It is a Ministry with overstretched resources in relation to the ambitions of the country. The PP government tried to merge the General Secretariat for Foreign Affairs and the General Secretariat for European Affairs into one, but Foreign Minister Josep Piqué had to return to the original structure in 2000 (Molina Alvarez de Cienfuegos and Rodrigo Rodriguez, 2002; Kennedy, 2000: 115–17) (see Figure 10.4 and Figure 10.5).

Institutionally, the Ministry of Foreign Affairs (MAE) had to adjust considerably to the transition from an authoritarian isolationist policy towards a democratic multilateral one. The successor socialist government created four state secretaries by separating the state secretary responsible for Latin America and Cooperation. The new structure has upgraded cooperation by becoming a state secretary on its own. The Zapatero government is committed to increasing the official development aid to 0.5 per cent of GDP by 2008, so that it becomes a central policy of the government. This led to a major restructuring of the Spanish Agency for International Cooperation. Moreover, a General Directorate for Security Issues, such as terrorism, nuclear proliferation and disarmament is part of the State Secretariat of Foreign Affairs. The reorganisation also meant a growing interest for other regions such as emerging China, Russia and the Asia-Pacific rim. There is some ambition from the Zapatero government to balance more the resources among different regions of the world. Naturally, the state secretariat for Latin America remains *primus inter pares* among the strategic regions of Spanish foreign policy (see Figure 10.3).

The Zapatero government set up a committee on the reform of the Spanish foreign service. The committee presented a report on 20 June 2005. The committee consisted of representatives from all ministries which are involved in international activities. The findings of the committee showed that there was scope for considerable improvement. Several problems of coordination and planning were identified which affected the quality of delivery of service to Spanish citizens abroad. Among these deficiencies the report mentions particularly, the scarce planning of external action, insufficient inter-ministerial coordination, inadequate management of human, administrative and financial resources in the external representations, lack of resources of the ministry of foreign affairs due to lower spending in comparison to most other European countries, apart from Portugal, Czech Republic and Poland.

In 2005, the budget of the ministry of foreign affairs was 0.56 per cent, it rises to 0.68 per cent if we include the official development aid which the ministry has

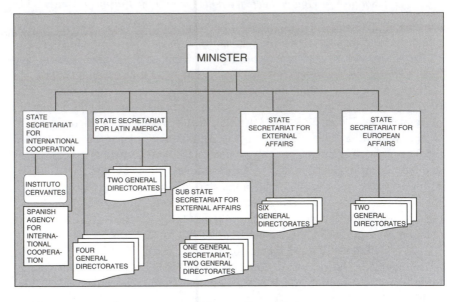

Figure 10.3 Structure of Ministry of Foreign Affairs (2006).

Source: Spanish Ministry of Foreign Affairs.

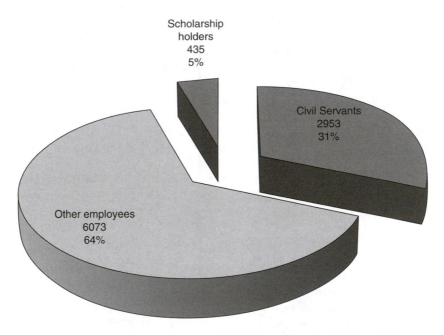

Figure 10.4 Staff employed by the Spanish Ministry of Foreign Affairs and Cooperation in 2005.

Source: Comisión para la Reforma Integral del Servicio Exterior Español, 2005: 21.

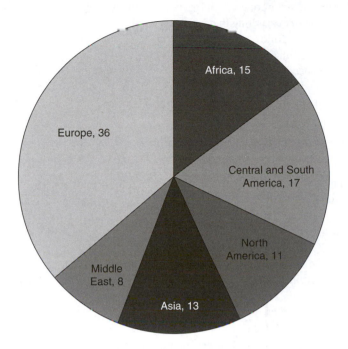

Figure 10.5 Distribution of staff employed by the Spanish Ministry of Foreign Affairs and Cooperation according to regions in 2005.

Source: Comisión para la Reforma Integral del Servicio Exterior Español, 2005: 22.

to distribute among the nongovernmental organisations responsible for development. In contrast, Ireland over 4.5 per cent, Sweden almost 4 per cent and the Netherlands about 3 per cent. Larger countries like the United Kingdom and France spend about 1.5 per cent, but Germany over 2 per cent. This means that the budget is inadequate for the kind of ambition has to play a central role in world affairs (Comisión para la reforma integral del servicio exterior, 2005: 40). Moreover, the report highlights that the modest resources are also inefficiently managed and spent. The financial process is quite bureaucratic, rigid and inadequate to meet the demands of a dynamic foreign service (Comisión para la reforma integral del servicio exterior, 2005: 42–4).

One of the most important aspects of the report are the proposed reforms, which among them emphasise improved coordination and simplication of procedures. This also includes proposals to finally modernise and create a common internet network for all Spanish missions scattered around the world. All this should be part of an overarching long-term 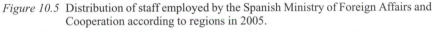 strategy to enhance the image of Spain in the world. The so-called 'marca España' (trademark Spain) should be part of the considerations of such an overarching strategy (Comisión para la reforma integral del servicio exterior, 2005: 48–53).

The report is also very keen to emphasise the need to invest in *diplomacia publica* (public diplomacy). Public diplomacy is meant as the collective efforts to disseminate a positive image of the country, and act counter any wrong perceptions. It means also the promotion of everything that is Spanish in the cultural, economic, political and social spheres. It follows the model developed by the United States Information Agency (USIA) in 1977. The image of Spain, also promoted by the Real Instituto Elcano, has become an important priority for Spanish governments. The report just recommends to make even bigger efforts in this direction. (Comisión para la reforma integral del servicio exterior, 2005: 233–7).

The Spanish presidencies of the European union in 1989, 1995 and 2002

The Spanish presidencies of the European Union were crucial for the enhancement of Spanish foreign policy. Nevertheless, the 1995 presidency must be regarded as the most successful of the three. The main reason is that Felipe Gonzalez was able to project Spain as a firm member of the European Union. The Euro-Mediterranean partnership approved in Barcelona in November 1995 has to be regarded as the biggest achievement of Spanish foreign policy since the transition to democracy. But we shall appraise the three presidencies individually before making a final assessment.

The presidency of the Council of Ministers of the European Union is an important event for any country. Each country is able to prepare an agenda which is implemented on behalf of the European Union. For a 6-month period the national interest has to be subordinated to the common interest. The presidency of the European Union is a very intense period of policy and agenda coordination for the staff of the Ministry of Foreign Affairs and the permanent representation (REPER). The country holding the presidency has to preside over 350 working group meetings, 100 permanent Representatives committee meetings (COREPER) and about thirty Council meetings.

The climax of such a presidency are generally the two European Councils bringing together all heads of state and prime ministers. While the Council of Ministers discusses according to area the more concrete technical aspects of policy and decision-making, the European Council is a forum to make broad decisions about the future of the European Union. It gives guidelines which are normally prepared by the European Commission. After 6 months a member-state is replaced by another member-state in the presidency. The smooth rotation of the presidency is assured by a trio of countries which is always changing and consists of the country holding the presidency, the country that held it before and the country that will hold it afterwards. Moreover, the small public administration of the Council supports the country in legal and other matters. The Constitutional Treaty agreed in 2004 and rejected in the French and Dutch referendums in 2005 was supposed to change this arrangement. The new arrangement is to have a president, nominated by the Council of the European Union, for a fixed term of $2^1/_2$ years, with the possibility of renewal. After the rejection of the Constitutional Treaty by the French and the Dutch and after a reflection period, the German presidency under Chancellor Angela Merkel revived the main principles of the Constitutional Treaty. After renegotiation and removal of the most critical issues for some of the member-states, especially the United Kingdom, France, the Netherlands and Poland, a Lisbon Treaty was agreed and signed under the Portuguese presidency in December 2007. In spite of the changes, the new kind of personalised presidency nominated for 2½ years is included in the new treaty. In this sense, our review of the previous Spanish presidencies of the European Union complete a cycle of European integration history, which is bound to be replaced by a new one.

Spanish diplomacy and administration started to prepare for the 1989 presidency of the European Union in 1987, just 1 year after joining the European Union. The main priorities were modernisation of the communications systems between the Spanish embassies and the upgrading of the qualifications of the personnel attached to the presidency. An organising committee of the EU presidency was established, so that the agenda could be implemented. In spite of the importance of the event, there was only an increase of thirty-nine posts, of which twenty positions were new and the rest related to postponed retirements (Grugel, 1991: 39). They regarded success in managing the presidency as a matter of prestige. The agenda-setting was very much controlled by the European Commission which wanted to push forward the issues related to the forthcoming Intergovernmental Conference, namely the establishment of Economic and Monetary Union. Moreover, Jacques Delors was also very keen to push the Charter of Fundamental Workers' Rights and to achieve the removal of border controls within the European Union. All these three aspects of European integration led only to modest results at the end of the presidency (Grugel, 1991: 34–5).

In spite of that, the Spanish presidency introduced with mixed success new elements into the overall external relations of the European Union. In 1989, the European Political Cooperation (EPC), the predecessor of CFSP, was the main way in which the different member-states worked together to come to a common position on matters related to world affairs. EPC was only designed to present common positions, but not to take any action.

Gonzalez was very interested in strengthening the link between the European Union and Latin America. This first attempt was quite difficult for Spanish diplomacy. Indeed, most of the initiatives were related to mediating in the process towards democracy in Central America, while relations with South America were not substantially improved. Spain was more successful in improving relations with North African countries, in particular Morocco. In this field, Spain emerged as a competitor to the long-established position of France (Grugel, 1991: 43–5).

In the 1995 presidency, Spanish diplomacy and public administration had already passed the level of institutional learning. Indeed, a more self-confident Spanish diplomatic corps prepared for the presidency of the European Union in the second half of the year. The agenda prepared in cooperation with the European Commission was certainly quite a breakthrough for the European Union and Spanish diplomatic priorities. First of all, the Secretary of State for European Affairs Carlos Westendorp was in charge of the Reflection Group for the intergovernmental conference of 1996, which led ultimately to the Treaty of Amsterdam. This clearly was a very prestigious task which was carried out with a high level of commitment. Westendorp made it clear that there was a need to include a chapter on employment coordination in the subsequent Amsterdam Treaty. There was pressure coming from the Spanish trade union confederations CCOO and the UGT as well as the European Trade Union Confederation (ETUC) (*El Diario Montañes*, 29 October 1995: 51; *El Pais*, 18 November 1995; *El Correo*, 18 November 1995: 40). Although the Treaty of Amsterdam was only approved in 1997 during the Dutch presidency and came into force in 1999, the Spanish input was certainly very important, because it forced other leaders such as Lionel Jospin and Tony Blair, after being elected in 1997, to support such a move. One of the big successes of Spanish diplomacy was the organisation of the European Council of Barcelona which led to the Euro-Mediterranean conference on 27 and 28 November 1995.

After years of joint diplomacy with Italy, Spain was able to achieve a restructuring of the relationship between the European Union and the Mediterranean. This conference set a new start for the European integration process, because the European Union began to see itself as a global player. This was possible, because of the collapse of the Soviet Union and the emerging power vacuum after the end of the Cold War. The conference led to the Euro-Mediterranean partnership which, following the model of the Organisation for Cooperation and Security in Europe (OSCE), also developed three levels of cooperation between the European Union and the Mediterranean partners: (1) a political and security partnership; (2) the establishment of a Euro-Mediterranean Free Trade Area, and (3) a partnership in social, cultural and human affairs. The ultimate aim is to achieve an integration of the northern single European market and the Mediterranean market into a huge market of 800 million persons, increasing after central and eastern European enlargement to over 1 billion. The date for completion of this huge market is 2010, which remains a very unrealistic date, due to the low level of progress made so far.

The Euro-Mediterranean partnership was also established to fight against the security risks coming from northern African countries which were already affecting all southern European countries. Among the security risks one can count illegal immigration, drug trafficking and the rise of Islamic fundamentalism and terrorism. Twenty-seven countries signed up to the Euro-Mediterranean partnership, the fifteen EU member-states and twelve Mediterranean countries (Morocco, Algeria, Cyprus, Egypt, Israel, Jordan, Lebanon, Malta, Palestine, Syria, Tunisia and Turkey). The figure of €4.7 billion for the period 1996–99 for the modernisation of Mediterranean economies, which had to be divided among the twelve countries, was quite insufficient. In spite of this, one can clearly count it as a major achievement for Spanish diplomacy. The conference was paralleled by other conferences related to the Euro-Mediterranean partnership such as the Alternative Mediterranean Conference and the conference of the Assembly of European Regions (AER) under the presidency of Generalitat president Jordi Pujol (*El Mundo*, 24 November 1995; *El Pais*, 27 November 1995; *El Pais*, 29 November 1995: 2).

The success of the Barcelona European Council strengthened the self-confidence of Spain as being a major player in the European integration process. The Madrid European summit led to several important conclusions, of which the most important was the relaunching of the Economic and Monetary Union (EMU) by announcing the final process towards full implementation of the new single currency. It was agreed to call the new currency the euro, giving it for the first time a name and concrete reality.

The European Council reinforced also the mechanisms for coordination of employment policies, by announcing that annual reviews of employment practices were to be introduced. The Madrid summit can be singled out as a new phase for the European integration process. Spanish diplomacy was also able to strengthen the relationship with South America by the signing of a EU–Mercosur agreement which started an ongoing process towards the creation of a free trade area between the two parts of the world. The same European Council pushed also forward the question of enlargement by giving a first tentative date for membership after 2000. The Spanish presidency was regarded as a major success by most representatives of other countries as well as by the President of the European Commission, Jacques Santer. The Spanish Foreign Minister Javier Solana became afterwards the new NATO secretary general and later on the High Representative for Common Foreign and Security Policy attached to the Council of the European Union, showing the growing importance of Spanish diplomats in Western institutions (*El Pais*, 17 December 1995; *Diario* 16, 17 December 1995; *El Pais*, Anuario, 1996: 62–3, 140–1). He has been instrumental in building the military and civilian capabilities of the new European Security Strategy.

Preparations for the Spanish presidency in the first half of 2002 also started quite early. Similar to previous presidencies, the personnel involved in the presidency went on several training programmes in several institutions including the European Institute of Public Administration (EIPA) in Maastricht. According to the EIPA 2000 report, Spain always sent the largest contingent to Maastricht. In 2000, there were 669 trainees from different parts of central and regional government. They represented 21 per cent of all national trainees which shows that all efforts to upgrade staff have been successful since accession. The high level of participation is explained by the fact that EIPA has a branch in Barcelona, the European Centre for the Regions (EIPA, 2001: 5). Nevertheless it shows that there is a huge demand for training in skills related to European integration.

The 2002 Spanish presidency was more subdued than the previous one. In terms of organisation the presidency had to organise sixty Council of Ministers meetings and an additional thirty-two meetings with Third World countries (Barbé, 2002: 91). The slogan of the presidency was *Mas Europa* (More Europe) but the overall enthusiasm presented by the Gonzalez administration could not be found under Prime Minister Aznar. One of the factors may be related to the divisive alliances that José Maria Aznar practised with prime ministers Tony Blair and Silvio Berlusconi against the traditional motor of the European integration, the Franco-German alliance (Barbé, 2002: 93–5). Furthermore, the 11 September

Table 10.3 Main dates of Spanish Presidency 2002

Month	Days and place		Meeting/Conference
JANUARY	8	Madrid	Meeting between Spanish Government and European Commission (Agenda setting)
	16	Strassbourg	Plenary Session of European Parliament
FEBRUARY	27–28	Granada	Ministerial meeting of EU and Gulf Council
MARCH	**15–16**	**Barcelona**	**European Council**
APRIL	4–6	Lanzarote	Ministerial Conference EU-Asia (ASEM) on migration flows
MAY	22–23	Valencia	Euromediterranean ministerial conference
	8	Madrid	EU–Canada Summit
	17	Madrid	Trojka Summit EU–Mercosur
	18	Madrid	Trojka Summit EU–Andean Community and Trojka Summit of EU–Mexico
JUNE	17–18	Madrid	EU-Latin America summit
	6–7	Madrid	Meeting of Foreign Affairs Ministers (ASEM)
	21–22	**Seville**	**European Council**

Source: *El Mundo, Anuario* 2003: 255.

attack on the twin towers in New York very much conditioned the agenda, which clearly was dominated by supporting the fight against terrorism and strengthening of the home and justice affairs pillars of the European integration process. Moreover, the Argentina crisis which exploded in November and December 2001 created problems for the continuing relationship between the European Union and Latin America. The 2002 presidency had to be considered as a transition presidency which was not able to present its own ambitious projects. This lack of ambition led to further developments and improvements in certain policy areas, but not to innovative ideas. One of the most important issues was the implementation of the euro in early 2002 and the successful transition period which was coincident with the Spanish presidency. The Barcelona European Council was not able to achieve a joint decision in social policy and the labour market, but it achieved approval for the Galileo project related to navigation by satellite which will compete directly with the American GPS (see Table 10.3).

Aznar's presidency was able to push forward the Euro-Mediterranean partnership by achieving association agreements with Algeria and Lebanon. This meant that only Syria was still awaiting conclusion of such an association agreement, prerequisite to taking part in the overall Euro-Mediterranean partnership. Nevertheless, he was not able to convince his counterparts of the necessity to create a Mediterranean Development Bank (Barbé, 2002: 100–1). In terms of the SEM, he achieved advancement in the liberalisation of the electricity and gas markets. There were some tentative moves to achieve consensus related to terrorism and illegal immigration, but this did not lead to any final agreement. For the first time, a Spanish prime minister took part in the G8 meeting in Canada. Aznar was acting on behalf of the European Union although Spain is very interested in becoming a member of G8 itself (Barbé, 2002: 101).

Parallel to the presidency, the European Convention started its work in March leading up to a European constitution in the summer of 2003. Although the presidency had not the same importance in chairing a reflection group like previous presidencies, Aznar upgraded his Ministry of Foreign Affairs with think tanks, such as the Royal Institute Elcano of International Relations (*Instituto Real Elcano de Relaciones Internacionales*) and other foundations, so that some reflective work could be done in Spain. In the end, the European Council ended with essentially five main conclusions: (1) it was agreed on further integration measures towards a common asylum and immigration policy including the penalisation of countries which do not take measures against illegal immigration; (2) the Council would be reformed by reducing the number of Council of Ministers area meetings from sixteen to nine and adopting a strategic pluri-annual plan by December 2003 for the next 3 years; (3) it was agreed to speed up the process of central and eastern enlargement until the end of the year; (4) it supported packages towards consolidation of budgetary policies and the liberalisation of markets such as energy and electricity; and (5) it developed and agreed a set of measures in the fight against terrorism. Indeed, ETA had been active during the presidency by perpetrating three car bomb attacks. The presidency was positively appraised by Javier Solana, the High Representative of the CFSP and Secretary General of the Council (*El Pais*, 19 June 2002: 3–7; *El Pais*, 23 June 2002: 2–6; *El Pais*, 30 June 2002: 6).

In this account, one can clearly see that Spanish diplomacy took the presidencies very seriously. All three presidencies played a major role in pushing the European integration forward. All three will be remembered for aspects related to external relations, economic and monetary union and justice and home affairs. The presidencies were also a catalyst for a reform of the Ministry of Foreign Affairs and Spanish foreign policy as a whole.

The priority areas of Spanish foreign policy

As already-mentioned, Spanish foreign policy was subject to a major transformation in the past two and a half decades. While Francoism relied very much on bilateral relations, Spanish democratic foreign policy gradually became more complex and multilateral. The Europeanisation of Spanish foreign policy pushed towards convergence with all other European countries. This became evident in the questions related to NATO membership as already-mentioned, which was linked to membership of the European Community. In the Suarez government, there were some attempts to define Spanish foreign policy as non-aligned. In 1979, Adolfo Suarez participated in the conference of non-aligned countries in Havana. This was pursued by the Foreign Minister of the first Socialist government, Fernando Morán.

Nevertheless, after accession the foreign policy of the Spanish government moderated considerably, particularly after the referendum on NATO in 1986. The climax of this change was the restoration of relations with Israel which was a demand of the Dutch government for support of Spanish accession. The normally pro-Arab Spanish governments since Franco came to power had to moderate towards a more balanced position in the question of the Middle East (Torreblanca, 2001: 486). This multilateralism and Europeanisation of Spanish foreign policy has remained a constant element up to today. In spite of different emphases, both the Socialist and the PP governments were very much in agreement on the ultimate aim which was the strengthening of Spain as a world power. In this sense, the key areas for Spanish foreign policy, the Mediterranean and Latin America, did not change very much. In the context of the Mediterranean, relations with Morocco are very important for Spanish foreign policy. The same can be said for Algeria, where gas and oil supply to Spain is of strategic importance.

Morocco: a difficult relationship

There are two main reasons why the relationship between Spain and Morocco is so difficult. First, Spain possesses the two small enclaves of Ceuta and Melilla, which are situated on the Moroccan coast. They are regarded as military priority in the fear that they may be taken over by the Moroccan army as both enclaves are quite small. According to the 2001 national census, Ceuta has a population of 71,505, while Melilla has 66,411 inhabitants. They are among the parts of Spain with the lowest GDP per capita (see Chapter 8). They are also gateways for illegal immigration.

In the past decade, many illegal immigrants are able to cross the border between Morocco and the enclaves and claim asylum. They are a major problem for the Spanish authorities. Second, Spain protested against the occupation of former Spanish Sahara by Morocco in 1975. Until the mid-1980s, Spain supported Polisario, the liberation movement of West Sahara. This naturally led to major tensions between Spain and Morocco. After accession to the European Union, the question of the independence of West Sahara has been delegated to the United Nations and the European Union as a whole. In this sense, Spain was able to transfer this problem to more powerful institutions. In spite of that, Spanish–Moroccan relations have been very tense, because of other issues such as the right to fish in Moroccan waters by Spanish fishermen. The negotiations of agreements were now transferred to the European Commission, which was able to offer subsidies and other aid development programmes in exchange for the right of Spaniards to fish in Moroccan waters. Nevertheless, the whole process can drag on for a long time like in 1995, leading to impatience among Spanish fishermen. There are also allegations that Morocco does not do very much to fight against drug trafficking (Gillespie, 1999b).

There was hope that the death of Morocco's King Hassan II in 1998 would lead to a democratisation and liberalisation of the regime. His son Mohammed VI succeeded him on the throne in 1999. In spite of that, misunderstandings between Spanish and Moroccan diplomats continued to create a very negative climate of relations. Such a negative atmosphere reached a climax in the autumn of 2001, when the foreign minister clearly presented an ambiguous position in relation to West Sahara. Morocco wanted to avoid an independence referendum by supporting the Baker plan which envisaged the granting of autonomy to West Sahara. France was supportive of the Moroccan position, but Foreign Minister Josep Piqué made clear that the position of Spain was the same as that of the United Nations, which envisaged a referendum. The Moroccan ambassador was withdrawn from Madrid as a protest against the Spanish attitude. It led to a reduction of cooperation in the different bilateral committees (*El Pais*, Domingo, 4 November 2001: 6; *El Pais*, Domingo, 16 December 2001: 9–11).

After the resignation of James Baker as special envoyee of the United Nations to the West Sahara, his plan which envisaged a possible road map to independence lost importance. Also successor Alvaro de Soto resigned after one year. In this sense, the process remains stagnated and without a perspective of being solved in the near future (Fernandez-Arias Menuesa, 2006: 154-60).

A further reinforcing reason for the attitude of Morocco was the fact, that the local and regional institutions of the autonomous community of Andalusia organised a mock referendum on the independence of West Sahara on 25 October in the same year, which led to an overwhelming support for it. This was regarded as interference in national affairs and added to the reasons, why Morocco withdrew its ambassador. As a consequence cooperation in important fields, such as international terrorism were blocked for the years to come. (Miguel, 2005: 43–4). The tensions escalated after the EU presidency in the first half of 2002, when Morocco invaded the small island of Perejil close to the Moroccan coast. Spain regarded the island as part of its territory and this led almost to a widescale military conflict between the two countries. It was easy for the Spanish army to recapture Perejil, but it became clear that the most vulnerable defence outposts were the two enclaves of Ceuta and Melilla (*El Pais*, 23 July 2002: 16). In a survey undertaken by the Spanish Centre for Sociological Investigations, 75.5 per cent of Spaniards were supportive of the intervention of the government in Perejil, while 20.2 per cent were against. It also seems that the majority of the population does not regard Morocco as an imminent threat to Spain in the future (*El Pais*, 27 July 2002: 21). The relations continued to be tense throughout the year. Morocco alleged that the Spanish secret services were destabilising the regime (*El Pais*, 3 November 2002: 23).

After the elections in September 2002 in Morocco, which were regarded as the first fair elections in the country, King Mohammed VI was able to strengthen his position due to the fact that the Assembly of Representatives (*Majiis al Nawab*) was very fragmented. Twenty-two parties were able to gain representation. The two main parties, the Socialist Union of People's Forces and the nationalist conservatives, Istiqal, were able to keep their hegemonic position. The rise of the moderate Islamic Justice and Development Party was quite problematic. Prime Minister Abderrahman Yusufi retained his position. This gave stability to the regime, although further democratisation and liberalisation will be necessary to make public administration more efficient (*El Pais*, Domingo, 22 September 2002: 1–3; Montabes, Parejo and Szmolka 2003). Relations between the two countries improved considerably in 2003, leading to new initiatives. The Moroccan ambassador returned to Madrid and the fisheries issue was discussed bilaterally between the two countries. The proposal was also made to create joint ventures, so that the Moroccan fisheries industry may profit from some transfer of technology.

During the height of the crisis, José Luis Zapatero visited officially King Muhammed VI and was cordially received. He was able to speak Spanish with the King. This attitude towards the opposition angered Foreign Minister Josep Piqué who, before Zapatero, had visited the Moroccan King and had to use an interpreter to conduct the conversation. The whole attitude of the Moroccan King towards the government of Prime Minister José Maria Aznar was quite negative.

The new Zapatero government was very keen to relaunch relations with Morocco. Prime Minister José Luis Zapatero launched with Turkey under the auspices of the United Nations the 'Alliance of Civilisations' project, which intends to contribute to the understanding of different cultures and overcome prejudices and fears between them. Good relations to Morocco is an important test case. One of the main reasons is that Morocco is undertaking major efforts to democratise its structures. Moreover, the Moroccan establishment is worried about the continuing importance of terrorist groups that operate from their territory or nationals that are operating in other countries, in particular Spain. Therefore, the first official visit abroad of José Luis Zapatero was to Morocco. There were attempts from right-wing elements within the army to discredit Zapatero as too soft in relation to the two Spanish enclaves in Ceuta and Melilla.

The Spanish government is also a strong supporter of the ambitious reforms that are taking place in Morocco. Among them, one has to highlight the reforms of the legal system in order to achieve gender equality in the country. This naturally is regarded as quite a difficult task, due to the existing cultural constraints that exist in the rural parts. Of interest is the commission 'Equity and Reconciliation', chaired by Dress Bezekri, which was in charge of investigating human rights abuses during the reign of Hassan II. A final report based on over 60,000 testimonials was drafted in June 2006. There has been also a considerable development towards genuine democratic structures. In spite of these developments there is still a long way to go. The Socialist government is interested in supporting such a process in order to undermine the danger of Islamic extremism. Cooperation in the fight against terrorism is a major priority of the Zapatero government. One of the big achievements of the emerging Moroccan democratic political system is the existence of a moderate Islamic party in parliament (Fernandez-Arias Menuesa, 2006: 160–2).

However, after a long period of cooperation until October 2007, tensions between Madrid and Rabat erupted again. The reason was the intention of Spanish King Juan Carlos and Queen Sofia to undertake their first visit to the enclaves of Ceuta and Melilla on 5 and 6 November 2007. This led again to the withdrawal of the Moroccan ambassador from Madrid as a protest against it. He returned only after 2 months (*El Pais*, 10 January 2008: 22).

In view of the forthcoming customs union with Morocco in 2012, the two enclaves, Ceuta and Melilla, want to give up on their special status within Spain and become integrated fully in the policies of the European Union. This means that

Ceuta and Melilla want to become part of the customs union, which will certainly contribute to a considerable reduction of the illegal trade between the enclaves and Morocco. Estimations of the value of the illegal trade (known under the euphemism in Ceuta of 'atypical trade') put it between €500 million to €1.5 billion annually. Morocco is worried that what has been regarded as 'occupied territory' and dispute with Spain, will become even more difficult, if the two enclaves become officially the southern border of the European Union (*El Pais*, 10 January 2008: 22).

The Mediterranean: the Euro-Mediterranean partnership

Despite a difficult relationship with Morocco, Spain is involved in the overall Euro-Mediterranean Partnership project. Since 1995, this ambitious project of the European Union is proceeding slowly, in spite of the problems related to the Middle East. In the past 8 years all countries have been signing association agreements with the European Union in order to kick-start in 2010 the Euro-Mediterranean Free Trade Area, which will comprise over 1 billion consumers. A general overview clearly shows that the main problem of the project is the still existing patrimonial democracies of the southern Mediterranean. Despite goodwill, the political systems and societies are still too closed and unaccountable to allow for a proper integration of the markets. One major problem has been the lack of integration among the markets of the southern Mediterranean. Conflict and distrust have prevented the creation of economies of scale in the region. In most of these patrimonial democracies, such as Algeria and Egypt, human rights are being violated. Moreover, corruption is a major problem for all these political systems. Algeria remains the main problem in the region, because it is an authoritarian dictatorship established after the victory of Islamic fundamentalists in 1992. Since then, the country has been in a permanent civil war which has caused major problems for foreigners living there (Gillespie, 1999b). In spite of all that, the fact that the European Union is present in the region provides a framework for the future.

Although the financial resources are far too low, they may become strategic catalysts for the establishment of basic infrastructures and other projects. Tunisia and Egypt became major tourist destinations and Jordan is moving slowly towards more open democratic structures and other countries may soon follow (Hamarneh, 2000; Martin-Muñoz, 2000). Spain, in this respect, was a catalyst for this project. Jointly with Italy it started at first with projects related to Mediterranean security which failed completely. It then contributed diplomatically to gain the other member-states to give a stronger role to the European Union in shaping the region. The main interest for Spain is to reduce the threats coming from the other side of the Mediterranean which are related to illegal immigration, Islamic fundamentalism and terrorism (Gillespie, 1997; 1999b). The review of the project in the second half of 2000 during the French presidency was rather disappointing (Jünemann, 2001). There were too many problems in the whole process of project management, and particularly in the ability to absorb the funding allocated to the Euro-Mediterranean partnership. There was a general concern about the sustainability of civil society, one of the aims of the overall package. The Valencia conference during the Spanish Presidency in the first semester of 2002 made some progress in pushing the Justice and Home Affairs agenda of the European Union, particularly the fight against terrorism. This was a reaction to the September 11, 2001 attacks against the twin towers in New York. In the end, the conference was able to produce a framework of cooperation for the implementation of several aspects of the Justice and Home Affairs of the European Union, including Islamic terrorism, fight against drug trafficking and illegal immigration (Gillespie, 2002: 111). Moreover, a contribution from Sweden was to establish a Euro-Mediterranean Foundation for the 'Dialogue of cultures and civilizations'. (Gillespie, 2002: 112). Already in 1998, Sweden had proposed such an institute. It was founded in 2000 in Alexandria, Egypt. The efforts in the Valencia conference was to transform the Alexandria institute into a Euro-Mediterranean Foundation for the 'Dialogue of cultures and civilizations'. Such an institute was established later on in Alexandria in Egypt and carried the name of the murdered swedish foreign minister, Anna Lindh, in 2005, who was instrumental in making it happen. (Schuhmacher, 2001: 93–7). The Presidency was also able to promote the free trade area initiative of the Agadir group, comprising Egypt, Morocco, Tunisia and Jordan. (Gillespie, 2002: 108).

After the conflictive foreign policy of former Prime Minister José Maria Aznar, the Socialist government presented a conciliatory approach towards the southern Mediterranean. As already-mentioned, the 'Alliance of the Civilisations' transformed the Euro-Mediterranean partnership approach into a global project. This was a quite original approach to the highly securitised issue in the relations between the West and the Muslim world. According to Isaias Barreñada, the new approach was thought out when Prime Minister José Luis Zapatero was flying over the Atlantic to make his first speech at the 59th General Assembly of the United Nations on 21 September 2004. It was then propagated at several other international gatherings until it was adopted by the United Nations one year later (Barreñada, 2006: 99). Spain was able to count on support from the French government and from Turkey of achieving a more global reach. In 2005, the Alliance of Civilisations chaired by High Representative Jorge Sampaio, who was the former president of Portugal, became another initiative of the United Nations. The Alliance of Civilisations was a clear anti-project to that of the Bush administration. Its scope is one of support of existing transcivilisational cooperation. Although the main priority is the relationship between the west and the muslim world, it has naturally a global reach. The High Representative is supported by a secretariat and several other forums in which different formations of civil society (national, transnational, global) are taking part. The Report of the High Level Group of the Alliance of Civilisations clearly emphasised the role as one of bridging the world's divides. The Alliance of Civilisations wants to focus on the youth as an important bridge for a more tolerant future. Moreover, it also wants to achieve a better more positive image of immigration. Last but not least, the media have an important role to change stereotypes and create more positive images of inter-civilisational cooperation (Barreñada, 2006: 101–2; 103–4). In spite of the success, Isaias Barreñada rightly questions the substance of the proposal which is still being developed. (Barreñada,

2006: 102–4). However, this became the first major initiative of the Zapatero government using instruments of public diplomacy to enhance of image of Spain abroad (Barreñada, 2006: 100).

A highlight of Spain's participation in the Euromediterranean Partnership was the organisation of the Barcelona conference in 2005, exactly a decade after its foundation. This was jointly organised with the United Kingdom, under the auspices of the British presidency. According to Richard Gillespie, the conference was overshadowed by events in the Middle East. Many governments of the southern Mediterranean sent only low-ranking representatives which were not able to make any final decisions. There is a continuing distrust about the real motives of the European Union, which wants to focus on security issues due to the international islamist terrorist threat (Gillespie, 2006: 273–4). The main reason for the failure was the ambition, particularly of Spain, to raise the stakes and the prominence of the conference. Moreover, the British wish to agree on a 'Code of Conduct in Countering Terrorism' was not accepted by the southern Mediterranean partners (Gillespie, 2006: 277).

Economically, the Euro-Mediterranean Partnership is stagnating. One of the main problems continues to be the very slow economic development. The southern Mediterranean is growing, but not sufficiently to catch up with the European Union or other emerging markets (Euro-Med Partnership, 2002: 11). Furthermore, there is now a general thrust of the European Union to water down the Euro-Mediterranean Partnership and replace it slowly with the new 'Neighbourhood Policy'. The latter requires from the EU neighbours to adopt most of the policies of the EU, particularly related to the Single European Market, Justice and Home Affairs and the Copenhagen criteria, even if in a less stringent way.

Latin America: the cultivation of Hispanidad, Ibero-American summits and Mercosur

Latin America has been always an important priority of Spanish foreign policy. *Hispanidad*, (Spanishness, or rather brotherhood) between the Spanish-speaking people due to cultural links, is regarded as a way to compensate for the loss of the empire in the world. After decades of rhetorical intentions, Spanish foreign policy became more involved in the whole process of strengthening the relations between Spain and Latin America. Indeed, accession to the European Union also provided an opportunity to establish stronger relations between Latin America and the European Union. Such a stronger relationship started in the early 1990s and is today characterised by a complex web of networks.

For Spain, the most important political forum is the Ibero-American Community of Nations (*Comunidad Ibero-Americana de Naciones*) which was established in 1991. It includes twenty countries, among them Portugal and Spain. The integration of Portugal was a major achievement of Spanish foreign policy, due to the fact Portugal itself has developed its own project of a Portuguese Speaking Community (*Comunidade de Paises de Lingua Portuguesa* – CPLP). The first meeting was held in July 1991 in Guadalajara, Mexico. In spite of many rhetorical intentions these Ibero-American summits did not lead to palpable results. In the meeting on 16–17 November 2002 in Mexico, it was agreed to reinforce the structures of the organisation and make it more efficient in terms of projects and international projection (*El Pais*, 17 November 2002: 2–3). The summit of 19–20 November 2004 in San José in Costa Rica, was quite important for the new foreign policy of Prime Minister José Luis Zapatero. After his speech at the United Nations, Prime Minister Zapatero presented his public diplomacy approach by speaking more about the 'Alliance of Civilizations' (*El Pais*, 21 November 2004: 5–6).

There is a quest by the member-states to strengthen the institutional structures of the Ibero-American Community of Nations. Such calls for a reinforcement of the institutional structures were already expressed by former Prime Minister José Maria Aznar. However, not until the 15th Ibero-American summit in Salamanca on 14–15 October 2005, was a General Ibero-American Secretariat created. Its main task was to function as a coordinating permanent structure. Enrique V. Iglesias became its first General-Secretary (EFE, 2006: 545). Several projects are being launched, such as a conference on immigration, cooperation in the fight against international Islamic terrorism and last but not least the establishment of an Ibero-American space of knowledge. Moreover, networks at the different levels of public administration and governments are being established between the member-states. For example, there have been efforts to achieve a better coordination and management of the Ibero-American network of Ministers of the Presidency and Equivalents, the establishment of a system of strategic information for the chiefs of government and the reinforcement of an Iberoamerican School of Government and Public Policies (IBERGOP) which was agreed in 1999 (EFE, 2006: 547–50).

Normally, relations between the countries taking part in the Ibero-American summits are quite cordial. The integration of Cuba in this forum is regarded by Spanish diplomacy as an important achievement. However, in the Ibero-American summit of November 2007, an exchange of harsh words between the King of Spain Juan Carlos, who has been a regular participant at these gatherings since they began, and President of Venezuela, Hugo Chavez, led to considerable coverage in the international news. Hugo Chavez was already speaking for longer than his allocated time, and he began to insult former Prime Minister José Maria Aznar. This led to the intervention of Prime Minister José Luis Zapatero who defended his compatriot, with whose opinions he did not agree, but whom he respected. Moreover, Zapatero said that Aznar was democratically elected. Chavez wanted to come back and respond to Zapatero, but suddenly the King just shouted at Chavez to 'shut up' ('*calla-te*'). This sudden outburst instantaneously made the headlines. It led also to major criticisms of King Juan Carlos inside his country. Many Spaniards found that the King should just represent the country, but not intervene in debates (*El Pais*, 18 November 2007; *El Pais*, 19 November 2007). However, end of July 2008 President Hugo Chavez visited King Juan Carlos of Mallorca and both made up, restoring their friendship.

As already-mentioned, Spain is engaged in pushing forward closer links between the European Union and Latin America. Indeed, in the past decade the European Union has created links with the Common Market of the

Southern Cone (Mercosur), the Andean Community and other economic communities in the Caribbean and Central America. From a Latin American perspective, there is the intention to develop in the long-term perspective a Latin American Economic Community. Mercosur is following closely the example of the European Union.[1] Naturally, the involvement of the European Union is creating some rivalry with the projects of the United States which are very keen to create a Free Trade Area of the Americas (FTAA).

Apart from culture, Spain has strong economic interests in Latin America. It is, after the United States, the main country investing in Latin America. Spanish investment has increased substantially over the past decade. In the European Union, it is the main country investing in Latin America. Due to the language, the Latin American market was excellent for the larger Spanish enterprises emerging from privatisation. Telefónica is now one of the main providers of telecommunications and other related products with participation in most privatised telecommunication companies of the region, including the vast market of Brazil. On 17 September 2007, President Luis Inacio Lula da Silva undertook an official visit to Spain in order to ask for support for his domestic Plan for the Acceleration of Development in Brazil. The plan envisages public investment of 250 billion US dollars in infrastructures, energy and communications over a four year period. Over 100 representatives of Spanish firms among them Telefonica, Iberdrola and Gas Natural attended the meeting. Both Prime Minister Luis Zapatero and President Lula da Silva want to establish a strategic partnership in the world economy, in order to accelerate the development of both countries. Such strategic alliance covers also a growing cooperation in the reform of the United Nations, support for the Alliance of the Civilizations and reinforcement of the Latin American economic integration. Representatives of the major Spanish firms were full of praise for the pragmatic and supportive role of the Brazilian government for investors. (*El Pais*, 18 September 2007: 20). Moreover, Spanish has become a compulsory module in the Brazilian school curriculum since 2005. (EFE, 2006: 551; 17 September 2006). This can be said also for the energy sector, where Endesa and Iberdrola have also strong stakes in energy and electricity companies. In the complementary energy sector other Spanish firms such as Repsol and Unión Fenosa were able to become major players in most countries. The banking sector expanded fast in most Latin American countries. Among the most successful are the Banco Bilbao y Viscaya Argentaria (BBVA) and Santander Central Hispano. The Argentina crisis clearly brought to light the risks that Spanish firms are facing. Nevertheless, they are committed to these long-term projects in Latin America where they have a privileged access through language. Moreover, their expansion in Latin America assured them that they could rise to be global players. In this context the best example is Telefónica, which clearly was able to profit from the dominant market position in Spain (*El Pais*, 11 February 2002: 4; *El Pais*, 28 January 2002: 10; *El Pais*, 6 June 2002: 56; Ontiveros and Fernandez, 2002).

The main difference between the Aznar and Zapatero governments, is that the latter tried to have good diplomatic relationship with all Latin American governments, including the ones characterised led by populist leaders such as

Hugo Chavez in Venezuela and Evo Morales in Bolivia. One of the most controversial decisions was to send a high-ranking junior minister to the Third World meeting organised by Cuba, in which North Korea, Venezuela and China took part. This was heavily criticised by Mariano Rajoy, the main leader of the opposition. However, this was part of the new open-minded public diplomacy of the new Socialist government. The limits of such cooperation with populist governments became clear when Spain tried to sell ten military transport C-295 planes and two maritime patrol CN-235 planes, costing €500 million in total, to Venezuela. The main problem was that these planes built by the Spanish firm EADS-CASA, included high technology components from US firms. This gave the right to the United States to veto the sale, which was particularly instigated by Vice-President Dick Cheney (*El Pais*, 13 January 2006: 15).

In sum, Spanish foreign policy and Spanish firms are more and more engaged in Latin America. This is the geographical area where Spanish firms were able to rise to become global players.

Gibraltar: the resistance of the population

One of the most important issues for Spanish foreign policy is the British enclave of Gibraltar. After Tony Blair came to power, Spanish–British negotiations started to achieve a compromise in relation to the status of Gibraltar. In spite of an agreement between the two governments to allow for a shared sovereignty solution, the 30,000-strong population of Gibraltar refused to accept this proposal and made strong representations in London, so that Gibraltar remains solely British (*El Pais*, 3 February 2002: 19; *El Pais*, 26 June 2002: 18; *El Pais*, 27 June 2002: 13). First Minister Daniel Caruana vehemently protested against the negotiations of the two countries and was very keen to keep the status quo for the enclave.

As a preventive action, Caruana called for a referendum in the autumn 2002 which led to an overwhelming support for the status quo. This naturally created major problems for the negotiations between Spain and the United Kingdom. Indeed, on 8 June 2003 comments made by Denis MacShane, the British Minister for European Affairs, upset Spanish diplomats. He compared Gibraltar with the two Spanish enclaves on the Moroccan coast, Ceuta and Melilla. He also expressed the opinion that an agreement over Gibraltar was not possible within the next 20 or 30 years. It meant that after the referendum, the United Kingdom changed its position from the original idea of shared sovereignty to the status quo (*El Pais*, 9 June 2003: 24). The political leadership in Spain was outraged about these comments.

The new Zapatero government started a new process in order to find a solution to the sovereignty of Gibraltar. The forum of dialogue, a tripartite committee consisting of representatives of Spain, United Kingdom and Gibraltar was established in October 2004 which acts as an important forum for continuing discussions. Also, Andalusia has become more integrated in the process at local level since March 2007, however any positive developments are still to be seen (*El Pais*, 28 December 2007). At the same time, more initiatives between Spain and Gibraltar were developed in order to achieve economic and movement advantages for both sides. The airport in Gibraltar is now open to Spanish citizens and Spain has liberalised the communications to Gibraltar. In September 2007, British Foreign Minister David Miliband paid an official visit to Spain. Moratinos confirmed that the process of dialogue was continuing, although there was no roadmap or timeframe for the question of Gibraltar (*El Pais*, 7 September 2007).

There is also some pressure from the United Nations to achieve a compromise on the issue (*El Pais*, 24 October 2007). However, in August 2007, *New Flame*, a ship full of scrap-iron coming from New York collided with *Tom Gertrud*, an oil tanker on the Gibraltar coast. Spain was only informed at a late stage, because the port of Gibraltar and the Spanish port of Algeciras, which is situated in the bay do not inform each other about the movement of their ships. The collision was due to this lack of communication between the two ports. While the *New Flame* had departed from Gibraltar, the *Tom Gertrud* left from Algeciras (*El Pais*, 27 August 2007). By February 2008, both the authorities in Gibraltar and Spain had still failed to rescue the ship. The ship broke in two. (*El Pais*.com, 21 February 2007). The accident was also a reason for Spain to protest in the European Union against the United Kingdom, of which Gibraltar is integral part (*El Pais*, 13 February 2008).

Spain and its European neighbours: Portugal, France and Italy

In the past 30 years, Spain has strengthened its linkages to its neighbours. Apart from the fact that Portugal, France and Italy are members of the European Union, the linguistic affinities between these four countries have allowed for more intensive cooperation.

The relationship of Portugal to Spain was always problematic due to the conflictive history since the twelfth century, when the country became independent. For Portuguese history it was quite a negative period when the Spanish King Philip II was able to unify the two Kingdoms, because the Portuguese King Sebastian had died in a battle in northern Africa. It meant that between 1580 and 1640, Portugal lost its independence. However, after a revolution in 1640, Portugal regained its independence and since then the relationship with Spain was always one of distance. Even when both Portugal and Spain were ruled by authoritarian dictators, both countries continued to live back to back. After the transition of democracy in Portugal and Spain relations between the two countries became much better. In spite of the competitive behaviour in relation to accession to the European Community between 1977 and 1986, both countries started to organise bilateral summits since 1982.

These luso-hispano summits at prime-ministerial level are used to resolve common problems in the peninsula, such as the use of rivers. Most rivers, such as the Douro and Tejo/Tajo/Tagus, originate in Spain and the water is used extensively, so that a regular complaint of the Portuguese authorities is that not enough water reaches the country. More than once the Portuguese government has demanded compensation for loss of water (*El Pais*, 6 June 2005: 29). Meanwhile, these summits have led to common projects, such as a high-technology research center at the University of Minho. Like Germany and France, the two Iberian countries became aware of common interests in the European Union, so that now they have strengthened the coordinating efforts between the two countries.

Such coordination spans many areas, in particular the Lisbon agenda and foreign policy (Freitas do Amaral, 2005). Spanish investment in Portugal has increased considerably over the past 30 years. In particular, Spanish banks are quite active in Portugal. Portuguese investment in Spain has been also increasing, although at a lower level (Corkill, 1999: 109–24). Luso-hispano relations became particularly important along the border of the two countries. After decades of neglect the socalled 'double periphery' (in relation to the national capital and Brussels), the EU-funded INTERREG programme became an important instrument to bring the two countries together. Although the development of cooperation is quite asymmetrical across the border, for example, more developed between Galicia and Norte de Portugal and Extremadura and Alentejo, the effects of integration between the two parts are being felt. It is interesting that many Portuguese students, particularly in medicine, now study in prestigious Spanish Universities, because the Portuguese public higher education system is not able to accommodate the large numbers of applicants. There is also a growing number of people in Spain learning Portuguese. It seems that about 9,000 people were learning Portuguese in 2004, a considerable rise from the 500 in 1996. About 40 per cent of those are in the border region in Extremadura. In this context, one should not fail to mention the hard work of the regional government of Extremadura in contributing to the cultural knowledge of Portuguese literature and history. In the past two decades, the regional government organised conferences, colloquia and other events to bring together the two countries.

Meanwhile, the regional government of Extremadura may be one of the main promoters of Portuguese culture through the publication of excellent books on the history, social sciences and culture of the two countries. It also watches closely the reports on Spain in Portugal and vice versa. Last but not least, an opinion survey among Portuguese undertaken by Portuguese newspaper *O Sol*, shortly before the visit of Portuguese president Anibal Cavaco Silva in Spain in November 2006, showed that the borders between the two countries were fading away. About 28 per cent of respondents supported unification with Spain, while 70 per cent were against it. Furthermore, 97 per cent agreed that the formation of one country through unification would benefit the economy. In such a case, the vast majority of 64 per cent would prefer a Republic, while 24 per cent a monarchy. The vast majority of supporters of a monarchy were very happy to have Juan Carlos as their King. Respondents were split over the question which of the two capitals, Madrid or Lisbon, should become the new centre of power (*El Pais*, 23 September 2006). This has to be regarded as a positive development in the emerging new relationship between the two countries.

The relationship between France and Spain has also established similar bilateral relations. Although Spain and France are rivals in the Mediterranean and other policy areas, overall there has been a similar integration of both countries. INTERREG played a major role in creating Franco-hispano projects along the Mediterranean coast. The so-called *Arco Latino* is a major project financed by

INTERREG to bring together local authorities from Italy, France and Spain. INTERREG cooperation exists also between the Basque country on both sides of the border. During the Aznar period, there were tensions between the two countries due to the support of the Spanish government for the Iraq War. Jacques Chirac and Gerhard Schröder, opponents, were confronted by British Prime Minister Tony Blair and Prime Minister José Maria Aznar, who supported the American approach. Another source of tensions was the different approaches to the issue of West Sahara. France wanted to preserve an area of interest in the region and this upset Spain. However, when Prime Minister José Luis Zapatero came to power, relations between the two countries improved considerably, because he withdrew the troops from Iraq and also was more constructive in the Constitutional Treaty. Zapatero's government was also the first to organise a successful referendum on the Constitutional Treaty in February 2005.

Spain and France have been working closely together in the fight against Basque terrorism. This anti-terrorism fight has been long-standing, but it gained new momentum during the Aznar period. After the attack on the twin towers on 11 September 2001, both countries reinforced their capabilities in order to defeat Basque terrorism. In spite of a ceasefire in 2006, the bombing of a car park in the airport of Barajas in late December 2006 reinforced the anti-terrorism fight. By June–July 2007 many important logistics centres were dismantled by the French police in cooperation with the Spanish authorities. Such raids and successes against ETA have become more often, suggesting that the organisation is weakening. There have been some suggestions that ETA is moving part of its logistics operations to Portugal. Therefore the Spanish–French police cooperation model may be also established between the two Iberian countries. Spanish–French summits are undertaken regularly. On 9 January 2008, such a summit took place in Paris between French Prime Minister Nicolás Sarkozy and Prime Minister José Luis Zapatero, in which the fight against ETA terrorism and the issue of immigration were the main points on the agenda. It was decided to establish permanent teams consisting of intelligence and police officers in the fight against ETA. This can be regarded as a stepping up of the cooperation in this particular issue. Moreover, the two countries were able to overcome their differences in relation to immigration policy. In 2005 and 2006, Zapatero had to endure criticisms from the French government because of the amnesty given to illegal immigrants and its subsequent more humane policies towards immigrants. In the summit, both countries agreed to support the reform of immigration policy at European Union level and coordinate their efforts. Probably, the most controversial aspect of the cooperation has emerged after Nicolás Sarkozy announced that it wanted to establish a Mediterranean Union. Sarkozy was able to gain the support of prime minister Zapatero as long as the new project did not create a doubling of structures to the stagnating Euro-Mediterranean partnership (*El País*, 10 January 2008).

This is the reason why the Spanish–Italian relations are becoming important now for Spain. The cooperation acts as a counterbalance to the ambitions of the French President Nicolás Sarkozy. There is a long-standing cooperation between the two countries, particularly after the end of the Cold War. Both countries were interested in creating a Mediterranean security zone through the establishment of a Conference of Mediterranean Security and Cooperation which would emulate the successful Organisation for Cooperation and Security in Europe (OSCE), Such diplomatic attempts all ended in failure, until in 1995 Spain was able to host the Barcelona conference which established the Euro-Mediterranean Partnership.

Similar to France and Portugal, Spanish–Italian meetings have been taking place during the new millennium. The close relationship between Prime Minister José Maria Aznar and Prime Minister Silvio Berlusconi allowed for excellent bilateral relations between the two countries. Again issues related to anti-terrorist police cooperation and the patrol of the border police were important topics discussed in such bilateral meetings. Similarly, the relationship between Italian Prime Minister Romano Prodi and Prime Minister Zapatero after 2006 were excellent. In 2007, both leaders met twice in order to discuss issues of common concern such as immigration and other EU policies. The meetings took place on 20 February 2007 in Ibiza and 15 December 2007 in Naples. Spanish interests in Italy have grown considerably in the past years. Telefonica has become a major investor in Italy.

The Spanish armed forces and the contribution of Spain to peacekeeping forces

Up until the coup attempt by Colonel Antonio Tejero on 23 February 1981, the so-called *tejerazo*, the Spanish armed forces were still divided among supporters of democracy and loyalists to the former authoritarian regime.

The difficult first years of democracy, the autonomy process, terrorism and disillusionment of the population with the UCD government were among the reasons for Colonel Tejero's desperate actions. The firm support of King Juan Carlos for the new constitutional monarchy led to the isolation of the conspirators, who believed that the King was on their side. This event finally established King Juan Carlos as the guarantor of democracy. His popularity rose considerably and has remained high ever since (*El Pais*, 22 November 2000: 4). After the Socialist Party came to power, Minister of Defence Narcis Serra started a much-needed reform and re-orientation of the Spanish armed forces. The reform was designed to modernise the armed forces, and after 1986 to make them compatible with the new tasks within NATO. Slowly, the orientation of the armed forces towards a broader European defence strategy was achieved. The strong cooperation between the European Union and the United Nations made participation in international missions important for the Spanish armed forces. The first Spanish blue helmets were sent in 1989 to Angola (UNAVEM), Namibia (UNTAG) and Honduras (ONUCA). The latter was led by a Spanish officer, General Agustin Quesada Gomez (*El Pais*, Anuario, 1990: 133). The number of troops was small, but clearly this was a sign of the reorientation of the Spanish foreign policy. Spanish troops took an active part in the international coalition in the first Gulf War in 1991.

The argument was that Spain was acting within the framework of the European Union and NATO. Although there was resistance against deployment in this first Iraq war, the argument put forward was able to convince the majority of the population (Kennedy, 2000: 117–18).

Throughout the 1990s, Spain has been contributing peacekeeping forces to different operations either spearheaded by NATO or the United Nations. Between 1989 and September 2006, Spain has been involved in thirty-two international humanitarian and/or military missions with contingents of at least more than ten military personnel. In 2002, the Spanish armed forces had deployed personnel in seven different places: Bosnia-Herzegovina; Kosovo; Macedonia; Afghanistan; Asia; Djibouti and the Horn of Africa (see Table 10.4).

Like many other armies around the world, the Spanish army is no longer reliant on compulsory conscription. The so-called *mili* (national service) was abolished in 1999, so that Spanish armed forces are now dependent on professional soldiers. This caused a major problem due to the fact that Spain is not able to recruit sufficient numbers. In January 2007, 79,128 men and women were in the active service (see Table 10.6). In 2005, The presence of women was 13.9 per cent, one of the highest in NATO, after the United States and Canada, but in 2007 it declined to 11.91 per cent (14,391). The major reason was a commitment of the government to achieve equality of opportunities in terms of gender in all sectors of society. In spite of this positive integration of women in the armed forces, adequate structures for such a move were not available. The lack of appropriate structures for the needs of women, particularly in cases of pregnancy and child care are still a major problem (Registro Central de Personal, 2007: 18;Gisbert, 2007b: 101–6). Since the *mili* was abolished the Spanish armed forces are facing a recruitment crisis. The number of soldiers has been declining since 2000. Former Defence Minister Federico Trillo Figueroa targeted Hispano-American immigrants and those from Equatorial Guinea to join several army services. He planned to recruit 2,000 foreigners into the armed forces. This naturally showed the level of desperation in recruiting enough soldiers. There was also a review of the defence strategy in line with the assessments coming from the United States, NATO and other European countries after September 11, 2001. The document was presented on 18 December 2002 in parliament and emphasised aspects related to fighting against international terrorism (*El Pais*, Anuario, 2003: 132).

Spain became a temporary member of the United Nations Security Council for the period 2002–4 and was clearly a strong ally of the United States and the United Kingdom in pursuing the agenda for a second war against Iraq. It contributed military forces to the Anglo-American coalition, in spite of considerable opposition inside the country. This was part of a strategy to upgrade the role of Spain as a middle-ranking power. Participation in military operations were regarded as an important instrument to gain more international recognition. Such power driven strategy of the Aznar government was replaced by a more multilateral strategy based on international legality of the Zapatero government. As already-mentioned, the Zapatero government withdrew the 1,300 troops in April–May 2004, alienating the close relationship with the US government. However, this was accompanied

Table 10.4 Deployment of Spanish troops and observers for peacekeeping and combat operations of the United Nations and the European Union in 2008

Country	Name of operation	Nature of deployment	Time frame
PRESENT INTERNATIONAL OPERATIONS			
Bosnia-Herzegovina	Althea-EUFOR (NATO)	258 soldiers out of 2,106 (reduction from originally overall 7,000 in 1992)	Since November 1992, but Althea-EUFOR only since 2004
Kosovo	KFOR (NATO)	585 soldiers out of 16,000	Since June 1999
Afghanistan	ISAF (NATO)	690 soldiers out of 37,000 + 52 instructors detached to the Afghan Army	Since August 2003
Libanon	UNIFIL/FINUL(UN) Policing Israelo–Lebanese border	1,100 soldiers out of 12,000 (UNIFIL just 2,000)	Since autumn 2006
MISSIONS WITH OBSERVERS			
Ex-Yugoslavia	Monitoring team of EU (ECMMY/ECMM/ EUMM)	4 (Higher-ranking officers)	Since 1991
Darfour, Sudan	Support mission of EU to African Union in Darfur (AMIS II)	2	Since 2005
Kosovo	UNMIK	2	Since 1999
Ethiopia, Eritrea	UNMEE Observing of demilitarise zone	3	Since 2003
Democratic Republic of Congo	MONUC-Observing of peace in the country and de-commissioning of arms among armed groups and their reintegration in society	2 out of 17,000 contingent	Since 2001

Source: Ministério de la Defensa, 2008, posted on website http://www.mde.es, accessed on 19 February 2008.

by a reinforcement of the Spanish contingent in Afghanistan, in order to strengthen the fight against the Taliban (Gisbert, 2007a: 35).

The defence policy of the Zapatero government stressed the continuity to the previous government. At the core of its policy was to continue on the path of reform, so that the Spanish armed forces could be adapted to the new challenges of the twenty-first century such as the proliferation of weapons of mass destruction, the threat of Islamic terrorism, shortage of strategic resources such as oil and gas

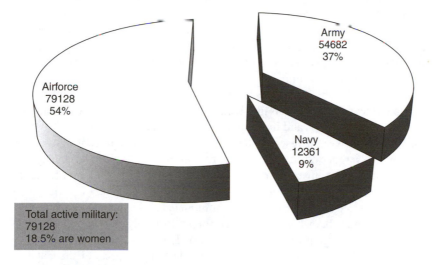

Figure 10.6 Spanish armed forces in 2007 (Estimates).

Source: Ministerio de la Defensa, 2007 quoted from El Pais, Anuario 2008: 133.

and the outbreak of local conflicts in different parts of the world. This led to the directive on national defence which was decided in December 2004 and followed up the review of defence strategy from the previous government. In November 2005, Parliament adopted the National Defence Law, which was designed to transform the Spanish armed forces in the next years. Although international legality, multilateralism and the role of Parliament in decision-making processes is emphasised, the new National Defence Law emphasises continuity rather than a break with the previous government.

The use of force for conflict resolution, even if it is not sanctioned by international organisations is an open option for the Spanish armed forces. Moreover, the Armed Forces continue to be supported by a research and development investment in military equipment. Among the projects, is the future fighter (*combatiente del futuro*) which led to the development of individualised high technology kits for the protection of soldiers in extreme conditions such as tropical climates (Gisbert, 2007a: 41). Since April 2006, a major restructuring plan has been implemented in order to make the Spanish armed forces more efficient and resolve the recruitment crisis. Among the measures there is also a plan to create different contracts in the military. A 6-year contract was introduced for those who want to get the security skills, but after the expiration of the period want to join the police or other domestic security forces. A second group who do not want to become permanent members of staff can serve until they reach 45 years of age. They will receive a yearly payment of €7,200 which they can top up with an additional job. The third group of permanent staff is able to get a pension when they reach 58 years of age. This flexible approach towards recruitment is accompanied by a considerable rise above inflation of armed forces personnel (Gisbert, 2007b: 91–2). As in many other countries, recruitment in the armed forces is related to the inability of the labour market to absorb newcomers. According to figures from Tomás Gisbert for the year 2002, 28.4 per cent of recruits came from Andalusia, 15.1 per cent from the Canary islands, 11.4 per cent from the Community of Madrid, 7.5 per cent from Castilla y León and 6.6 per cent from Galicia (Gisbert, 2007b: 92). All these autonomous communities have high levels of unemployment. It means also that sometimes commitment is low, leading to high levels of absenteeism and indiscipline (Gisbert, 2007b: 97–101).

Although in the past 30 years civilian power was able to gain control over the military, which was one of the pillars of the former Francoist authoritarian regime, the policies of the Socialist government alienated some parts of the more right-wing upper echelons of the military. Already in June 2004, General Luis Alejandre resigned from office due to the partisan appointments of the Socialist government at the top of the three branches of the armed forces. Probably, even more worrying for the Socialist government was the speech of Lieutenant-General José Mena on 5th January 2006, in which he criticised the negative aspects of the Catalan statute, including the continuing devolution process in terms of education and the use of language, and invoked the possibility for the armed forces to intervene using Article 8 of the constitution.[1]

Lieutenant-General Mena was relieved from his duty and put under house arrest for 8 days and at the end of this period forced into retirement. The reason for this swift reaction by minister of defence José Bono was that the military had to adhere to the principle of neutrality in relation to any government in power, and his comments were quite partisan in the context of the polarisation between PSOE and PP (*El Pais*, 13 January 2006: 16; Gisbert, 2007a: 35–6).

In sum, the Spanish armed forces underwent major changes to cope with tasks related to the post-Cold War period. Like many other west European armed forces they are overstretched both in technological as well as personnel terms.

11 September 2001, the Madrid bombings of 11 March 2004 and the fight against international Islamic terrorism: the Spanish contribution

As already-mentioned, Spain has revised its defence strategy up to 2015. The fight against international terrorism led by the United States is the major element in the strategy. This is the result of the terrorist attacks on the twin towers of the World Trade Center in New York, where almost 3,000 people died on 11 September 2001. Since then, Spain has been an important ally in the fight against international terrorism and former Prime Minister Aznar was able to link the problem of ETA with this ongoing struggle. He also ensured that ETA was recorded as a terrorist organisation in lists of illegal organisations in the European Union in 2001 and in the United States after the second Gulf War in April 2003. Moreover, Aznar pushed forward a proposal for such a list at the United Nations. This is part of an overall strategy in which the United Nations may be able to link anti-terrorism and access to development aid (*El Pais*, 7 May 2003: 27). Aznar was himself a target of terrorism in 1995 when ETA tried to assassinate him with a car bomb and he narrowly escaped. This might have compelled him to become one of the most prominent allies of the United States. The Seville European Council in June 2002 also reinforced the struggle against terrorism.

The main target of the international fight against terrorism is naturally the Islamic fundamentalist terrorist organisation Al Qaeda which perpetrated the terrorist attacks in New York. During the investigations, it was found out that Spain along with Germany were the two main countries, where Al Qaeda operatives prepared the terrorist attacks in the United States. Some weeks before the 11 September attacks, Mohamed Atta, one of the terrorists on board one of the planes which flew into the twin towers, was in Madrid and Tarragona respectively meeting several of the conspirators responsible for the attack. This news came as a shock for the Spanish secret services. Indeed, proximity to the southern Mediterranean countries and a vast illegal immigration population allowed for the preparation of operations inside Spain. There was also a Spanish–German connection of Al Qaeda operatives in preparing the attacks on the twin towers (*El Pais*, 14 October 2001: 31; *El Pais*, Domingo, 30 June 2002: 1–3; *El Pais*, 17 November 2002: 8).

On 24 January 2003, Spanish police undertook raids in Barcelona and Tarragona and was able to apprehend sixteen Algerians suspected of being members of Al Qaeda. Nevertheless, due to lack of evidence, these suspects had to be released, which was a major blow for the Spanish public prosecutor (*El Pais*, 22 June 2003: 24).

This ongoing international fight against terrorism under the leadership of the United States led to deployments of Spanish troops in Afghanistan and Iraq, where the American administration suspected links between the respective regimes and Al Qaeda. Such links could be proven in Afghanistan, but not in Iraq. In spite of the efforts of the international community, foreigners were targeted by five simultaneous car bomb attacks in Casablanca (Morocco) on 16 May 2003. Among the targeted buildings was the Spanish cultural centre, Casa de España. Forty-four people died in the explosions including two Spaniards. It clearly indicated that Al Qaeda had regained operative capability, creating major problems for the international coalition.

The Moroccan government condemned several Islamic extremists belonging to the Islamic fundamentalist group Salafia Jihadia. In total 134 persons were indicted of being directly or indirectly involved in the terrorist attacks. On 12 July 2003, the first thirty-four persons were sentenced by Moroccan courts. Ten of them were sentenced to death and the others received life sentences or very long sentences up to 20 years in prison. Some doubts, about the way the investigations were conducted, were presented by the lawyers of the accused. Nevertheless, it shows the determination of the Moroccan government to prevent Islamic fundamentalism from becoming a strong force in the country like in Algeria or Egypt (*El Pais*, 18 May 2003: 2–7; *El Pais*, 2 July 2003: 6; *El Pais*, 13 July 2003: 5).

One problem related to this anti-terrorist struggle is the fact that all European Union countries had to change their laws in order to introduce measures to combat alleged terrorism. This naturally included the restriction of some human rights which is very worrying, if this terrorist threat continues to be imminent (*El Pais*, 6 May 2003: 3).

Islamic terrorism gained a new dimension in the Spanish context after the Madrid bombings on 11 March 2004, 3 days before the crucial legislative elections. The '11 M' bombings, as they are referred to in Spain were not predicted by the Spanish secret services. As already-mentioned in previous chapters, some of the reasons for the failure to detect such a plot was an alienation between the government and the National Council of Inteligence (*Consejo Nacional de Inteligencia* – CNI). Just shortly before the 14 March 2004 legislative elections the government allegedly leaked classified secret information about a meeting between the Catalan *conceller en cap* (first minister) Albert Carod-Rovira with members of ETA in Perpignan in early January 2004, in which allegedly ETA would refrain from perpetrating acts of violence in Catalonia, in exchange for Catalan nationalist support for independence of the Basque country. Catalan President Pascual Maragall had no other option, but to ask for the resignation of Carod-Rovira, thereby weakening the Socialists before the crucial election of 14 March 2004 (Garcia-Abadillo, 2005: 169–73). Another factor that led to at least disruptions in the flow of information were the tensions between the Aznar government and Morocco in relation to the Western Sahara. In spite of the bombings in Casablanca and Marrakech in 2003, the flow of information between the secret services of the two governments suffered some delays, which contributed further to the failure to detect such a plot (Miguel, 2005: 43–4).

Although denied by the Aznar government, the support and participation of Spain in the Iraq War increased the risk for the country to acts of violence perpetrated by the Islamic terrorist organisation Al Qaeda. Al Qaeda is translated as the 'Network' and clearly it fits in the way they organise their terrorist actions. Although Osama bin Laden is regarded as the leader of the network, in reality it consists of several organisations that are only loosely connected through an anti-Western ideology and the dream of recreating an idealised caliphate which would unite the Arab world. Moreover, the ideology comprises a very archaic form of Islam. The geographic proximity of Spain to the Arab world, particularly the Maghreb, allows for many of these decentralised terrorist organisations to find refuge in the country, due to the high levels of police persecution to which they are subject in their own countries. Spain features as an important country for the imaginary of this terrorist organisations, because of the caliphate 'Al-Andaluz' that existed between the eighth and fifteenth centuries. Although there is a tendency to equate 'Al-Andaluz' with Andalusia, the reality is that these terrorist groups regard 'Al-Andaluz' as covering the whole of Spain. They have been successful in establishing cells in most European countries, in particular France, Spain, United Kingdom, Belgium and Germany, countries with large Islamic populations allow for the establishment of terrorist cells that can be activated at any time, when there is a planned terrorist attack. On the eve of the bombings there were at least three organisations with active cells in Spain: The Armed Islamic Group, Salaphist Group of Preaching and Combat, and the Moroccan Islamic Group of

Combat (de Aristegui, 2005: 310–11). While the Armed Islamic Group is active in Algeria, the two other groups are more keen to play an international role as a loose organisation in the network of Al Qaeda. The Salaphist Group of Preaching and Combat, which is well-entrenched in Spain is quite dangerous. The Moroccan Islamic Group of Combat is quite well-organised and has a vast infrastructure in Spain. Both belong to the more radical Salafyia Yihadia, which was involved in the bombings in Casablanca and Marrakech in 2003.

On 11 March 2004, Islamic terrorists detonated ten bombs with attached mobile phones in four trains which were arriving from the outskirts of the city at Madrid's Atocha station. Although not all bombs went off due to defected triggers, 191 persons died and 1,841 were hurt. Originally, the Aznar government blamed ETA. This was reinforced by the outright condemnation of the President of the Basque Country, Juan José Ibarretxe at 9.30 am. Soon, the president of the Basque Nationalist Party Josu Jon Imaz and the leader of the Catalan Republican Left Josep Carod i Rovira joined in condemning the Basque terrorist organisation (Garcia-Abadillo, 2005: 37–8). Only as the day progressed did it became clear that ETA was not the perpetrator, but Al Qaeda. Nevertheless, the government contacted all embassies and international missions blaming ETA for the terrorist acts. It led to the unanimous Resolution 1530 of the Security Council of the United Nations condemning the alleged act as being perpetrated by ETA, after considerable lobbying by the Spanish government. President George W. Bush also condemned ETA (Garcia-Abadillo, 2005: 47). However, at 1 pm Arnaldo Otegui, leader of the forbidden *Herri Batasuna*, the political arm of ETA, confirmed in a press conference that it was not the Basque terrorist organisation. He added that ETA does not target the working-class on their way to work (Garcia-Abadillo, 2005: 44). The discovery of a van with a video on which Islamic verses were recited further undermined the thesis that ETA was somehow involved.

In spite of the emerging evidence, several members of the Aznar government, such as Interior Minister Manuel Acebes and Foreign Affairs Minister Ana Palacios, continued to maintain that ETA as the perpetrator of the 11 March bombings. Although there was a growing number of indications that Al Qaeda was involved in the bombings, the Aznar government continued to hold on to just the ETA version. Such an explanation of events became problematic when the government held on to the ETA version in the subsequent days up until polling day. The opposition parties began to question this version of events. Particularly, main opposition leader José Luis Zapatero contacted the chief-editor of the newspaper *El Mundo* to say that he was sceptical of the governmental version of events and that his sources indicated Al Qaeda as being the main suspect (Garcia-Abadillo, 2005: 67–8). The Aznar government gave the impression that it wanted to cover up the emerging indications towards a plot perpetrated by Al Qaeda. Tensions between the two main parties, the Socialists and the People's Party, became quite evident on the eve of the polls, when normally campaigning is not allowed and there should be a day of reflection. As already-mentioned in Chapter 4, the behaviour of the government in the days after the most horrific terrorist act ever in Spain certainly contributed to the defeat in the 14 March 2004 elections. According to the journalist

Casimiro Garcia-Abadillo, the ETA version was propagated by Prime Minister José Maria Aznar, in order to prevent a connection of the population between the Spanish participation in the Iraq War and the Al Qaeda bombings (Garcia-Abadillo, 2005: 45–6).

After the victory of the Socialist party under the leadership of José Luis Zapatero in the general elections of 14 March 2004, one would assume that the People's Party under new leader Mariano Rajoy would work closely with the government to fight against the threat of Islamic terrorism. However, Rajoy continued to offer the theory, certainly influenced by former Prime Minister José Maria Aznar, that there was a link between ETA and Al Qaeda. Among the reasons for this new thesis was the fact that Etarras were serving in high security prisons with Al Qaeda terrorists. Therefore, the main opposition party PP continued a strategy of polarisation against the Socialist government. Rajoy maintained throughout the legislature period the theory that ETA was somewhat involved. Soon after Zapatero came to power, a parliamentary inquiry committee was set up to investigate the incidents which invited about 100 politicians, journalists, civil servants and other experts to give testimonials. The committee ended its work in December 2004, but its findings were only partially recognised by the PP. The thesis of involvement of ETA and allegations of manipulation of the electorate against the former government by the PP were expressed against the findings. This lack of consensus about 11-M between the two main parties has been a major problem for the fight against Islamic terrorism. The political divisions were not conducive to a more united front against the dangers of Islamic terrorism.

On 3 April 2004, the police were able to track down some of the leading perpetrators of the 11 March in the district of Lavapiés in Madrid. The attempt to storm the apartment by the police led to a collective suicide of the perpetrators by blowing themselves up. In total, six of the perpetrators killed themselves and seven other bodies were also found in the apartment (Garcia-Abadillo, 2005: 266).

After 2 years, finally the work of the police and judiciary were finished and the trial against twenty-nine indicted persons began. An informant of the Asturian police, called José Suarez Trashorras, who obtained the explosives for the terrorist cell was amongst those indicted. In early October 2006, top judge, Baltasar Garzón, found out, after cross-examining a team of police forensic experts, that they had done a forensic report linking ETA and Al Qaeda in terms of explosives used which was without scientific basis. It was a manipulation of the evidence. The politicisation of the investigation and the incrimination of forensic experts was a major twist in this version that ETA was somewhat involved (*El Pais*, 1 October 2006: 21–2; *El Pais*, 2 October 2006: 21–3). Such manipulation has to be understood in the context of the ongoing negotiations between the government and ETA towards negotiations after the declared truce by the terrorist organisation in March 2006. During this period The Association of Victims of Terrorism (AVT) staged demonstrations against the government in order to prevent negotiations with ETA (*El Pais*, 2 October 2006: 25).

Finally, the main trial came to an end on 24 July 2007 and sentencing took place in mid-October 2007. There were nineteen members of the terrorist group who were jailed with sentences reaching from 7 to 40 years. For the most important perpetrators such as the intellectual author Rabel Osman al Sayed, alias 'the Egyptian', and the real perpetrators, the Moroccans Jamal Zougam and Abdelmajid Bouchar, the prosecution had asked for a total of 38,952 years (*El Pais*, 25 July 2007: 16). The overall verdict, particularly in relation to Rabel Osman al Sayed, who had already been convicted for 10 years in Italy and therefore could not be convicted for the same crime in Spain, was disappointing for the victims.

In spite of withdrawal of the troops from Iraq, Islamic terrorism continues quite active in the country. At the end of July of 2007, there were more jihadists in preventive emprisonment than ETA terrorists. Islamic terrorism posed a greater threat to the country than the domestic Basque terrorism. The main reason was that Al Qaeda's ideological simplified model of Islam was attractive to many young people. According to figures from *El Pais*, there were 200 prisoners in preventive custody, out of 116 (58 per cent) were yihadists. Although it is always difficult to make generalisations about the yihadists in Spain, these figures show that there is a strong recruitment among the Moroccan and Algerian immigrant population. Spaniards are about 10 per cent of these detainees, which shows that such ideology has only a very limited impact on young Spaniards. (Figure 10.7.). If we take also the place of birth then only 4.3 per cent were born in Spain. Most yihadists were born in Morocco or Algeria. (Figure 10.8.). Last but not least, the age profile of

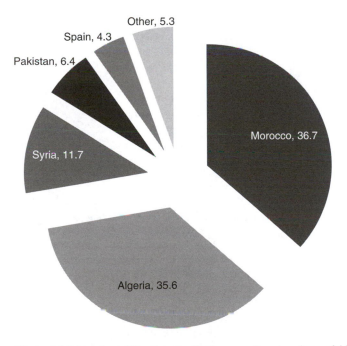

Figure 10.7 Detained Yihadists in Spain according to place of birth (2001–2005) in percentage.

Source: Dirección General de Instituciones Penitenciarias quoted from *El Pais*, 29 July 2007: 22.

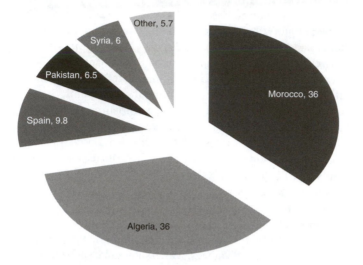

Figure 10.8 Detained Yihadists in Spain according to Nationality (2001–2005) in percentages.

Source: Dirección General de Instituciones Penitenciarias quoted from *El Pais*, 29 July 2007: 22.

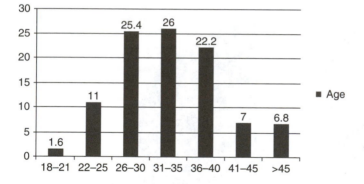

Figure 10.9 Detained Yihadists in Spain according to Age (2001–2005) in percentages.

Source: Dirección General de Instituciones Penitenciarias quoted from *El Pais*, 29 July 2007: 22.

these detainees shows that the vast majority are mature men. Over 63 per cent are aged between 26 and 40 years old (Figure 10.9.). The Iraq and Afghanistan wars have increased the level of recruitment for Al Qaeda-affiliated groups. In early January 2006, the Catalan police was able to capture the Moroccan, Oman Nakhcha, who is 33 years old. (*El Pais*, 13 January 2006: 21). Already during 2005, the national operation Tigris targeted this network of recruitment. In spite of the successes of the Spanish police, the threat alert continues high in the country. On 17–18 January Spanish police was able to dismantle a terrorist cell by arresting fourteen alleged Islamic terrorists, who planned to bomb one of the main buildings in Barcelona.

In spite of this fight against Islamic terrorism, the Zapatero government was very keen to create good relations with the Muslim community, in order to avoid their alienation from the Spanish political system. Apart from the fact that Spain is moving towards a multicultural society with all its advantages and disadvantages, the Muslim community in the vast majority is interested in isolating those who perpetrate acts of violence. This is also one of the reasons for the successes of the Spanish police against Islamic terrorism. In a survey on the Spanish Muslim community commissioned by the Ministry of Interior it shows that the vast majority feel integrated and are quite content to be in Spain. There is a general feeling that the Muslim community is treated equally in different institutions, such as hospitals. According to the figures, 83 per cent did not perceive any obstacles to practice its religion. Only about 13 per cent referred to some obstacles. However, the most important obstacle for the practice of religion are the lack of mosques (Ministerio del Interior, 2006) (see Figure 10.10).

Although there is still a lot to be done, the Spanish Muslim Community is well integrated in Spanish society. The integration policies of the Zapatero government were quite important in order to gain the trust of the vast majority of law-abiding Muslims. Moreover, the attempt of the government to push towards an aconfessional state, which gives equal attention to all religions has certainly contributed to a better integration of the spiritual leaders of the Muslim community. On the one hand, it is important to reduce the creation of cultural ghettos due to the lack of integration and allow Muslim men and women to be full citizens in a advanced society, on the other hand one has to prevent religious intolerance

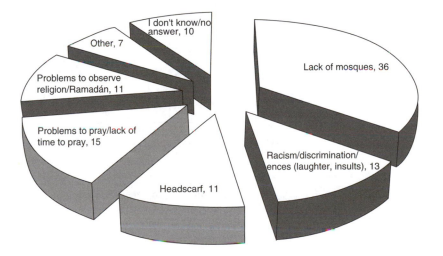

Figure 10.10 Perceived obstacles for the practice of religion among people who responded that there are such obstacles (2006).

Source: Ministry of Interior, 2006: Table 5.1.2.

in relation to traditional celebrations having any success. For example, Muslim protests against Christian celebrations of the *reconquista*, which were celebrated over centuries should not lead to change of lifestyles. On the contrary, the celebrations may highlight how historical enactment does no longer reflect the new multicultural Spanish society. Moreover, the introduction of Muslim celebrations, such as Ramadan or the feast of the lamb in regions such as Ceuta and Melilla, can only enrich Spanish society and increase tolerance for otherness thus undermining the position of Islamic fundamentalists (*El Pais*, 20 September 2007: 23).

One interesting finding of the above survey is that an overwhelming majority of the respondents think that Islam and Democracy are compatible. This is quite positive, because Spain and other European countries could show that their Muslim citizens are well integrated in their own national societies and able to influence political processes (see Figure 10.11).

In sum, the international war against terrorism is an open-ended, long-term operation. In Spain, the best ally is a well-integrated Muslim community which is able to separate religion as a private personal way of life and politics. This has to be accompanied by tolerance of otherness in overall society, so that fears based on ignorance are overcome. Successful Spanish governments have been quite successful in pushing forward an agenda of integration and tolerance, this is certainly paving the way for a richer qualitative democracy.

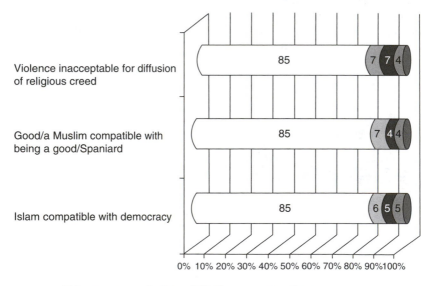

Figure 10.11 Different opinions on the relationship of religion and the political system (2006).

Source: Ministerio del Interior, 2006: Table 7.1.1.

Conclusions: a nation with international ambitions

Spanish foreign policy has made major transformations in the past three decades. After a long period of isolation during Francoism, Spain emerged as a country playing an important role in world politics. Between 1975 and 1985 one can characterise Spanish foreign policy as trying to find a place in the global order. After 1986, it became evident that Spain's future is at the heart of the European integration process. Such policy has been continuous in spite of different governments. The foundations for Spanish foreign policy both in institutional as well as substantial terms was laid down by the Gonzalez administration under foreign ministers Fernando Moran, Fernando Ordoñez and naturally Javier Solana. The self-confidence gained in the European arena led to a stronger engagement in the Mediterranean and Latin America.

There are slight differences between the foreign policy of the Gonzalez years and the Aznar years. The former was very keen to integrate itself completely in the projects of further European integration. The Franco-German axis was quite crucial for Spanish foreign policy. Aznar was more preoccupied with Spanish interests and has some reservations in supporting the Franco-German axis. Aznar found allies in the British Prime Minister Tony Blair and Italian Prime Minister Silvio Berlusconi. All three allied with the United States in the war against Iraq. Apart from the Iraq war, the conflict over Perejil and the disappointment with the British government in relation to Gibraltar showed that Aznar's foreign policy was very much still dominated by national interest. The foreign policy of the Zapatero government was a return to the multilateral approach of Felipe Gonzalez, whom Prime Minister Zapatero regards as a model and mentor.

The ambitions of Spain in world politics are limited by the fact that financially the country cannot afford a similar engagement as the United Kingdom, France or even Germany. This naturally makes it even more imperative that Spain uses its resources to reinforce the European integration process in the fields of security and foreign policy. Such a pattern has been re-emerging after the Iraq war. The Zapatero government pushed forward new initiatives such as the Alliance of Civilisations and initiated the process of reform of the Spanish foreign service.

In terms of defence policy, successive Spanish governments emphasised continuity. Problems of recruitment after the end of the conscription led to the introduction of reform, but it is still too early to tell, if this will lead to success. In terms of armament, Spain has become an exporter of weapons. The integration of Spanish firms such as CASA in international armaments networks allowed for the creation of a viable armaments industry, which is more and more part of an emerging long term European global strategy.

11 The quality of democracy in Spain
Some concluding remarks

One of the most quoted slogans during the authoritarian dictatorship to describe the then existing gap between Spain and most other west European countries was *España es diferente* (Spain is different) (Carr, 1999: 721). Throughout the past three decades the development of democracy and the narrowing of the cultural gap has made Spain similar to other west European democracies. Although the Spanish GDP per capita is still 80 per cent of the EU average, Spain changed qualitatively in the past two and a half decades, contradicting very much the slogan of the authoritarian regime. Nevertheless, whenever tourists come to Spain they realise that Spain is quite different from the rest of Europe. This is not related to economic development or the quality of democracy, but the way Spanish people live and think. Indeed, Spanish people did not converge in terms of the way they organise their daily life. The routine of Spanish life, that is predominantly that of the centre and in the south, is still characterised by late lunches (1.30–2pm) and late dinners (9–10pm). On hot summer days, there is almost no activity between 2 and 5pm. This different daily routine shows that Spain still retains many features of its inherited way of life. This rather superficial observation can be substantiated by other observations which led to the establishment of a vibrant peaceful democracy.

In contrast to Portugal and Greece, the Spanish transition to democracy was undertaken and controlled by the authoritarian elites of the regime in conjunction with the opposition. It was a consensual process towards a *ruptura pactada* (an agreed break). This lack of internationalisation of the Spanish transition to democracy makes it even more unique. It shows that the domestic actors were strong enough to make conscious decisions to move towards a better, more open regime without creating a divided country. The main reason for the success of Spanish democracy was the fact that the past was so full of historical failures – which ended in one of the most horrific civil wars of contemporary history. The fratricidal imagery shaped the transition of democracy and the way politics is done in Spain. The constitution has a very high symbolic value, so that it is quite difficult for the political class to make changes to it. It is a document that brought together the two Spains – the conservative, predominantly rural, Catholic and monarchic Spain and the progressive, urban, anti-clerical and republican Spain – and created a new political language and culture around it. The Spanish historical past, the successes and failures, are inherent in the way the Spanish political elite and the population think about themselves and the world.

The sense of failure created a solidarity among Spaniards with other people who are suffering around the world. It is an overwhelmingly peaceful society as the demonstrations against the Iraq war throughout early 2003 have shown. Former Prime Minister Aznar's support of the Iraq war even led to resignations of members of government who were not able to keep supporting the war against their conscience. After Prime Minister Zapatero came to power, a survey conducted by the prestigious Real Institute Elcano of International and Strategic Studies, a majority support a foreign policy based on 'disinterested internationalism', in spite of the fact that a quite strong minority was supportive of a foreign policy defending the national interest (see Chapter 10). It shows that there is a strong willingness to support international development cooperation, however one large part of the population is more conservative in this matter and its thinking is framed by a narrower view of the national interest. In short, Spanish society is divided along the left–right axis. The policies of the Aznar government and PP in general are more Atlanticist and dominated by the national interest, also in the European Union context. The PSOE and IU tend to advocate a more Europeanist foreign policy based on the already-mentioned 'disinterested internationalism'.

Another feature that makes Spain different from other countries is that it once had a large empire and knows that suffering can be caused when such an empire begins to decay until it is completely lost. This decline in the importance of Spain in the world was halted after 1978. Indeed, the new democratic regime re-created the foreign policy of the country. In this regard, the Socialist governments under Felipe Gonzalez opened up Spain to the world, both in economic as well as in political terms. The full commitment to European integration and the establishment of a Community of Ibero-American nations, which includes the always reluctant Iberian Portugal, re-established the importance of Spain in global terms. Spain became the European leader of investment in Latin America, thus creating a major transnational corporation, Telefonica. Aznar's foreign policy did not change very much in this respect, apart from the fact that he emphasised more on the special relationship with the United States. While all countries have a special relationship with the United States due to their superpower status, the network of relationships with Latin America (or Ibero-America as the Spaniards call it) is in European perspective unique. Portugal also has ambitions, but it is too small and again too focused on Brazil to match the Spanish efforts. This strong presence in Latin America has been consistent. The Zapatero government continued this policy towards Latin America, which includes also a growing interest in Brazil. The visit of the Brazilian President Lula da Silva to Spain in November 2007 was taken very seriously by the Spanish business community, which recognises the huge market that Brazil represents. A strategic alliance between these new democracies and important economies was forged in Madrid (see Chapter 10).

Even during the Argentina crisis in November–December 2001, the Spanish government and Spanish firms tried their best to help the country. This shows that the relationship with Latin America is something Spaniards are very proud of and want to make permanent and sustainable.

This international positive projection of Spain has to be understood in the context of domestic politics. The transition to democracy led to the establishment of a new pluralist Spain, in which different historic nations are living together. The constitutional compromise, related to the territorial structure of the country which was summarised in the formula of state of autonomies, led to an exciting adventure of decentralisation. It contributes to a very vivid and diverse country which is evolving towards an asymmetrical federalism, in spite of the fact that such a formula is not enshrined in the constitution. This state of autonomies is well liked by the vast majority of the population. Indeed, it has led to the creation of both regionalist-nationalist parties, such as the CiU in Catalonia and the PNV in the Basque Country, and mere regionalist small parties such as the UPN in Navarre or the PAR and the CHA in Aragon. Spain is a decentralised unitary state and unique in Europe in this respect. Neither Germany, nor Austria, nor Belgium – all three federal systems – can be compared with the Spanish case. Spain may have some similarities to German cooperative federalism, but it is still characterised partially by competitive federalism.

The main reason is that, apart from the constitutional limbo in terms of federalism, the whole system of multi-level governance between the different layers of government is still in the making. As Tanja Börzel (2000) revealed, Europeanisation has contributed to a transformation from competitive to cooperative federalism. In some way, Spain bears many similarities to the United Kingdom after devolution. Scotland, Wales and Northern Ireland can be compared easily to Catalonia, Galicia and the Basque Country. Both Northern Ireland and the Basque Country are characterised by a divisive society, of which parts may look to violence and terrorism to achieve their aims. The discussion on the establishment of English regions further confirms this trend towards decentralisation similar to the Spanish case. Similarities can be found to Italy, which since the mid-1990s is in the process of upgrading regionalisation in the direction of the Spanish example.

Prime Minister Zapatero was very keen to qualitatively change the relationship between the centre and the periphery. The conference of presidents became a new institution, which allows for a more regular exchange of information and common decision-making at the highest levels. After long negotiations in 2005 and 2006, the Catalan Statute was finally ratified, although the PP submitted an appeal to the Constitutional Court in this matter. Zapatero's negotiating skills led to a better relationship between centre and periphery in the Catalan case. This was facilitated by the historical coalition government of the Catalan Socialists with the historical Catalan Republican Party (ERC) and United Left-Greens (IC-V). The Catalan statute highlights also the importance of constitutionality in any review of regional institutions. CiU under the leadership of Artur Mas achieved an upgrading of the competences of Catalonia, but without transpassing the limits set by the constitution. In contrast, both PP and PSOE reject any calls for independence from the Basque government under Juan José Ibarretxe. The review of the Basque statute was rejected in February 2004 by Spanish Parliament, because of its unconstitutional wish to move to independence through an interim association agreement. It means that after three decades, Spanish law makers kept any advancement of autonomy of historical regions within the boundaries of the constitution. However, any attempts to impose rigidly independence claims is outrightly rejected by the main parties in Madrid. Moreover, independence may not have the majority necessary neither in the Basque Country nor in Catalonia. The quest for independence is even more complicated by the fact that it refers also to Navarre and parts of the southwestern French territories.

The establishment of a constitutional monarchy after democratic transition makes Spain also quite different from other countries which underwent similar transitions. The best example is naturally Greece, where the monarchy compromised with the previous authoritarian regime and was rejected by the population in a referendum in December 1974. King Juan Carlos I has been characterised by Charles Powell (1996) as the pilot of transition. Indeed, he was instrumental in pushing forward the agenda of democratisation with the prime minister of his choosing, Adolfo Suarez. They both surprised the world in achieving a successful transition to democracy. King Juan Carlos is extremely well-liked by the population. This became evident when he defended the democratic institutions against a coup attempt organised by Colonel Antonio Tejero on 23 February 1981. Today the King is still the 'institution' with the highest values.

In party-political terms, Spain is evolving more and more towards a two-party system, in spite of a proportional representation system based on a d'Hondt formula. The main reasons for this, as mentioned in Chapter 4, are the small constituencies which create the effect of a plural electoral system. In this sense, there is a growing polarisation between the two Spains. In the founding elections there were, at least, four main parties, the PSOE, the UCD, the AP-PP and the PCE. A four-party system remained up until 1993, due to the fact that Adolfo Suarez decided to create the CDS after 1982 with the remnants of the UCD. Today, there are only three parties: the PSOE, the PP and the IU. The latter is holding on with difficulties. Before the general elections of 9 March 2008, IU protested about the way surveys were undertaken which framed the whole electoral process in bipolarisation terms, ignoring other political parties (*El Pais*, 17 February 2008). It is difficult to predict if it will survive this continuing polarisation.

The Spanish party system is also unique, because it has created a centralist-regionalist divide. There are over ten regionalist parties in the Cortes and they represent in total 10–11 per cent of the electorate. They are important in the respective regions. In this sense, there are seventeen electoral Spains (*Españas electorales*) as defined by Vallés (1991). Similarities can be found again in the United Kingdom, although it created only three more distinctive electoral systems for Scotland, Wales and Northern Ireland in comparison to national elections. Although there is a lack of regionalist parties (with the exception of the Christian-Social Union (CSU) in Bavaria), Spain is closest to Germany with sixteen different regional party systems. These eighteen electoral arenas (seventeen regional and one national) influence each other. One could speak of a nationalisation of regional politics and a regionalisation of national politics, both processes feed each other. Probably, the clearest examples were during the last Gonzalez and the first Aznar governments, both highly dependent of support from regionalist parties in the Spanish parliament. There were also trade-offs at regional level, like between CiU and PP in Catalonia between 1999 and 2003.

One interesting characteristic of Spanish politics is the strong position of the prime minister, who is called in Spain *El presidente de gobierno* (president of government). The electoral system has normally created strong majorities, but even minority governments may survive, because of the constructive motion of censure which has to be submitted to parliament. It means that the prime minister can only be overthrown, if the opposition is able to name an alternative candidate for the job and eventually present a programme. This presidentialisation, which can be found in other countries such as the United Kingdom, Italy, Austria and Germany, allows for a high level of concentration of powers in the hands of the prime minister (van Biezen and Hopkin, 2005).

Spanish society is becoming similar to other European societies. In particular, individualisation is increasing fast, while the nuclear family, as well as the extended family, is beginning to be replaced or complemented by other lifestyles. According to the census of the population of 2001, the number of households with one member increased from 9.9 per cent in 1981 to 20.7 per cent. Such an increase was also registered in households with two people increasing in the same period from 20.9 per cent to 25.2 per cent. At the same time, there was a decrease in households with five members and more than six members from 14 per cent and 13.2 per cent to 7.7 per cent and 3.8 per cent respectively. The households with three members have increased only slightly from 19.5 per cent to 21.1 per cent (*El Pais*, 7 April 2003: 35). Divorce has increased substantially, although still not reaching the levels found in the Nordic countries and the United Kingdom (*El Pais*, 19 December 2001: 38). One of the most positive developments in Spanish society is the improved role of women in society and politics since democracy arrived. Indeed, after decades of authoritarianism where the family model was paternalist, women began to gain their place in public life in the 1960s. The Socialist government created in the 1980s the so-called Institute for Women (*Instituto de la Mujer*), which is regionalised, to promote the role of women in Spanish society and politics. Spanish women are slowly occupying important positions across the country. Spain has the largest number of female members in the lower house of parliament along with Austria, Germany, the Netherlands, Finland, Denmark and Sweden (see Chapter 4).

Although the role of Spanish women has improved considerably in the past three decades, there are still considerable inequalities in the labour market. Apart from the fact that the employment rate of women is lagging behind that of men, there is still discrimination of pay for the same job. Gender mainstreaming is still in the making and more efforts have to be made in order to increase the equality of opportunities. In the author's view, there is a big gap between the substantially improved position of women in politics and the reality in society in general. Today women remain disadvantaged in the labour market, including access to public administration higher-ranking positions (5 March 2005: 30).

One of the saddest aspects of Spanish society is the continuing high level of domestic violence against women. The number of tragic cases of women who are hurt and killed by their husbands is something negative in present Spanish society. The fast-track divorces approved by the Zapatero government were designed to protect such vulnerable women. In spite of the high number of such tragic incidents, one should not put this out of context (*El Pais*, Domingo, 25 March 2007). Domestic violence is a worldwide phenomenon that can be found in all societies from East Timor to Sweden.

One particular factor affecting democracy in Spain is the fact that income distribution has still high levels of inequality when compared to the EU average, the Nordic countries and the Continental European countries. In 2004, there was a difference of 5.1 times between the highest and lowest income. Taking Denmark as a comparison the difference is only 3.4 times, Germany 4.4 times and the United Kingdom 5.3 times. This becomes even more important, because about 20 per cent of the population in spite of being recipients of social security benefits is at risk of falling into the poverty trap. Spain falls into a group of countries which have a similar level of unequal income distribution and people living on the poverty line (European Commission, 2007a: 129). This is reinforced by the fact that anti-poverty programmes are tackled quite differently from region to region. The highest subsidies are paid in the Basque Country, Navarre and Madrid, which are also among the richest regions, while the southern regions have lower subsidies. The main reason is that decentralisation, which started in the 1980s, contributed to these differences in tackling poverty. Spain belongs to a group of EU countries such as Portugal, Greece, the United Kingdom and Ireland with the highest level of poverty. This is certainly a major obstacle for equality of opportunities and the quality of social and political citizenship for this part of the population (*El Pais*, 15 October 2001: 37). This certainly affects any attempts to empower this part of the population for the democratic project started in 1978.

According to a major study undertaken by the Fundación La Caixa which led to the compilation of a Social Yearbook of Spain in 2000 and 2001, there are still huge differences in welfare across Spain. The index of welfare includes data on wealth, health, the health service, levels of education, levels of employment, working conditions, housing, security and environment and shopping accessibility. The authors analysed over 406,737 data units comprising the 3,000 Spanish municipalities. In the end, an index was created which ranked the autonomous communities from 1 (minimum social welfare) to 10 (maximum social welfare). In spite of differences between 2000 and 2001, the division between richest and poorest Spanish regions is still quite wide (*El Pais*, 17 January 2002: 25). Such territorial inequalities continue to be a reality in Spain. It affects also the access to health, education and even to the media.

Another major aspect, which is less studied and is covered mainly by journalists, is informal politics. The networks of power have links to the authoritarian past and found some continuity between the old and new regimes. They involve prominent politicians, businessmen and naturally media tycoons. There are several networks that have considerable power in Spain and are part of the so-called power elite.

American-style lobbying has become an important phenomenon in contemporary Spanish politics. The privatisation of public enterprises during the 1980s and 1990s led to a vast economy of spoils used extensively by the Socialist and the PP governments (Tijeras, 2000). This is not a Spanish phenomenon, but clearly played a part in the enrichment of many people. The establishment of an Anti-Corruption Office (*Fiscalia Anti-Corrupción*) in 1996 was regarded as a major step in the right direction. Since then, the office under the leadership of Carlos Jimenez Villarejo has been able to investigate several cases of fraud that have led to convictions.

The success rate has been quite good: out of thirty-three cases investigated, twenty-nine led to convictions. The Fiscalia investigated cases related to Luis Roldán, the former Chief of the Civil Guard, Mario Conde, the Ex-president of Banesto, Luis Pascual Estevill, a judge involved in corruption, and the former Mayor of Marbella, Jesus Gil. The establishment of the Fiscalia was related to the emergence of so many corruption scandals during the last years of the Socialist government. Nevertheless, since 1997, the number of cases has been increasing again. In spite of that, the government with the support of the regionalist parties, the CiU, the PNV and the CC, introduced new legislation limiting the freedom of the prosecutors. Indeed, now the Anti-Corruption Office has to inform the person who is being investigated throughout the whole process. The process is now limited to 6 months. This means that the Anti-Corruption Office is not able to investigate without the knowledge of the alleged perpetrator. Moreover, the 6-month limit severely hinders any attempt of proper investigation, which as a rule-of-thumb lasts for years. The recent events in Madrid related to misappropriation of funds by the former PP mayor of Madrid José Maria Alvarez del Manzano and the alleged corruption of two Socialist MPs in the Madrid Community elections show that such an Anti-Corruption Office is very important to achieve high standards in Spanish democracy (*El Pais*, Domingo, 1 June 2003: 6–8; *El Pais*, 16 June 2003: 15).

The overall international thrust to step up the fight against corruption has led to some spectacular operations in Spain. Among the most prominent were Operation Malaya that led to the dismantling of the network of systemic corruption in Marbella, which had also links to international criminal organisations and Operation White Whale (*Ballena Blanca*) against money-laundering. The number of cases of municipal corruption that have come to light in the past five years has been substantial and shows that democratisation and the implementation of rule of law are still lagging behind at local level. Spain is an attractive place for all kinds of criminal organisations, *El Pais* refers to *la costa del crimen*, because most criminal organisations are based in the cities on the Mediterranean coast. Money laundering takes place in the tourism and construction industries (Sands, 2007; Gomez, 2005).

Islamic terrorism has become a preoccupation of Spanish governments. Shortly before the 9 March general elections, the Spanish government reinforced security in order to prevent a catastrophic event similar to that of 11 March 2004. The Zapatero government was very active in the fight against Islamic terrorism and has achieved to detained a considerable number of so-called Yihadists. The Socialist government was very keen to keep a positive dialogue with the Muslim community, so that it feels integrate and is supportive of the fight against terrorism.

A worrying sign in present Spanish politics is the high level of polarisation between the two main parties. The consensual style of politics which existed until the mid-1990s is less visible in the present. One example is the blocking of the re-appointment of judges in the Constitutional Court and the Higher Council of Judicial Power by the PP. Behind it, is the calculation of PP, that in the event that they come back to power after the general elections of 9 March 2008, that they will be able to impose a positive settlement for them. On the other side, the gay marriages law, the fast-track divorce and the reform of education have led to considerable opposition of the more conservative circles of society, particularly the Church. As Georgina Blakeley rightly analysed, there seems to be a gap emerging between the political elites and the population. While the population wants to initiate a process of reconciliation which includes a painful uncovering of the truth about the Republic, the Civil War and Francoism, the political elites still seem to be stuck in a discourse of the past, in which left and right tend to see what they like and ignore what they dislike (Blakeley, 2005). It may be, that after 30 years, that the political elite will now be taught by an emerging civil society the way forward to bring Spain to qualitative new level of democratic politics.

In sum, Spanish contemporary politics has converged towards other older European democracies. In the process it created a new political system that is quite original in its outcome. Somehow, Spaniards learned from history and decided to move towards a more diverse Spain, acknowledging all their different nationalities and groups. Socially and economically, Spain has a weaker economy than most other west European countries, but makes efforts to close the gap. In spite of all the difficulties encountered in redefining its identity, Spaniards looked forward without forgetting their glorious, but also painful, historical development. These are the ingredients that make contemporary Spanish politics more vibrant, lively and interesting than ever before. In 2008, the thirtieth anniversary of the original Spanish constitution, Spain has fulfilled some of the promises that such a new political system hoped to achieve. This became quite evident in the sport, particularly the crowning of the Spanish team as European champions in the football European championships and the victory of Rafael Nadal of Wimbledon, the first Spaniard to do so. All these success gives an indication of a new self-confident nation, which is slowly fulfilling all the hopes and promises that the fathers of the 1978 Constitution had for their country.

Biographical notes

King Juan Carlos I Borbón y Borbón. Born in Rome in 1938. He lived in exile until the late 1940s. He studied at the academies of the Spanish Army, Navy and Air Force. He completed his studies in law and economics at the Complutense University in Madrid. In 1969, he was nominated as the successor of dictator Francisco Franco. After Franco's death he became the new King of Spain and steered the democratic transition. The new constitution of 1978 legitimised the re-establishment of the monarchy and Juan Carlos I as the formal head of state, which he has been for the past 30 years.

José Maria Aznar. Born in Madrid in 1953. He studied law and later on became an inspector of state finances. He joined the People's Alliance in 1979 and became president of the regional government of Castilla León after the elections of 1987. In 1990, he became leader of the People's Party and led the party to victory on 3 March 1996. He became Prime Minister on 5 May 1996. He was able to achieve a second term with an absolute majority on 3 March 2000. He stepped down as Prime Minister in April 2004, and became President of the new Foundation for Social Studies (*Fundación para Estudios Sociales* – FAES) attached to the PP.

Leopoldo Calvo Sotelo. Born in Madrid in 1926. He was a civil engineer by profession. He was an MP (*procurador*) in the Cortes during the authoritarian regime. He was close to the monarchist movement during the dictatorship. He held several positions as a minister during Adolfo Suarez's governments between 1976 and 1981. He replaced Adolfo Suarez as Prime Minister on 26 February 1981. He stepped down after the defeat of the ruling party, the Union of Democratic Centre (UCD).

Santiago Carrillo. Born in Gijón (Asturias) in 1915 and was Secretary General of the PCE between 1960 and 1982. He became a crucial politician in the transition to democracy. He was instrumental in moderating the discourse of the Communist Party. He left the party in 1985 and joined the Socialist Party in 1990.

Manuel Fraga Iribarne. Born in Villalba in 1922. He studied law and political science and became a prominent politician of the Francoist regime. He was an

MP in the Francoist Cortes, a diplomat, a lecturer in several Spanish universities and occupied several positions in the Francoist bureaucracy. In 1962, he became Minister for Information and Tourism. He was instrumental in liberalising the press laws and promoting Spain as a tourist destination. He was Deputy Prime Minister in the Arias Navarro government of 1975–76. During the transition to democracy, he founded the People's Alliance which he led up until 1987. In 1989, he initiated the re-foundation of the AP, creating the People's Party. In the same year, he was elected with an absolute majority to the presidency of the regional government of Galicia between 1989 and 2005. In the June 2005 Galician elections, he achieved a strong relative majority, but had to step down, because the opposition was able to form a coalition.

Francisco Franco. Born in El Ferrol (Galicia) in 1892 and died in Madrid in 1975. He ruled as dictator between 1939 and 1975 and established an authoritarian regime, after defeating the Republicans in the Civil War. Until the mid-1950s, his policies were characterised by isolationism. The Cold War made him a vital ally of the American administration against the Soviet bloc. He initiated the process of economic and social development in the 1960s.

Felipe Gonzalez. Born in Seville in 1942. He studied law in Seville and became a labour lawyer. He became leader of the PSOE in September 1974 and became Prime Minister on 2 December 1982 with an overwhelming victory. He remained Prime Minister until 1996, when the PSOE was defeated by the PP of José Maria Aznar. He remained leader of the party until 1998 and was replaced by Joaquin Almunia. He remains an eminence grise in the PSOE.

Alfonso Guerra. Born in Seville in 1940. He became an industrial engineer and obtained a degree in philosophy and humanities. He became a member of the PSOE in 1960. He occupied several positions within the party since 1970. In 1982, he became Deputy Prime Minister in the Gonzalez government. Due to a corruption scandal involving his brother Juan, he had to resign as Deputy Prime Minister in 1991. Since then he has concentrated on work inside the party.

Gaspar Llamazares. Born in Logroño (La Rioja) on 28 November 1957. He studied medicine and became a doctor. He has been general coordinator of the United Left coalition since 2000.

Jordi Pujol. Born in Barcelona in 1930. Studied medicine in Barcelona. He became a member of the university Christian Catalan movement and took part in the clandestine Catalan opposition movement against Franco. He was the founding member of *Convergencia Democratica de Catalunya* in 1974 and president of the Catalan Generalitat (1980–2003). He was a major protagonist in strengthening the Europe of the Regions.

Mariano Rajoy Brey. Born in Santiago de Compostela on 27 March 1955. He studied law in the University of Santiago de Compostela. He became a civil servant in the land registry office. He became regional MP in 1981 and Secretary General of AP in Galicia. Between 1986 and 1987, he was Vice-President of the regional government in Galicia. Between 1989 and 1996 he was MP in the Congress of Deputies. Between 1996 and 2004 he was a crucial ally of Prime Minister José Maria Aznar. He was Minister of Public Administrations and later on Minister of Education and Culture. In the second Aznar government, he became Deputy Prime Minister and Minister of Interior. Since 3 September 2003 he has held the office leader of PP.

Adolfo Suarez. Born in Avila in 1932. He studied law and became a lawyer and was an important figure under Francoism. He was an MP (*procurador*) in the Cortes of the Franco regime, Director-General of the Spanish public television RTVE and Secretary General of the single-party National Movement. On 5 July 1976, he was nominated by King Juan Carlos I as Prime Minister and prepared the transition to democracy. His party, the Union of Democratic Centre, was pivotal in achieving a consensual constitutional settlement and transition between the old Francoist elites and the opposition. He resigned from office on 29 January 1981. Afterwards he founded a new party, the Democratic and Social Centre (CDS), which became the fourth largest party up until 1993, when it collapsed. Since then Suarez has been retired from politics.

José Luis Rodriguez Zapatero. Born on 4 August 1960. He studied law and became a lawyer and has been Secretary General of the PSOE since the thirty-fifth party conference in 2000. He was an MP between 1986 and 2004. He became Prime Minister after the general elections of 14 March 2004 and reelected after the elections of March 2008.

Notes

1 The transformation of Spanish politics

1 This first Carlist war became internationalised when the Holy Alliance, under the leadership of Prince Metternich, the Austrian Foreign Minister, and international supporters of the liberals intervened in the war. It was clearly an antecedent of the internationalisation of the Spanish Civil War between 1936 and 1939 (Bernecker, 1990: 64).
2 The term *cacique* is a derivation from *cacicato* and *caciquel*, words of Amerindian origin encountered by Spaniards in Santo Domingo in the late fifteenth century. A *cacique* was a chief or an owner of serfs in the New World, but in Spain the word quickly came to refer to royal agents. Later on, it applied to anyone with more than normal power or independence, although it continued to be related to persons being close to or having political power (see Kern, 1974: 14–15).
3 According to Sebastian Balfour the main mobilisation of electoral politics was in the larger cities, while the mainly rural society was detached from the whole political process. Society was largely immobile (Balfour, 1997: 104).
4 An excellent book on the ideological origins of Franco's state makes the point that actually many ideas were taken from right-wing monarchist theorists who wanted a re-installation of a conservative monarchy (Robinson, 1970; 1975).
5 According to surveys over 1.5 million persons emigrated to Switzerland, Germany and France between 1960 and 1972. This had naturally an impact on the country, because these emigrants were able to come back and speak about the way they lived in other countries (Garcia et al., 1996: 593–96).

2 The main features of contemporary political culture

1 This concept is taken from Kenneth Dyson and Kevin Featherstone (1996) who used it in relation to the way the European Union contributed as a vincolo esterno (external link) to push the Italian political elites to implement the Maastricht criteria, so that Italy would qualify for the first wave of Economic and Monetary Union. One can make a similar assessment for the Spanish case.

3 The core Spanish institutions

1 Alfonso XIII simply walked out of his job in 1931 allowing the vacuum to be filled by the Second Republic. He never formally abdicated until 1941 shortly before his death when he was forced to do so through ill health. His son Don Juan, Count of Barcelona, was the legitimate heir. Don Juan agreed to send his son, Juan Carlos, to be educated at school in Spain and then in the military academies as well as university. Because Don Juan was very intransigent in relation to Franco, the dictator began to prepare Juan Carlos

for succession. In the 1960s and 1970s Juan Carlos was well integrated into the structures of Francoism. In 1969 he was declared successor of Franco. This led to a major feud between Don Juan and Juan Carlos, which was only solved in 1977 when Don Juan formally renounced his claim to the throne.

2 In terms of power networks, the judiciary are not very well represented beyond the judiciary sector. There are very few judges among political and economic elites (Baena del Alcazar, 2002: 92–4).

4 Political parties and elections

1 The controversies over the law of political parties could be observed in the General Council of Judiciary Power (CGPJ) which was quite divided in its positive decision towards it. The overall vote was eleven for the law (mainly the conservative judges) and eight against (the so-called progressive votes) (El Pais, 16 April 2002: 17).

2 These figures are based on data provided by Mariano Torcal and Lucia Medina, 2002: 65.

3 For a study of the thirty-fourth party conference in June see the study by Mónica Mendez Lago and Julian Santamaria, 2001.

4 Felipe Gonzalez was offered the presidency of the party, but he rejected it to allow the new leader to have full powers in the transformation of the party (El Pais, 20 July 2000: 26).

9 The policy-making process

1 There are four European funds: the European Regional Development Fund (ERDF); the European Social Fund (ESF); the European Agricultural Guidance and Guarantee Fund (EAGGF) and the Financial Instrument for Fisheries Guidance (FIFG). Objective 1 is financed by ERDF, ESF, EAGGF and FIFG; objective 2 is financed by ERDF and ESF, while objective 3 is financed by ESF (European Commission, 2001a: 10).

2 INTERREG III promoted cross-border, transnational and inter-regional cooperation, through partnerships; LEADER brought together leading people in rural societies and economies to develop new strategies for sustainable development; URBAN 2 supported innovative strategies to regenerate cities and declining urban areas; EQUAL seeked to eliminate factors leading to inequalities and discrimination in the labour market (European Commission, 2001a: 12).

3 The main fish species that Spanish fishermen catch are tuna, mackerel and pilchard (European Commission, 2001g: 5).

4 During the Socialist governments several pieces of legislation were introduced to democratise access to education. Some of them had to be negotiated or led to conflicts with the Catholic Church. Among the pieces of legislation are: Law 8/1985 regulating the right to education (*Ley Organica del Derecho de Educación* – LODE); the Law of University Reform (*Ley de Reforma Universitaria* – LRU) also in 1985, the General Framework Law of the Education Sector (*Ley Organica General del Sistema Educativo* – LOGSE) which led to an expansion of compulsory education until 16 and abolished the dual system of academic vocational training towards a unified comprehensive system in secondary education. Last but not least, the Organic Law of Participation, Evaluation and Governance of the Teaching Centres (*Ley Organica de Participación, Evaluación y Gobierno de los Centros Docentes* – LOPEG) ensured more autonomy to the schools and also strengthened decentralisation of decision-making (Campo and Dura, 2002: 351).

10 Spanish foreign policy within the European Union

1 Mercosur was established on 26 March 1991 as an economic community and consists of four countries: Argentina, Brazil, Paraguay and Uruguay. Chile is an associate member and Venezuela became member in 2006.

2 Article 8 of the constitution   [Armed Forces]

(1) The Armed Forces, constituting the Land Army, the Navy and the Air Force, have as their mission the guarantee of the sovereignty and independence of Spain, the defence of its territorial integrity and the constitutional order.
(2) An organic law will regulate the bases of military organisation in conformity with the principles of the present Constitution.

References

Acuerdo Interconfederal para la Negociación Colectiva (ANC) (2003) Madrid website http://www.ceoe.es (accessed on 27 May 2003).

Adelantado, José, José Antonio Noguera and Xavier Rambla (1998) Las politicas de protección social: sistema de pensiones y prestaciones por desempleo. In: Ricard Gomá and Joan Subirats. *Politicas publicas en España. Contenidos, redes de actores y niveles de gobierno*. Barcelona: Ariel, pp. 200–22.

Agencia EFE (2006) *Anuario Iberoamericano 2006*. Madrod: Ediciones Piramide.

Agranoff, Robert and Gallarin Juan A. Ramos (1998) La evolución hacia una democracia federal en España: un examen del sistema de relaciones intergubernamentales. In: Robert Agranoff and Rafael Bañon i Martinez (eds), *El estado de las autonomias. ?Hacia un nuevo federalismo?*. Bilbao: Instituto Vasco de Administración Publica, pp. 55–103.

Agüero, Felipe (1995) *Militares, civiles y democracia: la España postfranquista en perspectiva comparada*. Madrid: Alianza Editorial.

Aguilar, Susana (1998) Las politicas de medio ambiente, entre la complejidad técnica y la relevancia social. In: Ricard Gomá and Joan Subirats (eds), *Politicas públicas en España. Contenidos, redes de actores y niveles de gobierno*. Barcelona: Ariel, pp. 249–68.

Aguilar Fernandez, Susana and Ana Ballesteros Peña (2004) Debating the concept of political opportunities in relation to the Galician social movement 'Nunca Mais'. In: *South European Society and Politics*, vol. 9, Number. 3, Winter, pp. 28–53.

Aguilera de Prat, Cesareo R. (2001) Los socialistas ante los pactos de gobernabilidad de 1993 y 1996. In: *Revista de Estudios Politicos*, 111, January–March, pp. 9–43.

Aguinaga Roustan, Josune (1997) Desarrollo e institucionalización del ambientalismo en España. In: José Felix Tezanos, José Manuel Montero and José Antonio Diaz (eds), *Tendencias de futuro en la sociedad española. Primer foro sobre tendencias sociales*. Madrid: Editorial Sistema, pp. 443–60.

Aja Eliseo (2003) *El Estado Autonomico. Federalismo y hechos diferenciales*. Madrid: Alianza.

Alberola Ila, Enrique (2002) La europeización de la politica macroeconómica. In: Carlos Closa (ed.), *La europeización del sistema politico español*. Madrid: Istmo, pp. 330–50.

Alcalde, Javier Villacampa (2003) Medios de comunicación como intermediarios del voto: la influencia de TV1 y Antena3 en las elecciones legislativas de 1993. In: *Revista Española de Investigaciones Sociológicas*, Number. 103–104, pp. 145–78.

Alcantara, Manuel and Antonia Martinez (eds) (1998) *Las elecciones autonómicas en España. 1980–1997*. Madrid: CIS.

Alcantara, Manuel and Antonia Martinez (2001) El Poder Judicial. In: Manuel Alcantara and Antonia Martinez (eds), *Politica y Gobierno en España*. Valencia: Tirant lo Blanch, pp. 243–65.

Alcubilla, Enrique Arnaldo (2002) Sobre la presentación y proclamación de candidaturas. In: *Revista de Estudios Politicos*, 117, July–September, pp. 145–71.

Alda Fernandez, Mercedes (2006) Los planes y programas conjuntos como instrumentos de cooperación intergubernamental. In: Lourdes Lopez Nieto (ed.), *Relaciones Intergubernamentales en la España Democrática. Interdependencia, Autonomia, Conflicto y Cooperación*. Madrid: Dykinson, pp. 133–46.

Alda Fernandez, Mercedes and Lourdes Lopez Nieto (2006) Los sistemas representativos y las relaciones intergubernamentales en el estado autonomico. In: Lourdes Lopez Nieto (ed.), *Relaciones Intergubernamentales en la España Democrática. Interdependencia, Autonomia, Conflicto y Cooperación*. Madrid: Dykinson, pp. 39–77.

Allué Buiza, Alfredo (2006) Relaciones gobierno-parlamento en el ambito autonomico. In: Pablo Oñate (ed.), *Organización y funcionamiento de los parlamentos autonómicos*. Valencia: Tirant lo Blanch, pp. 209–52.

Alonso, Rogelio (2007) La polarización en torno a la politica antiterrorist en España entre 2004 y 2006. In: Walther L. Bernecker and Günther Maihold (eds), *España: del consenso a la polarización. Cambios en la democracia española*. Frankfurt a. M.: Vervuert, pp. 119–44.

Alvarez-Miranda, Berta (1996) *El sur de Europa y la adhesión a la Comunidad. Los debates politicos*. Madrid: Centro de Investigaciones Sociologicas.

Amodia, José (1996) Spain at the polls: the elections of 3 March 1996. In: *West European Politics*, 19, 4 October, pp. 813–19.

Anduiza Perea, Eva (1999) *Individuos o sistemas? Las razones de la abstención en Europa occidental*. Madrid: CIS.

Anduiza Perea, Eva (2000) Los resultados electorales. In: Antonia Martinez and Monica Mendez (eds), *Las elecciones al parlamento europeo 1999*. Barcelona: Tirant lo Blanch, pp. 237–65.

Antoni, Michael (1981) *Spanien auf dem Weg zur parlamentarischen Demokratie. Parteien, Wahlen und politische Entwicklung 1975 bis 1980*. Frankfurt-am-Main: Peter D. Lang.

Anuario El Pais (2007). Madrid: El Pais.

Arahuetes, Alfredo (2002) Inversiones europeas en Iberoamerica, 1990–2000. In: *Perspectivas exteriores 2002. Los intereses de España en el mundo*. Edited by Fundación para las Relaciones Exteriores y el Dialogo Exterior (FRIDE). Madrid: FRIDE, pp. 251–71.

Associación para la Investigación de Medios de Comunicación (AIMC) (2007) *Audiencia de Internet* (November–December 2007). Madrid: AIMC.

Astudillo Ruiz, Javier (2001) Without unions, but socialist: the Spanish socialist party and first divorce from first union confederation. In: *Politics and Society*, 29, 2 June, pp. 273–96.

Atta, Sydney van (2003) Regional nationalist parties and new politics: the bloque Nacionalista Gallego and Plaid Cymru. In: *Regional and Federal Studies*, 13, 2, summer, pp. 30–56.

Badia, Miquel Caminal (1998) Catalanisme i autogovern. In: Miquel Caminal Badia and Jordi Matas Dalmases (eds), *El sistema politic de Catalunya*. Barcelona: Tecnos, pp. 25–53.

Badia, Miquel Caminal and Jordi Matas Dalmases (eds) (1998) *El sistema politic de Catalunya*. Barcelona: Tecnos.

Baena del Alcazar, Mariano (2002) Les élites espagnoles de la justice 1975–1982 et 1982–1996. In: *Pole Sud*, 16 May, pp. 79–94.

Balfour, Sebastian (1996) Bitter victory, sweet defeat. The March 1996 general elections and the new government in Spain. In: *Government and Opposition*, 31, 3, summer, pp. 275–87.

—— (1997) *The End of the Spanish Empire 1898–1923*. Oxford: Clarendon Press.

—— (2005) The reinventing of Spanish conservatism: the Popular Party since 1989. In: Sebastian Balfour (ed.), *The Politics of Contemporary Spain*. London: Routledge, pp. 146–68.

—— (2007) El Partido Popular a la busqueda de un nuevo papel politico. In: Walter C. Bernecker and Günther Maihold (eds), *España del consenso a la polarización. Cambios en la democracia española*. Madrid, Frankfurt a. M.: Iberoamericana, Vervuert, pp. 379–91.

Ballart, Xavier (2000) La administración de un presidente: Cataluña 1980–1997. In: Juan Luis Paniagua Soto (ed.), *Gobierno y administración en las comunidades autonomas. Andalucia, Canarias, Cataluña, Galicia y Pais Vasco*. Madrid: Tecnos, pp. 169–203.

Ballart, Xavier, Carles Ramió (2000) *Ciencia de la Administración*. Valencia: Tirant lo Blanch.

Banegas Nuñez, Jesus (2003) La TDT en España. Un reto superable. In: *Telos. Cuadernos de comunicación, tecnologia y sociedad*, Octubre–Diciembre, Number. 57.

Bañon, Rafael and Manuel Tamayo (1998) Las relaciones intergubernamentales en España: el nuevo papel de la administración central en el modelo de relaciones intergubernamentales. In: Robert Agranoff and Rafael Bañon i Martinez (eds), *El estado de las autonomias. ?Hacia un nuevo federalismo?*. Bilbao: Instituto Vasco de Administración Publica, pp. 105–59.

Bar, Antonio (1988) Spain. In: Jean Blondel and Ferdinand Müller-Rommel (eds), *Cabinets in Western Europe*. Basingstoke: Macmillan, pp. 102–19.

Baras, Montserrat and Jordi Matas Dalmases (1998) *Els partits politics i el sistema de partits*. In: Miquel Caminal Badia and Jordi Matas Dalmases (eds), *El sistema politic de Catalunya*. Barcelona: Tecnos, pp. 161–90.

Barbé, Esther (2000a) La PESC: desafios politicos y limites institucionales. In: Esther Barbé (ed.), *Politica exterior europea*. Barcelona: Ariel, pp. 107–28.

—— (2000b) Spain and CFSP: the emergence of a major player? In: Richard Gillespie and Richard Youngs (eds), *Spain: European and International Challenges*. Special Issue of *Mediterranean Politics*, 5, 2, pp. 44–63.

—— (2002) The Spanish presidency of the European Union 2002. In: *South European Society and Politics*, 7, 1 (summer), pp. 90–102.

Barnes, Samuel H. (1998) The mobilisation of political identity in new democracies. In: Samuel H. Barnes and Janos Simon (eds), *The Postcommunist Citizen*. Budapest: Erasmus Foundation, Institute of Political Science, Hungarian Academy of Sciences, pp. 117–37.

Barquero, Eugeni and Francesc Gusi (2007) La I+D Militar en el Estado Español (2000–2006). Arcadi Oliveres y Pere Ortega (eds), *El militarismo en España. Balance del ciclo armamentista español hasta 2007*. Barcelona: Icaria-Antrazyt, pp. 143–58.

Barrachina Lisón, Carles (2003) A retreat to the barracks: military and political changes in Spain (1976–1981). In: *BCN Political Science Debates*, pp. 67–117.

Barreiro, Belén (2002) La progresiva desmovilización de la izquierda en España: un analisis de la abstención en las elecciones generales de 1986 a 2000. In: *Revista Española de Ciencia Politica*, 6, April, pp. 183–205.

Barreñada, Isaias (2006) Alliance of civilizations, Spanish public diplomacy and cosmopolitan proposal. In: *Mediterranean Politics*, vol. 11, 1, pp. 99–104.

Basabe, Llorens Felipe and Maria Teresa Gonzalez Escudero (2001) The parliament of Spain: slowly moving onto the European direction? In: Andreas Maurer and Wolfgang Wessels (eds), *National Parliaments on their Ways to Europe: Losers or Latecomers?*. Baden-Baden: Nomos Verlag, pp. 199–222.

Baumer, Andreas (2007) De la polarización a la rupture: la derogación del consenso sobre la politica antiterrorista y el alto el fuego de ETA. In: Walter C. Bernecker and Günther Maihold (eds), España *del consenso a la polarización. Cambios en la democracia española*. Madrid, Frankfurt a. M.: Iberoamericana, Vervuert, pp. 145–66.

Bell, David S. (1983) The Spanish communist party in the transition. In: David S. Bell (ed.), *Democratic Politics in Spain*. New York: St Martin's Press, pp. 63–77.

Beltrán, Miguel (1993) The seventeen Spains. In: Richard Gunther (ed.), *Politics, Society, and Democracy*. Boulder, CO: Westview Press, pp. 214–32.

—— (2002) L'administration espagnole depuis la fin du franquisme. In: *Pôle Sud*, 16 May, pp. 65–77.

Ben-Ami, Shlomo (1983) *Fascism from Above. The Dictatorship of Primo de Rivera in Spain, 1923–1930*. Oxford: Clarendon Press.

Benton, Lauren (1989) *Invisible Factories and Industrial Development in Spain*. New York: State University of New York.

Beriain, Josetxo (1997) La construcción de la identidad vasca. In: Rafael Cruz and Manuel Perez Ledesma (eds), *Cultura y movilización en la España contemporanea*. Madrid: Alianza Editorial, pp. 137–68.

Bernecker, Walther L. (1982) *Colectividades y revolución social. El anarquismo en la guerra civil española, 1936–1939*. Barcelona: Critica.

—— (1984) *Spaniens Geschichte seit dem Bürgerkrieg*. Munich: Verlag C.H. Beck.

—— (1990) *Sozialgeschichte Spaniens im 19. und 20. Jahrhundert*. Frankfurt-am-Main: Suhrkamp.

—— (1998) Monarchie und Demokratie. Zur politischen Rolle von König Juan Carlos. In: Walther L. Bernecker and Klaus Dirscherl (eds), *Spanien heute. Politik, Wirtschaft, Kultur*. Frankfurt-am-Main: Vervuert, pp. 163–89.

—— (2002) Spanische Geschichte. *Von der Reconquista bis heute*. Darmstadt: Primus Verlag.

—— (2006) *Spanien-Handbuch. Geschichte und Gegenwart*. Opladen: UTB.

Blakeley, Georgina (2005) Digging up the Spain's past: consequences of truth and reconciliation. In: *Democratization*, vol. 12, 1, pp. 44–59.

Blanco, Valdés, Roberto L. (ed.) (2002) Galicia In: *Instituto de Derecho Publico, Informe de las comunidades Autonomas 2001*. Barcelona: Instituto de Derecho Publico.

—— (2003) Galicia. In: *Instituto de Derecho Publico, Informe de las Comunidades Autonomas 2002*. Barcelona: Instituto de Derecho Publico.

—— (2004) Galicia. In: *Instituto de Derecho Publico, Informe de las Comunidades Autonomas 2003*. Barcelona: Instituto de Derecho Publico.

—— (2005) Galicia. In: *Instituto de Derecho Publico, Informe de las Comunidades Autonomas 2004*. Barcelona: Instituto de Derecho Publico.

—— (2006a) Galicia. In: *Instituto de Derecho Publico, Informe de las Comunidades Autonomas 2005*. Barcelona: Instituto de Derecho Publico.

—— (2006b) *Introducción a la Constitución de 1978*. Madrid: Alianza.

Boix, Carles (1996) *Partidos politicos, crecimiento e igualdad. Estrategias economicas conservadoras y socialdemocratas en la economia mundial*. Madrid: Alianza Editorial.

Bonal, Xavier (1998) La politica educativa: dimensiones de un proceso de transformacion (1976–1996). In: Ricard Gomá and Joan Subirats (eds), *Politicas publicas en España. Contenidos, redes de actores y niveles de gobierno*. Barcelona: Ariel, pp. 153–75.

Bonet, Eduard, Irene Martín and José Ramón Montero (2006) Las actitudes politicas de los españoles. In: José Ramón Montero, Joan Font, MarianoTorcal (eds), *Ciudadanos, asociaciones y participación en España*. Madrid: CIS, pp. 105–32.

Borchert, Jens and Lutz Golsch (2003) Germany: from guilds of notables to political class. In: Jens Borchert and Jürgen Zeiss (eds), *The Political Class in Advanced Democracies*. Oxford: Oxford University Press, pp. 142–63.

Börzel, Tanja (2000a) From competitive regionalism to cooperative federalism: the Europeanization of the Spanish state of autonomies. In: *Publius. Journal of Federalism*, 30, 2, pp. 17–42.

Börzel, Tanja A. (2000b) Why there is no Southern European Problem: On Environmental Leaders and Laggards in the EU. *Journal of European Public Policy* 7(1), pp.141–62.

—— (2002) *States and Regions in the European Union. Institutional Adaptation in Germany and Spain*. Cambridge: Cambridge University Press.

Bosco, Anna (2000) *Communisti transformazioni di partito in Italia, Spagna e Portogallo*. Bologna: Il Molino.

Botella, Joan (1998) El sistema electoral español: formula electoral y umbrales de representación. In: *El sistema electoral a debate. Veinte anos de rendimientos del sistema electoral español, 1977–1997*. Madrid: CIS, pp. 91–100.

Bouzas Lorenzo, Ramón (2001) El personal politico en el marco del desarollo de la administración autonómica de Galicia. In: Jordi Matas (ed.), *El Control Politico de la Administración*. Barcelona: Institut de Ciencies Politiques i Socials, pp. 100–28.

Bradshaw, Roy P. (1972) Internal migration in Spain. In: *Iberian Studies*, 1, 2, pp. 68–75.

Brassloff, Audrey (1998) *Religion and Politics in Spain. The Spanish Church in Transition*. Basingstoke: Macmillan, pp. 1962–96.

Braudel, Fernand (1949) *La Mediterranée et le monde mediterranéen a' L'époque de Philippe II*. Paris: Librairie Armand Colin.

Brenan, Gerald (1995) *The Spanish Labyrinth. An Account of the Social and Political Background of the Spanish Civil War*. Cambridge: Canto.

Briole, Alain, Luis de la Torre, Richard Lauraire and Emmanuel Négrier (1993) *Les politiques publiques de telecommunication en Europe du sud. Service public et dynamiques territoriales des interets*. Montpellier: Université de Montpellier I-CEPEL.

Broughton, Andrea (2007) Comparative overview of industrial relations in 2005. Report posted on the website of European Observatory of Industrial Relations (EIRO). http://www.eiroline.com accessed 8 January 2008.

Bukowski, Jeanie (2002) A space for political choice? Regional development policy in Andalucia and Catalonia. In: *Regional and Federal Studies*, 12, 1, Spring, pp. 138–70.

Busquets, Gabriel (2003) España, Marruecos y Unión Europea. In: *Economia Exterior*, 24, Spring, pp. 69–76.

Bustamante, Enrique (2006) Un auténtico servicio público garantizado por el Consejo Audiovisual. In:*Telos, cuadernos de comunicación, tecnologia y sociedad*, Number. 68, Julio–Septiembre 2006. Online journal http://www.campusred.net/TELOS/anteriores/index50.html accessed 22 December 2007.

Caciagli, Mario (1984) The new mediterranean democracies: regime transition in Spain, Greece and Portugal. In: *The New Mediterranean Democracies: Regime Transition in Spain, Greece and Portugal*. London: Frank Cass, pp. 84–98.

—— (1993) La parabola de la Unión de Centro Democrático. In: José Felix Tezanos, Ramon Cotarelo and Andres de Blas (eds), *La transición democratica española*. Madrid: Editorial Sistema, pp. 389–413.

Cal, Rosa (1999) Apuntes sobre la actividad de la Dirección General de Propaganda del Franquismo. In: *Historia y Comunicación Social*, numero 4, pp. 15–33.

Caloghirou, Yannis, Yannis Voulgaris and Stella Zambarloukos (2000) The political economy of industrial restructuring: comparing Greece and Spain. In: *South European Society and Politics*, 5, 1, summer, pp. 73–96.

Calvo, Kerman (2007) Sacrifices that pay: polity membership, political opportunities and the recognition of same-sex marriage in Spain, *South European Society and Politics*, 12, 3, pp. 295–314.

Calvo, Kerman and José Ramón Montero (2002) Cuando ser conservador ya no es un problema: religiosidad, ideologia y voto en las elecciones de 2000. In: *Revista Española de Ciencia Politica*, 6, April, pp. 17–56.

Calvo, Kerman and José Ramon Montero (2005) Valores y religiosidad. In: Mariano Torcal Loriente, Laura Morales Diez de Ulzurrun, Santiago Pérez-Nievas Montiel (eds.) *España: sociedad y política en perspectiva comparada*. Valencia: tyrant lo blanch, pp. 147–71.

Campillo, Oscar (2004) *Zapatero. Presidente a la Primera*. Madrid: la esfera de los libros.

Campmany, Juan (2005) *El Efecto ZP. 1.000 dias de campaña a la Moncloa*. Barcelona: Planeta.

Campo, Esther del (2001) La emergencia de una pauta europeizada de agregación de intereses. In: Carlos Closa (ed.), *La europeización del sistema politico español*. Madrid: Istmo, pp. 68–84.

—— (2002) Los grupos de presión. In: Paloma Roman (ed.), *Sistema politico Español*. Madrid: McGraw-Hill, pp. 155–81.

Campo, Esther del and Jaime Ferri Durá (2002) Las politicas publicas. In: Paloma Román (ed.), *Sistema Politico Español*. Madrid: McGraw-Hill, pp. 339–63.

Capo Giol, Jordi (1994) Oposición y minorias en las legislaturas socialistas. In: *Revista Española de Investigaciones Sociologicas*, Number 66, pp. 91–113.

—— (2000) Sistema electoral y gobernabilidad española. In: *Revista Española de Ciencia Politica*, vol. 1. Number. 1, pp. 55–80.

Capo Giol, Jordi, R. Cotarelo, D. Lopez Garrido and J. Subirats (1990) By consociationalism to a majoritarian parliamentary system: the rise and decline of the Spanish Cortes. In: Ulrike Liebert and Maurizio Cotta (eds), *Parliament and Consolidation in Southern Europe. Greece, Italy, Portugal, Spain and Turkey*. London and New York: Pinter, pp. 92–129.

Carr, Raymond (1999) *España, 1808–1975*. Barcelona: Ariel.

Carr, Raymond and Juan Pablo Fusi (1979) *España: de la Dictadura a la Democracia*. Madrid: Planta Siglo XX.

Carrillo, Ernesto (2002) Los gobiernos locales. In: Paloma Román (ed.), *Sistema politico Español*. Madrid: McGraw-Hill, pp. 315 38.

Casas, Juan Gomez (1986) *Anarchist Organisation. The History of FAI*. Montreal: Black Rose Books.

Cascajo, José Luis and Rafael Bustos (2001) Constitución y forma de gobierno en España. In: Manuel Alcantara and Antonia Martinez (eds), *Politica y Gobierno en España*. Valencia: Tirant lo Blanch, pp. 99–120.

Castañer, Xavier (1998) La politica industrial. Ajustes, nuevas politicas horizontales y privatización: 1975–1996. In: Ricard Gomá and Joan Subirats (eds), *Politicas publicas en España. Contenidos, redes de actores y niveles de gobierno*. Barcelona: Ariel, pp. 79–112.

Castells, Manuel (2000) *The Power of Identity, Vol. II. The Information Age: Economy, Society and Culture*. Oxford: Blackwell.

Castillejo, Angel Garcia (2006) Una laguna fundamental del sistema democratico. El Consejo Estatal de Medios Audiovisuales. In: *Telos, Cuadernos de comunicación, tecnologia y sociedad*, Number. 68, Julio–Septiembre. Online journal http://www. campusred.net/TELOS/anteriores/index50.html accessed 22 December 2007.

Castillo, Pilar del (1985) *La financiación de partidos y candidatos en las democracias occidentales*. Madrid: CIS.

—— (1998a) El comportamiento electoral de los españoles en las elecciones al Parlamento Europeo de 1989. In: Pilar del Castillo (ed.), *Comportamiento Politico y Electoral*. Madrid: CIS, pp. 385–402.

—— (1998b) El sistema electoral: una revisión de las propuestas de reforma. In: Juan Montabes (ed.), *El sistema electoral a debate. Veinte anos de rendimientos del sistema electoral español, 1977–1997*. Madrid: CIS, pp. 71–6.

Castillo, Pilar del and Irene Delgado Sotillos (1998) Las elecciones legislativas de 1993: movilidad de las preferencias partidistas. In: Pilar del Castillo (ed.), *Comportamiento politico y electoral*. Madrid: CIS, pp. 125–48.

Castillo, Pilar del and Ismael Crespo (2000) *La opinión pública y el congreso de los deputados*. Barcelona: Tecnos, pp. 393–417.

Castillo, Pilar del, Antonio M. Jaime and José Luis Saez Lozano (2001) *El comportamiento electoral en la democracia española*. Madrid: Centro de Estudios Politicos y Constitucionales.

Castro, Consuelo Laiz (2002) Las elecciones y los sistemas electorales. In: Paloma Roman (ed.), *Sistema politico Español*. Madrid: McGraw-Hill, pp. 125–54.

Cazes, Georges, Domingo, Jean, and Gauthier, André (1985) *L'Espagne et le Portugal aux Portes du Marché Commun*. Montreuil: Real Editeur.

Cazorla Perez, José and Montabes Pereira, J. (1983) The social structure of Spain. In: David S. Bell (ed.), *Democratic Politics in Spain*. London: St. Martin's Press, pp. 180–97.

Centro de Investigaciones Sociologicas (CIS) (1985) La opinión pública ante la CEE, 1968–1985. In: *Revista Española de Investigaciones Sociologicas*, 29, pp. 287–376.

Centro de Investigaciones Sociologicas (CIS) (2007) website http://www.cis.es consulted throughout 2007.

Cervelló, Josep Sanchez (1993) *A Revolução Portuguesa e a sua influência na transição espanhola (1961–1976)*. Lisbon: Assirio e Alvim.

Chari, Raj S. (1998) Spanish socialists, privatising the right way? In: Paul Heywood (ed.), *Politics and Policy in Democratic Spain*. London: Frank Cass, pp. 162–79.

—— (2000) The March 2000 Spanish election: a critical election? In: *West European Politics*, 23, 3, July, pp. 207–14.

—— (2001) The EU 'dimensions' in economic policy making at the domestic level: evidence from labour market reform in spain. In: *South European Society and Politics*, vol. 6, Number. 1, summer 2001, pp. 51–74.

—— (2004) The 2004 Spanish elections:terrorism as a catalyst for change. In:*West European Politics*, vol. 27, Number. 5, November, pp. 954–63.

Chislett, William (2002) *The Internationalisation of the Spanish Economy*. Madrid: Real Instituto Elcano.

—— (2003) *La Inversión Española Directa en América Latina. Retos y Oportunidades.* Madrid. Real Instituto Elcano

Circuendez Santamaria, Ruth (2006) Las transferencias y subvenciones como instrumentos de las relaciones intergubernamentales en España. In: Lourdes Lopez Nieto (ed.), *Relaciones Intergubernamentales en la España Democrática. Interdependencia, Autonomia, Conflicto y Cooperación.* Madrid: Dykinson, pp. 205–38.

Cicuendez Santamaria, Ruth and Juan A. Ramos Gallarin (2006) La dimension intergubernamental del sistema de financiación autonomico. In: Lourdes Lopez Nieto (ed.), *Relaciones Intergubernamentales en la España Democrática. Interdependencia, Autonomia, Conflicto y Cooperación.* Madrid: Dykinson, pp. 175–203.

Clemente, Eloy Fernandez (1998) *El pensamiento y la obra de Joaquin Costa. Barcelona, Institut de Ciencies Politiques i Socials,* Working Papers no. 145.

Closa, Carlos (2000) La politica pesquera comun. In: Francesc Morata (ed.), *Politicas publicas en la Unión Europea.* Barcelona: Ariel, pp. 121–42.

Closa, Carlos and Paul Heywood (2004) *Spain and the European Union.* Basingstroke: Palgrave.

Coates, Crispin (2000) Spanish defence policy: Eurocorps and NATO reform. In: Richard Gillespie and Richard Youngs (eds), Spain: European and International Challenges. Special issue of *Mediterranean Politics,* 5, 2, pp. 170–90.

Collado Seidel, Carlos and Antonio Duato (2007) Ante una Iglesia diezmada. Doctrina católica en un Estado aconfesional y una sociedad secularizada. In: Walter L. Bernecker, Günther Maihold (eds), *España: del consenso a la polarización. Cambios en la democracia española.* Madrid, Frankfurt a. M.: Iberoamericana, Vervuert, pp. 339–77.

Colino, César (2001) La integración europea y el estado autonómico: europeización, estrategias y cambio en las relaciones intergubernamentales. In: Carlos Closa (ed.), *La europeización del sistema politico español.* Madrid: Istmo, pp. 225–60.

Collier, Xavier (2002) Continuidad y conflicto parlamentario en las comunidades autonomas españolas. In: Joan Subirats and Raquel Gallego (eds), *El estado de las autonomias. Veinte anos de autonomias en España. Leyes, politicas publicas, instituciones y opinion publica.* Madrid: Centro de Investigaciones Sociologicas, pp. 69–97.

Colomé, Gabriel, Benedicte Bazzana and Jesus Maestro (1998) Espagne. Guy Hermet, Julian Thomas Hottinger and Daniel-Louis Seiler (eds), *Les partis politiques en europe de l'ouest.* Paris: Economica, pp. 129–61.

Colomer, Josep M. (1999) The Spanish state of autonomies: non-institutional federalism. In: Paul Heywood (ed.), *Politics and Policy in Democratic Spain.* London: Frank Cass, pp. 40–52.

Comisión de Expertos para el Dialogo Social (2005) *Más y Mejor Empleo en un Nuevo Escenario Socio-economico: Por una Flexibilidad y Seguridad Laborales Efectivas.* Informe de la Comisión de Expertos para el Diálogo Social.

Comisión para la Reforma Integral del Servicio Exterior (2005) *Informe Sobre la Reforma del Servicio Exterior Español.* Madrid: Ministerio de la Presidencia, 20 June 2005.

Confederacion Española de Organizaciones Empresariales (CEOE) (2004) *Reseña del balance de la encuesta de CEOE sobre negociación colectiva 2002.* Madrid: CEOE.

Conferencia Episcopal Española (2006) El Nuevo Sistema de Asignación Tributaria en favour de la Iglesia Católica. Vicesecretaria de Asuntos Económicos. Posted on the website of the Spanish Archbishop Conference, http://www.conferenciaepiscopal.es, accessed on 27 January 2008.

Confederacíon Católica de Padres de Familia y de Padres de Alumnos (CONCAPA) (2008) website http://www.concapa.org accessed on 27 January 2008.

Congreso de Diputados (2007a) Parliamentary statistics website http://www.congreso.es accessed on 19 October 2007.

——— (2007b) Regimen economico y de ayuda a los señores diputados, 13 July 2006, pdf document posted in http://www.congreso.es, accessed 15 May 2007.

Consello Galego de Relacions Laborais (2002) *Informe sobre a Situacion Sociolaboral da Comunidade Auto noma Galega en 2001.* Santiago de Compostela: Consello Galego de Relacions Laborais.

Consejo General del Poder Judicial (CGPJ) (2007) The Spanish Justice System 2006. All the facts. Pdf file posted on the website of the Council of the Judiciary Power, http://www.poderjudicial.es, accessed on 19 October 2007.

Conversi, Daniele (1997) *The Basques, the Catalans and Spain. Alternative Routes to Nationalist Mobilisation.* London: Hurst.

Corkill, David (1999) *The Europeanization of the Portuguese Economy.* London: Routledge.

Coordinadora de las ONG de Desarollo (CONGDE) (2006) Informe de la CONGDE sobre el sector de las ONGD 2006. Madrid: CONGDE, posted on website of the coordinating organisation of the non-develoment organisations for international development, http://www.congde.org accessed on 27 January 2008.

Costa, Joaquin (1998) *Oligarquia y caciquismo. Como la forma actual de gobierno en España: urgencia y modo de cambiarla.* Madrid: Biblioteca Nueva.

Costa-Font, Joan and Rico, A. (2005) 'Power rather than path dependency? The dynamics of institutional change under health care federalism'. *Journal of Health Politics, Policy and Law* 30, Number. 1, pp. 231–52.

Cotarelo, Ramón (2002) Politica exterior española. In: Paloma Roman (ed.), *Sistema politico español.* Madrid: McGraw-Hill, pp. 365–80.

Cousins, Christine (2000) Women and employment in southern Europe: the implications of recent policy and labour market directions. In: *South European Society and Politics*, 5, 1, summer, pp. 97–122.

Crespo, Ismael and Fátima Garcia (2001) El sistema electoral. In: Manuel Alcántara and Antónia Martinez (eds), *Politica y Gobierno en España.* Valencia: Tirant lo Blanch, pp. 303–41.

Davis, Andrew (2004) The November 2003 elections in Catalonia: a landmark change in the Catalan political landscape. In: *South European Society and Politics*, vol. 9, Number. 3, Winter, pp. 137–48.

De Aristegui, Gustavo (2005) *La Yihad en España. La obsesión por reconquistar Al-Andalus* Madrid: La Esfera de los Libros.

Declaración para el Diálogo Social (2004) *Competitividad, Empleo Estable y Cohesión Social.* 8 July. Posted in European Industrial Relations Observatory (EIRO) online, http://eurofound.eu, accessed 28 December 2007.

Defensor del Pueblo (2003, 2008) website http://www.defensordelpueblo.es

De Pablo, Santiago, José Luis de la Granja and Ludger Mees (eds) (1998) *Documentos para la historia del nacionalismo vasco. De los Fueros a nuestros dias.* Barcelona: Editorial Ariel.

Delage, Fernando (2002) Globalización contra fundamentalismo: el mundo tras el 11 de septiembre. In: *Perspectivas Exteriores 2002. Los intereses de España en el mundo.* Edited by Fundación para las Relaciones Exteriores y el Diálogo Exterior (FRIDE). Madrid: FRIDE, pp. 21–34.

Delgado Sotillos, Irene (1997) *El comportamiento electoral municipal español, 1979–1995.* Madrid: CIS.

—— (2000) Elites politicas y vida parlamentaria: actividades y motivaciones de los diputados españoles. In: Antonia Martinez (ed.), *El congreso de los diputados en España: funciones y rendimiento.* Madrid: Tecnos, pp. 295–341.

—— (2007) Parlamentos y Parlamentarios. Rendimiento y Professionalización en Perspectiva Comparada. Paper presented at the Workshop Parliaments and Performance in a changing world. Eighth Conference of the Spanish Association for Political Science and Administration, University of Valencia, 18–20 September.

Delgado Sotillos, Irene, Antonia Martinez and Pablo Oñate (1998) *Parlamento y opinion pública en España. Opiniones y actitudes 19.* Madrid: Centro de Investigaciones Sociologicas.

Delgado Sotillos, Irene and Lourdes Lopez-Nieto (1995) Spain. In: *Political Data Yearbook 1995,* special issue of *European Journal for Political Research,* 28, 3–4, pp. 473–76.

—— (2001) Spain. In: *Political Data Yearbook 2000,* special issue of *European Journal for Political Research,* 40, 3–4, pp. 421–25.

—— (2002) Spain. In: *Political Data Yearbook 2001,* special issue of *European Journal for Political Research,* 41, 7–8, pp. 1084–88.

—— (2003) Spain. *Political Data Yearbook 2002.* In: Richard S. Katz (ed.), *European Journal of Political Research,* vol. 42, Number. 7–8, December 2003, pp. 1087–90.

Delgado, Irene and Lourdes Lopez Nieto (2003) Spain. *Political Data Yearbook 2002.* In: Richard S. Katz (ed.), *European Journal of Political Research,* vol. 42, Number. 7–8, December 2003, pp. 1087–90.

—— (2004) Spain. In: Ingrid van Biezen and Richard S. Katz (eds), *Political Data Yearbook 2003.* In: *European Journal of Political Research,* vol. 43, Number 7–8, December 2004, pp. 1138–1143.

—— (2005) Spain. In: Ingrid van Biezen and Richard S. Katz (eds), *European Data Yearbook 2004.* In: *European Journal of Political Research,* vol. 44, Number. 7–8: 1188–94.

—— (2006) Spain. In: Ingrid van Biezen and Richard S. Katz (eds), *European Data Yearbook 2005.* In: *European Journal of Political Research,* vol. 45, Number. 7–8: 1266–69.

Delgado, Irene and Miguel Jerez Mir (2007) *Mujer y politica en España en los albores del siglo XXI: un análisis comparado de la presencia femenina en las asambleas legislativas.* Xerocopied unpublished paper.

Diario de Sesiones de las Cortes Generales (2004) *Comisiones Mixtas, Para la Unión Europea,* Number. 7, 29.6.2004.

Diaz, José Antonio (1997) Tendencias de cambio en los valores de los españoles: un analisis prospectivo. In: José Felix Tezanos, José Manuel Montero and José Antonio Diaz (eds), *Tendencias de futuro en la sociedad española. Primer foro sobre tendencias sociales.* Madrid: Editorial Sistema, pp. 289–325.

Diaz-Nosty, Berardo (1976) *A comuna das Asturias. 15 Dias de poder proletario.* Lisbon: Libor.

—— (2006) Repensar la Comunicación. La huella es la mensaje. In: Fundación Telefónica (eds), *Tendencias '06.* Madrid: Fundación Telefónica, pp. 15–43.

—— (2007) El Nuevo continente virtual. In: Fundación Telefonica (ed.), *Tendencias '07. El escenario iberoamericano.* Madrid: Fundación Telefónica, pp. 13–86.

Diegues, Carlos Dias and José Luis Palmeiro Pinheiro (2006) A Galiza após Fraga. In: *Lusotopie,* vol. XIII, 1, Juin 2006, pp. 61–83.

Diez Peralta, Eva Maria (2001) La adaptación judicial: jueces y derecho comunitario. In: Carlos Closa (ed.), *La europeización del sistema politico español*. Madrid: Istmo, pp. 263–89.

Dowling, Andrew (2005) Convergencia i Unió, Catalonia and the New Catalanism. In: Sebastian Balfour (ed.), *The Politics of Contemporary Spain*. London: Routledge, pp. 106–20.

Dyson, Kenneth (2000) EMU as Europeanisation: convergence, diversity and contingency. In: *Journal of Common Market Studies*, 38, 4, pp. 645–66.

Dyson, Kenneth and Kevin Featherstone (1996) Italy and EMU as a vincolo esterno: empowering the technocrats, transforming the state. In: *South European Society and Politics*, 1, 2, Autumn, pp. 272–99.

Economic Bureau of the President (2007) *Economic Report of the President 2007*. Madrid: Presidencia del Gobierno.

Economic Policy Committee (2000) *Annual Report on Structural Reforms 2000. Report addressed to the Council and the Commission*. Brussels, 13 March 2000.

—— (2001) *Annual Report on Structural Reforms 2001*. Report addressed to the Council and the Commission. Brussels, 6 March 2001, ECFIN/EPC/171–01.

Eddles, Laura Desfor (1998) *Symbol and Ritual in the New Spain. The Transition to Democracy after Franco*. Cambridge: Cambridge University Press.

Eiroa San Francisco, Matilde (2007) Relaciones internacionales y estratégias de comunicación de la España de Franco ante la coyuntura de 1956. In: *Historia y Comunicación Social*, numero 12, pp. 5–22.

Ellwood, Sheelagh M. (1987) *Spanish Fascism in the Franco Era. Falange Española de las JONS 1936–1976*. London: Macmillan.

Espasa, Marta (2005) Puntos clave en torno al debate sobre saldos fiscales y solidariedad interterritorial. In: Núria Bosch and José Maria Durán (eds), *La financiación de las comunidades autonomas: politicas tributarias y solidariedad interterritorial*. Barcelona: Universitat de Barcelona, pp. 239–40.

Esteban, Jorge de (1989) El Proceso Constituyente Español, 1977–78. In: José Felix Tezanos and Roman Cotarelo and Andres de Blas (eds), *La Transición Democrática Española*. Madrid: Fundación Sistema.

Eurobarometer (2007) Public opinion in the European Union, survey conducted March–May 2006, Number. 65, January 2007. Luxembourg: Office of the Official Publications of the European Communities.

Euro-Med Partnership (2002) *Regional Strategy Paper 2002–2006 and Regional Indicative Programme 2002–2004*. Brussels:European Commission.

European Commission (1999) *The Structural Funds in 1997*. Ninth Annual Report. Luxembourg: Office of the official publications of the European Communities.

—— (2000a) *Common Support Framework (2000–6) for the Spanish Regions – Objective One*. Luxembourg: Office of the official publications of the European Communities.

—— (2000b) *Common Agricultural Policy – 1999 Review*. Luxembourg: Office of the Official Publications of the European Communities.

—— (2000c) *Regional Socio-Economic Studies on Employment and the Level of Dependency on Fishing*. February.

—— (2001a) *Working for the Regions*. Luxembourg: Office of the Official Publications of the European Communities.

—— (2001b) *The Structural Funds in 2000. Twelfth Annual Report*. Luxembourg: Office of the Official Publications of the European Communities.

—— (2001c) *Annual Report of the Cohesion Fund 2000*. Luxembourg: Office of the Official Publications of the European Communities, 2 vols.

—— (2001d) *Unity, Solidarity, Diversity for Europe, its People and its Territory. Second Report on Economic and Social Cohesion*. Luxembourg: Office of the official publications of the European Communities.

—— (2001e) *Organic Farming in the EU. Facts and Figures*. Brussels.

—— (2001f) *Green Paper on the Common Fisheries Policy After 2002*. Brussels, 20 March 2001, COM (2001) 135 final. Luxembourg: Office of the official publications of the European Communities.

—— (2001g) *Facts and Figures on CFP. Basic Data on Common Fisheries Policy*. Luxembourg: Office of the Official Publications of the European Communities.

—— (2001h) *Annual Report on structural Reforms 2001*. Report addressed to the Council and the Commission. Brussels, 6 March 2001, ECFIN/EPC/171-01.

—— (2002a) *The Social Situation in the European Union 2002*. Luxembourg: Office of the official publications of the European Communities.

—— (2002b) *Mid-term Review of the Common Agricultural Policy*. Communication from the Commission to the Council and the European Parliament. Brussels, 10 July 2002, COM (2002) 394 final.

—— (2002c) *Analysis of the Impact on Agricultural Markets and Incomes of EU Enlargement to the CEECs*. March.

—— (2002d) *Implementing the New EU Rural Development Policy: The Spanish Case*. Brussels, October.

—— (2002e) *Thirty First Financial Report, EAGGF Guarantee Section-2001* (COM 2002), 594 final.

—— (2002f) *The Economy EU: Review 2002*. Brussels, 11 December 2002, COM (2002) 712 final.

—— (2002g) *Employment Policies in the EU and in the Member States. Joint Report 2001*. Luxembourg: Office of the official publications of the European Communities.

—— (2002h) *The European Union Economy Review 2002*. In: European Economy, 6.

—— (2005a) *Working Together for Growth and Jobs. Integrated Guidelines for Growth and Jobs (2005–8). Communication to the Spring European Council*. Luxembourg: Office of the official publications of the European Commission.

—— (2005b) *Policy guidelines for regions falling under the new regional competitiveness and employment objective for the 2007–2013 period. Vol. II Country Report. Spain*. Brussels: European Commission.

—— (2006a) *Study On The Strengths, Weaknesses, Opportunities And Threats For Spanish Regions Within The Framework Of The Conclusions Of The Lisbon and Gothenburg European Councils*. Executive Summary. September 2006.

—— (2006b) *The EU Rural Development Policy 2007–2013. Fact Sheet*. Luxembourg: Office of the official publications of the European Communities.

—— (2006c) *Facts and Figures on CFP. 2006 Edition*. Luxembourg: Office of the official publications of the European Communities.

—— (2007a) *Social Situation of the European Union 2005–6*. Luxembourg: Office of the Official Publications of the European Communities.

—— (2007b) *Joint Report on Social Protection and Social Inclusion*. Luxembourg: Office of the Official Publications of the European Communities.

European Industrial Relations Observatory online (EIRO) website http://www.eiro. eurofound.eu.int

European Institute for Public Administration (EIPA) (2001) *Annual Report 2000.* Maastricht: EIPA.

Eurostat (2002) *Eurostat Yearbook. The Statistical Guide to Europe. Data 1990–2000.* Luxembourg: Office of the official publications of the European Communities.

Fandiño, Roberto G. (2003) El trasmisor cotidiano. Miedos, esperanzas, frustraciones y confusion en los rumores de una pequeña ciudad de provincias durante el franquismo. In: *Historia y Comunicación Social,* numero 8, pp. 77–102.

Feliu, Laura and Mónica Salomón (2000) La dimensión sur de la UE: politicas para el Mediterraneo. In: Esther Barbé (ed.), *Politica Exterior Europea.* Barcelona: Ariel, pp. 191–218.

Fernandez, Jorge (1998) La situación del debate de esta cuestión en el estado español. In: *La participación de las comunidades autonomas en los consejos de ministros de la unión europea.* Edited by the Instituto Vasco de Administración Publica. Bilbao: IVAP, pp. 19–25.

Fernandez-Arias Menuesa, Carlos (2006) Magreb. In: Instituto Español de Estudios Estratégicos, *Panorama Estratégico 2005–6.* Madrid: Ministerio de Defensa, pp. 148–70.

Fernandez Beaumont, José (2006) La refundación del sector audiovisual. In: Fundación Telefónica (2006) (ed.), *Tendencias '06. Medios de Comunicación,* pp. 221–42.

Ferrera, Maurizio, Anton Hemerijck and Martin Rhodes (2000) *O futuro da Europa social. Repensar o trabalho e a protecção social na nova economia.* Lisbon: Celta.

Ferri Durá, Jaime (2002) Las comunidades autonomas. In: Paloma Román (ed.), *Sistema Politico Español.* Madrid: McGraw-Hill, pp. 287–314.

Flores Gimenez, Fernando (1998) *La democracia interna de los partidos politicos.* Madrid: Congreso de los Diputados.

Fominaya, Cristina Flesher (2007) 'Autonomous movements and the institutional left: two approaches in tension in Madrid's anti-globalisation network', *South European Society and Politics,* 12, 3, pp. 335–58.

Font, Joan (2003) Local participation in Spain: beyond associative democracy. In: *BCN. Political Science Debates,* 1, pp. 43–64.

Font, Nuria (2001) La europeización de la politica ambiental: desafios y inercias. In: Carlos Closa (ed.), *La europeización del sistema politico español.* Madrid: Istmo, pp. 381–402.

Fossati, Fabio (2000) *Economia e politica estera: La Spagna é una media potenza?* Working Paper no. 180. Barcelona: Institut de Ciencies Politiques i Socials.

Fraile, Marta (2002) El voto económico en las elecciones de 1996 y 2000: una comparación. In: *Revista Española de Ciencia Politica,* 6, April, pp. 129–51.

Fuentes, Jorge (2002) La presidencia española de la UE y el futuro de Europa. In: *Perspectivas exteriores 2002. Los intereses de España en el mundo.* Edited by Fundacion para las Relaciones Exteriores y el Dialogo Exterior (FRIDE). Madrid: FRIDE, pp. 197–206.

Führer, Ilse Marie (1996) *Los sindicatos en España. De la lucha de clases a estrategias de cooperación.* Madrid: Consejo Economico y Social.

Fundación Encuentro (2004) *Informe España 2004. Una interpretación de la Realidad Social.* Madrid: Fundación Encuentro-Centro de Estudios del Cambio Social.

—— (2005) *Informe España 2005. Una interpretación de la Realidad Social.* Madrid. Fundación Encuentro-Centro de Estudios del Cambio Social.

—— (2006) *Informe España 2006. Una interpretación de la Realidad Social.* Madrid: Fundación Encuentro-Centro de Estudios del Cambio Social.

Fundación Telefónica (2006) (ed.), *Tendencias '06. Medios de Comunicación.* Madrid: Fundación Telefonica.

—— (2007) *La sociedad de información en España. Selección de indicadores 2006.* Madrid: Fundación Telefónica-Ariel.

Funes Rivas, Maria Jesus (1997) Evolución y tendencias de las asociaciones voluntarias en España: las organizaciones no gubernamentales como nuevo fenomeno en el panorama asociativo. In: José Felix Tezanos, José Manuel Montero and José Antonio Diaz (eds), *Tendencias de futuro en la sociedad españ ola. Pimer foro sobre tendencias sociales.* Madrid: Editorial Sistema, pp. 511–31.

Galduf, Josep M. Jordan (1997) Spanish-Moroccan economic relations. In: Richard Gillespie (ed.), *The Euro-Mediterranean Partnership. Political and Economic Perspectives.* London: Frank Cass, pp. 49–63.

Gangas, Pilar (2007) Representativeness of the social partners: agricultural sector-Spain. [ES0608019Q] Posted on website of European Industrial Relations Observatory http://www.eirofound. Accessed on 8 January 2008.

Garcia-Fernandez, Antonio Alfonso Bullón de Mendoza, Gomez de Valugera, Estibaliz Ruiz de Azua, Martinez de Ezquerecocha and Secundino José Gutierrez Alvarez (1996) *Documentos de historia contemporanea.* Madrid: Editorial Actas.

Garcia, Ferrando, Manuel, EduardoLopez-Aranguren and Miguel Beltrán (1994) *La conciencia nacional y regional en la España de las autonomias.* Madrid: Centro de Investigaciones Sociologicas.

Garcia-Abadillo, Casimiro (2005) *11-M La Venganza.* Madrid: Esfera de los Libros.

Garcia-Guereta Rodriguez, Elena Maria (2001) *Factores externos e internos en la transformación de los partidos politicos: el caso de AP-PP.* Madrid: Instituto Juan March de Estudios e Investigaciones-Centro de Estudios Avanzados en Ciencias Sociales.

Garcia-Nieto, Maria Carmen (1972) Introduccion: España en el ultimo tercio del siglo XIX. In: Maria Carmen Garcia-Nieto, Javier M. Donezar and Luis Lopez Puenta (eds), *Restauración y desastre 1871–1898. Bases documentales de la España contemporanea.* Madrid: Guadiana, pp. 11–37.

—— (1973) Introducción: viejas y nuevas fuerzas politicas. In: Maria Carmen Garcia-Nieto, Javier M. Donezar and Luis Lopez Puenta (eds), *La crisis del sistema canovista. 1898–1923. Vol. 5 of Bases Documentales de la España Contemporanea.* Madrid: Guadiana, pp. 11–40.

Genieys, William (1996) Les élites periphériques espagnoles face au changement de regime. In: Le processus d'institutionnalisation de l'etat autonomique. In: *Revue Française de Science Politique*, pp. 650–79.

—— (1998) Autonomous communities and the state in Spain. The role of intermediary elites. In: Patrick Le Gales and Christian Lequesne (eds), *Regions in Europe.* London: Routledge, pp. 166–80.

Gianmusso, Maurizio (1999) The Euro-Mediterranean decentralised network. In: *Mediterranean Politics*, 4, 1, pp. 25–52.

Gibbons, John (1999) *Spanish Politics Today.* Manchester: Manchester University Press.

—— (2001) Spain. In: Juliet Lodge (ed.), *The 1999 Elections to the European Parliament.* Basingstoke: Palgrave, pp. 185–98.

Gil, Olga (2002) *Telecomunicaciones y politica en Estados Unidos y España (1875–2002). Construyendo mercados.* Madrid: CIS.

Gillespie, Richard (1989) *The Spanish Socialist Party: A History of Factionalism.* Oxford: Oxford University Press.

—— (1990) The break-up of the socialist family: party-union relations in Spain, 1982–89. In: *West European Politics*, 13, pp. 47–62.

—— (1994) The resurgence of factionalism in the Spanish Socialist Workers' Party. In: David S. Bell and Eric Shaw (eds), *Conflict and Cohesion in Western European Social Democratic Parties*. London: Pinter, pp. 50–69.

—— (1997) Spanish protagonismo and the Euro-Med partnership initiative. In: Richard Gillespie (ed.), *The Euro-Mediterranean Partnership. Political and Economic Perspectives*. London: Frank Cass, pp. 33–48.

—— (1999a) Peace moves in the Basque country. In: *Journal of Southern Europe and the Balkans*, 1, 2, November, pp. 119–36.

—— (1999b) *Spain and the Mediterranean. Developing a European Policy towards the South*. Basingstoke: Macmillan.

Gillespie, Richard (2002) The Valencia conference: reinvigorating the Barcelona process? In: *Mediterranean Politics*, vol. 7, Number. 2, pp. 105–14.

—— (2006) Onward but not upward: The Barcelona conference of 2005. In: *Mediterranean Politics*, vol. 11, Number. 2, pp. 271–78.

Gilmour, John (2005) Losing its soul: the changing role of christian democracy in the development of Spain's new right. In: *South European Society and Politics*, vol. 10, Number. 3, November 2005, pp. 411–31.

Giordano, Benito and Elisa Roller (2001) A comparison of Catalan and Padanian nationalism: more similarities than differences? In: *Journal of Southern Europe and the Balkans*, 3, 2, November, pp. 111–30.

Gisbert, Tomás (2007a) La Politica de Defensa del Estado Español. In: Arcadi Oliveres y Pere Ortega (eds), *El militarismo en España. Balance del ciclo armamentista español hasta 2007*. Barcelona: Icaria-Antrazyt, pp. 13–42.

—— (2007b) Del Servicio Militar Obligatorio a la Tropa Professional. Una Professional-ización Repleta de Tensiones. In: Arcadi Oliveres y Pere Ortega (eds), *El militarismo en España. Balance del ciclo armamentista español hasta 2007*. Barcelona: Icaria-Antrazyt, pp. 85–111.

Gomez, Luis (2005) *España connection. La implacable expansion del crimen organizado en España*. Barcelona: RBA Libros.

Gomez Benito, Cristobal, Francisco Javier Noya and Angel Paniagua (1999) *Actitudes y comportamientos hacia el medio ambiente en España. Opiniones y Actitudes, 25*. Madrid: CIS.

Gomez Calderón, Bernardo (2006) Prensa: Bonanza económica frente a estancamiento de la diffusion. In: Fundación Telefonica (ed.), *Tendencias '06. Medios de Comunicación*. Madrid: Fundación Telefónica, pp. 69–76.

Gonzalez Gomez, Alfred (2006) La Cooperación multilateral institucionalizada: las conferencias sectoriales. In: Lourdes Lopez Nieto (ed.), *Relaciones Intergubernamentales en la España Democrática. Interdependencia, Autonomia, Conflicto y Cooperación*. Madrid: Dykinson, pp. 97–114.

Gonzalez Gomez, Alfredo and Lourdes Lopez Nieto (2006) Los partidos politicos en el desarollo autonomic: PSOE-AP/PP. In: Lourdes Lopez Nieto (ed.), *Relaciones Intergubernamentales en la España Democrática. Interdependencia, Autonomia, Conflicto y Cooperación*. Madrid: Dykinson, pp. 79–94.

Gonzalez Marrero, Secundino (1995) La constitución española de 1978. In: Paloma Román (ed.), *Sistema politico español*. Madrid: McGraw-Hill, pp. 31–51.

Gonzalez Sanchez, Carmen (2007) Comunidades Autónomas Españolas y la Politica de Cooperación al Desarrollo: Una Evaluación General. In: Mario Kölling, Stelios Stavridis and Natividad Fernández Sola (eds), *Las Relaciones Internacionales de las Regiones: Actores Sub-nacionales, para-diplomacia y gobernanza multinivel*. Actas de Congreso

Palacio de la Aljaferia, Zaragoza (Spain), Zaragoza; Servicio de Publicaciones de la Universidad de Zaragoza, 5–6 October 2006. pp. 259–86.

Graham, Robert (1984) *Spain: Change of a New Nation*. London: Michael Joseph.

Grugel, Jean (1991) The Spanish presidency of the European community: the external dimension. In: Jonathan Story and Jean Grugel (eds), *Spanish External Policies and the EC Presidency*. Centre for Mediterranean Studies, Occasional Papers, 2, April, Bristol: University of Bristol, pp. 33–48.

—— (1995) Spain and Latin America. In: Richard Gillespie, Fernando Rodrigo and Jonathan Story (eds), *Democratic Spain. Reshaping External Relations in a Changing World*. London: Routledge, pp. 141–58.

Guerrero Salom, Enrique (2000) *Crisis y cambios en las relaciones parlamentogobierno (1993–1996)*. Madrid: Tecnos.

—— (2004) El Parlamento. Qué es, cómo funciona, qué hace. Madrid: Editorial Sintesis.

Guia ONGs (2008) http://www.guiaongs.org accessed on 27 January 2008.

Guibernau, Montserrat (2000) Nationalism and intellectuals in nations without states: the Catalan case. In: *Political Studies*, 48, pp. 989–1005.

Guillén, Ana and Laura Cabiedes (1998) La politica sanitaria: analisis y perspectivas del sistema nacional de salud. In: Ricard Gomá and Joan Subirats (eds), *Politicas publicas en España. Contenidos, redes de actores y niveles de gobierno*. Barcelona: Ariel, pp. 176–99.

Gunther, Richard (1986a) The Spanish Socialist Party: from clandestine opposition to party in government. In: Stanley G. Payne (ed.), *The Politics of Democratic Spain*. Chicago: The Chicago Council of Foreign Relations, pp. 8–49.

—— (1986b) The parties in opposition: Prospects for change and for electoral success. In: *The Politics of Democratic Spain*. Edited by Stanley G. Payne. Chicago: The Chicago Council of Foreign Relations, pp. 50–110.

—— (1996) The impact of regime change on public policy: the case of Spain. In: *Journal of Public Policy*, 16, 2, pp. 157–201.

Gunther, Richard and Jonathan Hopkin (2002) A crisis of institutionalisation: the collapse of the UCD. In: Richard Gunther, José Ramón Montero, Juan J. Linz (eds), *Political Parties. Old Concepts and New Challenges*. Oxford: OUP, pp. 191–230.

Gunther, Richard and José Ramón Montero (1998) Los anclajes del partidismo: un analisis comparado del comportamiento electoral en cuatro democracias del sur de Europa. In: Pilar del Castillo (ed.), *Comportamiento politico y electoral*. Madrid: CIS, pp. 467–548.

—— (2001) The anchors of partisanship. A comparative analysis of voting behavior in four southern European democracies. In: P. Nikiforos Diamandouros and Richard Gunther (eds), *Parties, Politics, and Democracy in the New Southern Europe*. Baltimore: Johns Hopkins University Press, pp. 83–152.

Gunther, Richard, Giacomo Sani and Goldie Shabad (1988) *Spain after Franco. The Making of a Competitive Party System*. Berkeley: University of California Press.

Gunther, Richard, José Ramón Montero and José Ignacio Wert (1999) *The Media and Politics in Spain: From Dictatorship to Democracy*. Working Papers 176. Barcelona: Institut de Ciencies Politiques i Socials, Universitat Autonoma de Barcelona.

Gunther, Richard and José Ramón Montero, Joan Botella (2004) *Democracy in Spain*. New Haven:Yale University Press.

Hamann, Kerstin (1999) Federalist institutions, voting behavior, and party systems in Spain. In: *Publius: The Journal of Federalism*, 29, 1, Winter, pp. 111–37.

Hammann, Kerstin and John Kelly (2007) Party politics and the reemergence of social pacts in western Europe. In: *Comparative Political Studies*, vol. 40, Number. 8, pp. 971–94.

Hamarneh, Mustafa (2000) Democratisation in the Mashreq: the role of external factors. In: Alvaro Vasconcelos and George Joffe (eds), *The Barcelona Process. Building a Euro-Mediterranean Regional Community.* Special Issue of *Mediterranean Politics*, 5, 1, pp. 77–95.

Haubrich, Walter (1998) Die politische Kultur. In: Walther L. Bernecker and Klaus Dirscherl (eds), *Spanien heute. Politik, Wirtschaft, Kultur.* Frankfurt-am-Main: Vervuert, pp. 141–58.

Held, Gerd and Anna Sanchez-Velasco (2001) Spain. In: Hubert Heinelt and Randall Smith (eds), *Policy Networks and European Structural Funds.* Aldershot: Avebury, pp. 227–56.

Hernandez de Frutos, Teodoro (1997) *Identificaciones ciudadanas territoriales.* In: José Felix Tezanos, José Manuel Montero and José Antonio Diaz (eds), *Tendencias de futuro en la sociedad española. Primer foro sobre tendencias sociales.* Madrid: Editorial Sistema, pp. 363–88.

Herreros, Mariano Cebrian (2007) 50 años de television española. In: *Telos, Cuadernos de comunicación, tecnologia y sociedad*, enero–febrero.

Heywood, Paul (1990) *Marxism and the Failure of Organised Socialism in Spain 1879–1936.* Cambridge: Cambridge University Press.

—— (1991) Governing a new democracy: the power of the Prime-Minister in Spain. In: *West European Politics*, vol. 14, Number. 2, pp. 97–115.

—— (1993) Rethinking socialism in Spain: Programa 2000 and the social state. In: *Coexistence*, 30, pp. 167–85.

—— (1994a) Political corruption in Modern Spain. In: Paul Heywood (ed.), *Distorting Democracy: Political Corruption in Spain, Italy and Malta.* Bristol: Centre for Mediterranean Studies - University of Bristol. Occasional Paper 10, pp. 1–14.

—— (1994b) The Spanish left: towards a common home? In: Martin J. Bull and Paul Heywood (eds), *West European Communist Parties and the Revolution of 1989.* Basingstoke: Macmillan, St Martin's Press, pp. 90–118.

—— (1995a) *Government and Politics in Spain.* Basingstoke: Macmillan.

—— (1995b) Sleaze in Spain. In: *Parliamentary Affairs*, 48, 4, October, pp. 726–37.

—— (1998) Power diffusion or concentration? In search of the Spanish policy process. In: Paul Heywood (ed.), *Politics and Policy in Democratic Spain.* London: Frank Cass, pp. 103–23.

Heywood, Paul M. (2005) Corruption, Governance and Democracy in contemporary Spain. In: Sebastian Balfour (ed.), *The Politics of Contemporary Spain.* London: Routledge, pp. 39–60.

Hildenbrand, Andreas (1998) Regionalismus und Autonomiestaat (1977–1997). In: Walther L. Bernecker and Klaus Discherl (eds), *Spanien heute. Politik, Wirtschaft, Kultur.* Frankfurt-am-Main: Vervuert, pp. 101–39.

Holgado Gonzalez, Maria (2002) Financiación de partidos y democracia paritaria. In: *Revista de Estudios Politicos*, 115, January–March, pp. 129–53.

Hooghe, Liesbet and Gary Marks (2001) *Multilevel Governance and European Integration.* Lanham: Rowman and Littlefield.

Hopkin, Jonathan (1993) *La Desintegración de la Unión de Centro Democratico. Una interpretación organizativa.* Madrid: Centro de Estudios Constitucionales.

—— (1999) Political parties in a young democracy. In: David Broughton and Mark Donovan (eds), *Changing Party Systems in Western Europe.* London: Pinter, pp. 207–31.

—— (2001) Bringing the Members Back In? Democratizing Candidate Selection in Britain and Spain. In: *Party Politics*, 7: 343–61.

—— (2005) From census to competition; the changing nature of democracy in the spanish transition. In: Sebastian Balfour (ed.), *Contemporary Politics of Spain*. Basingstroke: Palgrave, pp. 6–26.

Huneeus, Carlos (1985) *La Unión del Centro Democrático y la Transición a la Democracia*. Madrid: Centro de Investigaciones Sociológicas.

Ibarra, Pedro (2000) Los estudios sobre los movimientos sociales: el estado de la cuestión. In: *Revista Española de Ciencia Politica*, 1, 2, April, pp. 271–90.

Inglehart, Ronald, Christian Welzel (2005) *Modernisation, Cultural Change and Democracy. The Human Development Sequence*. Cambridge: Cambridge University Press.

Institut de Ciencies Politiques i Socials (ICPS) (2002) *Observatório Politico Autonomico*. Ano 2001, 1. Barcelona: ICPS.

—— (2003) *Observatório Politico Autonomico. Año 2002*, 2. Barcelona: ICPS.

—— (2006) *Observatório Politico Autonomoico Año 2006*, 6. Barcelona ICPS.

Isbell, Paul and Alfredo Arahuetes (2005) *Indice Elcano de oportunidades y riesgos estratégicos para la economia española*. Madrid: Real Instituto Elcano, 26, pp. 34–7.

Issing, Otmar (2002) On macroeconomic policy coordination in EMU. In: *Journal of Common Market Studies*, 40, 2, pp. 345–58.

Jimenez, Fernando (1998) Political scandals and political responsibility in democratic Spain. In: Paul Heywood (eds), *Politics and Policy in Democratic Spain*. London: Frank Cass, pp. 80–93.

Jimenez, Fernando and Miguel Cainzos (2003) Political corruption in Spain. In: Martin J. Bull and James L. Newell (eds), *Corruption in Contemporary Politics*. Basingstoke: Palgrave, pp. 9–23.

Jiménez Sanchez, Manuel (2005) *El impacto político de los movimientos sociales. Un estudio de la protesta ambiental en España*. Madrid: Centro de Estudios Politicos y Constitucionales.

Jiménez, Manuel (2007) The environmental movement in Spain: a growing force of contention, *South European Society and Politics*, 12: 3, pp. 359–78.

Jones, Rachel (2000) *Beyond the Spanish State. Central Government, Domestic Actors and the EU*. Basingstoke: Palgrave.

Jordana, Jacint (1998) La politica de telecomunicaciones en España: del monopolio a la transición al mercado. In: Ricard Gomá and Joan Subirats (eds), *Politicas publicas en España. Contenidos, redes de actores y niveles de gobierno*. Barcelona: Ariel, pp. 270–92.

—— (2001) La politica de telecomunicaciones: ?una europeización necesaria, o la ausencia del debate publico? In: Carlos Closa (ed.), *La europeización del sistema politico español*. Madrid: Istmo, pp. 403–20.

Jünemann, Annette (2001) Die EU und Barcelona-Prozess-Bewertung und Perspektiven. In: *Integration*, 24 Jg., 1, pp. 42–57.

Jun, Uwe (2003) Great Britain: from the prevalence of the amateur to the dominance of the professional politician. In: Jens Borchert, Jürgen Zeiss (eds), *The political class in advanced democracies*. Oxford: Oxford University Press, pp. 164–86.

Kamen, Henry (2002) *Spain's Road to Empire. The Making of a World Power 1492–1763*. London: Penguin-Allen Lane.

Katz, Richard and Peter Mair (1995) Changing models of party organisation and party democracy: the emergence of the Cartel party, *Party Politics*, 1, 5–28.

Katz, Richard. S and Ruud Koole (2002) Political Data Yearbook 2001. In: *European Journal of Political Research*, 41, 7–8, pp. 885–96.

Kennedy, Paul (1999) The Spanish socialist workers'party. In: Robert Ladrech and Philippe Marliére (eds), *Social Democratic Parties in the European Union*. Basingstoke: Macmillan, pp. 176–88.

—— (2000) Spain. In: Ian Manners and Richard G. Whitman (eds), *The Foreign Policies of European Union Member-States*. London: Macmillan, pp. 105–27.

—— (2001) Spain's Third Way?: the Spanish Socialist Party's utilization of European Integration. In: *Journal of Southern Europe and the Balkans*, 3, 1, May, pp. 49–59.

Kern, Robert W. (1974) *Liberals, Reformers and Caciques in Restoration Spain (1875–1909)*. Albuquerque: University of New Mexico.

Kingdom of Spain (2000) *National Action Plan for Employment 2000*. Madrid.

Kraus, Peter A. and Wolfgang Merkel (1998) Die Konsolidierung der Demokratie nach Franco. In: Walther L. Bernecker and Klaus Dirscherl (eds), *Spanien heute. Politik, Wirtschaft, Kultur*. Frankfurt-am-Main: Vervuert, pp. 37–62.

Kreienbrink, Axel (2007) Immigración e integración social de los inmigrantes en España entre consenso y enfrentamiento politico. In: Walter C. Bernecker, Günther Maihold (ed.), *España del consenso a la polarización. Cambios en la democracia española*. Madrid, Frankfurt a. M.: Iberoamericana, Vervuert, pp. 239–64.

Kreuzer, Markus and Ina Stephan (2003) Enduring notables, weak parties, and powerful technocrats. In: Jens Borchert, Jürgen Zeiss (eds), *The Political Class in Advanced Democracies*. Oxford: Oxford University Press, pp. 124–41.

Lago, Ignacio and José Ramón Montero (2006) *The 2004 Election in Spain: Terrorism, Accountability and Voting*. Barcelona: Institut de Ciencies Politiques i Socials. Working Paper 253.

Lancaster, Thomas D. (1998) Nacionalismos, regionalismo e instituciones estatales: una evolución del caso español a partir de las opiniones de los ciudadanos. In: Robert Agranoff and Rafael Bañon i Martinez (eds), *El estado de las autonomias. ¿Hacia un nuevo federalismo?* Bilbao: InstitutoVasco de Administración Publica, pp. 245–68.

León Gross, Teodoro (2006) Radiografia de los grandes diarios. In: Fundación Telefonica (ed.), *Tendencias '06. Medios de Comunicación*. Madrid: Fundación Telefónica, pp. 119–27.

Ley para reforma politica (4 enero 1977) (1998) In: José Carlos Rueda (ed.), *Legislación electoral española (1808–1977)*. Barcelona: Ariel, pp. 203–5.

Liebert, Ulrike (1990) From polarisation to pluralism: regional-nationalist parties in the process of democratic consolidation in post-Franco Spain. In: Geoffrey Pridham (ed.), *Securing Democracy. Political Parties and Democratic Consolidation in Southern Europe*. London: Routledge, pp. 147–70.

Linz, Juan J. (1994) From great hopes to civil war: the breakdown of democracy in Spain. In: Juan J. Linz and Alfred Stepan (eds), *The Breakdown of Democratic Regimes*. Baltimore: Johns Hopkins University Press, pp. 142–214.

Linz, Juan J., Pilar Gangas and Miguel Jerez Mir (2000) Spanish *Diputados*: From the 1876 restoration to consolidated democracy. In: Heinrich Best and Maurizio Cotta (eds), *Parliamentary Representatives in Europe 1848–2000. Legislative Recruitment and Careers in Eleven European Countries*. Oxford: Oxford University Press, pp. 371–462.

Linz, Juan J., Miguel Jerez and Susana Corzo (2003) Ministers and regimes in Spain: from the first to the second restoration, 1874–2002. In: Pedro Tavares de Almeida, António Costa Pinto and Nancy Bermeo (eds), *Who Governs in Southern Europe? Regime Change and Ministerial Recruitment 1850–2000*. London: Frank Cass, pp. 41–116.

Llera, Francisco (1993) Conflict in Euskadi revisited. In: Richard Gunther (ed.), *Politics, Society, and Democracy. The Case of Spain*. Boulder, CO: Westview Press, pp. 169–95.

Llera, Josep Soler (1998) Las elecciones autonómicas en Cataluña (1980–1995). In: Manuel Alcantara and Antonia Martinez (eds), *Las elecciones autonomicas en España, 1980–1997*. Madrid: CIS, pp. 225–56.

Llera, Francisco J., José Ramón Montero and Francesc Pallarés (1998) Los partidos de ambito no estatal en España: notas actitudinales sobre nacionalismos y regionalismos. In: Robert Agranoff and Rafael Bañon i Martinez (eds), *El estado de las autonomias. ?Hacia un nuevo federalismo?* Bilbao: Instituto Vasco de Administración Pública, pp. 205–44.

—— (1998) Pluralismo y gobernabilidad en Euskadi (1980–1994). In: Manuel Alcantara and Antonia Martinez (eds), *Las elecciones autonomicas en España, 1980–1997*. Madrid: CIS, pp. 413–43.

—— (1999) *Pluralismo y gobernabilidad en Euskadi, 1980–1994*. Working Paper no. 162. Barcelona: Institut de Ciencies Politiques i Socials.

—— (2000) Gobierno y administración en Euskadi. In: Juan Luis Paniagua Soto (ed.), *Gobierno y administración en las Comunidades Autonomas. Andalucia, Canarias, Cataluña, Galicia y Pais Vasco*. Madrid: Tecnos, pp. 11–66.

—— (2002) La opinión pública: la diversidad de una nación plural. In: Joan Subirats and Raquel Gallego (eds), *Veinte años de autonomias en España. Leyes, politicas públicas, instituciones y opinion publica*. Madrid: Centro de Investigaciones Sociolo gicas, pp. 321–76.

—— (2006) La dimensión territorial e identitaria en la competición partidista y la gobernabilidad españolas. In: Francisco Murillo (ed.), *Transformaciones politicas y sociales en la España democrática*. Valencia: Tirant lo Blanch, pp. 239–317.

Llera, Fran J., A. Retortillo (eds) (2004) *Los español es y las victimas del terrorismo. 1° Encuesta nacional 'Percepción ciudadana sobre las victimas del terrorismo en España'.* Opiniones and Actitudes 50. Madrid: Centro de Investigaciones Sociologicas.

Lombardo, Emanuela (2003) La europeización de la politica española de igualdad de genero. In: *Revista Española de Ciencia Politica*, Number. 9, October, pp. 65–82.

—— (2004) *La europeización de la política española de igualdad de género*. Valencia: Tyrant lo Blanch.

Lopez Calvo, José (1996) *Organización y funcionamiento del gobierno*. Madrid: Tecnos.

Lopez Nieto, Lourdes (1986) *Alianza Popular: estructura y evolución electoral de un partido conservador (1976–1982)*. Madrid: CIS.

Lopez Nieto, Lourdes, Mercedes Alda, Esther del Campo, José Ramón Laorden, Eliseo Lopez, Teresa Lorenzo and Antonia Monteagudo (2002) Las relaciones entre parlamentos y gobiernos autonomicos: analisis preliminar de las funciones parlamentarias. In: Joan Subirats and Raquel Gallego (eds), *Veinte años de autonomias en España. Leyes, politicas publicas, instituciones y opinion publica*. Madrid: Centro de Investigaciones Sociologicas, pp. 31–68.

Lopez-Nieto, Lourdes (2001) Las Cortes Generales. In: Manuel Alcantara and Antonia Martinez (eds), *Politica y Gobierno en España* Valencia: Tirant lo Blanch, pp. 215–42.

—— (2006) Los convenios de colaboración en el Estado autonomico: intensidad, continuidad y multilateralidad de una relación casi desconocida. In: Lourdes Lopez Nieto (ed.), *Relaciones Intergubernamentales en la España Democrática. Interdependencia, Autonomia, Conflicto y Cooperación*. Madrid: Dykinson, pp. 147–71.

Lopez Pina, Antonio and Eduardo Aranguren (1976) *La Cultura Politica de Franco*. Madrid: Taurus Ediciones.

Magone, José M. (1996) *The Changing Architecture of Iberian Politics. An Investigation on the Structuring of Democratic Political Systemic Culture in Semiperipheral Southern European Societies*. Lewiston: Edwin Mellen Press.

—— (1998) The logics of party system change in southern Europe. In:Paul Pennings and Jan-Erik Lane (eds), *Comparing Party System Change*. London: Routledge, pp. 217–40.

—— (2001) *Iberian Trade Unionism. Democratization under the Impact of the European Union*. New Brunswick: Transaction.

—— (2002) Attitudes of southern European citizens towards European integration: before and after accession, 1974–2000. In: Antonio Costa Pinto and Nuno Severiano Teixeira (eds), *Southern Europe and the Making of the European Union*. New York: Columbia University Press, pp. 209–36.

—— (2003) *The Politics of Southern Europe. Integration into the European Union*. Westport: Praeger.

—— (2006) *The New World Architecture. The Role of the European Union in the Making of Global Governance*. New Brunswick, N.J.: Transaction.

—— (2007a) South European national parliaments and the European Union. An inconsistent reactive revival. In: John O'Brennan and Tapio Raunio (eds), *National Parliaments within the Enlarged European Union. From 'victims' of integration to competitive actors?*. London: Routledge, pp. 116–31.

—— (2007b) The southern European pattern of parliamentary scrutiny of EU legislation: emulating the French model. In: Holzhacker, Ronald and Erik Albaek (eds), *Democratic Governance and European Integration. Linking Societal and State Processes of Democracy*. Cheltenham: Edgar Elgar, pp. 229–48.

Maiz, Ramon and Antón Losada (2000) Institutions, policies and nation building: the Galician case. In: *Regional and Federal Studies*, 10, 1, Spring, pp. 62–91.

Maiz, Ramón, Pablo Beramendi and Mireia Grau (2002) La federalización del estado de las autonomias: evolución y deficit institucionales. In: Joan Subirats and Raquel Gallego (eds), *Veinte años de autonomias en España. Leyes, politicas publicas, instituciones y opinion pública*. Madrid: Centro de Investigaciones Sociologicas, pp. 379–424.

Maldonado Gago, Juan (2002) La cultura politica en España. In: Paloma Roman (ed.), *Sistema politico español*. Madrid: McGraw-Hill, pp. 81–99.

Mallen, Beatriz Tomas (2002) *Transfuguismo parlamentario y democracia de partidos*. Madrid: Centro de Estudios Politicos y Constitucionales.

Manuel, Villoria (2006) Spain. Country Report In: Transparency International, *Global Corruption Report*. Cambridge: Cambridge University Press. pp. 250–53.

Maravall, José Maria (1978) *Dictatorship and Political Dissent. Workers and Students in Franco's Spain*. London: Tavistock.

—— (1982) *Transition to Democracy in Spain*. London: Croom Helm.

Marks, Gary Richard Haesly and Heather Mbaye (2002) What do subnational offices think they are doing in Brussels. In: *Regional and Federal Studies*, vol. 12, Number. 3, pp. 1–24.

Marks, Gary and Ivan Llamazares (2006) Multilevel governance and the transformation of regional mobilization and identity in southern Europe, with particular attention to Catalonia and the Basque Country. In: Richard Gunther, P. Nikiforos Diamandouros and Dimitri A. Sotiropoulos (eds), *Democracy and the New State in the New Southern Europe*. Oxford:Oxford University Press, pp. 235–62.

Martin, Benjamin (1990) *The Agony of Modernization. Labor and Industrialization in Spain*. Ithaca: Cornell University Press.

Martin Ardiles, Antonio (2005a) The CEOE and the Ministry of Labour consider their positions on reforming the labour market. [ES0505201N] Posted on the website of European Industrial Relations Observatory http://www.eurofound. Accessed on 8 January 2008.

Martin Ardiles, Antonio (2005b) Union's electoral strength exceeds membership. [ES0501204F] Posted on the website of European Industrial Relations Observatory http://www.eurofound. Accessed on 8 January 2008.

Martin Ardiles, Antonio (2007) *Industrial Relations Developments 2006: Spain*. European Industrial Relations Observatory (EIRO) online http://eurofound.eu accessed on 28 December 2007.

Martin-Muñoz, Gema (2000) Political reform and social change in the Maghreb. In: Alvaro Vasconcelos and George Joffe (eds), The Barcelona Process. Building a Euro-Mediterranean Regional Community. Special Issue of *Mediterranean Politics*, vol. 5, Number. 1, pp. 96–130, 114–26.

Martinez, Antonia and Monica Mendez (2000) La representación politica en el congreso español. In: Antonia Martinez (ed.), *El congreso de los diputados en España: funciones y rendimiento*. Madrid: Tecnos, pp. 223–70.

Martinez Lucio, Miguel (1998) Spain: regulating employment and social fragmentation. In: Anthony Ferner and Richard Hyman (eds), *Changing Industrial Relations in Europe*. Oxford: Blackwell, pp. 426–58.

Martinez Lucio, Miguel and Paul Blyton (1995) Constructing the post-Fordist state? The politics of labour market flexibility in Spain. In: *West European Politics*, 18, 2, April, pp. 340–60.

Martinez-Herrera, Enric (2002) From nation-building to building identification with political communities: consequences of political decentralisation in Spain, the Basque Country, Catalonia and Galicia, 1978–2001. In: *European Journal for Political Research*, 41, 4, June, pp. 421–53.

Massot Marti, Albert (2004) España ante la reforma de la Politica Agricola Comun (PAC). Real Elcano Instituto de Estudios Internacionales y Estrategicos. Documento de Trabajo, Number. 50/2004.

Mata, José Manuel (1998) *Nationalism and Political Parties in the Autonomous Community of the Basque Country. Strategies and Tensions*. Working Papers 137. Barcelona: Institut de Ciencies Politiques i Socials.

Mata, José Manuel (2005) Terrorism and nationalist conflict. The weakness of democracy in the Basque Country. In: Sebastian Balfour (ed.), *The Politics of Contemporary Spain*. London: Routledge, pp. 81–105.

Matas Dalmases, Jordi (2001) El control politico de la administración en Cataluña. In: Jordi Matas (ed.), *El control politico de la administración*. Barcelona: Institut de Ciencies Politiques i Socials, pp. 35–75.

Matas Dalmases, Jordi and José Maria Reniu Vilalala (2003) La Politica delas Coaliciones en Cataluña. In: *Revista Española de Ciencia Politica*, Number. 9, October 2003, pp. 83–102.

Mateo, Manuel Cienfuegos (2001) Las cortes españolas ante la integración europea. In: Carlos Closa (ed.), *La europeización del sistema politico español*. Madrid: Istmo, pp. 198–224.

Matuschek, Peter (2003) Spain: A textbook case of partitocracy. In: Jens Borchert, Jürgen Zeiss (eds), *The Political Class in Advanced Democracies*. Oxford: Oxford University Press, pp. 336–51.

Maurice, Jacques (1990) *El anarquismo andaluz. Campesinos y sindicalistas, 1868–1936*. Barcelona: Critica.

Maxwell, Kenneth and Steven Spiegel (1994) *The New Spain. From Isolation to Influence*. New York: Council on Foreign Relations Press.

McDonough, Peter, Samuel H. Barnes and Antonio Lopez Pina (1998) *The Cultural Dynamics of Democratization in Spain*. Ithaca and London: Cornell University Press.

Meer, Marc van der (1996) Aspiring corporatism? Industrial relations in Spain. In: Joris van Ruysseveldt and Jelle Visser (eds), *Industrial Relations in Europe. Traditions and Transitions*. London: Sage, pp. 310–36.

Mendez Lago, Mónica (2000) *La estrategia organizativa del Partido Socialista Obrero Español (1975–1996)*. Madrid: CIS.

Mendez-Lago, Mónica (2005) The socialist party in government and in opposition. In: Sebastian Balfour (ed.), *The Politics of Contemporary Spain*. London: Routledge, pp. 169–97.

Mendez Lago, Mónica and Julian Santamaria (2001) La ley de la disparidad ideologica curvilinea de los partidos politicos: el caso de PSOE. In: *Revista Española de Ciencia Politica*, 4, April, pp. 35–69.

Mendez, Mónica and Fabiola Mota (2006) Las caracteristicas organizativas de las asociaciones en España. In: José Ramon Montero, Joan Font, Mariano Torcal (eds), *Ciudadanos, asociaciones y participación en España*. Madrid: Centro de Investigaciones Sociologicas, pp. 203–222.

Meny, Yves and Martin Rhodes (1997) Illicit governance: corruption, scandal and fraud. In: Martin Rhodes, Paul Heywood and Vincent Wright (eds), *Developments in West European Politics*. Basingstoke: Macmillan, pp. 95–113.

Menudo, Francisco Lopez (2002) Andalucia. In: *Instituto de Derecho Publico, Informe de las Comunidades Autonomas 2001*. Barcelona: Instituto de Derecho Publico.

—— (2003) Andalucia. In: *Instituto de Derecho Publico, Informe de las Comunidades Autonomoas 2002*. Barcelona: Instituto de Derecho Publico.

—— (2004) Andalucia. In: *Instituto de Derecho Publico, Informe de las Comunidades Autonomoas 2003*. Barcelona: Instituto de Derecho Publico.

—— (2005) Andalucia. In: *Instituto de Derecho Publico, Informe de las Comunidades Autonomoas 2004*. Barcelona: Instituto de Derecho Publico.

—— (2006) Andalucia. In: *Instituto de Derecho Publico, Informe de las Comunidades Autonomoas 2005*. Barcelona: Instituto de Derecho Publico.

Merkel, Wolfgang (1993) *Ende der Sozialdemokratie? Machtresourcen und Regierungspolitik im westeuropäischen Vergleich*. Frankfurt-am-Main: Campus.

Mesa del Olmo, Adela (2000) La politización de las estructuras administrativas de las comunidades autonomas. In: *Revista Española de Ciencia Politica*, 1, 2, April, pp. 211–35.

—— (2001) Problemas de articulación entre politica y administración en la Comunidad Autonoma Vasca. In: Jordi Matas (ed.), *El Control Politico de la Administracion*. Barcelona: Institut de Ciencies Politiques i Socials, pp. 79–98.

Miguel, Platón (2005) *11-M cómo la Yihad puso de rodillas a España*. Madrid: la esfera de los libros. pp. 43–4.

Military Capabilities Commitment Conference (2004) *Declaration on European Military Capabilities*. Posted on the website of the Council of the European Union. http://www.council.eu accessed on 7 January 2008.

Ministerio de Administraciones Publicas (MAP) (2000) *White Paper on the Improvement of Public Services. A New Administration at the Services of the Citizens*. Madrid: MAP, available online at www.map.es

—— (2005) *Conferencias Sectoriales. Reuniones en el año 2004*. Madrid: Ministerio de Administraciones Publicas.

—— (2006) *Conferencias Sectoriales. Reuniones en el año 2005*. Madrid: Ministerio de Administraciones Publicas.

—— (2007a) *Informe sobre la actividad de las conferencias sectoriales durante 2006.* Madrid: Ministerio de Administraciones Publicas.

—— (2007b) *Informe sobre los convenios de colaboración estado-comunidad autonomas tramitados durante 2006.* Madrid: Ministerio de Administracioes Publicas.

—— (2007c) *Traspasos Aprobados par alas Comunidades Autonomas y las Ciudades de Ceuta y Melilla.* Madrid: Ministerio de Administraciones Publicas, last stand 14 September 2007.

—— (2008), *Fondos de Compensación Interterritorial 2008.* Madrid: MAP Febrero 2008.

Ministerio de la Defensa (MDE) (2000) Libro blanco de la defensa española 2000. Madrid: MDE 2002 website http://www.mde.es accessed on 22 August 2003.

Ministerio de Educacion y Ciencia, (2007a) *Panorama de la Educación. Indicadores de la OCDE 2007. Informe Español.* Madrid: Ministerio de Educacion y Ciencia.

—— (2007b) Datos y Cifras 2007–8. Curso Escolar 2007–8. Madrid: Ministerio de Educacion y Ciencia.

—— (2007c) Pisa 2006. *Programa para la Evaluación Internacional de Alumnos de la OCDE. Informe Español.* Madrid: Ministerio de Educacion y Ciencia.

Ministerio del Interior (MIR) (2003) website http://www.mir.es accessed on 20 March 2003.

—— (2006) *La Comunidad Musulmana en España. Estudio de Opinion realizado por Metroscopia.* Madrid: Ministerio del Interior.

Ministerio del Trabajo y Asuntos Sociales (MTAS) (2001a) *Plan de acción para el empleo del reino de España.* Madrid: MTAS.

—— (MTAS) (2001b) Informes: II plan integral contra la violencia domestica. In: *Revista del Ministerio del Trabajo y Asuntos Sociales*, 40, pp. 125–34.

—— (MTAS) (2002) *Plan de acción para el empleo del reino de España.* Consejo de Ministros 26 April 2002. Madrid: MTAS.

Molas, Isidre and Oriol Bartolomeus (2003) Estructura de la competencia politica en España 1986–2000. In: Oriol Bartolomeus (ed.), *La competencia politica en la España de las autonomias.* Barcelona: Institut de Ciencies Politiques i Socials, pp. 17–42.

Molina, Óscar (2006) Trade union strategies and change in Neo-corporatist concertation: A new century of political exchange?, *West European Politics*, 29, 4, pp. 640–64.

—— (2007) State and regulation of industrial relations in Spain: old wine in a new governance bottle?', *South European Society and Politics*, 12, 4, pp. 461–79.

Molina Alvarez de Cienfuegos, Ignacio (1999) Spain: still the primacy of corporatism? In: Edward C. Page and Vincent Wright (eds), *Bureaucratic Elites in Western European States.* Oxford: Oxford University Press, pp. 32–54.

Molina, Ignacio (2000) Spain. In: Hussein Kassim, B. Guy Peters and Vincent Wright (eds), *The National Co-ordination of EU Policy. The Domestic Level.* Oxford: Oxford University Press, pp. 114–40.

Molina, Ignacio Alvarez de Cienfuegos (2001) La adaptación a la Unión Europea del poder ejecutivo Español. In: Carlos Closa (ed.), *La europeización del sistema politico español.* Madrid: Istmo, pp. 126–57.

—— (2002) La liberalización de la economia española (por efecto de la pertenencia a la Unión Europea). In: Carlos Closa (ed.), *La europeización del sistema politico español.* Madrid: Istmo, pp. 298–326.

Molina A. de Cienfuegos, Ignacio and Fernando Rodrigo Rodriguez (2002) Las transformaciones organizativas de la politica exterior española. In: *Revista de Estudios Politicos*, 117, July-September, pp. 173–221.

Molins, Joaquim M. and Alex Casademunt (1998) Pressure groups and the articulation of interests. In: Paul Heywood (ed.), *Politics and Policy in Democratic Spain*. London: Frank Cass, pp. 124–46.

Molins, Joaquim, Alexandre Casademunt (2001) Los Grupos de Interés. In: Manuel Alcantara y Antonia Martinez (eds), *Politica y Gobierno en España*. Valencia: Tirant lo Blanch, pp. 471–92.

Monferrer Tomás, Jordi M. (2004) La construcción de la protesta en el movimiento gay español: La Ley de Peligrosidad Social (1970) como factor precipitante de la acción colectiva. In: *Revista Española de Investigaciones Sociológicas*, Number. 102/103, pp. 171–204.

Montabes, Juan (2001) El Gobierno. In: Manuel Alcantara and Antonia Martinez (eds), *Politica y Gobierno en España*. Valencia: Tirant lo Blanch, pp. 165–213.

Montabes Pereira, Juana and Javier Torres Vela (1997) Elecciones, partidos y proceso politico en Andalucia (1977–1996). In: Manuel Alcantara, Antonia Martinez (eds), *Las elecciones autonómicas en España, 1980–1997*. Madrid: CIS, pp. 9–49.

Montabes, Juan, Maria Angustias Parejo and Inmaculada Szmolka (2003) La transitada transición: continuidades y cambios en la politica marroqui. In: *Economia Exterior*, 24, Spring, pp. 77–88.

Montabes Pereira, Juan and Carmen Ortega Villodres (2002) El voto limitado a las elecciones del Senado español: estrategias de nominación y rendimientos partidistas en las elecciones de marzo 2000. In: *Revista Española de Ciencia Politica*, Number. 7, October, pp. 103–30.

Montero, Feliciano (2007) Autocríticas del nacionalcatolicismo en los años cincuenta. In: Carolyn P. Boyd (ed.), *Religión y política en la España contemporánea*. Madrid: Centro de Estudios Politicos y Constitucionales, pp. 139–62.

Montero, José Ramón (1998a) Sobre las preferencias electorales en España: Fragmentación y polarización (1977–1993). In: Pilar del Castillo (ed.), *Comportamiento politico y electoral*. Madrid: CIS, pp. 51–124.

—— (1998b) Sobre el sistema electoral español: rendimientos politicos y criterios de reforma. In: Juan Montabes (ed.), *El sistema electoral a debate. Veinte años de rendimientos del sistema electoral español. 1977–1997*. Madrid: CIS, pp. 37–70.

—— (1998c) Stabilising the democratic order: electoral behaviour in Spain. In: *West European Politics*, 21, 4, pp. 53–79.

Montero, José Ramon and Mariano Torcal (1995) Cambio cultural, conflictos politicos y politica en España. In: *Revista de Estudios Politicos*, 74, pp. 9–33.

Montero, José Ramón and Kerman Calvo (2000) An elusive cleavage? Religiosity and Party Choice in Spain. In: David Broughton, Hans Martien Ten Napel (eds), *Religion and Mass Electoral Behaviour*. London: Routledge, pp. 118–39.

Montero, José Ramón and Richard Gunther (2002) Los estudios sobre los partidos politicos: una revisión critica. In: *Revista de Estudios Politicos*, 118, October–November, pp. 9–38.

Morán, Maria Luz and Jorge Benedicto (1995) *La cultura politica de los españoles. Un ensayo de reinterpretación*. Madrid: CIS.

Morales Diez de Ulzurrun, Laura (2006) *Instituciones, movilización y participación politica: El asociacionismo politico en las democracias occidentales*. Madrid: Centro de Estudios Politicos y Constitucionales.

Morales, Laura (2005) Existe una crisis participativa? La evolución de la participación politica y el asociacionismo en España. In: *Revista Española de Ciencia Politica*, number 13, pp. 51–87.

Morales, Laura and Fabiola Mota (2006) El Asociacionismo en España.In: José Ramon Montero, Joan Font, Mariano Torcal (eds.), *Ciudadanos, asociaciones y participación en España*. Madrid: Centro de Investigaciones Sociologicas, pp. 77–103.

Morata, F. (1995) L'Eurorégion et le reseau C-6: L'emergence du supraregionalisme en Europe du sud? In: *Pôle Sud*, 3, Autumn, pp. 117–27.

—— (1997) The Euro-region and the C-6 network: the new politics of subnational cooperation in the western Mediterranean. In: M. Keating and J. Loughlin (eds), *The Political Economy of Regionalism*. London: Frank Cass, pp. 292–305.

—— (1998) *La Unión Europea. Procesos, actores y politicas*. Barcelona: Ariel.

—— (2000) La politica regional y de cohesión. In: Francesc Morata (ed.), *Politicas publicas en la Union Europea*. Barcelona: Ariel, pp. 143–86.

Morata, Francesc and Dimitri Barua (2001) La europeización de las politicas de desarollo agricola y rural. In: Carlos Closa (ed.), *La europeización del sistema politico español*. Madrid: Istmo, pp. 461–85.

—— (2004) Politicas de cohesion y gobernanza europea: el caso de Cataluña. In: Francesc Morata (ed.), *Gobernanza Multiniveles en La Union Europea*. Valencia: Tirant lo Blanch, pp. 159–88.

—— (2007) La acción exterior de las comunidades autónomas: El Caso de Catalunya. In: Mario Kölling, Stelios Stavridis, Natividad Fernández Sola (eds), *Las Relaciones Internacionales de las Regiones: Actores Sub-nacionales, para-diplomacia y gobernanza multinivel*. Zaragoza: University of Zaragoza, pp. 305–09.

Moré, Iñigo (2004) The economic steps between neighbours: the case of Spain-Morocco. In: *Mediterranean Politics*, vol. 9, 2, summer, pp. 165–200.

Moreno del Rio, Carmelo (2000) Democracia, constitución y nacionalismo en Euskadi: tres discursos circulares para negar la existencia de una comunidad politica. In: *Revista Española de Ciencia Politica*, 3, October, pp. 125–48.

Mota, Fabiola and Joan Subirats (2000) El quinto elemento: el capital social de las comunidades autonomas. In: *Revista Española de Ciencia Politica*, 1, 2, April, pp. 123–58.

—— (2002) Capital social et capacité de gouvernement politique: leurs effets sur la satisfaction et le soutien au systéme politique autonomique espagnol. In: *Pôle Sud*, 16, May, pp. 107–24.

Mujal-León, Eusebio (1983) *Communism and Political Change in Spain*. Bloomington: Indiana University Press.

Murphy, Brendan (1999) European integration and liberalisation: political change and economic policy continuity in Spain. In: *Mediterranean Politics*, 4, 1, pp. 55–78.

Nagel, Klaus-Jürgen and Ferran Requejo (2007) El debate sobre la relación entre Centro y autonomias en España. In: Walter C. Bernecker and Günther Maihold (eds), *España del consenso a la polarización. Cambios en la democracia española*. Madrid, Frankfurt a. M.: Iberoamericana, Vervuert, pp. 265–95.

Nash, Elizabeth (1983) The Spanish socialist party since Franco: from clandestinity to government 1976–82. In: David S. Bell (ed.), *Democratic Politics in Spain*. New York: St Martin's Press, pp. 29–62.

Navarro Mendez, José Ignacio (2002) ?Pueden los partidos politicos expulsar Libremente a sus afiliados? In: *Revista de Estudios Politicos*, 107, January–March, pp. 269–95.

Navarro, Vicenç (2006) *El subdesarollo social de España. Causas y consecuencias*. Barcelona: Editorial Anagrama.

Newton, Mike (1983) Peoples and regions of Spain. In: David S. Bell (ed.), *Democratic Politics in Spain*. New York: St Martin's Press, pp. 98–131.

Newton, Michael and Peter J. Donaghy (1997) *Institutions of Modern Spain*. Cambridge: Cambridge University Press.

Nuñez Seixas, Xosé M.N. (1995) Os nacionalismos da Espanha contemporanea: uma perspectiva historica e algumas hipoteses para o presente. In: *Analise Social*, xxx, 2–3, pp. 489–526.

—— (1999) *Los nacionalismos en España contemporanea (siglos XIX y XX)*. Barcelona: Hipotesi.

Nuñez Seixas, Xosé M. (2007) El nuevo debate territorial en la España actual (2004–2006): ?Hacia un Estado Plurinacional? In: Walter C. Bernecker and Günther Maihold (eds), *España del consenso a la polarización. Cambios en la democracia española*. Madrid, Frankfurt a. M.: Iberoamericana, Vervuert, pp. 317–35.

Observatorio del Empleo, MISEP (2002) *La politica de empleo en España. Informe de base sobre instituciones, procedimientos y medidas de political de empleo*. Madrid: Secretaria General del Empleo.

Oficina de Justificación de la Difusión (2008) website at http://www.ojd.es accessed on 28 January 2008.

Oficina Economica del Presidente del Gobierno (2007) Dos años de INGENIO 2010. Posted on website of the Prime Minister's Office http://www.la-moncloa.es/programas/oep accessed 28 December 2007.

Oliet Palá, Alberto (2004) *La concertación social en la democracia española: crónica de un difícil intercambio*. Valencia: Tirant lo Blanch.

—— (2006) Del sindicalismo ideológico al clientelar. In: Francisco Murillo, José Luis Garcia de Serrana y otros (eds), *Transformaciones políticas y sociales en la España democratica*. Valencia: Tirant lo Blanch, pp. 333–98.

Oliveres, Arcadi and Pere Ortega (2007) (eds), *El militarismo en España. Balance del ciclo armamentista español hasta 2007*. Barcelona: Icaria-Antrazyt.

Oñate, Pablo Rubalcaba (1998) Las elecciones autonómicas de Aragón. In: Manuel Alcantara and Antonia Martinez (eds), *Las elecciones autonómicas en España, 1980–1997*. Madrid: CIS, pp. 51–79.

Oñate, Pablo (2000) Congreso, Grupos Parlamentarios y Partidos. In: Antonia Martinez (ed.), *El Congreso de los Diputados: Funciones y Rendimiento*. Madrid: Tecnos, pp. 95–139.

Oñate, Pablo and Francisco A. Ocaña (2005) Las elecciones generales de marzo de 2004 y los sistemas de partidos en Españatanto cambio electoral? In: *Revista Española de Ciencia Politica*, Number. 13, October 2005, pp. 159–82.

Oñate, Pablo and Irene Delgado (2006) Partidos, grupos parlamentarios y diputados en las asambleas autonomicas. In: Pablo Oñate (ed.), *Organización y funcionamiento de los parlamentos autonómicos*. Valencia: Tirant lo Blanch, pp. 135–72.

Oñate, Pablo Rubalcaba (2006) Elecciones, partidos y sistemas de partidos en la España democratica. In: Francisco Murillo, José Luis Garcia de la Serrana y Otros (eds), *Transformaciones y sociales en la España democratica*. Valencia: Tirant lo Blanch, pp. 399–431.

Ontiveros, Emilio and Yolanda Fernandez (2002) Flujos de inversión hacia America Latina. In: *Perspectivas Exteriores 2002. Los intereses de España en el mundo*. Edited by Fundación para las Relaciones Exteriores y el Dialogo Exterior (FRIDE). Madrid: FRIDE, pp. 273–313.

Organisation for Economic Development and Cooperation (OECD) (1964) *Economic Survey: Spain*. Paris: OECD.

Organisation for Economic Cooperation and Development (OECD) (2004) *Analisis de los resultados medioambientales*. Paris: OECD.

—— (1970) *Economic Survey: Spain*. Paris; OECD.

Otero, José Manuel, Nieves Lagares Diez, Alfredo Castro Duarte and Isabel Diz. Otero (1998) Las elecciones autonómicas en Galicia. In: Manuel Alcantara and Antonia Martinez (eds), *Las elecciones autonomicas en España, 1980–1997*. Madrid: CIS, pp. 285–307.

Ortuzar, Antoni (1998) La situación del debate de esta cuestió n en el estado español. In: *La participación de las comunidades autonomas en los consejos de ministros de la unión europea*. Edited by the Instituto Vasco de Administracio n Publica. Bilbao: IVAP, pp. 13–17.

Palacio, Luis (2006) Radiografia de los grupos de comunicación. In: Fundación Telefonica (ed.), *Tendencias'06. Medios de Comunicación*. Madrid: Fundación Telefónica, pp. 419–38.

Palacios, Simón Pedro Izcara (2007) Welfare benefits and social exclusion in southern Spain, *South European Society and Politics*, 12, 2, pp. 165–82.

Pallarés, Francesc (1998) Las elecciones autonómicas en España: 1980–1992. In: Pilar del Castillo (ed.), *Comportamiento politico y electoral*. Madrid: CIS, pp. 151–220.

Paniagua, Soto and Juan Luis (eds) (2000) *Gobierno y administración en las comunidades autonomas. Andalucia, Canarias, Cataluña, Galicia y Pais Vasco*. Madrid: Tecnos.

Parés i Maicas, Manuel (2006) La "telebasura": un fenómeno social preocupante. In: *Telós, cuadernos de comunicación, tecnologia y sociedad*, enero-Marzo, Number. 66. Online journal http://www.campursed.net/TELOS/anteriores/index50.html accessed 22 December 2007.

Payne, Stanley G. (1993) *Spain's First Democracy. The Second Spanish Republic*. Madison: University of Wisconsin Press.

Penas, Ignacio Lago and Santiago Lago Penas (2000) El sistema electoral español: una cuantificación de sus efectos mecanico y psicologico. In: *Revista de Estudios Politicos*, 107, January–March, pp. 225–68.

Pereira Castañares, Juan and Antonio Moreno Juste (2000) Il movimento per l'unitá europea e il processo di transizione e di consolidamento democratico in Spagna (1975–1986). In: Ariane Landuyt and Daniela Preda (eds), *I movimenti per l'unitá europea* 1970–1986. Bologna: Il Mulino, pp. 337–62.

—— (2002) Spain: in the centre or on the periphery of Europe? In: António Costa Pinto and Nuno Severiano Teixeira (eds), *Southern Europe and the Making of the European Union*. New York: Columbia University Press, pp. 41–80.

Pérez-Agote, Alfonso and José A. Santiago Garcia (2005) *La situación de la religion en España a principios del siglo XXI*. Opiniones and Actitudes, Number. 49. Madrid: Centro de Investigaciones Sociologicas.

Perez-Alcala, Gabriel M. (1998) Die spanische Wirtschaft auf dem Weg nach Maastricht. In: Walther L. Bernecker and Klaus Dirscherl (eds), *Spanien heute. Politik, Wirtschaft, Kultur*. Frankfurt-am-Main: Vervuert, pp. 224–65.

Perez-Diaz, Victor (1993) *The Return of Civil Society. The Emergence of Democratic Spain*. Cambridge: Cambridge University Press.

Petras, James F. (1990) Spanish socialism: on the road to Marbella. In: *Contemporary Crises. Law, Crime and Social Policy*, 14, 3, pp. 189–217.

—— (1993) Spanish socialism: the politics of neoliberalism. In: James Kurth and James Petras (eds), *Mediterranean Paradoxes. The Political and Social Structures of Southern Europe*. Providence: Berg Publishers, pp. 95–127.

Permanent Representation of France in the European Union (2006) *Guide to the European Security and Defence Policy (ESDP)*, Edition November 2006.

Piedrafita, Sonia, Federico Steinberg and José Ignacio Torreblanca (2006) *20 Años de España en la Unión Europea 1986–2006*. Madrid: Real Instituto Elcano.

Pino, Domingo del (2003) Marruecos-España: una nueva etapa. In: *Economia Exterior*, 24, Spring, pp. 37–50.

Polavieja, Javier G. (2002) Desempleo y castigo interbloques en las elecciones generales de 2000. In: *Revista Española de Ciencia Politica*, 6, April, pp. 97–127.

Porras, Antonio, Francisco Gutierrez and Maria Luisa Morillo (2002) La actividad legislativa de los parlamentos autonómicos, 1980–2000: agenda legislativa. In: Joan Subirats and Raquel Gallego (eds), *Veinte años de autonomias en España. Leyes, politicas publicas, instituciones y opinion publica*. Madrid: Centro de Investigaciones Sociologicas, pp. 167–201.

Porras Nadales, Antonio (1980) El Referendum de Iniciativa Autonomica del 28 Febrero en Andalucia. In: *Revista de Estudios Politicos*, Mayo–Junio 1980, pp. 175–94.

Powell, Charles T. (1990) The Tacito group and the transition to democracy 1973–77. In: Frances Lannon and Paul Preston (eds), *Elites and Power in Twentieth Century Spain*. Oxford: Clarendon Press, pp. 250–65.

—— (1995) Spain's external relations 1898–1975. In: Richard Gillespie, Fernando Rodrigo and Jonathan Story (eds), *Democratic Spain. Reshaping External Relations in a Changing World*. London: Routledge, pp. 11–29.

—— (1996) *Juan Carlos of Spain. Self-Made Monarch*. Basingstoke: Macmillan.

—— (2001) *España en democracia 1975–2000. Las claves de la profunda transformación de España*. Barcelona: Plaza Janes.

Pozo, Alejandro (2007) Los Ejércitos "Humanitários". Las Operaciones Españolas en el Exterior 1999–2005. In: Arcadi Oliveres y Pere Ortega (eds.), *El militarismo en España. Balance del ciclo armamentista español hasta 2007*. Barcelona: Icaria-Antrazyt, pp. 85–111.

Prego, Victoria (2000) *Presidentes. Veinticinco años de historia narrada por los cuatro jefes de gobierno de la democracia*. Barcelona: Plaza Janes.

Pridham, Geoffrey and José M. Magone (2006) The environment, socio-economic transformation and political change in the New Southern Europe. In: Richard Gunther and Nikiforos Diamandouros (eds), *The Changing Functions of the State in the New Southern Europe*. Baltimore, Oxford: Johns Hopkins University Press, Oxford University Press, (2006), pp. 262–304.

Programa Nacional de Reformas, PNR (2005) *Convergencia y Empleo*. Madrid: Oficina Economica del Presidente.

Programa Nacional de Reformas de España, PNR (2006) Informe Anual de Progreso 2006. Madrid: Oficina Economica del Presidente.

—— (2007) *Informe Anual de Progreso 2007*. Madrid: Oficina Economica del Presidente.

Putnam, Robert D. (with Robert Leonardi and Rafaella Nanetti) (1993) *Making democracy work. Civic traditions in modern Italy*. Princeton: Princeton University Press.

Radcliff, Pamela (2007) La iglesia católica y la transición a la democracia: un nuevo punto de partida. In: Carolyn P. Boyd (ed.), *Religión y política en la España contemporánea*. Madrid: Centro de Estudios Politicos y Constitucionales, pp. 209–28.

Ramio, Carles and Miquel Salvador (2002) La configuración de las administraciones de las comunidades autonomas: entre la inercia y la inovación institucional. In: Joan Subirats and Raquel Gallego (eds), *Veinte años de autonomias en España. Leyes, politicas publicas, instituciones y opinión pública*. Madrid: Centro de Investigaciones Sociologicas, pp. 99–133.

Ramirez, Manuel (1989) *Partidos políticos y constitución* (un estudio de las actitudes parlamentarias durante el proceso de creacion constitucional) Madrid: Centro de Estudios Constitucionales.

Ramirez, V., R. Perez Gomez and M. L. Marquez (1998) Proporcionalidad y bonificación al partido vencedor. Juan Montabes (ed.), *El sistema electoral a debate. Veinte años de rendimientos del sistema electoral español, 1977–1997*. Madrid: CIS, pp. 101–25.

Ramiro Fernandez, Luis (2000) Entre coalición y partido: la evolución del modelo organizativo de Izquierda Unida. In: *Revista Española de Ciencia Politica*, 1, 2, April, pp. 237–68.

—— (2003) Electoral incentives and organisational limits. The evolution of the Communist Party (PCE) and the United Left (IU). In: *Political Science Debates*, 1, pp. 9–39.

Ramiro Fernandez, Luis (2005) Programmatic Adaptation and Organisational Centralisation in the AP-PP. In: *South European Society and Politics*, vol. 10, Number. 2, July, pp. 207–23.

Ramos Gallarin, Juan A. (2006) Las Comisiones Bilaterales de Cooperación en el sistema español de relaciones intergubernamentales. In: Lourdes Lopez Nieto (ed.), *Relaciones Intergubernamentales en la España democratica. Interdependencia, Autonomia, Conflicto y Cooperación*. Madrid: Dykinson, pp. 115–31.

Real Instituto Elcano (2004) Barometro, June 2004, 6th survey Madrid: Real Instituto Elcano de Estudios Internacionales y Estrategicos 2004, p. 38 http://www.realinstitutoelcano.org accessed 17.9.2004.

Reif, Karl Heinz and Hermann Schmidt (1980) Nine second order national elections: a conceptual framework for the analysis of European election results. In: *European Journal of Political Research*, 8, 1, pp. 3–44.

Registro Central de Personal (2007) *Boletin Estadistico de Personal al Servicio de las Administraciones Publicas*. Extracto de la edición impresa in January posted on the Ministry for Public Administrations http://www.administración.es accessed on 18 October 2007.

Requena, Miguel (2005) The secularisation of Spanish society: Change in religious practice. In: *South European Society and Politics*, vol. 10, Number. 3, pp. 369–90.

Requejo, Ferrán (2007)*Federalismo plurinacional y pluralismo de valores El caso español*. Madrid: Centro de Estudios Politicos y Constitucionales.

Revenga Sanchez, Miguel and Maria de la Paz Sanchez Manzano (2002) El reparto del poder politico en el estado de las autonomias. Una fotografia de urgencia. In: *Revista de Estudios Politicos*, 116, April–June, pp. 321–45.

Rico, Ana Pablo Gonzalez and Marta Fraile (1998) Regional decentralisation of health policy in Spain: social capital does not tell the whole story. In: Paul Heywood (ed.), *Politics and Policy in Democratic Spain*. London: Frank Cass, pp. 180–99.

Ridao, Joan (2007) Les coalicions politiques a Catalunya. *El cas del govern Catalanista i d'esquerres*. Working paper number.257. Institut de Ciéncies Politiques i Socials, Universtat Autonoma de Barcelona.

Robinson, Richard A. H. (1970) *The Origins of Franco's Spain. The Right, the Republic and the Revolution 1931–1936*. Newton Abbot: David and Charles.

—— (1975) Genealogy and function of the monarchist myth of the Franco regime. In: *Iberian Studies*, II, 1, pp. 18–26.

Rodriguez Ibañez, José Enrique (1987) *Despues de una dictadura: Cultura autoritaria y transición politica en España*. Madrid: Centro de Estudios Constitucionales.

Rodriguez Cabrero, Gregorio (1998) El estado de bienestar en España: evolutivas y restruturación institucional. In: Ricard Gomá and Joan Subirats (eds), *Politicas Publicas en España. Contenidos, redes de actores y niveles de gobierno.* Barcelona: Ariel, pp. 135–52.

Rodrigo, Fernando (1995) Western alignment: Spain's security policy. In: Richard Gillespie, Fernando Rodrigo and Jonathan Story (eds), *Democratic Spain. Reshaping External Relations in a Changing World.* London: Routledge, pp. 50–66.

Roller, Elisa (2001) The March 2000 general election in Spain. In: *Government and Opposition,* 36, 2, pp. 209–29.

—— (2002a) The Basque Country and Spain. Continued deadlock? In: *Mediterranean Politics,* 7, 1, Spring, pp. 113–23.

—— (2002b) Reforming the senate? mission impossible. In: *West European Politics,* 25, 4, October, pp. 69–92.

Román Marugan, Paloma (2002) El Gobierno. In: Paloma Román (ed.), *Sistema politico español.* Madrid: McGraw-Hill, pp. 235–57.

—— (2002) Los partidos y los sistemas de partidos. In: Paloma Roman (ed.), *Sistema politico español.* Madrid: McGraw-Hill, pp. 101–24.

Ross, Chris (1996) Nationalism and party competition in the Basque Country and Catalonia. In: *West European Politics,* 19, 3, July, pp. 488–506.

Ross, George (1995) *Jacques Delors and European Integration.* Oxford: Oxford University Press.

Royo, Sebastian (2001) The collapse of social concertation and the failure of socialist economic policies in Spain. In: *South European Society and Politics,* vol. 6, 1, pp. 27–50.

Ruano, Pedro Ramirez (2001) Reflexiones acerca de la administración electoral. In: *Revista de estudios politicos,* 112, April–June, pp. 237–52.

Rubio, Antonio and Manuel Cerdán (1997) *El origen del GAL. Guerra sucia y crimen de estado.* Madrid: Temas de Hoy.

Ruiz Jimenez, Antonia Maria (2006) *De la necesidad, virtud. La transformación feminista del Partido Popular en perspective comparada.* Madrid: Centro de Estudios Politicos y Constitucionales.

Salmon, Keith (1995) *The Modern Spanish Economy. Transformation and Integration into Europe.* London: Pinter.

Salvador, Miquel (2002) Comunidades autonomas y orientación al ciudadano: el analisis de los puntos de encuentro. In: Joan Subirats and Raquel Gallego (eds), *Veinte años de autonomias en España. Leyes, politicas publicas, instituciones y opinion publica.* Madrid: Centro de Investigaciones Sociologicas, pp. 135–63.

Salz, Pavel, Erik Buisman, Jos Smit and Birgit de Vos (2006) *Employment in the Fisheries Sector: Current Situation (FISH/2004/4).* Final report, April 2006. Brussels: European Commission.

Sanchez-Albornoz, Sonsoles Cabeza (1998) *Los movimientos revolucionarios de 1820, 1830 y 1848 en sus documentos.* Barcelona: Ariel.

Sanchez de Dios, Manuel (1994) Executive parliamentary control. In: Amparo Almarcho Barbado (ed.), *Spain and EC Membership Evaluated.* London: Pinter, pp. 221–28.

—— (1995) Party discipline in the Spanish parliamentary parties. Paper presented at the ECPR workshop 'Party discipline and the organisation of parliaments', Bordeaux, April, 1995.

—— (2002) La justicia y el tribunal constitucional. In: Paloma Román (ed.), *Sistema politico español.* Madrid: McGraw-Hill, pp. 259–85.

Sands, Jennifer (2007) Organised crime and illicit activities in Spain: cause and facilitating factors. In: *Mediterranean Politics*, Vol.12, 2 July, pp. 211–32.

Saracibar, Rodolfo Perez (2002) *La participación regional en el proceso de decisión de la Unión Europea*. Brussels.

Sassoon, Donald (1996) *One Hundred Years of Socialism. The West European Left in the Twentieth Century*. London: Tauris.

Saz, Ismael (2007) Religión política y religion católica en el fascismo español. In: Carolyn P. Boyd (ed.), *Religión y política en la España contemporánea*. Madrid: Centro de Estudios Politicos y Constitucionales, pp. 33–55.

Schmitter, Philippe C. (1995) Organised interests and democratic consolidation in Southern Europe. In: Richard Gunther, P. Nikiforos Diamandouros and Hans-Jürgen Puhle (eds), *The Politics of Democratic Consolidation. Southern Europe in Comparative Perspective*. Baltimore and London: The Johns Hopkins University Press, pp. 284–314.

Schuhmacher, Tobias (2001) The mediterranean as a new foreign policy challenge? Sweden and the Barcelona process. In: *Mediterranean Politics*, vol. 6, Number. 3, pp. 81–102.

Seixas, Xosé M. Nuñez (1995) Os nacionalismos na Espanha contemporânea: uma perspectiva historica e algumas hipoteses para o presente. In: *Analise Social*, xxx, 2–3, pp. 489–526.

—— (1999) *Los nacionalismos en España contemporanea (siglos XIX y XX)*. Barcelona: Hipotesi.

Sevilla, Jordi Victor (2006) Saldos Fiscales y Solidariedad Interterritorial. In: Núria Bosch and Jose Durán (eds), *La financiación de las comunidades autonomas:Politicas tributarias y solidaridad interterritorial*. Barcelona: Universitat de Barcelona, pp. 251–62.

Share, Donald (1986) *The Making of Spanish Democracy*. New York: Praeger.

—— (1987) Transitions to democracy and transitions through transaction. In: *Comparative Political Studies*, 9, pp. 525–48.

—— (1989) *Dilemmas of social democracy. The Spanish Socialist Party in the 1980s*. Westport, CT: Greenwood Press.

Simon, Hipolito J. (2003) Que determina la afiliación a los sindicatos en España? In: *Revista del Ministerio de Trabajo y Asuntos Sociales*, 41, pp. 69–87.

Solé-Vilanova, Joaquim (1989) Spain: developments in regional and local government. In: Robert Bennett (ed.), *Territory and Administration in Europe*. London: Pinter, pp. 205–29.

Soriano, Ramón and Carlos Alarcon (2001) Las elecciones en España: votos iguales y libres. In: *Revista Estudios Politicos*, 114, October–December, pp. 115–29.

Spangenberg, Peter M. (1998) Die Liberalisierung des Fernsehens. Iberische Variationen über kulturelle, politische und wirtschaftliche Interessenlagen. In: Walther L. Bernecker and Klaus Dirscherl (eds), *Spanien heute. Politik, Wirtschaft, Kultur*. Frankfurt-am-Main: Vervuert, pp. 609–40.

Story, Jonathan (1991) Spanish external policies: towards the EC presidency. In: Jonathan Story and Jean Grugel (eds), *Spanish External Policies and the EC Presidency*. Centre for Mediterranean Studies, Occasional Papers, 2, April. Bristol: University of Bristol, pp. 1–31.

—— (1995) Spain's external relations redefined: 1875–1989. In:Richard Gillespie, Fernando Rodrigo and Jonathan Story (eds), *Democratic Spain. Reshaping External Relations in a Changing World*. London: Routledge, pp. 30–49.

Story, Jonathan and Jean Grugel (eds) (1991) *Spain's External Policies and the EC Presidency*. Occasional Papers 2, Bristol: Centre for Mediterranean Studies, University of Bristol.

Subirats, Joan (1998) El papel de las comunidades Autonomas en el sistema español de relaciones intergubernamentales. Quince años de estado de autonomias: luces y sombras de una realidad aun en discusión. In: Robert Agranoff and Rafael Banon i Martinez (eds), *El estado de las autonomias. Hacia un nuevo federalismo?* Bilbao: Instituto Vasco de Administracion Publica, pp. 161–80.

Subirats, Joan and Ricard Gomá (1998a) La dimensión sustantiva: los contenidos de las politicas publicas en España. In: Ricard Gomá and Joan Subirats (eds), *Politicas publicas en España. Contenidos, redes de actores y niveles de gobierno.* Barcelona: Ariel, pp. 365–87.

—— (1998b) La dimensión de estilo de las politicas publicas en España: entramados institucionales y redes de actores. In: Ricard Gomá and Joan Subirats (eds), *Politicas publicas en España. Contenidos, redes de actores y niveles de gobierno.* Barcelona: Ariel, pp. 388–406.

Szmolka, Inmaculada (1999) *Opiniones y actitudes de los españoles ante el proceso de integración europea. Opiniones y actitudes 21.* Madrid: Centro de Investigaciones Sociologicas.

Tamames, Ramón (1995) *La economia española 1975–1995.* Madrid: Temas de hoy.

Thomas, Hugh (1984) *The Spanish Civil War.* London: Penguin.

Threlfall, Monica (1997) Spain in social Europe: a laggard or compliant member state? In: *South European Society and Politics,* 2, 2, pp. 1–33.

Tijeras, Ramón (2000) *Lobbies. ? Como funcionan los grupos de presión españoles?* Madrid: Temas de hoy.

Tobes Portillo, Paloma (2002) El desarollo de las politicas activas de España: un analisis de los planes de acción para el empleo. In: *Revista del Ministerio de Trabajo y Asuntos Sociales,* 36, pp. 15–43.

Torcal, Mariano and Pradeep Chhiber (1995) Elites, cleavages y sistema de partidos en una democracia consolidada, España (1986–1992). In: *Revista Española de Investigaciones Sociologicas,* 69, pp. 7–38.

Torcal, Mariano and José Ramón Montero (1999) La formación y consecuencias del capital social en España. In: *Revista Española de Ciencia Politica,* 1, 2, April, pp. 79–121.

Torcal, Mariano and Lucia Medina (2002) Ideologia y voto en España 1979–2000: Los Procesos de reconstrucción racional de la identificación ideologica. In: *Revista Española de Ciencia Politica,* 6, April, pp. 57–96.

Torcal, Mariano, Richard Gunther and José Ramon Montero (2002) Anti-party Sentiments in Southern Europe. In: Richard Gunther, José Ramón Montero, Juan J. Linz (eds), *Political Parties. Old Concepts and New Challenges.* Oxford: OUP, pp. 257–90.

Torreblanca, Jose I. (2001) La europeización de la politica exterior española. In: Carlos Closa (ed.), *La europeización del sistema politico español.* Madrid: Istmo, pp. 483–511.

Transparency International (2006) *Global Corruption Report 2006.* London: Pluto Press.

—— (2007) *Global Corruption Report 2007* Cambridge: Cambridge University Press.

Trenzado, Manuel and Juan Nuñez (2001) Medios de Comunicación. In: Manuel Alcantara, Antonia Martinez (eds), *Politica y Gobierno en España.* Barcelona: Tirant lo blanch, pp. 493–530.

Tribunal de Cuentas (2007) *Informe de Fiscalización de los Estados Contables del Ejercicio 2004 de los Partidos Politicos con Representación Parlamentaria en las Cortes Generales o en las Asambleas Legislativas de las Comunidades Autonomas. Number. 762.* Madrid: Tribunal de Cuentas, 27 Junio posted on the website of the Audit Court, http://www.tce.es, accessed 15 October 2007.

Tusell Gomez, Xavier (1976) The functioning of the *cacique* system in Andalusia, 1890–1931. In: Stanley G. Payne (ed.), *Politics and Society in Twentieth Century Spain*. New York and London: New Viewpoints, pp. 1–28.

Tusell, Javier (2004) *El Aznarato. El Gobierno del Partido Popular*. Madrid: Aguilar.

Ulman, Joan Connelly (1988) *The Tragic Week. A Study of Anticlericalism in Spain. 1875–1912*. Cambridge: Harvard University Press.

Urquiza, José Manuel (2005) *Corrupción Municipal. Por qué se produce y cómo evitarla*. Cordoba: Almuzara.

Valenzuela, Manuel (1996) *Spain: the phenomenon of mass tourism*. In: Allan M. Williams and Gareth Shaw (eds), *Tourism and Economic Development. Western European Experiences*. London: Pinter, pp. 40–60.

Valiente Fernandez, Célia (2000) El feminismo del Estado y los debates politicos: la formación ocupacional en España. (1983–1998). In: *Revista Española de Ciencia Politica*, vol. 2, 1, pp. 127–47.

Valiente, Celia (2007) Are gender equality institutions the policy allies of the feminist movement? A contingent 'Yes' in the Spanish central state, In *South European Society and Politics*, 12: 3, pp. 315–34.

Vallés, Josep M. (1991) Entre la regularidad y la indeterminación: balance sobre el comportamiento electoral en España (1977–1989). In: *España debate la politica*. Madrid: Tecnos, pp. 27–43.

—— (1998) El numero de representantes y la dimensión de las circunscripciones. In: Juan Montabes (ed.), *El sistema electoral a debate. Veinte años de rendimientos del sistema electoral español. 1977–1997*. Madrid: CIS, pp. 77–90.

Vallés, Josep M. and Jordi Sanchez Picanyol (1998) Las elecciones municipales en España entre 1979 y 1991: balance provisional. In: Pilar del Castillo (ed.), *Comportamiento Politico y Electoral*. Madrid: CIS, pp. 365–81.

Vallés, Josep M. and Aida Diaz (2001) The March 2000 Spanish general elections. In: *South European Society and Politics*, 5, 3, Winter, pp. 133–42.

Beyers, Jan and Guido Dierickx (1998) The working groups of the Council of the European Union: supranational or intergovernmental negotiations? In: *Journal of Common Market Studies*, 36, 3, pp. 289–317.

Van Biezen, Ingrid (1998) Sobre o equilibrio interno do poder: as organizações partidárias nas novas democracias. In: *Análise Social*, 33, 4, pp. 685–708.

—— (2001) Party financing in new democracies: Spain and Portugal. In: *Party Politics*, 6, 3, pp. 329–42.

Van Biezen, I. (2003) *Political Parties in New Democracies. Party Organization in Southern and East-Central Europe*. Basingstroke: Palgrave.

Van Biezen, I. (2005) Terrorism and democratic legitimacy: conflicting interpretations of the Spanish elections, *Mediterranean Politics*, Vol. 10, 1, pp. 99–108.

Van Biezen, Ingrid and Jonathan Hopkin (2005) The presidentialisation of Spanish democracy: sources of prime ministerial power in Post-Franco Spain. In: Thomas Poguntke, Paul Webb (eds), *The Presidentialization of Politics. A Comparative Study of Modern Democracies*. Oxford: Oxford University Press, pp. 107–27.

Van Biezen, Ingrid and Richard S. Katz (2006) Political Data in 2005 In: Ingrid van Biezen and Richard S. Katz (eds), *Political Data Yearbook 2005*. In: *European Journal of Political Research,* vol. 45, Number. 7–8, December 2006, pp. 1023-1-33.

Varela, Jesus (2003) Relaciones pesqueras con Marruecos. In: *Economia Exterior*, 24, Spring, pp. 139-46.

Vasconcelos, Alvaro and George Joffe (eds) (2000) The Barcelona process. Building a Euro-Mediterranean regional community. Special Issue of *Mediterranean Politics, 5, 1.*

Vergopoulos, Kostas (1990) The political economy of democratic consolidation in Southern Europe. In: Diane Ethier (ed.), *Democratic Transition and Consolidation in Southern Europe, Latin America and South East Asia.* Basingstoke: Macmillan, pp. 139–54.

Viadel, Antonio Colomer (1989) *El sistema politico de la constitucion española de 1837.* Madrid: Congreso de los Diputados.

Vilas Nogueira, J. (2000) Gobierno y administración en la comunidad autonoma de Galicia. In: Juan Luis Paniagua Soto (ed.), *Gobierno y Administración en las Comunidades Autonomas. Andalucia, Canarias, Cataluña, Galicia y Pais Vasco.* Madrid: Tecnos, pp. 129–68.

Villacorta Mancebo, Luis (2000) La construcción del estado democratico español: algunas perspectivas. In: *Revista de Estudios Politicos*, 109, pp. 73–102.

Villoria Mendieta, Manuel (1999) El Papel de la burocracia en la transición ny consolidación de la democracia española: primera aproximacion. In: *Revista Española de Ciencia Politica*, 1, 1, October, pp. 97–125.

Wert, José Ignacio (1998) Elecciones autonomicas en España 1980–1996: una visión de conjunto. In: Manuel Alcantara and Antonia Martinez (eds), *Las elecciones autonomicas en España, 1980–1997.* Madrid: CIS, pp. 503–24.

Wessels, Wolfgang (2004) Die institutionelle Architectur der EU nach der Europaeischen Verfassung: Hohere Entscheidungsdynamik – neue Koalitionen? In: *Integration*, 3, pp. 161–75.

Whitehead, Lawrence (1991) Democracy by convergence and Southern Europe: a comparative politics perspective. In: Geoffrey Pridham (ed.), *Encouraging Democracy. The International Context of Regime Transition in Southern Europe.* London: Leicester University Press, pp. 45–61.

Williams, E. N. (1999) *The Ancien Regime in Europe. Government and Society in the Major States, 1648–1789.* London: Pimlico.

Youngs, Richard (2000) Spain, Latin America and Europe: the complex interaction of regionalism and cultural identification. In: Richard Gillespie and Richard Youngs (eds), *Spain: European and International Challenges.* Special issue of *Mediterranean Politics*, 5, 2, pp. 107–28.

Index

NEW Political Science eBooks Archive and Subscription Package from Routledge

INCLUDES FREE ACCESS TO BACKLIST CONTENT WORTH OVER £170,000 / $340,000

Routledge Research is renowned for cutting-edge, original research across the humanities and social sciences. Consisting of both single and multi-authored books and edited collections, the research program is characterized by dynamic interventions into established subjects and innovative studies on emerging topics.

Unlock this cutting-edge research with our new eBook Subscription Packages. Maximise your resources, access the right material where and when you want it.

Outstanding Offer! As an institution if you subscribe to our front list publishing program you are entitled to access our backlist archive of some 2,050 titles **completely free**!

- the politics collection consists of over 2,000 backlist titles, plus c.250 new books per year

- subscribe and you will also benefit from a huge saving on the list price

- pricing details and a full list of titles are available on request.

For further information on Taylor & Francis eBooks, purchasing options, and content for your library, please contact:

UK, Rest of the World
Carlos Gimeno, Taylor & Francis, 2 & 4 Park Square, Milton Park, Abingdon, Oxfordshire, OX14 4RN

Tel: +44 (0)7017 6062 | **Fax:** +44 (0)7017 6336
Email: online.sales@tandf.co.uk

US, Canada, Central & South America
Taylor & Francis, 270 Madison Avenue, New York, NY 10016, USA

Tel: 1-888-318-2367 | **Fax:** 212-244-1563
Email: e-reference@taylorandfrancis.com

Also available: Routledge Political Science eBooks Archive and Subscription Package

www.informaworld.com/ebooks

R Routledge
Taylor & Francis Group